Jonathan Edwards and the Psalms

A Redemptive-Historical Vision of Scripture

DAVID P. BARSHINGER

OXFORD
UNIVERSITY PRESS

OXFORD

UNIVERSITY PRESS

Oxford University Press is a department of the University of Oxford.
It furthers the University's objective of excellence in research, scholarship,
and education by publishing worldwide.

Oxford   New York
Auckland   Cape Town   Dar es Salaam   Hong Kong   Karachi
Kuala Lumpur   Madrid   Melbourne   Mexico City   Nairobi
New Delhi   Shanghai   Taipei   Toronto

With offices in
Argentina   Austria   Brazil   Chile   Czech Republic   France   Greece
Guatemala   Hungary   Italy   Japan   Poland   Portugal   Singapore
South Korea   Switzerland   Thailand   Turkey   Ukraine   Vietnam

Oxford is a registered trademark of Oxford University Press
in the UK and certain other countries.

Published in the United States of America by
Oxford University Press
198 Madison Avenue, New York, NY 10016

Quotations from *The Works of Jonathan Edwards Online* have been reprinted with
permission from the Jonathan Edwards Center, Yale University.

Quotations from Jonathan Edwards, *The Works of Jonathan Edwards* (© 1957–2008),
have been reprinted with permission from Yale University Press.

Library of Congress Cataloging-in-Publication Data
Barshinger, David P.
Jonathan Edwards and the Psalms: A Redemptive-Historical Vision of Scripture /
David P. Barshinger.
pages cm
Includes bibliographical references and index.
ISBN 978–0–19–939675–7 (cloth : alk. paper) 1. Edwards, Jonathan, 1703–1758.
2. Bible. Psalms.   I. Title.
BX7260.E3B37 2014
223'.2092—dc23
2014006208

1 3 5 7 8 9 6 4 2
Printed in the United States of America
on acid-free paper

to Allison,
whose love, patience, and support
sustained me through the
peaks and valleys
of this project

This book of Psalms has such an exalted devotion, and such a spirit of evangelical grace every[where] breathed forth in it! Here are such exalted expressions of the gloriousness of God, and even of the excellency of Christ and his kingdom; there is so much of the gospel doctrine, grace, and spirit, breaking out and shining in it, that it seems to be carried clear above and beyond the strain and pitch of the Old Testament, and almost brought up to the New. Almost the whole book of Psalms has either a direct or indirect respect to Christ and the gospel which he was to publish.

—JONATHAN EDWARDS, Sermon on Ps 89:6

Contents

Acknowledgments

SEVERAL PEOPLE HAVE helped make this book possible. I am especially grateful to Doug Sweeney for the many hours he spent providing insight into Edwards and his world, guiding me as I explored this topic, offering incisive feedback on my drafts, and giving the gracious support that has brought this work to completion. Many thanks to Scott Manetsch for his ongoing encouragement, careful readings of earlier drafts of this book, and assistance with some Latin translations. I'm thankful as well to Ken Minkema for making fruitful suggestions on earlier drafts, offering support in my research, and aiding me in deciphering Edwards' obscure handwriting. Gerald McDermott, Robert Brown, and two anonymous reviewers also provided beneficial feedback on the book that has strengthened the final version. Thanks also goes to the broad community of Edwards scholars, whose dedication to studying this New England divine and his life, theology, and significance has made it possible to dig into his biblical writings and discuss them in the context of his life and thought. A particular word of gratitude goes to Glenn Kreider, whose classroom rabbit trails on Edwards in my master's program first piqued my interest in this figure. Special thanks as well to Cynthia Read, Marcela Maxfield, and the Oxford University Press team for all their support in bringing this book to fruition.

Three libraries facilitated my research for this project, including the Rolfing Library of Trinity International University, the Beinecke Rare Book and Manuscript Library of Yale University, and the Richard J. Daley Library of the University of Illinois at Chicago. Special thanks to the Beinecke Library and their staff for providing access to Edwards' original sermon manuscripts on the Psalms.

Finally, I am truly grateful to my parents, Morris and Cathy Barshinger, not only for their constant support and affirmation during this book but also for nurturing an interest in thinking deeply about biblical, theological, and historical matters from an early age. My deepest thanks go to my wife, Allison, and our four children, Levi, Ian, Micah, and Noelle. They have sacrificed much for me to complete this project, but they have shown constant affection and encouragement—thank you for keeping life vibrant, joyful, and unpredictable during my years of working on this book.

Abbreviations

KJV   King James Version

WJE   *The Works of Jonathan Edwards*

WJEO   *The Works of Jonathan Edwards Online*

Note on the Text

THROUGHOUT THE BOOK, when I refer to the book of Psalms as a whole, I capitalize it, but when referring to an individual psalm or a defined selection of psalms, the word appears in lowercase. In addition, I discuss a number of Edwards' sermons on the Psalms from *The Works of Jonathan Edwards Online* (*WJEO*) that are available on the Jonathan Edwards Center at Yale University website. Instead of including the date I accessed each sermon, I have listed dates of accession in the bibliography and am listing the inclusive dates here: January 22, 2011–December 6, 2013.

Also, Edwards often wrote out his sermons using his own system of shorthand, and as I have used unpublished sermons from the *WJEO* and from manuscripts available at the Yale University Beinecke Rare Book and Manuscript Library or the Jonathan Edwards Center at Yale University, I have reproduced Edwards' writing literally, although I have spelled out abbreviations. His more common abbreviations include the following: "G." ("God"); "J. X." ("Jesus Christ"), "SS." ("Scriptures"), "Chh." ("Church"), "Relig." ("Religion"), "salva." ("salvation"), and "☉" ("world"). I have also added apostrophes (e.g., Edwards commonly used the contraction "ben't," meaning "be not," without the apostrophe) and other punctuation marks where the sense might otherwise be confusing, marking all emendations in square brackets.

In dealing with Edwards' unpublished sermons, portions of which I transcribed from the original manuscripts, I have omitted words or phrases that Edwards crossed out. I have also maintained the spelling in the original sources, especially in Edwards' unpublished manuscripts and in commentaries of the seventeenth- and eighteenth-century interpreters discussed, but I have converted the old style "ſ" to "s." In addition, in a number of cases, Edwards cited several passages from the Psalms to support a point, and when I have listed those out, I have retained the order in which he listed them, rather than placing them in canonical order.

In this book, I frequently cite the Yale University Press version of *The Works of Jonathan Edwards* (New Haven, CT: Yale University Press, 1957–2008) and *The Works of Jonathan Edwards Online* (Jonathan Edwards Center at Yale University, 2008). Throughout the book, I refer to the Yale printed edition of Edwards' *Works* as *WJE*, omitting the publisher's name or place, though citing the volume number and publication date, and I refer to the online *Works* as *WJEO* and omit the publisher's name and publication date, which remain constant for all *WJEO* volumes. Also, when referring to Edwards' "Blank Bible" and "Notes on Scripture" notebooks as his unpublished manuscripts, I set the titles in quotation marks, but when referring to them as the Yale University Press published editions, I set them in italics.

A special note should be made on Edwards' "Harmony of the Genius Spirit Doctrines and Rules of the Old Testament and the New." I used a transcription obtained from the Jonathan Edwards Center at Yale University when quoting this work, and the page numbers I cite refer to the page numbering used in the transcription of Edwards' "Harmony" that I received from the Center, even though the numbering of the three separate parts does not continue consecutively from part to part.

Finally, since the version of the Bible that Edwards used regularly in his ministry was the King James Version (KJV), I quote from the KJV whenever I quote from the Bible throughout the book.

Jonathan Edwards and the Psalms

Introduction

AS THE RELIGIOUS heat of the New England revivals cooled down in the mid-1740s, Jonathan Edwards (1703–1758) wrote his preeminent work reflecting on the true marks of a saint, *A Treatise Concerning Religious Affections* (1746), in which he argued that "[t]rue religion, in great part, consists in holy affections."[1] While so many in his own Northampton and throughout New England had experienced spiritual exercises of some kind during the height of the Great Awakening from 1740 to 1742, in *Religious Affections* Edwards considered those who had lapsed back to their old ways in the years following the widespread spiritual movement.[2]

To understand this phenomenon and discern the nature of true religion, Edwards turned to the Bible, and he found David, "the sweet psalmist of Israel" (2 Sam 23:1), to be one of the most eminent saints in Scripture who exhibited a life of holy affections and gave us "a lively portraiture of his religion, in the Book of Psalms."[3] Edwards said these "holy songs" were "nothing else but the expressions and breathings of devout and holy affections," expressions that "the Psalms of David are everywhere full of."[4] He described the nature of the Psalter as a book for the church of God at large:

> those Psalms are not only the expressions of the religion of so eminent a saint, that God speaks of as so agreeable to his mind; but were also, by the direction of the Holy Ghost, penned for the use of the church of God in its public worship, not only in that age, but in after-ages; as being fitted to express the religion of all saints, in all ages, as well as

---

1. Jonathan Edwards, *Religious Affections*, ed. John E. Smith, vol. 2 of *WJE* (1959), 95.

2. On the evidence that a "Great Awakening" did in fact occur in eighteenth-century New England, see Thomas Kidd, *The Great Awakening: The Roots of Evangelical Christianity* (New Haven, CT: Yale University Press, 2007).

3. Edwards, *Religious Affections*, 108.

4. Edwards, *Religious Affections*, 108.

the religion of the Psalmist. And it is moreover to be observed, that David, in the Book of Psalms, speaks not as a private person, but as the psalmist of Israel, as the subordinate head of the church of God, and leader in their worship and praises; and in many of the Psalms, speaks in the name of Christ, as personating him in these breathings forth of holy affection, and in many other Psalms, he speaks in the name of the church.[5]

In trying to make theological sense of the revivals, Edwards found that the Psalms offered the best distillation of holy affections available in one place, a sure guide for discerning between true and false religion—indeed, the Holy Spirit intended it as such. The Psalter reached beyond David's life and even the nation of Israel and brought forth divine songs that painted the ideal portrait of true religion for the church to use as its worship book in every age. And while Edwards spoke on the one hand about the historical person of David and his personal religion, he also spoke of the Christological and ecclesiological import of the Psalms, casting a broader net for interpreting the Psalter in a redemptive-historical framework.

As this selection from *Religious Affections* shows, the Psalms played a formative role in Edwards' life, informing his theology, his practice of worship, and his approach to interpreting Scripture. This appreciation for the Psalms corresponded to his love of the whole Bible, a passion he nurtured throughout his life. In his late teenage years, he drafted seventy resolutions to help keep his life focused on God and his glory, and to that purpose Edwards "[r]esolved, to study the Scriptures so steadily, constantly and frequently, as that I may find, and plainly perceive myself to grow in the knowledge of the same."[6] Edwards further described his love affair with the Bible years later in his "Personal Narrative" (December 14, 1740). Remembering his years as a young pastor in New York, he wrote: "I had then, and at other times, the greatest delight in the holy Scriptures, of any book whatsoever.... Used oftentimes to dwell long on one sentence, to see the wonders contained in it; and yet almost every sentence seemed to be full of wonders."[7] Edwards explained that throughout his life he "had an affecting sense of the excellency of the word of God, as a word of life; as the light of life; a sweet, excellent, life-giving word: accompanied with

---

5. Edwards, *Religious Affections*, 108–109.

6. Jonathan Edwards, "Resolutions," in *Letters and Personal Writings*, ed. George S. Claghorn, vol. 16 of *WJE* (1998), 755.

7. Jonathan Edwards, "Personal Narrative," in *Letters and Personal Writings*, ed. George S. Claghorn, vol. 16 of *WJE* (1998), 797.

a thirsting after that word, that it might dwell richly in my heart."[8] Even in his last days, Edwards had grand plans for writing a lengthy treatise on the Bible. On October 19, 1757, five months before his death, Edwards penned a letter to the Trustees of the College of New Jersey responding to their invitation that he take the place of his son-in-law Aaron Burr (1716–1757), who had just passed away, as president of the fledgling institution. Edwards explained why he saw himself unfit for the position, and, among his reasons, he disclosed his plans for two "great work[s]," the second of which he called "The Harmony of the Old and New Testament," a treatise that would provide "an explanation of a very great part of the holy Scripture," treating the prophecies of the Messiah, the types of the Old Testament, and the doctrinal harmony of the two testaments. He hoped its method would "lead the mind to a view of the true spirit, design, life and soul of the Scriptures, as well as to their proper use and improvement."[9] From his early years in college to the final days of his short presidency at the College of New Jersey, Edwards was a devout student of the Bible.[10]

But for all the ink devoted to Edwards over the past three centuries, this is not the Edwards that has been preserved.[11] Instead, a distorted portrait of Edwards remains the reigning image in scholarship today. While Edwards as an eclectic was interested in fields ranging from theology and philosophy to science and nature, he was at his core devoted to the glorious God of Scripture and to mining that Scripture for truth—an aspect left out of Edwards' scholarly portrait. This study aims to redress this unbalanced image of Edwards by examining his lifelong devotion to the Bible particularly through his engagement with the book of Psalms, exploring his theological engagement with the Psalms in the context of his interpretation, worship, and preaching.

The origin of the twenty-six–volume Yale University Press edition of *The Works of Jonathan Edwards*, completed in 2008, helps explain the predominant scholarly image of Edwards. Perry Miller launched the effort and served as the general editor for the first two volumes of the Yale *Works*, and, following Miller's lead, scholars focused primarily on Edwards as a philosopher, theologian, and revivalist. Stephen Stein explains that scholars neglected Edwards' biblical writings, following instead the "initial focus" of the Yale edition of

---

8. Edwards, "Personal Narrative," 798.

9. Jonathan Edwards to Trustees of the College of New Jersey, October 19, 1757, in *Letters and Personal Writings*, ed. George S. Claghorn, vol. 16 of *WJE* (1998), 727–729.

10. For more on Edwards' passion and undying interest in the Bible, see Douglas A. Sweeney, "The Biblical World of Jonathan Edwards," *Jonathan Edwards Studies* 3, no. 2 (2013): 207–211.

11. See M. X. Lesser, *Reading Jonathan Edwards: An Annotated Bibliography in Three Parts, 1729–2005* (Grand Rapids, MI: Eerdmans, 2008).

Edwards' *Works* on his published writings and giving little attention to his manuscripts. Miller's influence on the Yale edition set the "scholarly agenda" to focus on the philosophical and controversial aspects of Edwards. With this focus Miller's "attitude also biased readers against certain traditional theological concerns, including biblical interpretation."[12] In fact, Miller's biography of Edwards dedicated only three sentences to the "Blank Bible" (technically known as "Miscellaneous Observations on the Holy Scriptures") and "Notes on Scripture" manuscripts and even described their origin and relationship inaccurately.[13] As a result of all this, many significant twentieth-century works on Edwards have neglected his biblical manuscripts.[14]

In contrast, the evidence exhibits Edwards' extensive work in Scripture, as he worked out of what George Marsden calls "his biblicist and Calvinistic heritage."[15] And the later volumes in the completed Yale *Works of Jonathan Edwards* better testify to this reality. He dedicated his life to studying the Bible regularly, keeping voluminous notes on his observations in Scripture, and preaching his findings from the Bible two to three times every week to his congregation. The records Edwards left behind bear testimony that his resolution to focus on the Bible remained a priority throughout his life: Edwards' "Blank Bible" contains more than 5,500 entries; his "Notes on Scripture" 495 entries; and his extant corpus more than twelve hundred sermons.[16] Marsden, the preeminent Edwards biographer, observes that it is difficult to convey in a biography how foundational the Bible was for Edwards because his engagement with the

---

12. Stephen J. Stein, "Editor's Introduction," in Jonathan Edwards, *The "Blank Bible,"* ed. Stephen J. Stein, vol. 24 of *WJE* (2006), 98–101. See also Stephen J. Stein, "The Quest for the Spiritual Sense: The Biblical Hermeneutics of Jonathan Edwards," *Harvard Theological Review* 70 (1977): 100.

13. Perry Miller, *Jonathan Edwards,* the American Men of Letters Series (New York: William Sloane Associates, 1949), 127.

14. See George M. Marsden, "The Quest for the Historical Edwards: The Challenge of Biography," in David W. Kling and Douglas A. Sweeney, eds., *Jonathan Edwards at Home and Abroad: Historical Memories, Cultural Movements, Global Horizons* (Columbia: University of South Carolina Press, 2003), 7–8.

15. George M. Marsden, *Jonathan Edwards: A Life* (New Haven, CT: Yale University Press, 2003), 5.

16. Stein, "Editor's Introduction," in *The "Blank Bible,"* 1; and Jonathan Edwards, *Notes on Scripture,* ed. Stephen J. Stein, vol. 15 of *WJE* (1998), 610–613. While the last "Notes on Scripture" entry is Entry No. 507, there are a few gaps in the numbering, as well as some doubling. The gaps include nos. 114, 180–187, 245, 371–376, and the doubled entries include nos. 95, 138, 250, and 501, yielding a total of 495 entries. See Stephen J. Stein, "Editor's Introduction," in Jonathan Edwards, *Notes on Scripture,* ed. Stephen J. Stein, vol. 15 of *WJE* (1998), 36.

Bible was so "habitual that it gets obscured in accounts of more unique events and works that frame the narrative from day to day and year to year." Yet it was "constantly present," and one must not ignore "the paramount importance of Scripture for everything else in his thought."[17]

To peer into Edwards' "habitual" world of engaging the Bible, we will probe his interpretation and use of the book of Psalms—one of the most loved books of the Bible through the centuries. An exploration of Edwards on the Psalms reveals that the history of redemption gave structure to his theology and provided a framework for interpreting the Psalms. In fact, at the end of his life, in the same letter to the Trustees of the College of New Jersey mentioned above, Edwards described the other "great work" he hoped to write:

> A History of the Work of Redemption, a body of divinity in an entire new method, being thrown into the form of an history, considering the affair of Christian theology, as the whole of it, in each part, stands in reference to the great work of redemption by Jesus Christ; which I suppose is to be the grand design of all God's designs, and the *summum* and *ultimum* of all the divine operations and degrees.[18]

Edwards understood this history to envelop eternity past, God's work in human history through "successive dispensations," the great "affair of redemption," the church, and eternity future, including judgment for the reprobate and eternal bliss for the elect. He believed this "method" would be "the most beautiful and entertaining" way to show "the admirable contexture and harmony of the whole."[19]

His vision for this work had begun earlier in the "History of the Work of Redemption" sermon series he preached in 1739, and indeed, as we will see, he returned to these redemptive-historical themes throughout his life.[20] For Edwards, the history of redemption gave form to theology and a framework for reading Scripture, and thus I have organized this book by key theological themes in redemptive history because those themes rise to the surface when reading Edwards' engagement with the Psalms. Thus I suggest in this book

17. Marsden, *Jonathan Edwards: A Life*, 473.

18. Edwards to Trustees of the College of New Jersey, 727–728.

19. Edwards to Trustees of the College of New Jersey, 728.

20. See Jonathan Edwards, *A History of the Work of Redemption*, ed. John F. Wilson, vol. 9 of *WJE* (1989).

that the history of redemption provided the boundaries within which Edwards interpreted the Psalms.

The Central Place of the Psalms in Edwards' Life, Writings, and Culture

So why the focus on the Psalms?[21] As has been discussed above, no extensive work has been done on Edwards' engagement with the Psalms. Yet this book has historically played a constructive role in the development of theology and the rhythm of church life.[22] It has been a prominent book of the Bible for Christians throughout the history of the church, in part because of the Psalms' universal appeal to life experience but also because the earliest Christians— and Christians ever since—appropriated them for a Christian reading of the Old Testament.[23] Furthermore, for centuries the Psalter served as the song-book of the church, constituting perhaps the most well-known portion of Scripture for many people, especially the illiterate, and it has thus shaped the spiritual lives of countless Christians—not least of all the eighteenth-century New England Congregationalists.

More important for our immediate purposes, Edwards himself found the Psalms to be rich with theological depth and spiritual enrichment, and he used this book extensively and substantively in his writings and ministry. In fact, Edwards cited the Psalms more than any other book of the Bible in the twenty-six volumes of the Yale *Works of Jonathan Edwards*, which consti-tutes the best representative and searchable sample of Edwards' corpus. He cited the Psalms 4,204 times in these twenty-six volumes, and after that he

---

21. The material in this section has been adapted from my article, "Making the Psalter One's 'Own Language': Jonathan Edwards Engages the Psalms," *Jonathan Edwards Studies* 2, no. 1 (2012): 3–29. Used with permission from *Jonathan Edwards Studies*.

22. Quentin F. Wesselschmidt, ed., *Ancient Christian Commentary on Scripture: Old Testament: Psalms 51–150*, vol. VIII (Downers Grove, IL: InterVarsity, 2007), viii–xxii. Scholars have recently appeared increasingly interested in the Psalms' place in church his-tory: G. Sujin Pak and Herman J. Selderhuis independently examined Calvin on the Psalms; Michael Parsons studied Luther on the Psalms; and Beth Quitsland looked at the Psalter in the English Reformation era. G. Sujin Pak, *Judaizing Calvin: Sixteenth-Century Debates over the Messianic Psalms*, Oxford Studies in Historical Theology (New York: Oxford University Press, 2010); Herman J. Selderhuis, *Calvin's Theology of the Psalms*, Texts and Studies in Reformation and Post-Reformation Thought (Grand Rapids, MI: Baker Academic, 2007); Michael Parsons, *Martin Luther's Interpretation of the Royal Psalms: The Spiritual Kingdom in a Pastoral Context* (Lewiston, NY: Edwin Mellen, 2009); and Beth Quitsland, *The Reformation in Rhyme: Sternhold, Hopkins and the English Metrical Psalter, 1547–1603*, St. Andrews Studies in Reformation History (Aldershot: Ashgate, 2008).

23. Patrick D. Miller, Jr., *Interpreting the Psalms* (Philadelphia, PA: Fortress, 1986), 23.

cited the comparably sized book of Isaiah 3,852 times. His frequent use of the Psalms is due in part to its size as the largest book of the Bible, but the size of the Psalter cannot fully explain this pattern because Edwards cited the comparably large book of Jeremiah in the twenty-six volumes less than a third as often (1,183 times).[24] In fact, much about the book of Psalms resonated with Edwards, and he came back to it again and again.

---

24. I determined these figures using the "Scripture Lookup" search feature on *The Works of Jonathan Edwards Online* (hereafter, *WJEO*). This searching method, however, mixes much extraneous data in the results when searching for only a single book of the Bible without chapter and verse. I have thus eliminated from the results references to editorial introductions, footnotes, and notes within the volume; other references that did not come from Edwards; New Testament references (e.g., references to "psalms" in Eph 5:19 and Col 3:16); personal names (e.g., "John," "Isaiah," "Jeremiah"); references to works (e.g., a commentary on Isaiah); references to the same words not referring to the biblical book (e.g., "divine revelation"); and duplicate entries in the results list caused by the search feature's anomalies. I have also added a minimal number of occurrences missed in the search that I observed in my analysis. I have weeded out extraneous references only for the Psalms, the three books that represented a potentially higher number of references than the Psalms (Isaiah, the Gospel of John, and Revelation), and Jeremiah, a comparably large book that provides perspective on Edwards' citation of the Psalms. This analysis produced the following total references: Psalms, 4,204; Isaiah, 3,852; Gospel of John, 2,203; Revelation, 2,728; and Jeremiah, 1,183. To give one example of how the numbers on the "Scripture Lookup" feature can be misleading, a search on "John" totaled 7,924 hits in volumes 1–26 prior to eliminating extraneous material, a number inflated largely because the "Scripture Lookup" search feature captured the many personal names of "John" (e.g., John Stoddard, John Cotton, etc.). The Jonathan Edwards Center at Yale University, "WJE Online," http://edwards.yale.edu/ archive (accessed April 4, 2011).

The twenty-six printed volumes in the *WJE* as contained online represent the best sample of Edwards' works for comparative search capability for a number of reasons. First, they present a wide swath of material from every genre of Edwards' corpus, not to mention the segment deemed most worthy by the *WJE* project to commit to print. More important, these volumes have been largely standardized in their search capability online and thus are the best comparable set of Edwards' works at this time for searching purposes. Nearly each reference to a chapter or verse has been connected to the full name of the book of the Bible associated with it, even if Edwards did not state the full name himself (e.g., using abbreviations like "Ps." or mentioning a verse that referred back to a biblical book he mentioned a paragraph earlier). The editors of these volumes have also captured references when Edwards made no citation himself. The same cannot be said of the unprinted online volumes. Volumes 27–73 of the *WJEO* have not yet been fully standardized for searching for references to Scripture, meaning that more Scripture references get missed and making it difficult to speak with confidence about capturing comparable results for books of the Bible. With the limits of the search capabilities of the *WJEO*, searching volumes 1–26 produces the best current sample for comparing Edwards' use of various books of the Bible in his corpus.

These data suggest that Edwards gravitated to the Psalms often as he spent time in the Scriptures but not that it was his favorite book out of every book in the Bible. Edwards loved the Bible as a whole. Yet it is worthwhile to observe his clear interest in the Psalms suggested by these searching statistics. Furthermore, these statistics are not the only evidence of the Psalter's significance for Edwards, but they do indicate his ongoing interest in the Psalms.

Edwards gave the Psalms a prominent place in his Bible study. Not only did he grapple with the Psalter itself, but he also frequently turned to the Psalms to shed light on the other books of the Bible, employing the analogy of Scripture—interpreting Scripture with Scripture—as a key method of interpretation. Edwards devoted 388 entries to the Psalms in his "Blank Bible" manuscript, more than any other book, and more than twice as many as the comparably long books of Jeremiah (151 entries) and Ezekiel (132 entries).[25] While Edwards devoted only twenty-one entries to the Psalms in "Notes on Scripture"—far less than the eighty-eight entries on Genesis—he often cited the Psalms throughout the notebook, and looking at the total number of references to each book of the Bible in "Notes on Scripture" reveals that he cited the Psalms 558 times, more than any other book, including Isaiah, the second-most cited book (372 references), and Genesis, the third-most cited book (331 references).[26] The Psalms saturated his thinking, so that even when not his primary focus, they influenced his engagement with the rest of Scripture.[27]

Edwards worked from his voluminous notes on the Bible to develop his sermons, and he preached frequently on the Psalms—though none of his Psalms sermons were published in his lifetime.[28] His extant sermon corpus

---

The rest of this book offers further substantive evidence for the Psalms' significance in his thought.

25. Stein, "Editor's Introduction," in The "Blank Bible," 22. In comparison, after the book of Psalms, Edwards devoted 352 entries to Genesis, 336 to Isaiah, 293 to Job, 261 to Matthew, and less than 220 to the rest. It should be noted that the "Blank Bible" entries range in length from a three-word reference to several pages, so the total number of entries does not immediately indicate the amount of time and space he devoted to each book, though it does indicate to some degree the frequency with which he visited each book, and it is clear that he frequented the Psalms.

26. I calculated these figures using the search feature on the Jonathan Edwards Center website (http://edwards.yale.edu/archive; accessed March 23, 2011). Starting with the total number of references to each book in Notes on Scripture in the search results, I subtracted non-Edwards references occurring in the "Editor's Introduction" (pp. 1–46), in the editorial footnotes throughout the volume, and in duplicated hits in the search results that were caused by the Jonathan Edwards Center website's search engine anomalies. None of the remaining books' totals before removing such non-Edwards references were above 280 references.

27. In his "Catalogue" of reading, Edwards also demonstrated an interest in the Psalter, listing the Psalms amidst a number of biblical books, entries 106–126, that comprise, as Thuesen describes, "apparently a list…of biblical books to which he intended to devote special study" (Jonathan Edwards, "'Catalogue' of Reading," in Catalogues of Books, ed. Peter J. Thuesen, vol. 26 of WJE [2008], 140–141).

28. Edwards likely did not publish his Psalms sermons for the same reason that he did not publish the vast majority of his sermons: They constituted the core of his pastoral

of over twelve hundred sermons shows that he preached more sermons on the Psalms than any other book except the Gospel of Matthew. The top five books on which he preached most were Matthew (139), Psalms (108, including four sermons that are no longer extant), Luke (103), Isaiah (78), and Proverbs (59).[29] As elsewhere, Edwards continued to spring from text to text throughout the biblical canon in his development of the sermon doctrine, so the Psalms sprinkle his entire sermon corpus. These statistics collectively suggest that the Psalms saturated Edwards' writings and sermons; the remainder of this book will demonstrate Edwards' substantive use of the Psalms in his theological reflection and public ministry.

The frequency of the Psalms in Edwards' corpus as described above can be explained in part by the Psalter's size as the longest book of the Bible. Still, Edwards did not have to go to the Psalms as frequently as he did. All this to say that, while statistics do not paint the whole picture, they do demonstrate to a degree that Edwards had a special affinity for the Psalms. Taken alone, they are less meaningful, but when viewed in concert with the other substantive evidences of the Psalms' place in Edwards' corpus presented in this book, they support the significance of the Psalter for Edwards' life and thought.

The Psalms also constituted a central text in New England and in the lives of his people. In his *Faithful Narrative* of the 1734–1735 Northampton

ministry, not his publishing ministry. His Psalms sermons never saw the light of publication not because they were peculiar but because they were normative in his preaching ministry.

29. These figures were determined using The Jonathan Edwards Center at Yale University, "A Chronological List of Jonathan Edwards's Sermons and Discourses," 2007. Wilson Kimnach differs slightly for unclear reasons, perhaps because he is counting sermons that Edwards repreached, while I am not, or perhaps because he was working from an earlier, less complete list. While he claims that Edwards' "favorite sermon texts" in descending order were Matthew, Luke, Isaiah, Psalms, John, 1 Corinthians, Proverbs, and Romans, my research places the Psalms after Matthew and before Luke and Isaiah. See Wilson H. Kimnach, "General Introduction to the Sermons: Jonathan Edwards' Art of Prophesying," in Jonathan Edwards, *Sermons and Discourses 1720–1723*, vol. 10 of *WJE* (1992), 132. Also, Edwards preached at least four nonextant sermons on the following texts: Ps 94:6–10, in which Edwards "proved" the "Moral government of God over mankind"; Ps 2:11, cited in "Miscellanies" Entry No. 468, "Work of Humiliation"; Ps 90:11, mentioned in the "Blank Bible"; and Ps 18:25, preached at Sutton on February 1, 1742, as mentioned in Ebenezer Parkman's diary, which was extracted in Joseph Tracy's account of the Great Awakening. Jonathan Edwards, "Table to the 'Miscellanies,'" in The *"Miscellanies": Entry Nos. a–z, aa–zz, 1–500*, ed. Thomas A. Schafer, vol. 13 of *WJE* (1994), 141; Jonathan Edwards, The *"Miscellanies": Entry Nos. a–z, aa–zz, 1–500*, ed. Thomas A. Schafer, vol. 13 of *WJE* (1994), 510; Jonathan Edwards, The *"Blank Bible,"* ed. Stephen J. Stein, vol. 24 of *WJE* (2006), 520; Joseph Tracy, *The Great Awakening: A History of the Revival of Religion in the Time of Edwards and Whitefield* (Boston: Charles Tappan, 1845), 204.

awakening, Edwards described his congregants' scriptural reading habits and noted, "there was no book so delighted in as the Bible; especially the Book of Psalms, the Prophecy of Isaiah, and the New Testament."[30] In fact, the Psalter was the central book of worship at the Northampton congregation where Edwards preached, a practice his people adopted from their Puritan ancestors, making the Psalms a part of the very language of the people. Based on the New Testament precedent, Edwards held that the book of Psalms should be appropriated "as the language of Christ and the Christian church," for indeed it "was made use of in the public worship in Christian assemblies, from the beginning of the Christian church."[31]

The Psalms, no doubt, took on a life of their own among the laypeople, but while we have little knowledge of how the average layperson in Northampton used the Psalms in daily life, we can see more broadly that beginning in the mid-seventeenth century New Englanders commonly incorporated the Psalms into their lives. One place they used the Psalms was in conversion narratives, public accounts of one's journey to salvation that were sometimes required for full church membership.[32] As Patricia Caldwell notes, these narratives were inundated with quotations from and allusions to Scripture—even more so than their English Puritan counterparts. By making brief allusions to various biblical passages, they could "evoke a great range of scriptural meaning with only a few key words" through what Caldwell calls "the creative internalization of Scripture."[33] And these narrators employed the Psalms—along with the rest of the Bible—to explain their spiritual journey in terms that resonated with the language of Scripture, expressing their fear of God, shame for sin, hope of divine mercy, and comfort of assurances.

The Psalms show up often in relations given in Thomas Shepard's church that he recorded in his notebook. The narrators most often cited the Psalms to show how they gave them comfort. So when William Andrews came to a point where he believed he "could find no comfort," he found "much joy" in Ps

---

30. Jonathan Edwards, *A Faithful Narrative*, in *The Great Awakening*, ed. C. C. Goen, vol. 4 of *WJE* (1972), 184.

31. Jonathan Edwards, "Miscellanies" Entry No. 874, in *The "Miscellanies": Entry Nos. 833–1152*, ed. Amy Plantinga Pauw, vol. 20 of *WJE* (2002), 116. On the historic use of the Psalms in Puritan churches, see chapter 1, especially pp. 55–58, 66–71, and Horton Davies, *The Worship of the American Puritans, 1629–1730* (New York: Peter Lang, 1990), 43–44, 115–129.

32. For more on conversion narratives, see Patricia Caldwell, *The Puritan Conversion Narrative: The Beginnings of American Expression* (New York: Cambridge University Press, 1983); and Sarah Rivett, *The Science of the Soul in Colonial New England*, Omohundro Institute of Early American History and Culture (Chapel Hill: University of North Carolina Press, 2011).

33. Caldwell, *The Puritan Conversion Narrative*, 7, 29–31. Quotations on 29, 31.

16:6, "The lines are fallen unto me in pleasant places."[34] Likewise, Golding Moore "found the Lord drawing and endearing my heart to Himself, and thought there might be mercy for me," when he heard Ps 34:8, "O taste and see that the LORD is good."[35] And Jane Palfrey, when overwhelmed by her sin, was "encouraged…to go" to the Lord by Ps 25:11, "pardon mine iniquity; for it is great."[36] Later when she suffered from doubts, she was "encouraged" by the phrase in Ps 42:5 and 11, "hope thou in God."[37] The Psalms provided comforting language that sustained the faith of early American Puritans.[38]

The practice of delivering public conversion narratives continued into the early eighteenth century, and relations from the church of Timothy Edwards, Jonathan's father, show that converts used the Psalms to express various aspects of their faith journey, from regret over sin to delight in God's love. On the one hand, Esther Bissell, who related her conversion on July 24, 1700, described her prayer for "a sight of my heart" to "see and know myself" and my sinfulness, as she reflected on Ps 125:5, "As for such as turn aside unto their crooked ways, the LORD shall lead them forth with the workers of iniquity."[39] On the other hand,

---

34. Quoted in George Selement and Bruce C. Woolley, eds., *Thomas Shepard's Confessions*, vol. 58 of Publications of the Colonial Society of Massachusetts Collections (Boston: Colonial Society of Massachusetts, 1981), 113.

35. Quoted in Selement and Woolley, 122–123.

36. Quoted in Selement and Woolley, 151.

37. Quoted in Selement and Woolley, 152.

38. The Psalms constituted 15 percent of the Old Testament citations in Thomas Shepard's manuscript of his parishioners' public confessions (thirty-three of 226 occurrences), with only Isaiah being cited more frequently (31 percent, or sixty-nine of 226 occurrences). The New Testament appeared more frequently than the Old in narratives, a total of 318 times, with by far the heaviest reliance on the four Gospels (58 percent, or 184 occurrences). The Psalms constituted 6 percent of all biblical citations. Selement and Woolley, 213.

For more conversion narratives from Thomas Shepard's church that engaged the Psalms, see the narratives of Joanna Sill (Ps 139:1, 7); John Stedman (Ps 92:12); John Stansby (Pss 36:9; 64:7); Barbary Cutter (Pss 45:2; 140:7; 124:7); William Manning (Ps 50:15); Katherine (Pss 41:11; 16:5; 73:26; 119:57; 142:5); John Trumbull (Pss 8:1; 113:4); brother Jackson's maid (Ps 110:3); Joan Moore (Ps 130:1); Jane Wilkinson Winship (Ps 147:2); Henry Dunster (Psalm 40); Goodman Shepard (Pss 119:93; 81:10); John Fessenden (Ps 147:3); Widow Ann Errington (Pss 38:2; 45:5); Sir Jones (Ps 90:8); and an anonymous confessor (Ps 35:6). Quoted in Selement and Woolley, 50, 74, 87, 90–92, 97, 100–101; 107; 120; 135; 148; 161–163; 173–174; 177; 184; 199; 206. See also the relations of Goodwife Stevenson (Ps 90:8); John Shepard (Pss 38:4; 119:6; 90:8); and Mistress Gookin (Pss 18:25–26; 50:22; 51:9). Quoted in Mary Rhinelander McCarl, "Thomas Shepard's Record of Relations of Religious Experience, 1648–1649," *William and Mary Quarterly*, third series, 48, no. 3 (July 1991): 443, 445, 458, 463–465.

39. Quoted in Kenneth P. Minkema, "The East Windsor Conversion Relations, 1700–1725," *Connecticut Historical Society Bulletin* 51 (Winter 1986): 25.

in Ann Fitch's March 1700/1701 relation, she appropriated the language of the Psalms to express her communion with God. One night she could not sleep because she was captivated by "sweet" thoughts of "the wonderful love of Christ to sinners," and she thought that even if she fell asleep, she could "say with David" the words of Ps 139:18, "when I awake, I am still with thee."[40]

The Psalms also appeared in lay life in the prayer bids copied on scattered pages throughout Edwards' corpus, though these allusions are less clear than in the conversion narratives.[41] Within the prayer bids, several people spoke about the prayers of the "congregation" or that God will be praised in the "congregation," which could be a reference to several psalms that speak of the "congregation" (see, e.g., Pss 22:22, 25; 35:18; 40:9–10; 68:26; 107:32). This language reflects, on one level, the communal sense of supporting each other in prayer through affliction and, on another level, the psalmist's aim to relate God's deliverance publicly in the assembly of the faithful: "The widow Southwell Being sick of feavour desires the Prayers of ye Congregation"; "Increase Clark and his Wife desire the Prayers of the Congregation that god would Sanctify his Holy afflicting hand to them and theirs in taking away their daughter Rachel by Death that they may honour god under this Sore triel and improve it to their own Spirituel advantage"; "Dina Cors desiers that thanks may be given to god in this Congregation for his goodness to her in Preserving of her Life when grately Exposed By falling in to a River"; and "Ebennezar Sheldon of falltown and his Wife desires that thanks mite be Given to God in this Congregation for his wonderfullly preservating of them."[42]

---

40. Quoted in Kenneth P. Minkema, "The East Windsor Conversion Relations, 1700–1725," *Connecticut Historical Society Bulletin* 51 (Winter 1986): 41. For other testimonies from Timothy Edwards' church engaging the Psalms in similar ways, see Joshua Willis Junior's December 24, 1700, relation (Ps 42:1); Josiah Loomis' February 27, 1700/1701, narrative (Pss 139:7; 119:59); Daniel Skinner's late 1700 relation (Ps 130:7); Mary Elsworth's July 1725 relation (Ps 37:4); and Abigail Strong's September 14, 1725, narrative (Ps 127:1). Quoted in Minkema, "The East Windsor Conversion Relations," 31, 37–39; 46; 52–53; 56. See also the narratives of Martha Gowing and Abigail Gowing, who both quoted Ps 55:22, "Cast thy burden upon the LORD, and he shall sustain thee," as giving encouragement in coming to Christ, in Kenneth P. Minkema, "The Lynn End 'Earthquake' Relations of 1727," *New England Quarterly* 69, no. 3 (September 1996): 496, 498. And see Samuel Belcher's use of Ps 107:8 to express religious joys in his 1740 relation in Timothy Edwards' church in Kenneth P. Minkema, "A Great Awakening Conversion: The Relation of Samuel Belcher," *William and Mary Quarterly* 44, no. 1 (January 1987): 126.

41. For more on prayer bids, see Stephen J. Stein, "'For Their Spiritual Good': The Northampton, Massachusetts, Prayer Bids of the 1730s and 1740s," *William and Mary Quarterly*, third series, 37, no. 2 (April 1980): 261–285.

42. Jonathan Edwards, "The Day of Judgment" (Acts 17:31), in *Sermons and Discourses 1723–1729*, ed. Kenneth P. Minkema, vol. 14 of *WJE* (1997), 508; Jonathan Edwards, "433. Sermon on 2 Cor 9:15 (May 1737)," in *Sermons, Series II, 1737*, vol. 52 of *WJEO*, L. 1r.; Jonathan

Ephraim Marbl, a newcomer to the Northampton region, offers another example of applying the Psalms to his own life. He requested prayer because "almighty god in his holy & wise providence hath *Layd his hand heavy uppon me* not onely in multiplyd Deaths in my famely and Bodyly indispositions in my Self but also in outher Temporall Loses," including the loss of his house, furniture, looms, tackling, and store of Indian corn and grain.[43] This language reflects Ps 32:4, "For day and night thy hand was heavy upon me." Here we see how New Englanders appropriated the emotional language of the Psalms to express their own pain. Similarly, Sarah Osborn (1714–1796), a younger contemporary of Edwards, also exhibited a spiritual connection and personal interest in the Psalms, connecting her story and struggles with the language of the Psalter.[44] These various descriptions in conversion narratives and prayer bids remind us that Edwards lived in a culture that regularly applied the Psalms to one's personal life to shape one's theological conception of him or herself and the surrounding world.

Edwards encouraged that personal appropriation of the Psalms in daily life. As one example, he singled out the Psalter as a useful text in teaching children to read. While in Stockbridge, Edwards wrote to Sir William Pepperrell (November 28, 1751) to promote his belief that the best method of educating children was to use the Socratic method, rather than a rote method, so children would understand the meaning of what they read. In his discussion of children's early reading, he mentioned that after a child "begins to read in a Psalter, Testament or Bible, not only the words and phrases should be explained, but the things which the lesson treats of should be, in a familiar

---

Edwards, "Mary's Remarkable Act" (Mark 14:3), in *Sermons and Discourses 1739–1742*, ed. Harry S. Stout and Nathan O. Hatch with Kyle P. Farley, vol. 22 of *WJE* (2003), 384; Jonathan Edwards, "The Suitableness of Union in Extraordinary Prayer for the Advancement of God's Church" (Zech 8:20–22), in *Sermons and Discourses, 1743–1758*, ed. Wilson H. Kimnach, vol. 25 of *WJE* (2006), 204. See these quotations as well in Stein, "'For Their Spiritual Good,'" 271, 276, 273, 281. The idea that public testimony had a basis in the Psalms is found in the 1640 narrative of Henry Dunster, who served as president of Harvard College and explained in his own narrative the basis of giving public relations from Ps 40:10, "I have not hid thy righteousness within my heart; I have declared thy faithfulness and thy salvation: I have not concealed thy lovingkindness and thy truth from the great congregation." Quoted in Selement and Woolley, 161–163.

43. Jonathan Edwards, "Hebrew Idioms," Jonathan Edwards Collection, Beinecke Rare Book and Manuscript Library, Yale University, New Haven, CT, 6; available in Stein, "'For Their Spiritual Good,'" 280.

44. Catherine A. Brekus, *Sarah Osborn's World: The Rise of Evangelical Christianity in Early America*, New Directions in Narrative History (New Haven, CT: Yale University Press, 2013), 35, 88, 139, 151, 154.

manner, opened to the child's understanding."[45] Asking the child questions and giving the child an opportunity to talk through the issue would help him or her internalize the subject of the book. And if a child would internalize the content, such material ought to have good spiritual substance, as did the Psalms, which Edwards recommended as one of the first books a child should read.

Indeed, Edwards displayed a particular interest in the Psalms that his culture shared, and his use and interpretation of the Psalms deserves scholarly attention in understanding his biblicism—and by "biblicism," I mean his interest in and devotion to the Bible. Studying what Edwards said about the Psalms is valuable not only to correct our distorted image of the man and to give his biblical interpretation and manuscripts due attention but also because "America's theologian" had much to say about the book of Psalms.[46] Edwards made the sweetness of the Psalms his "own language," and this study probes what was in the Psalms that appeared so "excellent" and "sweet" to this learned New England divine.[47]

Historiographical Treatment of Edwards and the Bible

While no book or article has been published on Edwards and the Psalms, his reputation as a biblical interpreter in general has received attention, though scarcely to the degree it deserves.[48] In the decades after Edwards' death, the New Divinity theologians—as derisive opponents called his followers—promoted his thought to succeeding generations of Americans. His student Samuel Hopkins (1721–1803) and great-grandson Sereno E. Dwight (1786–1850) secured Edwards' status as an accomplished exegete. Hopkins wrote the first biography of Edwards, whom he described as "one of the greatest of divines,"

---

45. Jonathan Edwards to Sir William Pepperrell, November 28, 1751, in *Letters and Personal Writings*, ed. George S. Claghorn, vol. 16 of *WJE* (1998), 408.

46. On the label "America's theologian," see Robert W. Jenson, *America's Theologian: A Recommendation of Jonathan Edwards* (New York: Oxford University Press, 1988); Gerald R. McDermott, ed., *Understanding Jonathan Edwards: An Introduction to America's Theologian* (Oxford: Oxford University Press, 2009). Similarly, Avihu Zakai calls Edwards "the American Augustine." Avihu Zakai, *Jonathan Edwards' Philosophy of History: The Reenchantment of the World in the Age of Enlightenment* (Princeton, NJ: Princeton University Press, 2003), 1.

47. Edwards, "Personal Narrative," 798.

48. For a helpful summary of the state of the conversation about Edwards' biblicism, see Sweeney, "The Biblical World of Jonathan Edwards," 211–220.

and he attributed that greatness in large part to his dedication to and proficiency in biblical study: "he studied the Bible more than all other Books, and more than most other Divines do. His uncommon acquaintance with the Bible appears in his Sermons, and in most of his Publications: and his great pains in studying it are manifest in his Manuscript Notes upon it.... He took his religious Principles from the Bible, and not from any human System or Body of Divinity."[49] Dwight was the first to publish Edwards' "Notes on Scripture," though only in a partial, selective, and heavily edited form. He lauded Edwards' "regular and diligent study of the Sacred Scriptures" and observed his "highest veneration" for the Bible and his resolution to "possess himself, in every part of it which he read, of the true meaning of its Author."[50] Together, Hopkins and Dwight established Edwards' exegetical reputation, which largely remained "uncontested throughout the nineteenth century."[51] Edwards' facility with the Scriptures and reputation as a luminous exegete were in many ways simply assumed, not critically discussed either positively or negatively.[52]

Not until the mid-twentieth century did scholars again show a significant interest in Edwards and the Bible.[53] Some have focused on Edwards' belief in the truth and authority of Scripture.[54] Others have performed closer case

---

49. Samuel Hopkins, *The Life and Character of the Late Reverend Mr. Jonathan Edwards, President of the College of New-Jersey* (Boston: S. Kneeland, 1765), iii, 40–41. Kimnach comments on Hopkins' remark, noting, "[a]s usual, the precise and veracious Samuel Hopkins is closer to the truth than many more pretentious students of Edwards. . . the aptitude and penetration displayed in his use of scriptural passages are truly extraordinary. Any consideration of Edwards' literary qualities must give priority to his use of the Scripture." Kimnach, "Jonathan Edwards' Art of Prophesying," 207.

50. Sereno E. Dwight, ed., *The Works of President Edwards: With a Memoir of His Life*, vol. 1 (New York: S. Converse, 1829–1830), 57.

51. Stein, "Editor's Introduction," in *Notes on Scripture*, 31.

52. For example, the only nineteenth-century entry on Edwards' biblicism that Max Lesser lists in his bibliography of writings on Edwards is George B. Cheever's 1852 short review of Tryon Edwards' study of Jonathan Edwards' manuscripts. Cheever described several of Edwards' unpublished manuscripts on the Bible and noted Edwards' "indefatigable industry and thoroughness in the study of the Scriptures" and "his entire submission of all things to their authority." But mostly he discussed Edwards' theological and metaphysical writings. George B. Cheever, "The Manuscripts of President Edwards," *Independent* 4 (1852): 208; Lesser, *Reading Jonathan Edwards*, 87, 676.

53. Lesser's next entry on Edwards' "biblicism" after Cheever does not appear until 1949 with an article by Edwin Cady. That piece, however, dealt only with Edwards' biblical allusion as a subsidiary issue. Edwin H. Cady, "The Artistry of Jonathan Edwards," *New England Quarterly* 22 (1949): 61–72; Lesser, 191, 676.

54. For example, Ralph G. Turnbull, "Jonathan Edwards—Bible Interpreter," *Interpretation* 6 (1952): 422; John H. Gerstner, "The Church's Doctrine of Biblical Inspiration," in *The*

studies of his interpretation of the Bible, such as Stein's treatments of the book of Proverbs and the epistle of James; Glenn Kreider's study of Rev 4:1–8:1; William Tooman's treatment of Ezekiel chapters 1, 4–5, and 38–39; Jeongmo Yoo's analysis of Isaiah, Jeremiah, and Ezekiel; and Andrew Abernethy's case study of Isaiah 40–55.[55] But most scholars have centered not on the micro-level of unearthing the close details in Edwards' extensive manuscript and sermon material but on the macro-level of correcting the lopsided construction of an Edwards devoid of his biblicism.[56]

Stephen Stein has done the most to advocate that Edwards can only be understood through his constant engagement with the Bible. Stein provides lengthy, informative introductions for three volumes in the Yale edition of *The Works of Jonathan Edwards*, discussing Edwards' three most significant personal manuscripts on the Bible: "Notes on the Apocalypse," "Notes on Scripture," and the "Blank Bible."[57] In them Stein describes Edwards' biblical

Foundation of Biblical Authority, ed. James Montgomery Boice (Grand Rapids, MI: Zondervan, 1978), 23–58; John H. Gerstner, "Jonathan Edwards and the Bible," *Tenth* 9 (1971): 1–71; John H. Gerstner, "The View of the Bible Held by the Church: Calvin and the Westminster Divines," in *Inerrancy*, ed. Norman L. Geisler (Grand Rapids, MI: Zondervan, 1980), 383–410.

55. Stephen J. Stein, "'Like Apples of Gold in Pictures of Silver': The Portrait of Wisdom in Jonathan Edwards's Commentary on the Book of Proverbs," *Church History* 54 (1985): 324–337; Stephen J. Stein, "Cotton Mather and Jonathan Edwards on the Epistle of James: A Comparative Study," in *Cotton Mather and Biblia Americana—America's First Bible Commentary: Essays in Reappraisal*, ed. Reiner Smolinski and Jan Stievermann (Tübingen: Mohr Siebeck, 2010), 363–382; and Glenn R. Kreider, *Jonathan Edwards's Interpretation of Revelation 4:1–8:1* (Dallas, TX: University Press of America, Inc., 2004); William A. Tooman, "Edwards's Ezekiel: The Interpretation of Ezekiel in the *Blank Bible* and *Notes on Scripture*," *Journal of Theological Interpretation* 3, no. 1 (Spring 2009): 17–38; Jeongmo Yoo, "Jonathan Edwards's Interpretation of the Major Prophets: The Books of Isaiah, Jeremiah, and Ezekiel," *Puritan Reformed Journal* 3, no. 2 (2011): 160–192; Andrew T. Abernethy, "Jonathan Edwards as Multi-Dimension[al] Bible Interpreter: A Case Study from Isaiah 40–55," *Journal of the Evangelical Theological Society* 56, no. 4 (December 2013): 815–830.

56. See, e.g., Conrad Cherry, who briefly argues that "Jonathan Edwards was preeminently a biblical theologian" and that it is "precisely because of his commitment to biblical exegesis" that Edwards "contributed to the emergence of modern thought"; Karin Spiecker Stetina, who argues that "it's time for scholars to turn their attention back to the influence that Scripture and faith had on Jonathan Edwards" but does not delve deeply into his exegesis of Scripture; and the other scholars discussed below. Conrad Cherry, "*Symbols of Spiritual Truth*: Jonathan Edwards as Biblical Interpreter," *Interpretation* 39, no. 3 (1985): 263, 264; Karen Spiecker Stetina, *Jonathan Edwards' Early Understanding of Religious Experience: His New York Sermons, 1720–1723* (Lewiston, NY: Edwin Mellen, 2011), ix.

57. Stephen J. Stein, "Editor's Introduction," in Jonathan Edwards, *Apocalyptic Writings*, ed. Stephen J. Stein, vol. 5 of *WJE* (1977), 1–93; Stein, "Editor's Introduction," in *Notes on Scripture*; and Stein, "Editor's Introduction," in *The "Blank Bible."*

interpretive method, his sources, and the history and function of the manuscripts. He sets Edwards in the Protestant commentarial tradition and highlights his foundational use of typology.[58] Even with his overviews, Stein contends that Edwards' biblical manuscripts demand much closer study. In a statement that can be applied to Edwards' other manuscripts, Stein succinctly describes the value of "Notes on Scripture" to understanding Edwards' intellect and theology: "Without this biblical element the writings of Jonathan Edwards make little sense."[59] Elsewhere Stein challenges other scholars: "His biblical reflections—located in notebooks and commentaries, sermons and treatises—beg for closer examination than they have received to date. Much research remains to be done."[60]

Douglas Sweeney has furthered the conversation by describing Edwards' unfailing commitment to the Bible as the highest authority. Edwards himself "maintained an exceptionally high view of the Bible's inspiration," and while he believed much could be gained from the "book of nature" and from reason, still the Bible held priority and illuminated the human world.[61] Sweeney points out that Edwards' "most significant contribution to the history of exegesis" was his typological interpretation of Scripture. Yet Edwards was also committed to rooting meaning in the historical context of Scripture, and this commitment to both historicism and "hidden symbols" is what makes Edwards "a

---

58. Stein, "Editor's Introduction," in *Notes on Scripture*, 6, 18.

59. Stein, "Editor's Introduction," in *Notes on Scripture*, 46.

60. Stephen J. Stein, "Edwards as Biblical Exegete," in *The Cambridge Companion to Jonathan Edwards*, ed. Stephen J. Stein (Cambridge: Cambridge University Press, 2007), 193. See also Stein's repetition of these observations in 1977, 1988, and 1998, respectively: "few have taken seriously the place of the Bible in Edwards's thought"; there is "an amazing paucity of serious scholarship dealing with ['his biblical writings']"; and "Previous literature has often failed to reckon sufficiently with the scriptural principle in his thought, despite the widespread presence of biblical language, citations, and discourse throughout his writings." Stein, "Quest," 100; Stephen J. Stein, "The Spirit and the Word: Jonathan Edwards and Scriptural Exegesis," in *Jonathan Edwards and the American Experience*, ed. Nathan O. Hatch and Harry S. Stout (New York: Oxford University Press, 1988), 123; Stein, "Editor's Introduction," in *Notes on Scripture*, 21. On the recent increasing scholarly interest in Edwards' biblicism, see Kenneth P. Minkema, "Jonathan Edwards in the Twentieth Century," *Journal of the Evangelical Theological Society* 47, no. 4 (2004): 675.

61. Douglas A. Sweeney, "'Longing for More and More of It'? The Strange Career of Jonathan Edwards's Exegetical Exertions," in *Jonathan Edwards at 300: Essays on the Tercentenary of His Birth*, ed. Harry S. Stout, Kenneth P. Minkema, and Caleb J. D. Maskell (Lanham, MD: University Press of America, Inc., 2005), 27; Douglas A. Sweeney, "Edwards and the Bible," in *Understanding Jonathan Edwards: An Introduction to America's Theologian*, ed. Gerald R. McDermott (Oxford: Oxford University Press, 2009).

fascinating example of a modern thinker with premodern sympathies."[62] Even so, in Sweeney's assessment, "Three hundred years after Edwards's birth, and half a century into what some have called the Edwards renaissance, few have bothered to study Edwards's extensive exegetical writings," treating Edwards' biblicism as "an embarrassing family secret, one that would damage our reputations if widely known."[63] But Sweeney argues that Edwards' theology rested foundationally on how he interpreted Scripture, which highlights the necessity of studying his exegesis more carefully.[64]

A pioneering book-length treatment of Edwards' biblicism is Robert Brown's *Jonathan Edwards and the Bible*, which explores Edwards' engagement with and response to modern biblical criticism. Brown casts him as "modestly critical," a man of his time who on the one hand sought to uphold "conservative interpretation" but on the other aspired to be "critical," or "judicious," eagerly appropriating the new methods to create "a hybrid traditionalism, one modified in significant ways by his accommodations to the new learning."[65] Brown's description of Edwards as "modestly critical" rightly captures his interest in engaging the latest works on biblical interpretation without jettisoning his unwavering commitment to the supernatural. Nonetheless, Brown devotes little time to Edwards' interpretive methods or actual engagement with the Bible. He laments the lack of study on Edwards' biblical commentary: "Jonathan Edwards' biblical interpretation is the subject most neglected in the study of his writings and intellectual pursuits, and the subject most deserving of attention by scholars and admirers alike."[66] His exegetical writings are key to Edwards because the Bible was foundational in his writings, and "[t]he real measure of his hermeneutic, so richly and complexly delineated in the 'Miscellanies,' 'Notes on Scripture,' 'Blank Bible,' and sermons has yet to be taken."[67]

---

62. Douglas A. Sweeney, "Edwards, Jonathan (1703–1758)" in *Dictionary of Major Biblical Interpreters*, ed. Donald K. McKim (Downers Grove, IL: IVP Academic, 2007), 399.

63. Sweeney, " 'Longing for More,' " 26.

64. To highlight the centrality of Scripture in Edwards' ministry, Sweeney organizes his biography of Edwards around the Bible. Douglas A. Sweeney, *Jonathan Edwards and the Ministry of the Word: A Model of Faith and Thought* (Downers Grove, IL: IVP Academic, 2009). See also his forthcoming *Edwards the Exegete: Biblical Interpretation and Anglo-Protestant Culture on the Edge of the Enlightenment* (New York: Oxford University Press, in press).

65. Robert E. Brown, *Jonathan Edwards and the Bible* (Bloomington: Indiana University Press, 2002), xvii–xix.

66. Robert E. Brown, "The Bible," in *The Princeton Companion to Jonathan Edwards*, ed. Sang Hyun Lee (Princeton, NJ: Princeton University Press, 2005), 87.

67. Brown, *Jonathan Edwards and the Bible*, 199.

In an effort to take Edwards' biblical manuscripts seriously, Glenn Kreider conducted the first book-length research on Edwards' exegesis of a defined segment of Scripture: Rev 4:1–8:1. While others have emphasized Edwards' frequent use of typology, Kreider argues that his reigning method of interpretation is "a particular form of typology," namely "Christological typology."[68] He states, "ultimately what organizes and synthesizes the various types is Christ. It is Christ and his work of redemption on behalf of the church that provide the antitype to the various types, no matter where they are found," whether in Scripture or in history or nature. He also notes the vast need for further attention to Edwards' biblical interpretation, that "his view of Scripture and his hermeneutical method have received little attention," and adds that, "[s]ince the Bible was so important to Edwards, one cannot understand him adequately without dealing with his use of Scripture."[69] He recommends work be done in other genres of Scripture and in Edwards' sermons, which constitute the largest portion of his written corpus—"perhaps 80 percent of what he produced," according to Robert Brown.[70] Kreider's acknowledgement that so much remains to be done, however, raises a hesitancy about adopting his label for Edwards' method of biblical interpretation, "Christological typology." While he makes an arguable case for Rev 4:1–8:1, his thesis requires more extensive assessment for Edwards' interpretation of the rest of Scripture.

Three articles published in recent years have dug into Edwards' interpretation of the major prophets, and they illustrate both positive directions and limitations in current studies of Edwards' exegesis.[71] First, these scholars recognize Edwards' complex, layered approach to Scripture. Tooman observes Edwards' typological emphasis, belief in the harmony of the Bible, and multivalent interpretation of Ezekiel. Yoo also pushes scholars, from his examination of Isaiah, Jeremiah, and Ezekiel, to describe Edwards' interpretive approach in "a more comprehensive way," rejecting labels of literal, allegorical, typological, or Christological.[72] Similarly, in examining Edwards' exegesis of Isaiah 40–55, Abernethy argues that "Edwards recognizes multiple dimensions of meaning with the biblical text," drawing upon those various dimensions depending on

---

68. Kreider, *Edwards's Interpretation of Revelation 4:1–8:1*, 289.

69. Kreider, *Edwards's Interpretation of Revelation 4:1–8:1*, 289, 1, 22.

70. Kreider, *Edwards's Interpretation of Revelation 4:1–8:1*, 22, 290. Brown, "The Bible," 88.

71. See also my article "'The Only Rule of Our Faith and Practice': Jonathan Edwards' Interpretation of the Book of Isaiah as a Case Study of His Exegetical Boundaries," *Journal of the Evangelical Theological Society* 52, no. 4 (2009): 811–829.

72. Yoo, "Edwards's Interpretation of the Major Prophets," 184.

the contexts, such as the study or the pulpit.[73] As I describe Edwards' engagement with the Psalms, we will see his complex approach to interpretation in action. A second question that arises in these treatments of Edwards on the major prophets is his relationship to the Protestant exegetical tradition. Tooman ultimately argues that "in many ways Edwards departed from typical practices in Protestant exegesis," while Yoo claims that "he firmly stands in continuity with Reformation hermeneutical tradition."[74] But neither establishes this point by closely comparing Edwards with the actual exegesis of earlier interpreters—something I seek to do in this book. A third issue is the breadth of Edwards' sources treated. Both Tooman and Yoo constrain themselves to only two of Edwards' manuscripts, the "Blank Bible" and "Notes on Scripture" (no doubt very important ones). But these treatments miss how Edwards treated these passages in other places in his corpus—most significantly, in his sermons, as Abernethy does in his treatment of Isaiah 40–55, but also in treatises and elsewhere. This study examines Edwards' engagement with the whole book of Psalms and includes every type of work in his corpus in an aim to give a fuller understanding of Edwards' exegetical patterns.

Like these scholars who have studied Edwards on the major prophets, Brandon Withrow calls for acknowledging that Edwards "explored [Scripture] on many levels," and he also argues that "the spiritual reading of Scripture found in the writings of ancient Christians...clearly have a kindred spirit in the ideas of Edwards."[75] In Withrow's account, Edwards' thoroughgoing interest in the spiritual senses along with the incarnational emphasis in his theology connects him with the early church exegetes, especially those in the Eastern tradition. While Withrow's goal is not to discuss the Psalms at length, he does use the Psalms to highlight Edwards' fascination with the Christological meaning of the text, arguing that "while showing an appreciation of the poetic nature of Psalms," Edwards was "more interested in reading between the lines and looking for a christological message intended by the Spirit" and that in Edwards' "Blank Bible" and notes on typology, "the Psalms are repeatedly understood within a christological framework."[76] While Withrow makes suggestive arguments concerning Edwards' incarnational

73. Abernethy, "Edwards as Multi-Dimension[al] Bible Interpreter," 817.

74. Tooman, "Edwards's Ezekiel," 19; Yoo, "Edwards's Interpretation of the Major Prophets," 190.

75. Brandon G. Withrow, *Becoming Divine: Jonathan Edwards's Incarnational Spirituality within the Christian Tradition* (Eugene, OR: Cascade, 2011), 174, 204.

76. Withrow, *Becoming Divine*, 177, 185.

theology, his discussion of Edwards on the Psalms underscores the need for a more thorough and complex treatment of Edwards' exegesis in specific books like the Psalms to arrive at more nuanced ways of talking about Edwards' interpretation, as I seek to do in this book.

In their milestone volume on *The Theology of Jonathan Edwards*, Michael McClymond and Gerald McDermott weigh in on Edwards' exegesis, noting, like others, that despite an "enormous trove of biblical reflection" in his corpus, "[c]omparatively little has been done thus far on Edwards's biblical theology."[77] They observe three prominent themes in Edwards' biblical manuscripts: that the Old Testament is "a massive typological system," that the Bible along with all reality expresses "the Trinity's desire to communicate its beauty and being to others," and that "history is a massive story of redemption controlled by Christ and encompassing every atom and moment."[78] Also, similarly to Withrow's connection of Edwards with the ancient Eastern church fathers, their assessment of Edwards' biblical interpretation stresses "his thoroughgoing commitment to spiritual exegesis" that sets him apart from his peers and his "catholic tendency insofar as he embraced the medieval tradition of seeing multiple senses in scripture."[79] These claims demand further assessment, and I seek to provide a lens through which to view these descriptions by comparing Edwards' exegesis with his Reformed exegetical predecessors.

Stephen R. C. Nichols displays the continuing interest in Edwards' biblicism in his study of Edwards' notes for a work he planned to call "The Harmony of the Old and New Testament." In exploring prophecy, typology, and doctrine in Edwards' notes, Nichols argues that Edwards used a unified typological method and that his view of the Bible's harmony militates against Stein's argument that he was unrestrained in his interpretation of the Bible. Rather, Nichols rightly demonstrates that for Edwards the Bible stood as a unified whole because the Messiah, his kingdom, and his redemption draw together the diverse parts in doctrinal harmony—themes that resonate with Edwards' exegesis of the Psalms.[80]

As for Edwards' work on the Psalms, no monograph, journal article, or essay has been devoted to this topic. The most focused research is found in

---

77. Michael J. McClymond and Gerald R. McDermott, *The Theology of Jonathan Edwards* (New York: Oxford University Press, 2012), 717.

78. McClymond and McDermott, *The Theology of Jonathan Edwards*, 34–35.

79. McClymond and McDermott, *The Theology of Jonathan Edwards*, 175, 17.

80. Stephen R. C. Nichols, *Jonathan Edwards's Bible: The Relationship of the Old and New Testaments in the Theology of Jonathan Edwards* (Eugene, OR: Pickwick, 2013).

Stein's "Editor's Introduction" to The "Blank Bible" volume in the Yale edition, where he devotes eight pages to Edwards' approach to "Wisdom Literature" in the "Blank Bible." Stein describes the individual psalms as "multifaceted documents for him, inviting poetic musing, theological observation, and justification for partisan views" and supporting "his Christological interpretive scheme." Edwards' commentary on the Psalms is too complex, Stein observes, to categorize neatly, but he suggests that "a critical center," if there is one, is that "he regarded a great number of them to be prophetic of Christ—either of Christ himself, or of 'Christ mystical,' his body, the church." Stein further argues that this "Christological principle gave Edwards immense hermeneutical latitude in his interpretation of the psalms" and that "[a]t times his judgments appear to move beyond typology to allegory. His pursuit of spiritual meaning in the texts knew no bounds."[81] Stein makes this argument on a more sustained level in an earlier article in which he concludes that "the Bible did not function for him as a theological norm or source in any usual Protestant fashion because the literal sense of the text did not restrict him. On the contrary, the freedom and creative possibilities of the spiritual sense beckoned, and he pursued them with abandon."[82]

Stein's brief evaluation provides a helpful introduction to the topic of Edwards' work in the Psalms but is limited by both its brevity and its engagement with only Edwards' "Blank Bible" manuscript—understandably so, given the aim of his editor's introduction. But this again highlights the dearth of literature on Edwards' interpretation of the Psalms and the need for a fuller exploration of his use of the Psalms in sermons and theological writings. The need for further research also calls for a closer assessment of Stein's description of Edwards' "Christological principle" and his claim that Edwards took "immense hermeneutical latitude" that "knew no bounds" in the Psalms.

Project Aim and Methodology

What scholarship on Edwards and the Bible most needs at this point is detailed work in Edwards' extensive biblical writings to test and tweak the broader claims about Edwards' interpretation and use of the Bible. Only with close studies in Edwards' massive corpus of biblical material will we grasp his approach to the task of biblical interpretation and proclamation. This book focuses on the Psalms as an important portion of Edwards' biblical

---

81. Stein, "Editor's Introduction," in The "Blank Bible," 34–35, 40.

82. Stein, "Quest," 100–101, 113.

commentary, and in the following pages I explicate Edwards' development of theology from the book of Psalms in the context of the history of interpreting, preaching, and worshiping with the Psalms.

Herman Selderhuis, in his study of John Calvin's (1509–1564) theology of the Psalms, structures his work around Calvin's *Commentary on the Book of Psalms*, which gives his study both an easily definable primary source and period of time.[83] In contrast, this project must harvest material from varied sources over the course of Edwards' life because he never collected his writings or sermons on the Psalms in a systematic commentary like Calvin, nor are all of his manuscripts easily datable.[84] Thus to probe Edwards' engagement with the Psalms, I have examined every occurrence of the Psalms in the twenty-six printed volumes of the completed Yale edition of Edwards' *Works* using the Scripture indices in the volumes and the "Scripture Lookup" feature of the Jonathan Edwards Center website.[85] Examining various works and genres of Edwards' writings is necessary for grasping his overarching approach to the Psalms because when he wrote or preached on the Psalms, he did so for the occasion. So some psalms that he discussed at length in one manuscript received little mention in another. I have given particular attention to his biblical notebooks, where much of his commentary on the Psalms is located, because Edwards used them as a breeding ground for theological and sermonic fruit.[86] I also consulted a number of relevant unpublished pieces

---

83. Selderhuis, *Calvin's Theology of the Psalms*.

84. Correlating dates with Edwards' biblical manuscripts would prove impossible, particularly in the "Blank Bible." Stein calls the "Blank Bible" a "chronological puzzle" and describes the overbearing challenge of "[d]ating more than five thousand entries written randomly in the interleaved Bible in scattered fashion over a period of nearly three decades." Stein, "Editor's Introduction," in *The "Blank Bible,"* 104.

85. Except for volumes 2, 3, and 26, these two methods of research produced largely the same results, with minor variations in some volumes. I relied most heavily on the online search feature, which on occasion captured occurrences the printed indices missed. Rarely, I found a stray reference to the Psalms not captured by either method. The printed versions of volumes 2 and 3, *Religious Affections* and *Original Sin*, respectively, are the only two volumes that do not provide a Scripture index, and in volume 26, *Catalogues of Books*, the online search feature proved unreliable, failing to produce page number results that coincided with the printed book form, so I used only the printed volume's Scripture index in that instance.
New Testament quotations of the Psalms lie outside the scope of this project due to the plethora of material available in Edwards' corpus strictly on the book of Psalms proper and because the project seeks to understand Edwards' engagement with the book of Psalms itself, not the use of the Old Testament in the New.

86. On the significance of Edwards' notebooks for the development of his thought, see Wilson H. Kimnach, "Jonathan Edwards' Art of Prophesying," 42–74.

from the extant Edwards corpus, including "Harmony of the Genius, Spirit, Doctrines, and Rules of the Old Testament and the New," "Prophecies of the Messiah," "Supplement to Prophecies of the Messiah," "The Fulfillment of the Prophecies of the Messiah," "Subjects of Inquiry," and "Hebrew Idioms."[87] The dozens of sermons Edwards preached on the Psalms constitute one of the most significant sources of his engagement with the Psalms, so I have examined all of his sermons on the Psalms, most of which have not been published and over a third of which are yet to be transcribed. This method gives the priority due to Edwards' biblical manuscripts and sermons that they have rarely received and explores untapped sources in an effort to understand better both Edwards the man and Edwards on the Psalms.[88]

Furthermore, the project is not intended to reconstruct a verse-by-verse commentary on the Psalms. Stein observes that "Edwards never wrote a systematic commentary" on any book of the Bible, and he is right to note that Edwards was "more occasional and happenstance" in his exegetical work, in the sense that he did not write a verse-by-verse commentary on single books of the Bible.[89] At the same time, Edwards was disciplined and systematic in his exegesis in that he regularly immersed himself in Scripture and recorded his observations, in part because he had to prepare and preach sermons three times per week. How else could he have amassed such voluminous notes on the Bible? This study, then, seeks to determine the primary theological thrusts in Edwards' writings on the Psalms without suggesting that Edwards wrote an actual commentary on the Psalms. That means that I do not follow a chronological development of the Psalms in Edwards' life and works since that

---

87. Jonathan Edwards, "Harmony of the Genius, Spirit, Doctrines, and Rules of the Old Testament and the New," Beinecke Rare Book and Manuscript Library, Yale University, New Haven, CT; "The Miscellanies: Entry No. 1067: Prophecies of the Messiah," Franklin Trask Library, Andover Newton Theological School, Newton, MA; "Supplement to Prophecies of the Messiah," Franklin Trask Library, Andover Newton Theological School, Newton, MA; "The Miscellanies: Entry No. 1068: The Fulfillment of the Prophecies of the Messiah." Franklin Trask Library, Andover Newton Theological School, Newton, MA; "Subjects of Inquiry," in *Minor Controversial Writings*, vol. 28 of *WJEO*; and "Hebrew Idioms," Beinecke Rare Book and Manuscript Library, Yale University, New Haven, CT.

88. Cf. Brown, "The Bible," 98; Stetina, *Jonathan Edwards' Early Understanding of Religious Experience*, 47–50.

89. Stein, "Editor's Introduction," in *The "Blank Bible,"* 102. Stein critiques John Gerstner's "reconstruction" of Edwards' writings on the letter to the Hebrews for its resemblance to such a commentary. See John H. Gerstner, *The Rational Biblical Theology of Jonathan Edwards*, vol. 1 (Powhatan, VA: Berea, 1991), 247–479. In the path of Gerstner, David S. Lovi and Benjamin Westerhoff have more recently compiled Edwards' comments on the book of Romans in *The Power of God: A Jonathan Edwards Commentary on the Book of Romans* (Eugene, OR: Pickwick, 2013).

approach would miss the resonant theological themes in Edwards' engagement with the Psalms. Instead, the first chapter grounds Edwards' engagement with the Psalms through interpretation, worship, and preaching in his historical context.

It is also beyond the scope of this study to provide a detailed overview of the church's major commentaries on the Psalms prior to Edwards, because it does not allow space or time to do justice to the centuries of development. I thus devote time to Edwards' direct Reformed tradition stemming from Calvin to the New England Puritans. These works were selected primarily for prominence or for known influence on Edwards. Richard Muller warns that scholars studying Reformers' biblical interpretation often "discuss the thought of the Reformers in relative isolation," failing to note originality in interpretation or to identify "lines of influence."[90] Muller's caution applies equally to examinations of Edwards and other later theologians. Thus, in contrast to Tooman, who drew conclusions about Edwards' departure from Puritan exegesis in his treatment of Ezekiel without comparing his interpretations to earlier exegetes, this project assesses Edwards' originality against his own tradition by comparing his treatment of key texts with the actual exegesis of earlier interpreters. It also examines influences on his interpretation and grounds Edwards in his place and time by setting him in the Reformed Protestant traditions of interpreting the Psalms from Calvin through the English Puritans to the New England Puritan context in which Edwards developed his own interpretation of the Psalms.

The Psalms as Redemptive-Historical Songs

This study enters into the conversation about Edwards and the Bible by performing a close study of Edwards on the Psalms, which answers Brown's call for focused study on Edwards' biblical manuscripts and sermons and builds on Stein's work that has highlighted Edwards' biblical manuscripts as foundational yet neglected artifacts in understanding the man. In the process, I assess Stein's charge that Edwards does not remain within an orthodox tradition in his biblical interpretation, McClymond and McDermott's suggestion that Edwards' biblical exegesis is "catholic," and Kreider's claim that the best label for Edwards' interpretive method is "Christological typology." In

---

90. Richard A. Muller, "Biblical Interpretation in the Era of the Reformation: The View from the Middle Ages," in *Biblical Interpretation in the Era of the Reformation: Essays Presented to David C. Steinmetz in Honor of His Sixtieth Birthday*, ed. Richard A. Muller and John L. Thompson (Grand Rapids, MI: Eerdmans, 1996), 5.

exploring Edwards' engagement with the Psalms, I suggest some correctives to these propositions.

The bulk of the book aims to describe the theological themes Edwards developed using the Psalms, providing the first book-length volume to look at Edwards' exegetical approach to a full book of the Bible. The project shares both Kreider and Stein's recognition that Edwards often dealt thematically with the Bible.[91] In this project I set forth Edwards' theological engagement with the Psalms not only to help correct the distorted picture of Edwards that leaves out his biblicism but also to describe the details of how his commitment to Scripture colored his life and thought.

I argue that the Psalms provided Edwards with a rich, layered theological text for addressing the issues of his day. My thesis is that in a world experiencing major epistemological shifts and liturgical challenges, Jonathan Edwards appropriated the book of Psalms as a divinely inspired anchor to proclaim the gospel and rehearse the redemptive-historical work of the triune God. As the new "enlightened" learning changed the way people thought about the Bible, nature, and history, and as new concerns arose about the liturgical practices of the church in an era that increasingly questioned clerical authority and traditional forms of ecclesiastical order, Edwards faced these challenges head on using the Psalms as one key tool for keeping the church focused on what he believed constituted the core convictions of the Christian faith: The triune God's work of redemption to reconcile depraved humanity to himself for the sake of his glory.

Throughout the book we will see Edwards' continual emphasis on the history of redemption, which leads me to describe his interpretation as a "redemptive-historical approach" to the Psalms. With this phrase, I seek to describe the encompassing interpretive framework by which Edwards read the Psalms. While he used literal, typological, Christological, and other "methods" of interpretation, none of these methods orients all the others to his interpretive purpose or captures what he was actually doing in his work on the Psalms—which is why some scholars' labels of his interpretive method are misleading. Rather, when Edwards employed various methods— a term I use broadly—he used them as tools that were guided by his broad redemptive-historical understanding of the Psalms.

This study is organized so as to reflect Edwards' own theological emphases in the Psalms. Chapter 1, "The Psalter in Edwards' World," describes the context in which Edwards lived and the interpretive, liturgical, and homiletical issues

---

91. Kreider, *Edwards's Interpretation of Revelation 4:1–8:1*, 91; Stein, " 'Like Apples of Gold in Pictures of Silver,' " 336.

related to the Psalter that he faced. Edwards leaned on the Protestant-Puritan tradition of interpreting the Bible, especially Matthew Poole and Matthew Henry, and used their resources in his own approach to understanding the Psalms. He also spoke to the questions of the relationship between the Psalms and the gospel, of the Psalms' place in church worship, and of the proper use of the Psalms in the pulpit. This chapter provides the background for placing Edwards in his place and time as we move on to grasp his theological use of the Psalter.

The remaining chapters of the book delve into the theological themes that emerge from Edwards' dealings with the Psalms throughout his life, underscoring that the themes he emphasized in his treatment of the Psalms followed the lines of the history of redemption, the overarching paradigm of Scripture that guided him in his engagement with the Psalter. In chapter 2, "God and Scripture," we see Edwards' reflections on the foundation of the redemptive-historical story: God and his revelation. All things exist to promote God's glory because he alone is holy. As the sovereign, omniscient being, he orders everything according to his providence and foreknowledge to further his redemptive work in the world, though God's ways remain mysterious, beyond human comprehension. Perhaps the most mysterious work of God is his great mercy and grace toward humanity, which Edwards celebrated in his writings on the Psalms. How do we know this God? Primarily through the book of Scripture, by which God reveals himself and his purposes to humanity. Edwards used the Psalms, in fact, to describe the nature of Scripture and defend its reliability against some of the criticisms of his day.

Chapter 3, "Humanity and Sin," rehearses the problem of human depravity. Edwards used the Psalms to reflect on the nature of humanity in its feeble, post-Fall state but also to describe original sin and its deleterious effects on the human race. Edwards particularly noted the deceitfulness of sin and warned of the just consequence for humanity's sinful affront to its holy Creator: eternal death.

Chapter 4 is devoted entirely to the person of "Christ," the pivotal agent in God's redemptive-historical plan. Edwards used the Psalms to reflect on the prophecies and types of Christ, his earthly life of obedience and delight in God's will, his redemptive work on the cross, and his glorification and eschatological reign.

In chapter 5, "Spirit and Gospel," we see Edwards' interest in the proclamation of the gospel and the work of the Spirit to engender true religion in those undergoing conversion. For Edwards, the Psalms taught about the Holy Spirit's work, especially as the source of spiritual light, and they also proclaimed the Christian doctrine of salvation. In celebrating salvation, the

Psalter also expressed the need to rejoice in the Spirit's work of revival and gave guidance for discerning true and false religion. Here we discuss Edwards' preaching of the gospel from the Psalms as a means of the Spirit's gracious work and draw these themes together in his explicit emphasis on God's work of redemption.

In chapter 6, "Christian Piety," we see how his understanding of the work of redemption had significant implications for the life of the professing Christian. In fact, Edwards used the Psalms extensively to preach on pious living and promote holy affections in the individual members of Christ's body. He believed that God's people should make the Psalms their own language, which would help them to live out Christian virtues, relate in harmony with people, and live in right relationship with God.

In chapter 7, "Church and Eternity," we observe the corporate implications for the Christian church, exploring Edwards' ecclesiological interpretation of the Psalms. From the Psalms he spoke often of "Christ mystical," or the body of Christ, the church. In the Psalter Edwards also gleaned much about the future for Christ's body and for those outside of the Christian community, addressing Christ's coming kingdom, the end of the world, the future judgment of the wicked, and the future hope of the church.

In the conclusion, I assess how Edwards' treatment of the Psalms affirms and corrects what scholars have already said about Edwards and the Bible and suggest avenues for further research. I also outline the areas of continuity and discontinuity between Edwards and the Puritan-Reformed exegetical tradition. Finally, I speak to Edwards' place in the history of engagement with the Psalms and consider what his legacy with regard to the Psalms might be today.

Jonathan Edwards loved the Psalms in large part because their poetic, universal style proved so versatile that they could "express the religion of all saints, in all ages."[92] Edwards appropriated the Psalms as redemptive-historical songs to fulfill what he believed was his theological and ministerial duty, to promote true religion in his age. The history of redemption provided Edwards with a framework for interpreting the Psalms and worshipping with the Psalter as he proclaimed the gospel and the attendant doctrines of God's work of redemption directly from the book of Psalms.

---

92. Edwards, *Religious Affections*, 109.

I

The Psalter in Edwards' World

Open thou mine eyes, that I may behold wondrous
things out of thy law.
Psalm 119:18

My tongue shall speak of thy word:
for all thy commandments are righteousness.
Psalm 119:172

Praise ye the LORD. *Sing unto the* LORD *a new song,*
and his praise in the congregation of saints.
Psalm 149:1

THE PSALMS FUNCTIONED as a multifaceted book in Edwards' thought, experience, and ministry. For Edwards, the Psalter was a divinely inspired book of Scripture that should be read and interpreted, and it served as the songbook of the church from Edwards' boyhood through his pastorate. The Psalms also needed to be proclaimed from the pulpit as he carried out his ministerial duties to his congregation. Here we explore how Edwards engaged the Psalms within the context of the history of the church engaging the Psalms and the interpretive, homiletical, and liturgical issues in his day.

Interpretive Issues

To set the stage for Edwards' theological themes in the Psalms, I will explore the broader historical context for how interpreters approached the Psalter, outline some of the more significant interpretive issues raised in the Age of Enlightenment, describe how Edwards fits into those interpretive discussions through his own methods, and show how Edwards' sources reveal him to be a critically engaged interpreter of the Psalms.

Historical Approaches to Interpreting the Psalms

One of the best early Christian portraits of the Psalms comes from Athanasius' (c. 296–373) "Letter to Marcellinus," which illustrates the profound attention given to the Psalms early in church history. Athanasius quoted "a learned old man" as saying that the Psalms, in a way, contain the whole Bible: while each section of the Bible consists of particular material, including law, history, prophecy, and salvation, "the Book of Psalms is like a garden containing things of all these kinds."[1] The Psalms are "divinely inspired," and the divine author, the Spirit, unifies the books of the Bible; since the Spirit is "indivisible by nature," then "surely the whole is in each," and thus one can identify Christ in certain passages in the Psalms.[2] Athanasius also held that the Psalter "contains even the emotions of each soul," and unlike other parts of Scripture, the reader can hear and speak the words of the Psalms as his or her own words in prayer, worship, and life.[3] Athanasius' letter foreshadowed the ways much of the later Christian tradition would appropriate the Psalms.

In general, the early church employed the Psalms largely to establish its theology, especially Christ's divinity and messianic office. The Psalter also proved useful in arguing for the unity of the two testaments, in countering Christological, Trinitarian, and anthropological heresies, and in offering comfort and eternal hope in affliction.[4] Origen (185–232) employed an allegorical method of interpretation in the Psalms, identifying references to both Christ and Christ mystical (i.e., his body, the church), a practice based on his belief that Scripture interprets Scripture.[5] Augustine also gravitated to the Psalms, saturating his *Confessions* with the language of the Psalter and investing three decades in writing his lengthy *Expositions of the Psalms*. His most influential contribution for later interpretation was identifying in the Psalms the *totus Christus*, "a prophecy of the mystery of Christ in his totality—of Christ, head and body."[6] The interpretive stream that read the Psalms through a Christological

---

1. Athanasius, "A Letter of Athanasius, Our Holy Father, Archbishop of Alexandria, to Marcellinus on the Interpretation of the Psalms," in *The Life of Antony and the Letter to Marcellinus*, trans. Robert C. Gregg (New York: Paulist, 1980), 101–102. Italics original.

2. Athanasius, "A Letter of Athanasius," 126, 104–107.

3. Athanasius, "A Letter of Athanasius," 108–109, 112–123.

4. Quentin F. Wesselschmidt, ed., *Ancient Christian Commentary on Scripture: Old Testament: Psalms 51–150*, vol. VIII (Downers Grove, IL: InterVarsity, 2007), xix–xxii.

5. Ronald E. Heine, *Reading the Old Testament with the Ancient Church: Exploring the Formation of Early Christian Thought* (Grand Rapids, MI: Baker Academic, 2007), 154–163; Origen, "Commentary on Psalms 1–25, Fragment from Preface," in *Origen*, ed. and trans. Joseph W. Trigg, Early Church Fathers Series (New York: Routledge, 1998), 69–71; Origène, *Philocalie, 1–20 sur les Écritures*, ed. and trans. Margerite Harl (La Tour-Maubourg, France: Les Éditions du Cerf, 1983), 240–244.

6. Michael Fiedrowicz, "General Introduction," in *Expositions of the Psalms: 1–32*, trans. Maria Boulding and ed. John E. Rotelle, part III, vol. 15 of *The Works of Saint Augustine*

lens dominated much of Christian interpretation through the early and medieval church, though it should be noted that another lively stream advocated an emphasis on the literal, historical reading and moral application of the Psalter, visible in interpreters like Diodore of Tarsus (d. *c.* 390) and John Chrysostom (*c.* 347–407).[7]

The Psalms remained popular in the medieval era, when Psalms commentaries proliferated and the Psalter was "the most widely read book of the Old Testament."[8] The traditional fourfold sense of Scripture (*quadriga*) dominated Psalms studies, which included a discussion of the literal, allegorical (doctrinal), tropological (ethical), and anagogical (eschatological) senses. In the twelfth century, the school of St. Victor devoted more attention to the Hebrew language and the literal sense.[9] And in the thirteenth century, Thomas Aquinas (1224/25–1274) also emphasized the literal meaning as the basis for the spiritual senses.[10] Still, his concern for worship to retain its Christian character led him to emphasize the Christological content of the Psalter.[11] Echoing Athanasius, Thomas explained that the Psalter "has as a general topic the whole of theology" and "contains all of scripture," by extension

---

(Hyde Park, NY: New City, 2000), 13, 38, 43, 60 (quotation on 43); Susan E. Gillingham, *Psalms Through the Centuries*, vol. 1, Blackwell Bible Commentaries (Malden, MA: Blackwell, 2008), 39. For an example of the Psalms in Augustine's *Confessions*, see *The Confessions of St. Augustine*, trans. John K. Ryan (New York: Image Books, 1960), 210.

7. Gillingham, *Psalms Through the Centuries*, 31–33; Diodore of Tarsus, "Commentary on the Psalms, Prologue," in *Biblical Interpretation in the Early Church*, ed. Karlfried Froehlich, Sources of Christian Thought Series (Philadelphia, PA: Fortress, 1984), 85; Christopher A. Hall, *Reading Scripture with the Church Fathers* (Downers Grove, IL: InterVarsity, 1998), 93–101. Though he does not focus on the Psalms, Bradley Nassif offers a nuanced reading of Chrysostom's general exegesis in "Antiochene θεωρία in John Chrysostom's Exegesis," in *Ancient & Postmodern Christianity: Paleo-Orthodoxy in the 21st Century: Essays in Honor of Thomas C. Oden*, ed. Kenneth Tanner and Christopher A. Hall (Downers Grove, IL: InterVarsity, 2002), 49–67.

8. Beryl Smalley, *The Study of the Bible in the Middle Ages*, 3d ed. (1964; repr. Notre Dame, IN: University of Notre Dame Press, 1978), xi, 337. See also Karlfried Froehlich, "Christian Interpretation of the Old Testament in the High Middle Ages," in *Hebrew Bible / Old Testament: The History of Its Interpretation*, ed. Magne Sæbø (Göttingen: Vandenhoeck & Ruprecht, 1996), 499.

9. On the school of St. Victor, see Smalley, 83–195, and Gillingham, *Psalms Through the Centuries*, 87–90.

10. Karlfried Froehlich, "Thomas Aquinas (1224/25–1274)," in *Dictionary of Major Biblical Interpreters*, ed. Donald K. McKim (Downers Grove, IL: IVP Academic, 2007), 983.

11. James A. Weisheipl, *Friar Thomas D'Aquino: His Life, Thought, and Work* (Garden City, NY: Doubleday & Co., 1974), 368–369.

"the matter of this book is Christ and his members."[12] On the whole, the tradition of explaining the Psalms as prophecies of Christ held ascendency in the High Middle Ages, and "the consideration of the original historical sense was overshadowed by the thoroughgoing and total reinterpretation of the Psalter as a Christian book."[13]

The Psalms continued to be much admired in the Reformation era. Martin Luther (1483–1546) gravitated to the Psalms in part because he was so well acquainted with them as a monk who recited them daily but also because he saw his inner spiritual struggles, his *Anfechtungen*, contained in them.[14] As he interpreted the Psalms, Luther found, like Athanasius, "a summary of the entire Bible," he saw "Christ as the heart of the Psalter," and he interpreted the Psalms as a guide to the Christian life.[15] For John Calvin (1509–1564), "the Psalms assumed greater and greater significance in his theological development" over time.[16] Similarly to Athanasius, Calvin called the Psalms, "An Anatomy of all the Parts of the Soul," for the Psalter functions as a "mirror" reflecting every human emotion, and it redresses the agitations that distract the mind.[17] Like Luther, the Psalms strengthen the Christian in obedience for the "Psalms are replete with all the precepts which serve to frame our life to every part of holiness, piety, and righteousness."[18]

But Calvin also took a distinct approach to interpreting the Psalms. He concerned himself far less than his predecessors and even contemporaries

---

12. Thomas Aquinas, *The Gifts of the Spirit: Selected Spiritual Writings*, ed. Benedict M. Ashley and trans. Matthew Rzeczkowski (Hyde Park, NY: New City, 1995), 95, 96. See also Thomas Aquinas, *Sancti Thomae Aquinatis Doctoris Angelici Ordinis Praedicatorum Opera Omnia*, Tomus XIV, Parma ed. (1852–1873; repr., New York: Musurgia, 1949), 148–150.

13. Froehlich, "Christian Interpretation of the Old Testament," 501.

14. Roland H. Bainton, *Here I Stand: A Life of Martin Luther* (New York: Meridian, 1977), 262.

15. Robert Kolb, "The Doctrine of Christ in Nikolaus Selnecker's Interpretation of Psalms 8, 22, and 110," in *Biblical Interpretation in the Era of the Reformation: Essays Presented to David C. Steinmetz in Honor of His Sixtieth Birthday*, ed. Richard A. Muller and John L. Thompson (Grand Rapids, MI: Eerdmans, 1996), 313; Kenneth Hagen, "*Omnis homo mendax*: Luther on Psalm 116," in *Biblical Interpretation in the Era of the Reformation: Essays Presented to David C. Steinmetz in Honor of His Sixtieth Birthday*, ed. Richard A. Muller and John L. Thompson (Grand Rapids, MI: Eerdmans, 1996), 86; Martin Luther, *Reading the Psalms with Luther* (St. Louis, MO: Concordia, 2007), 14–15.

16. Herman J. Selderhuis, *Calvin's Theology of the Psalms* (Grand Rapids, MI: Baker Academic, 2007), 16.

17. John Calvin, *Commentary on the Psalms*, trans. from the Original Latin and Collated with the Author's French Version by James Anderson, vol. 1 (1843–1855; repr., Grand Rapids, MI: Eerdmans, 1963), xxxvii.

18. Calvin, *Commentary*, 1:xxxix.

with reading Christ in the Psalms and focused far more on the literal and historical meaning of each psalm, a mark of his humanist training. He pursued the goal of "comprehending the design of each of the writers" and held that God had exhibited in David and the other psalmists "an example for imitation."[19] As Wulfert de Greef explains, Calvin felt that the way early exegetes like Augustine "filled the Psalms with Christological content did violence to their historical context, and thus nullified what the psalmists experienced in their relationship to God."[20] In this emphasis, Calvin mirrored the Jewish method of rooting interpretation in the Hebrew text and historical context led by Abraham Ibn Ezra (*c.* 1089–*c.* 1164) and David Kimchi (1160–1235), which elicited Protestant accusations that he was a Judaizer.[21] This issue occupies G. Sujin Pak in her monograph, *The Judaizing Calvin*, in which she argues that "Calvin introduces a significant shift in the history of the interpretation of [the messianic] Psalms first and foremost concerning his identification of their 'literal sense'" not with Christological readings but with the human author's intention.[22] Calvin thus represents a pivot point because he spoke to the church through the Psalms by affirming Israel's history in the Old Testament, where God was "present in shadows and images," while upholding its continuity with the New Testament church.[23] This approach allowed him sometimes to connect the Psalms indirectly to Christ and the church, though he prioritized and elevated the Psalms' historical context in interpretation.[24]

Puritan interpretation of the Psalms in the seventeenth and early eighteenth centuries brings us nearer to the interpretive issues Edwards faced. Reformed exegetes of this time were interested in linguistics and textual criticism and were united around a literal reading of the text over and against excessive allegory, but "the diversity and breadth of the letter as made possible by typological and figurative exegesis and by interest in the prophetic and messianic meanings of passages yielded varied interpretations and varied

---

19. Calvin, *Commentary*, 1:xxxix, xl.

20. Wulfert de Greef, "Calvin as Commentator on the Psalms," trans. Raymond A. Blacketer, in *Calvin and the Bible*, ed. Donald K. McKim (New York: Cambridge University Press, 2006), 89.

21. De Greef, "Calvin as Commentator," 106.

22. G. Sujin Pak, *Judaizing Calvin: Sixteenth-Century Debates over the Messianic Psalms*, Oxford Studies in Historical Theology (New York: Oxford University Press, 2010), 8.

23. Wulfert de Greef, "Calvin's Understanding and Interpretation of the Bible," trans. David Dichelle, in *John Calvin's Impact on Church and Society, 1509–2009*, ed. Martin Ernst Hirzel and Martin Sallmann (Grand Rapids, MI: Eerdmans, 2009), 85.

24. De Greef, "Calvin as Commentator," 95–96. De Greef, "Calvin's Understanding," 71.

interests."[25] We gain a clearer sense of these concerns by looking at four of the more important Puritan commentators on the book of Psalms in the seventeenth century, to whom we will compare Edwards' exegesis in the remaining study: David Dickson, John Trapp, Matthew Poole, and Matthew Henry.[26]

David Dickson (1583–1663), a Scottish pastor and theologian, wrote *A Brief Explication of the Psalms*, published from 1653–1655. As a Puritan pastor, Dickson suffered deprivation and confinement for a year and a half under King James I and later lost his post as professor of divinity at Edinburgh under King Charles II's Act of Uniformity (1662).[27] In his approach to the Psalter, he had a broad, redemptive view of the Psalms' "scope," "not only to teach us the Grounds of Divinity," but also "to direct us how to apply Saving Doctrines practically to our selfe."[28] Dickson taught that Psalm 1 offers two paths, righteousness or wickedness, while Psalm 2 "giveth us God, in Christ, for a Captain and Leader to us" against wickedness.[29] The rest of the Psalms "hold forth the Examples of Christ and his Followers" to support believers as they endure "a life mixed with Crosses and sweet Comforts"—as Dickson himself had experienced.[30] All this looks forward to the "Joy unspeakable" celebrated in the final six Psalms that will come with the "full meeting of Christ, and all his Redeemed ones" at the second coming.[31] From these descriptions we

25. Richard A. Muller, *Holy Scripture: The Cognitive Foundation of Theology*, vol. 2 of *Post-Reformation Reformed Dogmatics: The Rise and Development of Reformed Orthodoxy, ca. 1520 to ca. 1725*, 2d ed. (Grand Rapids, MI: Baker Academic, 2003), 449.

26. These commentators were chosen from two lists of prominent commentaries on the Psalms compiled by Richard Muller and John Thompson. Richard A. Muller, "Biblical Interpretation in the Sixteenth and Seventeenth Centuries," in *Dictionary of Major Biblical Interpreters*, ed. Donald K. McKim (Downers Grove, IL: IVP Academic, 2007), 39–43; and John Thompson, "A Finding Guide to English Translations of Commentary Literature Written 1600–1700," Fuller Theological Seminary, http://purl.oclc.org/net/jlt/exegesis/ (accessed November 28, 2009). Dozens more could have been included; Thompson lists 111 English works on the Psalms from the years 1600–1700. Those included here were selected because of their prominence, the authors' Puritan commitments, the size of their works (many smaller tracts or sermons on the Psalms were printed during that century), and the fact that Edwards cited two of the works (Poole and Henry). See more on Edwards' sources on pp. 50–53 below.

27. Robert Wodrow, "Short Account of the Life of the Author" (1726), in David Dickson, *A Brief Explication of the Psalms*, vol. 1 (1726; repr., Glasgow: John Dow, 1834), xvii–xxv.

28. David Dickson, *A Brief Explication of the first Fifty Psalms* (London: T. M. for Ralph Smith…, 1652), 1–2.

29. Dickson, *First Fifty Psalms*, 2.

30. Dickson, *First Fifty Psalms*, 2–3.

31. Dickson, *First Fifty Psalms*, 3.

get a taste of Dickson's Christological and typological leaning, in contrast to Calvin's more restrained approach to the Psalms, and we also see his emphasis on "the chiefe Doctrines" of the Scriptures—God's work of redemption.[32]

An important English contemporary of Dickson was John Trapp (1601–1669), whom Muller calls "one of the best of the Puritan commentators."[33] Trapp devoted himself to writing commentaries on much of the Bible, including *A Commentary or Exposition Upon the Books of Ezra, Nehemiah, Esther, Job, and Psalms* (1657). He viewed the Psalms as a book of praises filled with treasures, a summary of the Scriptures in one place, and a collection of "Spiritual Songs" that the Holy Spirit "indited."[34] In his interpretation of the Psalms, he paid close attention to the Hebrew, compared the text with other parts of Scripture, exposited passages phrase by phrase, and shared stories and insights gleaned from such diverse sources as Pythagoras, Jerome, David Kimchi, and England's monarchical history. While he sometimes interpreted the Psalms Christologically, he was generally more reserved and preferred to make spiritual and devotional points from the literal sense in the Psalms' historical setting.

Matthew Poole (1624–1679) produced the *Synopsis Criticorum Aliorumque Sacrae Scripturae Interpretum* from 1669–1674, a work that would capture the attention of many exegetes, including Edwards.[35] Poole, a Presbyterian supporter of the Puritan establishment during the Commonwealth years in England (1649–1660), compiled critical data in his *Synopsis* from a diverse group of commentators, including English and continental Protestants, Roman Catholics, and rabbis.[36] As Gerald Bray observes, "[t]he commentary is a hybrid work, and very little of it can be attributed to Poole himself. However, it is the selections that struck a chord with his readers, most of whom were

---

32. Dickson, *First Fifty Psalms*, [i].

33. Muller, "Biblical Interpretation in the Sixteenth and Seventeenth Centuries," 42. On Trapp's life, see Bertha Porter, "Trapp, John (1601–1669)," in vol. 19 of *The Dictionary of National Biography*, ed. Leslie Stephen and Sidney Lee (London: Oxford University Press, 1917), 1082. For a laudatory account of Trapp, see Charles LeRoy Goodell, "A Puritan Commentator," *Methodist Review* 99 (January 1917): 63–74.

34. John Trapp, *A Commentary or Exposition Upon the Books of Ezra, Nehemiah, Esther, Job, and Psalms...* (London: T.R. and E.M. for Thomas Newberry..., 1657), 562.

35. Matthew Poole, *Synopsis Criticorum Aliorumque Sacrae Scripturae Interpretum* (London: Cornelius Bee, 1669–1676). Poole's colleagues also produced an English version of his commentary after his death, the two-volume *Annotations on the Holy Bible* (1683–1685), a distinct work in itself.

36. Gerald L. Bray, "Poole, Matthew (1624–1679)," in *Dictionary of Major Biblical Interpreters*, ed. Donald K. McKim (Downers Grove, IL: InterVarsity, 2007), 840.

preachers looking for suitable material."[37] Poole began by discussing critical questions including structure and authorship of the Psalms, arguing that some psalms dated to the exile and that Ezra collected them into one book.[38] He emphasized literal exegesis of the text, interpreting Scripture using Scripture, theological exposition, and practical application, and following Trapp and Calvin, he used spiritual interpretation cautiously.[39]

Matthew Henry (1662–1714) produced a commentary that has remained popular even in the twenty-first century, his *Exposition of the Old and New Testaments* (1708). His biblical interpretations are an expression of the religiously moderate reign of William and Mary, emphasizing application and devotion.[40] Henry called the Psalms "one of the choicest and most excellent Parts of all the Old Testament" for "so much is there in it of CHRIST and his Gospel, as well as of GOD and his Law, that it has been call'd the Abstract, or Summary, of both Testaments."[41] The book was "divinely inspir'd," and though the primary penman was David, it was "no doubt, deriv'd originally from the Blessed Spirit."[42] Its purpose is both to "assist the exercises of Natural Religion"—that is, to kindle "devout Affections"—and to "advance the Excellencies of Reveal'd Religion," with a focus on Christ, "the Crown and Center of Revealed Religion," who is "here clearly spoken of in Type and Prophecy."[43] Henry's approach to the Psalms emphasized the continuity between the Old and New Testaments with its implications for typology, the Messiah, and the church; "the improving of the biblical imagery," or elaborating on the metaphors and figures in Scripture; and the interpretation of Scripture by Scripture.[44] Unlike Calvin, Henry was very comfortable finding typological meanings in the Psalms. His *Exposition* is also characterized by an interest in promoting piety, which was of great use to pastors like Edwards who wanted to

---

37. Bray, "Poole, Matthew," 841.

38. Poole, *Synopsis*, 477–479.

39. Bray, "Poole, Matthew," 841–842.

40. Hughes Oliphant Old, "Henry, Matthew (1662–1714)," in *Dictionary of Major Biblical Interpreters*, ed. Donald K. McKim (Downers Grove, IL: InterVarsity, 2007), 520–524.

41. Matthew Henry, *An exposition of the five poetical books of the Old Testament; viz. Job, Psalms, Proverbs, Ecclesiastes, and Solomon's song...* (London: T. Darrack..., 1710), n.p. [introduction to the book of Psalms]. Henry's 1710 text did not include page numbers, so in all citations of Henry, I provide the Psalms text on which he was commenting to give a reference point.

42. Henry, *Exposition*, [introduction to book of Psalms].

43. Henry, *Exposition*, [introduction to book of Psalms].

44. Old, "Henry, Matthew," 523; Stephen J. Stein, "Editor's Introduction," in *The "Blank Bible,"* ed. Stephen J. Stein, vol. 24 of *WJE* (2006), 63.

spark revival in their congregations.[45] In fact, Henry influenced several revivalists of the mid-eighteenth century, most notably George Whitefield, and his commentary became a standard text for many New England pastors.[46]

These streams of interpretation demonstrate some breadth in approaches to the Psalms prior to Edwards and show a number of common emphases. Throughout all eras, the use of Scripture to interpret Scripture features prominently. The early and medieval church embraced a Christological and ecclesiological understanding of the Psalter, while during and after the Reformation, exegetes found more fruit in the historical David without abandoning Christological interpretation. The Reformation era saw a renewed interest in the original Hebrew and in linguistic background that lasted into the eighteenth century. Most important, this brief survey highlights a shift that took place in Calvin's biblical writings toward literal exegesis that resulted in a tension within Protestant exegesis about just what "literal" could entail. Should it follow the reserved approaches of Trapp and Poole, focusing on the historical David in the Psalms? Or should it lean into the typological approaches of Dickson and Henry, exalting Christ and his redemptive work figuratively intended by the divine author in the Psalms? These questions would be heightened as the world wrestled with the influx of Enlightenment-era thought and the unique challenges it brought to interpreting the Psalter.

Interpretive Issues in the Age of Enlightenment

During the last decades of the seventeenth century, as biblical scholars and divines were embracing the study of philology and the so-called oriental languages, a movement arose that historians would later describe by the word "Enlightenment."[47] Historians have applied this term in a variety of ways.

---

45. Old, "Henry, Matthew," 522–523; Stein, "Editor's Introduction," in *The "Blank Bible,"* 63.

46. David Crump, "The Preaching of George Whitefield and His Use of Matthew Henry's *Commentary,*" *Crux* 25, no. 3 (September 1989): 19–28. Crump argues for a strong Puritan continuity between Henry and Whitefield: "Puritan theology, passed on as it was through the writings of Matthew Henry, may well have enjoyed the period of its greatest influence during the ministry of George Whitefield." Quotation on 24.

47. Dorinda Outram describes the slow process that it took for terms like "Enlightenment," "les lumières," or "Aufklärung" to come into general use during the Enlightenment. As one example, Samuel Johnson included no entry for "Enlightenment" in his famous *Dictionary,* first published in 1755, until the later 1775 edition, far into the late eighteenth century. Dorinda Outram, *Panorama of the Enlightenment* (Los Angeles, CA: J. Paul Getty Museum, 2006), 24–28.

Some like Peter Gay described the "Enlightenment" as a unified seculariz-ing of society.[48] But most historians have abandoned that model for a more complex understanding of the time and movement. Dorinda Outram rejects the notion that "there was an entity called *the* Enlightenment," noting that "[t]here was never a stable, universally accepted definition of 'Enlightenment' during the Enlightenment."[49] At the very least, as Jonathan Yeager explains, "the overwhelming majority declares that we can no longer speak of 'The Enlightenment' as a unified movement."[50] Instead, we can speak of "one over-arching Enlightenment, but with specific 'hues' of religious beliefs—whether radical, Arminian, Calvinistic, Socinian, or evangelical—varying geographical locations, and spanning from the culmination of the Thirty Years' War [1618–1648] to the end of the eighteenth century."[51] What unified the various shades of the Enlightenment was what Josh Moody calls "the self-consciousness of the intellectual thrust of the period," even if this was a "developing" characteristic.[52]

Along the "Enlightenment spectrum," David Sorkin notes, many "religious enlighteners" aimed "to harmonize faith and reason."[53] In fact, as Gertrude Himmelfarb observes, while the Enlightenment in France took a markedly anti-religious stance, for both the British and American Enlightenments, "reli-gion was an ally, not an enemy," and it posed no "threat to enlightenment—to reason, science, and the life of the mind in general."[54] A secularizing force occurred but not uniformly in every area of life. Rather, as Gerald McDermott explains, "secularism as a principle of separation of church and state began to emerge" but "not a secular age in the sense that God was excluded from public

---

48. Peter Gay, *The Enlightenment: An Interpretation*, 2 vols. (New York: W. W. Norton, 1966–1969).

49. Dorinda Outram, *The Enlightenment*, 2d ed., New Approaches to European History (Cambridge: Cambridge University Press, 2005), 3; Outram, *Panorama of the Enlightenment*, 24.

50. Jonathan M. Yeager, *Enlightened Evangelicalism: The Life and Thought of John Erskine* (New York: Oxford University Press, 2011), 19.

51. Yeager, *Enlightened Evangelicalism*, 19.

52. Josh Moody, *Jonathan Edwards and the Enlightenment: Knowing the Presence of God* (Lanham, MD: University Press of America, 2005), 5.

53. David Sorkin, *The Religious Enlightenment: Protestants, Jews, and Catholics from London to Vienna* (Princeton, NJ: Princeton University Press, 2008), 6, 19.

54. Gertrude Himmelfarb, *The Roads to Modernity: The British, French, and American Enlightenments* (New York: Vintage, 2004), 18–19, 212–217. Quotations on 18, 212.

discussion."[55] Instead, God was very much a part of the age, an observation that is particularly visible in some evangelicals of that time who were sympathetic to aspects of the Enlightenment. As Catherine Brekus observes, while evangelicalism has often been portrayed as antagonistic to the Enlightenment, actually "the relationship between evangelicalism and the Enlightenment was fraught with tensions," and while evangelicals condemned certain aspects of the extreme skepticism and anti-Bible sentiment of the Enlightenment, they also "absorbed many Enlightenment ideas as their own" in trying "to adapt to a changing world."[56] To talk of the Enlightenment, then, requires that we speak of varying viewpoints vying for ascendency, ways of thinking that shared an intellectual edge but differed in often sharp ways, especially on religion.[57]

Following this more complex description of the Enlightenment, we can see that intellectuals of all religious shades embraced a hope in reason but to varying degrees. Some Enlightenment thinkers pushed to free mainstream thought from the shackles of traditional religion, calling into question traditional beliefs about the Bible. So writers such as Benedict de Spinoza (1632–1677) and Richard Simon (1638–1712) raised suspicion about the historical reliability of the biblical text, which contributed to the rise in Edwards' lifetime of the historical-critical method.[58] At the same time, to other Enlightenment-era thinkers, the emphasis on textual criticism and historical criticism raised not only new difficulties for interpretation but also new opportunities, since they believed that reason and faith would ultimately harmonize.

In England, one religious "hue" of the Enlightenment was the rise of deism, a system of thinking that sought to uphold the semblance of a deity that could be reconciled with human ratiocination, a belief structure that placed the Bible under the authority of reason and offered a religious alternative for the modern person. Publishing his influential *Essay Concerning Human Understanding* in 1689, John Locke (1632–1704), who declared his trust in the Bible's authority to his death, unwittingly laid the foundation for calling that authority into question through his ideas on empiricist thinking from

---

55. Gerald R. McDermott, *Jonathan Edwards Confronts the Gods: Christian Theology, Enlightenment Religion, and Non-Christian Faiths* (New York: Oxford University Press, 2000), 17–18.

56. Catherine Brekus, *Sarah Osborn's World: The Rise of Evangelical Christianity in Early America*, New Directions in Narrative History (New Haven, CT: Yale University Press, 2013), 7–12. Quotations on 9, 10.

57. On the Christian or religious Enlightenment, see Douglas A. Sweeney, "The Biblical World of Jonathan Edwards," *Jonathan Edwards Studies* 3, no. 2 (2013): 250n128.

58. Muller, *Holy Scripture*, 452–455.

experience and reason. The tools he developed provided an arsenal to those English philosophers who developed the religious system of deism. So John Toland (1670–1722), a disciple of Locke's, wrote his controversial *Christianity not Mysterious; or a Treatise shewing, That there is nothing in the Gospel contrary to Reason, nor above it: And that no Christian Doctrine can be properly call'd a Mystery* (1696). Toland aimed to revise epistemological assumptions by arguing that one could judge religious matters using nothing more than his God-given reason. Matthew Tindal (1653/57–1733), a thoroughgoing deist, captured the thrust of the movement in his book *Christianity as Old as the Creation: or, the Gospel, a Republication of the Religion of Nature* (1730), which has been called "the Bible of deism." Tindal argued that natural, not revealed, religion is evident to and sufficient for all people, leading to a belief in God's existence and a corresponding morality. The Bible is useful generally for its divine moral commands, but overall it is unreliable because the authors who gave it were largely immoral, the text has so many variants, and the proper interpretation is so widely debated. The Bible thus fell into the shadow of natural religion, and the debate between the deists and the "orthodox" was "finally a debate about the relationship between 'natural religion' based on abstract principles and 'revealed religion,' said to be rooted in the religious experience recorded in Scripture."[59]

These new debates affected the interpretation of the Psalms. Susan Gillingham notes that as critical theory spread, the eighteenth century witnessed an increase in Psalms commentaries detached from the church, which radically changed Psalms exegesis: "No longer was the interpreter constrained by a community of faith which had guarded the psalms in the history of tradition; gradually everything became open to question."[60] Scientific questions relegated the pious book of Psalms to a bygone era—a huge blow to a book that had pervaded church and society in earlier centuries. Rather, studies became more interested in the authorship and purpose of the Psalms, typology and prophecy fell under question, and the Psalter began to be studied less as a devotional hymnbook and more as a collection of ancient poetry, a text for gleaning historical data about the past. But even as criticism secured its foothold, "revivalist movements focused intensely on psalmody" as a means

59. McDermott, *Jonathan Edwards Confronts the Gods*, 18. See also Henning Graf Reventlow, "English Deism and Anti-Deist Apologetic," in vol. 2 of *Hebrew Bible, Old Testament: The History of Its Interpretation*, ed. Magne Sæbø (Göttingen: Vandenhoeck & Ruprecht, 2008), 851–874; Robert E. Brown, *Jonathan Edwards and the Bible* (Bloomington: Indiana University Press, 2002), 130; Sæbø, "From the Renaissance to the Enlightenment," 43.

60. Gillingham, *Psalms Through the Centuries*, 192–194. Quotation on 194.

of renewing the heart.[61] This impulse reveals again that eighteenth-century thinkers engaged Enlightenment ideas in diverse ways even in relation to the Psalter. In Edwards' day, the radical forms of the Enlightenment had by no means achieved hegemony, and while more interpreters were discussing new critical questions, many also continued to engage questions related to vital heart religion.

So while some exhibited a radical commitment to the individual's ability to reason divorced from any tradition, customs, or divine revelation, others lauded reason *within* a framework that upheld a tradition or maintained biblical authority. In fact, in the eighteenth century, many mainstream thinkers who embraced Enlightenment thinking rejected its radical elements. As Jonathan Yeager shows, because the radical form of the Enlightenment did not take center stage until the late eighteenth century, many British and American evangelicals "would not have viewed the Enlightenment as counterintuitive to faith, at least prior to the 1790s."[62] In fact, many Enlightenment thinkers sought to appropriate reason as a support for their theological endeavors, framing it as a tool that still had to submit to the authority of divine revelation.[63] Many Enlightenment-era Christians fully believed that the results of reasonable inquiry would harmonize with the truth already revealed in Scripture. They embraced reason but fought against what they believed was an inappropriate use of reason when the boundaries of faith were removed. As we will see, Edwards embraced reason while elevating revelation as the ultimate epistemological authority as he engaged the Psalms.[64] Others have argued as much for Edwards. For example, based on Edwards' engagement with and use of rational theological arguments for his defense of the orthodox doctrine of the Trinity, Steven Studebaker and Robert Caldwell have described Edwards

---

61. Gillingham, *Psalms Through the Centuries*, 195–199, 204. Quotation on 204.

62. Yeager, *Enlightened Evangelicalism*, 16.

63. As one example, Cotton Mather (1663–1728) was a key theologian who both valued typology, allegory, and even Gematria and also amassed all the data he could find from the church fathers, the Protestant tradition, Roman Catholic commentators, Jewish Midrash, classical Greek and Roman philosophers, history and customs, philology, and the natural sciences. See Cheryl Rivers, "Cotton Mather's *Biblia Americana* Psalms and the Nature of Puritan Scholarship" (PhD diss., Columbia University, 1977), 194–203; Jan Stievermann, "Cotton Mather and 'Biblia Americana'—America's First Bible Commentary: General Introduction," in *Cotton Mather and* Biblia Americana—*America's First Bible Commentary: Essays in Reappraisal*, ed. Reiner Smolinski and Jan Stievermann (Tübingen: Mohr Siebeck, 2010), 5–13.

64. For another example of an evangelical who embraced certain aspects of the Enlightenment while rejecting others, see Brekus, *Sarah Osborn's World*.

as "a Reformed participant in the Enlightenment."[65] We will see here that Edwards exhibited one "hue" of Enlightenment thought within the complex era we now call the Age of Reason.

Distinguishing Marks of Edwards' Interpretation of the Psalms

Edwards entered this context of new questions concerning the Psalms with a hunger for information that could shed light on the Psalms, tempered by a firm belief in their authority as divinely inspired Christian Scripture. While we will explore Edwards' theological themes in the remaining chapters, here we briefly identify four important ways that he approached the Psalms in the context of the history of interpreting the Psalms and the Enlightenment impact on New England: engaging the new learning, employing the analogy of Scripture, interpreting theologically, and using a dual authorship model.

The New Learning

Edwards demonstrated an interest in the latest scholarship and engaged Enlightenment thought for a number of motivations, including a desire to gain insight for his own exegesis of the Psalms and to counter new ideas that undermined the Bible's authority. Edwards' engagement with the new learning with respect to the Psalms confirms that he directly combatted the attempts to undermine biblical authority, while at the same time "he continued to feed his insatiable appetite for the latest in polite [or Enlightenment-related] reading."[66]

In employing the new learning in his interpretation, Edwards attended to lexical and historical data to shed light on the language and background of the Psalms. This pursuit of knowledge in many ways grew out of Reformed exegesis prior to any "new learning," yet new discoveries led to different insights and questions. As for linguistics, while Edwards only rarely interacted with the Hebrew in his writings, he had an understanding of Hebrew that allowed him to gain lexical insight for theological purposes.[67] And he suggested corrections

65. Steven M. Studebaker and Robert W. Caldwell, III, *The Trinitarian Theology of Jonathan Edwards: Text, Context, and Application* (Farnham, UK: Ashgate, 2012), 140.

66. Peter J. Thuesen, "Edwards' Intellectual Background," in *The Princeton Companion to Jonathan Edwards*, ed. Sang Hyun Lee (Princeton, NJ: Princeton University Press, 2005), 27.

67. See Edwards' discussion of יְכַחֲשׁוּ ("submit themselves") in Ps 66:3 in *Religious Affections*; שָׁפַט ("judge") in Ps 96:13 in the "Miscellanies"; נְעוּרִים ("from his youth") in Pss 71:5–6, 17–18, and 129:1–2 in *Original Sin*; מוֹצָא ("going out") in Pss 107:33, 35, 19:6, 65:8, and 89:34 in *Notes on Scripture*; מִשְׁפָּט in Ps 25:9 in the "Blank Bible"; and צֶדֶק

to the King James Version (KJV) a half dozen times in his notebooks, building from his knowledge of Hebrew yet always with a concern for the theological import of the text.[68] Edwards also explored the historical background to inform his interpretation, a practice that contextualizes him in the concerns of the day. The person of David was a particular flashpoint as many in Edwards' time sought to sever the link between David and Christ—especially the deists, who regularly derided the Old Testament as immoral and un-Christian.[69] While Edwards rejected this break, he nonetheless engaged the Psalms regularly on their historical level to understand David's situation. For example, in his reading of Ps 38:7, "For my loins are filled with a loathsome disease: and there is no soundness in my flesh," he considered the historical meaning for David and suggested, in an interpretive move that seems to tarnish Bathsheba's reputation, that David contracted some kind of sexually transmitted disease in his adultery with her. But Edwards still emphasized the consequence of

---

("to be righteous") and its derivatives in his " 'Controversies' Notebook." Jonathan Edwards, *Religious Affections*, ed. John E. Smith, vol. 2 of *WJE* (1959), 147–148; Jonathan Edwards, *The "Miscellanies": Entry Nos. a–z, aa–zz, 1–500*, ed. Thomas A. Schafer, vol. 13 of *WJE* (1994), 166; Jonathan Edwards, *Original Sin*, ed. Clyde A. Holbrook, vol. 3 of *WJE* (1970), 266–267; Jonathan Edwards, *Notes on Scripture*, ed. Stephen J. Stein, vol. 15 of *WJE* (1998), 594–596; Jonathan Edwards, *The "Blank Bible,"* ed. Stephen J. Stein, vol. 24 of *WJE* (2006), 489. Jonathan Edwards, " 'Controversies' Notebook: Justification," in *Writings on the Trinity, Grace, and Faith*, ed. Sang Hyun Lee, vol. 21 of *WJE* (2003), 345–354. On Edwards' facility with Hebrew, Goldman argues that while Edwards "never mastered the intricacies of Hebrew grammar and syntax," nonetheless "the references to Hebrew words, concepts, and texts in his writings reveal a growing familiarity with the Hebraic and Judaic traditions," and he "made use of his Hebrew knowledge and constantly endeavored to enlarge that body of knowledge." Shalom Goldman, *God's Sacred Tongue: Hebrew & the American Imagination* (Chapel Hill: University of North Carolina Press, 2004), 77–78, 87. See also Shalom Goldman, "Introduction," In *Hebrew and the Bible in America: The First Two Centuries*, ed. Shalom Goldman, (Hanover: University Press of New England, 1993), xi–xxx; Sweeney, "The Biblical World of Jonathan Edwards," 227. The Hebrew Bible that Edwards used was a 1609 Genevan edition of the Antwerp Polyglot Bible *Biblia Hebraica: eorundem Latina interpretatio Xantis Pagnini Lucensis, Benedicti Ariae Montani . . .*, (1569–1572) by Santi Pagnini (1470–1541) and Benedict Arias Montanus (1527–1598). In the early 1750s he indicated his interest in procuring a new edition of the Hebrew Bible by the Roman Catholic Father Charles-François Houbigant (1686–1783), *Biblia Hebraica: cum notis criticis et versione Latina . . .* (Paris, 1753). Jonathan Edwards, " 'Catalogue' of Reading," in *Catalogues of Books*, ed. Peter J. Theusen, vol. 26 of *WJE* (2008), 117, 171, 282–283, 423.

68. See Edwards' quibbling with the KJV rendering of Pss 84:3; 9:17; 60:8; 72:15; 73:4; 112:5; and 103:19. Edwards, *Notes on Scripture*, 335; Edwards, *The "Blank Bible,"* 480, 503, 509, 509–510, 528; and Jonathan Edwards, *The "Miscellanies": Entry Nos. 501–832*, ed. Ava Chamberlain, vol. 18 of *WJE* (2000), 381.

69. Gerald R. McDermott, *Jonathan Edwards Confronts the Gods: Christian Theology, Enlightenment Religion, and Non-Christian Faiths* (New York: Oxford University Press, 2000), 99, 105–106.

David's sin: "By this psalm it seems evident that David labored under some very painful and loathsome disease in his loins, that was brought upon [him] as a punishment of his sin with Bathsheba."[70] The history of David or Israel informed Edwards' exegesis on a number of occasions, yet he always kept his eye on the spiritual or theological import of the background data.[71]

Enlightenment thought manifested itself most clearly in Edwards' thinking through the critical questions he addressed concerning the Psalms—questions like authorship. Edwards rejected the notion that David was the sole author of the Psalms and instead held that "ten penmen" wrote the Psalms.[72] In a move to defend the whole of the Psalter as authoritative, Edwards claimed that even the titles of the Psalms were "part of the canon of the Scriptures."[73] He also engaged the new learning by questioning its conclusions about the veracity of the Bible and defending the divine inspiration of the Psalms.[74] Areas related to biblical authority vexed Edwards most, and we consider how he responded to the Enlightenment assaults on the Bible in more detail in chapter 2 on his discussion of Scripture from the Psalms.

The Analogy of Scripture

While Edwards attended to the original language and historical background of the Psalms, his *modus operandi* was to look into the rest of Scripture to understand the texts at hand. That is why Stephen R. C. Nichols notes that "[t]he degree to which he relies on this [principle that Scripture is its own interpreter] has been underestimated in previous accounts of his exegesis."[75]

---

70. Edwards, *The "Blank Bible,"* 493–494.

71. See also his notes on Pss 105:15; 78:43; 78:9; 18:7–15; 90:5–9; 105:28; and 63:1–2. Edwards, *Religious Affections,* 229; Edwards, *Notes on Scripture,* 204; Edwards, *The "Blank Bible,"* 484, 513, 521, 525–526, and 678.

72. Jonathan Edwards, "God's Excellencies" (Ps 89:6), in *Sermons and Discourses 1720–1723,* ed. Wilson H. Kimnach, vol. 10 of *WJE* (1992), 415.

73. Jonathan Edwards, "Like Rain upon Mown Grass" (Ps 72:6), in *Sermons and Discourses 1739–1742,* ed. Harry S. Stout and Nathan O. Hatch with Kyle P. Farley, vol. 22 of *WJE* (2003), 300.

74. Edwards, *Notes on Scripture,* 518–520, 522, 609–610.

75. Stephen R. C. Nichols, *Jonathan Edwards's Bible: The Relationship of the Old and New Testaments in the Theology of Jonathan Edwards* (Eugene, OR: Pickwick, 2013), 25. Nichols uses this point to argue, against Stein, that "surprising though some of his conclusions may be to modern sensibilities, Edwards's exegesis is not the flight of fancy that Stein contends, but is tightly constrained by his reading of Scripture." Nichols, *Jonathan Edwards's Bible,* 24–25. See also Jeongmo Yoo's discussion of Edwards' use of the analogy of Scripture in "Jonathan Edwards's Interpretation of the Major Prophets: The Books of Isaiah, Jeremiah, and Ezekiel," *Puritan Reformed Journal* 3, no. 2 (2011): 164–166.

The Psalter was one book in a divinely inspired collection, and the unity of the Bible gave him the grounds for employing the analogy of Scripture, the practice of interpreting Scripture with Scripture, a practice firmly upheld by the Westminster Confession.[76] Edwards even exhorted his congregation in November 1739 to adopt the practice, to *"compare one scripture with another. For the Scripture, by the harmony of the different parts of it, casts great light upon itself."*[77] Edwards repeatedly employed the analogy of Scripture to shed light on the Psalms. In his reflection on Psalm 119, for example, he compared several verses from that psalm with other passages to interpret the meaning, correlating Ps 119:142 with Isa 51:6; Ps 119:143 with Matt 5:18 and Ps 119:152; Ps 119:144 with Prov 16:21, 1 John 3:22, and Ps 119:142, 150, and 160; Ps 119:151 with Rom 10:6–8 and Deut 30:14; Ps 119:153 with Phil 1:28; and Ps 119:166 with Pss 33:18, 147:11, and Gal 5:6.[78] Edwards viewed Scripture as a harmonic whole and, over and over, too often to recount here, he moved from passage to passage throughout the Bible to open up the Psalms text at hand.

Theological Interpretation

Edwards regularly read the Psalms theologically, observing themes that transcended the historical context of the writer. For example, in "Notes on Scripture" Entry No. 17 on Ps 49:3–4, he noted the psalmist's quite raw description of the dark afterlife. He speculated that "perhaps a future state is here more plainly spoken of than anywhere else in the Old Testament; the Psalmist really speaks right down plain about it."[79] Yet "notwithstanding this certainty and unavoidableness of death," the psalmist compares the end of the wicked and godly by speaking of "a future state and the resurrection, which were great mysteries in Old Testament times."[80] Edwards detected hope of a resurrection even in the veiled world of the Old Testament because the psalmist says, "God

---

76. Chapter 1, article 9 of the Westminster Confession reads: "The infallible rule of interpretation of Scripture is the Scripture itself; and therefore, when there is a question about the true and full sense of any Scripture (which is not manifold, but one), it must be searched and known by other places that speak more clearly." *The Westminster Confession of Faith, A.D. 1647,* in *The Evangelical Protestant Creeds, with Translations,* vol. 3 of *The Creeds of Christendom, with a History and Critical Notes,* ed. Philip Schaff (New York: Harper & Brothers, 1877), 605.

77. Jonathan Edwards, "The Importance and Advantage of a Thorough Knowledge of Divine Truth" (Heb 5:12), in *Sermons and Discourses 1739–1742,* ed. Harry S. Stout and Nathan O. Hatch with Kyle P. Farley, vol. 22 of *WJE* (2003), 101. Emphasis added.

78. Edwards, *The "Blank Bible,"* 532.

79. Edwards, *Notes on Scripture,* 52–53.

80. Edwards, *Notes on Scripture,* 52–53.

will redeem my soul from the power of the grave: for he shall receive me" (Ps 49:15). His exegetical method freed him to read the psalm theologically, not merely historically, to connect the psalmist's words with the divine author's encompassing truths from all Scripture. The remaining chapters of this book will thoroughly demonstrate Edwards' theological interpretation.

Dual Authorship: Prophecy and Typology

Edwards' theological approach and its fuller understandings of the Old Testament were possible because he held to dual authorship, affirming the Holy Spirit's reigning intentions while still retaining the human author's individual contributions. This is why Brandon Withrow remarks that for Edwards, the "many potential meanings" in a biblical passage "are intended by the Spirit as the divine author and are essentially another type of literal meaning."[81] In his "Blank Bible" note on Ps 8:5–9, for example, Edwards observed a twofold reference to the creation of man and the incarnation of Christ, writing, "it is exceeding common for the Holy Ghost to speak of the shadow and the thing shadowed forth, of the lesser and the greater, of the same kind both under one. He speaks most directly and expressly of the first, but he has an ultimate and perhaps a principal respect to the latter."[82] The Bible itself validated this practice, for Paul applied Psalm 8 to Christ in Heb 2:6–9.[83]

In Edwards' view, we can see both the human author's viewpoint and the divine author's ultimate intention. He made this point clear in a sermon on Ps 40:6–8, where he recognized that the verses could be considered as relating either to David or to Christ. He described a general principle for interpreting the Psalms: "in many passages in the Psalms, the Psalmist has a more immediate respect to himself in those things which he speaks; but yet the Holy Ghost has a principal aim at the Christ, the son of David."[84] David may have been oblivious of the full meaning of his words, but no matter, for "the Holy

---

81. Brandon G. Withrow, *Becoming Divine: Jonathan Edwards's Incarnational Spirituality within the Christian Tradition* (Eugene, OR: Cascade, 2011), 179.

82. Edwards, *The "Blank Bible,"* 479.

83. Edwards, *The "Blank Bible,"* 479. See also Edwards, *The "Blank Bible,"* 864. Edwards used Psalm 8 to express this same concept in his "Apocalypse Series," in *Apocalyptic Writings*, ed. Stephen J. Stein, vol. 5 of *WJE* (1977), 150. See also Edwards' "Miscellanies" Entry No. 702, where he explored how the creation of man shadows forth the new creation. Edwards, *The "Miscellanies": Entry Nos. 501–832*, 284–289.

84. Jonathan Edwards, "The Sacrifice of Christ Acceptable" (Ps 40:6–8), in *Sermons and Discourses 1723–1729*, ed. Kenneth P. Minkema, vol. 14 of *WJE* (1997), 440–441.

Ghost might have a further aim in those words which he dictated to David, than David himself had."[85]

Edwards' affirmation of dual authorship allowed him to incorporate the new learning into his interpretation via accommodation. For example, Ps 148:4 calls two groups to praise Yahweh, "ye heavens of heavens, and ye waters that be above the heavens," and Edwards understood these to be metaphors for "ye people and multitudes."[86] However, he also accepted the scientific claim in his day that no waters resided above the heavens, so he explained that "the Holy Ghost intended it not so."[87] Of course, the psalmist believed waters really were there, for that was the reigning conception in his day. Using accommodation Edwards maintained a distinction between what the psalmist understood and what the Spirit intended, the latter of which always agreed with the ontological reality of creation.[88]

In affirming the unifying element of the Spirit's inspirational work in the Scriptures, Edwards also saw prophetic elements in the Psalms. In his "Notes on Scripture" entry on Ps 48:7, "Thou breakest the ships of Tarshish with an east wind," Edwards interpreted the passage to refer to God's use of the gospel to overthrow "Satan's pagan kingdom in Europe," a prophecy of Christendom's defeat of Roman paganism. The gospel, he explained, was a light that shone from the east to the west to accomplish this overthrow.[89] The dual authorship model also freed Edwards to make typological and Christological interpretations of the Psalms. Edwards believed that God commonly gave his revelation using typology in David's day: "it was the manner in those ancient times to

---

85. Edwards, "The Sacrifice of Christ Acceptable," 441. It is worth noting that Edwards did not hold to a strict theory of dictation but believed that the Spirit "indited" the Scriptures through the human authors, who left their imprint on the biblical text. See, for example, Edwards, *The "Blank Bible,"* 513, and Edwards, *The "Miscellanies": Entry Nos. 501–832,* 236. See also Douglas A. Sweeney, "Edwards and the Bible," in *Understanding Jonathan Edwards: An Introduction to America's Theologian,* ed. Gerald R. McDermott, (Oxford: Oxford University Press, 2009), 67–68.

86. Edwards, *Notes on Scripture,* 66.

87. Edwards, *Notes on Scripture,* 66.

88. In this "Notes on Scripture" entry, Edwards cited "Miscellanies" Entry No. 229, "Scripture," where he explained his view of accommodation: "God had a design and meaning which the penmen never thought of, which he makes appear these ways: by his own interpretation, and by his directing the penmen to such a phrase and manner of speaking, that has a much more exact agreement and consonancy with the thing remotely pointed to, than with the thing meant by the penmen," for God "condescended to their manner of speaking and thinking." Edwards, *The "Miscellanies": Entry Nos. a–500,* 347–348.

89. Edwards, *Notes on Scripture,* 52.

deliver divine instructions in general in symbols and emblems, and in their speeches and discourses to make use of types and figures and enigmatical speeches, into which holy men were led by the Spirit of God."[90] Psalm 49:4 and 78:2 even gave a basis for typology, for both speak of "parables" and "dark sayings"; as Edwards explained, with the coupling of "parable" and "dark sayings" the meaning of "parable" was not limited to "a set of discourse of things appertaining to divine wisdom," but rather more properly intended "a mystical, enigmatical speech signifying spiritual and divine things, and figurative and typical representations."[91] Because Scripture embraced typology, Edwards employed it liberally in his interpretation, especially in his Christological and ecclesiological readings of the Psalms.

Edwards' appreciation for Christological and ecclesiological interpretation certainly connects him with the early and medieval church, but the way he went about it was more akin to the seventeenth-century Puritans than to Augustine or Origen. The distinct qualities of Protestant typology emerged seminally in Calvin, who gave greater credence to the natural, historical reading of the text and transformed later Reformed exegesis. So while Edwards followed more in the stream of Dickson and Henry than Calvin, Trapp, and Poole, he was nonetheless indebted to Calvin's emphasis on the literal sense, and he regularly felt the need to establish the literal, historical sense of the Psalms and learn from David before moving to the sense that he said the Holy Spirit ultimately intended.[92]

Edwards, the Enlightenment, and the Christian Tradition

Edwards' typology provided him a means not only to discuss Christ from the Psalms but also to assert the radically supernatural character of the Scripture

---

90. Jonathan Edwards, "Types of the Messiah," in *Typological Writings*, ed. Mason I. Lowance Jr. with David H. Watters, vol. 11 of *WJE* (1992), 193.

91. Edwards, "Types of the Messiah," 217. Psalm 49:4 reads, "I will incline mine ear to a parable: I will open my dark saying upon the harp," and Ps 78:2 reads, "I will open my mouth in a parable: I will utter dark sayings of old." Edwards made the same point with Ps 78:2 in Jonathan Edwards, "Types," in *Typological Writings*, ed. Wallace E. Anderson, vol. 11 of *WJE* (1992), 153.

92. On Edwards' pursuit of both the literal meaning and the Christological, ecclesiological, or eschatological meanings of the text and his use of typology in interpreting Isaiah, Jeremiah, and Ezekiel, see Yoo, "Edwards's Interpretation of the Major Prophets," 166–179. Yoo similarly argues that Edwards' pattern of rooting typology in the literal meaning "clearly distinguished him from the allegorical interpretation of medieval exegesis" and placed him "in continuity with the typology of the sixteenth- and seventeenth-century biblical exegetes." Quotation on 179. For more on Edwards' Christological and ecclesiological interpretation in the Psalms, see chapters 4 and 7, respectively.

in a world that increasingly questioned its reliability. Edwards' typology, then, should be seen not merely as an outworking of his Puritan heritage but as a direct attack on criticism's assault on the Bible's authority. As Brown notes, Edwards "was in fact part of an international movement aimed at revising a constellation of issues pertaining to religious epistemology and typology."[93] So in "Miscellanies" Entry No. 1172, "Double Senses of Scripture," Edwards made note of William Warburton's (1698–1779) *The Divine Legation of Moses Demonstrated* (London, 1741), which defended the double sense of Old Testament prophecy against deist Anthony Collins' (1676–1729) claim that the Old Testament contained no prophecies of Christ.[94] As George Marsden points out, Scripture, not nature or reason, was "the key to reading the true meaning of everything else" for Edwards, and all the types of Scripture "pointed ulti-mately to the redemptive work of Christ," which meant that "[n]ature needed to be interpreted as containing this same message."[95]

Douglas Sweeney and Brandon Withrow describe Edwards' relationship to the Enlightenment in clear terms, noting that "Edwards's interest was to plunder the Egyptians while remaining guarded against Enlightenment extremes," a perspective based on his perception of his place in redemptive history. He believed that he both stood on "the foundation of the Reformation doctrines" while also standing at the dawn of a new age, seeking to unravel the intricacies of Reformed doctrines. So they conclude that Edwards "did engage the Enlightenment sources, even using their expressions, but was also just as eager to bring Scripture and his Reformed Calvinism to bear upon their excesses."[96] So Brown similarly concludes that "Edwards was actively embarked on a plan that would devote considerable attention to the critical historical study of virtually the entire corpus of biblical literature. Yet it is also the case that he strenuously resisted the most radical and negative judgments about the historical integrity and meaning of the biblical texts."[97]

---

93. Brown, *Jonathan Edwards and the Bible*, 148.

94. Jonathan Edwards, *The "Miscellanies": Entry Nos. 1153–1360*, ed. Douglas A. Sweeney, vol. 23 of *WJE* (2004), 88.

95. George Marsden, *Jonathan Edwards: A Life* (New Haven, CT: Yale University Press, 2003), 77.

96. Douglas A. Sweeney and Brandon G. Withrow, "Jonathan Edwards: Continuator or Pioneer of Evangelical History?" in *The Advent of Evangelicalism: Exploring Historical Continuities*, ed. Michael A. G. Haykin and Kenneth J. Stewart (Nashville, TN: Broadman & Holman Academic, 2008), 288.

97. Brown, *Jonathan Edwards and the Bible*, 94.

Edwards' approach to the Psalms likewise shows him to be critically engaged, but biblically grounded and theologically focused. He embodied a tension common among conservative theologians in his age, seeking the latest scholarship on the Bible but rejecting conclusions that questioned the Bible's historicity. And in the Psalms Edwards aimed to connect the new learning with ancient Christianity while never giving up the orthodox doctrines of Scripture's veracity and authority. As a man living on the hinge from the premodern to the modern eras (to use anachronistic terms), Edwards sought to harmonize critical-historical findings with the theological and typological interpretations that reflected the long Christian tradition and that were marked by the Puritan emphasis on heart religion, hammering home the redemptive message God the Spirit revealed through the whole of Scripture to humankind.[98]

Edwards' Sources on the Psalms[99]

As Edwards interpreted the Psalms, he worked within a tradition of exegesis and drew from the labors of others who had studied the Psalms. While we cannot be certain of all the sources Edwards had access to, or even how he used each one, the sources we have record of tell us something about his exegetical concerns, revealing his interest both in critical, historical, and background questions and in spiritual and theological reflection.

Edwards cited Matthew Poole's (1624–1679) *Synopsis Criticorum Aliorumque Sacrae Scripturae Interpretum* (1676) in relation to the Psalms more than any other source: seventy times in the "Blank Bible," ten times in "Prophecies of the Messiah," three times in "Harmony of the Genius Spirit Doctrines and Rules of the Old Testament and the New," twice in his treatise on *Original Sin*, and once in the "Miscellanies." In his use of Poole, Edwards most often merely cited the *Synopsis* with the abbreviation "SSS," leaving little clue what insight he gained from the commentary. The *Synopsis* provided all kinds of background and lexical data from a variety of sources that Edwards consulted to fill out his understanding of the Psalms in their world. One way the *Synopsis*

---

98. Edwards was not alone in his approach to enlightened thought; a number of New England pastors sought insight from the new learning while also stirring up devout affections in their congregations, evident from John Corrigan's study, *The Prism of Piety: Catholick Congregational Clergy at the Beginning of the Enlightenment* (New York: Oxford University Press, 1991).

99. Some of the material in this section is adapted from my article, "Making the Psalter One's 'Own Language': Jonathan Edwards Engages the Psalms," *Jonathan Edwards Studies* 2, no. 1 (2012): 3–29. Used with permission from *Jonathan Edwards Studies*.

served Edwards particularly well was by providing access to Jewish commentary. In *Original Sin* Edwards cited Jewish rabbis quoted in Poole, and in "Prophecies of the Messiah," he was primarily interested in the Jewish rabbis' testimony that certain psalms spoke prophetically of the Messiah, evidence from non-Christian authorities for his own argument that the Psalms foretold of the Christ. Edwards' use of Poole demonstrates his desire to incorporate a multitude of source materials into his exegetical decisions. He did not limit himself merely to Puritan sources but rather sought the best scholarly exegetical work available to someone on the colonial frontier who had limited access to the latest resources.

The second most cited source in Edwards' engagement with the Psalms is Matthew Henry's *Exposition of the Old and New Testaments*, which Edwards cited nineteen times in the "Blank Bible." Unlike Poole, Edwards always quoted Henry at some length, using the *Exposition* both for its background information about the biblical context and for its typological insight. For example, in Edwards' interpretation of Ps 51:7, "Purge me with hyssop," he quoted Henry's background on "the ceremony of cleansing the leper," which included the sprinkling of blood, and from that observation he followed Henry in concluding that purging with hyssop means "with the blood of Christ applied to my soul."[100] Edwards used Henry's historical discussion of Jewish ceremony but also moved to its Christological implication—two ways that he commonly benefited from Henry.

The other sources that Edwards cited on the Psalms in his corpus fall into two general categories. On the one hand, he cited tools or aids from which he gleaned historical, lexical, or technical information in making interpretive decisions.[101] These works included Johannes Buxtorf's (1564–1629) *Lexicon*

---

100. Edwards, *The "Blank Bible,"* 499.

101. In the "Blank Bible," Edwards cited the following sources: Johannes Buxtorf, *Lexicon hebraicum et chaldaicum* (Basil, 1615); Alexander Cruden, *A Complete Concordance to the Holy Scriptures of the Old and New Testaments* (London: D. Midwinter et al., 1738); Philip Doddridge, *The family expositor; or, a paraphrase and version of the New Testament. With critical notes...,* 6 vols. (London: John Wilson, 1739–1756); John Glas, *Notes on Scriptures-Texts, in Seven Numbers,* in vol. 3 of *The Works of Mr. John Glas,* 2d ed. (1748–1760; repr., Perth: R. Morison and Son, 1782), 1–344; Humphrey Prideaux, *The Old and New Testament Connected in the History of the Jews and Neighbouring Nations, from the Declension of the Kingdoms of Israel and Judah to the Time of Christ,* 9th ed. (London: R. Knaplock et al., 1725); Francis Roberts, *Clavis Bibliorum. The key of the Bible, unlocking the richest treasury of the Holy Scriptures...* (London: T. R. and E. M. for George Calvert, 1648); Samuel Shuckford, *The sacred and prophane history of the world connected...,* 3 vols. (London: R. Knaplock and J. Tonson, 1728–1730); and Edward Wells, *An historical geography of the Old Testament...,* 3 vols. (London: James Knapton, 1711–1712). Edwards, *The "Blank Bible,"* 494, 526; 476; 482; 528; 511, 537; 525; 512; and 525. Also, in his "Notes on Scripture" entries on the Psalms, Edwards drew background data from Arthur Bedford, *Scripture Chronology Demonstrated by Astronomical Calculations...* (London:

Hebraicum et Chaldaicum (1615), a standard Hebrew lexicon that Edwards employed to dig into the nuance of meanings in the Hebrew language. This tome was written by a stalwart Reformed Protestant who "had gained an academic reputation bordering upon legend" by the time of his death and whose *Lexicon* would be used by Christian (and even some Jewish) Hebraists for decades.[102] On the other hand, Edwards also found several theological works to be fruitful in informing his exegesis, both on theological and technical levels.[103]

James and John Knapton et al., 1730), in Entry No. 203 (Ps 90:10); Ephraim Chambers, *Cyclopaedia: or, An universal dictionary of arts and sciences...*, (London: J. and J. Knapton et al., 1728), in Entry No. 319 (Psalm 68); and Wells, *An Historical Geography*, in Entry No. 254 (Ps 78:43). Edwards, *Notes on Scripture*, 126–127, 298, and 204. It is also possible Edwards owned a copy of Henry Ainsworth's *Annotations upon the five bookes of Moses, and the booke of the Psalms. Wherein the Hebrew words and sentences are compared with, and explained by the ancient Greeke and Chaldee versions...*, 2 vols. (London, 1622), which he cited in his "Blank Bible" note on Num 22:28, though it is unclear whether or not he used it with the Psalms. Edwards, *The "Blank Bible,"* 272–273; see also Edwards, " 'Catalogue' of Reading," 171.

102. On Buxtorf's significant contribution to the field of Hebrew studies, see Stephen G. Burnett, *From Christian Hebraism to Jewish Studies: Johannes Buxtorf (1564–1629) and Hebrew Learning in the Seventeenth Century* (Leiden: E. J. Brill, 1996). Quotation on 4.

103. From the "Blank Bible," Edwards mentioned the following theological sources: John Evans, *Practical discourses concerning the Christian temper...*(London: John and Barham Clark..., 1723); Theophilus Gale, *The Court of the Gentiles: or, A Discourse Touching the Original of Human Literature, both Philologie and Philosophie, from the Scripture & Jewish Church, Part 1, Of Philologie*, 2d ed. (Oxon: H. Hall for Tho. Gilbert, 1672); Hugo Grotius, *De Veritate religionis Christianae* ([S.I.]: Excudebat L. L[ichfield] impensis G. Webb, 1639); James Hervey, *Theron, Paulinus, and Aspasio; or, Letters and Dialogues, upon the Nature of Love to God, Faith in Christ, Assurance of a Title to Eternal Life...*, 3 vols. (London, 1755); Richard Kidder, *Demonstration of the Messias: In Which the Truth of the Christian Religion Is Proved Especially against the Jews. In Three Parts*, 2d ed. corr. (London: John Osborn..., 1726); Richard Rawlin, *Christ the Righteousness of His People; or, The Doctrine of Justification by Faith in Him. Represented in Several Sermons, Preached at the Merchants Lecture at Pinner's-Hall* (London: R. Hett and J. Oswald, 1741); Isaac Watts, *The Glory of Christ as God-Man Display'd...* (London: J. Oswald and J. Buckland, 1746). Edwards, *The "Blank Bible,"* 517, 526, 525, 502, 528, 494, and 505. In "Notes on Scripture" Entry No. 319 (Psalm 68), he cited *Theoretica-practica theologia...*(Trajecti ad Rhenum: Ex officina Thomae Appels, 1699) by Peter Van Mastricht, his favorite theologian. Edwards, *Notes on Scripture*, 298. For more on Van Mastricht, see Jonathan Edwards to the Reverend Joseph Bellamy, January 15, 1747, in *Letters and Personal Writings*, ed. George S. Claghorn, vol. 16 of *WJE* (1998), 217; and Adriaan Neele, *Petrus Van Mastricht (1630–1706): Reformed Orthodoxy: Method and Piety*, Brill Series in Church History (Leiden: Brill, 2009). In his "Catalogue," Edwards mentioned two theological books related to the Psalms, which he may or may not have procured: John Howe, *The blessedness of the righteous opened, and further recommended from the consideration of the vanity of this mortal life: in two treatises, on Psal. 17.15, Psal. 89.47* (London: A. Maxwell..., 1673); and James Duchal, *Presumptive arguments for the truth and divine authority of the Christian religion...*(London: A. Millar, 1753), which included a sermon on Ps 98:9. Edwards, " 'Catalogue' of Reading," 184, 285. Edwards found John Owen's *A Practical Exposition on the CXXXth Psalm* (London, 1680) insightful on the topic of grace. Jonathan Edwards, "Table to the 'Miscellanies,' " in *The "Miscellanies": Entry Nos. a–z, aa–zz, 1–500*, ed. Thomas A. Schafer, vol. 13 of *WJE* (1994),

Of particular note in this category is Johann Friedrich Stapfer's *Institutiones Theologiae Polemicae Universiae*, which Edwards cited with regard to the Psalms six times in "Prophecies of the Messiah," once in his "Supplement to Prophecies of the Messiah," and once in his treatise on *Original Sin*. In each case he used Stapfer's quotation of Jewish rabbis to bear on his own discussion. In the "Messiah" manuscripts, he highlighted rabbinic commentary that certain Psalms, such as Psalm 72, speak prophetically of the Christ.[104]

All in all, Edwards did not view himself as a lone interpreter. As Marsden notes, "When Edwards studied Scripture, he did not simply sit in his study with the Bible and try to discern its meanings. Rather, he worked directly within a tradition of interpretation."[105] He sought out dozens of critical and theological sources to enlighten his understanding of the Psalms' background and their theological and practical import for the Christian. Recognizing the role of these sources in Edwards' thought also highlights that the influence of biblical interpreters exceeded that of philosophers like Locke, George Berkeley, or Isaac Newton, as Sweeney explains: These exegetical sources "rarely played as great a role in shaping his scholarly agenda. But they played a greater role in its execution."[106]

Homiletical Issues

For Edwards, interpreting the Psalms was tightly intertwined with proclaiming the Psalms from the pulpit, as it was for most interpreters in the previous centuries.[107] Because most of the homiletical issues were wrapped up with how rightly to interpret the biblical text, preaching reflected the ways

---

133. Also, as a young man, Edwards benefitted from Thomas Manton's *One hundred and ninety Sermons on the Hundred and Nineteenth Psalm* (London, 1681). Jonathan Edwards, "Resolutions," in *Letters and Personal Writings*, ed. George S. Claghorn, vol. 16 of *WJE* (1998), 758; Jonathan Edwards, "Personal Narrative," in *Letters and Personal Writings*, ed. George S. Claghorn, vol. 16 of *WJE* (1998), 774, 776.

104. Jonathan Edwards, "The Miscellanies: Entry No. 1067: Prophecies of the Messiah," Franklin Trask Library, Andover Newton Theological School, Newton, MA, §39, §46, §52, §61, §91, and §97[a]; Jonathan Edwards, "Supplement to Prophecies of the Messiah," Franklin Trask Library, Andover Newton Theological School, Newton, MA; Edwards, *Original Sin*, 430.

105. Marsden, *Jonathan Edwards: A Life*, 474.

106. Sweeney, "The Biblical World of Jonathan Edwards," 211.

107. For example, on the influential position of the sermon in New England culture, see Harry S. Stout, *The New England Soul: Preaching and Religious Culture in Colonial New England* (New York: Oxford University Press, 1986).

pastors interpreted the Psalms, and thus we will spend less time on homiletical issues since much of the section on interpretive issues applies to preaching the Psalms. Nonetheless, it is helpful to consider briefly the historical approaches to preaching the Psalms, the homiletical issues with the Psalms in Edwards' day, and Edwards' priorities in preaching the Psalms.

Historical Approaches to Preaching the Psalms

The practice of preaching the Psalms dates back to the early church as one of the most common ways of engaging the book. Most commentators carried pastoral duties and took their exegesis into the pulpit—such was the case for Origen and Augustine, who both preached homilies on the Psalms and wrote separate commentaries as well. Two major emphases tended to dominate Christian preaching of the Psalms in the early and medieval church: proclaiming Christ from the Psalms and challenging listeners to live spiritually devoted and morally upright lives.[108]

In the Reformation era, Calvin gave the Psalms a prized position in the pulpit. In his general practice, Calvin only preached from the New Testament on Sundays and reserved the Old Testament for weekdays. His only exception was the book of Psalms, which he started preaching on Sunday afternoons in the 1550s. He also treated the Psalter in his Friday Congregation gatherings with fellow pastors from 1555 to August 1559.[109] Calvin gave the Psalms a particular prominence in his preaching and teaching that many in the later Reformed tradition would adopt.

In fact, the Psalms were one of the Puritans' favorite books for homiletical treatment. During the seventeenth century, English pastors frequently preached on the Psalms and put their sermons into printed tracts, leaving a trail of Psalms homilies.[110] As an example, in his *One Hundred and Ninety Sermons on the Hundred and Nineteenth Psalm*, Thomas Manton exhibited a redemptive-theological interest and aimed to spur people to walk in the way of blessing described throughout

---

108. Gillingham, *Psalms Through the Centuries*, 28–29, 32–33, 58, 113, 141.

109. Selderhuis, *Calvin's Theology of the Psalms*, 14, 24.

110. John Thompson's "Finding Guide to English Translations of Commentary Literature Written 1600–1700" lists over three dozen published sermons on the Psalms from the century, in addition to several formal lectures on the Psalms and a number of other expositions, tracts, and treatises on the Psalms that likely were derived from sermonic material. John Thompson, "A Finding Guide to English Translations of Commentary Literature Written 1600–1700," Fuller Theological Seminary, http://purl.oclc.org/net/jlt/exegesis/ (accessed November 28, 2009).

Psalm 119.[111] In these sermons, Puritan and Anglican pastors preached from the Psalms for a range of occasions and purposes. The Psalms provided sermonic texts for thanksgiving days (Ps 118:17), funerals (Pss 17:15; 39:5; 73:26), royal functions (Pss 80:17; 121:8), political events such as battles (Ps 60:11–12), Parliament (Ps 72:1–3), the Parliamentary Army's victory during the English Civil Wars (Ps 118:17), the restoration of Charles II (Ps 21:1–5), and the unity achieved by the Glorious Revolution of William and Mary (Ps 133:1). Most published sermons, of course, arose from the minister's regular duty of preaching to his congregation. Pastors preached on Christ's kingdom and priesthood (Psalm 110), God's glory (Pss 19:2; 72:24–26; 73:24), and God's goodness to his church (Psalm 73). They also addressed affliction (Ps 94:12), plague (Psalm 91), and storms (Ps 148:8) and warned of human mortality (Psalm 90). And they emphasized individuals' spiritual state and God's redemptive work by laying open the choice of godly and natural men (Ps 4:6–8), exposing the inheritance of saints and the miserable portion of "worldlings" (Ps 17:14), describing the upright man (Ps 97:11), offering consolation for true repentance (Psalm 51), pointing to the refuge God provides to good men (Ps 40:17), exploring the mystery of redemption (Psalm 126), and outlining saints' personal and national duties (Ps 94:17). The Psalms provided seventeenth-century English pastors with a rich text for addressing the various social and political concerns of their time and also for preaching the gospel and proclaiming God's glorious goodness in a world of troubles.[112]

Historically, the Psalms featured as an important book for Christian proclamation. Preachers appropriated the Psalms to address a diversity of issues since it touched on a breadth of topics, from describing Christ and the core truths of the Christian religion to addressing corporate concerns for the church and society as a whole and encouraging piety and morality in individuals through the gospel.

Homiletical Issues with the Psalms in Edwards' Day

Matthew Henry, the Presbyterian whose commentary on the Bible enjoyed such approbation and popularity among preachers with a Puritan heritage, commended the Psalms as texts "to be read and opened by the ministers of Christ, as containing great and excellent truths, and rules concerning good

---

111. Thomas *Manton, One Hundred and Ninety Sermons on the Hundred and Nineteenth Psalm*, (London: Tho. Parkhurst...; Jonathan Robinson...; Brabazon Aylmey...; and Benjamin Alsop..., 1681).

112. Thompson, "A Finding Guide."

and evil," just as Christ himself opened them up to his disciples.[113] He believed the New Testament pattern of expositing the Psalms as Christian truths not only gave grounds for preaching the Psalms but indeed placed a mandate on Christian pastors to proclaim its most excellent truth faithfully in the pulpit.

But this common conviction, long held throughout the history of the church, was gradually coming into doubt. As critical learning leaned more and more into historicity as the epistemological ground of truth, more interpreters sought to explain the book of Psalms in its ancient Jewish context, which opened up questions about its application to the Christian church or to people living two to three millennia after it was written. While most New England pastors continued preaching from the Psalms, the underlying currents were in place to marginalize the Psalms in the pulpit, at least in circles beholden to the new learning. And Enlightenment-era thinking raised questions about how much of Christ should be seen in the Psalms and whether or not it should be preached as a Christian book.[114]

These questions led many pastors to dwell on the historical background of the Psalms. However, most New England pastors in the early- to mid-eighteenth century continued to preach the Psalms in traditional ways, focusing on the personal and spiritual needs of their people; the corporate needs of the society in the face of political, military, and meteorological uncertainties; and the need for a people to receive comfort in the wake of death's sting. So a pastor like Gilbert Tennent of New Brunswick, New Jersey, preached from the Psalms on a number of occasions to discuss different concerns, from preaching a thanksgiving day sermon (Ps 65:1) and calling on Christians to thank God for a British naval victory (Ps 136:3–4) to exhorting listeners to consider their ways and not forget God (Ps 50:22).[115] Thomas Prince of Boston chose Psalms texts to discuss God's providential judgment manifested in natural causes such as earthquakes (Ps 18:7) and to preach funeral sermons (Pss 116:15; 12:1), a common pastoral practice to help congregants deal with death.[116] The Psalms

---

113. Henry, *Exposition*, [introduction to the book of Psalms].

114. Gillingham, *Psalms Through the Centuries*, 194–203.

115. Gilbert Tennent, *A sermon preach'd at Burlington in New-Jersey, November 23, 1749*... (Philadelphia, PA: W. Bradford, 1749); Gilbert Tennent, *The necessity of thankfulness for wonders of divine mercies*... (Philadelphia, PA: William Bradford, 1744); and Gilbert Tennent, *The danger of forgetting God describ'd... In a sermon on Psalm L. 22*... (New York: John Peter Zenger, 1735).

116. Thomas Prince, *Earthquakes the works of God and tokens of his just displeasure: Two sermons on Psal. xviii. 7*... (Boston: D. Henchman, 1727); Thomas Prince, *Precious in the sight of the Lord is the death of his saints*... (Boston: S. Kneeland & T. Green, 1735); Thomas Prince,

provided a way to discuss political and military concerns from a providentialist standpoint. Thus Charles Chauncy's thanksgiving sermon from Ps 98:1 discussed the British victory at Cape Breton in 1745; George Whitefield preached on Britain's duties from Ps 105:45; and Peter Clark preached to British troops in 1755 on the need for fervency in religion during war.[117] New England pastors also preached on personal spiritual matters from the Psalms: Daniel Lewes sought to deter people from sin and its bitter remembrances (Ps 25:7), Mather Byles described the upright man from Ps 37:37, and John Tucker upheld God's goodness despite affliction (Ps 118:18–19).[118]

This survey of published sermons gives a taste of the sermons preached from the Psalms in New England, though it should be noted that unpublished sermons can reveal different emphases than printed sermons since many published sermons were printed for specific occasions. As Harry Stout observes, "The message and meaning of occasional sermons could and did change over time as New England's social and political circumstances changed, but regular preaching—the preaching colonists heard most of the time—remained consistently otherworldly."[119] Preachers utilized the sermon form to preach to all kinds of shifting concerns facing their congregations, including wars, natural disasters, and political upheaval, but their weekly focus never lost sight of the preeminent importance of a person's and society's relationship with God. Their "regular preaching" upheld gospel matters: "each generation of New England ministers invented and institutionalized a growing range of occasional sermons that allowed for pulpit commentary on social and political themes without corrupting the enduring concern of regular preaching, which was the salvation of the soul."[120] The gospel had been at the core of Puritan

---

The pious cry to the Lord for help when the godly and faithful fail among them...(Boston: T. Rand, 1746); Hughes Oliphant Old, *Moderatism, Pietism, and Awakening*, vol. 5 of *The Reading and Preaching of the Scriptures in the Worship of the Christian Church* (Grand Rapids, MI: Eerdmans, 2004), 246.

117. Charles Chauncy, *Marvellous things done by the right hand and holy arm of God in getting him the victory*...(Boston: J. Fleet, 1745); George Whitefield, *Britain's mercies and Britain's duty*...(Boston: S. Kneeland and T. Green, 1746); and Peter Clark, *Religion to be minded, under the greatest perils of life*...(Boston: S. Kneeland, 1755).

118. Daniel Lewes, *The sins of youth, remembred with bitterness: As represented in a sermon...upon Psalm XXV. 7* (Boston: S. Kneeland, 1725); Mather Byles, *The character of the perfect and upright man...In a discourse on Psalm XXXVII. 37* (Boston: S. Gerrish, 1729); and John Tucker, *God's goodness, amidst his afflictive providences, a just ground of thankfulness and praise: a discourse on Psalm CXVIII, 18,19*...(Boston: S. Kneeland, 1757).

119. Stout, *The New England Soul*, 6.

120. Stout, *The New England Soul*, 6.

preaching for more than a century when Edwards climbed into the pulpit, and even with the influx of the new learning, preachers held firmly to their commitment to preaching the gospel. In New England, homiletics continued this emphasis: "The primary function of the sermon was to proclaim the Gospel of the mighty acts of God culminating in the redemption accomplished in the atoning crucifixion and resurrection of Christ, which guaranteed absolution to the penitent and promised eternal life for men and women of faith and sanctity."[121] This commitment to gospel preaching found traction in the days of the Great Awakening, and many pastors like Edwards used the Psalms for proclaiming the good news of Jesus Christ in their towns.

Edwards' Homiletical Priorities in Preaching the Psalms

Sometime between the summer of 1722 and the spring of 1723, while stationed at his first pastorate in New York City, the teenaged Edwards preached two of his earliest extant sermons on the Psalms.[122] In "God's Excellencies," Edwards built from Ps 89:6, "For who in the heaven can be compared unto the Lord, and who among the sons of the mighty can be likened unto the Lord?" to argue that "God is infinitely exalted in gloriousness and excellency above all created beings," and to describe God in his grand glory.[123] He also pointed out that in this psalm Ethan the Ezrahite, "or rather the Spirit of God by Ethan, gives us a most glorious prophecy of Christ."[124] In his sermon on Ps 95:7–8, "The Duty of Hearkening to God's Voice," he preached an awakening message for his listeners to take heed and stop focusing on temporary "worldly baubles" and to listen to the voice of God "with the heart" immediately.[125] These sermons were just the beginning of a lifelong love of preaching the Psalms, foreshadowing his interest in preaching on God's glory, Christ, and revival in more than one hundred sermons on the Psalms.

---

121. Horton Davies, *The Worship of the American Puritans, 1629–1730* (New York: Peter Lang, 1990), 78, 100. Quotation on 78.

122. While we do not know the chronological order in which these sermons were preached, Thomas A. Schafer has dated them to the same period. See Wilson H. Kimnach, ed., "Appendix: Dated Batches of Sermons," in Jonathan Edwards, *Sermons and Discourses 1720–1723*, vol. 10 of *WJE* (1992), 645.

123. Edwards, "God's Excellencies," 416.

124. Edwards, "God's Excellencies," 415.

125. Jonathan Edwards, "The Duty of Hearkening to God's Voice" (Ps 95:7–8), in *Sermons and Discourses 1720–1723*, ed. Wilson H. Kimnach, vol. 10 of *WJE* (1992), 438–439.

In his homiletical approach to the Psalms, Edwards held much in common with his New England Puritan ancestors, not least of all a belief in the need to base his sermons on the authority of Scripture.[126] Wilson Kimnach observes that "all theology for Edwards was ultimately founded in Scripture."[127] Edwards often used various passages in the Bible to bear on his doctrinal arguments, layering scripture upon scripture to prove his points, but in this approach he still gave the Bible the authoritative position in his theology. As John Carrick observes, "Edwards demonstrates repeatedly that the Scriptures were at one and the same time both the source and the confirmation of his exposition."[128] Also, like his Puritan predecessors, Edwards was adept at employing both biblical and natural imagery to illustrate his theological arguments.[129] And he powerfully wielded the tool of logic, with the result that "[t]hose who listened would be left little room to escape his web of arguments."[130]

In developing sermons, Edwards followed the Puritan structure of text, doctrine, and application (or improvement or use). In his first relatively brief section he exposited the meaning of the text. Then he turned to state his doctrine and provide arguments and proofs in support of it. Finally, he drove home the implications of the doctrine by "improving" on it, that is, applying it or suggesting ways his people could make "use" of the doctrine.

In his exposition of the text, Edwards made it his practice to examine the sermon text, usually a verse or two, by starting with a discussion of the context. He constantly talked about the "occasion" that prompted the writing of whatever particular psalm he was addressing, and he often connected it with the setting in Israel's history or the life of David. So, for example, in his sermon on Ps 7:8, he considered the occasion of the writing intimated by the psalm's title, "Shiggaion of David, which he sang unto the LORD, concerning the words of Cush the Benjamite." Edwards understood "Cush" as referring to the Benjamite Shimei, who cursed David when he was fleeing Absalom.

---

126. On the American Puritans' devotion to Scripture as their foundation, see Davies, *Worship of the American Puritans*, 79–82, 92–94.

127. Wilson H. Kimnach, "General Introduction to the Sermons: Jonathan Edwards' Art of Prophesying," in Jonathan Edwards, *Sermons and Discourses 1720–1723*, vol. 10 of *WJE* (1992), 51.

128. John Carrick, *The Preaching of Jonathan Edwards* (Carlisle, PA: Banner of Truth Trust, 2008), 239.

129. Davies, *Worship of the American Puritans*, 87–92.

130. Marsden, *Jonathan Edwards: A Life*, 129. For fuller treatments of Edwards as preacher, see Kimnach, "General Introduction to the Sermons," 3–258; and Carrick, *The Preaching of Jonathan Edwards*.

In that instance, David appealed to God as the arbiter of truth to judge if he deserved such a curse. Edwards explained this context by looking at the historical account in 2 Samuel 16 and then returning to the Ps 7:8 text, "The LORD shall judge the people: judge me, O LORD, according to my righteousness, and according to mine integrity that is in me," to show David's confidence in God as his judge. From this exposition Edwards preached on the great hope that Christians should have in God as their judge.[131] As he moved from text to theology in his sermons, he regularly began by contextualizing the Psalms.[132]

What stands out in the application sections of Edwards' sermons is that he constantly hammered home the gospel. As he addressed his uses to the various segments in his congregation, he often gave applications for those who were obstinate sinners, those who were under awakenings but not repentant, and those who had been truly converted. This categorization by spiritual state reveals his burden for the unconverted men, women, and children sitting in the pews. In marshaling all his homiletic tools, Edwards sought to draw sinners to repentance and salvation in Christ. In this emphasis, Edwards stood on common ground with earlier New England Puritan preachers, whom Horton Davies describes in a way that fittingly represents Edwards: "Their own genius as preachers lay in combining fidelity to the Biblical record, with relevant and illuminating imagery, and a psychological penetration that would force the evasive soul ambushed in its own dark excuses and illusions out into a coruscating exposure to the Light of the World."[133] In a revealing passage from *Religious Affections*, Edwards described the preacher's duty to make an impression on people's affections so that God's Word might enliven them in the matters of religion:

> And the impressing divine things on the hearts and affections of men, is evidently one great and main end for which God has ordained, that his Word delivered in the holy Scriptures, should be opened, applied, and set home upon men, in preaching.... God hath appointed a particular and lively application of his Word, to men, in the preaching of

131. Jonathan Edwards, "'Tis a Blessed Thing to Some Persons That God Is to Be Their Judge" (Ps 7:8), in *The Glory and Honor of God: Volume 2 of the Previously Unpublished Sermons of Jonathan Edwards*, ed. Michael D. McMullen (Nashville, TN: Broadman & Holman, 2004), 55–56.

132. For a similar argument regarding Edwards' sermons on and interpretation of Isaiah 40–55, see Andrew T. Abernethy, "Jonathan Edwards as Multi-Dimension[al] Bible Interpreter: A Case Study from Isaiah 40–55," *Journal of the Evangelical Theological Society* 56, no. 4 (December 2013): 827–829.

133. Davies, *Worship of the American Puritans*, 81.

it, as a fit means to affect sinners, with the importance of the things of religion, and their own misery, and necessity of a remedy, and the glory and sufficiency of a remedy provided.[134]

In preaching to the affections, Edwards emphasized the gospel, setting men's miserable condition before them so they might accept the sure remedy offered by Christ. While he tended more toward a Christological and typological interpretation of the Psalms in his "Notes on Scripture" and "Blank Bible" manuscripts (though not exclusively), his sermons on the Psalms reveal his gospel thrust in preaching, using the Psalms to elicit responses to the gospel and to encourage renewed piety, a strategy especially visible in his applications.

Edwards' preaching habits on the Psalms in Stockbridge constitute no major departure from his earlier homiletical priorities. He preached twenty of his 104 extant sermons on the Psalms in Stockbridge, and he tended to preach them from shorter manuscripts or outlines, partly reflecting his need for extra time since he preached through a translator.[135] He liked to use the book of nature to connect to the natural habitat of the Indians, just as he had frequently used natural imagery in earlier sermons.[136] But it is striking that Edwards did not rely on natural imagery from the Psalms more often in his sermons to the Indians. What occupied Edwards most was his desire to warn the Indians of their sinful dilemma and proclaim the gospel of Christ as their only solution.

For example, he seemed particularly interested in describing the problem of sin that has its grip on every individual, preaching on the nature of humans as different from all creatures in their capacity to know God but who are infirm, naturally blind to the things of God, and more willing to trust men or riches than God.[137] He also explained what makes a man truly happy, appealing

---

134. Edwards, *Religious Affections*, 115.

135. On Edwards' sermons to the Indians at Stockbridge, see Kimnach, "General Introduction to the Sermons," 125–129; Wilson H. Kimnach, "Edwards as Preacher," in *The Cambridge Companion to Jonathan Edwards*, ed. Stephen J. Stein (New York: Cambridge University Press, 2007), 119–121; Rachel M. Wheeler "Edwards as Missionary," in *The Cambridge Companion to Jonathan Edwards*, ed. Stephen J. Stein (New York: Cambridge University Press, 2007), 204–206.

136. Wheeler, "Edwards as Missionary," 204–205.

137. Jonathan Edwards, "1004. Sermon on Ps 119:60(b) (September 1751)," Beinecke Rare Book and Manuscript Library, Yale University, New Haven, CT; Jonathan Edwards, "319. Sermon on Ps 90:5–6 (April 1734)," in *Sermons, Series II, 1734*, vol. 49 of *WJEO*; Jonathan Edwards, "1007. Sermon on Ps 119:18 (October 1751)," Beinecke Rare Book and Manuscript Library, Yale University, New Haven, CT; Jonathan Edwards, "1168. Sermon on Ps 118:6–9 (July 23, 1756)," Beinecke Rare Book and Manuscript Library, Yale University, New Haven,

to the innate human desire for happiness, and he equated the happy man with the godly man who loves God above all things and walks in a holy manner.[138] Edwards motivated the Indians to turn to Christ on the one hand by warning them of how little time they have in this temporal realm but on the other hand by reveling in the incomparable joys of being in God's house and God's presence and extolling the good gifts that come from God.[139] Throughout these sermons, Edwards' emphasis on the gospel, seen through the need for salvation from sin and the hope found only in Christ, served as the organizing theme for the Psalms sermons to the Stockbridge Indians.

We have record that Edwards preached on the Psalms every year between 1723 and 1756, except 1725, 1727, 1730, and 1732.[140] Because some sermons are datable only to a period that straddles two years (e.g., August 1731–December 1732), it is likely, though impossible to verify, that Edwards preached sermons on the Psalms in 1730 and 1732. Either way, the Psalms clearly served as Edwards' homiletical fare steadily throughout his life. He treated a number of doctrinal themes from the Psalms in the pulpit, including twenty-one sermons on Christian piety; sixteen on sin, wickedness, and judgment; fifteen on Christ and his benefits; thirteen each on God's nature and character, on human nature, and on spiritual benefits to the church; nine on awakening and repentance; and four on prayer. What is striking is that in any given year, he

---

CT; Jonathan Edwards, "1161. Sermon on Ps 37:16 (April 1756)," Beinecke Rare Book and Manuscript Library, Yale University, New Haven, CT.

138. Jonathan Edwards, "981. Sermon on Ps 112:1 (February 1751)," Beinecke Rare Book and Manuscript Library, New Haven, CT; Jonathan Edwards, "God the Best Portion of the Christian" (Ps 73:25), in vol. 4 of *Works of President Edwards* (Worcester ed.), 8th ed. (1778; repr., New York: Leavitt & Allen, 1852), 540–547; Jonathan Edwards, "1031. Sermon on Ps 27:4(b) (March 1752)," Beinecke Rare Book and Manuscript Library, Yale University, New Haven, CT; Jonathan Edwards, "1112. Sermon on Ps 119:1–6 (March 1754)," Beinecke Rare Book and Manuscript Library, Yale University, New Haven, CT; Jonathan Edwards, "1147. Sermon on Ps 1:1 (August 1755)," Beinecke Rare Book and Manuscript Library, Yale University, New Haven, CT.

139. Jonathan Edwards, "1071. Sermon on Ps 39:5 (March 1753)," Beinecke Rare Book and Manuscript Library, New Haven, CT; Jonathan Edwards, "1113. Sermon on Ps 119:59–60 [60–61] (March 1754)," Beinecke Rare Book and Manuscript Library, Yale University, New Haven, CT; Jonathan Edwards, "1038. Sermon on Ps 84:10 (May 1752)," Beinecke Rare Book and Manuscript Library, Yale University, New Haven, CT; Jonathan Edwards, "1175. Sermon on Ps 27:4(c) (October 1756)," Beinecke Rare Book and Manuscript Library, Yale University, New Haven, CT; Jonathan Edwards, "1096. Sermon on Ps 145:15–21 (Nov. 1, 1753)," Beinecke Rare Book and Manuscript Library, Yale University, New Haven, CT.

140. See Appendix 1, "Jonathan Edwards' Sermons on the Psalms," for a chart outlining the breakdown of the sermons on the Psalms. The categories discussed below are based on the general doctrinal thrust of the sermons, although it should be noted that Edwards' sermons were complex events, normally lasting about one hour, that spoke to a number of concerns.

preached from the Psalms to address various issues without confining himself to one particular doctrinal theme.

The thread that runs through Edwards' sermons is the preaching of the gospel. Even when Edwards preached directly on Christ from the Psalms—which represents a relatively small portion of his Psalms sermon corpus (14 percent)—he still turned that discussion in the improvement section to a call for people to turn to Christ because his glory, kingship, or benefits should motivate people to respond to the gospel. And while he was concerned to root his interpretation in the historical setting of the Psalms as Enlightenment thought spread its influence, Edwards—like his fellow New England pastors—still preached the Psalms theologically with an emphasis on the proclamation of the gospel.

Liturgical Issues

The Psalms have a long history of use in worship, a practice that reaches back to the days of David and has uniquely colored the church's approach to this book.[141] We move now to liturgical issues by briefly describing the historical use of the Psalms in worship, outlining the psalm singing controversies in New England, and considering how Edwards used the Psalms in worship and engaged the liturgical debates of his day.

Historical Use of the Psalms in Worship

The Christian practice of singing the Psalms in worship grew out of the Jewish custom of using the Psalter as their hymnbook, and it dates to the apostolic times of the church, when Paul told Christians in Col 3:16 that they should be "teaching and admonishing one another in psalms and hymns and spiritual songs, singing with grace in your hearts to the Lord." In the early centuries of the church, we have sparse details on Christians' use of the Psalms, but some communities clearly embraced the Psalms in Christian liturgy even in the first century.[142] That the Psalms were so widely quoted in the first two centuries of Christian writings also suggests their parallel use in early worship.[143]

---

141. On the use of the Psalms in ancient Israelite worship, see Sigmund Mowinckel, *The Psalms in Israel's Worship* (1962; repr., Grand Rapids, MI: Eerdmans, 2004).

142. Gillingham, *Psalms Through the Centuries*, 40.

143. Frank C. Senn, *Christian Liturgy: Catholic and Evangelical* (Minneapolis, MN: Fortress, 1997), 71. See also Tertullian, *On Prayer*, in Lawrence J. Johnson, *Worship in the Early Church: An Anthology of Historical Sources*, vol. 1 (Collegeville, MN: Liturgical Press, 2009), 135. Paul F. Bradshaw warns against assuming a widespread practice of psalm singing in

By the fourth century, Christians used the Psalter regularly in worship, in part due to the Constantinian Settlement (313), which made Christianity a legal religion. The resulting church-state establishment spawned a rise in both desert and urban monasticism, renewing psalm recitation and singing, which became "a regular feature of eucharistic services."[144] The desert fathers who removed themselves from mainstream society gravitated to the Psalms, citing the Psalms more than any Old Testament book in the collective *Sayings of the Desert Fathers.*[145] The monasteries organized their offices of prayer around both the repetition of selected psalms and the continuous reading of the whole Psalter. They emphasized the Psalms because "the psalms embraced all Scripture, and therefore to learn them by heart (along with parts of the New Testament) was to embrace the essence of the Gospel."[146] John Cassian's (c. 360–c. 435) *Institutes of the Cenobia* and Benedict of Nursia's (480–550) Rule both bore weighty influence on Western monasticism in instituting weekly recitation of the entire Psalter, and as James White explains, "[w]eekly recitation of the psalms throughout a lifetime of stable community life shaped the lives of thousands of men and women for centuries."[147]

The laity was also exposed to the Psalms in the singing of psalms and hymns, which often imitated psalms. Ambrose of Milan (337/339–397) championed psalmody, and when some denigrated the singing of psalms as "superfluous and less fitting for divine services," Nicetas of Remesiana (d. c. 414) wrote a tract, "On the Usefulness of Psalmody," arguing from the Old and

---

worship without stronger documentary evidence than we have. *The Search for the Origins of Christian Worship: Sources and Methods for the Study of Early Liturgy* (New York: Oxford University Press, 1992), 22–24, 138–139.

144. William T. Flynn, "Liturgical Music," in *The Oxford History of Christian Worship*, ed. Geoffrey Wainwright and Karen B. Westerfield Tucker (Oxford: Oxford University Press, 2006), 770.

145. Douglas Burton-Christie, *The Word in the Desert: Scripture and the Quest for Holiness in Early Christian Monasticism* (Oxford: Oxford University Press, 1993), 97. See also James McKinnon, "Desert Monasticism and the Later Fourth-Century Psalmodic Movement," *Music and Letters* 75 (1994): 505–521.

146. Gillingham, *Psalms Through the Centuries*, 40–42. Quotation on 42.

147. James F. White, *Introduction to Christian Worship* (Nashville, TN: Abingdon, 1981), 120; Hughes Oliphant Old and Robert Cathcart, "From Cassian to Cranmer: Singing the Psalms from Ancient Times until the Dawning of the Reformation," in *Sing a New Song: Recovering Psalm Singing for the Twenty-First Century*, ed. Joel R. Beeke and Anthony T. Selvaggio (Grand Rapids, MI: Reformation Heritage Books, 2010), 1–5; Benedict of Nursia, *Rule*, in Lawrence J. Johnson, *Worship in the Early Church: An Anthology of Historical Sources*, vol. 4 (Collegeville, MN: Liturgical Press, 2009), 31; Senn, *Christian Liturgy*, 200–202; Gillingham, *Psalms Through the Centuries*, 51–53.

New Testaments that "it is incorrect to believe that the practice of psalmody has now been abrogated just as many other practices of the Old Law have come to an end"—an issue that would resurface in New England debates over psalmody.[148]

In the medieval era, the Psalter continued to infuse Christian worship in both Eastern and Western traditions and in both monasteries and cathedrals. Patterns of usage differed by region; some sang only the Psalms, while some included hymns imitating the Psalms.[149] Throughout the medieval era, the Psalms took on special importance to the lay people since in most cases it was the only book of the Bible they were allowed to read or recite, and so the Psalms "were perceived to be the property of lay Christians in a way that the rest of the Scriptures were not."[150] In the late Middle Ages, however, psalmody fell to a low point. The laity participated less in church singing as the trained chanters and choir took over that role and as complex cathedral music drowned out psalmody; the Latin liturgy also became a barrier as lay knowledge of Latin dissipated.[151]

Naturally, then, one major issue of worship reform in the Reformation era was to include the laity in psalm singing. Luther restored congregational singing of psalms and hymns, and other Reformed churches followed suit.[152] Calvin particularly bolstered the development of psalmody by embracing the regulative principle, a belief that only the resources and practices of worship instituted and exemplified in Scripture were to be used in church. Thus Calvin promoted the translation of metrical, rhyming psalms and introduced the singing of only the Psalms in worship in unison with no musical instruments. Calvin taught that the Psalms provide "an infallible rule for directing us with respect to the right manner of offering to God the sacrifice of praise," and he added that "there is no other book in which we are more perfectly taught the

148. Gillingham, *Psalms Through the Centuries*, 37–38, 42; Ambrose of Milan, *Commentaries on Twelve Psalms of David*, in Lawrence J. Johnson, *Worship in the Early Church: An Anthology of Historical Sources*, vol. 2 (Collegeville, MN: Liturgical Press, 2009), 71–72; Nicetas of Remesiana, *On the Usefulness of Psalmody*, in Lawrence J. Johnson, *Worship in the Early Church: An Anthology of Historical Sources*, vol. 3 (Collegeville, MN: Liturgical Press, 2009), 207, 210.

149. Gillingham, *Psalms Through the Centuries*, 47–55.

150. William L. Holladay, *The Psalms Through Three Thousand Years: Prayerbook of a Cloud of Witnesses* (Minneapolis, MN: Fortress, 1993), 178.

151. Gillingham, *Psalms Through the Centuries*, 120–121.

152. Gillingham, *Psalms Through the Centuries*, 140.

right manner of praising God, or in which we are more powerfully stirred up to the performance of this religious exercise."[153]

Metrical psalmody served as perhaps the most innovative method for putting the Psalms in the laity's hands, and it also served as "one of [the Reformation's] most powerful weapons" for spreading and deepening the movement.[154] While Luther adapted psalms loosely for German hymns, those in the Swiss Reformation confined themselves to the biblical text as they put psalms to meter and rhyme. Metrical psalmody was introduced in England in the 1540s by Dutch Protestants fleeing persecution and gained increasing popularity during the latter half of the sixteenth century, especially among dissenters and nonconformists. The most well-known metrical psalter was Thomas Sternhold and John Hopkins' version, *The Whole Booke of Psalms*, published in 1549 with forty-four psalms, which was expanded to include the whole Psalter in 1562. That version became known simply as *Sternhold and Hopkins* and remained the most popular version into the eighteenth century, gradually yielding to the 1696 version by Poet Laureate Nahum Tate and royal chaplain Nicholas Brady, which offered smoother renderings and became known simply as *Tate and Brady*.[155]

During the Parliamentary reign in England, the Westminster assembly produced the *Directory for the Public Worship of God in the Three Kingdoms* (1644), which temporarily replaced the Puritan-abhorred Book of Common Prayer. The *Directory* admonished that "[it] is the duty of Christians to praise God publicly, by singing of psalms together in the congregation, and also privately in the family."[156] They aimed to transform not just the church but the basic unit of the family through the singing of psalms, and while they encouraged voices singing in tune, the "chief care" lay in engaged minds and changed hearts,

---

153. Calvin, *Commentary*, 1:xxxviii–xxxix.

154. Zoltan Haraszti, *The Enigma of the Bay Psalm Book* (Chicago: University of Chicago Press, 1956), 3.

155. Beth Quitsland, *The Reformation in Rhyme: Sternhold, Hopkins and the English Metrical Psalter, 1547–1603*, St. Andrews Studies in Reformation History (Aldershot: Ashgate, 2008), esp. 1–18, 273; Gillingham, *Psalms Through the Centuries*, 146–155; Holladay, *Psalms Through Three Thousand Years*, 198–206; Davies, *The Worship of the English Puritans* (Westminster: Dacre, 1948), 162–164. On the history and development of metrical psalmody, which in some forms predates the Reformation, see Allen Cabaniss, "Background of Metrical Psalmody," *Calvin Theological Journal* 20, no. 2 (1985): 191–206.

156. *A Directory for the Public Worship of God in the Three Kingdoms*, reprinted in *Scripture and Worship: Biblical Interpretation and the Directory for Public Worship*, by Richard A. Muller and Rowland S. Ward, The Westminster Assembly and the Reformed Faith Series, ed. Carl R. Trueman (1645; repr., Phillipsburg, NJ: P & R, 2007), 174.

singing "with understanding and with grace in the heart."[157] The *Directory* also established the practice, in places where congregants could not read, of "lining out" the psalm, whereby one person would "read the psalm, line by line, before the singing of it"—though this practice later contributed inadvertently to the degeneration of psalmody.[158]

Psalm Singing Controversies in New England

The Reformers' innovation in metrical psalmody encouraged lay internalization of the Psalter but also laid the groundwork for controversy. Those Reformers who so firmly upheld accurate translation of the Bible in the vernacular also translated the Psalms more freely to place them in memorable metrical settings—a move that paved the way for composing hymns that loosely paraphrased the Psalms.[159] But how far should one go in adapting the biblical text for lay worship? The tension between the regulative principle and the desire to nurture lay spiritual development in understandable terms led to a faceoff in the eighteenth century. Those who sang *Sternhold and Hopkins* did not automatically embrace Isaac Watts. So the eighteenth century had its own "worship wars"—not over hymns versus praise songs but over metrical psalms versus hymns.

In North America, from the beginning of English settlement the pioneers sang the Psalms. The English settlers at Jamestown in 1607 preferred *Sternhold and Hopkins*, and the English separatists who settled at Plymouth in 1620 brought the metrical version of Henry Ainsworth, *The Booke of Psalms: Englished both in Prose and Meeter.*[160] The New England Puritans used both *Sternhold and Hopkins* and Ainsworth's version for a time, though they were vexed by the former because of its inaccurate renderings of the Hebrew and disliked the latter because it employed too many meters and was identified with the separatists, who more radically distanced themselves from the Church of England. So their creation of a new metrical Psalter served as "an expression

---

157. *A Directory for the Public Worship*, 174.

158. *A Directory for the Public Worship*, 174; Davies, *Worship of the English Puritans*, 165. See also Davies, *Worship of the American Puritans*, 125–127. On the history of Puritan worship, see Harry S. Stout, "Liturgy, Literacy, and Worship in Puritan Anglo-America, 1560–1670," in *By the Vision of Another World: Worship in American History*, ed. James D. Bratt (Grand Rapids, MI: Eerdmans, 2012), 11–35.

159. Davies, *Worship of the English Puritans*, 162; Gillingham, *Psalms Through the Centuries*, 144; Holladay, *Psalms Through Three Thousand Years*, 206.

160. Davies, *Worship of the English Puritans*, 166.

of the colony's own brand of Calvinism," differentiating themselves from the Plymouth separatists and the Church of England.[161] The Massachusetts Bay Colony pastors' version was the first book to be printed in America, *The Whole Book of Psalmes Faithfully Translated into English Metre* (1640), which became known simply as the *Bay Psalm Book* and went through more than fifty editions over the next century.[162] In doing so, the Massachusetts Bay clergy who toiled to produce the *Bay Psalm Book*—including Peter Bulkeley, John Cotton, John Eliot, Richard Mather, Nathaniel Ward, Thomas Welde, Samuel Whiting, and John Wilson—employed their Hebrew skills to create an accurate metrical translation of the Psalms for the spiritual health of their churches.[163] Charles Hambrick-Stowe observes, "The massive undertaking of completing the *Bay Psalm Book* within the first ten years of settlement makes sense only if we recognize Puritanism as a popular devotional movement," aiming to promote conversion and piety.[164]

The *Bay Psalm Book* met with great success for over a century.[165] But gradually, the singing of psalms declined in quality as churches struggled

---

161. Haraszti, *Enigma of the Bay Psalm Book*, 7–10. Joanne van der Woude similarly argues that the *Bay Psalm Book* represented the Puritans' effort to assert themselves in the transatlantic context by "articulating a new, colonial identity within Anglo-American Protestantism," particularly by the claim that the *Bay Psalm Book* exhibited greater faithfulness to the text of Scripture than earlier psalters, though she suggests that their values of "simplification and homogenization" actually sacrificed both fidelity to the Hebrew and verbal elegance for "metrical regularity." Joanne van der Woude, "'How Shall We Sing the Lord's Song in a Strange Land?' A Transatlantic Study of the *Bay Psalm Book*," in *Psalms in the Early Modern World*, ed. Linda Phyllis Austern, Kari Boyd McBride, and David L. Orvis (Burlington, VT: Ashgate, 2011), 116, 120–121, 129–130. Quotations on 116, 129, 130.

162. Haraszti, *Enigma of the Bay Psalm Book*, 29. The *Bay Psalm Book* was modestly revised in 1651.

163. Haraszti makes the important corrective that several authors collaborated on this project and that some were quite adept at versification, including John Cotton and John Wilson. Haraszti, *Enigma of the Bay Psalm Book*, 12–27.

164. Charles Hambrick-Stowe, *The Practice of Piety: Puritan Devotional Disciplines in Seventeenth-Century New England* (Chapel Hill: University of North Carolina Press, 1982), 113. Davies, *Worship of the American Puritans*, 120–125; Gillingham, 158–159; Hambrick-Stowe, 103–104, 111–116; Karen B. Westerfield Tucker, "North America," in *The Oxford History of Christian Worship*, ed. Geoffrey Wainwright and Karen B. Westerfield Tucker (Oxford: Oxford University Press, 2006), 588–595. See also Allen Carden, *Puritan Christianity in America: Religion and Life in Seventeenth-Century Massachusetts* (Grand Rapids, MI: Baker Book House, 1990), 115–132, for a description of seventeenth-century Puritan practices with regard to worship, preaching, and personal piety.

165. On the mid-seventeenth-century controversies over psalm singing, see Haraszti, *Enigma of the Bay Psalm Book*, 19–27, and John Cotton's (1584–1652) preface to *The Bay Psalm Book* (1640; repr., Chicago: University of Chicago Press, 1956), esp. [4–5, 9–10] (the text omits printed page numbers). On Cotton's 1647 extended volume on the topic, see David W. Music,

to maintain knowledge of the tunes. One thorny problem precentors faced was keeping the congregation on the same tune. Poor congregational singing grated on the ears of many pastors and led to a unified ministerial movement to reform singing in New England in the 1720s and 1730s. Cotton Mather (1663–1728) promoted singing schools; Thomas Symmes (1678–1725) sought to abolish the oral tradition of lining out and replace it with reading music by note; and Thomas Walter hailed the practice of three-part harmony. Laypeople initially resisted the "New Way" of singing in part because they sensed it was an attack on their religious identity, since they associated these practices with "Popery."[166] But support for the New Way gained traction through a series of publications and discourses on the topic. Between 1720 and 1730, thirty-one ministers, including Benjamin Colman, Cotton Mather, and Thomas Prince, gave signature approval or preached in support of the New Way of singing. Pastoral concerns, however, were driven not by aesthetics but primarily by "the clergy's concern with irreligion, cultural decline, and their own status."[167] Pastors were deeply troubled that New England was slumping into increasing vice, and they promoted the singing of psalms as one strategy for reformation. The reforms made a lasting impact on New England culture, for by the 1740s most congregations in New England had adopted the New Way of singing.[168] However, throughout the singing controversies of the 1720s, "everyone agreed on the texts to be sung: psalms, and only psalms."[169] But that practice began to shift during the revivals. In essence, the psalm singing controversies of the 1720s and 1730s were a prelude to and contributing cause of both the religious revivals of the 1740s *and* the adoption of hymn singing in public worship.

Another key force behind the changes in psalmody was Isaac Watts (1674–1748), who rejected the regulative principle as blind acceptance of baseless tradition, saying that such a method brought darkness into the minds of worshipers, while it was better for worshipers to understand what they sang. So

---

" 'An Holy Duty of God's Worship': John Cotton's *Singing of Psalms a Gospel Ordinance,*" *The Hymn* 56, no. 1 (Winter 2005): 7–15.

166. Van der Woude, "A Transatlantic Study of the *Bay Psalm Book,*" 133–134.

167. Laura L. Becker, "Ministers vs. Laymen: The Singing Controversy in Puritan New England, 1720–1740," *New England Quarterly* 55 (March 1982): 79–80.

168. Becker, "Ministers vs. Laymen," 79–96; Haraszti, *Enigma of the Bay Psalm Book,* 69–71; Robert Stevenson, *Protestant Church Music in America: A Short Survey of Men and Movements from 1564 to the Present* (New York: W. W. Norton & Company, 1966), 16–31.

169. Christopher N. Phillips, "Cotton Mather Brings Isaac Watts' Hymns to America; or, How to Perform a Hymn without Singing It," *The New England Quarterly* 85, no. 2 (June 2012): 208.

Watts departed from literal translations and metrical versification to "imitate" the Psalms in his 1719 *The Psalms of David Imitated in the Language of the New Testament*.[170] He held that the Jewish Psalms needed to be fleshed out with the revelation received in Christ, and he sought to show *"how insufficient a strict translation of the psalms is to attain the designed end."*[171] Instead of speaking in the language of the types contained in the Psalms, Watts spelled out the antitype, celebrating the fullness of redemption secured in Christ, the ultimate sacrificial Lamb. Watts' "grand design" was *"to teach my author to speak like a Christian."*[172]

Watts did not stop with revolutionizing psalmody; he also insisted that "even the Christianized Psalter could not meet every need of New Testament worship," for Christians had liberty to sing out the fullness of Christian doctrine that was revealed in Christ long after the Psalms were composed.[173] The metrical Psalters made Watts' development possible because they moved one step away, with Protestant approval, from the strict literal rendering of the biblical text. The acceptance of Christian hymns was just a step away from imitating the Psalms, and Watts pioneered that development.[174] Davies argues that by defending "the right to paraphrase the songs of the Old Dispensation in the interests of the New," Watts freed Puritans from literalism and made the production of hymns possible.[175]

A number of English Calvinists rejected Watts' innovations, arguing that proper worship of God was to sing David's psalms, by which they meant *Sternhold and Hopkins*. Watts' hymns and psalter also met with resistance in New England, where people were committed to the *Bay Psalm Book*, *Sternhold and Hopkins*, and *Tate and Brady*. But the singing school movement and revivalism together loosened these psalters' hold on the people.[176] Cotton Mather

---

170. Esther Rothenbusch Crookshank, "'We're Marching to Zion': Isaac Watts in Early America," in *Wonderful Words of Life: Hymns in American Protestant History and Theology*, ed. Richard J. Mouw and Mark A. Noll, Calvin Institute of Christian Worship Liturgical Studies Series (Grand Rapids, MI: Eerdmans, 2004), 20.

171. Isaac Watts, *The Psalms of David imitated in the language of the New Testament, and apply'd to the Christian state and worship with the preface, or, an enquiry into the right way of fitting the Book of Psalms for Christian worship, and notes* (1719; repr., Boston: D. Kneeland, for Thomas Leverett, in Corn-Hill, 1770), viii. Italics original in all quotations from Watts.

172. Watts, *The Psalms of David imitated*, xviii.

173. Crookshank, "'We're Marching to Zion,'" 20.

174. See Watts, *The Psalms of David imitated*, xix. For more on Watts' hymns, see Madeleine Forell Marshall and Janet Todd, *English Congregational Hymns in the Eighteenth Century* (Lexington: University of Kentucky Press, 1982), 28–59.

175. Davies, *Worship of the English Puritans*, 176, 178.

176. Crookshank, "'We're Marching to Zion,'" 22, 25.

led the way in promoting Watts' hymns by appending them to the end of his published sermons. By 1740 nine other pastors had done the same, seeking to engender devotional piety by disseminating Watts' hymns. In doing so, they unwittingly set the stage for the shift from exclusive psalmody to exclusive hymnody in New England. One of these pastors was Edwards, who attached one of Watts' hymns to his sermon, *A Supernatural and Divine Light* in 1734.[177] The desire to promote warm-hearted religion through these hymns helped spark revival. As Mark Noll observes, "nothing was more central to the evangelical revival than the singing of new hymns written in praise of the goodness, mercy, and grace of God."[178] What made hymns so powerful was that they gave a voice to the people to sing in language that resonated with their hearts, stirred by the evangelical message of redemption. The themes they revisited time and again were the doctrines of God's redemptive work in the gospel: "the hymns that were most often reprinted held to their narrow focus on the great acts of redemption that disturbed complacent sinners, turned them with longing to Christ, encouraged them in the life of faith, and joined them to Christ eternally."[179]

Given the background of how important psalm singing was to seventeenth-century Puritans, we can better understand how controversial it was to move away from singing only the Psalms in public worship. Such a move could be understood as departing from the Bible itself. Yet of even greater importance to many eighteenth-century New England pastors than the literal words of the Bible was the life-changing message of the Bible that God had redeemed his people through Jesus Christ. Jonathan Edwards engaged the controversies over psalmody in worship in the midst of the revivalist impulse of the mid-eighteenth century.

Edwards and the Psalms in Worship

Edwards grew up singing the Psalms in his father's church and expressed an appreciation for the devotional discipline in his spiritual life. At age nineteen, he recorded a personal worship resolution in his "Diary": "To praise God, by singing psalms in prose, and by singing forth the meditations of my heart in

---

177. Phillips, "Cotton Mather Brings Isaac Watts' Hymns," 213–214, 217–218, 221.

178. Mark A. Noll, "The Defining Role of Hymns in Early Evangelicalism," in *Wonderful Words of Life: Hymns in American Protestant History and Theology*, ed. Richard J. Mouw and Mark A. Noll, Calvin Institute of Christian Worship Liturgical Studies Series (Grand Rapids, MI: Eerdmans, 2004), 4. See also Davies, *Worship of the English Puritans*, 179.

179. Noll, "The Defining Role of Hymns," 11.

prose."[180] This entry was written on September 22, 1723, at the time that the New England clergy were promoting the New Way of singing, and this resolution reflected two interests in Edwards' approach to worship, both the tradition of singing psalms and a desire to express heartfelt piety in song using his own words. These commitments would find fuller expression in the years to come.

Early on Edwards embraced the switch from lining out psalms to singing psalms in harmony.[181] Like the clergy calling for singing reform, Edwards was also deeply concerned about his congregation's worldliness and sought to vivify religion in their hearts through song. Northampton had transitioned to the New Way of singing under Edwards' grandfather Solomon Stoddard in the 1720s, and it is likely that during Edwards' pastorate "a good portion of the congregation had been through several singing schools."[182] He promoted singing in harmony with powerful results. The Northampton congregation experienced a revival in 1734–1735 that captured international attention through Edwards' *Faithful Narrative of the Surprising Work of God in the Conversion of Many Hundred Souls in Northampton* (1737). While the revival arose out of several causes—Edwards attributed it, in part, to a sermon series on justification by faith[183]—the singing reforms softened the people's hearts and gave them a means of enjoying the sweetness of revival:

> Our public praises were then greatly enlivened; God was then served in our psalmody, in some measure, in the beauty of holiness [Ps 96:9]. It has been observable that there has been scarce any part of divine worship, wherein good men amongst us have had grace so drawn forth and their hearts so lifted up in the ways of God, as in singing his praises. Our congregation excelled all that ever I knew in the external part of the duty before, generally carrying regularly and well three parts of music, and the women a part by themselves. But now they were evidently wont

180. Jonathan Edwards, "Diary," in *Letters and Personal Writings*, ed. George S. Claghorn, vol. 16 of *WJE* (1998), 781.

181. Mark A. Noll, "The Significance of Hymnody in the First Evangelical Revivals, 1730–1760," in *Revival, Renewal, and the Holy Spirit*, ed. Dyfed Wyn Roberts, Studies in Evangelical History and Thought (Milton Keynes, UK: Paternoster, 2009), 49–50.

182. David Music, "Jonathan Edwards and the Theology and Practice of Congregational Song in Puritan New England," *Studies in Puritan American Spirituality* 8 (2004): 118.

183. Jonathan Edwards, *A Faithful Narrative*, in *The Great Awakening*, ed. C. C. Goen, vol. 4 of *WJE* (1972), 148–149; Jonathan Edwards, "Preface to *Discourses on Various Important Subjects*," in *Sermons and Discourses 1734–1738*, ed. M. X. Lesser, vol. 19 of *WJE* (2001), 794–795.

to sing with unusual elevation of heart and voice, which made the duty pleasant indeed.[184]

During this period, Edwards showed an appreciation for Watts' psalmody. In his "Account Book" he noted that he lent Watts' *Psalms of David, imitated in the language of the New Testament* to Increase Clark in December 1735.[185] A decade later David Brainerd, another pro-revivalist, also used Watts' book to teach the Indians Psalm 127; Watts' version proved didactically useful with the Native population because it was memorable and understandable.[186] No doubt the effect of singing during the revivals in Northampton influenced Edwards' desire to hire a singing teacher for his Indian and English congregations in Stockbridge, as recorded in his June 4, 1753, letter to an unidentified singing teacher.[187] Edwards believed that "[m]usic, especially sacred music, has a powerful efficacy to soften the heart into tenderness, to harmonize the affections, and to give the mind a relish for objects of a superior character."[188]

Not only did Edwards embrace the New Way of singing to nurture congregants' affections for God, in the second wave of awakenings in the early 1740s he even accepted some hymns. While none appear to have objected to the singing shift, at least one man questioned the use of hymns. Edwards records that "Mr. Root" delivered a message allegedly from Benjamin Colman, pastor of Brattle Street Church in Boston: "Tell Mr. Edwards from me, that

184. Edwards, *Faithful Narrative*, 151.

185. Jonathan Edwards, "Account Book," in *Catalogues of Books*, ed. Peter J. Thuesen, vol. 26 of *WJE* (2008), 351; Jonathan Edwards, "Register of Persons to Whom Edwards Lent Books," in *Catalogues of Books*, ed. Peter J. Thuesen, vol. 26 of *WJE* (2008), 417. Edwards also expressed interest in obtaining Sir Richard Blackmore's (1654–1729) and Tate and Brady's versions of the Psalter and comparing the latter to the original Hebrew. Jonathan Edwards, "'Catalogue' of Reading," 178; Jonathan Edwards, "Subjects of Inquiry," in *Minor Controversial Writings*, vol. 28 of *WJEO*, 18–19 (accessed June 14, 2011).

186. Jonathan Edwards, *The Life of David Brainerd*, ed. Norman Pettit, vol. 7 of *WJE* (1985), 377.

187. Jonathan Edwards to a Singing Teacher, June 4, 1753, in *Letters and Personal Writings*, ed. George S. Claghorn, vol. 16 of *WJE* (1998), 596–597.

188. Jonathan Edwards to Sir William Pepperell, November 28, 1751, in *Letters and Personal Writings*, ed. George S. Claghorn, vol. 16 of *WJE* (1998), 411. For more on Edwards' promotion of singing in Northampton, see Jonathan Edwards, "344. Thanksgiving Sermon on Rev 14:2 (Nov. 7, 1734)," in *Sermons, Series II, 1734*, vol. 49 of *WJEO*; Jonathan Edwards, "398. Sermon on Col 3:16 (June 17, 1736)," in *Sermons, Series II, 1736*, vol. 51 of *WJEO*; and Music, "Jonathan Edwards and the Theology and Practice of Congregational Song," 103–133, who argues that Edwards was "among the musically progressive pastors of his time." Quotation on 128.

I desire that he would by no means sing Dr. Watts' Hymns."[189] In seeking to clear up the matter, Edwards wrote to Colman, a friend of Watts, to see if he indeed made such an unlikely remark. In the letter, Edwards explained that until 1742, the church sang only psalms during formal church gatherings. But while Edwards was traveling for itinerant ministry one week that January, the congregation began singing hymns, particularly those of Watts, under the leadership of Samuel Buell, the visiting minister. When Edwards returned, he approved of the moderate use of hymns because the people had "a very general inclination to it," but he was unwilling to depart from the use of the Psalms altogether or even marginalize them: "When I came home I disliked not their making some use of the hymns, but did not like their setting aside the Psalms." He thus made adjustments so that hymns could be sung only in the summer afternoon services.[190]

Edwards also defended hymns in *Some Thoughts Concerning the Revival* in language strikingly similar to Watts' apology for hymns and psalm imitations:

> I can find no command or rule of God's Word, that does any more confine us to the words of the Scripture in our singing, than it does in our praying; we speak to God in both.... And 'tis really needful that we should have some other songs besides the Psalms of David: 'tis unreasonable to suppose that the Christian church should forever, and even in times of her greatest light in her praises of God and the Lamb, be confined only to the words of the Old Testament, wherein all the greatest and most glorious things of the Gospel, that are infinitely the greatest subjects of her praise, are spoken of under a veil, and not so much as the name of our glorious Redeemer ever mentioned, but in some dark figure, or as hid under the name of some type.[191]

Yet while Edwards rejected the regulative principle confining Christian worship only to songs found in Scripture, he retained a high place for the Psalter in worship: "it should always be used in the Christian church, to the end of the world."[192]

---

189. Jonathan Edwards to the Reverend Benjamin Colman, May 22, 1744, in *Letters and Personal Writings*, ed. George S. Claghorn, vol. 16 of *WJE* (1998), 144.

190. Jonathan Edwards to Benjamin Colman, 144–145. Quotation on 144.

191. Jonathan Edwards, *Some Thoughts Concerning the Revival*, in *The Great Awakening*, ed. C. C. Goen, vol. 4 of *WJE* (1972), 407.

192. Edwards, *Some Thoughts*, 406–407.

In the Stockbridge years, Edwards witnessed the continuing controversy over singing Psalms versus hymns. On a trip home to Stockbridge after visiting his daughter Esther in Newark, Edwards spent time with some Presbyterians in New York City who were wrangling over the choice of a new pastor since one Scottish party insisted they sing only psalms.[193] For his own part, Edwards had made peace on that question, accepting hymns while upholding the primacy of psalmody. It is not difficult to understand why Edwards embraced hymnody along with psalmody because it was common across the evangelical spectrum—whether German Pietists, Methodists, Presbyterians, Baptists, or Congregationalists—to promote the use of new hymns for the purpose of reviving the hearts of people; these hymns were uniquely able to express the evangelical message of renewal in a way that deeply moved one's affections.[194] In this way Edwards marked an important religious transition to evangelicalism. Noll argues that "Watts became himself an all-important bridge between the older Puritanism and modern evangelicalism because he demonstrated that a freer, more expressive, more Christ-centred hymnody could actually advance the Puritan desire to secure the truths of the Bible in the minds and hearts of those who sang."[195]

An interest in furthering the gospel meant Edwards embraced both hymns and psalms in stirring the hearts of his people. Like other revivalists, he believed singing spiritual songs was a divinely endowed means of nurturing religious fruit in his congregation, for "the duty of singing praises to God, seems to be appointed wholly to excite and express religious affections."[196] By arousing people's religious affections through singing both hymns and psalms, Edwards believed he was participating in God's grand redemptive aims since in David's time God had furthered his redemptive work by "inspiring David to show forth Christ and his redemption in divine songs which should be for the use of the church in private and public worship throughout all ages."[197]

---

193. Marsden, *Jonathan Edwards: A Life*, 420.

194. Noll, "The Significance of Hymnody," 45–64.

195. Noll, "The Significance of Hymnody," 48. See Marsden's similar comment in *Jonathan Edwards: A Life*, 143.

196. Edwards, *Religious Affections*, 115.

197. Jonathan Edwards, *A History of the Work of Redemption*, ed. John F. Wilson, vol. 9 of *WJE* (1989), 209.

Conclusion

As we have observed in this chapter, Edwards stood within a long stream of people who interpreted, preached, and worshipped with the Psalms. Interpreters stretching back to the early church consistently showed the book of Psalms a great deal of attention, valuing its encompassing treatment of theological and devotional themes. The analogy of Scripture united these exegetes who also exhibited a firm commitment to finding Christ in the Psalms, though to varying degrees. Within the Protestant Reformed tradition, two major streams emerged, one emphasizing the literal-historical sense that accepted moderate use of typological readings and the other embracing a freer identification of typological readings grounded in the literal sense. The influx of Enlightenment ideas brought new insights to the interpretation of the Psalms but also raised new questions, particularly concerning the value of Christological and typological readings since many began to read the Psalms primarily, or solely, as historical documents and ancient poetry. Within this context, Edwards was critically engaged but biblically grounded and theologically focused as he interpreted the Psalms. His interpretive practices distinguished him as an exegete clearly invested in the critical-historical data available in his day but always reading within a theological framework that upheld the Bible as the supernatural revelation of God. His sources on the Psalms show that he placed a premium on understanding the literal and historical meaning of the Psalter but also interpreted the Psalms within both a theological framework and the context of the Christian tradition. Edwards used a typological and theological approach to interpretation that stood in line with that tradition while allowing him to address skeptical, naturalistic interpretations of his day and emphasize the redemptive message revealed in the whole of Scripture that found resonance in the Psalms.

In the history of Christian homiletics, preachers have also often chosen the Psalms as their sermonic text since its breadth of topics provided pastors with a wide array of messages to proclaim. From the early days of the church down to Edwards' own time, preachers spoke on the Psalms to discuss the core doctrines of Christianity, to deal with social and ecclesiological concerns, to nurture Christian piety, to comfort hurting believers, and to proclaim the gospel of Jesus Christ. Edwards likewise addressed many different issues as he preached from the Psalms, and he took measures to ground his doctrines in the text of the Psalms, which he contextualized in their historical setting. But as he moved from text to theology to application in his sermons, the theme that resonated throughout his Psalms sermons was the gospel. Even when the new Enlightenment learning began to push Christ and the Christian religion out of the Psalms, Edwards did not flinch in proclaiming the good news of God's grace and hope. Again and again, whether at Northampton or Stockbridge, Edwards proclaimed the redemptive message of Scripture from the Psalms both to nurture conversion and to stimulate Christian piety.

The Psalter has also held a prominent place in Christian worship beginning in the early church, and at many times it was the most well-known book of the Bible for the layperson, who repeatedly sang its songs in the regular rhythm of worship and life. The waning of psalm singing in the late Middle Ages led the Reformers to reappropriate the Psalter in worship, and they paved the way both for the high place of the Psalter in church order and—inadvertently through metrical psalmody—for the undermining of the Psalter in corporate worship. Also, while some resisted applying the Psalms directly to Christ, many defended the practice as appropriate for Christians. Edwards lived during a time when Isaac Watts wrote both psalm imitations and hymns because he sought to stir up heart religion and vital piety—a move that led to weighty debates and dissension in the mid-eighteenth century. For his part, Edwards loved the Psalms in both personal and corporate worship to the end, but loved the gospel more than anything, and so he was willing to depart with convention and welcome a moderate use of hymns if it might promote heart-felt devotion to God. So Edwards clearly stood within the long Christian tradition of singing the Psalms in worship and joined with those throughout the history of the church who believed it appropriate to adapt the Psalms to sing explicitly about Christ in worship. Just as he sang of the gospel using the Psalter, so Edwards also used the Psalms in his ministry and theology to show forth Christ and God's broad work of redemption.

2

God and Scripture

Not unto us, O LORD, not unto us,
but unto thy name give glory,
for thy mercy, and for thy truth's sake.
Psalm 115:1

IN LIGHT OF the diversity of themes treated in the book of Psalms, it is not surprising that Edwards developed several theological themes in his engagement with the Psalter. But this variety of topics does not imply chaos in Edwards' reading of the Psalms. Rather, the history of redemption guided him in his engagement with the Psalter, and at the fountainhead of all redemptive work in history stands God, from whom every severe judgment and every good grace flows. To speak of redemption, one must first speak of God. As Edwards delved into the Psalms, he found a deep reserve of instruction on the nature of God and his ways. His exegesis of the Psalms informed his understanding of God, as both an unknowable and a revelatory Being, and from God's revelation in the Psalms, Edwards saw God's glory upheld as his supreme aim in creation. He also detected God's merciful aims of redemption and his sovereign oversight of that redemptive history. His doctrine of inspiration, informed by the Psalter, gave him the theological grounds for exploring the Psalms for such truth about God. Thus Edwards never doubted the reliability of the Bible, and as he interpreted the Psalms, he soaked up all he could from the new critical learning, fully expecting it to harmonize with God's divinely inspired Word. This openness to the new learning only moderately affected his exegesis as he grounded himself in a redemptive-historical approach to the Psalms. In this chapter we see how Edwards, as he engaged the Psalms, discussed God's glory, sovereignty, mystery, mercy, and revelation.

The Glory of God

One of Edwards' favorite verses from the Psalms, one that he said "has often been sweet to me," was Ps 115:1, "Not unto us, O LORD, not unto us, but unto thy

name give glory, for thy mercy, and for thy truth's sake."[1] He preached on this
passage in the fall of 1723 to highlight the preeminence of God's glory. As was his
custom, he described the psalm's context, apparently a psalm of praise to God
for delivering Israel out of trouble. He observed that the psalmist offers praise
to the Lord in a manner that is "always most acceptable to God," namely by
"acknowledging [Israel's] insufficiency" and ascribing their success solely to "the
power and mercy of God."[2] Moving further into the psalm, Edwards noted the
contrast between the God of Israel and the pagan gods: Israel's God is the God
of the heavens who does "whatsoever he hath pleased" (Ps 115:3), while the heathen gods are the senseless "work of men's hands" (Ps 115:4–5).[3] So the psalmist
boasts, as all Christians ought, not in his own work but in God's glory. Edwards
made three observations on the text. First, as the psalmist repeats, "not unto
us," he "lays himself and his people low," so that even though God used the
people as a means of their own deliverance, the psalmist deflects all glory to God,
the source of the power and wisdom that led to salvation.[4] Second, the psalmist
exalts God, who "wholly and solely" deserves the glory, for only he can do whatever he pleases, while we "depend on him for his help."[5] And third, the psalmist
takes particular "delight" in "abasing himself and exalting God"; "[h]e has not the
least inclination to assume the glory to himself, but to abhor the thoughts of it
and delight in attributing all to God."[6] Thus Edwards preached this doctrine: "It
is the temper of the truly godly to delight to exalt God and to lay themselves
low."[7] The godly man lives to see God honored in his heart, by his life, and in
public, and he especially loves to attribute glory to God for his redemption:

> But especially it is the joy of his heart to give God all the glory of his
> spiritual enjoyment. He loves to give him the whole praise of his

---

1. Jonathan Edwards, "Personal Narrative," in *Letters and Personal Writings*, ed. George
S. Claghorn, vol. 16 of *WJE* (1998), 800.

2. Jonathan Edwards, "That It Is the Temper of the Truly Godly to Delight to Exalt God and
to Lay Themselves Low" (Ps 115:1), in *The Blessing of God: Previously Unpublished Sermons of
Jonathan Edwards*, ed. Michael D. McMullen (Nashville, TN: Broadman & Holman, 2003),
72.

3. Similarly, in his "Blank Bible" note on Ps 115:2, Edwards highlighted the contrast between
the heathen idols and Israel's imageless but glorious, sovereign God. Jonathan Edwards, *The
"Blank Bible,"* ed. Stephen J. Stein, vol. 24, part 1 of *WJE* (2006), 529.

4. Edwards, "That It Is the Temper," 72.

5. Edwards, "That It Is the Temper," 73.

6. Edwards, "That It Is the Temper," 73.

7. Edwards, "That It Is the Temper," 73.

redemption and salvation, admires of God's goodness in choosing him from all eternity. Admires that he should be of his distinguishing goodness, chosen out from among so many, to be made the vessel of honor and subject of glory. He wonders at God's goodness in sending his Son to redeem him. He likewise admires at his grace in calling of him to Christ by his Holy Spirit. He delights to acknowledge that his conversion is not at all owing in any respect to himself but to the grace of God alone.[8]

Paradoxically, while he exalts in God's glorious redemption, he also rejoices in humbling himself, not that he feels forced to abase himself but rather he is grieved that he cannot humble himself more, in light of his sin. As Edwards moved into the application, God's glory became the prism through which people could examine themselves to see if they were truly godly. God's glory is so infinite that the godly, when they see his grandeur, will humble themselves at his feet and cry, "not unto us, O Lord, not unto us, but unto thy name give glory."[9]

As this sermon illustrates, the exaltation of God featured prominently in Edwards' theology and ministry, and the Psalms provided a biblical basis for this focus. Using the Psalms to make a pronounced emphasis on God's glory fell in line with Edwards' Reformed predecessors. In commenting on Ps 115:1, Matthew Henry noted that "[b]oasting is here for ever excluded," for we ought to have "no opinion of our own Merits" but rather center on "God's Glory."[10] And Matthew Poole likewise noted that glory should be attributed to God alone, not to humans, who do not merit it.[11] John Trapp called this verse "the godly man's *motto*," and he pulled from Augustine to say, "In all thy good deeds give God the glory, and take up lowly thoughts of thy self."[12] While

---

8. Edwards, "That It Is the Temper," 76.

9. Edwards, "That It Is the Temper," 71–87.

10. Matthew Henry, *An exposition of the five poetical books of the Old Testament; viz. Job, Psalms, Proverbs, Ecclesiastes, and Solomon's song*...(London: T. Darrack..., 1710), [Ps 115:1].

11. The Latin reads: "Gloria miraculorum Ægyptiacorum tibi soli, xnon nostris meritis, tribuatur," and "gloriosam exhibe liberationem, quae tamen non nobis, sed tibi solum gloriosa sit." Matthew Poole, *Synopsis Criticorum Aliorumque Sacrae Scripturae Interpretum et Commentarum, Summo Studio et Fide Adornata*, vol. II: *Complectens Libros Jobi, Psalmorum, Proverbiorum, Ecclesiastis, & Cantici Canticorum* (Francofurti ad Moenum: Balthasaris Christophori Wustii, 1678), 1188.

12. John Trapp, *A Commentary or Exposition Upon the Books of Ezra, Nehemiah, Esther, Job, and Psalms*...(London: T. R. and E. M. for Thomas Newberry..., 1657), 867–868. Italics original.

Edwards did not cite Henry, Poole, or Trapp in his notes on this verse, he mirrored them all in his interpretation.[13]

Edwards defined God's "glory" as his "excellency...consisting either in greatness or in beauty, or as it were preciousness, or in both conjunctly," and he cited several psalms as supporting this concept (Pss 19:1; 45:13; 63:2–3; 66:2; 72:19; 87:3; 102:16; 145:5, 12–13).[14] Because of God's excellent greatness and beauty, he deserves all glory from humanity. In his treatise *Freedom of the Will*, Edwards pointed to Ps 29:1–2—"Give unto the LORD, O ye mighty, give unto the LORD glory and strength. Give unto the LORD the glory due unto his name; worship the LORD in the beauty of holiness"—and "many other psalms," to show that men are to be " 'giving unto him all the glory,' of the good which is done or received, rather than unto men;...he should be regarded as the being to whom all glory is due."[15]

Whether people honor him or not, God's glory will eventually be made manifest everywhere, as Edwards taught in his sermon on Ps 66:5, "Come and see the works of God: he is terrible in his doing toward the children of men." Edwards explained that great blessing awaits those who make the effort to "come and see" God's works and reflect on the glory contained in them: "[T]he Glory of them is so Great & wonderfull that we shall be well Rewarded for our taking the Pains to Go to see them."[16] By "terrible" the psalmist meant that "God is awfull in his works. [H]is works are such as not only tend to strike with admiration but also with Aw[e] & Dread to Possess us with fear & trembling."[17] Either way, whether eliciting admiration or dread, God's works bring glory to his name. Thus Edwards preached this doctrine: "That 'tis to the Glory of G[od] that he is terrible in his doings towards the Children of men."[18] God is "terrible" in his excellency, infinite power, abhorrence of sin, and works of creation and providence, but his doings toward humanity are especially terrible, whether his work of redemption—manifested in Christ's terrible suffering and in a terrible blow to Satan—or "his works of vengeance towards

---

13. N.B. In my comparison of Edwards with earlier exegetes throughout the book, it can be assumed that Edwards did not cite the interpreters unless I note otherwise.

14. Jonathan Edwards, *Dissertation I: Concerning the End for Which God Created the World*. In *Ethical Writings*, ed. Paul Ramsey, vol. 8 of *WJE* (1989), 514.

15. Jonathan Edwards, *Freedom of the Will*, ed. Paul Ramsey, vol. 1 of *WJE* (1957), 279.

16. Jonathan Edwards, "98. Sermon on Ps 66:5 (Spring–Fall 1729)," Beinecke Rare Book and Manuscript Library, Yale University, New Haven, CT, L. 1r.

17. Edwards, "98. Sermon on Ps 66:5," L. 1r.–1v.

18. Edwards, "98. Sermon on Ps 66:5," L. 1v.

the Children of men," specifically in his temporal, spiritual, and eternal judgments.[19] While Edwards' understanding of "terrible" as awe-inspiring stood in
continuity with the Reformed tradition, his view that God's "terrible" works
also had a dreadful, fear-inducing nature manifested his unique emphasis on
the passage.[20] He forwarded this idea in part because he wanted to connect
God's works with his glory, for God's terrible works are "a Great manifestation
of his Glory & excellency" that "will be forever to his honour."[21] While some
thought it unjust of God to judge humans with such powerful displays of his
might, Edwards held that it is God's glory to get the victory over his enemy,
vindicate his authority and majesty, manifest his justice and hatred of sin,
reveal his truth, display his sovereignty, and "make men see how valuable and
Precious [is] his mercy."[22] In his application, Edwards exhorted his people to
take notice of God's "Perfect Gloriousness[,] that he is Glorious without exception in all that he is and does," for "these works are no spots or blemishes that
obscure the Glory of G[od] but in Every one of them[—]even the most terrible
of them all[—]God[']s Glory does & forever will Gloriously shine forth."[23]

Edwards explained from the Psalms that God's infinitely glorious nature
demands that all humanity bow in homage to him. Preaching on Ps 89:6,
"For who in the heaven can be compared unto the LORD? who among the
sons of the mighty can be likened unto the LORD?" Edwards showed that the
writer portrays God's glory by comparing it to the highest of created beings,
whether the angels in heaven or the kings on earth, for "none, of the angels
or of those spotless, pure, wise, bright, and active spirits there, are worthy to be
compared with him," and "[t]he great kings, princes, emperors, and monarchs
of the world, that look like gods [to] the wondering and amazed eyes of men,

19. Edwards, "98. Sermon on Ps 66:5," L. 4v.

20. While Henry recognized that God's works have sometimes "frightened" God's enemies
into "a feigned submission," he defined "terrible" as "admirable," eliciting "Reverence" and
"an holy Awe." Henry, Exposition, [Ps 66:5]. Poole understood "terrible" to mean "reverendas"
(awe-inspiring) or possibly "formidabilis" (terrifying); he emphasized the contrast between
God's works and human efforts. Poole, Synopsis, 914. Trapp saw these works as God's "stu-
pendous proceedings," indicating his "care" and "providence." Trapp, Commentary, 753. John
Calvin likewise described these "terrible" works as God's "extraordinary providence in their
defence and preservation." John Calvin, Commentary on the Psalms, trans. from the original
Latin and collated with the author's French ver. by James Anderson, vol. 2 (1843–1855; repr.,
Grand Rapids, MI: Eerdmans, 1963), 469.

21. Edwards, "98. Sermon on Ps 66:5," L. 9v.

22. Edwards, "98. Sermon on Ps 66:5," L. 10v.–14r. Quotation on L. 14r.

23. Edwards, "98. Sermon on Ps 66:5," L. 14r.–14v.

are nothing to him."[24] Having encompassed all of creation and established that God is greater than the whole of it, Edwards declared his doctrine: "God is infinitely exalted in gloriousness and excellency above all created beings."[25] While he did not cite Henry in his sermon or notebooks on this verse, Edwards' sermon echoes Henry's observation: "If there be any Beings that can pretend to vie with GOD, sure they must be found among the Angels; but they are all infinitely short of him"; indeed, "[n]o angel, no earthly Potentate, whatsoever, is comparable to GOD."[26] As Edwards continued his sermon, he "set forth the greatness, gloriousness, and transcendent excellency of that God who made us," arguing that God's gloriousness is "the highest theme that ever man…entered upon yet."[27] To prove his doctrine he showed that God is infinitely exalted above all creatures in duration, greatness, loveliness, power, wisdom, holiness, and goodness. So foundational is the doctrine of God's glory that "the whole of Christianity follows as an improvement from this doctrine," from the dreadfulness of sin and the terribleness of his wrath to the wonder of the incarnation and the privilege and happiness enjoyed by those he makes holy—in short, God's redemptive-historical work.[28]

---

24. Jonathan Edwards, "God's Excellencies" (Ps 89:6), in *Sermons and Discourses 1720–1723*, ed. Wilson H. Kimnach, vol. 10 of *WJE* (1992), 416. Edwards re-preached this sermon at an unspecified place and time.

25. Edwards, "God's Excellencies," 416.

26. Henry, *Exposition*, [Ps 89:6]. For similar interpretations of this text that elevate God's glory above the heavenly angels, see Trapp, *Commentary*, 806; David Dickson, *A Brief Explication of the other fifty Psalmes, From Ps. 50 to Ps. 100* (London: T. R. and E. M. for Ralph Smith…, 1653), 310–311; and Calvin, *Commentary*, 3:423–424.

27. Edwards, "God's Excellencies," 416, 417.

28. Edwards, "God's Excellencies," 425. Similarly, to set God's glory in relief, Edwards compared it again to the angels in another sermon, building his argument from Ps 113:6, "Who humbleth himself to behold the things that are in heaven, and in the earth!" He insisted that these words show "God[']s Humbling himself to behold the things that are in Heaven," and that while the angels are "the most excellent & exalted in their nature of all things in the whole creation," when God "beholds" these creatures, he must come "down from the height of his glory" to these things in heaven that are "infinitely below" his "glory & dignity." Jonathan Edwards, "685. Sermon on Ps 113:6 (November 11, 1742)," Beinecke Rare Book and Manuscript Library, Yale University, New Haven, CT, L. 1r., 3r., 3v., 6r., 6v. Reformed exegetes also commonly touted God's condescension from Ps 113:6. Henry observed that "[c]onsidering the Infinite Perfection, Sufficiency, and Felicity of the Divine Nature, it must be acknowledg'd an Act of wonderful Condescension that GOD is pleased to take into the Thoughts of his Eternal Counsel…both the Armies of Heaven, and the Inhabitants of the Earth." Henry, *Exposition*, [Ps 113:6]. Trapp likewise noted, "Lo, it is a condescention in God to vouchsafe to look out of himself upon the Saints and Angels." Trapp, *Commentary*, 866. And Calvin stated, "[i]f in regard to angels he humble himself, what is to be said in regard to men, who, grovelling upon the earth, are altogether filthy?" Calvin, *Commentary*, 4:333–334. Edwards did not cite Henry, Trapp, or Calvin on Ps 113:6, but he did make a note in his

The Psalms speak often of God's glorious nature by upholding his name. Edwards taught that God's "name" represents his glory and perfections and that he created the world to make known his name, a teaching to which the Psalms frequently testify (Pss 23:3; 31:3; 109:21; 25:11; 79:9; 106:8; 76:1; 148:13; 135:13).[29] God's "name" refers to his reputation, so when Ps 9:10 states, "they that know thy name will put their trust in thee," it means they who know "thy name and fame which thou has gotten to thyself by thy faithfulness to thy people that have trusted."[30] People trust in God because the saints report him to be trustworthy, for God's name particularly refers to his reputation of faithfulness. So Ps 48:8, 10 testify: "As we have heard, so have we seen in the city of the LORD of hosts, in the city of our God.... According to thy name, O God, so is thy praise."[31] This psalm explains the meaning of Ps 138:2, "I will worship toward thy holy temple, and praise thy name for thy lovingkindness and for thy truth: for thou hast magnified thy word above all thy name"—"name" again referring to God's glory and acts in human history.[32]

The Psalms also speak of God's shekinah glory, particularly in Ps 36:9, "For with thee is the fountain of life: in thy light shall we see light." The image of light recalled to Edwards' mind Rev 21:23, "And the city had no need of the sun, neither of the moon, to shine in it: for the glory of God did lighten it, and the Lamb is the light thereof." Thus he said that "[t]he Psalmist seems to have the light of the Shekinah in the temple in his eye, for he is speaking here of the pleasures and good things of God's house," and this light refers both to God's glory and "the light that God enjoys, the light in which he is happy," a

---

"Blank Bible" to see Poole on this verse. However, he did not discuss the points he gleaned from Poole in the sermon. Poole observed, like these other exegetes, that "[i]n the presence of God all are humble, whether they may be terrestrial or celestial" ("Coram Deo cuncta sunt humilia, sive terrestria sint, sive coelestia"). He also discussed the grammar of the passage and explained that "in heaven" refers back to the verb "dwelleth," while "in earth" refers to the verb "beholds" ("*in caelo* referentur ad verb. *habitat*, &, *in terra*, ad verbum *videt*"). From Poole's discussion of the syntax, Edwards determined that the proper translation of Ps 113:5–6 is, "Who exalteth himself to dwell in heaven, and humbleth himself to behold on earth," moving the words "in heaven" earlier in the word order so that they coincide with the act of exaltation, which follows the parallelism common in Hebrew poetry. Edwards, *The "Blank Bible,"* 528; Poole, *Synopsis,* 1185. All translations of Poole are mine. Many thanks to Scott Manetsch for input regarding Latin translations in a handful of passages.

29. Edwards, *Concerning the End,* 493–495.

30. Edwards, *The "Blank Bible,"* 479.

31. Edwards, *The "Blank Bible,"* 479.

32. Edwards, *The "Blank Bible,"* 538.

light in which the saints can experience happiness themselves.[33] In fact, the saints only find happiness in God's glory. So in Ps 89:15, "Blessed is the people that know the joyful sound: they shall walk, O LORD, in the light of thy countenance," Edwards envisioned God's glory in his light-emitting countenance. Thus as Moses heard the joyful sound at Mt. Sinai and was granted to see "God's back parts," giving him a brightness of countenance, so for those who delight in God's glory, it will be "easy and sweet, that they may dwell in it and walk in it" for "God shall be their everlasting light."[34]

In a sermon reflecting on the benefits of God's presence, Edwards engaged the Psalms to explore further God's glorious acts. In November 1735, on the heels of the Northampton awakening, Edwards preached a thanksgiving sermon on Isa 12:6, "Cry out and shout, thou inhabitant of Zion: for great is the Holy One of Israel in the midst of thee," and called his people to rejoice for all the benefits they had seen from God's presence during the previous year. In this sermon Edwards made reference to the Psalms sixty-four times as he celebrated God's glorious nature and beneficent works toward Northampton.[35] Edwards weaved a number of Psalm texts together (Pss 148:13; 89:6; 95:1–3; 77:13; 99:2–3, 5) to establish God's glorious nature: "Because of his being so great and holy a God, he is worthy to be exceedingly rejoiced in and praised. The sum of the divine glory consists in his greatness, and in his holiness, and his goodness."[36] Edwards also intertwined several texts from the Psalms (Pss 24:8; 35:5; 91:1, 5–6; 48:11–14; 76:3; 125:2; 89:18; 46:1–3, 7; 47:1) to establish that those who have God in their midst "have a most sufficient and sure defense from evil."[37] The Psalms show further that when God is in a people's midst, they lack nothing since in his greatness he can supply all their needs. So Ps 34:10 teaches that "they that seek the LORD shall not want any good thing"; God is "the fountain of

---

33. Edwards, *The "Blank Bible,"* 492.

34. Edwards, *The "Blank Bible,"* 519.

35. M. X. Lesser observes that in this sermon Edwards "transcribes in whole or in part, in particular or in paraphrase, roughly seven scriptural texts per manuscript page, nearly 150 in all, attributing only half of them. Citations from seventeen books of the Old Testament, including two from Habakkuk, crowd out those from the New Testament by more than six to one, the nearly sixty excerpts from Psalms [Lesser's count is slightly low], twice those from Isaiah, forming a rich mosaic of intricate figures and tropes. His biblicism, always remarkable, if seldom on display like this, is nothing short of stunning here." M. X. Lesser, ed. *Sermons and Discourses 1734–1738,* vol. 19 of *WJE* (2001), 451.

36. Jonathan Edwards, "God Amongst His People" (Isa 12:6), in *Sermons and Discourses 1734–1738,* ed. M. X. Lesser, vol. 19 of *WJE* (2001), 456.

37. Edwards, "God Amongst His People," 458. See also Edwards, *The "Blank Bible,"* 476.

all good" and "an inexhaustible and infinite fountain"—"enough for the supply of everyone."[38] So with God as their shepherd, they "shall not want" (Ps 23:1), and God shall provide for their bodily and spiritual needs, for "no good thing will he withhold from them that walk uprightly" (Ps 84:11). Indeed, when God dwells in a people's midst, "he himself is the sum of all good," and because God embodies goodness for his people, they have all they need for happiness: "God is theirs, and therefore they are happy, if they have nothing else."[39]

To Edwards, God's glory was an all-encompassing concept for discussing Christian doctrine, embodying the whole purpose of God's creation with the history of redemption serving as the vehicle for reaching that end. In his harmonic view of Scripture, Edwards found echoes of this redemptive-historical thrust in the Psalms. In a note on Ps 3:8, "Salvation belongeth unto the LORD: thy blessing is upon thy people," he observed that "Salvation is spoken of throughout the Old Testament as a peculiarly glorious work, and is celebrated as one of the principal glories of the God of Israel."[40] Edwards developed this thought from Alexander Cruden, who explained that the Hebrews spoke of salvation not in "concrete terms" but in abstractions (e.g., "the joy of salvation") and showed how often "salvation" was used in the Old Testament to refer to God's deliverance of his people.[41] Also, in his "Miscellanies" notebook, he wrote an entry (no. 1080) on "GOD'S GLORY THE END OF THE CREATION," in which he cited dozens of scriptures attesting to God's glory as the proper end of creation, including twenty references to the Psalms.[42] Edwards pursued this thinking further in his posthumously published Concerning the End for Which God Created the World (1765), and he used the Psalms to establish his overarching claim that God created the world and conducted his redemptive work for his glory. He quoted Ps 79:9, "Help us, O God of our salvation, for the glory of thy name: and deliver us, and purge away our sins, for thy name's sake," as evidence that God's glory is "the end of the work of redemption in the Old Testament."[43] The Psalms testified in several places (Pss 8:1, 9; 104:31; 148:13) to

---

38. Edwards, "God Amongst His People," 461.

39. Edwards, "God Amongst His People," 462–463.

40. Edwards, The "Blank Bible," 476.

41. Alexander Cruden, A Complete Concordance to the Holy Scriptures of the Old and New Testaments (London: D. Midwinter et al., 1738), n.p. [entry for "Salvation"].

42. Jonathan Edwards, The "Miscellanies": Entry Nos. 833–1152, ed. Amy Plantinga Pauw, vol. 20 of WJE (2002), 462–464. The Psalms passages include Pss 106:8; 23:3; 72:17; 76:1; 111:9; 148:13; 149:3; 8:1, 9; 25:11; 31:3; 79:9; 115:1; 109:21; 143:11; 72:9; 97:6; 148:13; 90:16; and 102:15.

43. Edwards, Concerning the End, 488.

"the glory of God" being "the last end of many of God's works."[44] Edwards held that "divine goodness, particularly forgiveness of sin, and salvation" are often spoken of as being for the sake of God's goodness or name (Pss 25:7, 11; 6:4; 31:16; 44:26).[45] So Ps 106:8 summed up this concept that God accomplishes his works on earth to manifest his glory: "he saved them for his name's sake, that he might make his mighty power to be known."[46]

The Psalms functioned for Edwards both as a progenitor and corroborator of doctrine. As Edwards studied the Psalter and rehearsed it in worship, he observed God's work of redemption being revealed in history, from creation through judgment and deliverance, and all these events telescoped on God's glory, the goal of all God's works, which tempered Edwards' interpretation of the Psalms just as the Psalms guided him to such exegetical and theological conclusions. God manifested his unique glory particularly in his sovereignty, a theme Edwards also heard resonating in the Psalter.

The Sovereignty of God

In his vision of the Psalms, Edwards saw God standing as the supreme ruler of creation, the sovereign that orders all things to accomplish his redemptive purposes in the world. God's sovereignty is further fleshed out in the Psalms in describing his providence, his omniscience, and his unique role as judge and discerner of individuals' hearts.

Broadly speaking, when Edwards read Rev 19:6, "for the Lord God omnipotent reigneth," he saw the fulfillment of "that which is so often spoken of in the Psalms and Prophets, of God reigning over all nations."[47] He detected the all-encompassing sovereignty of God in several particular psalms, including Ps 95:4, "In his hand are the deep places of the earth: the strength of the hills is his also." God holds all, from the depths to the heights:

The deep and low places, and also the high places of the earth, are his and in his hand. And in the next verse it is said, both the sea and dry land

---

44. Edwards, *Concerning the End*, 491. Edwards similarly argued from Pss 145:5–10; 148; 103:19–22 that "God's *praise* is the desirable and glorious consequence and effect of all the works of creation." Edwards, *Concerning the End*, 502. Italics original.

45. Edwards, *Concerning the End*, 506.

46. Edwards, *Concerning the End*, 498. In like manner Ps 19:1 states that "[t]he heavens declare the glory of God." Edwards, *Concerning the End*, 499.

47. Jonathan Edwards, "Exposition on the Apocalypse," in *Apocalyptic Writings*, ed. Stephen J. Stein, vol. 5 of *WJE* (1977), 123.

is his, the sea which was west and the land which was east. By which is elegantly set forth how the whole earth is in God's right [hand] and possession, in its depth and height, in its length and breadth, in every part of its surface, in every part of its content, and everything of which the whole globe is composed.[48]

God's all-encompassing sovereignty meant that he could use the lightening as his "arrows," echoing both Ps 144:6, "Cast forth lightning, and scatter them: shoot out thine arrows, and destroy them," and Ps 18:13–14, "The LORD also thundered in the heavens, and the Highest gave his voice; hail stones and coals of fire. Yea, he sent out his arrows, and scattered them; and he shot out lightnings, and discomfited them." From this observation Edwards discern that "God fought against [his enemies] with thunder and lightning."[49] As the sovereign ruler over all creation, God does as he pleases: "Whatsoever the LORD pleased, that did he in heaven, and in earth, in the seas, and all deep places" (Ps 135:6). Here Edwards saw a reference to the wonders God performed for Israel in Egypt apart from any compulsion by other gods, "which shows him to be above all gods...and that his dominion is not limited to a particular people or country, and that he is not God only of a particular part of the world, but that he is supreme and absolute Lord of the whole universe."[50]

Two sermons on the Psalms further elucidate Edwards' emphasis on God's sovereignty from the Psalter. The first, preached in June 1735—the same month that his uncle, Joseph Hawley Sr., committed suicide, which led to the dying of the revivals—was on Ps 46:10, "Be still, and know that I am God." Edwards said this psalm was "a song of the church in a time of great revolutions and desolations in the world."[51] It cast God as a "refuge and strength" in times of trouble (Ps 46:1), as a source of comfort that "shall make glad the city of God" (Ps 46:4),

---

48. Edwards, *The "Blank Bible,"* 523.

49. Jonathan Edwards, *Notes on Scripture*, ed. Stephen J. Stein, vol. 15 of *WJE* (1998), 131–132. See also Edwards' use of Ps 18:14 to show that "God fought against them with thunder and lightning" in Entry No. 211, Judges 5:20, where he relied on Bedford's *Scripture Chronology* for this point. Jonathan Edwards, *Notes on Scripture*, ed. Stephen J. Stein, vol. 15 of *WJE* (1998), 140. For similar readings of God using nature to fight enemies from Ps 18:7–15, see Edwards, *The "Blank Bible,"* 484, and Edwards, *Notes on Scripture*, 152.

50. Edwards, *The "Blank Bible,"* 537.

51. Jonathan Edwards, "The Sole Consideration, that God Is God, Sufficient to Still All Objections to His Sovereignty," in vol. 6 of *The Works of President Edwards*, ed. Sereno E. Dwight (New York: S. Converse, 1829), 293. For more on the Joseph Hawley incident, see George M. Marsden, *Jonathan Edwards: A Life* (New Haven, CT: Yale University Press, 2003), 163–169.

and as the deliverer of the church who brings desolations on her enemies (Ps 46:6–9). This description of God for the church in troublesome times led to the sermon's text, in which, having "manifested his power and sovereignty," God commands all to be still.[52] From Ps 46:10, Edwards described our "duty" to be still before God, a duty grounded in God's divine nature, which implies a stillness of "*words*, not speaking against the sovereign dispensations"; a stillness of "*actions and outward behavior*, so as not to oppose God in his dispensations"; and a stillness of "*the inward frame of our hearts*, cultivating a calm and quiet submission of soul to the sovereign pleasure of God, whatever it be."[53] Edwards defended this doctrine: "the bare consideration *that God is God*, may well be sufficient to still all objections and opposition against the divine sovereign dispensations."[54]

Edwards stood in line with Reformed interpretations of this verse in upholding God's sovereignty but phrased his defense of God's sovereignty in a unique way by targeting not literal enemies of God and his church, but ideological enemies, people who consider God's sovereignty an affront to reason.[55] In establishing this claim, Edwards reflected on six implications from God being God. As God, he is "an absolutely and infinitely *perfect* being" and cannot err; "infinitely above all comprehension," rendering quarrels "unreasonable"; the owner of all things with "a right to dispose of them according to his own pleasure"; "*worthy* to be sovereign over all things," making it unfitting to leave things to chance; unstoppable for he is "the great and mighty God" who "will do all his pleasure"; and "able to avenge himself of those who oppose his sovereignty."[56] Edwards reproved the unregenerate who resented and questioned God's sovereign "disposals of his grace."[57] He charged that it is "from mean thoughts of God" that people believe they do not deserve God's eternal wrath and "quarrel against his justice in the *condemnation of sinners*, from the

---

52. Edwards, "The Sole Consideration," 294.

53. Edwards, "The Sole Consideration," 294. Italics original.

54. Edwards, "The Sole Consideration," 294.

55. Henry, for example, explained that God's enemies should be still and cease their threats and instead recognize that "*he is God*, one infinitely above them" and that "in spite of all their impotent Malice against his Name and Honour he will be *exalted among the Heathen* and not merely among his own People." Henry, *Exposition*, [Ps 46:10]. Italics original. Similarly, Trapp offered this explanation: "learn, by what ye have felt, that there is no contending with omnipotency. I will be exalted, asking you no leave." Trapp, *Commentary*, 707. Calvin and Poole both saw it as God telling those who wage war on God's people to stop. Calvin, *Commentary*, 2:204–205; Poole, *Synopsis*, 805.

56. Edwards, "The Sole Consideration," 294–299. Italics original.

57. Edwards, "The Sole Consideration," 299.

doctrine of original sin," and they foolishly trust in their own righteousness and "contend with him, because he bestows grace on some, and not on others."[58] At a time when his congregation was reeling from Hawley's suicide, Edwards reminded his people—perhaps in an attempt to keep the revivals alive—that God's sovereign dispensations are not up for debate, yet are fully righteous, and they elicit a response, for "God will make all men to know that *he is* God. You shall either know it for your good here, by submission, or to your cost hereafter."[59]

Twenty years later, Edwards revisited the doctrine of sovereignty while preaching from Ps 60:9–12: "Who will bring me into the strong city? who will lead me into Edom? Wilt not thou, O God, which hadst cast us off? and thou, O God, which didst not go out with our armies? Give us help from trouble: for vain is the help of man. Through God we shall do valiantly: for he it is that shall tread down our enemies." Edwards preached this sermon for a fast day in the wake of General Edward Braddock's defeat by the French and the Indians. The new commander-in-chief of the British forces in North America had led his army to attack France's Fort Duquesne only to be routed and Braddock mortally wounded. Wilson Kimnach calls this defeat the biggest event in the English colonies between the Great Awakening and the American Revolution.[60] Edwards found a striking parallel between the circumstances in David's time and those of his own. He observed from the context of Ps 60:1–3 that God's people had suffered great defeat in war, much like the English had suffered at Fort Duquesne. What the Israelites needed was "deliverance and victory" to get possession of the strongholds of Edom, just as the English sought to capture Fort Duquesne. But God did not help them because David and the English had depended on "the help of man," not on God.[61] But even in war, people must look to God for their help, for God is sovereign over all nations. He shows people through defeats that "'tis he and not they that determines the event," which is why he says "in his providence," "Be still, and know that I am God" (Ps 46:10).[62] As Psalm 46 displays God's power to make "desolations" in the earth, to cease wars, break bows, cut spears, and burn chariots (Ps 46:8–9),

---

58. Edwards, "The Sole Consideration," 300–302. Italics original.

59. Edwards, "The Sole Consideration," 303. Italics original.

60. Wilson H. Kimnach, ed., in *Sermons and Discourses 1743–1758*, vol. 25 of *WJE* (2006), 685.

61. Jonathan Edwards, "God's People Tried by a Battle Lost" (Ps 60:9–12), in *Sermons and Discourses 1743–1758*, ed. Wilson H. Kimnach, vol. 25 of *WJE* (2006), 688.

62. Edwards, "God's People Tried by a Battle Lost," 691.

so Psalm 60 displays God's people as coming to their senses only after defeat, realizing that "God alone can give victory."[63] God's sovereignty means that "*It becomes a people after defeats in war to relinquish all other dependence and to look to him for help.*"[64]

Edwards left no trace of consulting other interpreters on this passage, but his sermon mirrors other Reformed interpretations, and Henry provides a good example. Henry cast David as asking, "What Allies, what Auxiliaries, can I depend upon to make me Master of the Enemies['] Country and their Strong-holds?"[65] Not human ingenuities, for help comes only from God. When they suffered defeat, or "the Frowns of Providence," then they recognized that it was "because they had forfeited the gracious Presence of GOD with them."[66] Still, they flung themselves upon God's mercies, so that while "they own GOD's Justice in what was past, they *hope in his Mercy* for what was to come."[67] Both Henry and Edwards upheld God's sovereignty, yet Edwards applied his interpretation uniquely to New England's militaristic exploits. While Henry understood the warfare as a spiritual battle, Edwards related it to current geopolitical war with striking correspondence to the original battle imagery, appropriating it uniquely for his day.[68]

God's sovereign rule also implied his providence in ordering events, a theme Edwards found resounding in the Psalms. From one angle, Edwards affirmed that God willed evil events to accomplish his greater purposes. So as Edwards read Ps 105:25, "He turned their heart to hate his people, to deal subtilly with his servants," he concluded that "God willed that [the] Egyptians

---

63. Edwards, "God's People Tried by a Battle Lost," 691.

64. Edwards, "God's People Tried by a Battle Lost," 690–691. Italics original. Edwards went on in the sermon to interpret the defeat as "an awful rebuke of the Most High for our pride and vain confidence." He saw this as a call to reject the vain help of man and to become "earnest with God for his help in our expeditions." The English had greater hope for God's help because their enemy, the French, were devoted to the Roman Catholic Church, "members of the kingdom of Antichrist" and "enemies of the true church." Edwards believed they were on the right side but must still rely on God. Edwards, "God's People Tried by a Battle Lost," 696. For more on Edwards' approach to the Roman Catholic Church, see Marsden, *Jonathan Edwards: A Life*, 3–4, 414–417.

65. Henry, *Exposition*, [Ps 60:9–12].

66. Henry, *Exposition*, [Ps 60:9–12].

67. Henry, *Exposition*, [Ps 60:9–12]. Italics original.

68. See also Dickson, who explained, "It is God's absence from, or gracious presence with a people, which maketh the successe of the warres of his people against their enemies worse or better." Dickson, *Other fifty Psalmes*, 62. (N.B. When I use a short citation of Dickson's second volume on the Psalms, I retain the original case setting of the title, except for the first word of the short title.) Poole showed some debate over whether the enemy's "strong city" referred indefinitely to several cities or particularly to Rabbas, but he still emphasized

should hate God's people."[69] Joseph's story provided a perfect example of God ordering evil events for "good ends," as it is told in Ps 105:17, "He sent a man before them, even Joseph, who was sold for a servant." This passage, which interprets the event of Joseph's brothers selling him into slavery as God "sending" Joseph, confirmed Edwards' overall point: "That it is most certainly so, that God is in such a manner the disposer and orderer of sin, is evident, if any credit is to be given to the Scripture."[70] God's providential ordering of evil events did not preclude his merciful ordering of good events. For example, Ps 105:37 states that when the Israelites left Egypt, "there was not one feeble person among their tribes," and Edwards saw this as evidence of "a special care of providence over 'em, and a miraculous interposition with respect to such circumstances and state of the bodies of the people, as might make them incapable of such a journeying as God called them [to]."[71] Similarly, Edwards observed that amidst all the "overturnings of the world" from Babylon to Persia to Greece to Rome, God performed a "wonderful preservation of the church," which "gives light" to God's providential work in Ps 46:1–3.[72]

God's providence was most clearly visible in the provision for humanity's sustenance through nature's cycles, and on three occasions Edwards selected

---

the theological point that "neither by me nor by foreign human strength is it able to be done, but by God's help alone" ("Nec meis nec alienis humanis viribus hoc fieri potest, sed solius Dei auxilio"). Poole, *Synopsis*, 885. Trapp made a comparison to British history to show that human help is unreliable, noting the failure of Ætius, a Roman-appointed Gaul, to subdue the Britons, yet Trapp applied the military descriptions to "Spiritual warfare," observing that "[t]he Saints['] comfort is, that where human help faileth, divine beginneth." Trapp, *Commentary*, 743–744. Calvin focused on David's circumstances and held that God is the sole source of help and alone deserves honor for our successes; "[a]ll other resources of a worldly nature vanish before the brightness of thy power." Calvin, *Commentary*, 2:407–409. Quotation on 408.

69. Jonathan Edwards, *The "Miscellanies": Entry Nos. a–z, aa–zz, 1–500*, ed. Thomas A. Schafer, vol. 13 of *WJE* (1994), 204.

70. Edwards, *Freedom of the Will*, 399. In this point Edwards responded to the charge that God is "the author of sin," arguing that it depends on how one defines the phrase. In addition to Joseph, Edwards gave numerous other examples from Genesis through Revelation. See also Edwards' discussion of Ps 81:12 and what it means that God gives people over to sin in his argument against Daniel Whitby, who charged that men are innocent of sin if they do evil by necessity. Edwards, *Freedom of the Will*, 295–296.

71. Edwards, *The "Blank Bible,"* 526.

72. Jonathan Edwards, *A History of the Work of Redemption*, ed. John F. Wilson, vol. 9 of *WJE* (1989), 250. Ps 46:1–3 reads, "God is our refuge and strength, a very present help in trouble. Therefore will not we fear, though the earth be removed, and though the mountains be carried into the midst of the sea; Though the waters thereof roar and be troubled, though the mountains shake with the swelling thereof."

texts from the Psalms to discuss this providence. In a December 1752 sermon to the Stockbridge Indians, Edwards took as his text Ps 14:1, "The fool hath said in his heart, There is no God. They are corrupt, they have done abominable works, there is none that doeth good," preaching the doctrine, "There certainly is a G[od]."[73] To prove this doctrine to his Stockbridge Indian audience, Edwards turned not to the book of Scripture, with which they were less familiar, but to the book of nature, a "book" that in Edwards' view incontrovertibly testified to God's existence. Edwards' appeal to design in nature to prove the existence of God had biblical warrant (see Rom 1:19–20), but his move in this direction from Ps 14:1 was a unique development not shared by his Reformed predecessors.[74] How do we know there is a God? With all the predictability we observe in nature and all the provision we have in nature, it is unreasonable to expect anything except that God created and ordered it for our good. For example, Edwards explained that it would be impossible to live without the sun, but some Being knew we needed it and thus created it to give us warmth and light in just the right portions in all seasons. Not only did he create it, but he "Keeps it going" and has kept it working for "so many thous[ands of] years."[75] Edwards spoke similarly about the moon and stars; the earth, sea, rivers, and clouds; the leaves, vegetation, and fruits; the beasts, birds, and fish; and the human body with all its complexity and function. Since so many things work just right in nature, Edwards concluded that "nothing is more certain" and "nothing certain so many ways" than the existence of God, and thus, "How stupid & foolish are men" when they do not consider their state before their gracious Creator.[76]

Twenty-four years earlier, for a thanksgiving sermon on November 7, 1728, Edwards preached from Ps 65:11, "Thou crownest the year with thy goodness; and thy paths drop fatness." He observed that the psalm gives three reasons for praising God: "for spiritual blessings on his Church and People" (Ps 65:1–5); "for God[']s work of Creation" (Ps 65:6); and "for his Goodness in his Common Providence" (Ps 65:7–13).[77] The final section "beautifully sets forth the Bounty

73. Jonathan Edwards, "1059. Sermon on Ps 14:1(b) (December 1752)," Beinecke Rare Book and Manuscript Library, Yale University, New Haven, CT, L. 1r. See my discussion of Edwards' 1730 sermon on Ps 14:1 in chapter 3, pp. 143–147, 155–157.

74. See Henry, *Exposition*, [Ps 14:1]; Poole, *Synopsis*, 576–577; Trapp, *Commentary*, 601–602; David Dickson, *A Brief Explication of the first Fifty Psalms* (London: T. M. for Ralph Smith . . . , 1652), 66–67; Calvin, *Commentary*, 1:188–191.

75. Edwards, "1059. Sermon on Ps 14:1(b)," L. 1v.

76. Edwards, "1059. Sermon on Ps 14:1(b)," L. 4v.

77. Jonathan Edwards, "76. Sermon on Ps 65:11 (November 7, 1728)," in *Sermons, Series II, 1728–1729*, vol. 43 of *WJEO*, L. 1r.

of God bestowed upon mankind" in the agricultural cycles he has established to provide for their needs—a common Reformed interpretation of this psalm.[78] Edwards took the phrase "crowning the year with goodness" to mean that, during the harvest season, the fruits of men's labor represent God's crowning goodness; God "Rewards and Crowns all their Labour and toil."[79] He attributed all these things not to men's labor but ultimately to "Gods goodness" and thus preached the doctrine, "That we Ought to Praise God for Annual blessings."[80] By "annual blessings," Edwards meant God's "Common Bounty" over the course of the year, such as the sun, seasons, rain, fruits, and preservation, and he said we ought to praise God for these blessings because they are "as much the meer bounty of God as if they were Given never so Immediately."[81] Even secondary causes are created by God, for "Tis God and God Alone that Orders second Causes as to be a means of these blessings," and so, in his radical supernaturalism, Edwards explained that "we don[']t owe [these gifts] Partly to him and Partly to some other Cause."[82] This line of thinking led into Edwards' application that God deserves our utmost gratitude for his blessings.[83]

---

78. Edwards, "76. Sermon on Ps 65:11," L. 1r. See Henry, *Exposition*, [Ps 65:11]; Poole, *Synopsis*, 909–910; Dickson, *Other fifty Psalmes*, 87–89; Calvin, *Commentary*, 2:461–465.

79. Edwards, "76. Sermon on Ps 65:11," L. 1r.

80. Edwards, "76. Sermon on Ps 65:11," L. 1r., 1v. Henry likewise called people to praise God for the annual blessings of his providence: "Let all these common Gifts of the Divine Bounty, which we yearly and daily partake of, increase our Love to God as the best of Beings, and engage us to glorify him with our Bodies, which He thus provides so well for." Henry, *Exposition*, [Ps 65:6–13]. Similarly, Dickson upheld "God's providence" in nature by saying "the husbandry is all the Lord[']s." Dickson, *Other fifty Psalmes*, 88. Calvin also praised God's providence, noting that "the whole order of things in nature shows the fatherly love of God, in condescending to care for our daily sustenance." Calvin, *Commentary*, 2:463, 464.

81. Edwards, "76. Sermon on Ps 65:11," L. 1v., 4v.

82. Edwards, "76. Sermon on Ps 65:11," L. 6r., 7r. So Henry stated, "we must lift up our Eyes above the Hills, lift them up to the Heavens, where the original Springs of all Blessings are, out of sight." Henry, *Exposition*, [Ps 65:9]. Dickson also spoke of subordinating second causes: "Second causes, and the natural course of conveying benefits unto us, are not rightly seen, except when God, the first and prime cause, is seen to be nearest unto the actual disposing of them for producing the effect." Dickson, *Other fifty Psalmes*, 88. Calvin observed that "[i]t would seem as if the more perspicacity men have in observing second causes in nature, they will rest in them the more determinedly, instead of ascending by them to God," the true "origin" of natural blessings. Calvin, *Commentary*, 2:463.

83. Edwards' third sermon on this theme came in a thanksgiving sermon in November 1729, during a severe drought. Preaching on Ps 65:9, he considered that the psalm had likewise been written during a famine in Israel, and he developed a theological conclusion from the statement that "the river of God" is "full of water": "God, by the exercises of his common bounty towards men, shows that he has an all-sufficiency for the supply of their wants." Jonathan Edwards, "God's All-Sufficiency for the Supply of Our Wants" (Ps 65:9), in

This view of God's providence did not deny the need for human action. On the contrary, in Psalm 34 David praises God for delivering him, though he himself pretended to be a fool to escape Abimelech. Edwards explained the paradox:

> This psalm remarkably shows that a dependence on God for his protection and help should not cause us to neglect any proper endeavors, or the utmost use of our own strength and wisdom for our own preservation, deliverance, or any benefit we stand in need of. This psalm shows that David looked to God and trusted in him, when he was in such great danger in the land of the Philistines, and that God accepted his trust in him, and accordingly remarkably interposed and delivered him. "The angel of the Lord encamped round about him" [Ps 34:7]. And yet David made use of the utmost of his own contrivance and cunning for his own deliverance. "He changed his behavior," and "let his spittle fall down on his beard," and feigned himself distracted [1 Sam 21:13]; and God made use of this as the means of his deliverance.[84]

David's ingenuity was still a gift from God, and while it became a secondary means of deliverance, all praise for deliverance was due to God.

A further corollary of God's sovereignty that Edwards gleaned from the Psalms was his omniscience. As the sovereign ruler over the universe, God displays a knowledge of all things, even before they happen. God's complete knowledge of all things extends to eternity. In his reading of Ps 33:10–11—"the counsel of the Lord standeth for ever, the thoughts of his heart to all generations"—Edwards argued for God's foreknowledge of all things, that despite what is in men's hearts, "the whole scheme and series of his operations, are from the beginning perfectly in his view."[85]

In a September 1733 sermon on Ps 139:23–24, Edwards used the doctrine of God's omniscience as a basis for calling his people to examine their hearts for sinful ways. He described Psalm 139 as "a meditation on the omniscience of God," and he showed from the context how nothing the psalmist did was out of the purview of God's knowledge.[86] The "necessary *consequence* of this

Sermons and Discourses 1723–1729, ed. Kenneth P. Minkema, vol. 14 of *WJE* (1997), 474. On the context of the sermon, see Kenneth P. Minkema, ed., *Sermons and Discourses 1723–1729*, vol. 14 of *WJE* (1997), 471–473.

84. Edwards, *The "Blank Bible,"* 491.

85. Edwards, *Freedom of the Will*, 254.

86. Jonathan Edwards, "The Necessity of Self-Examination," in vol. 6 of *The Works of President Edwards*, ed. Sereno E. Dwight (New York: S. Converse, 1829), 328.

omniscience of God," is that "he will slay the wicked, since he seeth all their wickedness, and nothing of it is hid from him."[87] The psalmist "improves this meditation upon God's all-seeing eye" by asking God to search out his heart for any wicked way in him.[88] So he says, "Search me, O God, and know my heart: try me, and know my thoughts: And see if there be any wicked way in me, and lead me in the way everlasting" (Ps 139:23–24). Given the psalm's context, the psalmist clearly does not pray that God might gain knowledge, for God's omniscience has already been fully established. The psalmist hopes that God might reveal the depths of his heart to himself in "an act of mercy," so "that the *Psalmist* might see and be informed" by God's "discovering light"—a common Reformed interpretation.[89] David's end in this endeavor is clear: While the wicked are walking a path to condemnation and eternal peril, he wants to pursue the path that leads to everlasting life. He is not merely interested in "peace and quietness for the present" but the way "in which he may always have peace and joy."[90] So Edwards preached the doctrine, "All men should be much concerned to know whether they do not live in some way of sin."[91] That was the example of David in this psalm. Though he diligently searched his heart, he put minimal stock in his discernment, fearful that some wicked way "had escaped his notice," so he cried to God to shine his all-seeing light upon his soul, and he took comfort in God's omniscience to help him find the way of life.[92]

An interesting corollary to Edwards' understanding of God's sovereignty was his conviction that God alone can judge people and discern what is in their hearts. Because God alone is the sovereign ruler and he alone knows

---

87. Edwards, "The Necessity of Self-Examination," 328. Italics original.

88. Edwards, "The Necessity of Self-Examination," 328.

89. Edwards, "The Necessity of Self-Examination," 329. Italics original. Henry commented, "[t]hey that are upright can take comfort in God's Omniscience as a witness of their upright-ness, and can with an humble confidence beg of him to *search* and *try them*, to discover them to themselves." Henry, *Exposition*, [Ps 139:23–24]. Poole considered that the request may be either for David to have understanding of himself or that wrong perceptions of him might be corrected and David's sincerity vindicated. Poole, *Synopsis*, 1295. Trapp admonished that "[w]ee should not rest…in our heart[']s voice; nor accept its deceitful applause." Trapp, *Commentary*, 915.

90. Edwards, "The Necessity of Self-Examination," 329. Edwards noted in the "Blank Bible" that "way" here is a metonymy for those who walk in the way. Edwards, *The "Blank Bible,"* 538.

91. Edwards, "The Necessity of Self-Examination," 329.

92. Edwards, "The Necessity of Self-Examination," 330. In another sermon, Edwards also preached on God's omnipresence from Ps 139:7–10, defending the doctrine that "God is

all things, then he alone reserves the right to stand as the judge of people—a fundamental concept in Edwards' evaluation of the New England revivals. In *The Distinguishing Marks of a Work of the Spirit of God*, Edwards built from Ps 7:9–11 and Psalm 26 to argue that the "judging of hearts" and of a professing believer's state is "God's prerogative."[93] That God is the rightful judge of humanity is supported by the Psalms' frequent testimony to this truth (Pss 76:2–3; 14:7; 53:6; 20:2; 110:2; 128:5; 134:3).[94] And God is a fair and righteous judge, as Edwards gathered from Ps 11:7, "For the righteous LORD loveth righteousness; his countenance doth behold the upright." In a "Miscellanies" entry addressing objections to the idea that the doctrine of justification by faith is evident in the Old Testament, Edwards explained that the "main design" of this oft-misunderstood verse, Ps 11:7, is

> to declare the righteousness of God as judge, that he will thoroughly and impartially try the cause of the righteous, wherein the wicked contends with him and persecutes him without cause; and that he will condemn him whose cause is bad, or who is [in] the wrong; and that he will favor and approve of him who is right (as in the word translated "upright" signifies), or who has the right of the cause; and that because he is a righteous judge, one that delights in righteousness or in judging righteously, and abhors partiality and injustice.[95]

In an October 1736 sermon, Edwards explored the benefits and dangers of having God as one's inevitable judge. He chose as his text Ps 7:8, "The LORD shall judge the people: judge me, O LORD, according to my righteousness, and according to mine integrity that is in me." He interpreted "Cush

---

everywhere present." The psalmist communicated this reality by dividing "the whole infinite space" into three parts, "height and depth and parallel distance." "Heaven" represents the highest possible space, "hell" represents the lowest possible space, and "the uttermost parts of the sea" represent the farthest spaces possible to go in the parallel plane of the psalmist's universe. No matter where the psalmist might try to go, still "he should yet be in God's hand." Jonathan Edwards, "That God Is Everywhere Present" (Ps 139:7–10), in *The Blessing of God: Previously Unpublished Sermons of Jonathan Edwards*, ed. Michael D. McMullen (Nashville, TN: Broadman & Holman, 2003), 108–109.

93. Jonathan Edwards, *The Distinguishing Marks*, in *The Great Awakening*, ed. C. C. Goen, vol. 4 of *WJE* (1972), 283. See also Edwards' discussion of these two passages in his "Notes on Scripture" entry on Rom 2:29. Edwards, *Notes on Scripture*, 353–354.

94. Edwards, *Notes on Scripture*, 362–363.

95. Jonathan Edwards, *The "Miscellanies": Entry Nos. 1153–1360*, ed. Douglas A. Sweeney, vol. 23 of *WJE* (2004), 533.

the Benjamite" (from the psalm's title) as Shimei, a unique interpretive move
amongst the Reformed interpreters in our purview. While others identified
Cush as Saul (Poole, Henry, and Trapp), a "flattering courtier" (Dickson), or
"one of Saul's kindred" (Calvin), Edwards found it compelling that this psalm
referred to the time when Shimei cursed David as he fled from Absalom.[96] At
that point David faced serious opposition: His own son Absalom charged him
with ruling the people unjustly and sought to tear the kingdom from him;
the bulk of Israel followed Absalom and considered it just to take David's life;
and Shimei accused David of murdering the house of Saul. But despite the
many enemies "ready to judge and condemn," David's comfort was "that the
matter was not to go as they judged but as God judged."[97] God's judgment
did not frighten David, and so he was willing to expose his inner being to
"the all-seeing eye of God," that "God should search his heart and judge him
according to what he found there," for he felt confident if only "the one who
could see his heart should be his judge."[98] Edwards preached a two-part doctrine from this verse. First, for Christians, "[s]ince God is to be their judge, 'tis
impossible that they should miss of being acquitted and rewarded," for God is
an omniscient, righteous judge who loves them because his Son has redeemed
them.[99] Second, "'tis well for some that God is to be their judge, for by that

---

96. Only Poole recognized Shimei as a possible referent, but he preferred to identify Cush
as Saul, as did Henry and Trapp. Dickson preferred a "flattering courtier," an interpretive
option that Poole and Trapp both mentioned. Calvin rejected the notion that David spoke
of Saul "under a fictitious name"; he said Cush was "one of Saul's [contemporary] kindred."
Poole, *Synopsis*, 525–526; Henry, *Exposition*, [Ps 7:8]; Trapp, *Commentary*, 576; Dickson, *First
Fifty Psalms*, 34; Calvin, *Commentary*, 1:75–76.

97. Jonathan Edwards, "'Tis a Blessed Thing to Some Persons That God Is to Be Their
Judge" (Ps 7:8), in *The Glory and Honor of God: Volume 2 of the Previously Unpublished Sermons
of Jonathan Edwards*, ed. Michael D. McMullen (Nashville, TN: Broadman & Holman, 2004),
55. The notion of comfort from God's office as Judge resonated with Calvin, who said it is
"a continual stream of comfort" to believers. Calvin, *Commentary*, 1:83. Other interpreters
also distinguished God as the unique Judge of all. Henry cast God's court as "the proper
Court" and observed that since he is "the Judge of all the Earth," then "no doubt He shall *do
right* and all will be oblig'd to acquiesce in his Judgment." Henry, *Exposition*, [Ps 7:8]. Italics
original. And Poole showed David appealing to God to exercise his judgment: "You, Lord,
alone are near to those whom it concerns to proclaim among the peoples, you therefore are
Judge of my enemies. Judge the peoples, whom either you punish, or, if they are innocent,
you acquit" ("Tu, Domine, solus es ad quem pertinet pronunciare inter populos, tu igitur
Judex es adversariorum meorum. Judicas populos, eosque vel punis, vel, si innocentes sint,
absolves"). Poole, *Synopsis*, 530.

98. Edwards, "'Tis a Blessed Thing," 55–56.

99. Edwards, "'Tis a Blessed Thing," 56–59. Quotation on 56. Dickson likewise emphasized
the hope of reconciliation with God that one has "through the Sacrifice of the mediator."
Dickson, *First Fifty Psalms*, 36.

means the mouths of all who reproach and condemn them will be stopped."[100] While Edwards focused solely on the benefits of God as judge for the righteous in his doctrine section, he turned in the application to show the misery of the wicked who must one day face this all-seeing, righteous God as their judge.

For Edwards, the Psalms bore ample testimony to God's sovereignty, especially borne out in his all-powerful rule; his providential ordering of good and evil in the world to accomplish his purposes; his comprehensive knowledge of all things, past, present, and future; and his unique prerogative to discern the nature of people's hearts and stand as their final judge. As Edwards made particularly clear in his sermons on the Psalms, God's sovereignty explains his sure victory over sin and death through his ordering of events so Christ would secure redemption for his people, the outworking of his divine plan conceived in eternity past. From a corporate perspective, he is guiding all of human history to work out his redemptive-historical purposes. From an individual perspective, God's sovereignty and omniscience serve as a beckoning call to sinners to wake from their slumbers and take seriously his absolute rule and promised judgment. For the saints, God's sovereignty is a welcome comfort of the assurance of salvation, as the Psalter so readily testifies: "David, throughout the Book of Psalms, almost everywhere speaks without any hesitancy, and in the most positive manner of God as his God; glorifying in him as his portion and heritage, his rock and confidence, his shield, salvation, and high tower, and the like."[101] God's sovereignty, however, makes his ways unpredictable to the human observer.

The Mysterious Ways of God

Because he is the sovereign, omnipotent ruler of creation, God does as he pleases and thus works in ways that people do not expect. Humanity cannot put God in a box. His decisions are his and are sometimes mysterious. Thus Edwards argued from Ps 77:19 that God's providence is so unsearchable for finite humanity that we should not try to replace it with our limited reason: "The dispensations and events of providence, with their reasons, are too little understood by us to be improved by us as our rule, instead of God's Word; God has his 'way in the sea, and his path in the mighty waters, and his footsteps are not known.'"[102] In

---

100. Edwards, "'Tis a Blessed Thing," 59.

101. Jonathan Edwards, *Religious Affections*, ed. John E. Smith, vol. 2 of *WJE* (1959), 167–168.

102. Jonathan Edwards, *Some Thoughts Concerning the Revival*, in *The Great Awakening*, ed. C. C. Goen, vol. 4 of *WJE* (1972), 451.

another treatise, Edwards returned to Ps 77:19, noting again that "[t]he conduct of divine providence, with its reasons, is too little understood by us," and God "gives none account of any of his matters."[103]

As men are in no place to question the sovereign plan of God, they ought not question the means God uses to accomplish his purposes. Because God's "judgments are a great deep" (Ps 36:6), we can determine "an extraordinary influence or operation" to be the work of God no matter what circumstances, instruments, and methods he uses by his sovereign will and no matter what "effects may be wrought on men's bodies"—a statement Edwards made while assessing the New England revivals in *Distinguishing Marks* (1741).[104] In his further evaluation of the revivals in *Some Thoughts Concerning the Revival* (1743), Edwards criticized those who dismissed them a priori because he held that the revivals should be judged by their fruits, not their means. God's "judgments are a great deep" (Ps 36:6), and "he hath his way in the sea, and his path in the great waters, and his footsteps are not known" (Ps 77:19). So it is presumptuous of man to decide for God how he should work:

> To judge a priori is a wrong way of judging any of the works of God. We are not to resolve that we will first be satisfied how God brought this or the other effect to pass, and why he hath made it thus, or why it has pleased him to take such a course, and to use such and such means, before we will acknowledge his work, and give him the glory of it. This is too much for the clay to take upon it with respect to the potter.[105]

Again we see here Edwards' concern to place humanity in proper respect to its sovereign, righteous Creator, who is free to use means as he will. Edwards warned, " '[t]is a great fault in us to limit a sovereign all-wise God, whose 'judgments are a great deep' [Ps 36:6], and 'his ways past finding out' [Rom 11:33], where he has not limited himself, and in things concerning which he has not told us what his way shall be."[106] Edwards mirrored Henry's interpretation of Pss 36:6 and 77:19, for Henry also connected these two verses to discuss God's mysterious methods: "As his power is sovereign, which he owes not any

---

103. Jonathan Edwards, *An Humble Inquiry into the Rules of the Word of God, Concerning the Qualifications Requisite to a Complete Standing and Full Communion in the Visible Christian Church*, in *Ecclesiastical Writings*, ed. David D. Hall, vol. 12 of *WJE* (1994), 319.

104. Edwards, *Distinguishing Marks*, 258.

105. Edwards, *Some Thoughts*, 294.

106. Edwards, *Some Thoughts*, 304.

account of to us, so his method is singular and mysterious, which cannot be accounted for by us."[107]

God's mysterious ways also revealed his unpredictability toward enemies. In a number of places, Edwards spoke from the Psalms to show how God confounds the wicked, particularly in *An Humble Attempt*. For example, Ps 35:4 and 6 state, "Let them be confounded and put to shame that seek after my soul: let them be turned back and brought to confusion that devise my hurt. . . . Let their way be dark and slippery: and let the angel of the LORD persecute them." Edwards concluded that "[t]he Scripture teaches us, that God is wont in this way to defend his church and people from their crafty and powerful enemies."[108] For example, Edwards believed that after the Reformation, God would never allow the antichrist to prevail against the Protestant church again, in keeping with the Psalmistic language of God frustrating wicked attempts to undermine the church. Edwards stated:

> Upon the account of such defense of God's Protestant church, and disappointment and confusion of all the subtile devices, deep-laid schemes, and furious attempts of their antichristian enemies, to bring them under, and root them out, . . . in spite of all that they do, makes them as it were gnash their teeth, and bite their tongues for mere rage and vexation; agreeable to Psa. 112:9–10. "His righteousness endureth forever, his horn shall be exalted with honor: the wicked shall see it and be grieved, and gnash with his teeth and melt away: the desire of the wicked shall perish."[109]

In the post-revival era, Edwards observed that "the people of God are set on high," in many cases having the power of magistrates and princes to protect them, which is "greatly to their [enemies'] grief and vexation; who, though they from time to time exert their utmost, never are able to prevail against them, to bring them under any more, as they had done in former wars."[110] It

---

107. Henry, *Exposition*, [Ps 36:6]. Poole likewise described God's ways as "most profound and inscrutable" ("profundissima & inscrutabilia"). Poole, *Synopsis*, 733.

108. Jonathan Edwards, *An Humble Attempt to Promote Explicit Agreement and Visible Union of God's People in Extraordinary Prayer for the Revival of Religion and the Advancement of Christ's Kingdom on Earth, Pursuant to Scripture-Promises and Prophecies Concerning the Last Time*, in *Apocalyptic Writings*, ed. Stephen J. Stein, vol. 5 of *WJE* (1977), 384–385. Edwards developed these ideas originally in his "Apocalypse Series." Jonathan Edwards, "Apocalypse Series," in *Apocalyptic Writings*, ed. Stephen J. Stein, vol. 5 of *WJE* (1977), 194.

109. Edwards, *Humble Attempt*, 385. See also Edwards, "Apocalypse Series," 195.

110. Edwards, *Humble Attempt*, 391. See also Edwards, "Apocalypse Series," 211.

is in the Psalms that the safety of God's church from enemies is often represented as their "dwelling on high" or "set on high" (Pss 59:1, 69:29, 91:14, 107:41).[111] Ultimately, God would confound the church's greatest enemy, Satan himself, as taught in Ps 8:2, "Out of the mouth of babes and sucklings hast thou ordained strength because of thine enemies, that thou mightest still the enemy and the avenger." In his "Blank Bible," Edwards interpreted "the enemy and the avenger" as the devil and the "babes and sucklings" as mankind, and so when God "ordained strength" out of their mouths, it was "to pour contempt upon the great and proud enemy and avenger, to conquer him and obtain a glorious triumph by so weak and despicable an instrument, and thrusting him down below babes and sucklings, and subduing him under their feet, and so causing his glorying to cease."[112] At a separate time, Edwards cited Poole in this same "Blank Bible" note, and Poole likewise interpreted the "enemy" as "Satan" and saw God's unanticipated means of overthrowing Satan through human flesh: "Thus the Son of God, in order to overthrow this enemy, assumed not Angelic nature…but human nature, which grew strong from infancy."[113] The ways and means that God uses are unpredictable, though they always accomplish his purposes, especially visible in his work of redemption.

To further describe God's mystery, Edwards used the imagery of darkness and clouds as described in Ps 18:11, "He made darkness his secret place; his pavilion round about him were dark waters and thick clouds of the skies," and Ps 97:2, "Clouds and darkness are round about him: righteousness and judgment are the habitation of his throne."[114] Edwards explained, "As he is God, he is so *great*, that he is infinitely above all comprehension; and therefore it is unreasonable in us to quarrel with his dispensations, because they are mysterious," for "[i]t is fit that God should dwell in thick darkness, or in light to which no man can approach, which no man hath seen or can see."[115] The

---

111. Edwards, *Humble Attempt*, 391. See also Edwards, "Apocalypse Series," 211.

112. Edwards, *The "Blank Bible,"* 477–478. See also Edwards, *Notes on Scripture*, 77.

113. Edwards, *The "Blank Bible,"* 478; Poole, *Synopsis*, 538. The Latin reads, "Itaque Filius Dei, ut hunc hostem profligaret, naturum assumpsit, non Angelicum…sed humanum, quae ab infantia adolescit."

114. Edwards, *The "Blank Bible,"* 466. See also his "Blank Bible" entries on 2 Samuel 15–18 and Ps 81:7 and his "Notes on Scripture" Entry No. 393 on Ezek 1:4. Edwards, *The "Blank Bible,"* 369, 516; Edwards, *Notes on Scripture*, 387.

115. Edwards, "The Sole Consideration, that God Is God," 295, 296. Similarly, Henry stated, "His Glory is invisible, his Counsels are unsearchable, and his Proceedings unaccountable, and so, as to us, *Clouds and Darkness are round about him.*" Henry, *Exposition*, [Ps 18:11].

Psalmistic image of clouds illustrates the unknowable wonder of God's glory. Reflecting in "Notes on Scripture" on Exod 13:21 and the pillar of cloud and fire by which God led the Jews in the desert, Edwards turned to the Psalms to consider the significance of the cloud:

> Another [thing] signified by God's glorious appearing in a cloud was probably the mysteriousness of the divine essence and subsistence, and of the person of Christ and of the divine operations. Thus it is said, Ps. 97:2, "Clouds and darkness are round about him; righteousness and judgment are the habitation of his throne." 1 Kgs. 8:12, "The Lord said that he would dwell in the thick darkness." Ps.18:11, "He made darkness his secret place; his pavilion round about him were dark waters and thick clouds of the skies."…God's nature is unsearchable. 'Tis high as heaven; what can we do? 'Tis deeper than hell; what can we know? His judgments are a great deep which we cannot fathom, and a cloud that we can't see through.…In the cloud of glory there was an excellent luster, but it was veiled with a cloud. There was a darting forth of glorious light and an inimitable brightness. But if any over-curious eye pried into it, [it] would find itself lost in a cloud.[116]

It is this uncontainable God that Edwards saw portrayed in the Psalms. His greatness would always amount to a mystery that baffles the finite minds of people. Yet perhaps the greatest mystery of all was the mercy that this grand God bestowed upon his creatures.

The Mercy of God

Edwards reveled in God's lavish mercy as he read the Psalms. Psalm 136 particularly captures this theme in an artistic repetition of the phrase, "for his mercy endureth for ever," after every line. Edwards saw no blame in the psalmist's repetition given the rich blessing of God's mercy. He said "we need not wonder" at his repetition "as if he were in an ecstasy at the consideration of the perpetuity of God's mercy to his church, and delight to think of it and knew not how but continually to express it."[117] Rather, he called his own people "with like pleasure and joy" to "celebrate the everlasting duration of God's mercy and faithfulness to his

---

116. Edwards, *Notes on Scripture*, 554.

117. Edwards, *A History of the Work of Redemption*, 525–526. Trapp likewise said it is not "any idle repetition, but a notable expression of the Saints['] unsatisfiableness in praising God for his never-failing mercy." Trapp, *Commentary*, 908.

church and people."[118] So for a thanksgiving sermon in November 1736, Edwards took as his text Ps 136:1, "O give thanks unto the LORD; for he is good: for his mercy endureth for ever," and because the psalm captured the topic so well, he spent much longer than usual in the text portion of the sermon. Edwards argued that the subject of Psalm 136 is "The Eternity & Constancy of God[']s mercy to his People."[119] He discussed the attribute, object, and property of God's mercy. The attribute of God's mercy is one that God "delights to Glorify" and one "the Psalmist delighted Greatly to Celebrate in his Psalms"; the object of God's mercy is his church, for this psalm is filled with God's acts of mercy toward his church; and the property of God's mercy is that it is "from Everlasting to Everlasting."[120] Edwards went on to describe these works of God as manifesting the "Eternity & perpetuity of God[']s mercy," noting that since God exercised his mercy toward his people at the beginning of time, before the church was formed, his mercy must be from eternity.[121] Given God's work for the church in history, one can conclude that "God[']s mercy to his Ch[urc]h has never failed so far," and "hence the Psalmist declares his faith that it will never fail."[122] In his final observations about Psalm 136 in the text section, Edwards noted that as the psalmist begins and ends with thanksgiving, so the proper "Improvement" of seeing the manifestations of God's mercies is "to Call upon God[']s People to Give thanks."[123] So Edwards preached the doctrine, "That all Great works of G[od] from the beginning of the [world] to the End of it are works of mercy to his People."[124]

Edwards also discussed the perpetuity of God's mercies in his reading of Ps 89:1–2, "I will sing of the mercies of the LORD for ever: with my mouth will I make known thy faithfulness to all generations. For I have said, Mercy shall be

---

118. Edwards, *A History of the Work of Redemption*, 526.

119. Jonathan Edwards, "413. Sermon on Ps 136:1 (November 1736)," in *Sermons, Series II, 1736*, vol. 51 of *WJEO*, L. 1r.

120. Edwards, "413. Sermon on Ps 136:1," L. 1r., 1v. Edwards recognized that the term "endure" seems to speak of God's mercy going on forever into eternity future without speaking to it originating in eternity past. Edwards rejected this interpretation because the term "endure" does not occur in the original Hebrew. He translated the clause as "mercy is in Eternity," signifying "from Eternity to Eternity," which was validated by the psalmist's recitation of God's works. Edwards, "413. Sermon on Ps 136:1," L. 1v.

121. Edwards, "413. Sermon on Ps 136:1," L. 2v.–3v. Quotation on L. 2v.

122. Edwards, "413. Sermon on Ps 136:1," L. 3v., 4v. Quotation on L. 4v.

123. Edwards, "413. Sermon on Ps 136:1," L. 5r. Dickson likewise saw this psalm as a call to give God thanks for his everlasting mercy. David Dickson, *A Brief Explication of the last Fifty Psalmes, From Ps. 100 to the end* (London: T. R. and E. M. for Ralph Smith . . . , 1654), 292–293.

124. Edwards, "413. Sermon on Ps 136:1," L. 6r.

built up for ever: thy faithfulness shalt thou establish in the very heavens." From this passage Edwards found a great testament to God's unfailing mercy:

> God's mercy towards his people shall endure forever, not only as long as the earth lasts, but as long as the heavens endure. God's mercy towards his church shall be increasing; God will be always carrying on the design of his mercy and love towards his church to greater and greater perfection. That as long as the world stands, God in the course of his providence will be prosecuting the design of his mercy towards his church, so that God's love shall more and more appear, and the effects of it be carried to a greater height, like a building that rises higher and higher.[125]

For Edwards, the Psalms clearly witnessed to the unfailing, eternal nature of God's mercy.[126]

The Psalms also testified to the transcendent nature of God's mercy, as Edwards declared in a summer 1731 sermon on Ps 108:4, "For thy mercy is great above the heavens...." He observed that the psalmist's reflection upon this attribute of God led him to "Elegantly set forth" "the Riches & Glory of his divine mercy" using a natural metaphor of the height of God's mercy above the heavens.[127] While other Reformed interpreters discussed both God's mercy and his truth, joining the first half of the verse with the second, "and thy truth reacheth unto the clouds," Edwards preached only on the first half of the verse to develop an extended reflection on God's mercy.[128] Edwards used the metaphor to signify two particular characteristics of this attribute, the "superlative inexpressible & Incomprehensible Greatness & Excellency of the mercy of G[od]."[129] First, with respect to the greatness of God's mercy, as the human mind cannot conceive of anything higher than the heavens, so God's mercy is even higher than that great heavenly body. Second, not only is God's glory great, it is also infinitely excellent, for "here the Psalmist

---

125. Jonathan Edwards, "Harmony of the Genius Spirit Doctrines and Rules of the Old Testament and the New," Beinecke Rare Book and Manuscript Library, Yale University, New Haven, CT, 255–256.

126. Edwards listed Pss 100:5; 102; 106:1, 39–43; 107:1; 117:2; 118:1–4, 29; 136; 138:7–8 in support of this point. Edwards, "Harmony," 260, 262, 263, 264, 275.

127. Jonathan Edwards, "195. Sermon on Ps 108:4 (July–August 1731)," in *Sermons, Series II, 1731–1732*, vol. 46 of *WJEO*, L. 1r.

128. Henry, *Exposition*, [Ps 108:4]; Poole, *Synopsis*, 1158; Trapp, *Commentary*, 737–738, 859; Dickson, *Last Fifty Psalmes*, 96.

129. Edwards, "195. Sermon on Ps 108:4," L. 1r.

may signify the Infinite Greatness & Excellency of God[']s mercy by its being above the heavens[—]Heaven being the Highest thing that is finite."[130] Thus Edwards preached this doctrine: "G[od] is a being of Transcendent mercy."[131] In his doctrine section, he explained that God's mercy is "Transcendent in that tis sufficient to Extend itself to the sinfull," and even to "an Object of any degree of sinfullness," for "the mercy of G[od] is sufficient to surmount all" sins.[132] In having a transcendent mercy, God "is never weary of show-ing mercy," to which the Psalms bear frequent witness: "tis one thing often taken notice of in the Psalms as one thing that shows the wonderfullness of God[']s mercy that it Endures forever."[133] The infinite greatness of God's mercy is further evident in that God reserves no good thing as too great to bestow on the miserable objects of his mercy and in that "no means [are] too Condescending or Expensive for mercy to use for the Good of sinners," namely God's Son—again highlighting God's redemptive purposes from the Psalms.[134] In applying this doctrine, Edwards noted how "Inexcuseable" it is for people to refuse such infinite mercy, cautioning that "none Encourage themselves in sin" from God's infinite mercy, and he exhorted Christians to love and trust God because of his transcendent, all-sufficient mercy for the greatest sinners.[135]

Edwards pointed to the Psalms to show that though his children provoke him and grieve his Spirit by their sins (Pss 78:40, 42–43; 95:9–10), God in his mercy turns away his wrath and spares them (Ps 78:38–39). In Edwards' words, "Justice's displeasure throws a dart that is leveled at the heart; but Mercy interposes as a shield between, and causes it to glance aside, and the precious life is preserved. And therefore we read of God's turning away his anger."[136] God's justice is satisfied and mercy manifested in Christ, in whom "Mercy and truth are met together" (Ps 85:10), for Christ interposes and stands in the gap as Moses, a type of Christ, did, as Ps 106:23 records, "Therefore he said that he would destroy them, had not Moses his chosen stood before him

---

130. Edwards, "195. Sermon on Ps 108:4," L. IV.

131. Edwards, "195. Sermon on Ps 108:4," L. IV.

132. Edwards, "195. Sermon on Ps 108:4," L. 2r., 3r., 3v.

133. Edwards, "195. Sermon on Ps 108:4," L. 4v., 5r.

134. Edwards, "195. Sermon on Ps 108:4," L. 5v.–6r. Quotation on L. 6r.

135. Edwards, "195. Sermon on Ps 108:4," L. 7v.–10v. Quotations on L. 7v., 10v.

136. Jonathan Edwards, "Undeserved Mercy" (Ezek 20:21–22), in *Sermons and Discourses 1734–1738*, ed. M. X. Lesser, vol. 19 of *WJE* (2001), 635, 638. Quotation on 638.

in the breach, to turn away his wrath, lest he should destroy them."[137] So the sinner must throw himself wholly on the infinite mercy of God.[138]

The good news is that God loves to shed his mercy on repentant sinners. In fact, one of the most powerful ways that God displays his mercy and grace is in his eagerness to answer prayer. Edwards argued from the Psalms that "God is a prayer-hearing God," noting that God provides plenteous mercy to those who call on him (Pss 34:10; 50:15; 86:4–5; 145:18–19) and that "[t]here is scarce anything that is more frequently asserted of God in Scripture than this, that he stands ready to hear prayer."[139] So in one of the three Psalms sermons that Edwards preached on God answering prayer, he chose Ps 65:2 as his text: "O thou that hearest prayer, unto thee shall all flesh come." This January 1736 fast sermon responded to a rapidly spreading illness in the area. Edwards explained that this text teaches us about the nature of the one true God, as distinguished from false gods, and he preached the doctrine, "That it is the character of the Most High, that he is a God who hears prayer."[140] As Edwards fleshed out this doctrine, he emphasized that, despite the contrast between God, who is "infinitely above all," and humanity, God "is graciously pleased to take a merciful notice of poor worms of the dust," and "he is wont to hear their prayers."[141] By "hearing prayer," Edwards meant both that God accepts with approval their supplications as giving him honor by coming to him and that God will act "by dealing mercifully with them in his providence, in consequence of their prayers, and by causing an agreeableness between his providence and their prayers."[142] But why does God like to answer prayer? In

---

137. Edwards, "Undeserved Mercy," 640.

138. See also Edwards' discussion of God's grace as contrasted with man's unworthiness from Ps 25:11. Edwards, *The "Blank Bible,"* 489.

139. Jonathan Edwards, "Praying for the Spirit" (Luke 11:13), in *Sermons and Discourses 1739–1742*, ed. Harry S. Stout and Nathan O. Hatch with Kyle P. Farley, vol. 22 of *WJE* (2003), 215.

140. Jonathan Edwards, "The Most High a Prayer-Hearing God" (Ps 65:2), in *The Works of Jonathan Edwards*, ed. Edward Hickman, vol. 2 (1834; repr., Edinburgh: Banner of Truth Trust, 1974), 113. Edwards repreached this sermon in March 1752, most likely to the white congregation in Stockbridge. Also, his sermon bears little resemblance to Henry's commentary, except that they both emphasized that God is "a GOD hearing prayer," or to Poole's commentary. Henry, *Exposition*, [Ps 65:2]; Poole, *Synopsis*, 904. However, like Edwards, Calvin emphasized that what makes God stand out is not that he will answer some particular type of prayer but that answering prayer is part of his very "nature," that the name "hearer of prayer" is "what constitutes an abiding part of his glory." Calvin, *Commentary*, 2:452.

141. Edwards, "The Most High a Prayer-Hearing God," 114.

142. Edwards denied, however, that God's answering prayers in this way necessitates that he will do exactly what a person asks; rather, because God accepts their prayers, "from hence

a word, "[b]ecause he is a God of infinite grace and mercy," for "[i]t is indeed a very wonderful thing, that so great a God should be so ready to hear our prayers…that worms of the dust should have such power with God by prayer; that he should do such great things in answer to their prayers, and should show himself, as it were, overcome by them."[143] Here Edwards upheld the tension between humans actually having "power" in prayer yet God feigning to be overcome by prayers. The statements seem mutually exclusive, but for Edwards, they were not. He called our prayers "polluted things," and yet "God delights in mercy and condescension," and thanks to Christ, we have a "glorious Mediator, who has prepared the way, that our prayers may be heard consistently with the honour of God's justice and majesty."[144]

In another sermon on prayer, Edwards preached on Ps 10:17, "thou wilt prepare their heart, thou wilt cause thine ear to hear" (March 1735). Edwards observed in this psalm that preparation of men's hearts is "the work of God," and he especially emphasized from the text that the "cause" of God's hearing is God himself:

> We don't cause God's ear to hear, but he causes it. The mercy of God towards his people is not moved or drawn by them but 'tis self-moved. It has its beginning, its first spring, on God himself, and the cause of it is not to be sought in the creature. 'Tis not men's prayers, nor any thing in them that is the cause of God's mercy to them, but 'tis from his own sovereign pleasure.[145]

Edwards went on to state that "[t]he whole affair" of God answering prayer, from stirring those who pray to preparing them to receive his answer, "in its beginning and end is from free grace"—reflective of Dickson, who said, "[g]race to pray, and the fixing of the heart in prayer on the Lord, is his gift, no less than the answer of the prayer."[146] Thus Edwards preached this

---

they may confidently rest in his providence, in his merciful ordering and disposing, with respect to the thing which they ask." Edwards, "The Most High a Prayer-Hearing God," 114.

143. Edwards, "The Most High a Prayer-Hearing God," 116.

144. Edwards, "The Most High a Prayer-Hearing God," 116. Dickson likewise noted that the "hearing and granting of prayer" are God's "pleasure." Dickson, *Other fifty Psalms*, 83.

145. Jonathan Edwards, "God's Manner Is First to Prepare Men's Hearts and Then to Answer Their Prayers" (Ps 10:17), in *The Glory and Honor of God: Volume 2 of the Previously Unpublished Sermons of Jonathan Edwards*, ed. Michael D. McMullen, (Nashville, TN: Broadman & Holman, 2004), 78–79.

146. Edwards, "God's Manner is First," 79; Dickson, *First Fifty Psalms*, 55.

doctrine: "God's manner is first to prepare men's hearts and then to answer their prayers."[147] Specifically, God prepares people to accept and enjoy his answer; to acknowledge God rather than second causes as the true source of the blessing received; and to respond by praising, loving, and glorifying God with his gifts.[148] God prepares men's hearts before answering prayer both "to secure his own glory" and "to promote their good," for "if God should bestow blessings on an unprepared subject he would not be in a capacity to enjoy it or to receive the benefit of it."[149] Edwards demonstrated a striking similarity with Henry in this sermon, and while he did not mention Henry on this particular verse, he did cite him on an earlier verse in this psalm (Ps 10:10).[150] Henry, like Edwards (and Poole and Trapp), emphasized God's work of preparing the person praying to receive God's blessing, that he "makes us fit to receive it and use it well."[151] For Edwards, like Henry, Poole, and Trapp, prayer is "a means to prepare us for the mercies that we stand in need of."[152] This approach holds people accountable for engaging in prayer as God's means of offering mercies but prioritizes God as the sovereign actor in the prayer event.

The reality is that God loves to answer prayer, a theme Edwards proclaimed in his May 1738 sermon on Ps 21:4, "He asked life of thee, and thou gavest it him, even length of days forever and ever." He described Psalm 21 as a response of praise for God answering the king's prayer in Psalm 20. The king here refers "more immediately" to David, but "'tis plain that the Holy Ghost in David has a further meaning, and that David speaks in the person of Christ, and that 'tis he that is principally intended."[153] God's "superlative goodness" is

---

147. Edwards, "God's Manner is First," 79.

148. Edwards, "God's Manner is First," 79–84.

149. Edwards, "God's Manner is First," 84–85.

150. Edwards, *The "Blank Bible,"* 480.

151. Henry stated, "He first *prepares the Heart* of his People, and then gives them an Answer of peace.... He prepares the Heart *for Prayer* by kindling holy Desires, and strengthening our most Holy Faith, fixing the Thoughts, and raising the Affections, and then He graciously accepts the Prayer; He prepares the Heart for the *Mercy itself* that is wanting and pray'd for, makes us fit to receive it, and use it well, and then gives it in to us." Henry, *Exposition*, [Ps 10:17]. Italics original. Similarly, Poole held that God acts first in mercy by preparing people both for prayer and for the grace he will give in response, for grace is prerequisite to one acquiring grace. Poole, *Synopsis*, 562. Trapp as well stated that God prepares people's hearts "by putting them into a praying frame, and so fitting them for mercy." Trapp, *Commentary*, 595.

152. Edwards, "God's Manner is First," 85.

153. Jonathan Edwards, "The Terms of Prayer" (Ps 21:4), in *Sermons and Discourses 1734–1738*, ed. M. X. Lesser, vol. 19 of *WJE* (2001), 772. Earlier Reformed exegetes likewise saw this

manifested both in that the king asked for "the greatest blessing"—life—and in that God gave it to him "to the utmost degree that it was possible for him to desire it in," that is, "a life without end, a life infinite in its duration, 'length of days forever and ever.' "[154] Thus Edwards preached this doctrine: "God never begrutches his people anything they desire, or are capable of, as being too good for 'em."[155] As the psalm speaks of Christ, he is understood as the "Mediator and the representative of his people," and he receives prayer "not merely as God," but as the God-Man, eager to give this "superlative goodness" to his body, the church.[156] By this doctrine Edwards meant that God does not withhold blessings from his people as if he thought them unworthy. While people regularly refuse good things to others, out of envy, contempt, or resentment, God gives willingly because he wants people to find infinite happiness in him even though "they deserve that God should infinitely resent" their offenses against him.[157] As God's plan of redemption is his chief design, it makes sense that God desires to bestow his blessings on undeserving people in order to manifest his grace:

> We may argue from God's design in the whole of his contrivance and dispensation in the great affair of man's redemption, which is to manifest the infinite riches of his grace. God's intention of redeeming a number of the fallen children of men by Jesus Christ, is the chief [of] all God's designs that ever was made known in this world.[158]

God did not give his Son resentfully to sinners as too much for their redemption. And now that they have Christ for their Mediator, believers have

---

passage issuing forth in fulfillment in the lives of both David and Christ, including Henry, Poole, Trapp, and even Calvin. Henry, *Exposition*, [Ps 21:4]; Poole, *Synopsis*, 638–639; Trapp, *Commentary*, 629; Calvin, *Commentary*, 1:346–348. What is unique about Edwards in this passage, compared to other Reformed exegetes, is the extraordinary hope that he gave *individual Christians* in approaching God in prayer.

154. Edwards, "The Terms of Prayer," 772.

155. Edwards, "The Terms of Prayer," 772. Henry also exalted God's mercy: "See how GOD's Grants often exceed our Petitions and Hopes, and infer thence, how rich He is in Mercy to those that call upon him." Henry, *Exposition*, [Ps 21:4]. Trapp did as well: "God is better to his people than their prayers; and when they ask but one Blessing he answereth them, as *Naaman* did *Gehazi*, with, *Nay, take two*." Trapp, *Commentary*, 629. Italics original.

156. Edwards, "The Terms of Prayer," 773.

157. Edwards, "The Terms of Prayer," 773–775. Quotation on 775.

158. Edwards, "The Terms of Prayer," 775.

"great encouragement" to pray and "look to God for whatever blessings they need, and for as great happiness as they desire, and for all that is requisite in order to their complete and eternal felicity."[159] Indeed, God delights to answer prayer; he "stands ready to give 'em their hearts' desire," a reference to Ps 21:2, and "stands ready to fill them; yea, he would have them open their mouths wide," a reference to Ps 81:10.[160] For Edwards, the Psalms set forth God's lavish grace and infinite mercy in God's sovereignly designed means of prayer.

In Edwards' reading of the Psalms, God's mercy toward humankind rose to the surface. The psalmist did not lose sight of God's greatness and glory; in fact, these highlighted all the more the grandeur of God's mercy, seeing the sovereign Creator stooping to forgive the sins of humanity, to show them loving-kindness, and to graciously hear and answer their prayers as a means of displaying his redemptive grace. One of the greatest mercies of all that God granted to humanity was the revelation of himself in Scripture.

The Revelation of God

Edwards understood that God, in his nature, is a communicative being, which leads us to expect him to reveal himself in an authoritative way, as in the Bible, to guide humanity in understanding who he is and what he is doing in the world.[161] Because the Psalms spoke at length about the nature of Scripture, Edwards found them to be an important tool in his engagement with the Enlightenment issues of his day.

The Nature of the Bible

Not surprisingly, Edwards gravitated to Psalm 119 when considering the nature of God's revelation as recorded in Scripture, as did his predecessors.[162] In a

---

159. Edwards, "The Terms of Prayer," 783. See also Edwards, *Humble Attempt*, 315, where he says that "God himself is the great good desired and sought after," which is why the psalmist "desired God, thirsted after him, and sought him," as testified by Pss 63:1–2, 8; 73:25; and 143:6.

160. Edwards, "The Terms of Prayer," 784. Psalm 21:1 reads, "Thou hast given him his heart's desire, and hast not withholden the request of his lips," and Ps 81:10 reads, "I am the Lord thy God, which brought thee out of the land of Egypt; open thy mouth wide, and I will fill it."

161. On Edwards' understanding of God as a communicative being, see Douglas A. Sweeney, *Jonathan Edwards and the Ministry of the Word: A Model of Faith and Thought* (Downers Grove, IL: IVP Academic, 2009), 160–163; Marsden, *Jonathan Edwards: A Life*, 460–463.

162. Henry said the "General Scope and Design" of Psalm 119 is "*to magnify the Law, and make it honourable* to set forth the Excellency and usefulness of Divine Revelation, and to

1729 sermon on Ps 119:2, he said that Psalm 119 in its wide scope aims "to set forthe the excellency of the word & Law of G[od]."[163] Following Ps 119:18, "Open thou mine eyes, that I may behold wondrous things out of thy law," Edwards exclaimed that "[t]he word of God contains the most noble, and worthy, and entertaining objects of man's most noble faculty, viz. his understanding, the most excellent things that man can exercise his thoughts about."[164] From this same verse, Edwards observed that while some commonly read the histories of the Bible as if they are the "private concerns" of particular people, yet they are "accounts of vastly greater things, things of greater importance and more extensive concernment than they that read them are commonly aware of."[165] In fact, the Word has such a depth of truth about creation that it could entertain the minds of "the ablest divines to the end of the world" and even then not be exhausted.[166] So Ps 119:96 states, "I have seen an end of all perfection: but thy commandment is exceeding broad," which Edwards interpreted to mean that "[t]he Psalmist found an end to the things that are human; but he could never find an end to what is contained in the Word of God.... There is enough in this divine science to employ the understandings of saints and angels to all eternity."[167] In

---

recommend it to us, not only for the Entertainment, but for the Government, of ourselves." Henry, *Exposition*, [introduction to Psalm 119]. Italics original. Poole recognized that the psalmist used a variety of terms for God's law to treat divine doctrine with more reverence and dignity ("reverentiae & dignitatis"), and he exclaimed, "[s]o many nomenclatures of the word of God show its perfections of every sort and the chief reasons on account of which we search and believe this, by which we are allured, to which we cling" ("Tot nomenclaturae verbi Dei ostendunt omnimodam illius perfectionem, & maximas rationes propter quas id scrutemur & credamus, in eo deliciemur, ei hæreamus"). Poole, *Synopsis*, 1207. Trapp called it "a Poem of commendation afore the Book of God." Trapp, *Commentary*, 876. Dickson explained that God inspired David in Psalm 119 to teach "all the faithful after him, to have the Word of God in special regard, and to have respect unto it, as the only rule whereby they might find direction, consolation and salvation." Dickson, *Last Fifty Psalmes*, 160. Calvin held that the prophet has two primary aims in this psalm: "the exhorting of the children of God to follow godliness and a holy life; and the prescribing of the rule, and pointing out the form of the true worship of God, so that the faithful may devote themselves wholly to the study of the Law." Calvin, *Commentary*, 4:398.

163. Jonathan Edwards, "146. Sermon on Ps 119:2 (Summer–Fall 1729)," in *Sermons, Series II, 1729*, vol. 44 of *WJEO*, L. 1r.

164. Jonathan Edwards, "Heeding the Word, and Losing It" (Heb 2:1), in *Sermons and Discourses 1734–1738*, ed. M. X. Lesser, vol. 19 of *WJE* (2001), 46.

165. Edwards, *A History of the Work of Redemption*, 291.

166. Jonathan Edwards, "The Importance and Advantage of a Thorough Knowledge of Divine Truth" (Heb 5:12), in *Sermons and Discourses 1739–1742*, ed. Harry S. Stout and Nathan O. Hatch with Kyle P. Farley, vol. 22 of *WJE* (2003), 95.

167. Edwards, "The Importance and Advantage," 95.

fact, Edwards believed God intentionally made his ways "hard to be understood" so seekers might derive pleasure in discovery, following Ps 111:2, "The works of the LORD are great, sought out of all them that have pleasure therein"—which was one reason why God placed so many types in the Old Testament and in nature.[168]

Edwards found a number of images in the Psalms that expounded the nature of God's Word. From Ps 29:3, "The voice of the LORD is upon the waters: the God of glory thundereth," Edwards observed that "Lightning and thunder is a very lively image of the word of God upon many accounts. 'Tis exceeding quick, and exceeding piercing, and powerful to break in pieces, and scorch, and dissolve, and is full of majesty."[169] When Ps 36:6 says, "Thy righteousness is like the great mountains," it suggested to Edwards that "[t]he steadfastness and immutability of God's word is...compared to the stability of mountains."[170] Edwards also called God's commands "purer than gold tried in the fire," following Pss 19:7–9 and 119:128.[171] Perhaps the most significant image from the Psalms was light. In his sermon, "Light in a Dark World, a Dark Heart," Edwards observed that "divine revelation is called light in the Scriptures" (e.g., Ps 119:130), and he found this a fitting image for the heart that truly receives God's Word because to such a person, "[i]t is sweet, and pleasant, and refreshing to the eyes of the mind, and much more so than the light of the sun is to the eyes of the body."[172] And as Scripture

---

168. Jonathan Edwards, "Profitable Hearers of the Word" (Matt 13:23), in *Sermons and Discourses 1723–1729*, ed. Kenneth P. Minkema, vol. 14 of *WJE* (1997), 247. Edwards believed that "[t]ypes are a certain sort of language, as it were, in which God is wont to speak to us" and that the language is learned through training, practice, and developing perceptive senses. He wondered how we can stop at explicitly identified types when those types give us a pattern for God's typological language permeating Scripture: "God han't expressly explained all the types of Scriptures, but has done so much as is sufficient to teach us the language." Jonathan Edwards, "Types," in *Typological Writings*, ed. Wallace E. Anderson, vol. 11 of *WJE* (1992), 151. For more on Edwards' typology, see chapter 4, pp. 166–177.

169. Edwards, The *"Blank Bible,"* 490.

170. Edwards, The *"Blank Bible,"* 724.

171. Jonathan Edwards, "All God's Methods Are Most Reasonable" (Isa 1:18–20), in *Sermons and Discourses 1723–1729*, ed. Kenneth P. Minkema, vol. 14 of *WJE* (1997), 184. Similarly, speaking on Ps 19:7–10, Edwards observed that "[t]he good that is obtained by the word of G[od] lasts forever." Jonathan Edwards, "1179. Sermon on Ps 19:7–10 (undated, *c.* 1750s)," Beinecke Rare Book and Manuscript Library, Yale University, New Haven, CT, L. 1r. Ken Minkema notes on the transcription of this sermon fragment that "[a]t least one leaf is missing at the beginning. Ps. 19:7–10 is in all likelihood not the text of the sermon, but a proof text that [Edwards] cites in the course of it."

172. Jonathan Edwards, "Light in a Dark World, a Dark Heart" (2 Pet 2:19), in *Sermons and Discourses 1734–1738*, ed. M. X. Lesser, vol. 19 of *WJE* (2001), 725.

often describes trouble and sorrow as darkness, so it represents spiritual comfort and joy as "light" (Ps 97:11). The sweetness, purity, and loveliness of the Word of God is compared to light in the Psalms (Pss 19:8, 10; 119:140) because of "the divinity and holiness that is seen in it."[173] Though the godly may experience dark trials and doubts, "still God's word is as a light that shines in their heart: they have light in the midst of darkness" (e.g., Pss 112:4; 119:50, 54, 92).[174]

In *Religious Affections*, Edwards argued that "[a]s the beauty of the divine nature does primarily consist in God's holiness, so does the beauty of all divine things," including the Word of God, which is excellent and beautiful because "it is so holy," as testified by Pss 119:140, 128, 138; and 19:7–10.[175] Of particular importance was the doctrine of inspiration. Edwards held that "there is no restraint to be laid upon the Spirit of God as to what he shall reveal to a prophet, for the benefit of his church, who is speaking or writing under immediate inspiration," and in David's case, God's progressive revelation granted to him made the book of Psalms the fullest witness at that time to the Messiah and his kingdom:

> But it may be that greater revelation which God made to him of the Messiah, and the things of his future kingdom, and the far more clear and extensive knowledge that he had of the mysteries and doctrines of the gospel, than others; as a reward for his keeping God's testimonies. In this, it is apparent by the Book of Psalms, that David far exceeded all that had before him.[176]

Given Edwards' belief that God extensively revealed his redemptive work in the Psalms, it is easy to understand why he wanted to establish the divine inspiration of the book of Psalms particularly and the Bible as a whole. In a world witnessing increasing attacks on the Bible's authority and on the value of the Psalms to the Christian church, Edwards responded by asserting the inspiration of the Psalms and addressing new critical issues in interpretation to uphold its witness to the gospel.

---

173. Edwards, "Light in a Dark World, a Dark Heart," 725–726. Quotation on 726.

174. Edwards, "Light in a Dark World, a Dark Heart," 729, 730.

175. Edwards, *Religious Affections*, 258.

176. Edwards, *Religious Affections*, 330, 331.

Enlightenment Issues

George Marsden, in discussing the surviving parts of Edwards' "Harmony of the Old and New Testament," observes that

> they reveal how acutely concerned he was to defend traditional views of the Bible from attack.... Many of the secular dimensions of the Enlightenment depended on displacing biblical accounts of history and human nature. It is not surprising, then, that Edwards spent vast amounts of time preparing to answer biblical critics.[177]

Similarly, Edwards' notes on the Psalms in his "Notes on Scripture" and "Blank Bible" manuscripts reveal his concern for upholding the inspiration and authority of the Bible.

In three "Notes on Scripture" entries—Entry Nos. 434, 440, and 506—Edwards presented seven arguments to establish that "the penmen of these psalms did pretend to speak and write by the inspiration of the Spirit of God, as much as the prophets when they wrote their prophecies."[178] First, Edwards argued that "[s]inging divine songs was of old one noted effect of the inspiration of the Spirit of God in the prophets, insomuch that such singing was called by the name of prophesying," and he pointed to several examples of people who prophesied through song, including Miriam (Exod 15:20–21), Moses (Deut 31:19–21), and Jacob (Genesis 49).[179] Second, the Scriptures represent the musicians' singing of psalms as prophesying (1 Chr 25:1–3) and even identified the composer Asaph as a prophet. Third, in his last words David, described as "the sweet psalmist of Israel," says, "The Spirit of the LORD spake by me, and his word was in my tongue. The God of Israel said, the Rock of Israel spake to me" (2 Sam 23:1–3). By this proclamation Edwards concluded that all the psalms David wrote were divinely inspired, being "holy songs... sung by the inspiration of the Spirit of God."[180]

Fourth, Edwards explained that we know the psalmists spoke by a spirit of prophecy because "the psalms are full of prophecies of future events."[181] Fifth, this spirit of prophecy applies to the psalmists because "God in the psalms is

---

177. Marsden, *Jonathan Edwards: A Life*, 475.

178. Edwards, *Notes on Scripture*, 518.

179. Edwards, *Notes on Scripture*, 518.

180. Edwards, *Notes on Scripture*, 518–519. Quotation on 519.

181. Edwards, *Notes on Scripture*, 519.

very often represented as speaking, and the words are evidently represented as his words."[182] Edwards later added a sixth point to the argument in Entry No. 434, where he showed that "David very early was endowed with the spirit of prophecy and miracles"—the prophecy referring to the words he spoke against Goliath and the miracles to his slaying of the lion and bear.[183] Finally, in Entry No. 506, Edwards argued that the "songs of Zion" or "the LORD's song" (as in Ps 137:3–4) referred to the "sacred songs" of "Zion, or God's church" and that since they belonged to the Lord, "they had God for their author, and were consecrated by his authority as a 'word.' "[184] Edwards continued by using an argument from the lesser to the greater: Just as God detailed all the utensils, instruments, and forms for worship in the temple to "the most minute circumstances," so we would expect God's similar direction in "the very matter of the worship," for "it would be strange if the songs that they were to sing, the most material and essential thing of all, should not be of divine appointment but should be left wholly to human wisdom and invention."[185] It was nonsense to think that God would give specific directions for something as small as temple utensils and neglect to inspire the words of worship.

Edwards sought to defend the inspiration of the Bible using the Psalms in a number of other places. He argued in "Miscellanies" Entry No. 359, "Inspiration of the Scriptures," that the presence of the Psalms in the canon testifies to the Bible's divinely inspired status because "the church should have a book of divine songs, given by inspiration from God for the use of his church, wherein there should be a lively representation of the true spirit of devotion, of faith, of hope, of divine love, joy, resignation, humility, obedience, repentance, etc."[186] Also, in "Miscellanies" Entry No. 1349, Edwards defended Old Testament inspiration by discussing how the book of Hebrews quoted the Psalms in reference to Christ. As none would deny that God is speaking about Christ being exalted above the angels in Heb 1:5–12, which quotes from the Psalms, so none could deny that "the prophets and inspired penmen of the Old Testament spake by inspiration of [the] Spirit of the supreme God," for the affinity of the passages testified to the same divine author.[187]

---

182. Edwards, *Notes on Scripture*, 520.

183. Edwards, *Notes on Scripture*, 522.

184. Edwards, *Notes on Scripture*, 609.

185. Edwards, *Notes on Scripture*, 609–610.

186. Edwards, *The "Miscellanies": Entry Nos. a–500*, 433.

187. Edwards, *The "Miscellanies": Entry Nos. 1153–1360*, 422.

Edwards was also concerned about some of the critical approaches of his day as they related to the Psalms. In a "Blank Bible" entry on Num 21:14, Edwards engaged with Henry Winder's thesis in his *Critical and Chronological History of the Rise, Progress, Declension, and Revival of Knowledge, Chiefly Religious*, which suggested that the book of Psalms was collected out of the "Book of Jasher," a book mentioned in Josh 10:13 and 2 Sam 1:18 and a book that is identical with the "book of the wars of the LORD" mentioned in Num 21:14.[188] A more likely explanation, Edwards held, was that they were distinct volumes, one inspired and one not: "I should rather think it [the book of Psalms] was a distinct collection of songs of prophets and inspired persons, as the other was the songs of others uninspired."[189]

A particularly pressing issue in Edwards' day was the authorship of the Pentateuch. In fact, Edwards' longest entry in the "Notes on Scripture" manuscript was Entry No. 416, "Whether the PENTATEUCH was written by Moses."[190] Edwards marshaled evidence from all over the Bible, including the Psalms, to establish his argument that Moses penned the Pentateuch, just as "the received opinion, both of Jews and Christians," has held for centuries.[191] Edwards believed that "Moses, being commanded and inspired by God, wrote those books that are called the Pentateuch, excepting only some particular passages that were inserted afterwards by a divine direction for the better understanding the history."[192] The Psalms played a significant role in his defense, showing up 213 times in this entry, which amounts to over one-third of his Psalms references in "Notes on Scripture." In this entry, he especially used Psalms 78, 105, and 106, which poetically recount Israel's history.

Edwards argued that a record of the history of God's works was fundamental to the Pentateuch, for "[w]riting of those works of God that are worthy to be remembered and celebrated by praises to God, is spoken of as a proper way of conveying the memory of them to posterity for that end," which is what Ps 102:18 testifies: "This shall be written for the generation to come."[193] Using

---

188. Henry Winder, *Critical and Chronological History of the Rise, Progress, Declension, and Revival of Knowledge, Chiefly Religious*, 2d ed. (London: J. Waugh and W. Fenner at the Turk's-Head, in Lombard-Street, 1756), 2:46–47.

189. Edwards, *The "Blank Bible,"* 270.

190. Edwards, *Notes on Scripture*, 423. For more on Edwards' concern with the authorship of the Pentateuch, see Robert E. Brown, *Jonathan Edwards and the Bible* (Bloomington: Indiana University Press, 2002), 115–128.

191. Edwards, *Notes on Scripture*, 423.

192. Edwards, *Notes on Scripture*, 423.

193. Edwards, *Notes on Scripture*, 429.

this passage to assert the Mosaic authorship of the Pentateuch was unique to Edwards, compared to earlier Reformed exegetes.[194] Edwards went on to apply that principle to the Pentateuch: "the importance of remembering these works of God related in the Pentateuch, is mentioned not only in the Pentateuch itself, but also in other parts of Scripture, as in Ps. 105:5. 'Remember his marvelous works that he hath done.' "[195] The rest of Psalm 105 makes it clear that these "marvelous works" refer to God's works from calling Abraham to taking his children into the promised land, and so in Psalm 105 the psalmist follows the Mosaic pattern that "connects the wonderful works and the laws or judgments of God's mouth together."[196] Thus Edwards appealed to historical psalms like Psalm 105 to show that law and history were so tightly intertwined that they could not be separated, which made it natural to suppose the author of the law was the author of the Pentateuchal history, for "[t]here is such a dependence between many of the precepts and sanctions of the law and other parts of the Pentateuch...that they can't be understood without the history."[197] He also argued that the "abridgement" of the Pentateuchal history in places like Psalm 78, 105, and 106 "plainly supposes that a full account of them was already in being, and well-known, and established."[198]

Edwards also applied the analogy of Scripture to the problem of Pentateuchal authorship. He argued that the rest of the Bible recorded the Pentateuch history, confirming the Jews' "standing public record" of the reliability of these "facts." Edwards stated:

It is a plain and demonstrative evidence, that the Jews had all along some standing public record of the facts that we have an account of in the history of the Pentateuch, that these facts are so abundantly, and in such a manner mentioned or referred to all along in other books of the

---

194. Henry, *Exposition*, [Ps 102:18]; Poole, *Synopsis*, 1118; Trapp, *Commentary*, 830; Dickson, *Last Fifty Psalmes*, 15–16; Calvin, *Commentary*, 4:115–116.

195. Edwards, *Notes on Scripture*, 429.

196. Edwards, *Notes on Scripture*, 429.

197. Edwards, *Notes on Scripture*, 432. A key text in Edwards' argument was Ps 105:8–10: "He hath remembered his covenant for ever, the word which he commanded to a thousand generations. Which covenant he made with Abraham, and his oath unto Isaac; And confirmed the same unto Jacob for a law, and to Israel for an everlasting covenant." Edwards held that the "covenant" God made in history was "synonymous" with the "law," meaning that Moses wrote both the law and the history since both were integral to the thrust of the Pentateuch. Edwards, *Notes on Scripture*, 425, 434, 430, 431, 436, 445, and 454–456. Quotation on 434.

198. Edwards, *Notes on Scripture*, 454.

Old Testament. There is scarcely any part of the history, from the beginning of Genesis to the end of Deuteronomy, but what is mentioned or
referred in other books of the Old Testament, that were the writings of
after ages.[199]

Edwards went on to provide several pages of references from the Bible that
demonstrated the "agreeableness" of the history from the Pentateuch with the
record of the rest of the Old Testament, and the Psalms featured prominently,
appearing 171 times in the lists.[200] For example, Edwards said, "In these writings we have very often mention of God's creating the heavens and the earth,"
and he cited, among other texts, Pss 89:11–12; 102:25; 115:15; 121:2; 124:8; and
134:3.[201] He mentioned such details in creation as "[t]he manner of God's creating by speaking the word, Ps. 33:6, 9, 148:5"; "God's creating the light, Ps.
74:16"; "God's gathering together the waters, Ps. 33:7"; "God's creating the
sun, Ps. 19:1, 4, 74:16"; and "God's creating man, Ps. 8:5."[202] Edwards linked
the Psalms in a similar fashion to several chapters in the history of humanity's
earliest years and the history of Israel.[203]

Edwards meticulously detailed the Pentateuchal history in the Psalms,
which reveals his belief that Scripture interprets Scripture and that Scripture's
testimony was a valid evidence base for establishing Mosaic authorship of the

---

199. Edwards, *Notes on Scripture*, 443.

200. Edwards, *Notes on Scripture*, 443–453.

201. Edwards, *Notes on Scripture*, 443.

202. Edwards, *Notes on Scripture*, 443–444.

203. Specifically, Edwards saw retellings of the following Pentateuchal details in the
Psalms: the descendants of Noah; the heads of nations; God's covenant with Abraham,
Isaac, and Jacob; Melchizedek the priest and king; Jacob as the preferred brother; Joseph's
enslavement and provision for his family; the Israelites' population explosion and subsequent oppression in Egypt; God's great wonders through Moses and Aaron; God's redemption of his people out of Egypt; the plagues upon Egypt; the details of the Israelite exodus
out of Egypt; the dividing of the Red Sea and destruction of the Egyptians in the waters;
God's guidance by a pillar of cloud and pillar of fire in the desert; that generation's stubbornness and rebellion in the wilderness; God's doing such great things for the glory of his
name; the people's praise to God; God's provision of manna; God's provision of water at
the rock of Meribah; God's giving of the law; the golden calf; Moses' standing in the gap for
Israel; the people's complaints and God's wrath over their lusts; God's provision of quails;
the people's disbelief; the demise of Korah and his company; Moses' anger that kept him
out of the promised land; the smiting of Og, king of Bashan; Israel's joining themselves to
Baal-peor and Phinehas's stand for righteousness; Moses' faithfulness; the people's hardness of heart; God's repeated judgments; and God's continual pardon and mercy. Edwards,
Notes on Scripture, 444–453.

Pentateuch. It particularly shows that Israel had a "standing record" of its history, not just on oral tradition. As Edwards put it:

> He that can observe the facts of the history of the Pentateuch, after this manner mentioned and referred in the writings of the several ages of the Israelitish nation, and not believe that they had all along a great and standing record of these things, and this very history, can swallow the greatest absurdity.... It was impossible that this vast number of events, with so many circumstances, with names of persons, and places, and minute incidents, should be so particularly and exactly known, and the knowledge of 'em so fully, and distinctly, and without confusion or loss, kept up for so many ages, and be so often mentioned in so particular a manner, without error or inconsistence, through so many ages without a written record.... and the comparing the records of the Pentateuch with the innumerable citations and references, shows that this was in fact that record.[204]

Edwards' detailed and lengthy discussion of the authorship of the Pentateuch reveals his clear engagement with the Enlightenment questions of his day. And the fact that he used the Psalms so substantively in his overall defense of Mosaic authorship reveals his firm belief both in the value of the Psalms in interpretation and in the Bible as a single voice proclaiming God's redemptive-historical work from beginning to end.

Edwards connected with one other area of the new learning as he engaged the Psalms, what we call "comparative religion" today. Enlightened circles were fascinated by the discoveries of other religions and often took their existence as an indication that reason and natural science had greater authority than the seemingly limited book of Scripture. As people learned more about other religions, they sought to integrate that new knowledge into their understanding of the world, and while the Bible had not spread to many of these indigenous peoples, natural revelation existed universally. So what we can know from the senses and reason gradually gained greater authority than Scripture because it seemed to explain religion better as Westerners were confronted with religious diversity. Edwards was similarly fascinated by what he learned about other religions, but in contrast, he detected echoes of the one true God latent in other nations and religions, following the concept of a *prisca theologia* (ancient theology). This idea, developed by early Christians

---

204. Edwards, *Notes on Scripture*, 453–454.

such as Clement of Alexandria, Origen, and Eusebius, claimed that vestiges of Christian truth had been deposited in all religions as great thinkers borrowed from the Hebrew tradition.[205]

Edwards saw testimony to light in other nations in a handful of places in the Psalms. In his "Blank Bible" notebook entry on Ps 106:1, "Praise ye the LORD...," Edwards pondered the similarity of the Hebrew word for "Hallelujah" (literally, "praise the Lord") with exclamations from the heathen hymns to Apollo, such as "Eleleu Ie"—gleaning such insights particularly from Theophilus Gale.[206] In his "Blank Bible" entry on Ps 146:9, "The LORD preserveth the strangers; he relieveth the fatherless and widow," Edwards suggested that this verse formed the foundation of the thinking in a passage from Homer where Eumaeus entertained Odysseus as a poor stranger and exclaimed, "Guest of mine, it were an impious thing for me to slight a stranger, even if there came a meaner man than thou; for from Zeus are all strangers and beggars."[207] Also, in his "Notes on Scripture" Entry No. 404, on Exod 33:14–15, Edwards speculated that the Hebrew term for God's "presence," פָּנַי, relates to the heathen term for Pan, the god of the shepherds. He cited Gale, who argued that the term Pan originated with the Hebrew term פָּן, which was one point that supported his overall claim that "Pan, whom the Poets feign to be the *God of Shepherds*, was *parallel* to, and, as 'tis presumed, originally

---

205. For more on Edwards' appropriation of the *prisca theologia*, see Gerald R. McDermott, *Jonathan Edwards Confronts the Gods: Christian Theology, Enlightenment Religion, and Non-Christian Faiths* (New York: Oxford University Press, 2000), 93–109.

206. Edwards, *The "Blank Bible,"* 526; Theophilus Gale, *Court of the Gentiles: or A Discourse touching the Original of Human Literature, both Philologie and Philosophie, From the Scriptures & Jewish Church, Part 1, Of Philologie,* 2d ed. (Oxon: H. Hall for Tho. Gilbert, 1672), Bk. 2, 38–39; Bk. 3, 13–14. Edwards also cited John Taylor, *The Hebrew Concordance, Adapted to the English Bible; Disposed after the Manner of Buxtorf* (London: J. Waugh and W. Fenner, at the Turk's Head in Lombard-Street, 1754–1757), 1:n.p. (entry 447 on הלל).

207. Edwards, *The "Blank Bible,"* 541; Homer, *The Odyssey,* in *The Complete Works of Homer: The Iliad and The Odyssey,* trans. S. H. Butcher and Andrew Lang (New York: The Modern Library, 1935), 210–211. Edwards recorded the quotation from Homer in his "Blank Bible" entry on Deut 10:18, which he cited in his "Blank Bible" note on Ps 146:9, as follows: "O stranger! It is not lawful for me, though one should come more miserable than thou art, to dishonor or disregard a stranger; for strangers and poor belong to the care of God." Edwards, *The "Blank Bible,"* 293. Edwards may have used Alexander Pope's translation of Homer's *The Odyssey,* which he listed in his "Catalogue," though Pope's translation is less similar: "It never was our guise To slight the poor, or ought humane despise. For *Jove* unfolds our hospi-table door, 'Tis *Jove* that sends the stranger and the poor." Jonathan Edwards, "'Catalogue' of Reading," in *Catalogues of Books,* ed. Peter J. Theusen, vol. 26 of *WJE* (2008), 154. Alexander Pope, trans., *The Odyssey of Homer,* vol. 10 of *The Poems of Alexander Pope,* ed. Maynard Mack (New Haven, CT: Yale University Press, 1967), 38–39.

traduced from, the Jewish *Messias*, stiled the *Shepherd of Israel*."²⁰⁸ Edwards saw this concept present in Ps 68:7–8, "The earth shook, the heavens also dropped at the presence of God [מִפְּנֵי אֱלֹהִים]: even Sinai itself was moved at the presence of God, the God of Israel"; and Ps 97:4–5, "The hills melted like wax at the presence of the LORD [מִלִּפְנֵי יְהוָה], at the presence of the Lord [מִלִּפְנֵי אֲדוֹן] of the whole earth."²⁰⁹ Compared with earlier Reformed exegetes, all three of these associations of the Psalms—with Apollo, Eumaeus, and Pan—were unique to Edwards.²¹⁰ But in Edwards' view, these associations suggested that some valid notions about the one true God had influenced other religions and folklore.

In these ways, we can observe how the questions from the new learning affected the way Edwards interpreted the Psalms. He read that, in light of the diversity of religious beliefs that were being discovered, scholars doubted the inspiration of the Bible and its validity as a source of truth about God. But these new questions did not diminish his belief in the Bible as God's authoritative and divinely inspired Word, and he saw evidence in the Psalms to support the inspiration of Scripture and the notion that God's revelation of himself to the ancient Hebrews formed the basis for all truth about God, wherever it may appear. As Edwards felt pressure from the questions the new learning raised, he used the Psalms in prayer so he might stay faithful to God's Word. In a "Blank Bible" entry on Ps 119:43, "And take not the word of truth utterly out of my mouth; for I have hoped in thy judgments," Edwards made this plea: "let none of those reproaches and persecutions, spoken of in the preceding verse, and vv. 39, and 22–23, and 51, and other places, nor any temptation whatsoever, prevail with me to forsake the profession of the truth, an open bold adherence to the word of thy truth, or the true religion."²¹¹

Conclusion

This discussion of God from the Psalms reveals Edwards' continuity with the broad contours of the Reformed exegetical tradition. He differed mostly either

208. Gale, *Court of the Gentiles*, Pt. 1, Bk. 2, 70. Italics original. Gale's work was essentially a massive work defending the *prisca theologia*. McDermott, *Jonathan Edwards Confronts the Gods*, 94.

209. Edwards, *Notes on Scripture*, 412–413.

210. On connecting Ps 106:1 with Apollo, see Henry, *Exposition*, [Ps 106:1]; Poole, *Synopsis*, 1143; Trapp, *Commentary*, 924; Dickson, *Last Fifty Psalmes*, 61. On connecting Ps 146:9 with the story in Homer, see Henry, *Exposition*, [Ps 146:9]; Poole, *Synopsis*, 1324; Trapp, *Commentary*, 689; Dickson, *Last Fifty Psalmes*, 359. On connecting Pss 68:7–8 and 97:4–5 with Pan, see Henry, *Exposition*, [Pss 68:7–8; 97:4–5]; Poole, *Synopsis*, 922, 1101; Trapp, *Commentary*, 757, 822–823; Dickson, *Other Fifty Psalmes*, 103–104, 383.

211. Edwards, *The "Blank Bible,"* 531.

in the way he described theological principles from the Psalms in his context, whether addressing a military loss, using the natural elements surrounding the Stockbridge Indians, or answering objections to God's sovereignty based on human reason, or in the way he engaged the critical questions of his day, whether the authorship of the Pentateuch or comparative religion. These critical interests illustrate the changing times in which Edwards lived and how those times changed him. Some have argued that Edwards was a "precritical" interpreter, including Stephen Stein, Glenn Kreider (at least with respect to the book of Revelation), and Jeongmo Yoo (at least with respect to Isaiah, Jeremiah, and Ezekiel).[212] But while Edwards certainly shared a great deal of continuity with the precritical tradition, as these scholars rightly point out, his approach to the Bible from the Psalms suggests that, as Robert Brown puts it, Edwards was "modestly critical," for he embraced a "hybrid traditionalism" that gleaned from the new learning while retaining "a high degree of confidence in the integrity of scriptural history."[213] As Douglas Sweeney puts it, Edwards is "a fascinating example of a modern thinker with premodern sympathies."[214]

Edwards' differences did not constitute a departure from Reformed exegesis. Like his predecessors, he affirmed the doctrine of inspiration based on the Psalter's testimony, and then this doctrine guided his interpretation of the Psalms. Because he believed that God had revealed himself and his plan of redemption in the divinely inspired Scriptures, that meant the Psalms revealed truth about God and his ways. Edwards was a theological interpreter whose theology directed his exegesis, which in turn informed his theology. In this chapter we have seen that Edwards read the Psalms specifically from a theocentric perspective, elevating God's glory as the grand purpose of his creation and underscoring God's sovereign activity in the outworking of his redemptive plan in history to accomplish his ends of glorifying his name. As he engaged with the new learning, he never lost sight of the theological parameters that God's glory and redemptive aims placed on his interpretation of the Psalms.

---

212. Stephen J. Stein, "The Spirit and the Word: Jonathan Edwards and Scriptural Exegesis," in *Jonathan Edwards and the American Experience*, ed. Nathan O. Hatch and Harry S. Stout (New York: Oxford University Press, 1988), 119; Glenn R. Kreider, *Jonathan Edwards's Interpretation of Revelation 4:1–8:1* (Dallas: University Press of America, 2004), 283; Jeongmo Yoo, "Jonathan Edwards's Interpretation of the Major Prophets: The Books of Isaiah, Jeremiah, and Ezekiel," *Puritan Reformed Journal* 3, no. 2 (2011): 164, 192.

213. Brown, *Jonathan Edwards and the Bible*, xvii–xviii.

214. Douglas A. Sweeney, "Edwards, Jonathan (1703–1758)" in *Dictionary of Major Biblical Interpreters*, ed. Donald K. McKim (Downers Grove, IL: IVP Academic, 2007), 399.

While the Psalter upheld the mystery of God, his unpredictability, and ultimately the impossibility of knowing him fully, it also upheld that what we do know about God is found in his revelation of himself in Scripture, a reliable witness to his character, acts, and purposes. It shows him to be the sovereign ruler over all creation, ordering human history in such a way as to accomplish his redemptive purposes, even through the mystery of prayer, and to spread his mercy and grace upon undeserving creatures—all to the praise of his name, "for his name alone is excellent; his glory is above the earth and heaven" (Ps 148:13).

3

Humanity and Sin

The fool hath said in his heart, There is no God.
They are corrupt, they have done abominable works,
there is none that doeth good.
Psalm 14:1–2

THE GOD OF infinite glory is also a God of infinite love who willingly condescends to his creation, especially showing his love toward humans, despite our low position and sinful state. In his sermon on Ps 113:6, in which Edwards contrasted God's infinitely high nature with the angels (discussed in chapter 2), he went on to show how different humans are from God by showing how much lower they are than the angels. For if God must humble himself to behold the glorious angels in heaven, how much more must he humble himself to behold the wicked creatures that inhabit the earth? Edwards explained, "There is a great difference as to the dignity & capacity & excellency of our natures & that of the angels. How greatly their strength exceeds men[']s—so their wisdom—their activity[,] their brightness & glory."[1] The nature of humanity is that they are "from dust & ashes" and are "feeble" and "dry stubble," and to make matters worse, man is also "a sinfull creature," a "Rebel" who "forsakes G[od]"—all of which together reveals "the Exceeding folly & vanity of men[']s self-righteousness."[2] And yet God "humbles hims[elf] on the notice he takes of them," especially in "the Condescension of J[esus] [Christ] the Et[ernal] Son," so that he might redeem them and bring such low, sinful creatures to himself to dwell with him eternally.[3]

These themes of the lowliness of human nature and the depth of sin in humanity, along with their connection to the history of redemption, featured prominently in Edwards' interpretation of the Psalms. His exegesis of

---

1. Jonathan Edwards, "685. Sermon on Ps 113:6 (November 11, 1742)," Beinecke Rare Book and Manuscript Library, Yale University, New Haven, CT, L. 12r.

2. Edwards, "685. Sermon on Ps 113:6," L. 11r., 12v.

3. Edwards, "685. Sermon on Ps 113:6," L. 13r., 14r.

the Psalms in relation to the doctrines of humanity and sin followed largely established patterns of interpretation, though, compared to earlier Reformed exegetes, he more emphatically emphasized the low state of humanity to exalt the glory of God and underscored the deep depravity of humanity to highlight the need for God's grace. Also, in his treatment of one of the key themes in his life's work—original sin—the Psalms served as a theological foundation for developing that doctrine. Edwards explored the Psalms for authoritative teaching on humanity and sin so he could awaken people to the basic problem facing humanity and to the solution in the gospel. We first discuss Edwards' treatment of human nature and then his understanding of human depravity from the Psalms, closing with two Psalms sermons on sin that illustrate his homiletical practice of guiding his hearers on the path from sin to hope.

Human Nature

Edwards believed that the Psalms teach us much about our nature as God's creatures. We can understand our nature better by positioning ourselves in relation to other created beings, and that is exactly what the psalmist does in Ps 8:4–5, "What is man, that thou art mindful of him? and the son of man, that thou visitest him? For thou hast made him a little lower than the angels, and hast crowned him with glory and honour." Edwards preached on this passage in February 1745 to show that "man is a creature who in his nature is vastly Inferior to the Angels," as he stated in his doctrine.[4] Edwards noted that the psalmist praises God for "the wonder of God & the Condescension of G[od] to man in advancing the Human nature to such dignity & Honour," a dignity that refers to both the first and second Adam.[5] In the first place, God bestowed honor on humans by giving them dominion over creatures and the lower world, while "[t]he second Exaltation of the nature of man which was vastly greater than this & of which this was but a type is that which is Performed in God[']s second work in actually uniting the Human nature to the divine In the 2d Adam."[6] Like Edwards, Reformed exegetes commonly identified Christ in this passage using the analogy of Scripture, comparing Ps 8:4–5 with Heb 2:6–7.[7] The phrase "made him a little lower than the angels"

---

4. Jonathan Edwards, "769. Sermon on Ps 8:4–5 (February 1745)," Beinecke Rare Book and Manuscript Library, Yale University, New Haven, CT, L. 3v.

5. Edwards, "769. Sermon on Ps 8:4–5," L. 1r.

6. Edwards, "769. Sermon on Ps 8:4–5," L. 1v.

7. Matthew Henry, *An exposition of the five poetical books of the Old Testament; viz. Job, Psalms, Proverbs, Ecclesiastes, and Solomon's song…* (London: T. Darrack…, 1710), [Ps 8:3–9]; Matthew

thus takes on two meanings. On the one hand, they refer to the exaltation of the first Adam and his descendants, but on the other hand, they refer to Christ's great humiliation in taking on human flesh. Edwards may have gleaned this argument from Matthew Poole, whom he cited, without further comment, in his "Blank Bible" on Ps 8:5.[8] Poole quoted a number of interpreters who recognized Christ in this passage, in large part because Paul applies it to Christ in Heb 2:6–7. One question that Poole raised was whether Ps 8:5 refers to humanity in its pristine state before the Fall, in its fallen state, or in its restored state. Most of the interpreters he quoted leaned toward both the pristine and the restored state; for example, Poole described the view that "this can be understood of man composed in the first place, Gen. 1,26. or after the fall it is peculiarly of Christ, & Christians, in whom this dignity is restored through Christ."[9] This led to another question, whether the passage speaks of Adam or Christ or both. Poole argued that "man" in Ps 8:4 does not refer to "the whole human race collectively" but certainly to the one man Christ, though at the same time, it refers to the elect by synecdoche—the head of the body for its members.[10] Poole used a common principle of interpretation that Edwards also employed, that many passages have "a double sense," both "the simple and the prophetic."[11]

Where Edwards was unique in his exegesis of these verses was the way he emphasized human sin. He focused his discussion on the first Adam, observing "[t]he Honourable Circumstance that G[od] placed Man in" by "giving him Honour little short" of the angels, which is so wonderful because "man in

---

Poole, *Synopsis Criticorum Aliorumque Sacrae Scripturae Interpretum et Commentarum, Summo Studio et Fide Adornata*, vol. II: *Complectens Libros Jobi, Psalmorum, Proverbiorum, Ecclesiastis, & Cantici Canticorum* (Francofurti ad Moenum: Balthasaris Christophori Wustii, 1678), 540. John Trapp, *A Commentary or Exposition Upon the Books of Ezra, Nehemiah, Esther, Job, and Psalms...*(London: T. R. and E. M. for Thomas Newberry..., 1657), 587–588; David Dickson, *A Brief Explication of the first Fifty Psalms* (London: T. M. for Ralph Smith..., 1652), 40; John Calvin, *Commentary on the Psalms*, trans. from the Original Latin and Collated with the Author's French Version by James Anderson (1843–1855; repr., Grand Rapids, MI: Eerdmans, 1963), 1:103–105.

8. Jonathan Edwards, *The "Blank Bible,"* ed. Stephen J. Stein, vol. 24 of *WJE* (2006), 478.

9. Poole, *Synopsis*, 541. The Latin reads, "Intelligi hoc potest de homine primum condito Gen. 1,26. at post lapsum peculiare est Christo, & Christianis, quibus per Christum haec dignitas restituitur."

10. Poole, *Synopsis*, 540–543. The Latin reads, "*Homo* hîc sign. non totum genus humanum collectivè, sed individuum hominem, nempe Christum, ut docet Ebr. 2,6. Vel, sign. electos, per synecdochen generis, ut patet ex Ebr. 2,6."

11. Poole, *Synopsis*, 541. The Latin reads, "Sic plura loca sunt quae duplicem habent sensum," both "simplicem, & propheticum."

hims[elf] or in his nature is so little & so much below the angels."[12] In other words, by saying man is "a little lower than the angels," the psalmist's aim is "not to Represent man[']s nature as very high but very low," for the text aims to show how great God's exaltation of man is in that he would pay mind to him.[13] While other Reformed exegetes noted humanity's low position, they discussed it by highlighting God's condescension to visit humanity, not by arguing that humans are so far below the angels. Matthew Henry illustrates how they took the phrase, "a little lower than the angels," more literally: "by his Soul, which is spiritual and immortal, he is so near akin to the Holy Angels, that he may be truly said to be but a *Little lower* than they, and is in order next to them."[14] Edwards established his view using the analogy of Scripture, showing throughout the Bible the angels' high position, evidenced by their appellations (e.g., "sons of God" [Job 38:7]); their strength; their office as "Chief ministers"; their great acts; their representation as great beings in order to demonstrate how much greater is something else, such as God's word or the work of redemption; and their ability to overpower man simply by appearing (Matt 28:2–4).[15] By looking at the Bible's discussion of angels elsewhere, Edwards deduced that humanity is far lower than the angels. In applying the doctrine, he pointed his congregants to the glory of God, evident merely in deigning to create them. Then he contrasted fallen angels and fallen humanity, for the passage shows "[h]ow manifest is the free grace of G[od] to fallen man that he should be redeemed Rather than the Fallen angels," and "[h]ow wonderful it is that when G[od] had a design of uniting hims[elf] to a crooked nature for his glory & the Benefit & Blessedness of that Crea[ture]," that the "nature of man should be chosen."[16] The incarnation of Christ thus turned the

---

12. Edwards, "769. Sermon on Ps 8:4–5," L. 3v.

13. Edwards, "769. Sermon on Ps 8:4–5," L. 4v.

14. Henry, *Exposition*, [Ps 8:4]. Reformed interpreters recognized humanity's weakness but did not establish the point by saying humanity was so much lower than the angels. Henry described humanity as "sinful, weak, miserable Man, a Creature so *forgetful* of thee, and his Duty to thee." Henry, *Exposition*, [Ps 8:4]. Poole noted, "How small a thing is man!" ("Quantula res est homo!"), for man is "weak & fragile & unsound" ("infirmus & fragilis & æger"). Poole, *Synopsis*, 540. Trapp described man as "*Sorry, sickly man*, a Mass of Mortalities, a Map of Miseries, a mixture or compound of Dirt and Sin." Trapp, *Commentary*, 587. Dickson pointed out "[t]he weakness and unworthiness of man." Dickson, *First Fifty Psalms*, 40. Calvin described humans as "vile and contemptible creatures, and utterly unworthy of receiving any good from God." Calvin, *Commentary*, 1:101. Edwards only cited Poole.

15. Edwards, "769. Sermon on Ps 8:4–5," L. 5r.–9r.

16. Edwards, "769. Sermon on Ps 8:4–5," L. 11r., 17r. Calvin similarly emphasized God's glory in the exaltation of humanity rather than angels: "God's wonderful goodness is displayed the more brightly in that so glorious a Creator, whose majesty shines resplendently in the

tables for humanity as God joined his nature to human nature—an emphasis Edwards' Reformed predecessors shared.[17] So despite humans being so much lower than angels, in the end Edwards rejoiced in "[h]ow wonderf[ul] is the grace of G[od] to the saints that they should be Priviledged in so many Respects above the Elect angels."[18]

This sermon shows how Edwards, as he reflected on human nature in its fallen state while engaging the Psalms, also reflected on humanity in its redeemed state, which naturally led to considering Christ, the God-Man who joined human nature to the divine nature to redeem humanity from sin. Edwards wrote similarly in "Miscellanies," Entry No. 702, noting from Psalm 8 that while man is "so vile an original," God crowned him with glory and honor and gave him dominion over all brute creatures, and since Heb 2:6–8 applies this passage to Christ, we find here "a type of the glorious and exalted state that man is brought into—particularly Jesus Christ the head of man, and they in him as their head."[19]

Still, the Psalms had much to say simply about human nature apart from its redeemed state. Edwards described "human nature" by saying it "is as the grass, a shaking leaf, a weak withering flower," images of humanity derived from Pss 37:2; 90:5–6; 102:11; 103:15–16; from Isa 64:6; and from Ps 103:15–16, respectively.[20] He developed an extended comparison between men and

---

heavens, graciously condescends to adorn a creature so miserable and vile as man is with the greatest glory, and to enrich him with numberless blessings. If he had a mind to exercise his liberality towards any, he was under no necessity of choosing men who are but dust and clay, in order to prefer them above all other creatures, seeing he had a sufficient number in heaven towards whom to show himself liberal." Calvin, however, preferred to translate the passage, "little lower than God," since the Hebrew אלהים can be translated "angels" or "God." Calvin, *Commentary*, 1:100, 102–103.

17. Henry likewise commented that "it is certain that the greatest favour that ever was shew'd to the Human Race, and the greatest Honour that ever was put upon the Human Nature was by the Incarnation and Exaltation of the Lord JESUS." Henry, *Exposition*, [Ps 8:3–9]. Poole noted that the restoration occurred "in the members of Christ" ("in membris Christi"). Poole, *Synopsis*, 542. Trapp observed the great blessing to saints who are united with Christ: "whatsoever is spoken here of man, is applied to Christ, and so is proper to the Saints, by vertue of their union with Christ; in which respect they are more glorious, saith one, than Heaven, Angels, or any Creature." Trapp, *Commentary*, 588. Dickson stated, "Look unto man in our Head Christ Jesus, God incarnate, and there man is wonderfully exalted." Dickson, *First Fifty Psalms*, 40. Calvin called Christ "the restorer of mankind"; God bestows his blessings "upon us by him." Calvin, *Commentary*, 1:104.

18. Edwards, "769. Sermon on Ps 8:4–5," L. 20v.

19. Jonathan Edwards, *The "Miscellanies": Entry Nos. 501–832*, ed. Ava Chamberlain, vol. 18 of *WJE* (2000), 288. For more on Edwards' discussion of Christ and redeemed saints from the Psalms, see chapters 4 and 7, respectively.

20. Jonathan Edwards, *Some Thoughts Concerning the Revival*, in *The Great Awakening*, ed. C. C. Goen, vol. 4 of *WJE* (1972), 302.

mown grass in a sermon on Ps 72:6, "He shall come down like rain upon the mown grass: as showers that water the earth." In the doctrine section, Edwards argued that humans "are fitly compared to grass on account of their weakness and frailty."[21] Using Pss 72:6 and 103:15–16, he explained that both men and grass depend on the heavens' influences: "'Tis the sun and rain that causes the grass to grow and flourish. If the rain be withheld, it soon withers. So it is with the soul of man. Its prosperity depends wholly on the influences of the Sun of righteousness and on spiritual showers."[22] Humans had become so enervated in the first place because they had fallen by sin, which not only wounded them but cut them down to the ground, for "Satan was the mower and sin was the scythe, and he was cut down at one stroke. He at once lost all his glory. He wholly lost that image of God, and all holy and excellent principles were banished out of his heart. He wholly lost his spiritual life and became dead in sin."[23] We discuss sin at greater length below, but it is important to remember that Edwards dealt with topics fluidly, showing the theological connections between each. And he embraced biblical imagery as a means of exploring theological themes like humanity, a practice his Reformed predecessors also employed, though in this passage they focused on the typological implications for Christ more than humanity.[24] Edwards, however, found the imagery illuminating for both humanity, as we have seen here, and Christ, as we will see in chapter 4.

These images of human weakness join with several passages in the Psalms that speak specifically of the brevity and frailty of human life, and Edwards preached on this topic from the Psalms on five particular occasions. In the spring of 1728 he delivered a sermon on Ps 90:12, "So teach us to number our days, that we may apply our hearts unto wisdom." Life lasts for so short a time that he wondered how those who either do not believe in an afterlife or live as if there were none manage to make it through a day, for if the present enjoyments are all we have, then that reality would "be Enough to damp

---

21. Jonathan Edwards, "Like Rain upon Mown Grass" (Ps 72:6), in *Sermons and Discourses 1739–1742*, ed. Harry S. Stout and Nathan O. Hatch with Kyle P. Farley, vol. 22 of *WJE* (2003), 303.

22. Edwards, "Like Rain upon Mown Grass," 304.

23. Edwards, "Like Rain upon Mown Grass," 304. See Edwards' similar comment in his "Blank Bible" entry on Ps 72:6. Edwards, *The "Blank Bible,"* 508.

24. Henry, *Exposition*, [Ps 72:6]; Poole, *Synopsis*, 966; Trapp, *Commentary*, 769; David Dickson, *A Brief Explication of the other fifty Psalms, From Ps. 50 to Ps. 100* (London: T. R. and E. M. for Ralph Smith…, 1653), 146; Calvin, *Commentary*, 3:107.

and discourage the hearts," even "in the midst of the Greatest Prosperity."[25] Wiser heathens gave this unknown future greater consideration, to the disheartening of their souls, and under the Old Testament dispensation, "when life and Immortality were not so Cl[ear]ily brought to light" as they were with Christ, many holy men stumbled without knowing the plain truth of everlasting life with God (e.g., Job 7:6; Ps 39:5–6; Eccl 3:18).[26] Looking at Moses' life, Edwards thought that the troubles of Israel in Egyptian bondage or in the wilderness may have elicited Moses' prayer in Psalm 90, as he reflected on the frailty, uncertainty, and vanity of human life. Thus Edwards preached this doctrine: "that Our time here is so short and Uncertain that we had Great need wisely to Improve it."[27] This life is so short on a number of accounts, considering how long men like Adam and Job used to live; considering the great work we have to do here of mortifying our lusts; and considering "how long the future life is."[28] This life is so uncertain because death is no respecter of persons but rather takes people at all ages, for "the Arrows of death fly Every where and fly unseen."[29] We ought to improve our time because it is "the only opportunity for that Great work which we have to do," and "a Whole Eternity depends upon the Good or ill improvement of this short life."[30] In his application, Edwards directed his hearers "Chiefly [to] mind spiritual things," and to avoid being "so Carefull about Earthly things as to be diverted from the affairs of your soul."[31] He sought a transformative response: "Live Every day as much according to the Rules of God[']s Word as if you were assured it was your Last. [I]f this Rule were observed almost all sorts of men would live very differently from what they now do."[32] Edwards' interpretation and exhortations stood in line with his Reformed predecessors, who emphasized that the "Divine Arithmetick" of numbering our days requires God to teach us so that we might make good on our short lives by preparing for eternity.[33]

---

25. Jonathan Edwards, "67. Sermon on Ps 90:12 (Spring 1728)," in *Sermons, Series II, 1728–1729*, vol. 43 of the *WJEO*, L. 1r.

26. Edwards, "67. Sermon on Ps 90:12," L. 1r.

27. Edwards, "67. Sermon on Ps 90:12," L. 3r.

28. Edwards, "67. Sermon on Ps 90:12," L. 3v.–5v. Quotation on 5v.

29. Edwards, "67. Sermon on Ps 90:12," L. 6v.

30. Edwards, "67. Sermon on Ps 90:12," L. 8r., 8v.

31. Edwards, "67. Sermon on Ps 90:12," L. 12r.

32. Edwards, "67. Sermon on Ps 90:12," L. 12v.

33. The phrase "Divine Arithmetick" comes from Trapp, *Commentary*, 902. Henry also spoke of the "doctrine Arithmetick" of God and exhorted his readers to "live under a constant

A year later, on May 28, 1729, Edwards preached a sermon that he may have delivered in light of the Massachusetts elections at that time, and he was especially concerned to establish that even rulers are mortal. The text he chose was Ps 82:6–7, "I have said, Ye are gods; and all of you are children of the most High. But ye shall die like men, and fall like one of the princes."[34] Edwards lived at a time when rulers were considered especially deserving of honor.[35] He upheld this tradition, arguing that rulers are given a special title and position, but warned that they are still subject to mortality. In the context of Psalm 82, God stands in the congregation of the rulers and reproves them for their injustice. He then commands them to rule justly and honorably, and he "Puts them in mind of their mortality to Ensure his Reproofs & Commands & that they may be sensible that however they are exalted above others death will set them on a level with other men."[36] Edwards made two observations about these

Apprehension of the Shortness and Uncertainty of Life and the near Approach of Death and Eternity," which engenders wise living. Henry, *Exposition*, [Ps 90:12]. Poole described the petition as asking God to make us know "the power of your anger" ("irae tuae vis") and the brevity of this life in comparison to life eternal, noting that "nothing is more difficult than to number our days" ("Nihil difficilius est quam dies nostros numerare"). He explained that this numbering of days refers not to "the custom of arithmetic" ("more Arithmeticorum") but to meditating on life's brevity, for the cause of the brevity is our sin and God's anger, and the penalty for sin is approaching. Poole, *Synopsis*, 1078–1079. Dickson lamented the folly of looking upon "the indefinitenesse of the time of continuance of it, as if the duration of it were infinite and our yeares were innumberable," and he said we must ask God to "reveal to our mindes the mystery of grace and reconciliation" and move us to apply the remedy to ourselves. Dickson, *Other fifty Psalmes*, 336, 337. Calvin lamented how "shameful is our stupidity in never comprehending the short term of our life," and he reminded readers that "[n]o man then can regulate his life with a settled mind, but he who, knowing the end of it, that is to say death itself, is led to consider the great purpose of man's existence in this world, that he may aspire after the prize of the heavenly calling." Calvin, *Commentary*, 3:473–474.

34. It appears from the manuscript that Edwards originally planned to preach this sermon from Ps 146:3–4, "Put not your trust in princes, nor in the son of man, in whom there is no help. His breath goeth forth, he returneth to his earth; in that very day his thoughts perish." But he crossed out the reference and preached instead on Ps 82:6–7.

35. At the same time, Edwards also witnessed the undermining of such authority toward the end of his life, most personally evident in the disrespect that the young people of his congregation showed him during the proceedings of the "young folks' Bible case" or "bad book case," when Timothy Root called him, disparagingly, "a wig." Marsden notes that the incident revealed "a young people's underground that was consciously defiant of church authority." George Marsden, *Jonathan Edwards: A Life* (New Haven, CT: Yale University Press, 2003), 291–305. Quotation on 298.

36. Jonathan Edwards, "99. Sermon on Ps 82:6–7 (Spring–Fall 1729)," in *Sermons, Series II, 1729*, vol. 44 of the *WJEO*, L. 1r. In his "Blank Bible," Edwards used the analogy of Scripture to shed light on this verse, noting 1 Chr 29:23 and 2 Chr 13:8, which both speak of kings as representing God, and Luke 1:32, which places Christ in the seat of these earthly kings. Edwards, *The "Blank Bible,"* 516. See also Edwards' "Notes on Scripture," Entry No. 482, on John 10:34–36, where Jesus quotes Ps 82:6; Edwards copied an extensive quotation from

rulers. On the one hand they are like gods because God has advanced them above other men and appointed them to rule over his fellow creatures; the appellation "gods" is applied "metaphorically" to represent "their being in authority like God and being as Judges in his Place for the Present."[37] On the other hand, they are on the same level of men and will die as all men do. So Edwards preached the doctrine "that Great men are as Liable to death as others."[38] In fleshing out this doctrine, he explained that all humans have the same nature in soul and body; so Ps 33:14–15 says that "He fashioneth their hearts alike." Still, God has so ordered the world that men are of "different ranks" and have different levels of ability with the same human faculties, and he has ordained these "outward distinctions" "for the sake of the order and wellbeing of the [world]."[39] Still, those who are great like this must nonetheless face death like the rest of humanity, for "their Greatness no way secures them from death," and "Their Riches won[']t buy off death."[40] Neither does their authority in temporal matters exempt them from being subject to the eternal laws for mortals, nor will their power in war over-come this war with death, nor will their education and political cunning elude death. In his application, Edwards exhorted those who are advanced above others to hold "honour & advancement" in contempt for they are "shadows," and as all flowers fade and die, even the most beautiful, so shall all men fade and die, even the greatest.[41] Edwards' interpretation of the passage mirrored his Reformed predecessors, who similarly interpreted these verses as warning earthly rulers to humble themselves as mere mortals.[42] If Edwards was unique, it was in the way

---

John Glas to explain in what ways the word "gods" could apply to ancient Hebrew rulers and how they typified Christ, who is God. Edwards, *Notes on Scripture*, 578–580; John Glas, *Some Notes on Scripture-Texts, Shewing the Import of these* NAMES *of* JESUS CHRIST, THE SON OF GOD AND THE WORD OF GOD; *With an Account of The Image of God in Man* (Edinburgh: W. Sand, A. Murray, and J. Cochran, 1747), 11–12.

37. Edwards, "99. Sermon on Ps 82:6–7," L. 1r.

38. Edwards, "99. Sermon on Ps 82:6–7," L. 1v.

39. Edwards, "99. Sermon on Ps 82:6–7," L. 1v.–2r.

40. Edwards, "99. Sermon on Ps 82:6–7," L. 5v., 6r.

41. Edwards, "99. Sermon on Ps 82:6–7," L. 7r., 7v.

42. Some of the Reformed interpreters' distinctive ways of bringing out this truth are illus-trated in what follows. Henry exhorted, "let the Consideration of their *Mortality* be both *mortifying* to their Pride, and *quickening* to their Duty," for "Kings and Princes, and Judges of the Earth tho' they are *Gods to us*, are Men to GOD, and shall *dye like Men*, and all their Honour shall be laid in the Dust." Henry, *Exposition*, [Ps 82:6–7]. Poole noted that God bestows honor upon them by sharing his own name—"I have deemed you worthy by my appellation" ("Ego dignatus sum vos mea appellatione")—while also warning that they are not immortal. Poole, *Synopsis*, 1032–1033. Trapp emphasized the duty of princes by quoting

he turned the sermon on its head in an effort to preach the gospel, making the great people of the earth nothing compared to the great people in heaven. He exhorted all his congregants: "let us not Eagerly Pursue to be Great in this [world] but let us seek heavenly Greatness," an exaltation above earthly kings that promises riches, honor, "high birth," the "best Learning," the "truest wisdom," "the noblest disp[osition]," and the opportunity to be "Kings with [Christ]."[43]

Indeed, for Edwards the brevity of life served as a motivator for getting people to think about the next life. If everyone is going to die and nobody knows when, then why put off the most crucial of questions, one's response to the gospel of Christ? In July 1733 Edwards returned to this theme by preaching on Ps 39:4, "LORD, make me to know mine end, and the measure of my days, what it is; that I may know how frail I am." Edwards noted that David likely wrote this psalm when he was being pursued by his enemies, most notably Saul. The pursuit on his life led him into "meditations of his frailty & mortality," and from this "musing upon his mortality" he prayed that God might "make him Know the nature of his Great Change & the shortness & uncertainty of Life."[44] Other Reformed interpreters deliberated over whether or not David was making a death wish, but Edwards was not concerned with that detail.[45] Instead, he emphasized that David's request to know his end was asking God

---

a Spanish friar who was known to say, "there were but few Princes in hell; for why? there were but few in all." Trapp, *Commentary*, 796. Dickson recognized that God grants rulers honor, power, and revenues "for the better discharge of their office under him," yet "[g]reat places among men do not exempt any from God[']s power, justice and judgement." Dickson, *Other fifty Psalmes*, 259. Calvin succinctly explained, "Forgetting themselves to be men, the great ones of the earth may flatter themselves with visionary hopes of immortality; but they are here taught that they will be compelled to encounter death as well as other men." Calvin, *Commentary*, 3:335.

43. Edwards, "99. Sermon on Ps 82:6–7," L. 8v.

44. Jonathan Edwards, "289. Sermon on Ps 39:4 (July 1733)," in *Sermons, Series II, 1733*, vol. 48 of the *WJEO*, L. 1r., 1v.

45. Poole gave the interpretive option that this was a death wish, that David wanted the end of his troubles to come and exclaimed, "why is it not better to release the bonds of this mortality?" ("cur non potius solvor vinculis mortalitatis hujus?"). Poole, *Synopsis*, 755. Trapp, citing Calvin as support, reproved David in this statement in which he wished for death and "grudged against God; considering the greatnesse of his grief, and the shortnesse of his life." Trapp, *Commentary*, 685. Dickson likewise saw this verse as David's death wish, but had more compassion on him as a man suffering trial. He deduced that "[t]he shortnesse of this life is a mitigation of the troubles thereof unto the godly; and the fear that life should continue longer then [sic] the afflicted man would, augmenteth the trouble; and this is the fountaine of this passionate and curious wish." Dickson, *First Fifty Psalms*, 263. Calvin was harder on David, arguing that he "was transported by an improper and sinful excess of passion" to blame God for his suffering; here "he complains, that, being a mortal man, whose life is frail and transitory, he is not treated more mildly by God." Calvin, *Commentary*, 2:76–77.

not to reveal the exact day he would die but rather to show "how uncertain the time of his death was" and to know "in the General how very short & uncertain human Life was."[46] Thus Edwards preached this doctrine: "It would be a thing that would tend much to men[']s Spiritual profit & advantage if they would be much on Considering their own mortality."[47] Edwards sought to help his people reflect on their mortality by painting a vivid picture of them lying on their deathbed with a physician giving them up for death and friends weeping around them. As humans are liable to any number of accidents or diseases, that moment could come to anyone unannounced, and thus "we should Consider what it is to Go into a boundless Endless Eternity where our state & Condition never shall be altered."[48] Such meditations can make people sober, humble, and sensible of how vain this world is, which should stir them up to "Get an Interest in [Christ]."[49] Edwards reproved his people for devoting so little time to thinking about their mortality, and he exhorted all "to be much in meditating on their Own mortality," for although it may seem like a "melancholy unpleasant theme," it could be that "acquainting your self with death may be your having Eternal Life."[50] Edwards made a particular appeal to young people, who are "very apt to flatter thems[elves] with hopes of Long Life"—an appeal that would seem prophetic nine months later.[51]

In April 1734, nine months after the Ps 39:4 sermon, a young man in the town of Northampton contracted pleurisy and died two days later. His death, in connection with Edwards' funeral sermon, became one impetus for the 1734–1735 Northampton awakening.[52] He chose as his text Ps 90:5–6, "Thou carriest them away as with a flood; they are as a sleep: in the morning they are

---

46. Edwards, "289. Sermon on Ps 39:4," L. iv.–2r. Edwards' reading of this verse was similar to Henry's, who likewise observed that David "doth not mean, LORD, let me know how long I shall live, and when I shall die; we could not in Faith pray such a Prayer, for GOD has no where promis'd to let us know, but has in Wisdom lock'd up that Knowledge among the secret Things which belong not to us, nor would it be good for us to know it." Henry, *Exposition*, [Ps 39:4]. Poole also recognized a devotional interpretation: David asked that, with "the brevity of this life properly considered and carefully weighed" ("probè consideratà ac perpensa vitae hujus brevitate"), he might rightly establish his life. Poole, *Synopsis*, 754–755.

47. Edwards, "289. Sermon on Ps 39:4," L. 2r.

48. Edwards, "289. Sermon on Ps 39:4," L. 3v.

49. Edwards, "289. Sermon on Ps 39:4," L. 10r.

50. Edwards, "289. Sermon on Ps 39:4," L. 15v.–16r.

51. Edwards, "289. Sermon on Ps 39:4," L. 18r.

52. Marsden, *Jonathan Edwards: A Life*, 153–155.

like grass which groweth up. In the morning it flourisheth, and groweth up; in the evening it is cut down, and withereth." Edwards noted that Moses wrote the psalm from his reflections on mortality probably toward the end of the thirty-eight years of wandering in the desert—a narrowing in on the context from his 1728 sermon on Ps 90:12 (see above). Because of that generation's disobedience, God swore in his wrath that he would not let them enter the promised land (Ps 90:9, 15), resulting in an "Extraordinary mortality" amongst the people, for in thirty-eight years' time, all the congregation twenty years and older—about 600,000 people—died.[53] Edwards went on to review the "various Lively Representations of the mortality of m[an]" contained in the psalm, and especially in the sermon text.[54] Humans are "dust," turned back to their original substance by the mere word of God (Ps 90:3), and their lives are as short as "a tale that is told" (Ps 90:9). Other Reformed interpreters likewise explored the metaphors in these verses to describe human weakness and call for examining one's life, the length of which is clearly unascertainable.[55] Edwards preached a parallel doctrine: "man is fitly Compared to Grass that in in the morning [is] Green & flourishing but in the Evening [is] Cut down & withered."[56] While in the morning the fields may greet us with "Green Grass Interspersed with beutifull flowers seeming to smile," in the evening it may be "suddenly mown down & dead & witherd having Lost Its beutifull Colour & cheerfull Lively aspect," and "so it is with man," for "He for awhile is flourishing & makes a fair show but in a very little time is Cut down & withered."[57]

---

53. Jonathan Edwards, "319. Sermon on Ps 90:5–6 (April 1734)," in *Sermons, Series II, 1734*, vol. 49 of the *WJEO*, L. 1r. Edwards repreached this sermon in July 1753 to the Stockbridge Indians and also in July 1757. See also Edwards, *The "Blank Bible,"* 521.

54. Edwards, "319. Sermon on Ps 90:5–6," L. 1v.–2r.

55. All these interpreters expounded on the psalm's metaphors and made observations similar to Edwards'. Henry described "the Frailty of Men, and his Vanity, even at his best Estate," for "[a]s soon as we are Born we begin to Die, and every Day of our Life carries us so much nearer Death." Henry, *Exposition*, [Ps 90:5–6]. Poole observed that "their life is short and vanishing" ("Vita eorum brevis est & evanida"). Trapp described "the vanity and misery of man[']s life." Trapp, *Commentary*, 901. Dickson reflected on "the mortality and misery of men" and noted that this warning demands a fitting response, so that "death may not drown both soul and body." Dickson, *Other fifty Psalmes*, 334. Calvin drew a hortatory conclusion: "This doctrine requires to be continually meditated upon; for although we all confess that nothing is more transitory than our life, yet each of us is soon carried away, as it were, by a frantic impulse to picture to his own imagination an earthly immortality. Whoever bears in mind that he is mortal, restrains himself, that instead of having his attention and affections engrossed beyond measure with earthly objects, he may advance with haste to his mark." Calvin, *Commentary*, 3:467.

56. Edwards, "319. Sermon on Ps 90:5–6," L. 2v.

57. Edwards, "319. Sermon on Ps 90:5–6," L. 2v.

A man has his business in the world, but when death comes, as it comes for all, "he has no more forever any thing to do" on earth.[58] Edwards heightened the situation by constricting the time between life and death: "There is but a little space between man[']s flourishing & his being Cut down & withering."[59] In a statement that foreshadowed his own death, he noted, "How many are taken away that die with acute diseases & han[']t many days['] warning."[60] Grass is an appropriate metaphor because men are so liable to being cut down in their youth, and here Edwards took advantage of the sorrowful occasion that brought them together, the young man's death, and made clear the frailty of life in striking, if not gruesome, terms:

> this the Person that so little a while ago was abroad amongst m[en] active & lively & Pleasant. [B]ut now how his Comeliness is turned into Corruption. [H]ow the mouth is Closed in Everlasting silence. [H]ow the Eyes are darken'd with Everlasting night[.] [H]ow those Limbs that were so active are now stiff & Immoveable. [T]he blood that was so warm & brisk in his veins is now Cold stagnated & Corrupted.[61]

Edwards then directly charged young people "to forsake youthfull vanity & with the Greatest seriousn[ess] & dilig[ence] to mind the Concern of their salva[tion]."[62] In Edwards' mind, nothing more could be done for the young deceased man, but if his death could direct others to consider their state, it could result in the salvation of many. Indeed, how unreasonable it is to pursue the fleeting pleasures of youth and put off preparation for death, for "[h]ow do you Know that you shall Live till your youth is past[?] [W]hat agreem[en]t have you made with death & what better Guard or security have you from it more than others that have died in youth[?]"[63] In contrast, those who have an interest in Christ are happy and flourishing even while young, for even if you die in youth, "if you have an Int[erest] in [Christ] it will do you no hurt for your soul will flourish in a thousand times Greater beuty in the Perfect Image of [Christ]

58. Edwards, "319. Sermon on Ps 90:5–6," L. 5v.

59. Edwards, "319. Sermon on Ps 90:5–6," L. 9r.

60. Edwards, "319. Sermon on Ps 90:5–6," L. 10v. On the circumstances of Edwards' death, caused by complications from a small pox vaccination, see Marsden, *Jonathan Edwards: A Life*, 490–498.

61. Edwards, "319. Sermon on Ps 90:5–6," L. 12r.

62. Edwards, "319. Sermon on Ps 90:5–6," L. 12r.

63. Edwards, "319. Sermon on Ps 90:5–6," L. 16v.

& in a more Glorious vigour & Cheerfulln[ess]."[64] And one day the body will flourish too, for "the decaying & withering of your body will only be in order to a more Glo[rious] flourishing" in the resurrection.[65] As Edwards described the grisly details of death so fresh on his people's minds, he led them to consider the lasting glory and beauty of a life vivified by the Son of God.[66]

For Edwards, the nature of humanity is weak and liable to death at any moment, and from this theme, which the Psalms addressed at length, Edwards returned to his deepest concern: the proclamation of the gospel for the salvation of sinners. Humans must be awakened, for in their fallen state they lack a natural interest in the things of God. Edwards observed that "men that are prudent for their temporal interest, act as if they were bereft of reason," as Ps 32:9 testifies: "Be ye not as the horse, or as the mule, which have no understanding."[67] Even those with great light about God, such as those in Northampton, pay God little attention. While discussing Ps 10:4, "The wicked, through the pride of his countenance, will not seek after God: God is not in all his thoughts," Edwards wondered at this too frequent reality that men do not give more frequent thought to the future state after death—"[s]ome scarcely ever think anything about it."[68] How strange, he thought, that "where the Sun of Righteousness shines right in his eyes, yet they shut their eyes against the light."[69] But the nature of humanity in its fallen state is to resist spiritual light.

---

64. Edwards, "319. Sermon on Ps 90:5–6," L. 19r.

65. Edwards, "319. Sermon on Ps 90:5–6," L. 20v.

66. In his fifth sermon on the brevity of life, Edwards preached in March 1753 on Ps 39:5, "Behold, thou hast made my days as an handbreadth; and mine age is as nothing before thee: verily every man at his best state is altogether vanity." In this sermon, of which we have a one-page outline, Edwards preached this doctrine: "The Time men have to spend in this [world] is very short"—short in comparison to how long he will have in the next world, to how much time he once had, to his desires, and to the "great works men have to do." Jonathan Edwards, "1071. Sermon on Ps 39:5 (March 1753)," Beinecke Rare Book and Manuscript Library, Yale University, New Haven, CT, L. 1r. Henry, Poole, and Dickson likewise emphasized that the brevity of human life as compared to a handbreadth should lead us to prepare for eternity. Henry, Exposition, [Ps 39:5]; Poole, Synopsis, 755–756; Dickson, First Fifty Psalms, 263. Trapp and Calvin, however, saw in this passage that David made an unjustified complaint against God. Trapp, Commentary, 688; Calvin, Commentary, 2:77–79.

67. Jonathan Edwards, Original Sin, ed. Clyde A. Holbrook, vol. 3 of WJE (1970), 155. Edwards cited Mark 8:18 and Jer 8:7 as well.

68. Jonathan Edwards, "The Importance of a Future State" (Heb 9:27), in Sermons and Discourses 1720–1723, vol. 10 of WJE (1992), 370. Edwards used Ps 10:4 to develop this same concept in his sermon, "Practical Atheism" (Ps 14:1), in Sermons and Discourses 1730–1733, ed. Mark Valeri, vol. 17 of WJE (1999), 52.

69. Edwards, "The Importance of a Future State," 370.

Edwards explored the theme of spiritual blindness in fallen humanity in a February 1740 sermon on Ps 94:8–11, "Understand, ye brutish among the people: and ye fools, when will ye be wise? He that planted the ear, shall he not hear? he that formed the eye, shall he not see? He that chastiseth the heathen, shall not he correct? he that teacheth man knowledge, shall not he know? The LORD knoweth the thoughts of man, that they are vanity." Edwards observed that some people suffer from a "spiritual *disease*," which is denoted as a "*blindness* of mind," and this disease is of such a "great *degree*" that it renders the subjects as fools, being characterized by a deep-rooted "obstinacy."[70] The nature of the blindness pertains to God and divine things, and their blind notion of God is characterized by "*unreasonableness* and *sottishness*" in that they suggest that the Creator of the eye would not be able to perceive with his own eye and that he would lack some knowledge, though he was "the *fountain and original* of all knowledge."[71] While other Reformed interpreters understood this text to apply to subsets of humanity, Edwards applied it to the whole human race, explaining that though the psalmist began considering that only some men are characterized by this disease, he ended up seeing that "this vanity and foolishness of thought is *common* and *natural to mankind*."[72] Edwards thus preached this doctrine: "That there is an extreme and brutish blindness in things of religion, which naturally possesses the hearts of mankind."[73] But he carefully distinguished from the outset that this blindness was not owing to a lack of capacity, faculties, or opportunity in man; Edwards found no fault in man's natural faculties. Rather, the blindness originated from a spiritual

---

70. Jonathan Edwards, "Man's Natural Blindness in the Things of Religion," in vol. 7 of *The Works of President Edwards*, ed. Sereno E. Dwight (New York: S. Converse, 1829), 3, 4. Italics original.

71. Edwards, "Man's Natural Blindness," 4. Italics original.

72. Edwards, "Man's Natural Blindness," 4. Italics original. Henry's approach to this passage emphasized the folly of atheists: "[t]he Atheistical, tho' they set up for Wits, and Philosophers and Politicians, yet are really the *brutish of among the People*." Henry, *Exposition*, [Ps 94:8–9]. Poole thought it could refer to this or that population or to the stupidest of Israel's people. Poole, *Synopsis*, 1091. Trapp saw this brutishness as characteristic of certain leaders: "Ye that are ringleaders to the rest, but no wiser than the reasonlesse creatures: yea, therefore worse, because ye ought to be better." Trapp, *Commentary*, 818. Dickson, like Henry, discerned a rebuke against "Atheisme," and he focused on describing wicked oppressors, who are "notwithstanding all their honour nothing in God['s] estimation, but as the meanest of the people; yea, as the beasts that perish." Dickson, *Other fifty Psalmes*, 361. Calvin understood that in this passage the psalmist sought to "arouse" the people from their "stupidity" and the pride of their self-importance, though Calvin narrowed in on subsegments of the human race, whether Jews or deluded rulers. Calvin, *Commentary*, 4:16–20; quotation on 17.

73. Edwards, "Man's Natural Blindness," 4.

principle that had gone awry: "There is a principle in his heart, of such a blinding and besotting nature, that it hinders the exercises of his *faculties* about the things of religion: exercises for which God has made him well capable, and for which he gives him abundant opportunity."[74] So Edwards pointed to the problem of original sin, upholding his distinction between moral and natural necessity. In his doctrine section he described the "brutish blindness" of men visible both in their open professions and in their life practice.[75] In his improvement section, Edwards noted the ruinous effects of the Fall, the need for divine revelation to open blind men's eyes, and the great blessing of God sending his Son as the light of the world. As for humanity in its fallen state, "we may learn the misery of all such persons, as are under the power of that darkness which naturally possesses their hearts."[76] Edwards preached that God in his grace gives wisdom and light to awaken fallen humans, but humanity by nature dwells in a state of severe spiritual blindness.

People in their natural state are also faithless and untrustworthy, as Ps 116:10–11 shows, "I believed, therefore have I spoken: I was greatly afflicted: I said in my haste, All men are liars." Edwards explained that the psalmist called out to the Lord in his distress (Ps 116:4) because he believed God was trustworthy, while he also knew trusting in men was futile: "I said, All men are liars, i.e. not fit to be trusted in, those that will fail and deceive the hopes of them that trust in them, agreeable to Ps. 62:8–9."[77] Edwards later added a reference to Poole without comment in his "Blank Bible" entry on these verses. He was probably most interested in the four interpretive options Poole presented for the phrase, "All men are liars" (כָּל־הָאָדָם כֹּזֵב). First, it could mean that David was thinking of everyone who deserted him (e.g., Saul, Absalom). Second, in a weak moment David could have meant Samuel, who was only a mere man and could have been mistaken about the kingdom promised to him. Third, it could mean more generally that "every man is deceitful with respect to God" for "salvation is to be expected by no one, but only by God."[78] Fourth, the

---

74. Edwards, "Man's Natural Blindness," 5. Italics original.

75. Edwards, "Man's Natural Blindness," 5–21. Quotation on 5.

76. Edwards, "Man's Natural Blindness," 25.

77. Edwards, *The "Blank Bible,"* 529. Ps 62:8–9 reads, "Trust in him at all times; ye people, pour out your heart before him: God is a refuge for us. Selah. Surely men of low degree are vanity, and men of high degree are a lie: to be laid in the balance, they are altogether lighter than vanity."

78. Poole, *Synopsis,* 1190. The Latin reads, "Omnis homo respectu Dei mendax est," and "A nullo homine speranda est salus, sed tantum a Deo."

meaning could be contextualized in David's life: "I have chiefly believed God to be conveying the truth in the promise of a kingdom, but I have said, all men are deceitful who are declaring otherwise."[79] Poole's third interpretive option affirmed Edwards' comments on human nature from these verses.

Edwards' theology of human nature as gleaned from the Psalms was by no means a flattering portrait. Humanity is weak and feeble, liable to die unexpectedly at any moment, prone to sickness, spiritually blind, stubborn in his condition, foolish in considering himself immune to death, and untrustworthy. It is important to note that his view of human nature as sifted through the Psalms, as we have already seen, was a view primarily of *fallen* humanity, though also of *redeemed* humanity. He did not address pre-Fall humanity from the Psalms, and as he focused on post-Fall human nature, he aimed particularly at awakening slumbering souls, who are so apt to spiritual blindness and obstinacy, so they might participate in Christ, the light of the world who enlightens and redeems people so they might enjoy the post-Redemption state that he has obtained by joining the divine nature with the human nature in himself. But in a fallen world, the issue of sin presents a serious problem that must be addressed in its fullness, and Edwards found much teaching about sin in the Psalms.

Original Depravity and Our Besetting Sin

At the core of Edwards' ministry was answering the question, what constitutes true religion? He sought to locate religion in the heart, much like Jesus said, "But those things which proceed out of the mouth come forth from the heart" (Matt 15:18). If people professed to be Christians, they could expect to see a love of the things of God in their heart. But if they saw no change in their affections, their profession was suspect. In the same way, Edwards located the problem of sin *in the heart*. As Ps 95:7–10 reports historically that "[t]he wickedness of that perverse rebellious generation in the wilderness, is ascribed to the hardness of their hearts," so Edwards observed that "the Scriptures place the sin of the heart very much in hardness of heart," which demonstrates that "true religion...lies very much in the affection of the heart."[80] And so the sin that dwells in the heart, the problem of original sin, places humanity in a state that threatens to corrupt them eternally, and from that heart issue stems a

---

79. Poole, *Synopsis*, 1191. The Latin reads, "maximè credidi Deum esse veracem in promissione Regni, omnes autem homines dixi esse mendaces qui secus dicerent."

80. Jonathan Edwards, *Religious Affections*, ed. John E. Smith, vol. 2 of *WJE* (1959), 116.

besetting sin in the way they deceive themselves about their state and continue to engage in sin—theological themes that Edwards emphasized in his reading of the Psalms.

Original Sin

Edwards liked to cast the maiden in Psalm 45 as a type of the church (see chapter 7), and the maiden's story of leaving her father's house for the house of her groom also typified the church leaving sin behind. In his "Blank Bible" note on Ps 45:10, "Hearken, O daughter, and consider, and incline thine ear; forget also thine own people, and thy father's house," Edwards interpreted the "father's house" as a reference to the sin that is "naturally dear to us" that the church must relinquish as it goes to Christ; this sin "may well be compared to our father's house and natural kindred, both because sin and corruption is what we have naturally, that which we are born with, and that we derive from our parents."[81]

This doctrine of natural-born sin was falling out of favor in Edwards' day, and he aimed to defend the "great important doctrine" of original sin especially in light of the recent opposition by the notable theologian John Taylor (1694–1761), whose *Scripture-Doctrine of Original Sin Proposed to Free and Candid Examination* (1740) had unsettled New England Calvinists.[82] In Edwards' treatise on *Original Sin*, the Bible served as a bedrock authority for his defense of the doctrine, and he employed the Psalms in several places to establish his argument. Sometimes he used them as proof-texts with other biblical citations, as when he quoted Ps 143:2 to support this assertion: "That every one of mankind, at least of them that are capable of acting as moral agents, are guilty of sin (not now taking it for granted that they come guilty into the world) is a thing most clearly and abundantly evident from the holy Scriptures."[83] He also cited Pss 115:4–8 and 135:15–18 to support his claim that "[t]he Scriptures are

81. Edwards, *The "Blank Bible,"* 495–496. Edwards later added an observation that "father's house" may refer to "this world" or "our native country," for "[w]e are naturally, and by our first birth, of the earth, earthly. We must forsake this country in our hearts for Christ. See Eph. 5:30–32." Edwards, *The "Blank Bible,"* 496. Edwards also cited this note in his "Blank Bible" notes on Gen 12:1 and 24:25, observing similarities with Abram leaving his "father's house" and Rebekah welcoming Abraham's servant out of the world to have a room in her father's house. Edwards, *The "Blank Bible,"* 155, 167.

82. Edwards, *Original Sin*, 102. For more on Edwards' treatise on *Original Sin* and the context of its publication, see Douglas Sweeney, *Jonathan Edwards and the Ministry of the Word* (Downers Grove, IL: IVP Academic, 2009), 154–160, and Marsden, *Jonathan Edwards: A Life*, 447–458.

83. Edwards, *Original Sin*, 114.

abundant in representing the idolatry of the heathen world as their exceeding wickedness, and their most brutish stupidity."[84]

In other places Edwards dealt with specific Psalms passages in greater detail. In Part I, Section 6 of *Original Sin*, he gave evidence for the corruption of human nature in its tendency toward "an extreme degree of folly and stupidity in matters of religion."[85] One clear example is "how cold, lifeless and dilatory" men are when it comes to matters of eternity, especially given the uncertain nature of this temporal world, as described in Ps 49:11–14: "Their inward thought is, that their houses shall continue for ever, and their dwelling places to all generations; they call their lands after their own names. Nevertheless man being in honour abideth not: he is like the beasts that perish. This their way is their folly."[86] While preachers plead and use every means possible to convince people that "things which are eternal, are infinitely more important than things temporal," listeners ignore the calls and attend to their temporal interests.[87] Edwards lamented:

> Though men are so sensible of the uncertainty of their neighbors' lives, when any considerable part of their estates depends on the continuance of them; how stupidly senseless do they seem to be of the uncertainty of their own lives, when their preservation from immensely great, remedy-less and endless misery, is risked by a present delay, through a dependence on future opportunity?[88]

Such common disregard for one's soul shows how sin is so deeply rooted in human hearts.

One particular objection that Taylor raised against the traditional view of original sin was that the Scriptures often describe sin as corporate where interpreters have misread it as individual and general. To make his point Taylor discussed Ps 14:1–3: "The fool hath said in his heart, There is no God. They are corrupt, they have done abominable works, there is none that doeth good. The LORD looked down from heaven upon the children of men, to see if there were any that did understand, and seek God. They are all gone aside, they

---

84. Edwards, *Original Sin*, 152.

85. Edwards, *Original Sin*, 147.

86. Edwards, *Original Sin*, 154.

87. Edwards, *Original Sin*, 155

88. Edwards, *Original Sin*, 155.

are all together become filthy: there is none that doeth good, no, not one." Taylor argued that in this place, the Spirit does not speak of "any Depravity of Nature derived from *Adam*, but manifestly of the Habits of Wickedness, which Men had contracted by their *own* evil Doings."[89] In fact, verse 5 speaks of "the generation of the righteous," which suggested to Taylor that "there were Men at that time in the Nation to whom that bad Character did not belong."[90] In Taylor's view, the people David complained about in the Psalms referred to "a strong Party disaffected to his Person and Government," a party synonymous with David's phrase, "the children of men."[91] He concluded that "none of the Texts here quoted out of the Psalms have reference to any Corruption common to all Mankind, but only to such Wickedness wherein several of the *Jewish* Nation were involved, but with which sundry Persons were not chargeable," which indicates that "the *Psalmist* cannot intend a Corruption of Nature derived from *Adam* to ALL Mankind."[92]

Edwards responded to this interpretation with his own detailed reading. First, even if the corruption of David's time referred to a particular party, still all the "new and extraordinary means" used in that period to promote godliness failed to produce any lasting spiritual change: "it appears that all those great means used to promote and establish virtue and true religion, in Samuel's, David's and Solomon's times, were so far from having any general abiding good effect in Israel" that even Solomon succumbed to corruption, openly tolerating idolatry in his kingdom.[93] Such corruption under such great means of grace suggested a deeper heart issue of indwelling sin. And Ps 14:2–3 plainly testifies to the doctrine of original sin: "Original depravity may well be argued from wickedness being often spoken of in Scripture as a thing *belonging to the race of mankind, and as if it were a property of the species.* So in Ps. 14:2, 3."[94] Edwards rejected Taylor's objection that the phrase, "the generation of the righteous" (Ps 14:5), means some individuals are not subject to original sin, "[f]or who ever supposed, that no unrighteous men were ever changed by

89. John Taylor, *The Scripture-Doctrine of Original Sin Proposed to Free and Candid Examination* (London: J. Wilson, at the Turk's-Head in Gracechurch-street, 1740), 103–104. Quotation on 103.

90. Taylor, *Scripture-Doctrine*, 104, 105.

91. Taylor, *Scripture-Doctrine*, 105.

92. Taylor, *Scripture-Doctrine*, 107.

93. Edwards, *Original Sin*, 179.

94. Edwards, *Original Sin*, 262. Italics original.

divine grace, and afterwards made righteous?"[95] According to Edwards, "The Psalmist is speaking of what men are as they are the children of men, born of the corrupt human race; and not as born of God, whereby they come to be the children of God, and of the generation of the righteous," and he pointed to Paul's use of this passage in Rom 3:10–12 "to prove the universal corruption of mankind; but yet in the same chapter he supposes, these same persons here spoken of as wicked, may become righteous, through the righteousness and grace of God."[96] These emphases on original depravity, sin's universality, and God's regenerating grace as the only true agent of change were regularly rehearsed in Reformed readings of this passage.[97]

---

95. Edwards, *Original Sin*, 262. Neither Henry, Trapp, nor Dickson discussed verse 5 as an objection to the universality of innate sin. Henry, *Exposition*, [Ps 14:5]; Trapp, *Commentary*, 604; Dickson, *First Fifty Psalms*, 68. Poole mentioned that the "generation of the righteous" was an argument against the universality of the verse, though he presented counter arguments, largely from the analogy of Scripture, citing Isaiah 64; 6:7; Jer 5:1; and Mic 7:2–4. Poole, *Synopsis*, 578. Calvin also offered an explanation: When David describes a remnant of godly people later in the psalm, it is because "there is a manifest difference between the children of God who are created anew by his Spirit, and all the posterity of Adam, in whom corruption and depravity exercise dominion." Calvin, *Commentary*, 1:195.

96. Edwards, *Original Sin*, 262. See also 284–291.

97. Henry commented on these verses that "Sin is the Disease of Mankind, and it appears here to be *Malignant* and *Epidemical*"; indeed, "it has infected the whole Race of Mankind," for "the Apostacy is universal." Also, he understood "children of men" as referring to the whole human race, interpreting this passage to teach original sin, for it shows "the Corruption in our own Nature" and indicates that only "the free and mighty Grace of God" can institute a change of nature. Henry, *Exposition*, [Ps 14:1–3]. Trapp likewise saw sin as a universal human problem, noting that David, who was a man after God's own heart, did not except himself from this indictment of a "universal community of declinations" ("universitas declinantium"), and he used the analogy of Scripture to support this judgment on humanity, citing Rom 3:10–12 and Isa 53:6. Trapp, *Commentary*, 602–603; quotation on 602. Dickson also located sin in the heart for "the heart is full of Atheisme," and he understood "children of men" to refer to "the state of nature" of all humanity, for while men may be more or less offensive, yet all "unrenewed" men have "corrupt hearts" and perform "vile and loathsome" actions in God's sight. Dickson located the change from sin to righteousness in the Spirit's work of regeneration. Dickson, *First Fifty Psalms*, 66–67. Calvin stated that these verses speak "on the subject of human depravity." While he described David's context of indicting "the children of Abraham," who were God's chosen people and yet so corrupt, Calvin also saw this as describing the whole of humanity, especially as Paul picked it up in Rom 3:10–12. He concluded: "Whence it follows, that all of us, when we are born, bring with us from our mother's womb this folly and filthiness manifested in the whole life, which David here describes, and that we continue such until God make us new creatures by his mysterious grace." Calvin, *Commentary*, 1:192–195.
  Poole recorded a lengthy discussion of this passage in his *Synopsis*. He presented the view that "children of men" refers to "the heirs of Adam" ("Haeredes Adami") and that "all" ("omnes") are characterized by "death in sins" ("mortis in peccatis"). The repetition of the phrase "there is none that doeth good" in verses 1 and 3 is made "on account of the certainty of things and the miserable weight of corruption" ("ob rei certitudinem, deploratamque

On the phrase, "the children of men," Edwards believed its frequent use in the Psalms indicated humanity's universal sinful nature: "So wickedness is spoken of in other places in the book of Psalms, as a thing that belongs to men, as of the human race," and he quoted Pss 4:2; 57:4; and 58:1–2 to this effect.[98] He rejected Taylor's "disaffected party" interpretation because the phrase is universal in scope, and he asked, why should the psalmist

> denote the wickedest and worst men in Israel by this name? Why he should choose thus to disgrace the human race, as if the compellation of sons of men most properly belonged to such as were of the vilest character, and as if all the sons of men, even every one of them, were of such a character, and none of them did good; no, not one?...It is a good, easy and natural reason why he chooseth to call the wicked sons of men, as a proper name for 'em, that by being of the sons of men, or of the corrupt ruined race of mankind, they come by their depravity. And the Psalmist himself leads us to this very reason (Ps. 58 at the beginning). "Do ye judge uprightly, O ye sons of men? yea, in heart ye work wickedness, ye weigh out the violence of your hands. The wicked are estranged from the womb, etc."[99]

In Edwards' view, a full reading of the Psalms led to an interpretation that sin infects every human being. While Taylor used a historical approach of

---

corruptionis gravitatem"). Using the analogy of Scripture by pointing to Rom 3:10–12, Poole also recognized that "the Apostle wants to effect a universal law concerning the constitution of man always" ("Apostolus legem universalem de cujusque hominis constitutione efficere vult"), so that both Paul and David "understand a universal fall of all people" ("universali omnium hominum labe intelligunt"). In fact, he added the observation that "this corruption of the human race is described, not only by actual sins, but also by original" ("Describitur hic corruptio generis humani, non tantum per peccata actualia, sed & originale") and indicates the condition of humanity "post-Fall" ("post lapsum"). The phrase "children of men" suggested to Poole not a subset of humanity but humans "in kind" ("in genere") and, again, "all mortals altogether" ("omnes omnino mortales"). While he described other viewpoints that suggested the psalmist's judgment refers to a local subset, Poole went on at length about the universality of sin that this verse indicates, based largely on the analogy of Scripture and the support of the early church fathers. Poole, *Synopsis*, 577–579.

Edwards did not cite any of these interpreters on this passage. He did mention Stephen Charnock's *Several discourses upon the existence and attributes of God* (London: D. Newman..., 1682), on Ps 14:1, in "Miscellanies" Entry No. 1002, but he did not talk about Ps 14:1 in that entry. Jonathan Edwards, *The "Miscellanies": Entry Nos. 833–1152*, ed. Amy Plantinga Pauw, vol. 20 of *WJE* (2002), 327.

98. Edwards, *Original Sin*, 262–263.

99. Edwards, *Original Sin*, 263.

contextualizing these phrases in David's time to apply sin to collective bodies, Edwards interpreted the Psalms theologically in light of both David's time and the full canon of Scripture to apply sin individually. While Taylor held that no Scripture passages "prove that *all* Mankind to a Man, *every single* Man over all the World, every Man that comes into the World, and as he comes into the World, is naturally corrupt," Edwards actually found that the argument from individuality compels one to uphold the universality of sin because it asserts the particularity of sin in conjunction with Scripture passages that say, "there is none righteous, not one."[100]

Another key Psalms passage on original sin was Ps 51:5, "Behold, I was shapen in iniquity; and in sin did my mother conceive me." Taylor argued that "shapen in iniquity" should be translated "born in sin" and that this phrase is metaphorical, for "'tis an hyperbolical Form of aggravating Sin," not a literal description of the natural generation of sin.[101] In contrast, Edwards asserted that humans are born with a moral impurity deserving of God's severe judgments: "without doubt, David has respect to this same way of derivation of wickedness of heart" in Ps 51:5.[102] Edwards rejected Taylor's reading, arguing instead that "[t]here is nothing else visible in David's case, to lead him to take notice of his being born in sin, but only his having such experience of the continuance and power of indwelling sin, after so long a time, and so many and great means to engage him to holiness; which shewed, that sin was inbred, and in his very nature."[103] Like Taylor, other Reformed interpreters saw this as an "aggravation" of his sin, but in contrast, they linked it with a depraved nature, aggravating the guilt of the sinner as a sinner by nature without excuse.[104]

---

100. Taylor, *Scripture-Doctrine*, 107. For example, see Edwards' discussion of the nature of sin as individual rather than corporate in Pss 32:3–4 and 143:2 to argue a universal infection from particular cases. Edwards, *Original Sin*, 289.

101. Taylor, *Scripture-Doctrine*, 131–139. Quotation on 135.

102. Edwards, *Original Sin*, 270.

103. Edwards, *Original Sin*, 271.

104. Henry understood that in this verse David "confesseth his Original Corruption" as having "an Adulterous Murtherous Nature," for "[s]in was twisted in with it, not as it came out of GOD's Hands, but as it comes through our Parents['] Loins." This is no excuse, but is an "Aggravation of Sin" within a natural-born sinner. Speaking on original sin, Henry explained: "It is to be sadly lamented by every one of us, that we brought into the World with us a corrupt Nature, wretchedly degenerated from its primitive Purity and Rectitude....This is what we call *Original Sin,* because it is as ancient as our Original, and because it is the Original of all our Actual Transgressions." Henry, *Exposition*, [Ps 51:5]. Poole presented various views on the translation and interpretation of the verse, but he promoted the view that this verse refers to original sin, stating, "my mother bore me having sin in the womb" ("me peccatum habentem gestavit utero mater mea"). He presented views against Pelagius, the

Edwards also argued from medieval rabbis that the doctrine of original sin had been an ancient tenet of the Jewish religion. He retrieved quotations of Jewish interpreters on Ps 51:5 from Protestant theologians Johann Friedrich Stapfer and Matthew Poole. He quoted "Eben-Ezra" (Abraham ben Meir Ibn Ezra; 1089–1164) as stating, "Behold, because of the concupiscence which is innate in the heart of man, it is said, 'I am begotten in iniquity.' And the sense is, that there is implanted in the heart of man *jetzer harang*, an evil figment, from his nativity."[105] He also gleaned from Manasseh ben Israel (1604–1657) that whether David referred to Eve or to his biological mother conceiving him in sin, "he would signify, that sin is as it were natural, and inseparable in this life. For it is to be observed, that Eve conceived after the transgression was committed; and as many as were begotten afterwards, were not brought forth in a conformity to the rule of right reason, but in conformity to disorderly and

---

Socinians, and Grotius, saying it is not able to be esteemed as hyperbole ("Nec probari potest hyperbole è locis designatis"). While he presented objections, he also presented several cases for his preferred view, that "this verse is understood concerning original sin" ("Intelligitur hic versus de peccato originali"). Poole showed that David "aggravates his sin by duration because concupiscence is fixed in the heart, even as if it is formed in it" ("Aggravat peccatum suum à duratione; quia concupiscentia est in corde fixa, & quasi formatur in illo"), and he presented arguments against the idea that original sin as described in this verse extenuates or excuses David's actual sins. Poole, *Synopsis*, 828–829. Trapp recognized in the phrase "shapen in iniquity" not an excuse but "an aggravation of his actual abominations," but only as they "were committed out of the vile viciousness of his nature," for his whole point in this verse was to allege "his original pravity." Trapp, *Commentary*, 722. Dickson likewise recognized that this phrase functioned "not to extenuate, but to aggravate their sin," but at its heart, it spoke of original depravity: "As original sin is common to all men by natural propagation from their parents, so is it not abolished out of the most holy in this life." Dickson, *Other fifty Psalmes*, 5. Calvin similarly rejected the notion that this verse is David's excuse for sin and rather saw that it "refers to original sin with the view of aggravating his guilt, acknowledging that he had not contracted this or that sin for the first time lately, but had been born into the world with the seed of every iniquity," for he confesses that "his nature was entirely depraved." In fact, for Calvin, this passage "not only teaches the doctrine" of original sin "but may assist us in forming a correct idea of it," namely the hereditary nature of sin's transmission. Calvin, *Commentary*, 2:290. Edwards did not cite Henry in Ps 51:5 but did cite him on verses 4 and 7. He also cited Poole on verse 5 in a footnote in *Original Sin*, as discussed below. He cited none of the others.

105. Edwards, *Original Sin*, 430. This is Edwards' translation. The Latin reads, "Ecce propter concupisceniam innatam cordi humane dicitur, in iniquitate genitus sum, atque sensus est, quod à nativitate implantatum sit cordi humano *jetzer harang*, figmentum malum." Stapfer noted that in Ps 51:7, "David spoke concerning the sin that is common and original to all humans" ("De peccato hoc omnibus hominibus communi & originali D AVID dixit, Psalmo LI. 7"). Johann Friedrich Stapfer, *Institutiones Theologiæ Polemicæ Universæ, Ordine Scientifico dispositæ*, vol. 3, 3d ed. (Tiguri: Heideggerum et Socios, 1757), 36. See also Jonathan Edwards, "Miscellanies" Entry No. 1325, in *The "Miscellanies": Entry Nos. 1153–1360*, ed. Douglas A. Sweeney, vol. 23 of *WJE* (2004), 298–302, where he quoted Stapfer discussing original sin and R. Levi Ben Gersom's discussion of Ps 51:7.

lustful affections."[106] From Poole, he quoted Eben-Ezra again as interpreting Ps 51:5 to mean "that evil concupiscence is implanted in the heart from child-hood, as if he were formed in it," and understanding "my mother" to refer to "Eve, who did not bear children till she had sinned."[107] Again, he quoted Manasseh ben Israel, who "from this place (Ps. 51:5) concludes, that not only David, but all mankind, ever since sin was introduced into the world, do sin from their original."[108] These Jewish writers gave Edwards support from those outside the Christian faith that further bolstered his argument.

A final proof from the Psalms for the doctrine of original sin in his trea-tise was the inevitability of death. Edwards asserted that "[u]niversal mortality proves original sin."[109] As Ps 17:9 testifies that "deadly enemies" are "the most bitter and terrible enemies," so "[d]eath is spoken of in Scripture as the chief of calamities, the most extreme and terrible of all those natural evils, which come on mankind in this world," and if death is so horrible, then it follows that its cause is equally odious.[110] Edwards pointed to Moses' psalm, Ps 90:3, 5–12, to observe "[h]ow plain and full is this testimony, that the general mortal-ity of mankind is an evidence of God's anger for the sin of those who are the subjects of such a dispensation?"[111] For when God shortens a man's life, he expresses judgment on sin, since any "hastening" of death manifests God's "great displeasure" over sin.[112] Edwards held that the shortening of men's years and the inevitability of death as taught in Psalm 90 provided incontrovertible evidence of God's anger over the general sin that infects humanity, and he developed his thinking in part from Arthur Bedford's *Scripture Chronology*, a

---

106. Edwards, *Original Sin*, 430. This is Edwards' translation. The Latin reads, "significare voluit, esse peccatum quast naturale, & inseparabile in hac vita. Ideo & post commissum delictum Eva concepit, & quotquot postea geniti sunt, non juxta regulam, recte rationi con-formem, sed affectus perturbatos, & libidinosos producti sunt." Stapfer, *Institutiones*, 3:36–37.

107. Edwards, *Original Sin*, 431. This is Edwards' translation. The Latin reads, "Concupiscentia mala est in corde à pueritia plantata, ac si formatus erat in ea. Per *matrem* indicat Evam, quae non peperit antequam peccabat." Poole, *Synopsis*, 529. Trapp quoted this same statement from Aben-Ezra; his Latin version reads, "Eve, qua non parturiebat antequam peccabat." Trapp, *Commentary*, 723.

108. Edwards, *Original Sin*, 431. This is Edwards' translation. The Latin reads, "Ita & Manasses Ben Israel, qui hinc concludit, *non solum Davidem sed omnem humanam speciem post peccatum in mundum introductu, ab origine sua peccare.*" Poole, *Synopsis*, 829.

109. Edwards, *Original Sin*, 206.

110. Edwards, *Original Sin*, 207.

111. Edwards, *Original Sin*, 209.

112. Edwards, *Original Sin*, 208.

portion of which he recorded in "Notes on Scripture" Entry No. 203. Bedford used the Pentateuch and Psalm 90 to describe the shortening of people's years, connecting God's anger with the decreased human lifespan. Bedford observed that "as Sin at first brought Death into the World; so Sin did afterward shorten the Age of Man."[113] Edwards explained that God had cut short the regular human lifespan throughout time, taking away the chance of immortality, cutting off more than eight hundred years of his life, and subjecting him to disease, wars, and calamities that often usher in death much earlier, even in infancy. Edwards concluded:

> If those particular and comparatively trivial calamities, extending perhaps not to more than a thousandth part of the men of one generation, are clear evidences of God's great anger; certainly this universal vast destruction, by which the whole world in all generations is swallowed up, as by a flood, that nothing can resist, must be a most glaring manifestation of God's anger for the sinfulness of mankind. Yea, the Scripture is express in it, that it is so.[114]

In fact, since divine chastisements in this life are "certain evidences that the subjects are not wholly without sin," then death is especially sure evidence of the general nature of sin in humanity.[115] Even though chastisements might result in benefit for us, as David describes in Ps 30:5, they issue forth as "the fruit of God's anger for his sin."[116] The Psalms make this point clear, namely that "slaying, or delivering to death, is often spoken of as in general a more awful thing than the chastisements that are endured in this life" (Pss 118:17–18; 88:15; 78:38–39; 103:9, 14–15; 30:2–3, 9; 13:3; 6:1–5; 88:9–11; 143:7; also Job 33:22–24; 10:9).[117] So Edwards understood the Scriptural sense of "death" to

113. Arthur Bedford, *The Scripture Chronology Demonstrated by Astronomical Calculations, and also by The Year of Jubilee, and the Sabbatical Year among the Jews: or, An Account of Time From the Creation of the World, to the Destruction of Jerusalem; as it may be proved from the Writings of the Old and New Testament* (London: James and John Knapton et al., 1730), 395; Jonathan Edwards, *Notes on Scripture*, ed. Stephen J. Stein, vol. 15 of WJE (1998), 126–127.

114. Edwards, *Original Sin*, 208–209.

115. Edwards, *Original Sin*, 214.

116. Edwards, *Original Sin*, 213. Ps 30:5 reads, "For his anger endureth but a moment; in his favour is life: weeping may endure for a night, but joy cometh in the morning." Edwards also pointed to Ps 119:67, 71, 75, which all speak of God's rightful afflictions given for the psalmist's good but particularly administered because he "went astray."

117. Edwards, *Original Sin*, 214.

mean "the proper wages of the sin of mankind," proving that it is a punishment or recompense for man's sin.[118]

In addition to his biblical arguments, Edwards used the metaphysical concepts of ontological realism, continuous creation, and humanity's participation in Adam's sin to help resolve some of the theological difficulties with the doctrine of original sin.[119] While the Psalms did not play a major role in his development of those ideas, Edwards nonetheless believed that they were consistent with God's revelation in the Psalms. In "Miscellanies" Entry No. 346, "Creation. Providence," for example, Edwards argued that his doctrine of continuous creation, "to suppose creation to be performed new every moment," was "most agreeable to the Scripture," for "[t]he Scripture speaks of it not only as past but as a present, remaining, continual act," as seen in Ps 65:6, "Which by his strength setteth fast the mountains; being girded with power," and Ps 104:4, "Who maketh his angels spirits; his ministers a flaming fire."[120] Similarly, in a sermon on Ps 139:7–10, Edwards used this passage to present the doctrine, "God is everywhere present," and in expounding that doctrine, he described "God's preservation of the world" as "nothing but a continued act of creation" and argued that, with respect to the preservation of sinners, "God has also created them, and he creates them every moment."[121] Also, in his sermon on Ps 40:6–8, Edwards recognized that as Adam was our representative in whom we die, so Christ is our representative in whom we live, though he did not use the Psalms to develop this point.[122]

In other contexts, Edwards returned to the Psalms to understand sin, emphasizing sin's connection with judgment, a relationship that reveals God's anger over human rebellion. So Edwards paraphrased God from Ps 50:21 as saying, "I won't let thy sins pass as little things not worthy to be taken notice

---

118. Edwards, *Original Sin*, 239. The Psalms confirm this definition, as David uses the word "death" to refer to "the proper wages and issue of sin" (Ps 34:21), "a certain thing" (Ps 139:19), and "a thing wherein the wicked are distinguished from the righteous" (Ps 69:28). Edwards, *Original Sin*, 240–241.

119. For more on the philosophical and theological aspects of Edwards' doctrine of original sin, see Michael J. McClymond and Gerald R. McDermott, *The Theology of Jonathan Edwards* (New York: Oxford University Press, 2012), 339–356; Sweeney, *Jonathan Edwards and the Ministry of the Word*, 154–160.

120. Edwards, *The "Miscellanies": Entry Nos. a–500*, 418.

121. Jonathan Edwards, "That God Is Everywhere Present," in *The Blessing of God: Previously Unpublished Sermons of Jonathan Edwards*, ed. Michael D. McMullen (Nashville, TN: Broadman & Holman Publishers, 2003), 109, 111, 116.

122. Jonathan Edwards, "The Sacrifice of Christ Acceptable," in *Sermons and Discourses 1723–1729*, ed. Kenneth Minkema, vol. 14 of *WJE* (1997), 453.

of, as thou thyself didst, and was ready to think that I did, because 'I kept silence.' But I will by no means clear the guilty, or acquit the wicked."[123] And since "God is angry with the wicked every day" (Ps 7:11), Edwards deduced that "[t]hey are in a miserable condition, for they have nothing to ease them, or defend them; they can't comfort themselves and say, 'those afflictions are from a father,' for they are inflicted by him whom they have made their dreadful enemy, and is angry with them every day."[124] The judgment theme is discussed further in chapter 7, but the issue of sin is only rightly understood, in Edwards' view, when connected to the devastating consequences facing all humans who remain in the fallen state caused by original sin.

The Deceitfulness of Sin

The sinful disposition in the hearts of humans wields its influence in such a way, Edwards believed, that it blinds people to their precarious state, and again, the Psalms served as a basis for this thinking. In his comment on Ps 119:163, "I hate and abhor lying: but thy law do I love," Edwards explained that "lying" referred especially to "those fallacious reasonings with which men are wont to excuse and justify themselves in crooked ways," a foolish hypocrisy that would only comfort them in their sin but ultimately result in their own harm.[125] Edwards fleshed out this concept in four sermons from the Psalms.

In an undated sermon, Edwards preached on human delusion from Ps 36:1–2, "The transgression of the wicked saith within my heart, that there is no fear of God before his eyes. For he flattereth himself in his own eyes, until his iniquity be found to be hateful."[126] He observed that the wicked man's folly is to consider himself in a safer position than he actually enjoys. He does not fear God because he does not believe God's threats of punishment will ever come to fruition, for "[i]f he were afraid of these he could never go on so securely in his sin, as he doth."[127] Instead he "flatters himself," making the grounds of his

---

123. Edwards, The "Blank Bible," 499.

124. Jonathan Edwards, "Christian Safety" (Prov 29:25), in Sermons and Discourses 1720–1723, vol. 10 of WJE (1992), 461. Edwards also used Ps 7:11 to place before sinners that "[t]he flames of God's wrath, that are as hot as hell fire, bear against you," in "The Threefold Work of the Holy Ghost" (John 16:8), in Sermons and Discourses 1723–1729, ed. Kenneth P. Minkema, vol. 14 of WJE (1997), 386.

125. Edwards, The "Blank Bible," 532.

126. The sermon is listed as being on Ps 36:2, but Edwards really preached on vv. 1–2.

127. Jonathan Edwards, "The Vain Self-Flatteries of the Sinner" (Ps 36:2), in vol. 4 of Works of President Edwards (Worcester ed.), 8th ed. (1778; repr., New York: Leavitt & Allen, 1852), 322.

hope something other than Christ, something that allows those like him to "persuade themselves that they shall escape those judgments," so that they put judgment day far from their minds—a common Reformed interpretation.[128] But such self-flattery does not last. Eventually, the wicked man will realize his "foundation of encouragement" rested on false grounds, and when he wakes to find his iniquity "hateful," he will realize that "it is a more dreadful thing to sin against God, and break his commandments, than he imagined."[129] By "experience" he will find his "sweet" sin to be "as bitter as gall and wormwood," and the fruit of his sin will convince him of its "hatefulness" and "terribleness."[130] So Edwards preached this doctrine: "Wicked men generally flatter themselves with hopes of escaping punishment, till it actually comes upon them."[131] This text and doctrine explained for Edwards why so many people stay in their sinful slumber despite the awakening sermons that vividly display the miseries of hell:

> Hence we learn the reason why awakening truths of Scripture, and awakening sermons, make no more impressions upon men. It is a wonderful and surprising thing, that God's denunciations of eternal misery, and threatenings of casting sinners into the lake that burneth with fire and brimstone forever and ever, do not affect them, do not startle them. But the truth is, they flatter themselves, by such means as we have mentioned, that this dreadful misery is not for them.[132]

---

128. Edwards, "The Vain Self-Flatteries," 322. Henry observed that if a person did fear God, "he would not talk and act so extravagantly as he doth," for such people deceive themselves by putting a "Cheat" "upon their own Souls." But the day will come when "the Sinner will be undeceiv'd" and his sin will be hateful to him because its consequences will be made manifest. Henry, *Exposition*, [Ps 36:1–2]. Poole likewise observed the deception of sin: "Collusion drove smoothly toward it, so that he began to satisfy himself by his shameful acts" ("Prævaricatio blandè egit apud illum, ut placer incipiat ipse sibi flagitiis suis"). Poole, *Synopsis*, 731. Trapp also noted the self-deception described here; this self-flatterer "stroketh himself on the head, and saith, I shall have peace, though I walk in the stubbornness of mine heart." Trapp, *Commentary*, 674. Dickson said that "the man that feareth not God, doth gull and deceive his own conscience, till he have gotten the iniquity accomplished." Dickson, *First Fifty Psalms*, 237. Calvin recognized that people flatter themselves "that they may not be dissatisfied with themselves in sinning." Calvin, *Commentary*, 2:4.

129. Edwards, "The Vain Self-Flatteries," 322. Calvin, in contrast, interpreted "until his iniquity be found to be hateful" to mean "hateful to all men," since their evil has grown so great in extent. Calvin, *Commentary*, 2:5.

130. Edwards, "The Vain Self-Flatteries," 322.

131. Edwards, "The Vain Self-Flatteries," 322.

132. Edwards, "The Vain Self-Flatteries," 327.

Edwards concluded by calling people to examine themselves to see whether or not they were flattering themselves—and if so, to stop living in delusion.[133]

Similarly, in the summer or fall of 1729, Edwards preached on Ps 10:6, "He hath said in his heart, I shall not be moved: for I shall never be in adversity." Psalm 10 describes the wicked man's evil ways, withholding from the poor and refusing to seek God. This verse, Edwards said, records the account of "that which upholds in him those wicked practices."[134] For a man to stay on a path that leads to self-destruction, he must convince himself that he travels no such path—which is exactly what the wicked man does. Though he may hear warnings that vividly portray the terrors of hell, he convinces himself that he will never be moved. He imagines that his life will never change, for he tells himself, "I shall never meet with any punishment for my wickedness."[135] How else can a man pay no heed to calls for repentance except by believing the warnings of punishment are as substantive as air? For the wicked, "God's judgments are far above out of his sight," and so Edwards preached this doctrine: "That wicked men be not apt to be sensible but that it will always be with them as it is now."[136] Though judgment looms, the wicked "think so little of it," and their "self-flattering disposition" leaves them with a sense of freedom from seriously considering the "approaching changes."[137] Reformed interpreters likewise interpreted this passage to describe the arrogance of the ungodly, who delude themselves about their spiritual state.[138] Edwards was

---

133. Edwards, "The Vain Self-Flatteries," 327–328.

134. Jonathan Edwards, "That Wicked Men Be Not Apt to Be Sensible but That It Will Always Be with Them As It Is Now" (Ps 10:6), in *The Glory and Honor of God: Volume 2 of the Previously Unpublished Sermons of Jonathan Edwards*, ed. Michael D. McMullen (Nashville, TN: Broadman & Holman, 2004), 67.

135. Edwards, "That Wicked Men Be Not Apt," 67.

136. Edwards, "That Wicked Men Be Not Apt," 67, 68.

137. Edwards, "That Wicked Men Be Not Apt," 68.

138. Henry stated that the wicked person "proudly sets Trouble at defiance, and is confident of the continuance of his own Prosperity." Henry, *Exposition*, [Ps 10:6]. Poole noted, "He boasts in his innocence, and on account of this stability, he promises happiness to himself" ("Gloriatur de sua innocentia, & ob eam stabilem sibi felicitatem pollicetur"), but "[t]his is an occasion of arrogance" ("Haec superbiae occasio"). Poole, *Synopsis*, 556. Trapp contrasted the wicked and the believer, for a believer can say he will never be moved because of "that good estate in which Christ hath set him," but for the wicked, who "conceiteth himself that he is innocent," it is "the vain vaunt of presumption." Trapp, *Commentary*, 593. Dickson noted that the wicked "promise to themselves perpetuity of prosperity, and do not fear evil." Dickson, *First Fifty Psalms*, 52. Calvin, like Trapp, distinguished between a Christian and a wicked person, "who, enjoying prosperity today, is so forgetful of the condition of man in this world, as through a distempered imagination to build his nest above the clouds, and

unique in creating an extended reflection on this verse to awaken people from their vain fantasies. Edwards blamed this delusion both on a "preference" for the present world and on "the stupefying nature of sin," as Pss 49:20 and 32:9 testify.[139] In his application, Edwards explained that so many men go to hell because they resist being made sensible of their danger and the means to escape it. He exhorted the wicked

> to consider that it won't always be with them as it is now. Ye who don't mind the sermons you hear and warning given you, ye who think yourselves well enough out in the enjoyment of the world. Ye who now give the reins to your carnal opportunities. The present state that you are ready to imagine to be, all will soon pass away, and there are vast alterations coming.[140]

As a concerned pastor, Edwards preached from the Psalms to awaken his congregation to the impending danger they convinced themselves would not come.

During that same summer or fall, Edwards preached a sermon on sin's power to deceive the soul about God's very existence, for if people could convince themselves that God did not really exist, then they would not fear having to stand before him as their judge. Edwards chose as his text Ps 14:1, "The fool hath said in his heart, There is no God"—a text that David Brainerd, years later, would use to describe his pre-conversion state: "scores of times in this case my heart has wished 'there was no God' (Ps. 14:1)."[141] Edwards interpreted "heart" as referring to "the whole soul" and concluded that "[a]s sin has dominion over the whole soul, so atheism is what taints all the faculties," for sin corrupts the mind to accept lies about God in order to live in ease.[142]

---

who persuades himself that he shall always enjoy comfort and repose." Calvin, *Commentary*, 1:143.

139. Edwards, "That Wicked Men Be Not Apt," 74. Ps 49:20 reads, "Man that is in honour, and understandeth not, is like the beasts that perish," and Ps 32:9 reads, "Be ye not as the horse, or as the mule, which have no understanding."

140. Edwards, "That Wicked Men Be Not Apt," 76.

141. Jonathan Edwards, *The Life of David Brainerd*, ed. Norman Pettit, vol. 7 of *WJE* (1985), 115.

142. Edwards, "Practical Atheism," 47. While Edwards did not describe what the "faculties of the soul" are in this sermon, he later explained in *Religious Affections* that the soul has two faculties: the understanding, by which it perceives and discerns things, and the inclination, which is also called the will and the heart, by which it is inclined or disinclined toward things and by which it exercises its approval or rejection of those things. Edwards, *Religious Affections*, 96.

Thus Edwards developed the doctrine, "A principle of atheism possesses the hearts of all ungodly men."[143] He expanded "atheism" from mere mental disbelief to practical acting out, from the mind to the heart, defining it as "any kind of rejecting, renouncing, or opposing the divine existence or the being of a God with whatever faculty."[144] This "practical atheism" stood in line with Reformed interpreters, who likewise employed this phrase to describe the passage.[145] For example, as Poole explained, the fool denies God's existence not primarily as the "chief Being" (primum Ens) but as "Judge and Governor" (Judicem & Gubernatorem) signified by the psalmist's use of the Hebrew אֱלֹהִים rather than יְהוָה, and so denying God's existence is essentially denying that one will be called to account for his life, which is why atheism is described as "the origin of all evil" (de origine omnium malorum).[146] Edwards likewise took this passage in the direction that what is really at the heart of practical atheism is the denial that God will judge a person's actions: "Ungodly men are prone practically to deny the being of God; that is, to live as if there was no God, to live without any respect or regard to him, as if he were not, or had nothing to do with them, or were any way concerned about the government and ordering of the world."[147] Edwards identified three causes of this atheistic principle: "the benumbing, stupefying nature" of sin; sinners' "aversion to divine and spiritual things"; and "an habitual dependence on their senses."[148] The third cause emerged powerfully in Edwards' day when men were wont to "believe nothing" or "realize nothing, but what is the object of sense."[149] Here he pinpointed

---

143. Edwards, "Practical Atheism," 47.

144. Edwards, "Practical Atheism," 48.

145. Henry said, "there is something of practical Atheism at the bottom of all Sin." Henry, Exposition, [Ps 14:1]. Trapp recognized that "there are practicall Atheists as well as Dogmaticall." Trapp, Commentary, 602. Dickson stated that "all the un-regenerate" are "practically Atheists." Dickson, First Fifty Psalms, 66. Calvin did not use the phrase "practical atheism" but described the concept; while people may not hold to "drawn out arguments or formal syllogisms," they deny God's position as judge: "As if the time would never come when they will have to appear before him in judgment, they endeavour, in all the transactions and concerns of their life, to remove him to the greatest distance, and to efface from their minds all apprehension of his majesty." Calvin, Commentary, 1:190–191.

146. Poole, Synopsis, 576. Edwards did not cite Poole or any other interpreters in his notes on this verse.

147. Edwards, "Practical Atheism," 53. Similarly, Henry stated, "there is no Man will say, There is no God, till he is so harden'd in Sin, that 'tis become his Interest there should be none to call him to Account." Henry, Exposition, [Ps 14:1].

148. Edwards, "Practical Atheism," 51–52.

149. Edwards, "Practical Atheism," 52.

the epistemological direction of Enlightenment thinking, which relied on the
natural senses and undermined the supernatural. In his application, Edwards
explained that because men are not apt to choose pain for themselves, the wicked
must be practical atheists, for "if men were not in a considerable measure atheists, it would be utterly impossible that they should go on and live so peaceably
and quietly in every wickedness and commit sin so boldly as they do under such
warnings as they have."[150] That people willingly deceive themselves to such an
extent so they do not have to change their wicked ways reveals "[t]he dismal waste
that the fall has made in man's soul: that he should be so separated and removed
from God that he should question his being, that the light of his mind should be
so put out, that he should question the very being of that only being and author
of all things, that he should be without the knowledge that is the main end of the
faculty of reason."[151] The fall into sin had so warped man's thinking that he had
grown accustomed to deluding himself about the most important issues related
to his soul, all in a (futile) effort to ease his soul from its inner turmoil.

Edwards again preached on the human sluggishness to recognize one's sin
in a September 1739 sermon on Ps 19:12. He first described the psalm's purpose
of extolling the excellency and purity of God's Word and the benefits of keeping
God's law. Thinking upon these things turned the psalmist to "self reflextion
& to consider how far he was Conformed to this Excellent pure Law of G[od],"
which led to his outcry, "Who can understand his errors? cleanse thou me
from secret faults" (Ps 19:12).[152] The term "errors" includes "every deviation"
from God's perfect word, but understanding these errors is no simple task, for
"[']tis exceeding difficult & indeed impossible without divine help for a m[an]
to understand his own Errours," which is why the psalmist asks for God's discerning help.[153] The phrase "secret faults" refers not to sins he had done privately but to sins of which he was unaware.[154] David offered Christians a good

---

150. Edwards, "Practical Atheism," 54.

151. Edwards, "Practical Atheism," 56.

152. Jonathan Edwards, "517. Sermon on Ps 19:12 (September 1739)," in *Sermons, Series II, 1739*, vol. 54 of the *WJEO*, L. 1r.

153. Edwards, "517. Sermon on Ps 19:12," L. 1v.

154. Henry and Trapp recognized that these "secret faults" could validly refer to being secret either from the world or from the self. Henry, *Exposition*, [Ps 19:12]; Trapp, *Commentary*, 626. But Calvin interpreted it, like Edwards, only as secret from the self, for these secret sins are "those with respect to which men deceive themselves, by thinking that they are no sins, and who thus deceive themselves not only purposely and by expressly aiming at doing so, but because they do not enter into the due consideration of the majesty of the judgment of God." Calvin, *Commentary*, 1:329.

model, for he was fully aware of how deceitful his own heart could be, and he was "much afraid of living in some way that was displeasing to G[od] insensibly to hims[elf]," so throughout the Psalms he often asked God to search his heart (e.g., Pss 26:2; 139:23–24).[155] Thus Edwards preached the doctrine, "[']Tis an Exceeding hard thing for men to be sensible that are sinfull & offensive to G[od]."[156] Original sin has made the human by nature spiritually blind so that "man is naturally totally Ign[orant] of G[od] in his divine Excellency & next to him he is most Ign[orant] of hims[elf]"[157] In this assertion Edwards quite clearly, if unwittingly, reflected Calvin's teaching in the *Institutes of the Christian Religion* that knowledge of oneself is predicated upon knowledge of God. For Calvin knowledge of God and knowledge of ourselves are necessarily bound together, and true wisdom consists of both forms of knowledge. Without one our knowledge is incomplete, and Calvin illustrated this by describing the human who deceives himself by not giving due thought to God:

> it is certain that man never achieves a clear knowledge of himself unless he has first looked upon God's face, and then descends from contemplating him to scrutinize himself. For we always seem to ourselves righteous and upright and wise and holy—this pride is innate in all of us—unless by clear proofs we stand convinced of our own unrighteousness, foulness, folly, and impurity. Moreover, we are not thus convinced if we look merely to ourselves and not also to the Lord, who is the sole standard by which this judgment must be measured.[158]

Like Calvin, Edwards understood how hard it is for people to sense their sin because sin is such a blinding darkness that perverts the inclination, which in turn "tends by a Reflex act to prejudice & further to Decieve the Understanding."[159] Because humans cannot bear to live with tension in

155. Edwards, "517. Sermon on Ps 19:12," L. 2r. Other Reformed interpreters emphasized God's mercy more than Edwards in their commentary on this verse. Henry, Poole, Trapp, Dickson, and Calvin all viewed this statement in Ps 19:12 as a recognition that humanity can never live up to God's law and must run to God for his mercy. Henry, *Exposition*, [Ps 19:12]; Trapp, *Commentary*, 626; Dickson, *First Fifty Psalms*, 106; Calvin, *Commentary*, 1:329. Poole summarizes it well: "This exclamation declares the mercy of God to be necessary" ("Hac exclamatione declarat misericordiam Dei necessariam esse"). Poole, *Synopsis*, 632.

156. Edwards, "517. Sermon on Ps 19:12," L. 2v.

157. Edwards, "517. Sermon on Ps 19:12," L. 3r.

158. John Calvin, *The Institutes of the Christian Religion*, ed. John T. McNeill and trans. Ford Lewis Battles, vol. 1 (Louisville, KY: Westminster John Knox, 2006), 37.

159. Edwards, "517. Sermon on Ps 19:12," L. 10r.

their minds and hearts, they "bring their principles & their practices to Agree together" to "Ease" their souls, "for they find that to live with principles and practices at variance under such light is to live a very uncomfortable disquieted Life."[160] And if their practices and principles do not agree, they often change their principles to agree with their practices, settling into a deluded complacency to convince themselves—against reason—that everything is okay, for "their self love prejudices against thinking their state to be so miserable[.] They would feign have it that they are in a pretty Good Estate."[161] So Edwards exhorted his people to examine their hearts and ask God to reveal their hidden faults, for people's hidden sins "often prove their Eternal undoing" since "your heart & ways are finally to be tried by him who can[']t fein of understanding your Err[ors]."[162]

Edwards believed that this deeply rooted sin corrodes and corrupts the heart, accomplishing its destructive aim by hiding its work of decay from the unsuspecting victim—a victim who happily complies because he does not want to know the truth about his sorry state, even though his sin should be quite clear in his mind since it is so blatantly obvious for all to see. Still, the blinding work of sin did not nullify all hope for the sinner.

A Path from Sin to Hope

Edwards was not interested in sin merely for sin's sake, to reflect on the gruesome nature of it as an end in itself. For Edwards the odiousness of sin highlighted the grandeur of God and the infinite kindness of his grace. It is fitting, then, as we close this chapter to mirror Edwards' homiletical practice and consider two sermons on the Psalms that lay out the path from his view of sin to his view of God's grace.

In March 1752 Edwards preached a sermon to the Stockbridge Indians on the subject of "the Infinite Evil of Sin" from Ps 5:4–5, "For thou art not a God that hath pleasure in wickedness: neither shall evil dwell with thee. The foolish shall not stand in thy sight: thou hatest all workers of iniquity."[163] In the doctrinal section of the sermon, Edwards contrasted humanity's despicable

---

160. Edwards, "517. Sermon on Ps 19:12," L. 10v.

161. Edwards, "517. Sermon on Ps 19:12," L. 11v.

162. Edwards, "517. Sermon on Ps 19:12," L. 17r., 18v., 24v. See Edwards' similar comment on Ps 19:12 in "Notes on Scripture" Entry No. 360. Edwards, *Notes on Scripture*, 345.

163. Jonathan Edwards, "1030. Sermon on Ps 5:4–5 (March 1752)," Beinecke Rare Book and Manuscript Library, Yale University, New Haven, CT, L. 1r.

sin with God's excellency—a rather unique emphasis from this passage.[164] Sin is made all the worse because it is against our Creator, who is "so good a G[od]" and "so excellent & Lovely" and who has "shown so much mercy."[165] In his application, Edwards explained that because sin is committed against such a good God, it is strictly forbidden and deserves God's severe punishment, which is why we see so many calamities, wars, and death—even hell itself. God's excellency also explains how great the gospel is, for such great sin shows that men cannot satisfy the price of their own sins but that the blood of Christ is necessary to make satisfaction—thus how "great a mercy is the forgiveness of sin."[166] Edwards thus sought to awaken sinners by showing them their sorrowful state without Christ for "all sins are infinitely Evil."[167] He exhorted them to stop sinning, to confess their iniquities regularly, and to ask God to reveal their sinfulness. Then he brought the sermon back full circle to God's greatness, for God's greatness not only implicates men in their evil but draws them out of their sinfulness. So he called them to pray that God would "open your Eyes to see his glory."[168] For Edwards, God's glory explained both why sin is infinitely evil and why God's work of redemption is so gracious.

Edwards brought together the depth of human sin and the weight of God's glorious grace in an undated sermon on Ps 25:11, "For thy name's sake, O LORD, pardon mine iniquity; for it is great." The last stanza of the psalm (vv. 15–22) suggested to Edwards that David wrote it to plead for God's deliverance from his enemies. All his distresses caused him to reflect on and confess his sins, and David gave two seemingly contrary reasons for why God should pardon him: God's glory and his own sin. First, he pled for the sake of God's name. David recognized his own unworthiness and looked not to men but appealed to God's honor, begging God to pardon him "for his own glory, for

---

164. Henry also saw this passage as a testimony of God's excellency, pointing out "[t]he *Holiness* of GOD's Nature" in that he is "a GOD that *hatest* [sin], as directly contrary to thine infinite Purity and Rectitude, and Holy Will." Henry, *Exposition*, [Ps 5:4–6]. In contrast, neither Poole, Trapp, Dickson, or Calvin followed that line of thought, instead focusing on God's disgust for sin and the wicked. Poole, *Synopsis*, 516; Trapp, *Commentary*, 576–577; Dickson, *First Fifty Psalms*, 25–26; Calvin, *Commentary*, 1:55–57. Poole emphasized, for example, how "mad" or "insane" ("insanos") are these foolish people who work iniquity. Poole, *Synopsis*, 516.

165. Edwards, "1030. Sermon on Ps 5:4–5," L. 1r.

166. Edwards, "1030. Sermon on Ps 5:4–5," L. 2r.

167. Edwards, "1030. Sermon on Ps 5:4–5," L. 2v.

168. Edwards, "1030. Sermon on Ps 5:4–5," L. 4v.

the glory of his own free grace, and for the honor of his own covenant faithfulness."[169] Second, he pled for mercy not because of the smallness and insignificance of his sins but because they were so offensive. David denied that the good he had done could "counterbalance" his sin but rather, as a beggar makes known the greatness of his tragedy, so David heightened the seriousness of his sin to make the case for his need of mercy.[170] It was as if to say, "my case will be exceedingly miserable, unless thou be pleased to pardon me," and God entertained such a plea, not because sinners "are worthy, but because they need his pity."[171] Thus Edwards preached the doctrine, "If we truly come to God for mercy, the greatness of our sin will be no impediment to pardon."[172] In fact, God's pardon of great sin only raises up the glory of his grace all the more—an emphasis regularly repeated by Reformed commentators on this verse.[173] So from a Psalms text on sin, Edwards launched into a discussion of our need to come to God for mercy, to be made aware of our misery and unworthiness, and he exhorted his people to approach God "as beggars, not as creditors," to "come for mere mercy, for sovereign grace, and not for anything that is due."[174] That means they can only come through Jesus Christ, for God's mercy is sufficient for the greatest of sins because "his mercy is infinite" and

---

169. Jonathan Edwards, "Great Guilt No Obstacle to the Pardon of the Returning Sinner" (Ps 25:11), in vol. 4 of *Works of President Edwards* (Worcester ed.), 8th ed. (1778; repr., New York: Leavitt & Allen, 1852), 422.

170. Edwards, "Great Guilt No Obstacle," 422.

171. Edwards, "Great Guilt No Obstacle," 422. See Edwards' similar discussion on Ps 25:11 in *The "Blank Bible,"* 489.

172. Edwards, "Great Guilt No Obstacle," 422.

173. Henry recognized that "the greater [iniquity] is, the more will Divine Mercy be magnify'd in the forgiveness of it. 'Tis the Glory of a Great GOD to forgive great Sins." Henry, *Exposition*, [Ps 25:11]. Poole argued that "it is fitting to a great God, that he remits great sins" ("Convenit Deo magno, ut magna peccata remittat"), and "it is rightly called *great* [or *many*]; for this sin is not singular or simple, but multitudinous and complex" ("rectè id vocat *multum*; nam peccatum illud non unicum aut simplex fuit, sed multiplex"). Poole, *Synopsis*, 674. Trapp also described God as one who "delighteth in mercy, and makest thy power appear in pardoning *the many and horrid sins* of thy poor penitents," for "[t]he more desperate was my disease, the greater is the glory of my Physician, who hath fully cured mee." Trapp, *Commentary*, 643. In the same way, Dickson exclaimed, "the Lord counts it a glory to be mercifull." Dickson, *First Fifty Psalms*, 144. And Calvin recognized in this verse that God pardons people "from no other cause than his own good pleasure," for it is as though David said, "My sins are, indeed, like a heavy burden which overwhelms me, so that the multitude or enormity of them might well deprive me of all hope of pardon; but, Lord, the infinite glory of thy name will not suffer thee to cast me off." Calvin, *Commentary*, 1:426.

174. Edwards, "Great Guilt No Obstacle," 423.

"the *satisfaction of Christ* is as sufficient for the removal of the greatest guilt, as the least."[175] This Psalms text spoke, in Edwards' view, of God's great glory in the work of redemption, for "[h]erein doth the *glory of grace* by the redemption of Christ much consist, viz., in its sufficiency for the pardon of the greatest sinners."[176] From eternity past God planned to glorify his free grace in this manner, for indeed, "[t]he whole contrivance of the way of salvation is for this end."[177] And so Edwards again preached the gospel from the Psalms, encouraging "sinners whose consciences are burdened with a sense of guilt, immediately to go to God through Christ for mercy."[178]

Conclusion

In Edwards' reading of the Psalms, he saw humanity depicted primarily in its fallen state—weak, feeble, liable to death, obstinately blind, and resistant to God's grace. Yet Christ, by joining human nature to divine nature, offers humanity a new nature; rather than remaining in a post-Fall state, humanity can find redemption in Christ and can become like him in his glorified state. Sin is a serious barrier that must be overcome, for it is innate to the human heart as a result of the Fall. Original sin infects the entire human race, and sin so deceives people that they believe themselves immune to God's judgment. But sin is no small thing; it is an infinite evil that God rightly punishes though, at the same time, God offers humanity redemption from its sinful state to glorify his grace.

This interpretation of the Psalms followed the contours of Reformed understandings of human nature and sin as presented in the Psalms, differing only on minor interpretive points. If Edwards carried a unique emphasis on human nature, it was on a lower view of humanity than his Reformed predecessors, placing humans far below angels and more quickly applying spiritual blindness universally to the whole human race. And where Edwards stood out on the discussion of sin in the Psalms lay not in his doctrinal convictions but in his pastoral practice of developing extended reflections on Psalms texts to arouse deaf sinners. Earlier Reformed interpreters shared this interest, but Edwards especially emphasized preaching on sin from the Psalms to probe at the dull consciences of his people more than attending to exegetical details.

---

175. Edwards, "Great Guilt No Obstacle," 423, 424. Italics original.

176. Edwards, "Great Guilt No Obstacle," 425. Italics original.

177. Edwards, "Great Guilt No Obstacle," 425.

178. Edwards, "Great Guilt No Obstacle," 425–426.

He also highlighted God's excellency and glory more often when encountering human sin in the Psalms.

Edwards' exegesis of the Psalms with regard to humanity and sin shows that he interpreted the Psalms literally and theologically, constrained by the analogy of Scripture, to describe the problem of human weakness and depravity and that he grounded his doctrine of original sin in the Psalms. This is not to deny Edwards' philosophical creativity in his doctrine of original sin. But it does highlight the Bible's foundational place in his theology; his doctrine was not simply philosophically driven. As he engaged exegetical arguments against original sin, he developed his counterarguments from his detailed exegesis of debated Psalms texts. His engagement with the Psalms on these theological themes also manifests his resounding emphasis on the gospel from the Psalter. For Edwards, discussing humanity and sin in the Psalms served to set the stage for God's great work of redemption, which brought glory to his name. With this gospel-saturated interpretation of the Psalms, it is no wonder that he spoke at length about the person and work of Christ.

4

Christ

Sacrifice and offering thou didst not desire;
mine ears hast thou opened:
burnt offering and sin offering hast thou not required.
Then said I, Lo, I come:
in the volume of the book it is written of me,
I delight to do thy will, O my God:
yea, thy law is within my heart.
Psalm 40:6–8

WHEN JONATHAN EDWARDS identified the person of Jesus Christ in the Psalms, he was not doing anything radically new in the Christian church. For centuries theologians had identified Christ in the Old Testament generally and in the Psalms particularly. Augustine understood the Psalms as "a prophecy of the mystery of Christ in his totality—of Christ, head and body (the *totus Christus*)."[1] Thomas Aquinas likewise held this "rule" for the Psalms: "The things related are to be interpreted as prefiguring something about Christ or the Church."[2] Even Calvin connected the Psalms with Christ, looking for the fulfillment of God's promised unending royal line to David in Jesus Christ, a son of David, and casting David's house and kingdom as "a shadow image of Christ's authority as Lord."[3] Edwards' contemporary, Cotton Mather, stated

---

1. Michael Fiedrowicz, "General Introduction," in *Expositions of the Psalms: 1–32*, trans. Maria Boulding and ed. John E. Rotelle, part III, vol. 15 of *The Works of Saint Augustine* (Hyde Park, NY: New City, 2000), 43. On Augustine seeing Christ (and the church) in the Psalms, see Fiedrowicz, 45–60.

2. Thomas Aquinas, *The Gifts of the Spirit: Selected Spiritual Writings*, ed. Benedict M. Ashley and trans. Matthew Rzeczkowski (Hyde Park, NY: New City, 1995), 100. Thomas explained: "Prophecies were, of course, sometimes pronounced about things of that time, but they were not said principally about them, except insofar as they were a prefiguration of future things. The Holy Spirit ordained that when such things were spoken of, certain things were included that surpassed the condition of the event." Aquinas, *The Gifts of the Spirit*, 100.

3. Wulfert de Greef, "Calvin's Understanding and Interpretation of the Bible," trans. David Dichelle, in *John Calvin's Impact on Church and Society, 1509–2009*, ed. Martin Ernst Hirzel

this reigning principle succinctly: "In short, Jesus Christ is the key that unlocks all the Scriptures. We have searched the Scriptures, and know them to good purpose, when we have dug so far into them, as to find them all testifying of the Lord Jesus Christ."[4]

In Edwards' day, however, some interpreters began reading the Old Testament strictly in its ancient historical context without reference to Jesus Christ. Anthony Collins (1676–1729) foreshadowed this thinking by accepting only one literal fulfillment of Old Testament prophecy, most often accomplished in the prophet's own day, not in Christ. And Thomas Morgan (1680–1743) embraced it by emphasizing the Old Testament as a historical Jewish religion and by completely rejecting it as part of the Christian Bible. Morgan cut the typological cord linking the Old Testament with the New.[5] That is why Susan Gillingham notes that the eighteenth century was a time when "gradually everything became open to question" and when "it became fashionable to bypass the difficult questions of the contemporary relevance of psalmody and to analyse instead the texts of the psalms as examples of ancient poetry."[6]

Edwards was unconvinced. He believed that severing the Psalms' connection to Christ constituted a misreading of the Scriptures. Of the Old Testament books, the Psalms stood out as a stellar witness to Christ. Edwards revealed his approach to the Psalms in a sermon on Ps 21:4, which says of the "king" that "[h]e asked life of thee, and thou gavest it him, even length of days forever and ever." While the king refers on one level to David, the Holy Spirit intended it to refer on another level to Christ, and Edwards observed that this dual meaning was "very common in the psalms of David" and that the New Testament

---

and Martin Sallmann (Grand Rapids, MI: Eerdmans, 2009), 84. Calvin sought to use the New Testament as his guide for finding Christ in the Old, and while he was more reserved than others, he held that failing to recognize Christ in the Old Testament would cause one to "remain in the dark." De Greef, 88. See also G. Sujin Pak, *Judaizing Calvin: Sixteenth-Century Debates over the Messianic Psalms*, Oxford Studies in Historical Theology (New York: Oxford University Press, 2010), 134, 138.

4. Cotton Mather, *Addresses to Old Men, and Young Men, and Little Children* (Boston: R. Pierce, for Nicholas Buttolph, 1690), 9–10.

5. Henning Graf Reventlow, "English Deism and Anti-Deist Apologetic," in vol. 2 of *Hebrew Bible, Old Testament: The History of Its Interpretation*, ed. Magne Sæbø (Göttingen: Vandenhoeck & Ruprecht, 2008), 862–864, 867–869.

6. In this "historically oriented reading," exegetes read the psalms "for their own sake." Johann David Michaelis thus produced a commentary on the Psalms in 1745, for example, that primarily offered historical and linguistic notes. Susan E. Gillingham, *Psalms Through the Centuries*, vol. 1, Blackwell Bible Commentaries (Malden, MA: Blackwell, 2008), 199.

appropriation of the Psalms confirms that they often apply to Christ.[7] As Edwards engaged the Psalms, then, it is no surprise that he frequently interpreted them as teaching about Christ.

As Edwards read the Psalms, the unity of Scripture provided the basis for his typological, prophetic, and Christological interpretation of the Psalms. As one who believed that the Bible is inspired by the Holy Spirit, who brought the disparate parts together into a harmonic whole, and that the Old Testament points to Christ, who purchased salvation for the world, then it only made sense to seek parallels between the Psalms and the Gospels. For Edwards the Bible was unified by the history of redemption, which provided him the exegetical framework for reading the Psalms. From this theological vantage point, Edwards highlighted the person and work of Christ in the Psalter because he is the central figure in the history of redemption. While Edwards' Christological interpretation of the Psalms at times may seem like a stretch to some modern interpreters, he was not boundless in his interpretation, but in fact, like most in the Reformed tradition preceding him, he used the analogy of Scripture as a guide and model for exploring the life and work of Christ in the Psalms, and the history of redemption provided the boundaries for his Christological interpretation of the Psalter.

We first explore the Old Testament foretelling of Christ, examining both types and prophecies of the Messiah. Then we move to particular aspects of Christ's life as described in the Psalter, especially his voluntary obedience to God's will as a devoted servant. From there we discuss Christ's redemptive work, a key emphasis in Edwards' engagement with the Psalms, followed by his glorification and kingly reign.

Foretelling of Christ

Edwards described the temporal relationship between the Psalms and Christ primarily in terms of typology and prophecy. Types prefigure Christ and his gospel in historical persons or events, representing him in shadows and veiled images that find their full embodiment in Christ and his times. Prophecies foretell specific details about the Messiah and his gospel, and while they are rooted in an ancient historical setting, they point to a future time when the fullness of their meaning will be fulfilled in Christ.

It is clear that Edwards recognized a distinction between these two modes of discourse because he planned "The Harmony of the Old and New

---

7. Jonathan Edwards, "The Terms of Prayer" (Ps 21:4), in *Sermons and Discourses 1734–1738*, ed. M. X. Lesser, vol. 19 of *WJE* (2001), 771–772. Quotation on 771.

Testament" to include separate sections on prophecies of the Messiah, the fulfillment of those prophecies, and types of the Messiah.[8] At the same time, as
Wallace Anderson explains, this plan for the "Harmony" demonstrates Edwards'
belief that prophecy and typology were integral to each other, for "[t]he trustwor-
thiness of the Old Testament and its prophetic content was essential to his view
of typology."[9] In practice Edwards sometimes blurred the distinction between the
two categories, but both types and prophecies formed a foundation for Edwards'
Christological vision of the Psalms—that the Psalms were a reliable testimony to
the person and work of Christ because the Bible speaks in a unified voice.

Types of the Messiah

Edwards kept a notebook on "Types of the Messiah," which he planned to integrate into one section of his "The Harmony of the Old and New Testament."
As Marsden explains, based on his notes for the "Harmony," Edwards simply
rejected "the premise of the critics that Scripture was to be interpreted like
other books. If Scripture were in some sense a revelation of God—as most
of the critics still allowed—then its design must contain excellencies that far
transcended the vicissitudes of the historical circumstances or the limits of
the language in which it happened to be revealed."[10] So Edwards amassed all
manner of typological and Christological evidence to show the uniqueness
and the unity of the Bible. He aimed, as Kenneth Minkema notes, to show
both "the authenticity and unity of the Scriptures" and "that biblical prophecies, types, and harmonies find their ultimate meaning in the person of the
incarnate Logos as Messiah."[11] Messianic types were critical to Edwards' view

---

8. Mason Lowance, Jr. and David Watters note: "We must be careful to distinguish *prophecy*
as a mode of discourse from *typology* as Edwards understood them." Mason I. Lowance,
Jr., and David H. Watters, "Editor's Introduction to 'Types of the Messiah,'" in Jonathan
Edwards, *Typological Writings*, ed. Wallace E. Anderson and Mason I. Lowance Jr. with David
H. Watters, vol. 11 of *WJE* (1992), 159.

9. Wallace E. Anderson, "Editor's Introduction to 'Images of Divine Things' and 'Types,'" in
Typological Writings, ed. Wallace E. Anderson and Mason I. Lowance, Jr., with David Watters,
Vol. 11 of *WJE* (1992), 13.

10. George M. Marsden, *Jonathan Edwards: A Life* (New Haven, CT: Yale University Press,
2003), 480.

11. Kenneth P. Minkema, "The Other Unfinished 'Great Work': Jonathan Edwards, Messianic
Prophecy, and 'The Harmony of the Old and New Testament,'" in *Jonathan Edwards's
Writings: Text, Context, Interpretation*, ed. Stephen J. Stein (Bloomington: Indiana University
Press, 1996), 53. For more on Edwards' "Harmony," see Minkema, "The Other Unfinished
'Great Work,'" 52–65, where he contextualizes this work as a polemical piece defending the

of the Bible, and he ruminated on them both in his "Types of the Messiah" notebook and throughout his corpus.

Space does not permit a full treatment of how Edwards engaged the Psalms in "Types of the Messiah," but this notebook does illustrate his desire to demonstrate the unity of the Bible through a robust treatment of types, and it particularly shows how he understood the Psalms to typify Christ and his gospel.[12] In his approach to this notebook, Edwards frequently used the analogy of Scripture and often turned to the Psalms for insight into the meaning of images from other parts of the Bible, and vice versa.[13] Edwards developed a thick description of types—too many to recount here—that relied heavily on the whole Bible and used the Psalms extensively to accomplish his goals of identifying shadows of the Messiah. As Stephen R. C. Nichols, explains, "In the scheme of God-glorifying redemption history, types shadow forth spiritual substance in a relationship thought of by God."[14]

In "Types of the Messiah," Edwards observed a typological correlation between events in Israel's history as recorded in the Psalms and the Messiah and his times. For example, Edwards said that as Ps 68:6–9 records God's deliverance of Israel out of Egypt, so it also points to the Messiah's deliverance of his people from their chains. As Edwards summarized it, "These things do abundantly confirm that the redemption out of Egypt, and the circumstances and events that attended it, were intended by the Great Disposer of all things to be types of the redemption of God's people by the Messiah, and of things appertaining to that redemption."[15] Another event typifying the Messiah was God's preservation of Noah, his family, and the animals from the flood, which showed "remarkable agreement" with his "preservation and salvation of the

---

Bible; and Stephen R. C. Nichols, *Jonathan Edwards's Bible: The Relationship of the Old and New Testaments in the Theology of Jonathan Edwards* (Eugene, OR: Pickwick, 2013).

12. The types Edwards discussed in this notebook did not always lead to Christ. For example, David's miraculous ability to kill the lion and bear and save his sheep was "plainly and evidently to be a type, sign and encouragement" that God would enable David to deliver his people. Jonathan Edwards, "Types of the Messiah," in *Typological Writings*, ed. Mason I. Lowance Jr. with David H. Watters, vol. 11 of *WJE* (1992), 200.

13. For example, when he explained that the twelve fountains of water at Elim in Exod 15:27 were types of the twelve patriarchs, he looked to Ps 68:26, which identifies the Lord as "the fountain of Israel," to establish that "fountain" often refers to the "paternity" of a tribe or nation. Edwards, "Types of the Messiah," 196.

14. Nichols, *Jonathan Edwards's Bible*, 93. Nichols holds that, ultimately, "Edwards's typology is a unitary approach agreeable to his metaphysical commitments and guided by Scripture." Nichols, *Jonathan Edwards's Bible*, 94.

15. Edwards, "Types of the Messiah," 210, 212–214. Quotation on 214.

church by the Messiah" and which Ps 46:1–3 captured by speaking of the mountains being carried into the midst of the sea.[16]

The primary way that Edwards used Psalms-based typology in his "Types of the Messiah" manuscript was pointing to individuals, such as Samson, David, and Solomon. Edwards saw Samson's strength as a type of the Messiah's great strength, following Ps 89:19, "Then thou spakest in vision to thy holy one, and saidst, I have laid help upon one that is mighty," and Ps 45:3, "Gird thy sword upon thy thigh, O most mighty, with thy glory and thy majesty."[17] But in a less expected manner, he also connected Samson's taste in women with the Messiah's choice of a spouse, that is, his church. As Samson married a Philistine and as "all the women that he loved were of that people that were his great enemies," so the Messiah marries "an alien from the commonwealth of Israel, as Ps. 45," typifying "the many prophecies that speak of Christ's calling the Gentiles and his saving sinners."[18]

Edwards saw "a more remarkable, manifest and manifold agreement between the things said of David in his history and the things said of the Messiah in the prophecies."[19] For example, as 2 Sam 22:51 says, "He is the tower of salvation for his king," that is, David, so Ps 2:6 says of the Messiah, "I have set my king on my holy hill in Zion."[20] As this example shows, in "Types of the Messiah" Edwards often spoke of the type using the historical books of the Bible and referred to the antitype, the Messiah, using the Psalms.[21] Outside of "Types of the Messiah," Edwards also described David as "the ancestor and great type of Christ," and because of the special favor God showed toward David by anointing him king and by committing his church to be in David's family forever, "his anointing may in some respects be looked on as an anointing of Christ himself"—so Ps 89:20 records, "I have found David my servant; with my holy oil have I anointed him."[22] Indeed, Edwards observed that many

---

16. Edwards, "Types of the Messiah," 222. Edwards also quoted Pss 32:6 and 91:7. See Edwards' similar discussion of Ps 69:14–15 in "Types of the Messiah," 237–238.

17. Edwards, "Types of the Messiah," 255–256.

18. Edwards, "Types of the Messiah," 255.

19. Edwards, "Types of the Messiah," 259.

20. Edwards, "Types of the Messiah," 259.

21. As another example of this method, see Edwards' comparison between 2 Sam 23:1 and Pss 89:19, 27; 45:6; and 110:1. Edwards, "Types of the Messiah," 270.

22. Jonathan Edwards, *A History of the Work of Redemption*, ed. John F. Wilson, vol. 9 of *WJE* (1989), 204–205. See also Edwards' "Miscellanies" Entry No. 769, where he used the Psalms to identify Moses and David as types of Christ from the Scriptures, pointing to Pss 106:23

"eminent persons" were plainly spoken of as types of the Messiah, including David in Psalm 89, "where the name of David is mentioned once and again, and yet the psalm evidently looks beyond David to the Messiah," and Solomon in Psalm 72, "which the title declares to have respect to Solomon, and yet the matter of the psalm most evidently shows that it has respect to the Messiah, many things in it being true of the Messiah and peculiar to him, and not true of Solomon."[23] Other Reformed interpreters also recognized these types.[24] These short descriptions give only a taste of how Edwards showed individuals typifying the Messiah.[25]

Outside "Types of the Messiah," Edwards identified types of Christ in structures, such as the temple and Noah's ark, and substances.[26] One distinctive type of Christ that Edwards developed was the manna God provided to the children of Israel in the Sinai wilderness. He based this type on Ps 78:25, "Man did eat angels' food: he sent them meat to the full." In "Miscellanies" Entry No.

---

and 78:67–72, respectively. Jonathan Edwards, The "Miscellanies": Entry Nos. 501–832, ed. Ava Chamberlain, vol. 18 of WJE (2000), 415.

23. Edwards, "Types of the Messiah," 304–305. See also, e.g., Edwards' development of Solomon as a type of the Messiah from Pss 2:2–6; 118:22; 96:10–13; 97:1, 8, 12; 98:4–9; 100:1–2; 89:2–3, 20–21, 25, 36–37; 45:6; 110:1, 4. Edwards, "Types of the Messiah," 279, 281, 284.

24. Henry, Trapp, and Dickson all identified David as a type or figure of Christ in Psalm 89, while Poole and Calvin recognized that Christ was the ultimate fulfillment of this promise but did not use the language of "type." As for Psalm 72, Henry, Poole, Trapp, and Dickson identified Solomon as a type or shadow of Christ. Calvin saw it as typical of Christ's kingdom but warned against interpreting it "simply as a prophecy of the kingdom of Christ" because that puts "a construction upon the words which does violence to them" and gives "the Jews occasion of making an outcry." John Calvin, Commentary on the Psalms, trans. from the Original Latin and Collated with the Author's French Version by James Anderson (1843–1855; repr., Grand Rapids, MI: Eerdmans, 1963), 3:100, 422; Matthew Henry, An exposition of the five poetical books of the Old Testament; viz. Job, Psalms, Proverbs, Ecclesiastes, and Solomon's song...(London: T. Darrack..., 1710), [Psalm 72; 89]; Matthew Poole, Synopsis Criticorum Aliorumque Sacrae Scripturae Interpretum et Commentarum, Summo Studio et Fide Adornata, vol. II: Complectens Libros Jobi, Psalmorum, Proverbiorum, Ecclesiastis, & Cantici Canticorum (Francofurti ad Moenum: Balthasaris Christophori Wustii, 1678), 963, 1062; John Trapp, A Commentary or Exposition Upon the Books of Ezra, Nehemiah, Esther, Job, and Psalms...(London: T. R. and E. M. for Thomas Newberry..., 1657), 768, 806; David Dickson, A Brief Explication of the other fifty Psalmes, From Ps. 50 to Ps. 100 (London: T. R. and E. M. for Ralph Smith..., 1653), 143, 306.

25. See also, e.g., Edwards' use of the Psalms to describe Jonah and Joseph as types of Christ. Jonathan Edwards, Notes on Scripture, ed. Stephen J. Stein, vol. 15 of WJE (1998), 78–79; Jonathan Edwards, The "Blank Bible," ed. Stephen J. Stein, vol. 24 of WJE (2006), 512.

26. On Edwards' use of Ps 78:69 to show that Christ is that "antitype" of the temple and thus explains how "the temple in effect remained forever," see Edwards, The "Blank Bible," 514. On his use of the Psalms to show that Noah's ark was "a type of the church in Christ," see "Notes on Scripture" Entry No. 297 on Gen 7:1–8:12. Edwards, Notes on Scripture, 269–270.

120, "Angels," written between March and May 1724, Edwards extrapolated from this verse that just as the Father communicates himself to fallen man by his Son, so he communicates himself to angels—"hence the manna, as it typified Christ, is called angels' food."[27] This identification was rare amongst Reformed interpreters; instead, they focused on the excellent quality of the manna since it would be fit for angels (if they ate substance), on their possible ministry of delivering it, and on the thankfulness that the angels would have for it that the Jews did not. Only Calvin recognized the potential for a type since Paul describes manna as "a figure and symbol of Christ" in 1 Cor 10:3, though he did not pursue it.[28]

Edwards, however, did explore the manna's typological significance in a sermon on this text between August 1731 and December 1732. Reflecting on the meaning of "angels' food," he deduced from the New Testament that it typified Christ. In what way could manna—called "bread of heaven" in Ps 105:40—be called "angels' food" when angels are "Pure spirits" who do not eat any "material substance"?[29] Edwards found clarification in John 6, where Jesus identified "the true bread from heaven" as "he which cometh down from heaven, and giveth life unto the world" (vv. 31–33) and contrasted the manna in the desert with himself, "the living bread" that can make people "live for ever" (vv. 49–51). As manna typified "angels' food," so Edwards compared manna to the sacramental bread of the Lord's Supper, representing both Christ and his benefits. Thus he preached the doctrine, "Those that [spiritually feed on] [Christ,] they Eat Angels['] food."[30] Feeding on Christ means, first, beholding Christ's

---

27. Jonathan Edwards, *The "Miscellanies": Entry Nos. a–z, aa–zz, 1–500*, ed. Thomas A. Schafer, vol. 13 of *WJE*, (1994), 284.

28. Henry explained that manna is like angels' food either in the sense that if angels ate food, they would eat the manna thankfully, or in the sense that they ministered this food to Israel. Henry, *Exposition*, [Ps 78:25]. Poole recognized that manna is called angels' food because either it is formed and given through the angels' ministry, it descends from the habitude of angels, or it is very excellent bread since it would be what angels ate, if they needed food. Poole, *Synopsis*, 1009. Trapp explained angels' food as "such delicate bread as might beseem Angels to eat, if they did eat at all." Trapp, *Commentary*, 786. Dickson likewise emphasized that manna is given this name to indicate "the excellency of the food, that it might have served for food to Angels, if they had any need of food." Dickson, *Other fifty Psalmes*, 207. Calvin highlighted that this verse speaks primarily of Israel's ingratitude, not only for food from the earth but even for bread rained down from heaven. Calvin, *Commentary*, 3:247.

29. Jonathan Edwards, "206. Sermon on Ps 78:25 (August 1731–December 1732)," in *Sermons, Series II, 1731–1732*, vol. 46 of the *WJEO*, L. 1v. Edwards repreached this sermon in July 1757, most likely for his white Stockbridge congregation since he did not mark it, as he usually did, for his Indian congregation.

30. Edwards, "206. Sermon on Ps 78:25," L. 2r. In the manuscript, Edwards crossed out the words "spiritually feed on," but in his outline of the doctrinal section, he said, "1. we would Explain what it is to feed on [Christ]. & 2. Show how they that do so do Eat angels['] food." It

glory and beauty for its "Comfort & Pleasure," and second, "partaking of the benefits which he Purchased," namely God's favor, adoption as a child of God, and eternal life.[31] As Edwards turned to the application, he highlighted God's gracious redemption, calling all "to admire at the Grace of G[od] in advancing us to such an honour & happiness as the feeding upon [Christ] that we who dwell in Houses of Clay & have our foundation in the dust & are such poor sinfull Creatures should have Angels['] food."[32]

Another category of types Edwards observed in the Psalms was types from nature. Scholars like to point out that he was innovative in using typology in nature, perhaps most famously casting the silkworm as a type of Christ.[33] But as Edwards explored natural typology in ways that stretched the art of Puritan typology in new directions, he did so on the basis of a natural typology he saw first in Scripture. He explicated three particular types in the Psalms from nature that point to Christ: the rock, the sun, and the river. In comparing Christ to a rock, Edwards described him as our defense against enemies and our refuge from the flood waters that rage beneath us using Ps 62:6–7 and 61:2.[34] And since the "Sun of righteousness," or Christ, in Mal 4:1–2, paralleled the imagery of the sun in the Psalms, Edwards determined, largely from Ps 19:4–6, that the course of the sun from morning to evening typified Christ's resurrection, ascension, and second return, while the light and predictability

---

is not clear why Edwards crossed out the words "spiritually feed on," but the doctrine needs a verb for it to make sense, and since it is clear that he intended to speak about feeding on Christ, I have retained the phrase.

31. Edwards, "206. Sermon on Ps 78:25," L. 2v., 4r. In "Miscellanies" Entry No. 744, Edwards argued that angels have "eternal life" through the bread of Christ, just as man also does, for it is "a tree of life to them, as well as to us." Edwards, The "Miscellanies": Entry Nos. 501–832, 387.

32. Edwards, "206. Sermon on Ps 78:25," L. 9r.

33. On the silkworm as a type of Christ, see Edwards' Entry Nos. 35 and 142 of "Images of Divine Things," in Typological Writings, ed. Wallace E. Anderson, vol. 11 of WJE (1992), 59, 100. On Edwards' natural typology, see Anderson, "Editor's Introduction to 'Images of Divine Things' and 'Types,'" 1–33; and Janice Knight, "Typology," in The Princeton Companion to Jonathan Edwards, ed. Sang Hyun Lee (Princeton, NJ: Princeton University Press, 2005), 190–209.

34. See Edwards' discussion of Christ as a rock of defense from Ps 62:6–7; his sermon on Christ as our rock of refuge from Ps 61:2; his discussion of the "rock of defense" in the Psalms generally; and his treatment of Ps 105:41 in "Notes on Scripture" Entry No. 213. Jonathan Edwards, "Honey from the Rock" (Deut 32:13), in Sermons and Discourses 1730–1733, ed. Mark Valeri, vol. 17 of WJE (1999), 133–134. Jonathan Edwards, "867. Sermon on Ps 61:2 (July 1747)," in Sermons, Series II, 1747, vol. 65 of the WJEO, L. iv. Edwards, The "Blank Bible," 358; Edwards, Notes on Scripture, 144.

of the sun typified his enlightening work in the hearts of humanity and his faithfulness.[35] Space confines us to discuss in depth only the river as a type.

To describe Christ using the type of a river, Edwards preached twice on Ps 1:3, "And he shall be like a tree planted by the rivers of water, that bringeth forth his fruit in his season; his leaf also shall not wither; and whatsoever he doeth shall prosper." The first occasion was in Northampton *c.* 1742 and the second in Stockbridge to the Indians in 1751.[36] The two sermons are distinct but essentially the same in content and structure. As Edwards began preaching to the Stockbridge Indians, the natural image of a river offered a clear bridge to their world.[37] In this 1751 sermon Edwards connected Ps 1:3 with Jer 17:8, which also compares a blessed man to "a tree planted by the waters," and with Isa 33:21, which identifies the Lord with the image of "broad rivers and streams." He preached this doctrine: "Christ is to the heart of a true saint like a river to the roots of a tree that is planted by it."[38] Reformed interpreters did not compare the river directly to Christ but did recognize in the metaphor of the rivers the constant flowing strength and influences of grace derived from God.[39]

---

35. See Edwards' discussion of the sun as a type of Christ's life and light—and of the revivals as the beginning of God's grand work—from Ps 19:4–6 in Jonathan Edwards, *Some Thoughts Concerning the Revival*, in *The Great Awakening*, ed. C. C. Goen, vol. 4 of *WJE* (1972), 357; Edwards, *Notes on Scripture*, 312–313; and Jonathan Edwards, "Christ the Spiritual Sun" (Mal 4:1–2), in *Sermons and Discourses 1739–1742*, ed. Harry S. Stout and Nathan O. Hatch with Kyle P. Farley, vol. 22 of *WJE* (2003), 53–54. See Edwards' discussion of the sun's predictability as a type of Christ's faithfulness from Ps 89:37 in Edwards, *The "Blank Bible,"* 520.

36. Jonathan Edwards, "693c. Sermon on Ps 1:3(a) (*c.* 1742)," Franklin Trask Library, Andover Newton Theological School, Newton, MA, L. 1r.–2v.; Jonathan Edwards, "Christ Is to the Heart Like a River to a Tree Planted by It" [Ps 1:3(b)], in *Sermons and Discourses 1743–1758*, ed. Wilson H. Kimnach, vol. 25 of *WJE* (2006), 600–604.

37. Rachel Wheeler notes that Edwards' sermons to the Stockbridge Indians accented the use of imagery, a point his Stockbridge Psalms sermons confirm. Rachel Wheeler, "'Friends to Your Souls': Jonathan Edwards' Indian Pastorate and the Doctrine of Original Sin," *Church History* 72, no. 4 (2003): 750–751.

38. Edwards, "Christ Is to the Heart Like a River," 602.

39. Henry recognized that a man is placed near these rivers "by the Means of Grace" and that from them he "receives supplies of Strength and Vigor, but in secret undiscern'd ways." Henry, *Exposition*, [Ps 1:3]. Poole noted how necessary the waters were in the Ancient Near East, and he further observed that "in accommodation to the pious, these rivers are flowing graces & the Spirit & the word of God, etc., from which sap and vigor are supplied continuously," for "the waters are a symbol of the regeneration and sap [or vitality] which we derive from Christ" ("Rivi hi accommodatione ad pium sunt fluenta gratiae & Spiritus & verbi DEI, &c. ex quibus eidem perpetuo subministratur succus & vigor"; "Aquae sunt symbolum regenerationis, & succi quem trahimus à Christo"). Poole, *Synopsis*, 484. Trapp understood the rivers as a metaphor for "those never-failing influences of grace and consolation" in a person that bubble up to eternal life (John 4:14). Trapp, *Commentary*, 563. Dickson saw them

Edwards made the link to Christ more explicit as he laid out five points of comparison in his doctrine section. First, like a river runs freely and is freely available, so Christ's love is available without cost, and his blood flows freely from his wounds. Second, as a tree planted by a river needs no other source of water, so Christ gives sufficient love, happiness, grace, and benefits to the true saint, for in Christ is "enough to supply a great multitude of persons with drink to satisfy all their thirst."[40] Third, unlike a brook that relies on rain showers, a great river does not dry up; in the same way, Christ's love is constant, and his grace and Spirit will continue to all eternity and will not dry up. Fourth, the soul receiving the river of Christ is united with Christ, for "[a]s the water enters into the roots, so Christ enters the heart and soul of a godly man and dwells there."[41] Fifth, as water refreshes and gives life to a tree, so Christ refreshes and enlivens the heart, for as a tree planted by a river remains green in a drought, thriving while other trees die, "[s]o the soul of a true saint [is sustained by Christ] in time of affliction, at death [and even] at the end of the world."[42] In his application, Edwards challenged his listeners to examine whether or not they were true saints, for if they were, they would experience a drastic change, like a tree in dry ground transplanted to the banks of a great river. They would find Christ "sweet and refreshing," and their religion would become vibrant.[43] Then Edwards exhorted sinners to "seek an interest in Jesus Christ," for even if they are green trees for the time being, they will eventually wither and die without Christ.[44]

As this sermon illustrates, Edwards grounded his typology in the Bible but embraced typology's imaginative facet, which allowed him to reflect on the multitudinous ways any natural image from the Psalms might enlighten and

---

as "the influence of Grace from Christ, for the entertaining of Spiritual Life in him." David Dickson, *A Brief Explication of the first Fifty Psalms* (London: T. M. for Ralph Smith..., 1652), 6. And Calvin likewise interpreted the "metaphor" of the rivers as imaging God's children as "always watered with the secret influences of divine grace, so that whatever may befall them is conducive to their salvation." Calvin, *Commentary*, 1:5–6.

40. Edwards, "Christ Is to the Heart Like a River," 603.

41. Edwards, "Christ Is to the Heart Like a River," 603. In his *c.* 1742 sermon, Edwards stated it this way: "[Christ] in those Gracious Communications is united vitally with the Heart of a saint," just as "the water unites into the Roots." Edwards, "693c. Sermon on Ps 1:3(a)," L. IV.

42. Edwards, "Christ Is to the Heart Like a River," 603. In his *c.* 1742 sermon, Edwards made three additional points, that like a river Christ flows "Constantly," that he flows "Irresistably," and that "The saint is near to [Christ]." Edwards, "693c. Sermon on Ps 1:3(a)," L. II., IV.

43. Edwards, "Christ Is to the Heart Like a River," 604.

44. Edwards, "Christ Is to the Heart Like a River," 604.

enrich our understanding of Christ. He viewed the natural world as endowed with typology that teaches us about the person and work of Christ, but he based that typology on natural imagery from the Bible that gave him grounds for making such comparisons. As Edwards approached the Psalms, then, he drew from his familiarity with the natural world and its processes to elaborate on the types made by the psalmists. While he located authority in the Bible as God's inspired Word, he employed all the tools at his disposal—whether in the book of Scripture or the book of nature—to elucidate the pregnant types he saw in the Psalms.

One Psalms passage to which Edwards devoted special attention as typifying Christ was Ps 82:6–8, "I have said, Ye are gods; and all of you are children of the most High. But ye shall die like men, and fall like one of the princes. Arise, O God, judge the earth: for thou shalt inherit all nations." We have already seen that Edwards preached on this passage to describe the mortality of human princes. He also reflected on the princes in this passage as a type of Christ in the "Blank Bible," in a *c.* 1750 entry in "Notes on Scripture," and in a December 1, 1757, letter to Joseph Bellamy.[45] The letter, his final correspondence with his friend and protégé, offers Edwards' fullest treatment of the passage. Apparently, Bellamy asked Edwards to give some insight into Christ's argument in John 10:34–36, which quotes from Ps 82:6.[46] Edwards first identified the historical meaning of "gods" in Psalm 82 as referring to Israel's princes in contradistinction to the surrounding nations' princes. Then he argued that these Jewish princes were "figures" of "the true King of the Jews and Prince of God's people, who is to rule over the house of Jacob forever, the Prince and Savior of God's church or spiritual Israel, gathered from all nations of the earth; who is God indeed."[47] These "gods" were "appointed types and remarkable representations of the true Son of God, and in him of the true God."[48] As Ps 82:8 spoke of one who would "inherit the nations," Edwards concluded this could only be Christ, "who is truly God, the true and just Judge and Savior (who is to be King over Gentiles as well as Jews)" and who "would

---

45. On the dating of the "Notes on Scripture" entry, see Stephen J. Stein, "Editor's Introduction," in *Notes on Scripture*, ed. Stephen J. Stein, vol. 15 of *WJE* (1998), 45.

46. John 10:34–36 reads, "Jesus answered them, Is it not written in your law, I said, Ye are gods? If he called them gods, unto whom the word of God came, and the scripture cannot be broken; Say ye of him, whom the Father hath sanctified, and sent into the world, Thou blasphemest; because I said, I am the Son of God?"

47. Jonathan Edwards to Joseph Bellamy, December 1, 1757, in *Letters and Personal Writings*, ed. George S. Claghorn, vol. 16 of *WJE* (1998), 733–734.

48. Jonathan Edwards to Joseph Bellamy, 734.

come and reign."[49] Interestingly, while some Reformed interpreters concurred that verse 8 spoke of Christ's coming reign, none of our five representatives identified the "gods," or magistrates, in verse 6 as types of Christ.[50] Edwards found support elsewhere, showing clear reliance on John Glas' *Some Notes on Scripture-Texts*, a portion of which he quoted in his "Notes on Scripture" entry. Glas likewise distinguished between the princes of the surrounding nations and the princes of Israel, who are called "gods," and he explained that the rulers of Israel "prefigured him who was to rule over the House of Jacob for ever; and they stood in that Office as his Types."[51] Furthermore, "the Scripture calling them so, is not broken; because what is said of these Types, holds fully true in their Antitype; who is plainly enough pointed at in the same Psalm."[52] Edwards used Glas as a foundation for identifying this text as typifying Christ.

For Edwards, the book of Psalms was a storehouse of types that foreshadowed Christ and his gospel. These types could be found in individuals, physical structures, nature, substances, and historical events. Edwards happily explored the various images for all their parallels with the Messiah for he believed that the Holy Spirit was the "Great Disposer of all things" and thus ordered history with symbolic meaning for the work of redemption, enshrining these types for

---

49. Jonathan Edwards to Joseph Bellamy, 734. This point is what occupied Edwards in the "Blank Bible" and "Notes on Scripture," where he made the typological connection even more explicit. In his "Blank Bible" entry on Ps 82:8, he explained that the princes "are no gods, nor are the true Son of God, but mere men, and no more than images and shadows" of Christ, the "antitype." Edwards, *The "Blank Bible,"* 516. See also Edwards, *Notes on Scripture*, 579.

50. Dickson did not identify Christ in this passage at all. Dickson, *Other fifty Psalmes*, 259–260. Others saw some possible intimation of Christ. Henry and Trapp noted that the clause, "thou shalt inherit the nations" (Ps 82:8) has respect to Christ's kingdom and second coming, especially in light of Ps 2:8. Henry, *Exposition*, [Ps 82:8]; Trapp, *Commentary*, 796. Poole recognized that verse 8 can speak of Christ rising to judge or inheriting the nations, yet even here he presented the likelihood that it pertains not to Christ's reign but to the general providence of God as he governs by his supreme authority. Poole, *Synopsis*, 1033. Like Poole, Calvin preferred the interpretation that it was too narrow to ascribe the inheriting of the nations to Christ rather than to God generally. Calvin, *Commentary*, 3:334–336.

51. John Glas, *Some Notes on Scripture-Texts, Shewing the Import of these NAMES of JESUS CHRIST, THE SON OF GOD AND THE WORD OF GOD; With an Account of The Image of God in Man* (Edinburgh: W. Sand, A. Murray, and J. Cochran, 1747), 12. Edwards received this booklet from his Scottish correspondent, John Erskine, and in a letter thanking Erskine for this piece (and others), he said, "There were various things pleasing to me in Glas's Notes, tending to give some new light into the sense of Scripture. He seems to be a man of ability, though I can't fall in with all his singularities." Jonathan Edwards to the Reverend John Erskine, July 5, 1750, in *Letters and Personal Writings*, ed. George S. Claghorn, vol. 16 of *WJE* (1998), 348.

52. Glas, *Some Notes on Scripture-Texts*, 12.

all ages in the worship book of the Jews and the church.[53] As McClymond and
McDermott note, "[t]ypology gave him the tool he needed to unify the biblical testaments, particularly at those junctures where the literal sense by itself
could not fulfill the theological vision which he believed united the Scriptures,"
the history of redemption.[54] Edwards emphasized Christ particularly because
he is the lynchpin of God's redemptive-historical work in the world, to which
the many types described above bear witness, testifying to Christ as the true
David, the verification of God's Word, the sustenance of angels and men, the
Sun that offers all manner of spiritual benefits, the defense and refuge of his
people, the nourishment of souls, the Savior of the church, the Son of God,
and the eternal king.

Prophecies of the Messiah

In his "Types of the Messiah" notebook, Edwards expressed his desire to look
into what "evidence" he could find showing that "the book of Psalms in general
relates to the Messiah, or that he and things pertaining to him are the grand
subject of those sacred songs of the church of Israel."[55] He developed his findings in his "Prophecies of the Messiah" and "Fulfillment of the Prophecies of
the Messiah" notebooks. He also discussed prophecies of the Messiah from
the Psalms elsewhere in his corpus, but these two notebooks provide the
best look into his approach to Christological prophecy in the Psalms.[56] They
demonstrate that Edwards read the Psalms with a view ultimately toward the
redemption accomplished in Christ. As Stephen R. C. Nichols shows, "[w]ith
pre-critical assumptions regarding the authorship and provenance of the biblical texts, Edwards argues that only by reading the prophecies as a persistent
anticipation of the Messiah, his redemption and kingdom, can the disparate
and temporally distinct texts cohere."[57]

In "Prophecies of the Messiah," Edwards employed the Psalms extensively
as he sought to demonstrate how thoroughly the Old Testament testified to

---

53. Edwards, "Types of the Messiah," 214.

54. Michael J. McClymond and Gerald R. McDermott, *The Theology of Jonathan Edwards*
(New York: Oxford University Press, 2012), 119.

55. Edwards, "Types of the Messiah," 203–203.

56. For example, see Edwards' discussion of Ps 97:7 in Edwards, *The "Blank Bible,"* 1137;
Psalm 69 in Edwards, *The "Miscellanies": Entry Nos. 501–832,* 273; and several other psalms
in Edwards, *The "Miscellanies": Entry Nos. 1153–1360,* 418.

57. Nichols, *Jonathan Edwards's Bible,* 50.

the coming Messiah. Space does not allow us to rehearse fully his frequent discussion of the Psalms in this manuscript, but that is unnecessary since his treatment followed clear patterns. As an "occasional theologian," Edwards wrote not *on* occasion but *for* the occasion, and the occasion in this manuscript was to identify the prophecies of the Messiah in the Old Testament and show the harmony of these prophecies by using the analogy of Scripture. Edwards' "Prophecies" notebook almost looks like a glorified cross-reference manual on passages referring to the Messiah, for his *modus operandi* was to compare passages at hand with the many other similar passages in Scripture for the purpose of sounding forth the harmonic voice of the Old Testament about the Messiah.[58] Oftentimes Edwards used the Psalms to give support for other messianic passages, but he also devoted thirty-one sections in "Prophecies" to expositing full psalms or large segments of psalms on the Messiah.[59] We will examine his treatment of Psalm 45 as exemplary of his engagement with the Psalms in this notebook, as well as his two sections detailing how the whole book of Psalms relates to the Messiah, followed by a short discussion of his "Fulfillment" notebook.

In §46 of "Prophecies of the Messiah," Edwards argued that Psalm 45, the marriage song of the Psalms, does not have chief respect to either David or Solomon but to Christ and that the bride in the psalm images the bride of Christ, the church, since sundry passages in Scripture suggest that the church should appear as a bride.[60] Edwards found a key to interpreting Psalm 45 in verse 13, "The king's daughter is all glorious within," noting that "this does in effect explain the whole song, and shows that the song is not about external, but about spiritual things."[61] Edwards concluded that the psalm is intended to be interpreted spiritually of Christ and his church, an interpretation shared by

---

58. It is important to recognize that Edwards' "Prophecies of the Messiah" notebook discussed not only passages foretelling about the person of Christ but also those about his gospel and times, and some of these sections are discussed in other chapters of this book.

59. The Psalms that Edwards gave special treatment with a full section include the following: Psalms 118 (§23); 50 and 96–100 (§36); 72 (§39); 110 (§45); 45 (§46); 46 (§47); 47 (§48); 48 (§49); 102 (§50); 14 and 53 (§51); 2 (§52); 20 and 21 (§53); 16 (§54); 22 (§55); 132:11–18 (§56); 89:1–37 (§57); 68 (§58); 87 (§59); 60 and 108 (§75); 67 (§76); 138 (§77); 85 (§78); 69 (§79); 86 (§80); 58 (§81); 65 (§82); 66 (§83); 80 (§84); 24 (§85); 145–150 (§86); and 40:6–10 (§97[a]). Note that §23 and §36 are in "Miscellanies" Entry No. 922, a shorter "Miscellanies" entry to which the longer Entry No. 1067 is appended.

60. The other references include Isa 62:4–5; Zeph 3:17; Isa 54:1–6; Jer 3:14; 30:31–33; and Hos 2:14–23. Jonathan Edwards, "The Miscellanies: Entry No. 1067: Prophecies of the Messiah," Franklin Trask Library, Andover Newton Theological School, Newton, MA, §46.

61. Edwards, "Prophecies of the Messiah," §46.

most Reformed exegetes. Noting several additional parallels, Edwards distinguished the nature of this psalm, saying,

> And 'tis worthy to be noted that the style used in this last verse of the Psalm shows plainly that it is no common love song, for it is the style of God promising everlasting honor and glory; and it seems from such a conclusion of the Psalm, as though we were to take the whole that had been said from the second verse, to be the words of God to the person that is the subject of the Psalm. And in the conclusion of v. 2, 'tis said, "God hath blessed thee for ever."[62]

In fact, Edwards made this same point in a number of other places in his corpus, arguing that "this psalm is no epithalamium relating to any marriage of David or Solomon" in his "Blank Bible" entries on Psalm 45 and on the Song of Solomon.[63] In his last entry in "Notes on Scripture," Entry No. 507—an entry that reveals the day's challenge to biblical authority—Edwards compared Psalm 45 and the Song of Solomon to show that these songs were authoritative Scripture and that they spoke of Christ and the church. Edwards stated:

> The great agreement between the BOOK OF SOLOMON'S SONG and the 45th psalm, and the express and full testimonies of the New Testament for the authority and divine inspiration of that psalm in particular, and that the bridegroom there spoken of is Christ, whose bride, the New Testament abundantly teaches us, is the church, I say, this agreement with those full testimonies are a great confirmation of the constant tradition of the Jewish church, and the universal and continual suffrage of the Christian church for the divine authority and spiritual signification of this song, as representing the union and mutual love of Christ and his church, and enervates the main objections against it. They agree in all particulars that are considerable, so that there is no more reason to object against one than the other.[64]

Edwards delineated the parallel elements between the two songs, showing that both represented the bridegroom as a king and the bride as a king's

---

62. Edwards, "Prophecies of the Messiah," §46.

63. Edwards, *The "Blank Bible,"* 495, 608.

64. Edwards, *Notes on Scripture*, 610.

daughter (Ps 45:13; Cant 7:1); the bridegroom as delighting in the bride's beauty (Ps 45:11; Cant 4:9); the bridegroom as "exceeding excellent and pleasant" (Ps 45:2; Cant 5:16); and the bridegroom's excellencies as perfumed ointment (Ps 45:7; Cant 1:3).[65] Edwards defended the Song of Solomon against those who objected to its vivid conjugal imagery by showing how similar it was to Psalm 45. Since no one would remove Psalm 45 from the canon, he pointed out a suggestive reading of Psalm 45 to argue for the authority of the Song of Solomon:

> 'Tis supposed by many to be very liable to a bad construction that the beauty of the various parts of the body of the spouse is mentioned and described in Solomon's Song. But perhaps these are no more liable to a bad construction than the 13th verse of the 45th psalm, where there is mention of the beauty of the bride's clothes, and her being "glorious within," where setting aside the allegory, or mystical meaning of the song, what is most naturally understood as the most direct meaning would seem to be, that she had not only glorious clothing, but was yet more glorious in the parts of her body within her clothing, that were hid by her clothing.[66]

Reformed interpreters resisted any association with a sexual reading.[67] But in Edwards' reading of Psalm 45, its similarity to the Song of Solomon and its prophetic description of Christ and the church together formed a powerful argument for the authoritative nature of the Song and Scripture as a whole.

In his discussion of Psalm 45, Edwards cited medieval rabbis, via Johann Friedrich Stapfer and Matthew Poole, as testimony that the psalm referred to the Messiah—a practice he repeated in his treatment of a number of psalms

---

65. Edwards, *Notes on Scripture*, 611.

66. Edwards, *Notes on Scripture*, 613.

67. Henry argued that verse 13 indicates that "[t]he Glory of the Church is spiritual Glory." Henry, *Exposition*, [Ps 45:13]. Poole gave four interpretive options for the bride being "all glorious within": (1) being in the presence of the king, (2) innate beauty, (3) a golden garment underneath her outer garments, or (4) the spiritual ornaments of virtue. He also quoted an interpreter who said that this psalm does not speak of "obscene affections" (*obscœnis amoribus*) but speaks figuratively of Christ's union with the church. Poole, *Synopsis*, 789, 800. Trapp also noted that verse 13 speaks spiritually of "the Inner-man" or "the hidden man of the heart." Trapp, *Commentary*, 705. Dickson used verse 13 to explain that this psalm speaks of "things spiritual, not discernable by the uptaking of the natural man." Dickson, *Other fifty Psalmes*, 311. Calvin explained verse 13 as signifying either that the queen is gloriously robed even in her "ordinary and daily attire" or that she derives all her glory from being within the presence of the king. Calvin, *Commentary*, 2:191–192.

in "Prophecies of the Messiah." From Stapfer, Edwards quoted Eben-Ezra on Psalm 45, who said, "There are those who say, this Psalm speaks of David or his son the Messiah; for this is even his name, just as also David my servant will be a King to them forever."[68] Edwards also cited "the Rabbies' opinion of the subject of this Psalm" from Poole's *Synopsis*.[69] Poole noted that Rabbi "Meir Arama says that all (the Rabbis) agree that this Psalm speaks of the Messiah."[70] One reason given for the spiritual reading of this psalm is "from the consensus of interpreters, not only of Jews...but also of Christians."[71] Poole also quoted a number of other interpreters, including several Christian exegetes who understood the passage to refer spiritually or typically of Christ and the church, as the Holy Spirit intended it, and he observed that "scarcely is there one who doubts but that it speaks of Christ," for "this psalm is prophetic, and it contains an epithalamium in which is celebrated the marriage of Christ with the Church."[72] Edwards read Psalm 45 largely in continuity not only with the Reformed tradition but even with the Jews, though they saw it referring to a Messiah who had not yet arrived. In fact, it was not unusual even for Puritan laypeople in New England to associate Psalm 45 with Christ; in Thomas Shepard's church a century before Edwards, Barbary Cutter saw "the excellency of person of Christ" from several passages, including Ps 45:2, which showed that "grace was poured out on His lips."[73] One striking difference between Edwards and the Reformed-Puritan tradition was that while they resisted identifying this psalm as a song for Solomon's wedding to Pharaoh's daughter, Edwards saw in that historical detail a redemptive symbol: As Psalm 45 spoke historically of Solomon marrying Pharaoh's

---

68. The Latin reads, "Sunt qui ajunt, hunc Psalmum de Davide loqui vel Messia filio ejus; nam & hoc ejus nomen, quomodo & David servus meus erit iis Dux in perpetuum." Johann Friedrich Stapfer, *Institutiones Theologiæ Polemicæ Universæ, Ordine Scientifico dispositæ*, vol. 3, 3d ed. (Tiguri: Heideggerum et Socios, 1757), 154.

69. Edwards, "Prophecies of the Messiah," §46.

70. "Meir Arama ait consentire omnes (Rabbinos) hunc Psalmu de Messia loqui." Poole, *Synopsis*, 788.

71. "Ex consensu interpretum, tum Judæorum...tum Christianorum." Poole, *Synopsis*, 790.

72. "Vix est qui dubitet quin de Christo loquatur"; "Hic Psalmus Propheticus est, continetque Epithalamium quo Christi cum Ecclesia nuptiae celebrantur." Poole, *Synopsis*, 788–790. Quotation on 788.

73. Quoted in George Selement and Bruce C. Woolley, eds., *Thomas Shepard's Confessions*, vol. 58 of Publications of the Colonial Society of Massachusetts Collections (Boston: Colonial Society of Massachusetts, 1981), 90.

daughter, so it spoke prophetically of "the calling of the Gentiles," pointing to the redemptive-historical nature of God's work.[74]

In addition to the several individual psalms Edwards engaged in "Prophecies of the Messiah," he also showed that "THE BOOK OF PSALMS IN GREAT PART RELATES TO THE MESSIAH" in two sections, §60 and §87.[75] In these sections, Edwards revealed that he understood the Psalms to be prophetic not merely of Christ but of God's offer of salvation through Christ to the whole world—his work of redemption at large. Parts of these sections thus appear in chapters 5 and 7 as they deal with the gospel and the church.

To provide proof of his claim, Edwards pointed to David's last words in 2 Sam 23:1–5, where "the sweet psalmist of Israel" states, "The Spirit of the LORD spake by me, and his word was in my tongue," and "he hath made with me an everlasting covenant, ordered in all things, and sure: for this is all my salvation, and all my desire." Based on this passage, Edwards said that "it seems as though the Messiah, and things appertaining to his times and his kingdom,

---

74. Edwards, "Types of the Messiah," 285. He particularly quoted Ps 45:10 and 13: "Hearken, O daughter, and consider, and incline thine ear; forget also thine own people, and thy father's house.... The king's daughter is all glorious within: her clothing is of wrought gold." In keeping with this theme of so many outsiders coming to the Messiah, Edwards pointed to the many Gentiles who visited Solomon, including the queen of Sheba (Ps 72:9–10, 15) and the ships of Tarshish (Ps 72:10). Edwards, "Types of the Messiah," 292.

Henry was adamant that this psalm is "an illustrious Prophecy of *Messiah the Prince*," arguing that 'tis all over Gospel, and points at *him only*, as a Bridegroom espousing the Church to himself, and as a King ruling in it, and ruling for it." He went so far as to say that "[w]e have no Reason to think it it [sic] has any reference to *Solomon*'s Marriage with *Pharaoh*'s Daughter," for "I take it to be purely and only meant of Jesus Christ." Throughout his exposition, Henry made comparisons between Psalm 45 and Christ and his gospel, and he called the marriage celebrated in this psalm a "Type of this Mystical Marriage between CHRIST and his Church." Henry, *Exposition*, [Psalm 45]. While Trapp recognized that this is an "*Epithalamium* or nuptial verse, made at the marriage of *Solomon* and the Shulamite," not Pharaoh's daughter, he also noted that it sets forth "Christ in his glory, and his Church in her beauty," describing "the mystical marriage of Christ and his Church." Trapp, *Commentary*, 702. Dickson, like Henry, set aside the historical referents of the psalm and argued that it is "altogether spiritual," speaking of "the mystical marriage of the *Messiah Christ Jesus* our Lord, and his Kirk." He recognized, like Edwards, that the psalm makes some statements that "cannot be verified in any person save in Jesus Christ alone," and he explored several parallels between Psalm 45 and Christ's marriage to the church. Dickson, *Other fifty Psalmes*, 303–304. Calvin spoke of a twofold meaning in Psalm 45, recognizing that it describes "the grace and beauty of Solomon, his virtues in ruling the kingdom, and also his power and riches," but is also a "figure" of "the majesty, wealth, and extent of Christ's kingdom," and Calvin explored the parallel meanings between the psalm and Christ and his church throughout his commentary. Calvin, *Commentary*, 2:173.

75. Similarly, the title of §87 is "The Book of Psalms, in General, in Great Part Relates to the Messiah."

are the chief subject of the Psalms of David."[76] Since these were David's last words, they describe his "main drift and *ultimum*," and they contain "the sum and main substance of those many other words or songs that he had uttered as sweet Psalmist, that were all spoken by the Spirit of God revealing to him great future things in vision and prophecy."[77] Edwards then made the prophetic relationship to Christ explicit:

> IN THE BOOK OF PSALMS in general, the Psalmist speaks either in the name of Christ, or in the name of the church. And this is to be observed concerning a very great part of this book, that the Psalmist speaks in the name of Christ most comprehensively taken, viz. as including his body or members, or in the name of Christ mystical; and even in some of those psalms that seem to be the most direct and plain prophecies of Christ, some parts of which are most applicable to the head or Christ, other parts to the body or the church.[78]

Edwards saw that Christ and the church were closely united in the Psalms because the psalmist was often viewed in "very many of the psalms" as "the head of the people of God…whose interest was the same with theirs, and they most nearly concerned in his sufferings, deliverance and exaltation."[79] These important statements show how Edwards conceived of the Psalter's nature. It foretold of Christ in his fullness, whether as head or as his body, the church. We discuss the church at greater length in chapter 7. At this point, it is crucial to point out that these statements should not be misread as if Edwards thought of the Psalms only as Christological, even in the broad sense of Christ and the church. He said that this is how the Psalms are to be read "in general," not universally. Also, he purposed in the "Prophecies of the Messiah" notebook to show that the Old Testament is full of prophecies of the Messiah, and in his characteristic hyperbole, he made an extreme statement to establish his point. As his interpretation of the book of Psalms throughout his corpus shows, Edwards read the Psalms with a wider lens, incorporating God's whole work of redemption in history, while the person of Christ and his ministry to his body play central roles in that larger story.

---

76. Edwards, "Prophecies of the Messiah," §60.

77. Edwards, "Prophecies of the Messiah," §60.

78. Edwards, "Prophecies of the Messiah," §60.

79. Edwards, "Prophecies of the Messiah," §60.

Edwards continued his discussion about the book of Psalms in §87 of "Prophecies," summing up his basic argument for this section in the beginning of the entry:

> This is a great argument the book of Psalms is, a great part of it, prophetical, and also that very much of it relates to the times of the Messiah, even in those parts of it where the speech is in the present or preter tense, viz. that God's people are so often spoken of as being in captivity, and the temple, city and land in desolation, or as being restored from a state of captivity and desolation, in psalms that were penned at a time when no such thing was, nor had lately been.[80]

Edwards determined composition dates largely from psalms' titles attributed to David or those in David or Solomon's era, such as Asaph or the sons of Korah. If a psalm attributed to David spoke of captivity, he reasoned that it could not describe Israel in David's lifetime but must be prophetic of a future time in the church when the Messiah will once and for all free his broad people from captivity to sin. Where biblical scholars today might reject David's authorship of a psalm that speaks of captivity, earmarking it as an exilic psalm, Edwards saw grounds for prophetic intention. He made such observations for twenty-one psalms.[81]

For Edwards the Psalms were saturated with prophecies of the Messiah and his times, so as Edwards turned to his manuscript, "The Fulfillment of the Prophecies of the Messiah," he continued to engage the Psalms in his discussion of Christ. The "Fulfillment" notebook was intended to draw together the Old Testament prophecies about the Messiah with the New Testament fulfillment of those specific prophecies, and one gets the sense from the manuscript that the Old Testament can tell the life of Christ from start to finish and proceed to its fruit in the work of redemption in later history all through its sundry prophecies. Edwards thus used this manuscript closely together with his "Prophecies of the Messiah" to manifest the

---

80. Edwards, "Prophecies of the Messiah," §87.

81. Such psalms include Psalms 9, 14, 44, 53, 60, 66, 68, 69, 74, 79, 80, 85, 102, 107, 108, 145–150. Edwards, "Prophecies of the Messiah," §87. Edwards also argued that the Psalms refer to the Messiah because of their musical inscriptions, which show the Psalter was intended for public worship. When David, Asaph, or others wrote in the first person, they "speak in the name of the Messiah, or of the church of God," for we would not expect their private complaints and prayers to be used "as the voice of the whole congregation of Israel to God, in their most public and solemn worship." Edwards, "Prophecies of the Messiah," §87.

harmonic relationship between the two, though he dealt with the Psalms differently in "Fulfillment" than in "Prophecies" because his starting point was the New Testament. The Psalms thus functioned more as proof-texts for his theological points rather than launching points for discussion. As one example, in §17 of "Fulfillment" Edwards set forth the theological point, "It was foretold that in the days of the Messiah there should be a very extraordinary exercise and display of divine mercy and grace," and he went on to give several proof-texts from throughout the Bible, including Ps 108:4, "For thy mercy is great above the heavens"; Ps 48:9, "We have thought of thy lovingkindness, O God, in the midst of thy temple"; and Ps 145:7, "They shall abundantly utter the memory of thy great goodness, and shall sing of thy righteousness."[82] Edwards identified several specifics of prophecy, but I provide examples later in this chapter and in chapters 5 and 7 as a brief sampling of Edwards' use of the Psalms in "Fulfillment of the Prophecies," which will give a sense of his intention with and general use of the Psalms in this particular notebook. It suffices at this point to note that Edwards read the prophecies of the Messiah in the Psalms as referring not only to Christ but also to God's whole work of redemption through Christ stretching throughout all history.

For Edwards, typology and prophecy constituted central ways of understanding the nature of the Psalms in relationship to the rest of the Bible and particularly to the New Testament. They provided a way to view the Scripture as a unified whole and to mine the depths of the Holy Spirit's intention in inspiring the complete book of Holy Writ. So it is no surprise that as Edwards engaged the individual books of the Bible and the smaller sections of those books—like the Psalter and its individual psalms—he read them with the purpose of the Bible as a whole in mind. He read them in light of the history of redemption, the paradigm that gave structure and meaning to the individual parts. The central figure in that history was Christ, and as we turn now from the lenses of typology and prophecy to particular aspects of Christ's life, redemptive work, and glorification, we do not leave these lenses behind but continue to see Edwards' unified view of the Old and New Testaments at play as he emphasized specific details in the person and work of Christ from the Psalms.

---

82. Jonathan Edwards, "The Miscellanies: Entry No. 1068: The Fulfillment of the Prophecies of the Messiah," Franklin Trask Library, Andover Newton Theological School, Newton, MA, §17.

Christ's Life of Obedience

As Edwards engaged the Psalms, several details about the life of Jesus emerged, from his incarnation and miracles to his transfiguration and prayer in Gethsemane. Edwards believed it was important to identify these descriptions in the Psalms for insight into the Scriptures and the person of Christ. One particular aspect of Christ's life that captivated Edwards was his willing obedience to God by becoming a humble servant. We examine the details regarding his life and voluntary servitude below.

Edwards capitalized on the psalmistic imagery of "descent" to describe the incarnation of Christ. In a number of places the Psalms speak of God coming down or the heavens bowing, and Edwards found in this language a reference to God coming to earth in human form. In "Notes on Scripture" Entry No. 271, on Rev 12:1, Edwards commented on Ps 18:9, "He bowed the heavens also, and came down," explaining that this verse describes Christ's "coming out of heaven to dwell amongst the people."[83] He similarly observed a reference to Christ's incarnation in Ps 144:5, "Bow thy heavens, O LORD, and come down: touch the mountains, and they shall smoke," commenting in his "Blank Bible":

> This was never so remarkably fulfilled as in the incarnation of Jesus Christ, when heaven and earth were as it were brought together. Heaven itself was as it were made to bow that it might be united to the earth. God did as it were come down and bring heaven with him. He not only came down to the earth, but he brought heaven down with him to men and for men.[84]

Edwards was unique in making any connection to Christ here compared to earlier exegetes.[85]

More narrowly, Edwards saw a reference to Christ's birth in Ps 22:9–10, "But thou art he that took me out of the womb: thou didst make me hope when I was upon my mother's breasts. I was cast upon thee from the womb: thou art

---

83. Edwards, *Notes on Scripture*, 227.

84. Edwards, *The "Blank Bible,"* 539. See also Edwards' comment on Ps 96:13, that it "cannot be meant any otherwise than by an incarnation." Edwards, *The "Miscellanies": Entry Nos. a–500*, 166.

85. Neither Henry, Poole, Trapp, Dickson, nor Calvin made a connection to Christ's incarnation in this passage. Henry, *Exposition*, [Ps 144:5]; Poole, *Synopsis*, 1315; Trapp, *Commentary*, 920; David Dickson, *A Brief Explication of the last Fifty Psalmes, From Ps. 100 to the end* (London: T. R. and E. M. for Ralph Smith . . . , 1654), 343; Calvin, *Commentary*, 5:263–264.

my God from my mother's belly." Edwards thought this verse referred to "the manner of Christ's birth being in a stable" because it demonstrated Mary's great dependence on God in that circumstance.[86] For it was in the stable where "the blessed Virgin," alone and without midwives to help her, "committed herself and the fruit of her womb to God, and received strength to bring forth by faith," and committed the baby Jesus to God when Herod pursued him, manifesting her dependence.[87]

The Psalms also described the miracles Jesus performed during his ministry in Israel. In "Miscellanies" Entry No. 512, Edwards argued for the divine nature of Christ's miracles since they mirrored Old Testament accounts of God accomplishing similar acts. He made a case for Christ's divinity by pointing to several psalms that describe the very miracles that Christ performed, including calming the sea (Pss 65:7; 107:29; 89:8–9; 93:4); casting out devils (Ps 74:13–14); feeding a multitude in the wilderness (Pss 78:19, 20, 23–25; 146:7); raising the dead (Ps 68:20); opening the eyes of the blind (Ps 146:8); raising one bound by a spirit of infirmity (Ps 146:7–8); and healing the sick (Ps 103:3).[88] Edwards concluded that the Psalms "prophesied" Christ would perform these miracles, that these miracles were "works of mercy and love," and that they were "lively types of the great spiritual works of God and the Redeemer."[89] The Psalms' prophetic and typological relationship to Christ revealed their greater purpose of foreshadowing God's loving work of redemption.

Edwards read another prophecy in Ps 104:2, "Who coverest thyself with light as with a garment," arguing that this verse foretold of Christ's transfiguration, where his raiment was described as "white as the light" (Matt 17:2)—an interpretation unique among Reformed interpreters.[90] This divine figure also had a zeal for God's ways that led to his own travail, which Edwards saw described in Ps 69:9, "For the zeal of thine house hath eaten me up, and the reproaches of them that reproached thee are fallen upon me." He applied this

---

86. Edwards, *The "Blank Bible,"* 485.

87. Edwards, *The "Blank Bible,"* 485.

88. Edwards, *The "Miscellanies": Entry Nos. 501–832*, 55–56. See his similar argument for Christ's divinity from the Psalms in *The "Miscellanies": Entry Nos. 1153–1360*, 615–616. See also his "Blank Bible" note on Ps 65:7, where he argued that the Old Testament mentioned many of Christ's miracles as "the peculiar works of God." Edwards, *The "Blank Bible,"* 503–504. Quotation on 504.

89. Edwards, *The "Miscellanies": Entry Nos. 501–832*, 57.

90. Edwards, *The "Blank Bible,"* 855; Neither Henry, Poole, Trapp, Dickson, nor Calvin linked Ps 104:2 to the transfiguration. Henry, *Exposition*, [Ps 104:2]; Poole, *Synopsis*, 1125–1126; Trapp, *Commentary*, 834; Dickson, *Last Fifty Psalms*, 32–33; Calvin, *Commentary*, 4:145.

verse, as John 2:17 does, to Christ's clearing the temple of moneychangers, which provoked the Pharisees and led to his sufferings: "it has so prevailed as entirely to govern me, and swallow me up, and caused me to renounce myself, and has caused me willingly to expose myself to be consumed by mine enemies, and hath actually been an occasion of my being devoured by them."[91]

One final event from Christ's earthly life prior to his death that Edwards saw in the Psalms was Christ's prayer in the Garden of Gethsemane. In "Notes on Scripture" Entry No. 225, on Luke 22:44, Edwards reflected on Ps 69:14–15, "Deliver me out of the mire, and let me not sink: let me be delivered from them that hate me, and out of the deep waters. Let not the waterflood overflow me, neither let the deep swallow me up, and let not the pit shut her mouth upon me." Edwards believed this psalm explains Luke 22:44, "And being in an agony he prayed more earnestly," for Christ prayed this psalm that night, asking "that he might be 'saved from death'; that though he must drink the cup, and pass through death, that he might not be swallowed up, that he might not fail and sink in so great a trial, but might overcome, as Christ is represented praying, Ps. 69:14–15."[92] While the Reformed tradition widely recognized that Psalm 69 was prophetic or typical of Christ and his sufferings, it was rare to identify verses 14–15 specifically with Christ's prayer in the Garden of Gethsemane, as Edwards did.[93] By connecting the Psalms with Christ's prayer, though, Edwards opened a window into the humanity of Christ.

Christ's zeal for the things of God led him to place himself in willing subjection in order to uphold God's honor and accomplish his plan of redemption. In "Notes on Scripture" Entry No. 163, Edwards commented on Ps 45:7, "Thou lovest righteousness, and hatest wickedness: therefore God, thy God, hath anointed thee with the oil of gladness above thy fellows." Christ demonstrated his love of righteousness and hatred of wickedness in "his humiliation and death, whereby he exceedingly manifested his regard to God's holiness and law, that when he had a mind that sinners should be saved, he was freely willing to suffer so much rather than it should be done with any injury unto that holiness and law."[94] In

---

91. Edwards, The "Blank Bible," 506.

92. Edwards, Notes on Scripture, 174.

93. Of our five interpreters, only Trapp observed that the church fathers read this psalm as "prophetical touching the passions of Christ, and his praying then to the Father," and noted that some apply verse 14 to Christ. Trapp, Commentary, 762–763. Henry, Poole, Dickson, and Calvin all recognized that Psalm 69 is prophetic or typical of Christ, but none applied verses 14–15 to Christ's prayer in the garden. Henry, Exposition, [Ps 69:14–15]; Poole, Synopsis, 946–947, 951; Dickson, Other fifty Psalmes, 116, 122; Calvin, Commentary, 3:45, 61–62.

94. Edwards, Notes on Scripture, 97.

Edwards' view, Christ willingly went to the cross because he would rather do harm to himself than to God's law and holiness. Edwards explored this theme of Christ as a willing servant extensively in his treatment of Ps 40:6–8, a passage he entertained often in his corpus. These verses served as a go-to passage in sermons to show that Christ willingly delighted to do God's will because Christ held "an infinite regard to the glory of God in dying for sinners," for he was more willing to pay the penalty of the law out of his love for men and out of his "infinite regard to the will or command of God."[95] He used this passage similarly in the "Miscellanies" manuscript, upholding Christ as the willing, cheerful servant who fulfilled God's law.[96] And in his treatise on *Freedom of the Will*, Edwards employed the passage to uphold Christ as an example of one whose holiness was determined but whose obedience also merited praise and reward.[97] Similarly, in a "Notes on Scripture" entry, Edwards observed that in saying the law was in Christ's heart, Ps 40:8 indicated that "he satisfied the law by his sufferings, for it was out of regard to the honor of God's law that, when he would save them that had broken it, he had rather himself suffer the penalty of the law than that their salvation should be inconsistent with the honor of it."[98]

Edwards treated the passage at greater length in two "Notes on Scripture" entries, a "Blank Bible" entry, and his sermon on Ps 40:6–8, all of which we examine. The passage reads, "Sacrifice and offering thou didst not desire; mine ears hast thou opened: burnt offering and sin offering hast thou not required. Then said I, Lo, I come: in the volume of the book it is written of me, I delight to do thy will, O my God: yea, thy law is within my heart." In "Notes on Scripture" Entry No. 62, Edwards interpreted Ps 40:6, "mine ears hast thou opened," or "bored," as a reference to Christ's servanthood, and he looked back to Exod 21:5–6, which set out the procedures for a servant who chose to

---

95. Jonathan Edwards, "Christ's Sacrifice an Inducement to His Ministers" (Acts 20:28), in *Sermons and Discourses 1743–1758*, ed. Wilson H. Kimnach, vol. 25 of *WJE* (2006), 667. See also Jonathan Edwards, "Serving God in Heaven" (Rev 22:3), in *Sermons and Discourses 1730–1733*, ed. Mark Valeri, vol. 17 of *WJE* (1999), 257; and Jonathan Edwards, "Glorious Grace" (Zech 4:7), in *Sermons and Discourses 1720–1723*, ed. Wilson H. Kimnach, vol. 10 of *WJE* (1992), 394.

96. See "Miscellanies" Entry Nos. 449, "Blood of Christ Washes Away Sin. Christ's Righteousness"; 845, "Justification. Blood of Christ. Obedience of Christ"; and 1106, "Righteousness of Christ." Edwards, *The "Miscellanies": Entry Nos. a–500*, 496–497; Jonathan Edwards, *The "Miscellanies": Entry Nos. 833–1152*, ed. Amy Plantinga Pauw, vol. 20 of *WJE* (2002), 66, 488.

97. Jonathan Edwards, *Freedom of the Will*, ed. Paul Ramsey, vol. 1 of *WJE* (1957), 281, 287, 290–293.

98. Edwards, *Notes on Scripture*, 245.

remain with his master rather than be set free: "And if the servant shall plainly say, I love my master, my wife, and my children; I will not go out free: Then his master shall bring him unto the judges; he shall also bring him to the door, or unto the door post; and his master shall bore his ear through with an aul; and he shall serve him for ever." Edwards argued that in the same way,

> Christ has his ear bored for the sake of his people, who are his wife and his children. He, by the assumption of a body, appears in the form of a servant for them (Heb. 10:5). Christ's ear is as it were bored thereby to the door of God's house (his church) forever. The ear is that whereby the servant hears his master's commands; hearing is the same with obeying in Scripture phrase. And the door is that by which he goes in and out in execution of them, and where he waits to know them.[99]

Edwards' reliance on the analogy of Scripture is evident in the way he drew together Exod 21:5–6 and Heb 10:5–7, the latter of which quotes Ps 40:6–8, to exposit the passage.[100] The Old Testament act of indenturing oneself for life to a master typified for Edwards Christ's act of devoting himself to accomplishing God's plan of redemption and joining himself to the church forever. Edwards explored the parallels further in "Notes on Scripture" Entry No. 171, where he tied the act of being a servant with the act of sacrifice. The psalmist delighted in obedience to God's law over ritual worship for "God often declared that willing obedience was better than sacrifice."[101] Thus the willing servant who bores his ear demonstrates his devotion by cheerful obedience. In the same way, the psalmist "speaks here prophetically" of Christ and specifically of his "becoming incarnate," for the words "mine ear hast thou bored" are rendered "a body hast thou prepared me" in the Heb 10:5 quotation of the verse.[102] Edwards explained that as the servant learned obedience through the suffering of having his ear bored, "[s]o did Christ learn obedience by the things that he suffered by the sacrifice of his body," that is, by taking on the body God had prepared for him and enduring the suffering inflicted on him, and thus Edwards paraphrased verse 6 as, "These sacrifices of beasts, etc., are

99. Edwards, *Notes on Scripture*, 67.

100. Similarly, Edwards made a note in his "Blank Bible" to compare this passage with Isa 50:5–6, which similarly says, "The Lord GOD hath opened mine ear..." Edwards, *The "Blank Bible,"* 495.

101. Edwards, *Notes on Scripture*, 99.

102. Edwards, *Notes on Scripture*, 100.

insignificant in themselves, but my crucifixion is the true sacrifice that God delights in."[103]

To develop this exposition, Edwards relied on a number of sources, cited in his "Blank Bible." On the meaning of the Hebrew word, כָּרָה ("opened"), he cited Richard Rawlin, who argued that this term can mean "to *adapt, fit, or make ready*," a translation supported by Buxtorf's *Lexicon Hebraicum et Chaldaicum* and Taylor's *Hebrew Concordance*.[104] Edwards read in Rawlin that "[a]lmost all our commentators seem to be agreed, that the Psalmist in this passage had his eye upon the custom, that was directed under the Jewish law, concerning menial servants having their *ear bored* in token of perpetual servitude," yet he also would have seen that Rawlin preferred the rendering

> *mine ears hast thou hollowed*, or fashioned, expressing the way and manner, in which that curious organ of the body is framed: and so by an easy and common figure of a part for the whole, by Christ's having his ear *hollowed* or framed, we are to understand his having a proper human body given him, in which he might offer up that sacrifice for the expiation of sin, which was so much wanted, and of which all the sacrifices of the Jewish law were but mere figures.[105]

Edwards sought to make the best of both worlds, building on the two meanings of the term, "to bore" and "to fit," and argued that they "more naturally signify Christ's incarnation or taking on him the human nature, of which the Apostle interprets; for by that he willingly 'took on him the form of a servant' [Phil. 2:7], and has his ear bored as such, and by that he had an ear prepared or fitted, by preparing a proper nature for him to receive and obey

---

103. Edwards, *Notes on Scripture*, 100.

104. Edwards, *The "Blank Bible,"* 494. Richard Rawlin, *Christ the Righteousness of his People; or, The Doctrine of Justification by Faith in Him. Represented in several Sermons, Preached at the Merchants Lecture at Pinner's-Hall* (London: R. Hett and J. Oswald, 1741), 87. John Taylor gave as possible meanings, "[t]o prepare, to make ready, to provide," though he interpreted Ps 40:6 "[f]iguratively" as meaning "[t]o prepare the Ears for Obedience." John Taylor, *The Hebrew Concordance, Adapted to the English Bible; Disposed after the Manner of Buxtorf* (London: J. Waugh and W. Fenner, at the Turk's Head in Lombard-Street, 1754–1757), 1:n.p. [entry 890 on כָּרָה]. Buxtorf offered the possible meanings, "he digs, he digs out, he bores: he prepared a banquet: he obtains" ("Fodit, Effodit, Perfodit: Convivium apparavit: Emit"). Johannis Buxtorf, *Lexicon Hebraicum et Chaldaicum Complectens Omnes Voces, Tam Primas quam Derivatas, quae in Sacris Bibliis, Hebraea, & ex parte Chaldea*…(Basileae: Francisci Plateri & Joh. Philippi Richteri, 1698), 374.

105. Rawlin, *Christ the Righteousness of his People*, 86, 87.

God's commandments in."[106] Edwards read this psalm in light of the Heb 10:5 quotation and explained how the two passages spoke consistently based on his unified conception of the Bible.[107]

In Edwards' sermon on Ps 40:6–8, "The Sacrifice of Christ Acceptable," he spent longer than usual in the exposition because he said it is "so remarkable a text."[108] Much of his sermon exposition mirrored his personal notebooks—the allusion to the servant being marked by an awl, David's preference of practice over formal sacrifices, the Holy Spirit's ultimate intention of the passage in Christ's willing obedience, the Heb 10:5 quotation that explicitly links it to the incarnation, and Christ's crucifixion as the true sacrifice in which God delights. Edwards preached this doctrine: "The sacrifice of Christ is the only sacrifice that is upon its own account acceptable to God."[109] As Edwards fleshed out the doctrine in his sermon, he contrasted the Old Testament sacrifices under the law with the sacrifice of Christ. The legal sacrifices were "not in themselves and upon their own account any way acceptable to God," for they possessed no moral goodness by nature, they could not make any satisfaction, and they were not "meritorious of God's favor or any positive blessing."[110] Their purpose

---

106. Edwards, The "Blank Bible," 494.

107. In addition, in his "Blank Bible" note on Heb 10:5, Edwards cited Bishop Richard Kidder and John Owen in explaining Heb 10:5, which quotes Ps 40:6. Edwards, The "Blank Bible," 1151. Kidder refuted the Jews' objection that the author of Hebrews corrupted the Ps 40:6 text for his own purposes, arguing that while the author used a different expression, it communicated the same sense, that "obedience is better than sacrifice." Furthermore, the author used the words from the common translation of the time, the Greek Septuagint, which interpreted the custom of marking a servant who chooses to stay with his master in words that the people of a new age would better understand. Richard Kidder, A Demonstration of the Messias. In which The Truth of the Christian Religion Is Proved, against all the Enemies thereof; But especially against the Jews. In Three Parts. 2d ed. corr. (London: John Osborn and Thomas Longman..., 1726), 2:89–92. Owen understood the Heb 10:5 quotation of Ps 40:6 as inspired by the Holy Spirit with a consistent purpose in both places: "The words, therefore, in this place are the words whereby the apostle expressed the sense and meaning of the Holy Ghost in those used in the psalmist, or that which was intended in them." Owen went so far as to say that even though the words mirrored the Septuagint, we should not deduce from that that the apostle was dependent on the Greek translation; rather, he interpreted the Psalms passage himself under the guidance of the Spirit: "This is certain, that the sense intended by the psalmist and that expressed by the apostle are the same, or unto the same purpose," and "[t]he end of it is, that the Son might be fit and meet to do the will of God in the way of obedience." John Owen, An Exposition of the Epistle to the Hebrews: Hebrews 8–10, vol. 23 in The Works of John Owen, D.D., ed. William H. Gould (London: Johnstone and Hunter, 1855), 458–459.

108. Jonathan Edwards, "The Sacrifice of Christ Acceptable" (Ps 40:6–8), in Sermons and Discourses 1723–1729, ed. Kenneth P. Minkema, vol. 14 of WJE (1997), 443.

109. Edwards, "The Sacrifice of Christ Acceptable," 443.

110. Edwards, "The Sacrifice of Christ Acceptable," 443–445. Quotations on 443, 445.

was to call the people to obedience, remind them of their sin, teach them that sin must be satisfied by suffering, and reveal "God's willingness to be reconciled."[111] Most important, they were "to typify the sacrifice of Jesus Christ and to lead men to trust in him," for "Christ was the end of all the ceremonial observances of the law; he was the sum and substance of all. By this ceremonial law, the gospel was preached to them; though they had not the direct light of the sun of righteousness, yet they had it reflected from those typical ordinances," which is why Edwards held that the sacrifices are "full of gospel doctrine."[112] As Edwards turned to describe the sacrifice of Jesus Christ, he showed how it was "in itself and upon its own account acceptable unto God," for it had "a transcendent holiness in it" since Christ offered his infinitely holy soul to vindicate God's holiness, which human sin had injured.[113] Christ's sacrifice was also "properly propitiatory" because he willingly offered a sacrifice that was "equivalent to what justice demanded of us for our sins" and was "a meritorious sacrifice" for it secured "positive blessings."[114] In his application, Edwards took this gospel message preached to the Jews and presented it to his congregation: "Let this sacrifice be acceptable unto us," and "let it be that which we look to and trust in."[115] Though Edwards did not cite anyone else on this passage, his interpretation was largely consistent with that of Reformed exegetes, except for Calvin, who was more reserved in his approach to the passage. What Edwards included that other Reformed interpreters did not was his claim that this passage depicts Christ defending God's honor in his voluntary servitude, perhaps indicating a shifting trajectory toward a moral government theory of the atonement.[116]

---

111. Edwards, "The Sacrifice of Christ Acceptable," 446–448. Quotation on 448.

112. Edwards, "The Sacrifice of Christ Acceptable," 448.

113. Edwards, "The Sacrifice of Christ Acceptable," 449–450. Quotation on 449.

114. Edwards, "The Sacrifice of Christ Acceptable," 452, 454.

115. Edwards, "The Sacrifice of Christ Acceptable," 456, 457.

116. Both Henry and Dickson said that this passage referred to the great work of "redemption" by Christ. Henry, Poole, Trapp, and Dickson all recognized that it shows the insufficiency of the Old Testament sacrifices to atone for sin but that they were types pointing to Christ, who atoned for sin in his body. Henry, Poole, and Dickson all recognized that the description of the opened ear refers back to the custom under the law of a servant boring his ear (though Poole offered other options too), and they all showed how the passage describes the willing obedience of Christ and connected the passage to Heb 10:5–7. Henry, *Exposition*, [Ps 40:6–8]; Poole, *Synopsis*, 763–766; Trapp, *Commentary*, 690–691; Dickson, *First Fifty Psalms*, 266, 269–270. Calvin was more reserved. Rejecting the allusion to the custom of a servant boring his ear, he interpreted the psalm as referring primarily to David and the clause, "Thou hast bored my ears," to mean that David's ears had been "cleansed" resulting in his ability to interpret the law better. When considering the Heb 10:5–7 quotation, Calvin

In Edwards' view, the Psalms teach us about Christ's life, from his incarnation to his prayer in Gethsemane, showing that he was truly God and truly human and that he had a deep zeal for God's ways. Most important, they teach of his willing obedience to take on the body God prepared for him so that in that body he might uphold God's honor and justice and might make atonement for sin in a manner that would satisfy God's wrath and reputation. As Christ delighted to do God's will, Edwards delighted to understand Christ's life of obedience from the Psalms so that, through that book, he might preach the gospel.

Christ's Redemptive Work

As Edwards reflected on Christ as refracted through the Psalms, one particular beam shone through with greater brightness: Christ's redemptive work. As McClymond and McDermott observe, "the primary focus of Edwards's Christology" was "Christ's satisfaction, which comprised all of his life but reached its apex in his death."[117] For Edwards, the Psalms described Christ's death and resurrection, which atoned for sins, redeems sinners, and secures benefits for the saints. These teachings brought into focus the purpose of the types and prophecies of the Messiah and of Christ's incarnation and obedient life on earth.

Psalm 22, Edwards believed, spoke at length about the death of Christ, which was a common conviction among Reformed exegetes.[118] Even the Jews interpreted this as a psalm of the Messiah, as he read in Poole.[119] Speaking in a

---

argued that the apostle took up the passage in a new direction than David intended, though under the Spirit's guidance. Calvin, *Commentary*, 2:98–104.

117. McClymond and McDermott, *The Theology of Jonathan Edwards*, 249.

118. Henry remarked, "The Spirit of CHRIST, which was in the Prophets, testifies in this Psalm, as clearly and fully as any where else in all the Old Testament, the Sufferings of CHRIST, and the Glory that should follow," and thus "[i]n singing this Psalm, we must keep our Thoughts fix'd upon CHRIST." Henry, *Exposition*, [Psalm 22]. Poole noted that the sense "more eminently respects the Messiah" ("sublimiore Messiam respicit") and also that "most apply this psalm of David likewise to a type of Christ" ("Plerique hunc Psalmum Davidi quoque, tanquam typo Christi accommodant"). Poole, *Synopsis*, 642–643. Trapp also read in this psalm the suffering of both David and Christ. Trapp, *Commentary*, 630–631. Dickson called Psalm 22 "a Prophecy of Christ[']s deepest sufferings, whereof *David[']s* exercise is a Type." Dickson, *First Fifty Psalms*, 116. Calvin explained that David "sets before us, in his own person, a type of Christ, who he knew by the Spirit of prophecy behoved to be abased in marvellous and unusual ways previous to his exaltation by the Father." Calvin, *Commentary*, 1:356.

119. In his "Prophecies" notebook, Edwards turned to Poole to observe "the rabbies interpreting this Psalm of the Messiah." Edwards, "Prophecies of the Messiah," §55; Poole, *Synopsis*, 642–643.

"Blank Bible" note on Ps 22:14, Edwards explained that the phrase "all my bones are out of joint" was "spoken of Christ in the time of his crucifixion," and was probably "literally fulfilled" in "his limbs being so stretched forth, and bearing all his weight on them so long, and his nerves and other ligatures so weakened and relaxed with extremity of pain, that it probably drew his bones out of joint."[120] Edwards not only identified prophecies but also found it important to show why the fulfillment of those prophecies was reasonable, as is evident in his comments on this and other verses in Psalm 22.[121] He further argued that the phrase "my heart is like wax" in verse 14 was fulfilled in John 19:34, when a soldier pierced his side, and "forthwith came there out blood and water."[122] In an August 1736 sermon Edwards explained the theological meaning of this verse using the language of atonement:

> Revenging justice then spent all its force upon him, on account of our guilt that was laid upon him; he was not spared at all; but God spent the arrows of his vengeance upon him, which made him sweat blood, and cry out upon the cross, and probably rent his vitals, broke his heart, the fountain of blood, or some other internal blood vessels, and by the violent fermentation turned his blood to water: for the blood and water that issued out of his side, when pierced by the spear, seems to have been extravasated blood.[123]

So Christ upheld God's moral government by substituting himself for sinners: "Christ stood up for the honor of God's justice, viz. by thus suffering its terrible executions. For when he had undertaken for sinners, and had substituted himself in their room, divine justice could have its due honor, no other way than by his suffering its revenges."[124] Edwards employed both the substitutionary and moral government models of the atonement as he interpreted the Psalms.[125]

---

120. Edwards, *The "Blank Bible,"* 486. See also Edwards' treatment of Psalm 22 in "Prophecies of the Messiah," §55.

121. Edwards worked out a similar explanation for why Christ's bones were stretched out of joint in "Fulfillment of the Prophecies," §67. He also made several similar comparisons between the Psalms and Christ's death in his "Fulfillment" notebook. See Edwards, "Fulfillment of the Prophecies," §63, §64, and §65.

122. Edwards, *The "Blank Bible,"* 962.

123. Jonathan Edwards, "The Excellency of Christ" (Rev 5:5–6), in *Sermons and Discourses 1734–1738*, ed. M. X. Lesser, vol. 19 of *WJE* (2001), 577–578.

124. Edwards, "The Excellency of Christ," 578.

125. Bruce Stephens describes Edwards' doctrine of the atonement as emphasizing satisfaction and moral government models of atonement and details the continuing focus on

Turning to verse 15, "My strength is dried up like a potsherd," Edwards said this was "remarkably fulfilled in Christ, whose body was drained of its moisture and animal spirits by a gradual shedding of blood, and want of sleep, and continual pains of body and agonies of mind, from the beginning of his agony in the garden till he expired on the cross."[126] Here Edwards quoted Henry's observation that Christ's tongue cleaving to his jaws (Ps 22:15) was a symptom of his approaching death.[127] Edwards also held that Ps 22:16, "they pierced my hands and my feet," referred to Christ's crucifixion. Looking at verse 17, "I may tell all my bones: they look and stare upon me," and verse 18, "They part my garments among them," Edwards saw evidence that Christ hung on the cross "stripped of his garments so that naked body appeared."[128] Again, he quoted Henry, who said, "His Blessed Body was lean and emaciated with Labor, Grief, and Fasting, during the whole Course of his Ministry, which made him look as if He were near Fifty Years old."[129] Also, he read "my darling" (or "my only one") as a reference to the church in Ps 22:20, "Deliver my soul from the sword; my darling from the power of the dog": "by his 'only one' here is doubtless meant the church. In Christ's soul's being delivered, the church was delivered, for he was not delivered as a private person."[130] Keeping sight of the redemptive aim of Christ's sufferings, Edwards argued that the Psalm 22 prophecies foreshadowed his redemption of the church.

In fact, Edwards positioned Christ's death in the history of redemption in his August 1750 sermon on Ps 45:3–5, "Gird thy sword upon thy thigh, O most mighty, with thy glory and thy majesty. And in thy majesty ride prosperously

---

government and law in his theological successors. Bruce M. Stephens, "An Appeal to the Universe: The Doctrine of the Atonement in American Protestant Thought from Jonathan Edwards to Edwards Amasa Park," *Encounter* 60, no. 1 (Winter 1999): 55–72. As seen in our discussion, though, it should be remembered that Edwards did not relinquish the language of substitution in his discussion of the atonement. McClymond and McDermott observe that Edwards endorsed both a substitutionary and moral government view of the atonement. McClymond and McDermott, *The Theology of Jonathan Edwards*, 250–251.

126. Edwards, *The "Blank Bible,"* 486.

127. Henry observed that "[t]he clamminess of his Mouth" is "a usual Symptom of approaching Death." Henry, *Exposition*, [Ps 22:15].

128. Edwards, *The "Blank Bible,"* 486.

129. Edwards, *The "Blank Bible,"* 486; Henry, *Exposition*, [Ps 22:17]. Perhaps Edwards felt justified from this description of Christ's scrawny body since his own dietary regimen left him looking gaunt. He had resolved "to maintain the strictest temperance in eating," so that, as Marsden notes, "observers commented on his strict eating habits and often emaciated appearance." Jonathan Edwards, "Resolutions," in *Letters and Personal Writings*, ed. George S. Claghorn, vol. 16 of *WJE* (1998), 754; Marsden, *Jonathan Edwards: A Life*, 51.

130. Edwards, *The "Blank Bible,"* 486.

because of truth and meekness and righteousness; and thy right hand shall teach thee terrible things. Thine arrows are sharp in the heart of the king's enemies; whereby the people fall under thee." Edwards observed from this text that "The Character of the Person [is] most mighty & glorious" and that the affair in which God will manifest his glory is "war," and he preached the doctrine, "The L[ord] J[esus] [Christ] is a glorious Conqueror."[131] He went on to set the background of this war in the fall: "when sin entered into the creation of G[od] there there [*sic*] began to be in the [world] Enemies to God and all that is good," with both angels and humans becoming enemies of God.[132] Since the fall, God's enemies have exalted themselves and proliferated their evil, yet God had a "design" in all these things for redeeming "an elect part of the world & bringing them out of a state of bondage & captivity under their Power to great & glo[rious] Honour & glory."[133] God gave Christ a "commission" and he "sent Him forth to this End to oppose & Conquer these Enemies & Evils in the great W[ork] of Redemption."[134] With this background, Edwards returned to the mighty warrior in the text, depicting Christ as a glorious conqueror in two ways. First, Christ procured redemption in his last sufferings when he opened "a glo[rious] conquest over Satan" and his evils, and in his resurrection he triumphed over all these evils—Satan, guilt, corruption, affliction, and death—so that "nothing of em could be found," just "like a boundless ocean that swallowed them up."[135] Second, Christ appears as a glorious conqueror "in the applica[tion] of R[edemption]" to the saints.[136] Edwards closed by exhorting sinners to yield to this conqueror, for by his death Christ will conquer individuals one way or the other, whether he conquers the sin in their hearts or their very beings; the option is either to "yield to the golden scepter of his Gr[eatness]" or be destroyed by his "rod of iron" (Ps 2:9).[137]

How is it that Christ's death obtains redemption? Edwards argued that it can only be understood in relation to the Old Testament sacrificial system, which reveals God's design that sin is atoned for only by blood sacrifice. Thus

---

131. Jonathan Edwards, "963. Sermon on Ps 45:3–5 (August 1750)," Beinecke Rare Book and Manuscript Library, Yale University, New Haven, CT, L. 1r. Edwards repreached this sermon three times, at Stockbridge, Canaan, and Mr. Morehead's in Boston.

132. Edwards, "963. Sermon on Ps 45:3–5," L. 1r.

133. Edwards, "963. Sermon on Ps 45:3–5," L. 3v.

134. Edwards, "963. Sermon on Ps 45:3–5," L. 3v.

135. Edwards, "963. Sermon on Ps 45:3–5," L. 5v., 6r.

136. Edwards, "963. Sermon on Ps 45:3–5," L. 8r.

137. Edwards, "963. Sermon on Ps 45:3–5," L. 10v.

Ps 118:27, "bind the sacrifice with cords, even unto the horns of the altar," reveals a type of Christ, who "when substituted for sinners, was bound by divine justice to suffer and be offered up a sacrifice."[138] Again, for Edwards, atonement included both substitution for sinners and satisfaction of divine justice. He addressed the issue of Christ's sacrifice further in his "Harmony of the Genius Spirit Doctrines and Rules of the Old Testament and the New," a manuscript by which Edwards hoped to establish the unity of the Bible.[139] Discussing this notebook, Nichols argues that the history of redemption and the covenant of grace provide the framework for Edwards' belief in the doctrinal harmony of the two testaments; Christ's redemptive work in the incarnation is "the crux of history," and all history, prior to and after Christ, is "a grand scheme divinely directed to God's own glory through the redemption of Christ."[140] In the "Harmony," Edwards argued from Psalm 50 that God required sacrifice for sin: "A sacrifice is absolutely necessary. There is no having any covenant interest in God without it.... 'Tis essential in the character of all true saints, that they are reconciled and united to God as their God by sacrifice."[141] However, God planned all along to abolish legal sacrifices and establish spiritual sacrifices as the only obligation of saints. So we are taught in Ps 51:16–17, "For thou desirest not sacrifice; else would I give it: thou delightest not in burnt offering. The sacrifices of God are a broken spirit: a broken and a contrite heart, O God, thou wilt not despise." For Edwards, verse 16 showed that "[t]he legal sacrifices of the Law of Moses were not sufficient to atone for sin; God never appointed them as expecting any such thing from them, nor does he require or desire [']em as of any value on their own account."[142] Instead, Christ fulfilled God's sacrificial requirement in his death. Thus, in his "Blank Bible" entry on Ps 51:18–19, "Do good in thy good pleasure unto Zion: build thou the walls of Jerusalem. Then shalt thou be pleased with the sacrifices of righteousness, with burnt offering and whole burnt offering: then shall they

---

138. Edwards, *The "Blank Bible,"* 531.

139. Edwards structured his "Harmony" notebook with two sections: First, he made theological statements followed by scriptural evidence from either or both testaments supporting those statements. Second, he walked through the Bible in canonical order, commenting specifically on certain passages that related to his topic of harmony. In this second section, he only made it through the Psalms before he died.

140. Nichols, *Jonathan Edwards's Bible*, 115.

141. Jonathan Edwards, "Harmony of the Genius Spirit Doctrines and Rules of the Old Testament and the New," Beinecke Rare Book and Manuscript Library, Yale University, New Haven, CT, 237.

142. Edwards, "Harmony," 239.

offer bullocks upon thine altar," Edwards said that the Holy Spirit was looking forward to "the accomplishing the work of redemption by Jesus Christ," since the sacrifice of bulls was a type of the perfect sacrifice that "indeed should be pleasing to God, and sufficient to atone for such sins as David's."[143] The legal sacrifices had a "typical accomplishment" in the multitude of sacrifices offered at the dedication of Solomon's temple, but the "ultimate and proper accomplishment" was found in "the redemption of Christ."[144]

In fact, Edwards argued that the Psalms taught that the coming Messiah would accomplish the work of atonement for he would be a priest after the order of Melchizedek (Ps 110:4).[145] Edwards developed this theme in a sermon on "Christ[']s Priestly office," taken from Ps 110:4, "The LORD hath sworn, and will not repent, Thou art a priest for ever after the order of Melchizedek."[146] The linking of Psalm 110 with Christ's priesthood was a common Reformed interpretation, and Edwards noted in his "Prophecies" notebook that even "the rabbies interpret it of the Messiah."[147] In his sermon, he first looked back into

---

143. Edwards, *The "Blank Bible,"* 500.

144. Edwards, *The "Blank Bible,"* 500. See also Edwards' discussion of Ps 72:3, 7 as prophetic of Christ's redemptive work in his "Blank Bible" entry on Jer 33:6. Edwards, *The "Blank Bible,"* 721.

145. Jonathan Edwards, "'Controversies' Notebook: Justification," in *Writings on the Trinity, Grace, and Faith*, ed. Sang Hyun Lee, vol. 21 of *WJE* (2003), 398.

146. Jonathan Edwards, "746. Sermon on Ps 110:4 (June 1744)," in *Sermons, Series II, 1744*, vol. 62 of the *WJEO*, L. IV. This sermon is the third in a three-part series on the prophetical, kingly, and priestly offices of Christ. The "prophetical" office is taken up in a sermon on Deut 18:18; the kingly office in a sermon on Ps 2:6 (discussed below); and the priestly office in this sermon on Ps 110:4. Jonathan Edwards, "743. Sermon on Deut 18:18 (June 1744)," in *Sermons, Series II, 1744*, vol. 62 of the *WJEO*. Jonathan Edwards, "745. Sermon on Ps 2:6 (June 1744)," in *Sermons, Series II, 1744*, vol. 62 of the *WJEO*. Edwards repreached this three-part series in March 1755, presumably at Stockbridge. See also Edwards' treatment of Psalm 110 in "Prophecies of the Messiah," §45.

147. Edwards, "Prophecies of the Messiah," §45. Poole noted that the old Hebrews were not doubtful but that it was to be understood of the Messiah; so Rabbi Obadiah states concerning Psalm 110, "The musician composed this psalm concerning the Messiah" ("Hunc Psalmum composuit Psaltes de Messia"). Poole also identified this psalm as describing Christ's priestly office. Poole, *Synopsis*, 1166–1169, 1175–1176. Quotation on 1166. As for other interpreters, Henry said that "[t]his Psalm is pure Gospel; 'tis only and wholly concerning CHRIST, the Messiah," and it particularly speaks of Christ's office as priest in verse 4, in which he was appointed "[t]o make Atonement for our Sins." Henry, *Exposition*, [Ps 110:4]. Trapp maintained that this psalm is "[c]oncerning Christ" and that verse 4 specifically addresses "Christ[']s Priestly Office." Trapp, *Commentary*, 852–853. Dickson argued that "[t]his Psalm containeth the doctrine of Christ, God and man in one person, concerning his everlasting Kingdom and Priesthood," and in his office of priest Christ reconciles humans to God "by his propitiatory sacrifice." Dickson, *Last Fifty Psalmes*, 108, 110–111. Calvin held that this psalm sets forth "the perpetuity of Christ's reign, and the eternity of his priesthood," for

Old Testament history to show that the only legitimate priesthood mentioned besides the line of Aaron is Melchizedek. But Edwards essentially used Ps 110:4 as a spring text to Hebrews, which guided him in outlining the many differences between the two priesthoods. Edwards described the priestly office of Christ as the "office of [Christ] in the Execution of which he makes attonement for the sins of men & procures for them the Favour of G[od]"—that is, both satisfying God's justice and obtaining spiritual benefits for the church by his merits.[148] In his priestly office, Christ completely performed "the work of Redemption strictly so called," which is why his priestly office "seems to be the principal office of the Redeemer."[149] Christ executes this office by offering a "divinely Holy" sacrifice that satisfied the wrath of God and by interceding with his Father to bless those he has redeemed.[150] In his application, Edwards urged poor sinners to come boldly to God because he is ready to accept not their offering but the offering of Christ as priest—an offering planned from eternity, prefigured in the ancient sacrifices, completed by Christ, accepted by God through "Remarkeable Testimonies," including the resurrection, ascension, kingdom, and coming judgment.[151]

As Edwards mentioned briefly in the application of this sermon, the resurrection of Christ presents one of the key evidences that Christ's atoning work on the cross was satisfactory and acceptable to God, and Edwards saw several parallels between the Psalms and the resurrection of Christ. In "Miscellanies" Entry No. 691, Edwards read a foretelling of Christ's resurrection in Ps 69:14–15, the passage that Edwards believed Christ prayed in Gethsemane. Since Christ prayed, "let not the pit shut her mouth upon me," and since the "pit" commonly means the "grave" in Scripture, "what he prays for is that he mayn't continue in the grave," for the resurrection was the "appointed and promised"

---

one must "admit that the truths here stated relate neither to David nor to any other person than the Mediator alone." Calvin, *Commentary*, 4:295–296.

148. Edwards, "746. Sermon on Ps 110:4," L. 2r.–3v. Quotation on L. 2r.

149. Edwards, "746. Sermon on Ps 110:4," L. 2r.–2v. In "Miscellanies" Entry No. 1035, "SATISFACTION OF CHRIST," Edwards described how Christ completely satisfied God's justice in an unusual exegesis of Ps 69:5, "O God, thou knowest my foolishness; and my sins are not hid from thee." He explained that God "forgives nothing to the Messiah, [but] beholds all his guiltiness by imputed sin, has set all in the light of his countenance, and don't cover or hide the least part of it," thus implying his complete satisfaction for sins. Edwards, *The "Miscellanies": Entry Nos. 833–1152*, 375–376.

150. Edwards, "746. Sermon on Ps 110:4," L. 4v.–5r. Quotation on L. 4v.

151. Edwards, "746. Sermon on Ps 110:4," L. 6v.–7r.

deliverance that he "expected."¹⁵² In "Miscellanies" Entry No. 958, Edwards explained that in "his second birth," Christ was again "begotten of God" and "born of the womb of the earth" in his resurrection, which is what is meant by Ps 2:7, where "God the Father says to Christ, with respect to his resurrection," "Thou art my Son; this day have I begotten thee."¹⁵³ Similarly, in "Notes on Scripture" Entry No. 328 on Ps 19:4–6, which compares the sun to a bridegroom coming out of his chamber, Edwards argued that "the Holy Ghost, in these expressions which he most immediately uses about the rising of the sun, has an eye to the rising of the Sun of Righteousness from the grave."¹⁵⁴ He compared Old Testament times to the night and argued that "the commencing of the gospel dispensation, as it was introduced by Christ, is called the Sun of Righteousness rising."¹⁵⁵ When does this begin? Edwards pinpointed the resurrection of Christ as the starting point of this new dispensation, using Psalm 19 as imaging Christ's spiritual marriage to the church: "Therein the Sun of Righteousness rises from under the earth, as the sun appears to do in the morning, and comes forth as a bridegroom. He rose as the joyful glorious bridegroom of his church."¹⁵⁶

As we have seen, in Edwards' view, the redemptive work of Christ included not only his satisfaction of God's justice but also his procurement of benefits for the saints. He described an array of benefits obtained using the Psalms. In a "Blank Bible" note on Ps 8:5–9, Edwards discussed "the wonderful goodness and condescension of God to man in advancing the human nature to such dignity and honor" by uniting humanity with God in Christ.¹⁵⁷ He further explored the benefits of Christ's redemptive work in two sermons on the Psalms. We have already encountered one of these when Edwards compared

---

152. Edwards, *The "Miscellanies": Entry Nos. 501–832*, 273. Edwards used the resurrection as one of several arguments for celebrating the Sabbath on the first day of the week, rather than the seventh.

153. Edwards based this Christological reading on Heb 5:5, which cites Ps 2:7 in relation to Christ. Edwards, *The "Miscellanies": Entry Nos. 833–1152*, 236–237. See also his similar observation that Ps 2:7 is "applied to Christ's resurrection" in Acts 13:33 in *Original Sin*, ed. Clyde A. Holbrook, vol. 3 of *WJE* (1970), 364.

154. Edwards, *Notes on Scripture*, 311.

155. Edwards, *Notes on Scripture*, 311.

156. Edwards, *Notes on Scripture*, 311. In addition, Edwards cited Poole in his "Blank Bible" entry on Ps 19:5. Edwards, *The "Blank Bible*," 485. Poole described the bridegroom as having splendid garments and gleaming rays that turn all eyes to him and gladden his friends. The passage speaks particularly of the marriage to the elect, which issues in great felicity for all. Poole, *Synopsis*, 628.

157. Edwards, *The "Blank Bible*," 478.

the frailty of human nature to grass, a January 1741 sermon for the sacrament on Ps 72:6, "He shall come down like rain upon the mown grass: as showers that water the earth." Here Edwards repeated one of his principles of interpreting the Psalms, that "the Holy Spirit, in some of the Psalms, has a twofold aim and intendment.... They have respect more immediately to some person that is an eminent type of Christ. But their principle and more ultimate respect is to Christ himself."[158] Edwards found support for this reading in Stapfer and Poole, who both testified that the Jews read Psalm 72 of the Messiah.[159] In Edwards' exposition of Psalm 72, he compared several verses that referred both to Solomon and to Christ and even noted some verses that could really only apply "in any proper sense" to Christ alone (Pss 72:5, 8, 11, 17), concluding that the words of the sermon text, Ps 72:6, are "much more applicable to Christ than they are to Solomon...and doubtless they are principally intended of Christ."[160] Observing that Christ is often depicted by natural types in Scripture, Edwards argued that Christ is here represented by rain coming down from heaven, which images his dispensing of benefits on humanity and is compared to mown grass. Edwards thus preached this doctrine: "Christ, in communicating himself and dispensing his benefits, does as it were come down as the rain on the mown grass."[161] He explored the parallels of this imagery with Christ through three points in the doctrinal section. First, he showed how, like rain, Christ is said to come down from heaven—namely in his incarnation, at the day of judgment, in glorious displays of his power, and in the Spirit's saving influences on sinners' hearts. Second, he compared the subjects of Christ's benefits to mown grass (see pp. 129–130). Finally, he compared rain on mown grass to Christ's communication of himself to his subjects: "in descending upon them he refreshes, revives and restores them as the rain doth the grass after it is mown."[162] In his application, Edwards

---

158. Jonathan Edwards, "Like Rain upon Mown Grass" (Ps 72:6), in *Sermons and Discourses 1739–1742*, ed. Harry S. Stout and Nathan O. Hatch with Kyle P. Farley, vol. 22 of *WJE* (2003), 300. See also Edwards' similar treatment of Psalm 72 in "Prophecies of the Messiah," §39.

159. Edwards, "Prophecies of the Messiah," §39. Stapfer stated, "Most of the Jews explain part of Psalms 72 concerning the Messiah" ("Plurima Judæorum pars Psalmum LXXII de Messia exponunt"). Stapfer, 62. Poole also noted that "the old Hebrew scholars nevertheless recognize these things in this passage to pertain more eminently in a sense to the Messiah" ("Sublimiori tamen sensu pertinere haec ad Messiam agnoscunt vetus Scholiastes Hebraeus hoc loco"), as Rabbis Saadia Ben Joseph Gaon (892–942) and Solomon Ben Isaac Jarchi (1104–1180) testify. Poole, *Synopsis*, 963.

160. Edwards, "Like Rain upon Mown Grass," 301–301. Quotations on 300.

161. Edwards, "Like Rain upon Mown Grass," 301.

162. Edwards, "Like Rain upon Mown Grass," 308.

called people to see if they had ever experienced the refreshment of Christ, exhorted those seeking salvation to become like mown grass by recognizing the inadequacy of their works, and invited "those whose souls are wounded with a sense of their sins and miserable state to come to Christ."[163] Applying Psalm 72 to Christ was common in Edwards' day. In "Miscellanies" Entry No. 1227, Edwards recorded a segment of a Samuel Davies (1723–1761) sermon, in which he compared the description of Solomon in Psalm 72 to Christ: "Thus the reign of Solomon is celebrated in such exalted language, as can fully agree to none but a greater than Solomon, who now reigns over his spiritual Israel (Ps. 72)."[164] This Christological parallel was a standard comparison in the Reformed tradition.[165]

Edwards explored another benefit of Christ's redemptive work in an April 1747 sermon on Ps 84:3, "Yea, the sparrow hath found an house, and the swallow a nest for herself, where she may lay her young, even thine altars, O Lord of hosts, my King, and my God." He noted that what the psalmist longed for was "The Place where God[']s altars were" because they are near to "his G[od] & Redeemer."[166] In "Notes on Scripture" Entry No. 349, Edwards made a similar observation, for while the birds have a nest as their home, David was an exile who was "banished from God's house," and this verse captures his "ardent exclamation, expressing the longing of David's soul after God's

---

163. Edwards, "Like Rain upon Mown Grass," 318. See also Edwards' similar discussion in *Religious Affections*, 154, and in his entry on Ps 72:6 in *The "Blank Bible,"* 507–509.

164. Edwards, *The "Miscellanies": Entry Nos. 1153–1360*, 159. Samuel Davies, *A Sermon, Preached before the Reverend Presbytery of New-Castle, October 11, 1752* (Philadelphia, PA: B. Franklin and D. Hall, at the New Printing Office, in Market street, 1753), 4.

165. Henry explained that Christ comes down "by the Graces and Comforts of his Spirit," for "[t]he Gospel of CHRIST distills as the Rain, which softens the Ground that was hard, moistens that which was dry, and so makes it green and fruitful." Henry, *Exposition*, [Ps 72:6]. Poole identified the rain as a referent to Christ and presented different times in his work when it might refer to him, whether when he descended to the earth, when he descended into the virgin's womb, or when he will descend in his eschatological reign. He recognized a double meaning that it referred to both Solomon and Christ. Poole, *Synopsis*, 966. Trapp stated that this imagery of rain indicates that Christ "shall bee very dear to us, and much delighted in," for he shall make "his Church to grow and flourish." Trapp, *Commentary*, 769. Dickson said that no matter what condition the church be in, even as "a mowen down meadow," still "Christ by his Word, Spirit, and effectual blessing shall revive and recover them: as grass cut down being watered by rain, is made to grow again." Dickson, *Other Fifty Psalmes*, 146. Even Calvin said that this prophecy received "its highest fulfilment in Christ, who, by distilling upon the Church his secret grace, renders her fruitful." Calvin, *Commentary*, 3:107.

166. Jonathan Edwards, "860. Sermon on Ps 84:3 (April 1747)," Beinecke Rare Book and Manuscript Library, Yale University, New Haven, CT, L. 1r.

altars."[167] He cited Poole in his "Blank Bible" entry on this verse, and Poole described how the birds could make their nests in the top of the temple or in the trees near the tabernacle and that, as David was in exile at the time, it is understandable how he might envy the birds. Poole also compared the nest, where a bird finds rest, with God's altars, where the spirit finds rest, and showed that God's altars thus symbolize refuge, sweetness, and security.[168] In Edwards' sermon he took the verse further by identifying the place believers long for as Christ himself—a unique interpretation.[169] As David "longs after it as his Home," so Edwards preached the doctrine, "[Christ] is the Believer[']s Home."[170] Christ is the believer's home in that he is the believer's "Refuge & shelter" and his "Resting Place"—the place "where He ordinarily abides" and "where He enjoys what is his own," the place where he "has his daily entertainm[en]t" and "is at Liberty," and the place "where he meets his nearest Friends" and loves his children.[171] In his application Edwards challenged people to examine whether they truly longed after Christ as their home, for a "Hypocrite don[']t make [Christ] his home" but instead "The [world] is his Home."[172] He exhorted people "To seek that you may have [Christ] for your home," for Christ is a "Paradise" of "unspeakable delights."[173]

As Edwards read the Psalms in light of the Bible's unity, he heavily emphasized Christ's role as Savior, the Redeemer who atoned for sin on the cross, satisfied God's justice, merited spiritual benefits for those he redeemed and

---

167. Edwards, *Notes on Scripture*, 335.

168. Poole, *Synopsis*, 1039–1040.

169. None of these five Reformed interpreters made a link between God's altars and Christ as the believer's home, though they all recognized in this verse the strong desires of the psalmist for God's altars and for communion with God. Henry, *Exposition*, [Ps 84:3]; Trapp, *Commentary*, 799; Dickson, *Other fifty Psalmes*, 268; Calvin, *Commentary*, 3:355–357.

170. Edwards, "860. Sermon on Ps 84:3," L. 1r., 1v.

171. Edwards, "860. Sermon on Ps 84:3," L. iv.–5r.

172. Edwards, "860. Sermon on Ps 84:3," L. 6v.

173. Edwards, "860. Sermon on Ps 84:3," L. 7r., 8v., 9r. In addition to the benefits discussed here, see Edwards' discussion from Psalm 23 of the benefit of Christ as our shepherd and his rod as our comfort. Jonathan Edwards, "The Sweet Harmony of Christ" (John 10:4), in *Sermons and Discourses 1734–1738*, ed. M. X. Lesser, vol. 19 of *WJE* (2001), 438; and Edwards, *The "Blank Bible*," 487, 488. In his "Blank Bible" entries on Ps 23:2 and 4, Edwards also cited three other entries discussing the staff. Edwards, *The "Blank Bible,"* 271; Edwards, *Notes on Scripture*, 106–108, 524–525. See also Edwards' March 1751 sermon on Ps 36:7, which he repreached later that same year and in which he explored God's excellent lovingkindness in Jesus Christ. Jonathan Edwards, "989. Sermon on Ps 36:7 (March 1751)," Franklin Trask Library, Andover Newton Theological School. Newton, MA.

united to himself, and was vindicated in the resurrection. The vast benefits he secured for believers range from refreshment and peace to refuge and security in a glorious home of love. In Edwards' unified understanding of the Bible, he argued that the Psalms—and the whole Old Testament—make it plain that "[t]he WORK OF SALVATION is often spoken of as peculiar to God," as Pss 37:39; 3:8; 25:5; 27:1; and 68:30 testify.[174] By comparing the Psalms' anticipation of God's salvation with the New Testament revelation of Christ, Edwards concluded that "now nothing is more evident by the express and abundant doctrine of Scripture than that Jesus Christ is most eminently and peculiarly the Savior of God's people and the Savior of mankind, the Savior of the world."[175]

Christ's Glorification and Kingly Reign

In the history of redemption, the story does not end with Christ's securing redemption but continues through the outworking of that redemption in the church and the eschaton. In the person of Christ, God displays his pleasure with Christ's work by glorifying his Son from his ascension to his dominion over all things as king.

Edwards taught that the Psalms prophesied of Christ's ascension and exaltation to the throne room of God—what McClymond and McDermott call his "enthronement theology"—in a number of places, but he gravitated to two particular passages in discussing Christ's ascension.[176] The first was Ps 24:7–10:

> Lift up your heads, O ye gates; and be ye lift up, ye everlasting doors; and the King of glory shall come in. Who is this King of glory? The LORD strong and mighty, the LORD mighty in battle. Lift up your heads, O ye gates; even lift them up, ye everlasting doors; and the King of glory shall come in. Who is this King of glory? The LORD of hosts, he is the King of glory. Selah.

In his "Blank Bible," Edwards placed the words, "Lift up your heads, O ye gates," into the mouth of God the Father, who "himself opened the gates of heaven to receive his Son after his passion in token of his great acceptance

---

174. Edwards, *The "Miscellanies": Entry Nos. 1153–1360*, 617.

175. Edwards, *The "Miscellanies": Entry Nos. 1153–1360*, 619.

176. McClymond and McDermott, *The Theology of Jonathan Edwards*, 287–291. See also Edwards' discussion of Christ's ascension from Ps 8:1; the title of Psalm 30; Pss 47:9; 113:3–4; and 115:2–3. Edwards, *The "Blank Bible,"* 477, 491, 496; Edwards, *The "Miscellanies": Entry Nos. 833–1152*, 169, 496.

of what he had done."[177] The lifting of the doors "has respect to God's, or Christ's, triumphant ascension into heaven after a battle and victory over his enemies here on earth," as if entering through a "vault" that leads from earth to "the pavement of heaven," and the doors open "when the King of Glory [approaches], as most readily receiving the King of Glory as a most proper inhabitant, the rightful owner of the house, one infinitely worthy to be received."[178] In this "Blank Bible" entry, Edwards cited Poole, who recognized that this passage can be understood "concerning the ascension of Christ" and explained that while the gates can refer to the gates of Zion or the gates of the temple when the ark was brought up to Jerusalem, they have greater respect to Christ's work, whether the "gates of the heavenly Jerusalem" where the angels are guards, or "authority and power," or "Christian people, who are the Temple of God."[179] Poole's exegetical discussion reflected the general approach of the Reformed tradition, which mostly affirmed a reference to Christ's ascension in this passage—Calvin standing out as the exception.[180]

Edwards preached a sermon on this passage in January 1739, which closely mirrored his "Notes on Scripture" entry on the passage (Entry No. 308). Edwards set the sermon in the context of the question of verse 3—who can ascend God's holy hill?—and he used the geography of Israel to establish a typology. Under David's reign the holy hill of God referred to Mount Zion, where the ark of the covenant had been placed, and under Solomon's reign

177. Edwards, The "Blank Bible," 489.

178. Edwards, The "Blank Bible," 489.

179. Edwards, The "Blank Bible," 489. The Latin reads, "de ascensione Christi"; "portarum coelestis Jerosolymae"; "imperia & regna"; "homines Christianos, qui sunt Templum Dei." Poole, Synopsis, 667–668.

180. Henry recognized that while this psalm describes the bringing of the ark into the temple, that historical event typifies "the Ascension of CHRIST into Heaven" as "the Gates of Heaven" are opened to him. Henry went on to say that it also typifies "CHRIST's entrance into the Souls of Men by his Word and Spirit, that they may be his Temples." Henry, Exposition, [Ps 24:7–10]. Trapp observed that Ps 24:7–10 celebrates "Christ['] ascension" as the angels look on with admiration and his opening "the way to all his Members," though it also has reference to bringing up the ark and to saints opening the gates of their hearts. Trapp, Commentary, 638–640. Dickson argued that the ascent of the ark offered a "shadow" of Christ, who after securing "our redemption" through "his great battels" did "ascend to heaven, and make way for his subjects to come up after him." Dickson, First Fifty Psalms, 138–139. Calvin did not apply this passage to Christ's ascension. He interpreted it at length as referring to the ark being taken up to the temple on Mount Zion, and only toward the end of his exposition did he show that Christ is the king of glory who now dwells in our midst instead of in a temple. Calvin, Commentary, 1:409–413.

to Mount Moriah, where the temple was built—both hills typifying heaven.[181] Thus in the sermon text, Ps 24:7–10, the gates to the holy hill represent the gates to heaven, and the king of glory refers to Jesus Christ, and so the psalm speaks of Christ's ascension into heaven. When the psalmist says that "he that hath clean hands and a pure heart" can ascend God's holy hill, it has a double meaning: "In one sense all [Christ']s sincere disciples & followers are such[;] they are pure in Heart & hands with a purity of sincerity [and] universal Obedience[.] [B]ut in another sense [Christ] alone is so who was perfectly free from all defilem[ent] of Heart & hands."[182] Thus Edwards determined that "[t]his Psalm treats of the Ascension of both head & members of the Ch[urc]h of [Christ] into Heaven."[183] In describing Christ's ascension, Edwards commented that this psalm signifies "with what Joy & wellcome [Christ] was receivd in Heaven by His F[ather] & all the Heavenly Inhabitants" for "Tis Probable that the day of [Christ']s ascension into H[eaven] was the most Joyfull day that ever was seen there."[184] Then Edwards developed a typological connection between David's victory over Goliath and Christ's victory over Satan. As David killed Goliath with his own sword, then carried the head of Goliath into Jerusalem and elicited the question from Saul, "whose son is this youth?" (1 Sam 17:55), so likewise Christ defeated Satan with his own sword, the cross, then "ascended into Heaven in triumph as it were with the Head of saatan in his hand" and so elicited the question, "Who is this King of glory?"[185] Edwards explained this phrase to indicate not the inquirers' ignorance, but their admiration, and thus Edwards came to his doctrine, "Jesus [Christ] Entring his Glory after he suff[ered] was a sight worthy to be beheld with Great Admiration," for Christ is himself wonderful and infinitely glorious, and "the Glory he enterd into was wonderfull Glory."[186]

Edwards also discussed Psalm 68 at greater length with reference to Christ's ascension. He held that it speaks of both the ark's ascension to Mt. Zion and the ascension of the Messiah; it deals with "the subject of Christ's ascension" as it speaks twice of God riding on the heavens (68:4, 33).[187] In his

---

181. Jonathan Edwards, "499. Sermon on Ps 24:7–10 (January 1739)," in *Sermons, Series II, 1739*, vol. 54 of the *WJEO*, L. 1r.

182. Edwards, "499. Sermon on Ps 24:7–10," L. 1v.–2r. See Edwards, *Notes on Scripture*, 281.

183. Edwards, "499. Sermon on Ps 24:7–10," L. 2r. See Edwards, *Notes on Scripture*, 281.

184. Edwards, "499. Sermon on Ps 24:7–10," L. 2r., 2v. See Edwards, *Notes on Scripture*, 282.

185. Edwards, "499. Sermon on Ps 24:7–10," L. 3r. See Edwards, *Notes on Scripture*, 282.

186. Edwards, "499. Sermon on Ps 24:7–10," L. 3v., 7r.

187. Edwards, "Types of the Messiah," 219; Edwards, *The "Blank Bible,"* 315.

treatment of Ps 68:18–20, Edwards spoke of Christ's ascension to his throne in heaven within the purview of his redemptive work:

> That the divine Redeemer of the church and people of God, and the Savior of sinners, should ascend into heaven and fix his throne there, after he has obtained the most signal victory over their enemies, is a most suitable manifestation of his glory as a triumphant conqueror and all-sufficient Redeemer; and is greatly for the advantage of his people, and what they have cause to rejoice in, being needful in order to his receiving those gifts which they most need, and wherein their greatest happiness consists; and giving the greatest advantage for his saving them from death, and bestowing on them eternal life.[188]

Edwards was especially interested in verse 18: "Thou hast ascended on high, thou hast led captivity captive." While this passage referred on one level to the ascending of the ark of the covenant, it referred chiefly to "God's ascending on high" for four reasons: (1) verse 15 says the hill ascended is a "high hill," but "Mt. Zion in Jerusalem was not so"; (2) the Old Testament regularly uses the expression "on high" (v. 18) to refer to heaven; (3) the ark was carried on the Levites' shoulders, while the chariots described in v. 17 are identified as thousands of angels; and (4) the psalm itself describes the one ascending as "him that rideth upon the heavens by his name JAH" (v. 4) and "him that rideth upon the heavens of heavens," for "his strength is in the clouds" (vv. 33–34).[189] Edwards concluded, "Therefore what must be chiefly intended, must be God's ascending when he shall appear visibly as the Savior of his people in the Messiah's days, agreeably to many prophecies…and therefore this is a prediction of the Messiah's ascending into heaven."[190] This application to Christ's ascension and completion of the work of redemption was standard in Reformed exegesis.[191]

---

188. Edwards, "Harmony," 244. Ps 68:18–20 reads, "Thou hast ascended on high, thou hast led captivity captive: thou hast received gifts for men; yea, for the rebellious also, that the LORD God might dwell among them. Blessed be the Lord, who daily loadeth us with benefits, even the God of our salvation. Selah. He that is our God is the God of salvation; and unto GOD the Lord belong the issues from death."

189. Edwards, "Prophecies of the Messiah," §58.

190. Edwards, "Prophecies of the Messiah," §58.

191. Henry recognized that "CHRIST's ascending on high is here spoken of as a thing past, so *sure* it was" and that "[i]t may include his whole Exalted State, but points especially at his Ascension into Heaven, to the Right Hand of the Father." Henry, *Exposition*, [Ps 68:18]. Poole considered how this verse applies to David, to God, and to Christ, and speaking of Christ, he said, "You, our incarnate God, after you completed the work of redemption on earth, you

Edwards developed the typology of Psalm 68 more extensively in "Notes on Scripture" Entry No. 319, on Psalm 68, which he titled, "The Removal of the Ark and Christ's Ascension."[192] In this entry, which is the longest "Notes on Scripture" entry on the Psalms, Edwards pointed to a number of parallels between the bringing up of the ark and the ascension of Christ, stating, "The bringing up the ark of God out of the house of Obed-edom the Gittite, into the city of David on the top of Mt. Zion, on which occasion this psalm was penned, was the most remarkable type of the ascension of Christ that we have in the Old Testament."[193] Edwards noted that as the ark was attended by the princes of the tribes of Israel (Ps 68:27), so "Christ was attended with multitudes of angels in his ascension into heaven" (Ps 68:17–18).[194] The most "probable" location for all these angels meeting Christ was, following Acts 1:9, "in the upper parts of the earth's atmosphere, beyond the region of the clouds," and Edwards speculated that "Christ's human nature there had its transformation into its glorious state" because, theologically, the disciples could not have perceived Christ in his glory and lived, and, scientifically, "[a]n earthly body might subsist as far as the region of the clouds, but it could not subsist further."[195] While Christ ascended slowly for the disciples to see him gradually go, once he reached the clouds, "he mounted with inconceivable swiftness, answerable to the agility of an heavenly glorious body."[196] As the return of the ark was a time to "rejoice before

---

ascended into heaven, having triumphed over sin, death, the devil, idols, etc. Thus Paul interprets, Eph 4:8" ("Tu, Deus noster incarnate, post peractum opus Redemptionis in terris, ascendisti in coelum, de peccato, morte, Diabolo, idolis, &c. triumphans. Ità interpretatur Paulus Ephes. 4,8"). Poole, *Synopsis*, 932–935. Quotation on 933. Trapp recognized that Paul "teacheth us to understand it of his wonderful Ascension." Trapp, *Commentary*, 759. Dickson likewise saw in verse 18 a reference to Christ's ascension as affirmation that he had perfected "the work of Redemption," for "here the Lord[']s Spirit led his people to look through the shadow of the ascending of the Ark toward the city of *David*, unto the ascending of God incarnate (represented by the Ark) into heaven." Dickson, *Other fifty Psalmes*, 107. Italics original. Calvin, after discussing how this verse applied to David's rise to the throne, showed that, following Eph 4:8, it describes Christ's ascension with an eye to "the result and fruit of it, in his subjecting heaven and earth to his government." Calvin, *Commentary*, 3:25–27. Quotation on 26.

192. Edwards, *Notes on Scripture*, 297n7. This "Notes on Scripture" entry held importance to Edwards, who referred to it in his "Blank Bible" entries on 2 Sam 6:12–23; 6:19; 6:20–23; Psalm 68; Acts 1:9; and Heb 12:1. Edwards, *The "Blank Bible,"* 362, 504, 968, 1160.

193. Edwards, *Notes on Scripture*, 297.

194. Edwards, *Notes on Scripture*, 298.

195. Edwards, *Notes on Scripture*, 299–300.

196. Edwards, *Notes on Scripture*, 300.

God" (Ps 68:3) and a time for "singers" and "players on instruments" (Ps 68:25) so "Christ's ascension is represented as an exceeding joyful occasion."[197] Edwards also showed parallels to Christ from the historical accounts of the ark's return, including David's sacrifice in the tabernacle and Christ's sacrifice of blood; David's blessing of his household and Christ's blessing of his church by sending the Spirit; and David's rejection of Michal, his wife who despised him for his humbling show, and Christ's rejection of the Jewish church, which despised him for humbling himself in his incarnation.[198] As Edwards summarized the parallels between Psalm 68 and Christ's ascension, God's work of redemption rose to the surface:

> The glorious attendants and consequents of Christ's ascension are livelily represented in this psalm, and other divine songs that seem to be penned on occasion of the recovering the ark, as particularly Christ's glorious victory over his enemies (vv. 1–2, 18), the destruction of Satan's kingdom and his church's enemies that followed (vv. 12, 14, 16, 23, 30), a terrible manifestation of wrath against obstinate sinners (vv. 6, 21), the publishing [of] the gospel in the world (vv. 11, 33), a remarkable pouring out of the Spirit (v. 9), a great increase of the privileges of the church and a more abundant measure of spiritual blessings (vv. 3, 10, 13, 18, 19, 24, 29, 34–35), the calling of the Gentiles (v. 6, 29, 31–32), a glorious salvation from slavery and misery for sinners and enslaved (vv. 6, 13, 20, 22).[199]

Edwards included passages from all over the Bible to establish his argument, from Israel's history books to the Gospels and epistles, all working in concert with Psalm 68 to describe Christ's ascension as one key aspect of God's work of redemption in history.

When Christ ascended on high, God crowned him as king and established him on the throne of heaven: "As in the 16th Psalm, 'tis foretold that God would show the Messiah the way to his blissful and glorious presence, and his right hand, so Ps. 110[:1], it is said, God would bid him sit on his right hand."[200] In fact, Edwards saw much in the Psalms that described Christ's kingly position and dominion, and in June 1744 he preached a sermon on the "Kingly office

---

197. Edwards, *Notes on Scripture*, 300.

198. Edwards, *Notes on Scripture*, 301.

199. Edwards, *Notes on Scripture*, 302.

200. Edwards, "Fulfillment of the Prophecies," §94.

of [Christ]" from Ps 2:6, "Yet have I set my king upon my holy hill of Zion."[201] He defined Christ's kingly office as "that office by which he Governs & dispenses all things with supream power so as to subserve to the Great design of his Redemption."[202] Christ's kingly dominion "extends over all things & nothing is exempt but he that put all things under him," and the "End" or purpose of his dominion is "to Promote the Great design of his Redeeming Love towards his Elect."[203] In fact, Christ always works with the plan of redemption guiding his exercise of this office, for from the beginning, he "Govern[ed] the [world] in subordination to the great designs of his Redemption," and so in his application Edwards exhorted all to receive Christ as their king.[204]

The reality is that Christ's dominion is unassailable, a point Edwards established from a July 1744 sermon on Ps 2:3–4, "Let us break their bands asunder, and cast away their cords from us. He that sitteth in the heavens shall laugh: the Lord shall have them in derision." Edwards called this psalm "one of the plainest Prophecies of [Christ] in this Book of Ps[alms]," and his Christological treatment of the psalm resonated with the Reformed tradition.[205] In his "Prophecies of the Messiah" manuscript, he showed that even the Jews interpreted this psalm of the Messiah by pointing to Stapfer and Poole. Stapfer stated that, "formerly none of the Jews doubted that this psalm is to be explained of the Messiah."[206] Edwards

---

201. This sermon was the second in a three-part series on the prophetical, kingly, and priestly offices of Christ (see footnote 146 above). See also Edwards' treatment of Psalm 2 in "Prophecies of the Messiah," §52; and his comment on Ps 89:27 in *The "Blank Bible,"* 519.

202. Edwards, "745. Sermon on Ps 2:6 (June 1744)," L. 2r.

203. Edwards, "745. Sermon on Ps 2:6 (June 1744)," L. 3v., 7r.

204. Edwards, "745. Sermon on Ps 2:6 (June 1744)," L. 9v., 11v. Quotation on L. 9v.

205. Jonathan Edwards, "747. Sermon on Ps 2:3–4 (July 1744)," Beinecke Rare Book and Manuscript Library, Yale University, New Haven, CT, 1r. See also Edwards, "Prophecies of the Messiah," §52. Henry argued that the "primary Intention and Scope" of Psalm 2 is "the Kingdom of the Messiah the Son of David," and he suggested that "there is less in it of the Type, and more of the Anti-type, than in any of the Gospel-Psalms, for there is nothing in it but what is applicable to CHRIST." Henry, *Exposition*, [Psalm 2]. Trapp explained from Psalm 2 that "[t]he Lord Christ of whom *David* was both a *Father* and a *Figure*, (as here appeareth) shall surely reign, maugre all the rage and resistance of his enemies." Trapp, *Commentary*, 5. Italics original. Dickson argued that "this Psalme doth mainly, if not only, concern Christ" and shows that "[t]hough Christ's Enemies promise to themselves success in their opposition to Christ, and that they shall surely overturne his Kingdome, yet shall their imaginations prove folly." Dickson, *First Fifty Psalms*, 7–8. Calvin interpreted the psalm with respect to David but noted that "[a]ll this was typical, and contains a prophecy concerning the future kingdom of Christ," and that "all who do not submit themselves to the authority of Christ make war against God." Calvin, *Commentary*, 1:9–13. Quotations on 9, 11, 12.

206. The Latin reads, "Hunc Psalmum de Messia explicandum esse nemo olim Judæorum dubitavit." Edwards, "Prophecies of the Messiah," §52; Stapfer, 142.

also made a note to see Poole "[c]oncerning the Jews interpreting this Psalm of the Messiah, and the evidences that it indeed respects the Messiah."[207] In Poole Edwards read that Rabbi David Kimchi said the old rabbis understood this psalm to refer to the Messiah; that Rabbi Eben Ezra said this psalm concerns either David or the Messiah; and that Rabbi Obadiah Haggaon stated, "In this Psalm the author surveys the things of the days of the Messiah."[208] Poole cited other rabbis as well and showed that while the psalm speaks of David, he is a type of Christ and his reign.[209]

In Edwards' sermon he observed that wicked men aim to throw off God's government but that such attempts are vain because "God[']s son in the Heaven out of their Reach is above all & Rules over all."[210] More than that, "their attempts should prove for their own vexation," for God's laughter at their futile attempts will only increase their exasperation.[211] Edwards thus preached the doctrine, "However wicked men oppose God[']s Rule over them & Endeavour to cast it off[,] all their attempts will be in vain for G[od] will still Rule over them."[212] In the end God will still have his way and will dispose events according to his own purposes, despite the attempts of the wicked to thwart him. If they refuse to submit to God's Law, he will be their Judge, for "if they won[']t make his Law their Rule of action he will make it his Rule of Judgm[en]t."[213] In his application, Edwards called professors of religion to reveal their true colors, arguing that if you hold onto any sin, if there be "any one dear lust that you Refuse wholly to cast off," "if you will not be universally Holy" (i.e., in every area of life), then "you are one of those spoken of in the text & doc[trine] & one of those that he that sits in the Heavens has in derision."[214] For those who yield to Christ's rule, "G[od] Exercises his governing power over them as

---

207. Edwards, "Prophecies of the Messiah," §52. See also his similar reference to Poole in *The "Blank Bible"* 476.

208. The Latin reads, "In hoc Psalmo recenset autor res dierum Messia." Poole, *Synopsis*, 487.

209. Poole, *Synopsis*, 486–490.

210. Edwards, "747. Sermon on Ps 2:3–4," L. 1r. In "Miscellanies" Entry No. 702, Edwards read the "kings" in Ps 2:2 as having two referents, both the kings of the earth who rebel against Christ and the "heavenly principalities" who rebelled against God when he decreed that he would exalt human flesh to the position of sonship. Edwards, *The "Miscellanies": Entry Nos. 501–832*, 301–302.

211. Edwards, "747. Sermon on Ps 2:3–4," L. 1r.

212. Edwards, "747. Sermon on Ps 2:3–4," L. 1v.

213. Edwards, "747. Sermon on Ps 2:3–4," L. 5v., 6r.

214. Edwards, "747. Sermon on Ps 2:3–4," L. 11r.–11v.

a Loving F[ather] as for their Good"; his is "the Governm[en]t of Love."²¹⁵ But
for all others, Christ's rule will mean eternal, intolerable suffering. Edwards
exhorted all to yield willingly to God's government, for the only question is
what kind of rule you will experience: "if you are willing & obedient those
bands will be no other than the silken Cords of his Love but if other wise
they will be Iron chains & Fetters of Brass."²¹⁶ So Edwards called his people to
"hearken to the sweet call of [Christ]."²¹⁷

Edwards discussed Christ's dominion in other treatments of the Psalms
as well, giving particular attention to Psalm 110. In a sermon on Mal 4:1–2,
Edwards described the diverse experiences of those who will be under Christ's
powerful rule using the Psalms: While it will result in salvation for one, it will
be "exercised in tormenting and destroying the other."²¹⁸ Christ, the Sun of
righteousness, "will rule over believers with a golden scepter of grace and love,
making them willing in the day of his power"—a reference to Ps 110:3—"but
he will rule over unbelievers in wrath and with a rod of iron, dashing them
in pieces as a potter's vessel"—a reference to Ps 2:9.²¹⁹ In another sermon,
he used Ps 110:3, "Thy people shall be willing in the day of thy power," to
argue that Christ rules his subjects not with external force, as earthly princes
do. Instead, "he rules their hearts," and "He governs their wills and inclinations, and turns them as the rivers," for Christ's "power" refers to "a gracious,
almighty influencer, whereby Christ guides and governs the inclinations and
actions of the heart."²²⁰ That Christ will rule is irrefutable, but how one will
experience his rule depends completely on the disposition of the individual,
either a joyful acceptance or a vexed resistance. For those who willingly submit
to God, Christ's kingdom rule would bring "a spiritual happiness, consisting

---

215. Edwards, "747. Sermon on Ps 2:3–4," L. 10r.

216. Edwards, "747. Sermon on Ps 2:3–4," L. 12v.

217. Edwards, "747. Sermon on Ps 2:3–4," L. 12v.

218. Edwards, "Christ the Spiritual Sun," 61.

219. Edwards, "Christ the Spiritual Sun," 61. See also Edwards' note on Zeph 1:7–8, where he
commented on Ps 2:9, observing that, "Christ is the person to whom the Father hath committed the destruction of his enemies as well as the salvation of his elect people." Edwards,
The "Blank Bible," 808.

220. Jonathan Edwards, "The Threefold Work of the Holy Ghost" (John 16:8), in *Sermons
and Discourses 1723–1729*, ed. Kenneth P. Minkema, vol. 14 of *WJE* (1997), 422. Edwards
made this same point in "Glorying in the Savior" (Isa 45:25), in *Sermons and Discourses 1723–
1729*, ed. Kenneth P. Minkema, vol. 14 of *WJE* (1997), 465–466. See also Jonathan Edwards,
"The Justice of God in the Damnation of Sinners" (Rom 3:19), in *Sermons and Discourses
1734–1738*, ed. M. X. Lesser, vol. 19 of *WJE* (2001), 361.

in righteousness and holiness, and the favor and worship and enjoyment of God" (Pss 110:3; 89:14–29; 72:2–3, 5, 7; 132:16–17; 45:4).[221]

Edwards gave a fuller exposition of Psalm 110 and Christ's kingly rule in a May 1733 sermon on Ps 110:2, "The Lord shall send the rod of thy strength out of Zion: rule thou in the midst of thine enemies." Edwards interpreted the psalm as "Prophetical" of Christ's "Exaltation and the success of this Gospel & Glory of his Kingd[om]," a common Reformed interpretation.[222] After Christ died, rose from the grave, and ascended into heaven, God told him to "Sit thou at my right hand, until I make thine enemies thy footstool" (Ps 110:1). At the time of Christ's ascension, his kingdom was inaugurated, and he "began the actual administration of his Regal Power with Conspicuous & unveiled Glory."[223] Edwards observed that Christ rules over both his enemies and his people. His power over his enemies is testified by the phrases, "until I make thine enemies thy footstool" (Ps 110:1) and "rule thou in the midst of thine enemies" (Ps 110:2), while his rule over his people is cited in verse 3, "Thy people shall be willing in the day of thy power, in the beauties of holiness from the womb of the morning: thou hast the dew of thy youth." This description was fulfilled, Edwards held, in the early days of the church after Christ's ascension. He speculated that "thy youth" refers to Christ's youth, which was likely a reference to "the Primitive times of the Ch[urch]," or the "Youth of the [Chris]tian Church Mystical."[224] In this framework, Edwards rejected

---

221. Edwards, *The "Miscellanies": Entry Nos. 833–1152*, 148–149. Quotation on 148.

222. Jonathan Edwards, "282. Sermon on Ps 110:2 (May 1733)," in *Sermons, Series II, 1733*, vol. 48 of the *WJEO*, L. 1r. Henry presented Christ's kingdom as being "maintained and set up in the World in despite of all the Opposition of the Power of Darkness." Henry, *Exposition*, [Ps 2:2]. Poole described Ps 110:2 as "a word about Christ, or his most powerful Reign" ("verbum Christi, sive Regni ejus, potentissimum"). Poole, *Synopsis*, 1169. Trapp likewise read the psalm as referring to Christ's rule and noted, "those that will not stoop to thy Government, let them feel thy power." Trapp, *Commentary*, 853. Dickson explained Ps 110:2 saying, "How many enemies soever shall oppose the Kingdome of Christ, and how powerful soever they shall be, yet Christ shall bear rule." Dickson, *Last Fifty Psalmes*, 109–110. Calvin understood Ps 110:2 to confirm that "Christ's kingdom shall be vastly extended." Calvin, *Commentary*, 4:300.

223. Edwards, "282. Sermon on Ps 110:2," L. 1r.

224. Edwards, "282. Sermon on Ps 110:2," L. 1v. In Edwards' thinking, the "dew" in this passage could refer to "the multitude of saints as souls sanctified by the word of G[od] which drops as Rain and distills as the dew on the tender Herb in the morning of the Gospel & upon the first Rising of the sun of righteousness." Edwards cited Mic 5:7, which identifies "the remnant of Jacob" as "a dew from the Lord, as the showers upon the grass." Edwards, "282. Sermon on Ps 110:2," L. 1v. See also Edwards' two entries on Ps 110:3 in the "Blank Bible," where he made a similar comparison to Christ but also argued that, in addition to the saints, the dew refers to "the word of God" and "the Spirit of God." Edwards, *The "Blank Bible,"* 527–528.

the interpretive option that the "enemies" in verse 2 were converted, instead identifying them with the enemies in the rest of the psalm (Ps 110:1, 5, 6), enemies that never accepted Christ's rule but were forced to become subject to Christ's "rod" of power.²²⁵ Edwards explained that Christ "shall Rule over not only some but all his Enemies but not all are made willing in the d[ay] of his Power."²²⁶ Thus Edwards preached the doctrine, "[Christ] shall Rule in the midst of his Enemies," by which he meant that Christ rules "in spite of his Enemies" and "over his Enemies."²²⁷ God decreed that Christ have a "universal dominion," reflecting Ps 2:7, because he is his "son & heir," giving him a "nat[ural] Right to Inherit the Kingd[om] of the F[ather]," and because it is a "suitable Reward" for the "Glorious W[ork] of Redem[ption]" that he wrought here on Earth."²²⁸ In his application, Edwards called all "To Accept of [Christ] as your King & Entirely Yield your self to his Rule," warning that if people opposed his government, it will nonetheless be established and will only promote their misery, but if they submit to his government, they will be happy and will even reign with Christ in his kingdom.²²⁹

As Edwards looked down the halls of time, he saw an eschatological role for Christ in Ps 75:3, "The earth and all the inhabitants thereof are dissolved: I bear up the pillars of it." Here "Christ speaks of himself as the restorer of the world after it has been destroyed" and the creator of the new heavens and new earth.²³⁰ In the end, when Christ's work of redemption and judgment is completed, Edwards believed that Christ will hand the kingdom to the Father and present the church. At that time, the Father will smile upon his Son with "infinitely sweet manifestations of his acceptance," and Christ shall put on "the glory of that infinitely sweet divine love, grace, gentleness and joy, and shall shine with this sweet light far more brightly than ever he did

---

225. In his "Blank Bible" entry on Ps 110:2, Edwards explored the basis for the name "rod of strength," recognizing on the one hand that the rod was "a token of power, might, or rule" and on the other hand that it might be an allusion to Moses' rod, through which God wrought great works. Edwards, *The "Blank Bible,"* 527.

226. Edwards, "282. Sermon on Ps 110:2," L. 2r.

227. Edwards, "282. Sermon on Ps 110:2," L. 2r., 3v.

228. Edwards, "282. Sermon on Ps 110:2," L. 6v., 7r.

229. Edwards, "282. Sermon on Ps 110:2," L. 8v., 12r. Quotation on L. 8v. See also Edwards' discussion of "Christ's dominion over the world" from Psalm 8 in *Original Sin*, 415.

230. Edwards, *The "Blank Bible,"* 694. Edwards made this point in conjunction with Isa 65:17–18, "For, behold, I create new heavens and a new earth...."

before," a fulfillment of Ps 21:6, "For thou hast made ['the king'] most blessed for ever: thou hast made him exceeding glad with thy countenance."[231]

From Christ's ascension to his kingly reign even to the moment when he will hand over the kingdom to the Father, indicating the completion of his work, the glorification of Christ to the right hand of the Father featured prominently in Edwards' engagement with the Psalms. Christ's exaltation served as a crowning moment in the history of redemption because it vindicated him in his humiliation and servitude and confirmed his meritorious work to redeem humanity through his death and resurrection. The glorification of Christ ensures that the outcome of world history is already determined and that Christ himself will finally bring his people home to him and stamp out the rebellion once and for all.

Conclusion

In his sermon "The Excellency of Christ," Edwards argued that Christ displays the most beautiful and perfect combination of seemingly opposing attributes, which constitutes his unique excellence. Edwards believed this concept is captured in Ps 85:10, "Mercy and truth are met together, righteousness and peace have kissed each other."[232] Christ manifested God's infinite, strict justice in his willingness to endure suffering rather than allow the honor of God's justice to suffer insult. Yet at the very moment of upholding God's strict justice, Christ at the same time expressed God's infinite mercy: "what glorious and ineffable grace and love have been, and are exercised by him, towards sinful men! Though he be the just judge of a sinful world, yet he is also the Savior of the world: though he be a consuming fire to sin, yet he is the light and life of sinners."[233]

As Edwards read of Christ in the Psalms, what organized his thoughts was the history of redemption, which casts Christ, the central figure of redemption, as both Savior and judge—two appellations that summarize his relationship to the two categories of humanity, saved and condemned. The history of redemption best frames the various aspects of Christ's person and work as portrayed in the Psalms, a book that witnesses to his incarnation and life of voluntary servitude, to his death that atones for sins by substituting himself

---

231. Edwards, *The "Miscellanies": Entry Nos. 833–1152*, 233. See also Edwards' comment on Ps 110:1 and 1 Cor 15:25–26 that Christ's reign at the right hand of God will continue until he has subdued all his enemies, specifically "Antichrist, and Mahometanism, and heathenism." Then he shall "resign up the kingdom to the Father, as having done his work." Edwards, *The "Blank Bible,"* 1062.

232. Edwards, "The Excellency of Christ," 572.

233. Edwards, "The Excellency of Christ," 572.

for sinners and by upholding God's justice, to his resurrection that expresses God's acceptance of his atoning work, to the spiritual benefits he obtains for his bride, to his glorification in his ascension and coronation, to his righteous rule defending the saints and judging the wicked, and even to the completion of his work as he hands the kingdom to the Father. Edwards developed a robust understanding of the Psalms' testimony concerning Christ's role in the history of redemption through his unified understanding of the Old and New Testament, characterized by his employment of typology and prophecy. For Edwards the history of redemption was the reigning motif that unified the Scripture and provided the exegetical framework for reading the Psalms. Theologically speaking, the person and work of Christ was central to Edwards' understanding of the Psalms because he is the central figure in the unfolding of God's plan of redemption, and, conversely, the Psalms provided extensive, authoritative material for developing his Christology. And while some have disparaged Edwards' exegesis as too typological and free, it is important to remember that he was working within a long tradition of reading Christ in the Psalms based on a shared belief in the unity of the Bible and the analogy of Scripture. While Edwards was more exploratory in his use of types—observing types of Christ in the Psalms that earlier Reformed interpreters did not, such as the manna and the river—and while he made more connections between the Psalms and Christ than his Reformed predecessors—particularly regarding such details of Christ's life as the incarnation or transfiguration—Edwards was not unique or unconventional to envision Christ in the Psalms but rather stood on firm ground within the Reformed exegetical tradition.[234] Neither was his Christological reading of the Psalms haphazard or unbounded; rather, the history of redemption provided the boundaries for interpretation, and the analogy of Scripture provided the accepted basis for interpreting the Psalms as Christological songs.

Speaking on Psalm 2 in "Miscellanies" Entry No. 1349, Edwards exhibited just how explicitly he believed the Psalms spoke of Christ: "Men are abundantly called upon to trust in Christ, not only in the New Testament, but the Old, as in the end of the second Psalm and elsewhere."[235] Just as Edwards read of Christ in the Psalms, he similarly saw in the Psalms the sounding of the gospel and the application of Christ's work by the Holy Spirit. It is these theological themes within the history of redemption that we consider next.

---

234. As McClymond and McDermott state, "Edwards saw even more typological import in the Old Testament than did many of his predecessors," an observation my study corroborates—although Edwards' continuity with the Reformed tradition should not be minimized. McClymond and McDermott, *The Theology of Jonathan Edwards*, 126.

235. Edwards, *The "Miscellanies": Entry Nos. 1153–1360*, 415.

5

Spirit and Gospel

They shall be abundantly satisfied
with the fatness of thy house;
and thou shalt make them drink of the river of thy pleasures.
For with thee is the fountain of life:
in thy light shall we see light.
Psalm 36:8–9

THE HISTORY OF redemption constituted an organizing theme for Edwards' interpretation and use of the Psalms. And while Christ was central to Edwards' understanding of redemptive history, the Holy Spirit also played a critical role, in contrast to some earlier Reformed theologians.[1] Edwards read in the Psalms a full-orbed redemptive-historical theology that incorporated the Holy Spirit's work, influenced his doctrine of salvation, and informed his outworking of those doctrines in his pastoral duties of promoting revivals, discerning individuals' religious experiences, and preaching the gospel.

In this chapter we will see that Edwards' exegesis of the Psalms was driven by his redemptive-historical understanding of Scripture. He had such a unified understanding of the Bible that he believed one could discuss a variety of theological topics from the Psalms, extrapolating truths about the Holy Spirit's nature and work, discussing soteriological matters of regeneration and justification, describing the proper effects of the Spirit's work in revival, discerning an authentic work of God, and proclaiming the gospel. And the degree to which Edwards discussed the Holy Spirit and the broad work of God's redemption in the Psalms militates against scholars' claims that his interpretation of the Psalms was "Christological."[2] We begin this chapter by

---

1. Michael J. McClymond and Gerald R. McDermott, *The Theology of Jonathan Edwards* (New York: Oxford University Press, 2012), 262–264.

2. For a similar argument against viewing Edwards' exegesis as "Christological," see Andrew T. Abernethy, "Jonathan Edwards as Multi-Dimensional Bible Interpreter: A Case Study from Isaiah 40–55," *Journal of the Evangelical Theological Society* 56, no. 4 (December 2013): 824–827.

examining what Edwards said concerning the person and work of the Spirit from the Psalms. From there we delve into themes that Edwards developed from the Psalms that revolve around the gospel, including the doctrine of salvation, the public promotion of salvation in revivals, the discernment of what constitutes a true converting work of the Spirit, and the duty of gospel preaching. The chapter closes with a discussion of Edwards' explicit elaboration of God's work of redemption in the Psalms.

The Holy Spirit

In the Psalms Edwards saw teaching both on the Trinity as a whole and on the three Persons of the Godhead.[3] As he discussed the Holy Spirit particularly in the Psalms, he spoke of types and descriptions of the Spirit's nature, and he emphasized the Spirit's work of giving light to spiritually blind people and inspiring the Psalms with gospel doctrine.

In discussing the person of the Holy Spirit, Edwards pointed to Ps 51:11–12, "Cast me not away from thy presence; and take not thy holy spirit from me. Restore unto me the joy of thy salvation; and uphold me with thy free spirit." Noting that "the original" Hebrew phrase, וְרוּחַ קָדְשְׁךָ, literally means, "the Spirit of thy holiness," he explained that the Spirit receives the appellation of "Holy" not because of his own personal holiness but "chiefly because God's holiness consists in him."[4] In making this distinction, Edwards showed that God's very essence is holiness, an attribute shared among the three persons of the Trinity, for the Spirit is not holier than the Father or Son but is holy in that he is God.

From the Psalms' imagery Edwards described all kinds of types related to God's redemptive work, including the Holy Spirit. So in Ps 110:7, "He shall drink of the brook in the way: therefore shall he lift up the head," Edwards interpreted the "brook" as referring to "the Holy Ghost, which is often

---

3. Besides discussing the individual members of the Trinity in the Psalms, Edwards recognized some intimation of the doctrine of the Trinity in the Psalms. In "Miscellanies" Entry No. 1241, titled "Trinity," Edwards noted that in Ps 58:11, "verily he is a God that judgeth in the earth," the Hebrew אֱלֹהִים שֹׁפְטִים, or literally, "Elohim, Judges," occurs in the plural, suggesting plurality in the oneness of God. Jonathan Edwards, *The "Miscellanies": Entry Nos. 1153–1360*, ed. Douglas A. Sweeney, vol. 23 of *WJE* (2004), 175. See also Jonathan Edwards, "Of God the Father" (1 Cor 11:3) in *Sermons and Discourses 1743–1758*, ed. Wilson H. Kimnach, vol. 25 of *WJE* (2006), 150. For two perspectives on Edwards' Trinitarianism, see Steven M. Studebaker and Robert W. Caldwell, III, *The Trinitarian Theology of Jonathan Edwards: Text, Context, and Application* (Farnham, UK: Ashgate, 2012) and Amy Plantinga Pauw, *The Supreme Harmony of All: The Trinitarian Theology of Jonathan Edwards* (Grand Rapids, MI: Eerdmans, 2002).

4. Jonathan Edwards, *The "Miscellanies": Entry Nos. 833–1152*, ed. Amy Plantinga Pauw, vol. 20 of *WJE* (2002), 389.

compared to water, to a spring, a river, etc."[5] He also saw an image of the Spirit in the "dove" described in Ps 68:13, "Though ye have lien among the pots, yet shall ye be as the wings of a dove covered with silver, and her feathers with yellow gold." Edwards connected the imagery to the Spirit by saying God's excellency is "like the light reflected in various beautiful colors from the feathers of a dove, which colors represent the graces of the heavenly dove," for such "beautiful colors do well represent the Spirit, or the amiable excellency of God, and the various beautiful graces and virtues of the Spirit."[6] Thus from the nature of the Spirit as God's excellency emerges the work of the Spirit in the grace he sheds on humanity, a theme Edwards repeated elsewhere. Similarly, while Edwards connected the river with Christ in Ps 1:3, "And he shall be like a tree planted by the rivers of water, that bringeth forth his fruit in his season" (see pp. 173–175), he also likened these "ever-flowing" rivers to "the goodness of God," or "[t]he Spirit communicated and shed abroad," which meant that the Spirit influences Christians as the river nourishes trees: "the trees that grow and flourish by the river's side through the benefit of the water represent the saints who live upon Christ and flourish through the influences of his Spirit."[7]

In the same way, reading Ps 133:3, "As the dew of Hermon, and as the dew that descended upon the mountains of Zion: for there the LORD commanded the blessing, even life for evermore," Edwards argued that the "dew" "doubtless meant spiritual and divine influences, communications of the Holy Spirit from above."[8] Edwards cited Poole in his note on Ps 133:3, and it appears he was mainly interested in Poole's discussion of geography, grammar, and poetry to determine in what way the dew of Mount Hermon descends on Mount Zion.[9] Poole showed that the verse indicates, in part, the abundance of dew on Mount

5. Jonathan Edwards, *The "Blank Bible,"* ed. Stephen J. Stein, vol. 24, part 1 of *WJE* (2006), 528.

6. Jonathan Edwards, "Discourse on the Trinity," in *Writings on the Trinity, Grace, and Faith,* ed. Sang Hyun Lee, vol. 21 of *WJE* (2003), 138.

7. Jonathan Edwards, "Images of Divine Things," in *Typological Writings,* ed. Wallace E. Anderson, vol. 11 of *WJE* (1992), 54–55. See also 58, 63, 74, 82–84, 85, 100, 120, 129, 129–130.

8. Edwards, *The "Blank Bible,"* 536.

9. Some possible explanations Poole described were that Mount Hermon poetically represents Mount Zion; that Mount Hermon is a synecdoche, a part of the mountains of Israel that represent the whole of them; and that the passage speaks of a communion, as if the dew from heaven irrigates both mountains and makes them one. Matthew Poole, *Synopsis Criticorum Aliorumque Sacrae Scripturae Interpretum et Commentarum, Summo Studio et Fide Adornata,* vol. II: *Complectens Libros Jobi, Psalmorum, Proverbiorum, Ecclesiastis, & Cantici Canticorum* (Francofurti ad Moenum: Balthasaris Christophori Wustii, 1678), 1270–1271.

Hermon and its fertility being shared with Mount Zion; Edwards similarly noted in his entry that "Hermon was an high mountain, and in such places the dews are in great plenty, and perhaps in some parts of it, full of it, very fertile as to this."[10] Still, toward the end of Poole's discussion, he briefly mentioned a connection to "Zion, where the Holy Spirit descended on the Apostles" and recognized that the good which God gives is "the remission of sins and eternal life," a reading consonant with Edwards' Spirit-focused interpretation.[11]

The most important image Edwards used from the Psalms to describe the Holy Spirit's nature was oil, which signified that the nature of the Spirit is excellency, joy, and love. Reading Ps 45:7, "Thou lovest righteousness, and hatest wickedness: therefore God, thy God, hath anointed thee with the oil of gladness above thy fellows," Edwards argued that the "oil of gladness" here "signifies the Holy Ghost, with which Christ is anointed," for "[t]he Holy Ghost is God's delight and joy."[12] Similarly, Edwards described the Spirit as Christ's anointing in Ps 133:2, "It is like the precious ointment upon the head, that ran down upon the beard, even Aaron's beard: that went down to the skirts of his garments." Edwards explained that "[t]he Spirit was poured forth upon Christ, the head of the church," yet this ointment proceeded from the head "down to the church, which is Christ's body," exhibiting the "fullness" of grace that Christians receive in the Spirit.[13] It was common in the Reformed exegetical tradition to link the oil to God's grace flowing from Christ to his body but not to identify the oil with the Spirit, as Edwards did.[14] In another context, Edwards identified oil as representing "excellence and

---

10. Edwards, *The "Blank Bible,"* 536.

11. The Latin reads, "Sion, ubi Spiritus Sanctus in Apostolos descendit," and "remissione peccatorum, & vitam aeternam." Poole, *Synopsis,* 1271.

12. Jonathan Edwards, *The "Miscellanies": Entry Nos. a–z, aa–zz, 1–500,* ed. Thomas A. Schafer, vol. 13 of *WJE* (1994), 368. See Edwards' similar comment in *The "Miscellanies": Entry Nos. a–500,* 342.

13. Edwards, *The "Blank Bible,"* 536. Edwards held that this running oil shows how "inexhaustible" is the Holy Spirit's communication of himself. Jonathan Edwards, *Notes on Scripture,* ed. Stephen J. Stein, vol. 15 of *WJE* (1998), 209. See also, Edwards, *Notes on Scripture,* 244.

14. Only Trapp compared the oil to the Spirit. However, Trapp, Dickson, and Calvin made an explicit link between the head and body of Aaron and that of Christ. Trapp stated that "the Spirit of grace, that oil of gladness, *Psal. 45.7,* poured out abundantly, even to a *redundancy,* upon Christ the head, runneth down upon all the members of his body mysticall, even to the meanest." John Trapp, *A Commentary or Exposition Upon the Books of Ezra, Nehemiah, Esther, Job, and Psalms…*(London: T. R. and E. M. for Thomas Newberry…, 1657), 906. Dickson noted that the blessing of Christian concord "is not to be expected by any, but through Christ, on whom the oile of gladnesse, and all the graces of the Spirit are first poured out, and then from him are carried to the meanest member of his body." David Dickson, *A Brief*

love" because the Hebrews used oil for its "flowing smoothness" to "make the face shine" (Ps 104:15). Indeed, as the experiences of Moses and Stephen show, a shining face is "the proper effect of an extraordinary effusion of the Holy Spirit and exercise of divine grace," for a shining face represents "beauty, excellence and joy," as well as God's "love and favor."[15]

In his "Discourse on the Trinity," Edwards drew together Pss 133:2 and 36:7–9 to envision the Holy Spirit as "the Deity in act" as "the divine essence itself flows out and is as it were breathed forth in love and joy."[16] Casting oil as a type of the Holy Spirit confirmed this description of the Spirit's nature, for oil comes from the olive tree and the olive branch signifies "love, peace and friendship."[17] As the dove after the flood was "a token for good, a sign of God's love and favor," so "[t]he olive branch and the dove that brought it were both the emblems of the same, viz. the love of God; but especially did the holy anointing oil, the principal type of the Holy Ghost, well represent the divine love and delight by reason of its excellent sweetness and fragrancy," as described in Ps 133:2.[18] Psalm 36:7–9 made it even more "plain" that "God's love, or his lovingkindness, is the same with the Holy Ghost."[19] The passage reads, "How excellent is thy lovingkindness, O God! therefore the children of men put their trust under the shadow of thy wings. They shall be abundantly satisfied with the fatness of thy house; and thou shalt make them drink of the

---

Explication of the last Fifty Psalmes, From Ps. 100 to the end (London: T. R. and E. M. for Ralph Smith…, 1654), 281. Calvin did not identify the oil with the Spirit but held that true concord always "takes its rise in the true and pure worship of God" and that this peace "springs from Christ as the head" and "is diffused through the whole length and breadth of the Church." John Calvin, Commentary on the Psalms, trans. from the Original Latin and Collated with the Author's French Version by James Anderson (1843–1855; repr., Grand Rapids, MI: Eerdmans, 1963), 5:165. While Henry and Poole did not link the verse to the Spirit or Christ, both recognized that the oil, designating brotherly love, comes from God's grace. As Henry put it, this love is like ointment for it is "a Grace of his working in us." Matthew Henry, An exposition of the five poetical books of the Old Testament; viz. Job, Psalms, Proverbs, Ecclesiastes, and Solomon's song…(London: T. Darrack…, 1710), [Ps 133:2]. Poole described the flowing oil as the "communion of grace between the head and the members" ("communio gratiae inter caput & membra"). Poole, Synopsis, 1269.

15. Edwards, The "Miscellanies": Entry Nos. a–500, 347. See also Entry No. 330, "Holy Ghost," where Edwards again used the oil in Psalm 133 as an image of the Spirit. Edwards, The "Miscellanies": Entry Nos. a–500, 409.

16. Edwards, "Discourse on the Trinity," 121. Edwards cited this discussion in his "Blank Bible" entry on Ps 36:7–9. Edwards, The "Blank Bible," 492.

17. Edwards, "Discourse on the Trinity," 127.

18. Edwards, "Discourse on the Trinity," 127–128.

19. Edwards, "Discourse on the Trinity," 128.

river of thy pleasures. For with thee is the fountain of life: in thy light shall we see light." Edwards argued that the images of fatness (anointing oil), a river, and a fountain all referred to the lovingkindness in verse 7, and he used the analogy of Scripture (citing Ezekiel 47; John 4:14; 7:38–39; and Revelation 22) to draw these images together with the Holy Spirit. He concluded that when these passages were taken together, "we cannot doubt but that it is the same happiness that is meant in this Psalm."[20] Earlier Reformed exegetes did not identify the images of oil, river, or fountain with the Spirit.[21] But in Edwards' conception, the Psalms' imagery of oil and water represented the Holy Spirit particularly as joy, excellency, and love. As McClymond and McDermott explain, Edwards' belief that the Holy Spirit is the love of God shed on us, or the "thing purchased" in the atonement, while developed from Augustinian thought, was "an original contribution to Christian theological reflection."[22]

Edwards not only spoke of the Spirit's nature but also described his work, which connects us more directly with the grace of the gospel. Edwards gravitated toward the image of light in the Psalms to describe what the Holy Spirit communicates to people. Building again from Ps 36:8–9, Edwards explained that God's operation on those who have true religious affections is of a "spiritual" nature, for it shows saints "seeing light in God's light, and being made to drink of the river of God's pleasures."[23] Psalm 119 especially brought out the Spirit's work of imparting light. In his August 1733 sermon, "A Divine and Supernatural Light," Edwards taught that the Holy Spirit gives "spiritual light" to the mind of the

---

20. Edwards, "Discourse on the Trinity," 128–129.

21. Neither Henry, Poole, Trapp, Dickson, or Calvin identified these images with the Spirit. Henry, *Exposition*, [Ps 36:8–9]; Poole, *Synopsis*, 734; Trapp, *Commentary*, 676; David Dickson, *A Brief Explication of the first Fifty Psalms* (London: T. M. for Ralph Smith..., 1652), 240; Calvin, *Commentary*, 2:11–12.

22. McClymond and McDermott, *The Theology of Jonathan Edwards*, 262–263. From this idea Edwards developed the notion that the Holy Spirit is the bond between the Father and the Son, the bond between the human and divine natures of Christ, and the bond that unites the believer with God in spiritual union. McClymond and McDermott, *The Theology of Jonathan Edwards*, 272. See also Robert W. Caldwell, III, *Communion in the Spirit: The Holy Spirit as the Bond of Union in the Theology of Jonathan Edwards*, Studies in Evangelical History and Thought (Eugene, OR: Wipf & Stock, 2007).

23. Jonathan Edwards, *Religious Affections*, ed. John E. Smith, vol. 2 of *WJE* (1959), 203. See also Edwards' general comment on the Psalms where he noted that "[t]he things that we find David comforting himself in, in the Book of Psalms, are not his being a king, or a prophet, but the holy influences of the Spirit of God in his heart, communicating to him divine light, love and joy." Edwards, *The Distinguishing Marks*, in *The Great Awakening*, ed. C. C. Goen, vol. 4 of *WJE* (1972), 279.

believer "immediately."[24] Edwards showed from the Psalms that God enlightens the Christian's understanding of the Bible supernaturally: "The Scripture also speaks plainly of such a knowledge of the Word of God, as has been described, as the immediate gift of God; Ps. 119:18, 'Open thou mine eyes, that I may behold wondrous things out of thy law.' "[25] Could the psalmist not read the "wondrous" stories of creation, the flood, and the exodus with his natural eyes? Of course he could, but "[d]oubtless by 'wondrous things' in God's law, he had respect to those distinguishing and wonderful excellencies, and marvelous manifestations of the divine perfections, and glory, that there was in the commands and doctrines of the Word, and those works and counsels of God that were there revealed," for such excellencies are not visible to everyone, but are "peculiar to the saints, and given only by God," following Ps 25:14, "The secret of the LORD is with them that fear him; and he will shew them his covenant."[26]

In his October 1751 sermon on Ps 119:18, Edwards preached a three-part doctrine contrasting people in their natural state and people under the Spirit's gracious influences, an interpretation that only some in the Reformed tradition identified.[27] First, he showed that "men are naturally blind so that they don[']t [see] the main things in the word of G[od]."[28] While natural men may understand some things in God's Word, they do not grasp "the greatest things," such as God's "glory & Excellency," Christ's sufficiency to be their Savior, or the things of the next world.[29] Second, he described the Spirit's role

24. Jonathan Edwards, "A Divine and Supernatural Light" (Matt 16:17), in *Sermons and Discourses 1730–1733*, ed. Mark Valeri, vol. 17 of *WJE* (1999), 417.

25. Edwards, "A Divine and Supernatural Light," 418.

26. Edwards, "A Divine and Supernatural Light," 418. See Edwards' similar use of Ps 119:18 in Jonathan Edwards, "False Light and True" (2 Cor 11:14), in *Sermons and Discourses 1734–1738*, ed. M. X. Lesser, vol. 19 of *WJE* (2001), 138.

27. Henry, Trapp, and Dickson all explained that humans are blind to spiritual things unless God opens their eyes by his supernatural grace but did not identify the Holy Spirit as the source of this spiritual enlightenment. Henry, *Exposition*, [Ps 119:18]; Trapp, *Commentary*, 878; Dickson, *Last Fifty Psalmes*, 170. Poole and Calvin, however, did identify the Spirit as the illuminator. Poole argued that the Messiah is "the marrow of the Law, which is not able to be comprehended without revelation and the Spirit of God, because *folly* is in humanity" ("medulla Legis, quaeque sine revelatione & Spiritu Dei comprehendi nequit, cum *stultitia* sit homini"). Poole, *Synopsis*, 1210. Calvin likewise read this verse as a reference to the Holy Spirit's work of illumination, noting that "every man is blind," leaving him "unable to discern the light of the heavenly doctrine, until God, by the invisible grace of his Spirit, opens [his eyes]." Calvin, *Commentary*, 4:413.

28. Jonathan Edwards, "1007. Sermon on Ps 119:18 (October 1751)," Beinecke Rare Book and Manuscript Library, Yale University, New Haven, CT, L. 1r.

29. Edwards, "1007. Sermon on Ps 119:18," L. 1r.–1v.

in giving them divine light: "G[od] by giving them his grace & his Sp[irit] to make em holy opens their Eyes to see those things."[30] And finally, it is only "when men by God's Sp[irit] are brought to see those things," such as the glory, excellency, and mercy of God, that they "see em to be wonderful."[31] Edwards exhorted his people to ask God to open their eyes since no one can open his or her own eyes, and he warned that if the Spirit never opens their eyes, they will not only live miserably in this life but "will End in eternal darkness."[32]

Edwards made the connection between this light in Psalm 119 and the Holy Spirit's impartation of it even clearer elsewhere. This spiritual sight comes from the Holy Spirit and is something that "natural men cannot have," for God's children live in Christian holiness "from an holy heavenly disposition, which the Spirit of God gives them."[33] In Edwards' view, "[t]he sanctifying influence of the Spirit of God rectifies the taste of the soul, whereby it savors those things that are of God," and all of these influences by the Spirit are manifest in the psalmist's longing for God's statutes in Psalm 119:

> The leading of the Spirit which God gives his children, which is peculiar to them, is that teaching them his statutes, and causing them to understand the way of his precepts, which the Psalmist so very often prays for, especially in the 119th Psalm; and not in giving of them new statutes, and new precepts. He graciously gives them eyes to see, and ears to hear, and hearts to understand.[34]

Edwards taught from the Psalms that a person could understand and live the Christian life only with the supernatural light and grace granted by the Holy Spirit.

Edwards described the special grace of the Holy Spirit in other ways using the Psalms. From Ps 50:21 he read a description of the Spirit's convicting work: "The Holy Ghost makes men [sensible] how sinful their lives are, brings sin to remembrance. They little regarded how many sins they had committed, but now they are brought to reflect."[35] And in his "Harmony of the Genius Spirit Doctrines

---

30. Edwards, "1007. Sermon on Ps 119:18," L. IV.

31. Edwards, "1007. Sermon on Ps 119:18," L. IV.

32. Edwards, "1007. Sermon on Ps 119:18," L. 2V.

33. Jonathan Edwards, *Some Thoughts Concerning the Revival*, in *The Great Awakening*, ed. C. C. Goen, vol. 4 of *WJE* (1972), 436.

34. Edwards, *Some Thoughts*, 437.

35. Jonathan Edwards, "The Threefold Work of the Holy Ghost" (John 16:8), in *Sermons and Discourses 1723–1729*, ed. Kenneth P. Minkema, vol. 14 of *WJE* (1997), 382.

and Rules of the Old Testament and the New," he engaged the Psalms to argue that the Word is not sufficient alone to save but that we need special grace from the Holy Spirit to experience salvation. In reading Ps 27:11, "Teach me thy way, O Lord, and lead me in a plain path, because of mine enemies," Edwards argued that it is God's Spirit who communicates this special grace to people: "We need not only external instruction, but the teachings of God's Spirit, to make us rightly to understand God's way, and to lead us in it."[36] And following Ps 143:10, "Teach me to do thy will; for thou art my God: thy spirit is good; lead me into the land of uprightness," Edwards saw further evidence that "[b]esides the teachings of God's word, we need the teachings of his Spirit in order to a right knowing God's will and our duty, and in order to our becoming truly Holy."[37]

Clearly, as Edwards discussed the Holy Spirit in the Psalms, he focused on the supernatural grace and light given to sinful men in a natural state. However, we cannot talk about how Edwards described the Holy Spirit's work from the Psalms without mentioning his inspiration of the Psalms because time and again, as we have seen, Edwards noted that the Spirit intended multivalent meanings when he inspired the psalmists to write. Edwards explained the Spirit's work of inspiring the Psalms and imbuing them with gospel truth in his treatment of Ps 78:2, where he observed that the "dark sayings" mentioned there indicate that the Holy Spirit was speaking of things that transcended the events in Israel's day, for God's wonderful works in Israel's history "are called a 'parable' and 'dark sayings,' because all these things are typical of gospel things. And with an eye to gospel things, this psalm (as almost all the rest) was indited by the Spirit of God."[38] This interpretation of Ps 78:2 was unique to Edwards in the Reformed tradition, but in Edwards' view, the Psalms were replete with gospel revelation because of the Holy Spirit's inspirational work.[39]

---

36. Jonathan Edwards, "Harmony of the Genius Spirit Doctrines and Rules of the Old Testament and the New," Beinecke Rare Book and Manuscript Library, Yale University, New Haven, CT, 226.

37. Edwards, "Harmony," 277. See Edwards' similar comments on Pss 4:8; 23:3; 25:4–5, 8–9, 12, and 14; 86:11. Edwards, "Harmony," 218, 224, 225, 255. To show that we need spiritual light for salvation, Edwards also cited several verses from Psalm 119, including Ps 119:12, 18–19, 26–27, 33–34, 64, 66, 68, 73, 102, 108, 124–25, 135, 144, 169, 171. Edwards, "Harmony," 268.

38. Edwards, The "Blank Bible," 513.

39. Henry did not explicitly say the Spirit endowed these "dark sayings" with gospel things but recognized generically, in light of Matt 13:35's correlation of these "dark sayings" with Christ's parables, that they were "Representations of the State of the Kingdom of God among Men." Henry, Exposition, [Ps 78:2]. Neither Poole, Trapp, Dickson, nor Calvin connected these "dark sayings" to the Spirit or the gospel. Poole, Synopsis, 1005; Trapp, Commentary,

In his engagement with the Psalms, Edwards spoke explicitly about the Spirit's nature and work, gravitating to the two images of oil and light. He described the Spirit as God's excellency, love, and joy, and what he emphasized in the Spirit's work was his impartation of divine light and saving grace and his inspiration of the Psalms with the gospel message. As we explore the doctrine of salvation, the revivals, the discernment of true religion, and the proclamation of the gospel, we continue to see the Holy Spirit's role in the promotion of gospel doctrine in Edwards' reading of the Psalms.

The Doctrine of Salvation

The doctrine of salvation was a priority early in Edwards' thought as he engaged with heterodox teachings concerning humanity's role in the salvation process. This controversy heated up at the 1722 Yale commencement when Timothy Cutler, Rector of Yale, closed his commencement prayer with a phrase from the Book of Common Prayer, which signaled his defection to Anglicanism. At the following year's commencement, Edwards, who needed to deliver a disputation to complete his master's degree, boldly chose to enter the controversy by defending "Reformed religion" against Anglican-Arminian notions of self-determination and proclaimed that "A Sinner Is Not Justified in the Sight of God Except Through the Righteousness of Christ Obtained by Faith."[40] He continued to emphasize the doctrine of salvation throughout his writings, even attributing the success of the 1734–1735 revival in large part to his sermon series on "Justification by Faith Alone."[41] As we consider his theological ruminations on salvation in the Psalms, it is important to note, as McClymond and McDermott show, that Edwards understood salvation as inclusive of conversion, justification, sanctification, and divinization, with two underlying principles, grace and faith.[42] Edwards used the Psalms to discuss the various aspects of salvation.

784; David Dickson, *A Brief Explication of the other fifty Psalmes, From Ps. 50 to Ps. 100* (London: T. R. and E. M. for Ralph Smith…, 1653), 198; Calvin, *Commentary*, 3:227–228.

40. Jonathan Edwards, "Quæstio: Peccator Non Iustificatur Coram Deo Nisi Per Iustitiam Christi Fide Apprehensam," in *Sermons and Discourses 1723–1729*, ed. Kenneth P. Minkema and trans. George G. Levesque, vol. 14 of *WJE* (1997), 60. On the background to Edwards' Quæstio, see George G. Levesque, "Introduction" to Edwards' "Quæstio," in *Sermons and Discourses 1720–1723*, ed. Kenneth P. Minkema, vol. 14 of *WJE* (1997), 47–52, and George M. Marsden, *Jonathan Edwards: A Life* (New Haven, CT: Yale University Press, 2003), 82–93.

41. Jonathan Edwards, *A Faithful Narrative*, in *The Great Awakening*, ed. C. C. Goen, vol. 4 of *WJE* (1972), 148–149. See also Jonathan Edwards, "Justification by Faith Alone" (Rom 4:5), in *Sermons and Discourses 1734–1738*, ed. M. X. Lesser, vol. 19 of *WJE* (2001), 143–242.

42. McClymond and McDermott, *The Theology of Jonathan Edwards*, 357.

In addressing conversion, Edwards argued that infancy typified the conversion process. In one instance, he compared the conversion of sinners to the weaning of a child, as testified by Ps 131:2: "Surely I have behaved and quieted myself, as a child that is weaned of his mother: my soul is even as a weaned child."[43] Yet in another context, Edwards compared "the formation of Christ in the soul" to "the formation of a child" in the womb, basing the comparison on Ps 139:14–15, "I will praise thee; for I am fearfully and wonderfully made: marvellous are thy works; and that my soul knoweth right well. My substance was not hid from thee, when I was made in secret, and curiously wrought in the lowest parts of the earth."[44] While Psalm 139 refers to the "new creature" that the Spirit forms, this regeneration occurs "in secret," which is why Edwards concluded that "[w]e know not the works of God, that worketh all," and why, in part, he rejected the Puritan morphology of conversion:

> some have gone too far towards directing the Spirit of the Lord, and marking out his footsteps for him, and limiting him to certain steps and methods. Experience plainly shows, that God's Spirit is unsearchable and untraceable, in some of the best of Christians, in the method of his operations, in their conversion. Nor does the Spirit of God proceed discernibly in the steps of a particular established scheme, one half so often as is imagined.[45]

Using Ps 139:14–15 as a type of spiritual regeneration—a unique interpretation compared to the earlier Reformed tradition—allowed Edwards to free conversion from the oppressive morphology of conversion of his forefathers and put it in the hands of the Holy Spirit.[46]

But while the conception of a child could typify spiritual regeneration, Edwards argued in his treatise on *Original Sin* from Ps 139:14–15 that it can also signify our "first birth or generation," when we were created in the womb.[47] Since birth could refer to a creation, he claimed that being born again indicates a person is "created

---

43. Edwards, *Some Thoughts*, 367.

44. Edwards, *The "Miscellanies": Entry Nos. 833–1152*, 156.

45. Edwards, *Religious Affections*, 161–162.

46. On the Puritan morphology of conversion and Edwards' rejection of it, see Marsden, *Jonathan Edwards: A Life*, 26–29; and Douglas A. Sweeney, *Jonathan Edwards and the Ministry of the Word: A Model of Faith and Thought* (Downers Grove, IL: IVP Academic, 2009), 117–120. Earlier interpreters focused on the wonderful work of God in creating the natural body but did not see that creation as a type of spiritual regeneration. Henry, *Exposition*, [Ps 139:14–15]; Poole, *Synopsis*, 1289–1290; Trapp, *Commentary*, 914; Dickson, *Last Fifty Psalmes*, 315; Calvin, *Commentary*, 5:214–217.

47. Jonathan Edwards, *Original Sin*, ed. Clyde A. Holbrook, vol. 3 of *WJE* (1970), 369.

again," and so when Ps 51:10 speaks of "creating a clean heart," it signifies God's "giving a new heart," the event of regeneration or being born again.[48] Edwards earlier discussed Ps 51:10 in a "Miscellanies" entry, arguing that regeneration in a sense was "often renewed" or "continued through the whole life," even after the Holy Spirit's initial work of grace in a person's life.[49] David's penitential prayer after his adultery with Bathsheba and murder of Uriah provided an example of a repeated conversion. David had already been initially converted when he prayed that God would "create" in him a clean heart and "renew a right spirit" in him (Ps 51:10). Yet the language of "creating" and "renewing" suggested a similar work to that initial regeneration: "The first clear discovery of God and Christ to the soul, when it follows the more obscure dawnings of grace and feebler actings of faith in holy desires after Christ and holiness, seem to be sometimes represented as their conversion."[50] But as McClymond and McDermott observe, Edwards' notion of repeated conversions indicated not a synergistic model of regeneration but "a continual concurrence of God's active power" in the believer's life.[51]

The power that an individual experiences is the gracious influence of the Holy Spirit, and to explain this grace, Edwards looked to Ps 110:3, "Thy people shall be willing in the day of thy power, in the beauties of holiness from the womb of the morning: thou hast the dew of thy youth." In "Miscellanies" Entry No. 665, "IRRESISTIBLE GRACE," he used Ps 110:3 to argue that when divine grace enters into the human heart, it destroys the will's opposition to God's commands and makes the man willing to obey, so "[t]he effect that is wrought by grace is on the will itself, to incline and bring it to a compliance."[52] Later, in "Miscellanies" Entry No. 1029, "INFUSED GRACE. TEXTS OF SCRIPTURE," Edwards cited Ps 110:3 among several other texts to highlight God's promises in Scripture to "produce" of his own "arbitrary, efficacious operation" the heart change "by which men become gracious and holy."[53] In

---

48. Edwards, *Original Sin*, 369.

49. Edwards, *The "Miscellanies": Entry Nos. 833–1152*, 68.

50. Edwards, *The "Miscellanies": Entry Nos. 833–1152*, 68–73. Quotation on 72.

51. McClymond and McDermott, *The Theology of Jonathan Edwards*, 386–388.

52. Jonathan Edwards, *The "Miscellanies": Entry Nos. 501–832*, ed. Ava Chamberlain, vol. 18 of *WJE* (2000), 211.

53. Edwards, *The "Miscellanies": Entry Nos. 833–1152*, 366. While the sixteenth-century reformers avoided "infusion" language when articulating the doctrine of justification, seventeenth- and eighteenth-century Reformed theologians retrieved it, as did Edwards. For Edwards, it did not imply God's assistance of natural human ability but rather imaged "the Spirit's pouring himself into the human soul and taking up residence there" McClymond and McDermott, *The Theology of Jonathan Edwards*, 381–382. Quotation on 382. See also

two "Blank Bible" entries on Ps 110:3, Edwards made the connection to the Spirit more explicit by identifying the "dew" with "the word of God" and "the Spirit of God," "for the Spirit of God, which is a Spirit of love, is compared to the dew, Ps. 133."[54] Building from the dew as a type of the Spirit, Edwards portrayed regeneration in vivid imagery. The multitudes of converts in those early days of the church could be seen as the "spires of grass watered, refreshed, adorned, and crowned, each one with a drop of this heavenly dew."[55] The result of the Spirit's dew upon the grass was a new nature: "these drops of dew is [sic] made up of that water that descends from heaven and gathers on the grass into a drop. So the new nature in the saints is created and as it were constituted of the Holy Spirit."[56] Using the Psalms, Edwards highlighted the primacy of God's act of grace communicated by the Spirit as prior to any human act of goodness.

In a later addition to this "Blank Bible" entry, Edwards mentioned both Poole and John Glas without commenting on their works.[57] Poole noted that the phrase, "from the womb of the morning: thou hast the dew of thy youth," is "a difficult passage," one of the most obscure in the Psalms, and it can refer to Christ, divinity, or God's people.[58] Speaking of Christ, it refers to the graces God gave to Christ in the incarnation; speaking of divinity, it refers to "the eternal generation of Christ" in his deity; and speaking of the people of Christ, the dew can be compared to "grace and virtue," to a multitude dense like the early morning dew, or to God's supernatural regeneration, for "the offspring will be begotten and brought forth entirely new by Christ, in an uncommon and wonderful manner, clearly by God regenerating them by the word and Spirit."[59] Poole also noted a metaphor for God's grace apart from human works: "As the morning dew is brought forth in a wonderful and invisible manner, without human power . . . thus from the grace of God, in a distant secret manner, is brought forth the youth of the Messiah, that is, that people of

---

Hyun-Jin Cho, *Jonathan Edwards on Justification: Reformed Development of the Doctrine in Eighteenth-Century New England* (Lanham, MD: University Press of America, 2012).

54. Edwards, *The "Blank Bible,"* 527.

55. Edwards, *The "Blank Bible,"* 527.

56. Edwards, *The "Blank Bible,"* 527.

57. Edwards, *The "Blank Bible,"* 528.

58. Poole, *Synopsis,* 1172. The Latin reads, "Locus hic difficilis est."

59. Poole, *Synopsis,* 1172, 1174. The Latin passages read: "æternam Christi generationem"; "gratiam & decorum"; and "Christo soboles nascetur & crescet prorsus novo, inusitato & mirabili modo, Deo videlicet per verbum & Spiritum eos regenerante."

devotion."[60] While Poole did not associate the dew explicitly with the Spirit, he made a clear link between Ps 110:3 and God's regenerating work, emphasizing its portrait of a multitude of saints—the interpretive path that characterized the Reformed tradition on this passage.[61] Glas, however, quibbled with the "generally supposed" reading that the dew refers to willing people; instead, by drawing on several biblical passages discussing dew, Glas argued that the dew refers to "Christ's gracious and powerful influence upon his people, by his word and Spirit," which falls upon them as dew and makes them willing.[62] Glas went on to show that Christ's power through the Spirit's grace is "fitly" compared to dew because "however gently and imperceptibly it fall upon men, as the dew; yet it is effectual to overcome their natural aversion, and irresistibly incline their hearts and will unto him."[63] The comparison of Edwards with his sources and other Reformed interpreters in their interpretation of Ps 110:3 shows that Edwards did not depart from the Reformed tradition in their emphasis on God's regenerating work in new converts, though he did uniquely develop the imagery of the dew as a reference to the Spirit.

Edwards also devoted a notebook to reflecting on "Faith," and he used the Psalms to illuminate his understanding of the nature of saving faith. He observed that many passages in the Old Testament speak of "trusting in God as the condition of his favor and salvation," but "especially" Ps 78:21–22,

---

60. Poole, *Synopsis*, 1174. The Latin reads, "Ut ros mirabili & invisibili modo ex Aurora nascitur, sine ope humana…sic ex gratia Dei, modo longe abstrusiori, nascitur Messiae *juventus*, i.e. *populus ille devotionum.*"

61. While Henry did not associate the dew with the Spirit, he did say that the passage displayed "[t]he Conversion of a Soul," and he identified the "*particular Power*" as "the Power of the Spirit, going along with the Power of the Word, to the People of CHRIST, which is *effectual* to make *them* willing." Also, for Henry the dew, not the grass, referred to an "abundance of young Converts." Henry, *Exposition*, [Ps 110:3]. Trapp thought the imagery of the dew meant "the influence of his Spirit" and that the early morning dew was "an apt similitude" expressing both "the multitude of Christ's converts, and the manner of their heavenly generation." Trapp, *Commentary*, 853. Dickson saw a picture of conversion, for God's elect "are made most willing Converts by his Omnipotent power, effectually inclining their hearts, and making them willing," while the dew represents an "abundance of Converts." Dickson, *Last Fifty Psalmes*, 110. Calvin recognized a reference to the "vast multitudes" that are "regenerated by the Spirit of Christ and by the word," though he did not link the Spirit with the dew. Rather, the dew represented new converts: "As men are struck with astonishment at seeing the earth moistened and refreshed with dew, though its descent be imperceptible, even so, David declares that an innumerable offspring shall be born to Christ, who shall be spread over the whole earth." Calvin, *Commentary*, 4:303–304.

62. John Glas, *Notes on Scriptures-Texts, in Seven Numbers*, in vol. 3 of *The Works of Mr. John Glas*, 2d ed. (Perth: R. Morison and Son, 1782), 226.

63. Glas, *Notes on Scriptures-Texts*, 227.

"Therefore the LORD heard this, and was wroth: so a fire was kindled against Jacob, and anger also came up against Israel; Because they believed not in God, and trusted not in his salvation."[64] While this passage described the severe judgment experienced by the faith-less, Edwards also used several phrases from the Psalms to speak positively about the nature of true faith: stretching out hands to Christ (Ps 68:31); trusting God under the shadow of his wings (Pss 17:8; 36:7; 57:1; 63:7; 91:1); loving God's salvation (Pss 70:4; 40:16; 78:22; 119:166); running to God as a refuge (Pss 62:7–8; 91:2; 71:1, 3); waiting on the Lord or his salvation (Pss 25:2–3, 5, 21; 37:3, 5, 7, 9, 34; 27:13–14; 39:7; 52:8–9; 59:9; 62:1–2, 5–8; 130:5–8; 33:18–20; 40:1, 3–4); hoping in God or in his mercy (Pss 78:7; 146:5; 39:7; 71:5; 22:8–9; 38:14–15; 33:18–22; 147:10–11; 119:49, 114; 130:3–8; 119:74, 166); looking to or for God (Pss 133:1–2; 34:4–5; 141:8; 25:15); rolling oneself on the Lord (Pss 22; 37:5); and committing oneself to God (Ps 31:1–6).[65] These descriptions all centered on God and his power and underscored humanity's dependence on the Lord. Edwards further highlighted that "the nature of true faith in Christ" requires dependence on him in a discussion of Ps 50:5, "Gather my saints together unto me; those that have made a covenant with me by sacrifice."[66] Edwards explained his meaning:

> believers do therein by the sincere full act of their minds and hearts appoint Christ to be their sacrifice, as such bring him and offer him to God; i.e. they entirely concur [with] what was done in his offering himself a sacrifice for sinners as a real sacrifice, sufficient and proper for them, trusting in this sacrifice, coming to God and giving himself up to God, hoping for acceptance by this sacrifice and taking God for his God, hoping for an interest in him as such by this sacrifice, that so God may be his God and he one of his people.[67]

Here Edwards sought to make good on the Old Testament practice of sacrifice as an expression of faith in God for the Christian under the new covenant, so he cast the Christian as expressing faith by bringing Christ "as such" to offer him as their sacrifice. Still, Edwards did not emphasize the bringing but the "concurring," "trusting," and "hoping." He was constantly engaging Scripture

---

64. Jonathan Edwards, "Faith," in *Writings on the Trinity, Grace, and Faith*, ed. Sang Hyun Lee, vol. 21 of *WJE* (2003), 419.

65. Edwards, "Faith," 443, 445, 449–456.

66. Edwards, "Faith," 468.

67. Edwards, "Faith," 468.

in his formation of doctrine, even exploring fine terminological and theological details to make sense of the nature of saving faith. Edwards applied the unity of the two testaments to the Psalms and thus appropriated the Psalms for an all-encompassing doctrine of faith.

Discussions of faith naturally lead into the aspect of the doctrine of salvation that Edwards spent the greatest time discussing in the Psalms, justification by faith. Edwards used the Psalms to treat justification in two "Miscellanies" entries, in which he was especially concerned with how to understand justification in the Old Testament within the framework of the whole Bible. In Entry No. 861, "JUSTIFICATION. HOW WORKS JUSTIFY," Edwards connected the ideas of trust and obedience to argue that true trust demands evidence of works. The New Testament concept of "faith," he explained, is "equivalent" to the Old Testament concept of trust, and the Old Testament often connected trust with action so that "[c]leaving to God in practice, as having our expectations of happiness and well-being from him, as our portion and chief good, and serving him in dependence on his sufficiency for us and faithfulness to us in that way, is implied and very much intended in the Old Testament notion of trusting in God."[68] Here Edwards emphasized dependence on God as humans act out their trust in service, and he noted several psalms as evidence of this concept: Ps 2:11–12 connects the command to "[s]erve the LORD with fear" with a promised blessing to those who "put their trust in him"; Ps 4:4–5 links "trust in the LORD" with the command to "sin not"; and Psalm 37 issues commands like "Trust in the LORD, and do good" (Ps 37:3) and "Commit thy way unto the LORD; trust also in him" (Ps 37:5).[69]

Edwards dealt with this issue at length in "Miscellanies" Entry No. 1354, "JUSTIFICATION: OBJECTION against the doctrine of JUSTIFICATION by faith alone from the conditions of God's favor chiefly insisted on in the OLD TESTAMENT."[70] In this entry Edwards explored Old Testament passages that seemed to suggest that God required obedience to be saved, in contrast to the New Testament requirement of faith in Christ. He presented several arguments to show that God has always required faith as the ground of justification, whether in the Old or New Testament. Part of his argument rested on the Psalms. Edwards sought to show that the language of "fearing God" (e.g., Pss 15:12–14; 31:19; 85:9; 103:11–13, 17; 115:13) was used to describe the condition of the covenant of grace, an expression akin to worshipping the true God and rejecting idols.

---

68. Edwards, *The "Miscellanies": Entry Nos. 833–1152*, 85.

69. Edwards, *The "Miscellanies": Entry Nos. 833–1152*, 85–86.

70. Edwards, *The "Miscellanies": Entry Nos. 1153–1360*, 506–543.

Edwards linked the Old Testament expressions of "fearing God" and "knowing God" but added that they also included "observing all prescribed moral duties," just as the New Testament describes true faith as being expressed in keeping moral duties: "We are there taught that God will own no other faith as true but that which works by love and shows itself in deeds of charity (Jas. 1:27 and 2:14–16)."[71] While justification is based solely on Christ's work, true saving faith in Christ issues forth in moral obedience to God's commands. So "when serving and obeying God and keeping his commands is spoken of as the special terms of his covenant and favor, it is so spoken of as an expression of trust and hope in God," a teaching upheld by numerous Old Testament passages, including several from the Psalms.[72] In fact, Edwards held that the book of Psalms and Psalm 119 especially show "[w]hat manner of obedience was the condition of God's favor, and with regard to what in the nature of this obedience it was that it was the condition of justification."[73] That is, obedience is not a condition proper but is the outworking of the cleaving to God described as faith.

Edwards provided another argument by engaging Ps 24:3–4, which reads, "Who shall ascend into the hill of the LORD? or who shall stand in his holy place? He that hath clean hands, and a pure heart; who hath not lifted up his soul unto vanity, nor sworn deceitfully."[74] Here he found a description not of "the grand qualification" for entry onto God's holy hill but of the distinguishing marks of someone who has been justified by faith.[75] Moral works are the fruit of the Spirit's work in a person's life, while the righteousness that ushers them to the holy hill of God rests in Christ, not them. So "[t]his may well be understood as only giving the character of such as should be admitted to those privileges," and "the mentioning these don't at all imply that this is that

---

71. Edwards, *The "Miscellanies": Entry Nos. 1153–1360*, 522.

72. Edwards, *The "Miscellanies": Entry Nos. 1153–1360*, 522–523. The Psalms passages he listed include, in cited order, Pss 37:3–9, 27, 34, 37, 39–40; 4:5; 4:3–5; 5:10–12; 16:1; 17:3–7; 25:1–5, 10, 12, 20–21; 26:1–6; 31:6, 23–24; 32:10–11; 33:18; 34:7–22; 36:7–10; 37; 52:7–8; 55:22–23; 62; 64:10; 73:27–28; 84:11–12; 112:7; 119:41–49, 113–120, 145–148, 166; 147:11.

73. Edwards, *The "Miscellanies": Entry Nos. 1153–1360*, 523. See also Edwards' use of the Psalms in his word study of צדק, "he is righteous," and its derivatives to argue that these words are "properly judicial or forensic terms … in their original and most common signification," meaning that describing Old Testament saints as "righteous" does not controvert the doctrine of "justification by Christ's righteousness alone received by faith." Jonathan Edwards, "'Controversies' Notebook: Justification," in *Writings on the Trinity, Grace, and Faith*, ed. Sang Hyun Lee, vol. 21 of *WJE* (2003), 345–354.

74. He also discussed the parallel passage Ps 15:1–2: "LORD, who shall abide in thy tabernacle? who shall dwell in thy holy hill? He that walketh uprightly, and worketh righteousness, and speaketh the truth in his heart."

75. Edwards, *The "Miscellanies": Entry Nos. 1153–1360*, 524–525.

righteousness, that virtue, whose value it is that primarily recommends 'em to be received to a title to these privileges."[76] Rather, as Ps 24:6 states, "This is the generation of them that seek him, that seek thy face, O God of Jacob," so this psalm signifies all the more that those who are accepted are those who "seek" God, an expression used in the Bible to describe the nature of *faith*. Thus Psalm 24 leads us to understand these moral duties "only as signs of that faith which is the more primary condition of acceptance."[77] Using this passage as a basis for discussing the doctrine of justification by faith was fairly unusual compared to earlier Reformed exegetes, who focused more on the characteristics of true worshipers while still differentiating hypocrites who perform external works from true worshipers whose hearts have been changed by God.[78]

That Edwards spoke of "the more primary condition of acceptance" alerts us to his notion that there are other conditions of salvation, as he stated in his published sermon on "Justification by Faith Alone." There he explained that the term "condition" is "ambiguous" and interpreted differently, and he particularly addressed the diverse ways that Scripture speaks of "conditions" of salvation, noting that in one sense,

faith is not the only condition of salvation or justification, for there are many things that accompany and flow from faith, that are things

---

76. Edwards, *The "Miscellanies": Entry Nos. 1153–1360*, 525.

77. Edwards, *The "Miscellanies": Entry Nos. 1153–1360*, 525.

78. Henry did not specifically address the question of justification by faith in this passage, but while he focused on explaining the characteristics of a righteous person, he did mention that a "blessing from the LORD" (Ps 24:5) is justification and salvation, noting that "Righteousness is Blessedness, and 'tis *from God* only that we must expect it, for we have no Righteousness of our own." Henry, *Exposition*, [Ps 24:3–6]. Poole recognized that not all are counted a part of God's family and that this passage distinguishes between hypocrites who worship only in an external show and true worshipers who are pure in heart. The psalmist also "notes holy affections . . . as it were prior to holy works" ("Notat hoc sanctos affectus, Act. 15,9. sicut prius, sancta opera"). Poole, *Synopsis*, 665–666. Quotation on 665. Trapp did not address justification by faith, but did mention that there are only "a select number . . . who shall be everlastingly happy" and receive salvation from God. Trapp, *Commentary*, 938–939. Quotation on 938. Dickson came the closest to Edwards' discussion of justification by faith, though he did not speak of it in the detail that Edwards did. He spoke of "the marks and priviledges of the true subjects of this Kingdome" and distinguished "true Converts" from the visible church, and he explained that one must first "[Covenant] with God by Faith" and then be "cleansed by the blood of sprinkling for justification," for "[t]he holy life of the true believer, is not the cause of his justification before God. . . . But he shall receive justification, and eternall life, as a free gift from God, by vertue of the Covenant of Grace." Dickson, *First Fifty Psalms*, 136–137. Calvin did not focus on justification by faith, but noted from the outset that while David made "only a tacit reference to this subject," it is clear that God's people become accepted through the "pure grace" of God and that David here "insists principally" on "distinguishing true Israelites from the false." Calvin, *Commentary*, 1:404–405.

with which justification shall be, and without which it will not be, and therefore are found to be put in Scripture in conditional propositions with justification and salvation in multitudes of places: such are "love to God," and "love to our brethren," "forgiving men their trespasses," and many other good qualifications and acts.[79]

In Edwards' view, that godly love "flow[s] from faith" implies something different than saying that godly love precedes justification. As Sweeney explains, "Edwards taught what he did for largely exegetical reasons," seeking to be faithful to the teaching in both Romans and James, and thus in his understanding, "godly love is implied in saving faith and so is spoken of in Scripture as a condition of salvation—not a condition that secures justification before God, but a condition without which one does not have genuine faith."[80] That explains why Edwards in the same sermon series used David and the penitential Psalm 32 as an example of one who was justified by faith and not works. In this psalm, David expressed sorrow over the sin that he committed *after* his justification. Since Paul quoted David's words from Ps 32:1–2 as an example of one "unto whom God imputeth righteousness without works" (Rom 4:6), Edwards understood that "David was not justified by works of the ceremonial law," and "therefore men's own obedience is not that by which they are justified."[81]

Edwards also dealt with the doctrine of justification by faith using the Psalms in his "Harmony" notebook. He argued that the Old Testament gives ample evidence that "THE GRAND CONDITION OF GOD'S SALVATION, PROTECTION, DELIVERANCE, ETC." is "FAITH IN GOD," citing dozens of passages from the Psalms as support.[82] Later in the notebook, Edwards commented that passages like Ps 5:11–12 make the condition for justification one of faith, not of works or lineage, for "[t]rust in God [is] the grand condition of salvation," and "[f]aith, or trust in God, is the spring of comfort and joy and light from darkness

---

79. Edwards, "Justification by Faith Alone," 152.

80. Douglas A. Sweeney, "Justification by Faith Alone? A Fuller Picture of Edwards's Doctrine," in *Jonathan Edwards and Justification*, ed. Josh Moody (Wheaton, IL: Crossway, 2012), 143, 151. For a helpful discussion of the language of "conditions" in Edwards' doctrine of justification, see especially 140–150.

81. Edwards, "Justification by Faith Alone," 181. See also 203, 226, and 230, where Edwards also used Psalm 32 to further his doctrine.

82. Edwards, "Harmony," 1–3. The Psalms passages Edwards cited include Pss 5:11; 7:1; 11:1; 16:1; 18:30; 21:7; 22:4–5; 25:2–3, 20; 26:1; 27:13–14; 28:7; 31:1–6, 14, 19–20, 24; 33:18–22; 34:22; 37:3, 5–7, 40; 39:7–8; 40:1; 52:7–9; 56:3–4, 11; 57:1; 62:1–2, 5–10; 71:1, 5; 78:21–22, 32–33; 86:2; 91:2–4; 106:24; 115:9–10; 116:10; 118:8–9; 119:41–42; 125:1–2; 141:8; 143:8; and 144:2.

to fallen man."[83] Edwards made a similar comment that trust in God or faith is "the grand condition" of salvation in several other psalms in this notebook.[84] In several places in the Psalms, he saw the teaching that men depend on God and God alone for their salvation and happiness.[85] Edwards' exposition of Psalm 62 is representative of his understanding of faith as God's "grand condition" for salvation with works as the fruit of such faith: "In saving faith, men trust in God, make God their refuge,…set their heart on God as their portion and their glory (vv. 7, 10); trust in God entirely and perseveringly (v. 8); and their faith is fruitful in good works and a holy practice (v. 12)."[86] For Edwards works are not prior to trust in God, but faith necessarily issues forth in good works, and Edwards saw plentiful evidence from the Psalms that justification by faith has always been God's *modus operandi* in every age.[87]

We have not exhausted Edwards' doctrine of salvation, and many scholars continue to debate whether or not he strayed from the Reformed faith in his outworking of the doctrine.[88] But we have seen that Edwards directly engaged controversial questions surrounding the doctrine of salvation, and the Psalms played a

---

83. Edwards, "Harmony," 218. Psalm 5:11–12 reads, "But let all those that put their trust in thee rejoice: let them ever shout for joy, because thou defendest them: let them also that love thy name be joyful in thee. For thou, Lord, wilt bless the righteous; with favour wilt thou compass him as with a shield."

84. The texts Edwards mentioned include Pss 4:5; 7:1; 9:9–10; 10:14; 11:1–2; 13:5; 14:5–7; 16:1; 17:7; 18:2–3, 30; 20:7–9; 21:4, 7; 22:4–5, 26; 25:1–5, 15, 20–21; 26:1; 27:13–14; 28:7–8; 31:1–6, 14–20, 24; 32:10; 33:18–20; 34:4–6, 8, 10, 22; 37:3–7, 9, 34, 40; 38:15–16; 40:1–4, 16; 42:5, 11; 43:5; 55:22–23; 56:3–4, 9–11, 13; 57:1–3; 59:9–10; 61:3–6; 62; 65:2, 5; 69:6, 32–33; 70:4–5; 71:1–7, 14–16; 84:8–9, 12; 86:1–7; 91:1–16; 115:8–11; 116:4–11; 118:8–9; 119:41–44, 49, 114; 121:1–2; 125:1–2; 130; 143:6–9, 10; 147:10–11. Edwards, "Harmony," 217–229, 231–234, 240–246, 254, 255, 257, 266, 267, 270, 272–274, 277, and 278.

85. Edwards mentioned Pss 21:4; 22:29; 62:11; 68:34–35; 71:14–16; 84:5–7, 8–9; 116:4–11; and 146:1–5. Edwards, "Harmony," 223, 224, 241, 244, 246, 253, 254, 267, 278.

86. Edwards, "Harmony," 241.

87. See also Jonathan Edwards, "390. Sermon on Ps 127:2 (May 1736)," in *Sermons, Series II, 1736*, vol. 51 of *WJEO*, L. 2r., 2v.

88. On this debate, see especially Sweeney, "Justification by Faith Alone?" 129–154, where he summarizes the state of the discussion and offers a fresh perspective on the topic by showing how Edwards addressed justification by faith in his understudied sermons and personal manuscripts. See also John J. Bombaro, "Jonathan Edwards's Vision of Salvation," *Westminster Theological Journal* 65 (2003): 45–67; Cho, *Jonathan Edwards on Justification*; McClymond and McDermott, *The Theology of Jonathan Edwards*, 389–404; Josh Moody, ed., *Jonathan Edwards and Justification* (Wheaton, IL: Crossway, 2012); Anri Morimoto, *Jonathan Edwards and the Catholic Vision of Salvation* (University Park, PA: Penn State Press, 1995); Stephen R. C. Nichols, *Jonathan Edwards's Bible: The Relationship of the Old and New Testaments in the Theology of Jonathan Edwards* (Eugene, OR: Pickwick, 2013), 142–187; and Sweeney, *Jonathan Edwards and the Ministry of the Word*, 114–121.

key role in how he explained the various aspects of salvation—particularly justifi-cation by faith—and how he presented a reasonable defense of the doctrine in the face of theological debates. For Edwards, because the Bible is a unified whole, the Psalms exhibited a richness of gospel doctrine that made it an illuminating book for understanding God's salvation, from the gracious influences of the Holy Spirit to the dependent faith of believers in Christ and his justifying grace.

Revival

While Edwards is sometimes caricatured as a hermetic bookworm who burned away twelve to thirteen hours a day alone in his study, he was actually deeply concerned for the souls of his people, and while he did not follow the common pastoral practice of visiting his parishioners in their homes, he spent countless hours with them in his study, helping them discern their spiritual condition. He devoted much of his time to using means to create the best conditions for the Holy Spirit to wield his gracious influences on people. Said another way, while Edwards reflected on and fine-tuned his doctrine of salvation, he also applied those thoughts by fanning the spiritual flames in his congregation.

For this revivalist, who shepherded two internationally renowned revivals in his lifetime, the Psalms helped him describe what was happening in the renewed hearts of the Northamptonites. In Edwards' *A Faithful Narrative*, he adapted the language of Ps 40:2–3 to describe the experiences of those in the 1734–1735 revival: "From day to day, for many months together, might be seen evident instances of sinners brought out of darkness into marvellous light, and delivered out of an horrible pit, and from the miry clay, and set upon a rock with a new song of praise to God in their mouths."[89] He also put words to the revival using the Psalms by noting, "[t]here were remarkable tokens of God's presence in almost every house. It was a time of joy in families on the account of salvation's being brought unto them....The goings of God were then seen in his sanctuary [Ps 68:24], God's day was a delight, and his tab-ernacles were amiable [Ps 84:1]."[90] One evidence of the movement of God's Spirit was the joy with which the people sang the psalms during meetings:

> Our public praises were then greatly enlivened; God was then served
> in our psalmody, in some measure, in the beauty of holiness [Ps 96:9].
> It has been observable that there has been scarce any part of divine

---

89. Edwards, *Faithful Narrative*, 150–151.

90. Edwards, *Faithful Narrative*, 151.

worship, wherein good men amongst us have had grace so drawn forth and their hearts so lifted up in the ways of God, as in singing his praises.... now they were evidently wont to sing with unusual elevation of heart and voice, which made the duty pleasant indeed.[91]

This joy in singing psalms was not unique to Northampton but appears to have been a common feature in the transatlantic revivals. Fred van Lieburg observes, for example, that singing the Psalms was a defining part of the revival services in Nijkerk, Holland in 1750.[92]

As the 1734–1735 revival died down, Edwards preached a Thanksgiving sermon on Isa 12:6 calling his people to rejoice for all the benefits of having seen God in their midst, a sermon that featured sixty-four references to the Psalms. In this November 1735 sermon Edwards recognized that while the "progress made" was not as bright as it had been, God was still in their midst, and the Psalms gave them words to describe these revivals:

How many poor, sinful creatures, poor, miserable, distressed souls amongst us, have of late been brought together to Mount Zion, to a glorious feast prepared there, to sing and rejoice in God. God hath sent "a plentiful rain amongst us, whereby he has refreshed his inheritance, when it was weary" [Ps 68:9]. We have seen the goings, "even the goings of God, our King, in his sanctuary" [Ps 68:24], here. "Mercy and truth have here met together; righteousness and peace have kissed each other. Truth has sprung out of the earth; and righteousness has looked down from heaven" [Ps 85:10–11]. "God's work is honorable and glorious, and his righteousness endureth forever. He hath made his wonderful works to be remembered, because he is gracious and full of compassion.... The works of his hands are verity and judgment.... They stand fast forever and ever, and are done in truth and uprightness. He hath sent redemption to his people: he hath commanded his covenant forever: holy and reverend is his name" [Ps 111:3–9].[93]

Similarly, the Psalms provided the language for attributing the revivals to God alone. Because the revivals touched the "most unlikely" subjects and began

---

91. Edwards, *Faithful Narrative*, 151.

92. Fred van Lieburg, "Interpreting the Dutch Great Awakening (1749–1755)," *Church History* 77, no. 2 (June 2008): 318–336. Quotation on 321.

93. Jonathan Edwards, "God Amongst His People" (Isa 12:6), in *Sermons and Discourses 1734–1738*, ed. M. X. Lesser, vol. 19 of *WJE* (2001), 465–466.

simultaneously in three unrelated towns (Northampton, Massachusetts; Windsor, Connecticut; and York, Maine), "'tis unreasonable to ascribe it to any other than an immediate divine power that works arbitrarily where and when God will," and thus we should "give all the praise to God, and say, as Ps. 72:18–19, 'Blessed be the Lord God, the God of Israel, who only doth wondrous things. And blessed be his glorious name forever and ever."[94] In the same way, Edwards appealed to Ps 115:1 as the language that he and his people must appropriate in discussing the revivals; they must give glory to God alone for his work of awakening souls and cities. Edwards preached, "If it be asked, why he should show such favor to this people; the right answer is, he loved us because he loved us. And to God we ought to say, 'Not to us, not to us, O Lord, but thy name be the glory' [Ps 115:1]."[95] By describing the revivals using the Psalms, Edwards aimed to give them greater credibility as a true work of the Holy Spirit because he believed they were.

As the 1735 revival passed, a troubled Edwards lamented a resuscitated spiritual apathy in the town while continuing to preach for people to respond to the gospel. With the arrival of George Whitefield in the American colonies in November 1739, a new longer revival broke out across the colonies, including in Northampton. In his September 1741 commencement address at Yale, later published as *The Distinguishing Marks of a Work of the Spirit of God*, Edwards compared the latest revival with the earlier revival, arguing that the current revival was "more purely spiritual" because, in contrast to the 1735 revival when people got too comfortable with God and "did too much forget their distance from God," in the 1741 revival they "rejoice with a more solemn, reverential, humble joy; as God directs the princes of the earth, Ps. 2:11."[96] It appears that Edwards spoke too soon, for only a couple years later he would denounce this very issue in the 1740–1742 revival using the same passage. In *Some Thoughts Concerning the Present Revival of Religion in New England* (1743), Edwards acknowledged that errors accompanied the revivals and argued that "the worst cause of errors that prevail in such a state of things, is spiritual pride."[97] He warned that many sins are difficult to discern, just as the psalmist observes in Ps 19:12, "Who can understand his errors? cleanse thou me from secret faults," but "spiritual pride is the most secret of all sins. The heart is so deceitful and unsearchable in nothing in the world, as it is in this matter,

---

94. Edwards, "God Amongst His People," 466.

95. Edwards, "God Amongst His People," 467.

96. Edwards, *Distinguishing Marks*, 270.

97. Edwards, *Some Thoughts*, 414.

and there is no sin in the world, that men are so confident in, and so difficultly convinced of."[98] Edwards warned that spiritual pride can produce "a certain unsuitable and self-confident boldness before God and men," and he rebuked those who rejoiced in God without heeding Ps 2:11, "Serve the LORD with fear, and rejoice with trembling," for "they han't rejoiced with a reverential trembling, in a proper sense of the awful majesty of God, and the awful distance between God and them."[99] Edwards thought some of the more radical elements of revivalists were getting too comfortable with God, and while he promoted the revivals, he sought to maintain hierarchy and a proper respect for God.[100]

Psalm 2 served as a paradigm for describing God's work in the revivals and people's response to it. Edwards used the picture of God setting his king on his holy hill from Ps 2:6 as a metaphor for the revival work: "So it always is when God, in any great dispensation of his providence, does remarkably set his king on his holy hill of Zion, and Christ in an extraordinary manner comes down from heaven to the earth, and appears in his visible church in a great work of salvation for his people."[101] In fact, setting up his king was exactly what God was doing in the revivals.[102] But while Edwards was so optimistic about the relationship of the revivals to the establishment of Christ as king, many in his day were skeptical or even downright critical. Edwards employed the Psalms in his response to those denunciations and turned the tables by warning those who criticized the revivals that they stood in a dangerous position. During particular seasons of glorification, as Edwards believed they were experiencing, God pours out his Spirit to advance his kingdom, and "God declares his firm decree that his Son shall reign on his holy hill in Zion: and therefore those that at such a time don't kiss the Son, as he then manifests himself, and appears in the glory of his majesty and grace, expose themselves to perish from the way, and to be dashed in pieces with a rod of iron."[103] By paraphrasing Ps 2:6, 9, and 12, Edwards held that, as Christ is deserving of all honor and as his wrath will shatter those who do not acknowledge his honor, it is incumbent upon

---

98. Edwards, *Some Thoughts*, 416.

99. Edwards, *Some Thoughts*, 426.

100. See Thomas Kidd, who argues persuasively that Edwards staked out a moderate position on the revivals, in contradistinction both to anti-revivalists and radical revivalists. Kidd, *The Great Awakening: The Roots of Evangelical Christianity* (New Haven, CT: Yale University Press, 2007), 117–120, 137.

101. Edwards, *Some Thoughts*, 349.

102. Edwards, *Some Thoughts*, 370. See his similar comments from Ps 2:6 on 350, 369, 371.

103. Edwards, *Some Thoughts*, 350. See his reiteration of this point on 369.

all who name the name of Christ to rejoice in the revivals. To slander the revivals is to slander Christ and kindle his wrath.[104]

In fact, a major theme in *Some Thoughts* was Edwards' argument that true Christians needed to rejoice in the revivals, while those who opposed them put themselves in a precarious place, and he employed the Psalms in establishing this argument. Edwards pointed to Ps 118:22, "The stone which the builders refused is become the head stone of the corner" (quoted in Matt 21:42 and 1 Pet 2:7), to warn those who criticize the revivals:

> This shows how dangerous it is to continue always stumbling at such a work, forever doubting of it, and forbearing fully to acknowledge it and give God the glory of it: such persons are in danger to go, and fall backward, and be broken, and snared and taken, and to have Christ a stone of stumbling to them, that shall be an occasion of their ruin; while he is to others a sanctuary, and a sure foundation.[105]

The opportunity to partake in the Spirit's work would eventually pass, and Edwards warned his fellow New England Congregationalists not to miss it.[106]

---

104. Edwards' use of such strong language from the Psalms shows that he believed these revivals were a unique event that could only be finally explained by the Spirit's work, contra the claims of historians Jon Butler, Joseph Conforti, and Frank Lambert. Jon Butler, "Enthusiasm Described and Decried: The Great Awakening as Interpretive Fiction," *The Journal of American History* 69, no. 2 (1982), 305–325; Joseph Conforti, "The Invention of the Great Awakening, 1795–1842," *Early American Literature* 26, no. 2 (1991), 99–118; Frank Lambert, *Inventing the "Great Awakening"* (Princeton, NJ: Princeton University Press, 1999). See also Kidd, *The Great Awakening*, xiii–xix, 321–324, where he argues convincingly that there was indeed a widespread awakening, though it was "a long Great Awakening" that lasted for the greater part of the eighteenth century and "produced a new variation of Protestant Christianity: evangelicalism." Quotation on 322.

105. Edwards, *Some Thoughts*, 351.

106. See also Edwards' discussion of Psalm 68, written for the return of the ark of the covenant to Zion, to show that "the exceeding rejoicings of Israel" over "the return of God to a professing people, in the spiritual tokens of his presence, after a long absence from them," represents a type of "the joy of the church of Christ on his returning to it, after it has been in a low and dark state, to revive his work." To further develop this theme, Edwards drew on the historical accounts in 1 Chr 13:2–5; 15:28; 16:2–3; and 2 Sam 6:16, 19–23, which contrasts the widespread rejoicing over the return of the ark against the scorn of Michal, David's wife and Saul's daughter, over David's dancing. By casting David as a type of Christ, Edwards compared the spouse of David with the bride of Christ, admonishing, "let us take heed, in this day of the bringing up of the ark of God, that while we are in visibility and profession the spouse of the spiritual David, we don't shew ourselves to be indeed the children of false-hearted and rebellious Saul, by our standing aloof, and not joining in the joy and praises of the day...and so bring the curse of perpetual barrenness upon our souls." Edwards, *Some Thoughts*, 365–366.

Edwards particularly called on civil rulers to support the revivals, appealing again to Psalm 2. As the passage describes the king's solemn entry into the royal city, "it is expected that all, especially men in public office and authority, should manifest their loyalty, by some open and visible token of respect by the way, as he passes along; and those that refuse or neglect it are in danger of being immediately struck down."[107] Edwards warned of punishment threatened against spiritual and civic rulers who did not rejoice in God's kingdom advance, paraphrasing Ps 2:10, 12 for the rulers of his day: "Be wise now, ye rulers; be instructed, ye judges of New England: kiss the Son, lest he be angry, and ye perish from the way."[108]

Instead of opposing the revivals, Edwards encouraged New England's civic and spiritual leaders to promote the revival of religion in moderate ways, and the Psalms helped him stake out this moderate position. Edwards explained that, "at such a day as this, God does especially call his people to the exercise of extraordinary meekness and mutual forbearance," for "when Christ rides forth in his glory and his majesty, it is 'because of truth, meekness and righteousness'" (Ps 45:3–4).[109] He also argued that those who experienced a true work of God's Spirit would "abound in deeds of charity, or almsgiving," and he criticized his fellow Christians that "[w]e generally in these days seem to fall far below the true spirit and practice of Christianity with regard to this duty."[110] Psalm 112:4–9 gives quite a different picture, describing a "good man" as one who "hath given to the poor" and making it manifest that "giving to the poor is the way to receive spiritual blessings."[111]

As Edwards developed his moderate stance on the revivals—a position that promoted revivals while seeking to avoid what he considered the excesses of more radical revivalists, such as social egalitarianism and disregard for hierarchy—he used the Psalms to warn both those who remained neutral or

---

107. Edwards, *Some Thoughts*, 371.

108. Edwards, *Some Thoughts*, 373. See his similar comments on Pss 110:5–6 and 45:3–4. Edwards, *Some Thoughts*, 371. See also his use of Pss 2:7–9; 9:6–8; and 110:1–7 in his December 1741 sermon on Judg 5:23 to warn people that remaining neutral on the revivals was tantamount to opposing them and would elicit God's judgment. Jonathan Edwards, "The Curse of Meroz" (Judg 5:23), in *Sermons and Discourses 1739–1742*, ed. Harry S. Stout and Nathan O. Hatch with Kyle P. Farley, vol. 22 of *WJE* (2003), 498–499. Also see Edwards' comparison of ministers to a "flaming fire" (Ps 104:4), calling on them to seek "a double portion of the Spirit of God at such a time as this." Edwards, *Some Thoughts*, 507.

109. Edwards, *Some Thoughts*, 498–499. Edwards likewise pointed to Pss 37:11 and 76:9.

110. Edwards, *Some Thoughts*, 524.

111. Edwards, *Some Thoughts*, 525.

opposed the revivals altogether and those who became proud about their religious awakening or failed to join ecstatic experiences with faithful Christian duty. All in all, Edwards longed to have the Spirit's presence among his people, and he looked for signs that what was happening in his revival context mirrored the descriptions of God's gracious influences on his people as recorded in the Psalms.

Discerning True and False Religion

With the rise of revival critics and the ups and downs of the two revivals in Northampton, Edwards sought to make sense of the religious experiences he observed. Much of his career was wrapped up with the spiritual revivals throughout New England and a biblically and theologically driven explanation of what happened. Why had so many who were seemingly moved by the Holy Spirit and who had professed awakenings in the heat of the revivals later return to spiritually apathetic living? Edwards thought deeply about this issue of discerning between true and false experiences of religion, which is why McClymond and McDermott claim that his "project of spiritual discernment was among the most penetrating and subtle in Christian history."[112] As Edwards explored the depths of the human heart and the unreliability of external appearances, he turned to the Psalms to help him articulate what he observed in the religious experiences of Northampton.

One of the issues Edwards addressed from the Psalms was the bodily effects of the spiritual revivals. Were such physical manifestations a true sign of the Spirit's work on souls? Edwards pointed to places in the Psalms that linked spiritual influences with bodily effects to show that the Spirit's work can, though does not necessarily, entail physical effects. In *Distinguishing Marks*, Edwards quoted Ps 32:3–4: "When I kept silence, my bones waxed old through my roaring all the day long. For day and night thy hand was heavy upon me: my moisture is turned into the drought of summer," and he argued that indeed the Scriptures gave evidence of extreme bodily reactions to spiritual conviction: "The Psalmist gives an account of his crying out aloud, and a great weakening of his body under convictions of conscience, and a sense of the guilt of sin.... We may at least argue so much from it, that such an effect of conviction of sin, may well in some cases be supposed."[113] In *Religious*

---

112. McClymond and McDermott, *The Theology of Jonathan Edwards*, 320.

113. Edwards, *Distinguishing Marks*, 233. See also Edwards' similar comment on Ps 119:131: "I opened my mouth, and panted: for I longed for thy commandments." Edwards, *Some Thoughts*, 303.

Affections, Edwards argued that strong religious affections can influence both the soul and the body from Ps 84:2, "My soul longeth, yea, even fainteth for the courts of the LORD: my heart and my flesh crieth out for the living God." Edwards explained from this and other passages that "the Scripture often makes use of bodily effects, to express the strength of holy and spiritual affections; such as trembling, groaning, being sick, crying out, panting, and fainting."[114] While earlier Reformed exegetes did not deny the physical experiences recorded in these passages, Edwards alone used these passages to make the explicit argument that holy religious affections can be accompanied with bodily manifestations.[115] But Edwards also warned that these effects "oftentimes arise from great affections about temporal things, and when religion is no way concerned in them."[116] That is why he ultimately pointed to "sincerity and soundness in religion" as the best evidence of God's work, citing forty passages from the Psalms.[117] In fact, we prove our sincerity to ourselves by Christian practice, as taught in Ps 119:6, "Then shall I not be ashamed, when I have respect unto all thy commandments"; as Edwards paraphrased, "then shall I be bold and assured and steadfast in my hope."[118] On the one hand, Edwards wanted critics to stop maligning God's work, even if it issued in strange bodily effects like those recorded in the Psalms. On the other hand, he wanted people to be honest about their spiritual state and find the surest evidence for their hope.

As Edwards continued to observe people's experience of religious exercises, he realized how hard it is for one person to assess the authenticity of another's experience. In fact, one key point in Edwards' understanding of discerning true and false religion was that people can very easily fool other people. Some may seem genuine when in fact they are wicked to the core. The paradigm passage that Edwards used to show this reality was Ps 55:12–14: "For it was not an enemy that reproached me; then I could have borne it: neither was it he that hated me that did magnify himself against me; then I would have hid myself from him: But it was thou, a man mine equal, my guide, and

---

114. Edwards, *Religious Affections*, 134, 135.

115. Henry, *Exposition*, [Pss 32:3–4; 84:2;]; Poole, *Synopsis*, 707–708; 1038–1039; Trapp, *Commentary*, 660–661, 799; Dickson, *First Fifty Psalms*, 209–210; Dickson, *Other fifty Psalmes*, 207; Calvin, *Commentary*, 1:527–530; 3:354–355.

116. Edwards, *Religious Affections*, 132.

117. Edwards, *Religious Affections*, 397.

118. Edwards, *Religious Affections*, 421.

mine acquaintance. We took sweet counsel together, and walked unto the house of God in company."

The topic of misjudging the hearts of others was at the forefront of Edwards' mind in September 1741 for he addressed this topic using Ps 55:12–14 in his *Distinguishing Marks* commencement address and also preached a sermon from Ps 55:12–14 that month. In his sermon Edwards explained the story behind this passage by identifying David's sweet friend as Ahithophel, who had served as David's personal counselor. But when Absalom drove his father, David, out of Jerusalem and took the kingdom in a coup, he recruited Ahithophel to serve as his advisor. Ahithophel thus betrayed David and advised Absalom on how to destroy his father's kingdom (2 Sam 15:1–17:23). Edwards observed from this passage how David had placed "confidence" in Ahithophel and yet "[h]ow he was decieved in him."[119] Edwards held that Ps 55:12–14 represented David's lament of Ahithophel, and he employed this passage frequently because it served as a quintessential representation of the human inability to judge another person's character, even a close friend and advisor with whom one has shared spiritual joys. In this sermon, he thus preached the doctrine, "men are not sufficient to positively determine the state of the souls of others that are of God[']s visible People."[120]

In David's case, he was "a great divine" and "a very understanding wise man" who had a remarkable degree of spiritual wisdom, evident in his contributions in the Psalms, and he was an "Eminently holy man" who had experienced diverse circumstances to give him a deep understanding of people.[121] He had spent much time with Ahithophel, who was "one of the most familiar friends he had," and by appointing Ahithophel his counselor, even in spiritual matters, Edwards showed that "[h]e had a high esteem of him not only as a Good man but Eminently so."[122] But while David savored Ahithophel's "sweet counsel," he discovered that "he was not only no saint but a notoriously wicked man, a murderous vile wretch."[123] Edwards exclaimed that "such an unfathomable deceit is there in the Heart of man."[124] He also showed how judging the heart is a task

---

119. Jonathan Edwards, "633. Sermon on Ps 55:12–14 (Sept. 1741)," Beinecke Rare Book and Manuscript Library, Yale University, New Haven, CT, L. 1r.

120. Edwards, "633. Sermon on Ps 55:12–14," L. 1r.

121. Edwards, "633. Sermon on Ps 55:12–14," L. 1v.

122. Edwards, "633. Sermon on Ps 55:12–14," L. 2r.

123. Edwards, "633. Sermon on Ps 55:12–14." L. 2r.–2v. Edwards made this same verbatim statement in Edwards, *Distinguishing Marks*, 286.

124. Edwards, "633. Sermon on Ps 55:12–14," L. 2v.

that belongs to God alone, for " '[t]is spoken of very often as God[']s prerogative to Judge the state of others['] hearts," as Ps 7:8–11 testifies, "[t]he Lᴏʀᴅ shall judge the people."¹²⁵ Edwards reasoned that, "If it be God[']s Prerogative then tis a good Reason that men should not meddle with it," for even Christians are ill-adept at judging the hearts of others given their own warped hearts.¹²⁶ In his application, Edwards warned that while ministers had a pastoral duty to deal with people's consciences, no one—not even ministers—had the discernment to make "an open publick separation between the Converted & unconverted."¹²⁷ He also exhorted individuals not to rest their hope of salvation on the judgment of another human but encouraged people to judge the state of their soul by depending on God's Word and God's Spirit, which "never go alone," but "must both go together."¹²⁸ The confirming witness of the Spirit mixed with the abiding fruits of converting grace described in the Word (abandoning sin and practicing righteousness) together form the best arbiter between true and counterfeit grace.¹²⁹

Edwards continued to employ Ps 55:12–14 in later writings to show that discerning another's spiritual state is so elusive.¹³⁰ But he was not the first to observe the deceptive nature of the soul from Ps 55:12–14. In fact, Calvin turned to this passage to describe his own experience of being accused by "brethren" and even fellow "preachers of the gospel" who waged "nefarious war against me," because David's description gave words to his experience.¹³¹ In his commentarial treatment of the passage, though, Calvin rejected the identification of this person as Ahithophel, and, instead of using this passage to discuss the difficulty of discerning another's spiritual state, he reiterated the pain of being betrayed by such a close, intimate friend.¹³² Henry, Poole, Trapp, and Dickson, on the other hand,

---

125. Edwards, "633. Sermon on Ps 55:12–14," L. 5r.

126. Edwards, "633. Sermon on Ps 55:12–14," L. 5v.

127. Edwards, "633. Sermon on Ps 55:12–14," L. 7r. Here Edwards seems to have been responding to those like Gilbert Tennent and George Whitefield who were publicly identifying some ministers as being unconverted. See Kidd, *The Great Awakening*, 59–61; Marsden, *Jonathan Edwards: A Life*, 210–211.

128. Edwards, "633. Sermon on Ps 55:12–14," L. 7v.

129. Edwards, "633. Sermon on Ps 55:12–14," L. 7v.–8v.

130. See Edwards' use of Ps 55:12–14 in "Miscellanies" Entry No. 1000, "Jᴜᴅɢɪɴɢ. Dɪsᴄᴇʀɴɪɴɢ Oᴛʜᴇʀs," (late 1742–early 1743), in Edwards, *The "Miscellanies": Entry Nos. 833–1152*, 326; Edwards, *Religious Affections*, 184; Edwards, *Notes on Scripture*, 355–356.

131. Calvin, *Commentary*, 1:xlvi.

132. Calvin, *Commentary*, 2:335–337.

all identified Ahithophel as the traitor, while Henry and Dickson also observed that the visible church is a mixed body.[133] Edwards, however, presented the most thorough treatment of this passage with reference to the difficulty of discerning others' spiritual state.

Discerning true and false conversions led to a more contentious issue as Edwards applied his theology of true religious experience to his doctrine of the church in *An Humble Inquiry into the Rules of the Word of God, Concerning the Qualifications Requisite to a Complete Standing and Full Communion in the Visible Christian Church*, the public defense of his policy to examine converts prior to being accepted as full members. Why did Edwards take such a strong position on membership, which became the presenting issue for his expulsion from Northampton? While the question is complex, at the core of his action was a desire to help his parishioners evaluate whether or not they had experienced true conversion, especially since he had observed so many whose experiences had proved abortive.[134]

His pastoral desire to nurture true confessions came to the surface in his *Humble Inquiry* as he engaged the Psalms. In the course of his work, Edwards argued that people should own the covenant publicly and that "none ought to be admitted to the privileges of adult persons in the church of Christ, but such as make a profession of real piety," since the covenant is God's covenant, which unites us spiritually with him.[135] He believed there must be some proof of inward piety if a person were to be welcomed into the visible church, and

133. Henry reminded people that "[t]here has always been, and will always be a mixture of good and bad, found and unfound in the visible Church, between whom perhaps for a long time we can discern no difference; but the searcher of Hearts doth." He also noted that "[w]e must not wonder if we be sadly deceiv'd in some that have made great Pretensions to those two Sacred things, *Religion* and *Friendship; David* himself, tho' a very wise Man, was thus impos'd upon, which may make our *like* Disappointments the more *tolerable*." Henry, *Exposition*, [Ps 55:12–14]. Italics original. Dickson noted the possibility for deception: "A godly and wise man may be deceived in his choice by the close carriage of an hypocrite, who because he hath no sound principles of stedfastnesse in a good cause, may both disappoint his friend, and deceive him also." Dickson, *Other fifty Psalmes*, 30. See also Poole, *Synopsis*, 846–848; Trapp, *Commentary*, 732.

134. Perhaps the weightiest factor was Edwards' concern that the visible church maintain a purity as the Bride of Christ. See Rhys S. Bezzant, *Jonathan Edwards and the Church* (New York: Oxford University Press, 2013), 169–190; McClymond and McDermott, *The Theology of Jonathan Edwards*, 451–464, 476–479, 487–493. Douglas A. Sweeney, "The Church," in *The Princeton Companion to Jonathan Edwards*, ed. Sang Hyun Lee (Princeton, NJ: Princeton University Press, 2007), 167–189.

135. Jonathan Edwards, *An Humble Inquiry into the Rules of the Word of God, Concerning the Qualifications Requisite to a Complete Standing and Full Communion in the Visible Christian Church*, in *Ecclesiastical Writings*, ed. David D. Hall, vol. 12 of *WJE* (1994), 199, 205. Quotation on 205.

he showed that God distinguishes between sincere and false professions, just as Ps 51:6 states, "Behold, thou desirest truth in the inward parts," and as Ps 11:7 says, "For the righteous LORD loveth righteousness; his countenance doth behold the upright."[136] Psalm 78:36–37 further demonstrated God's demand for sincerity, for he rejects those who "flatter him with their mouth" though their heart is not right within them.[137] Edwards feared that the churches of New England would fall into the same state of insincerity as the generation of Israel in the wilderness, that their "owning the covenant" was becoming "mere form and ceremony," since people commonly neglected owning the church covenant until they got married, "and then to do it for their credit's sake, and that their children may be baptized."[138] He argued that churches ought not confirm people in "knowingly" making "a lying promise," like the Israelites in Ps 78:36 who "did flatter [God] with their mouth" and "lied unto him with their tongues."[139] God saw through such insincerity, and the wicked had no place in God's visible church, as taught in Ps 50:16, "But unto the wicked God saith, What hast thou to do to declare my statutes, or that thou should-est take my covenant in thy mouth?" This psalm particularly demonstrated that the wicked did not belong in God's visible church, for "they reject the very covenant, which they with their mouths profess to own and consent to," as in Ps 50:17, "Seeing thou hatest instruction, and castest my words behind thee."[140] So Edwards concluded, "Therefore, I think, it follows, that they who know it is thus with them, have nothing to do to take God's covenant into their mouths; or in other words, have no warrant to do this, until it be otherwise with them."[141] For ultimately hypocrites are like "[a] deceitful bow, that appears good, but fails the archer," as in Ps 78:57, and Edwards saw no place for them in the visible church.[142] The Psalms helped Edwards defend the importance of a pure visible church and show how deceitful and hypocritical people were in

---

136. Edwards, *An Humble Inquiry*, 208. Edwards also cited Ps 51:6 in *Misrepresentations Corrected and Truth Vindicated*, in *Ecclesiastical Writings*, ed. David D. Hall, vol. 12 of *WJE* (1994), 412.

137. Edwards, *An Humble Inquiry*, 212–213. Edwards also discussed Ps 78:34–37 in *Misrepresentations*, 432–433.

138. Edwards, *An Humble Inquiry*, 213.

139. Edwards, *An Humble Inquiry*, 215–216.

140. Edwards, *An Humble Inquiry*, 218.

141. Edwards, *An Humble Inquiry*, 219.

142. Edwards, *An Humble Inquiry*, 222.

seeking the benefits of church membership without exercising the fruits of the Spirit's grace.

Edwards also addressed this question while preaching on the Psalms in a December 1751 sermon on Ps 78:36–37, "Nevertheless they did flatter him with their mouth, and they lied unto him with their tongues. For their heart was not right with him, neither were they stedfast in his covenant." In this sermon to the Stockbridge Indians and Mohawks, Edwards described the nature of false religion. One cannot help but wonder if he was thinking of his Northampton congregation, which had ejected him after two seasons of revival, a church he worried was filled with false professors. He preached the doctrine: "Tis hanous wickedness to make a false Profession of Relig[ion] when the Heart is not Right[eous] & so not to be steadfast in God[']s Cov[enant]"—a doctrine well in line with the Reformed exegetical tradition.[143] While it is "the duty of all men to be the friends of G[od]" and while it is good to profess religion when one is "willing to forsake all" for Christ, "a solemn Profession is great wickedness" when people are "not truly the Friends" of God.[144] In fact, "G[od] hates such Professions worse than the Heathen," and ultimately, no one can fool God with their lips since "G[od] sees the Heart & that is what he requires."[145] In his application, Edwards charged the people to "see to it you don[']t make a false Profes[sion] without giving your Hearts," and he especially targeted those who do it "only to get your Chil[dren] baptized"—a reminder that the membership controversy at Northampton was still fresh on his mind.[146]

---

143. Jonathan Edwards, "1013. Sermon on Ps 78:36–37 (December 1751)," Beinecke Rare Book and Manuscript Library, Yale University, New Haven, CT, L. 1r. Elsewhere Edwards observed on this verse (Ps 78:36) that "certainly it is absurd to suppose that men can make up for the want of sincere respect by fallacy and guise, or that they can make up for the want of truth by falsehood and lying." Jonathan Edwards, *Charity and Its Fruits*, in *Ethical Writings*, ed. Paul Ramsey, vol. 8 of *WJE* (1989), 180. As for the Reformed tradition, Henry likewise interpreted these verses as showing that "[t]hey were not sincere in this Profession." Henry, *Exposition*, [Ps 78:36–37]. Poole called it a "feigned repentance" ("Ficta erat poenitentia"). Poole, *Synopsis*, 1010. Trapp said these verses describe "Hypocrisie," for "[s]ure it is that many men[']s devotion is meer dissimulation." Trapp, *Commentary*, 788. As Dickson likewise commented, "Profession of faith and repentance, which doth forsake sin and seek God onely for temporal reasons, is but a lying unto God." Dickson, *Other fifty Psalmes*, 211. Calvin observed from this passage "that we ought to beware of a species of hypocrisy which is more hidden, and which consists in this, that the sinner, being constrained by fear, flatters God in a slavish manner, while yet, if he could, he would shun the judgment of God." Calvin, *Commentary*, 3:253.

144. Edwards, "1013. Sermon on Ps 78:36–37," L. 1r.

145. Edwards, "1013. Sermon on Ps 78:36–37," L. 1v.

146. Edwards, "1013. Sermon on Ps 78:36–37," L. 2v.

Edwards charged: "Take Heed you ben[']t deceived by taking up a notion that you are friends without good Reason."[147]

As Edwards reflected on the experiences of his people in the revivals, he used the Psalms to emphasize the priority of discerning between true and false religion. The Psalms exhibited that a genuine work of the Spirit may produce bodily effects, though it need not do so. They provided Edwards with the key passage that shows the inability of a person to judge another's spiritual state, as well as how easy it is for the wicked to deceive others. Edwards also turned to the Psalter to establish the importance of examining people's spiritual state for a pure visible church and to warn people of the heinous sin of feigning religion. As we have seen here, the Psalms formed a significant portion of the biblically authoritative basis Edwards used to establish his theology of discerning a true work of the Spirit of God.

Preaching the Gospel

Edwards was first and foremost a pastor concerned for the souls of his congregation. He took his duties very seriously and considered himself a "watchman for souls" who "must give an account" for "the souls of men committed to [his] care by the Lord Jesus Christ."[148] He identified himself and other pastors as "ministers of the gospel," emphasizing that in their care for souls, ministers must proclaim the good news of salvation above all.[149] They must help spiritually resistant people deal with the most important issue facing their soul.[150] While it is no surprise

---

147. Edwards, "1013. Sermon on Ps 78:36–37," L. 2v. See also Edwards' sermon on Ps 66:3, in which he observed that God's power and terror instill fear in his enemies, so that "tho[ugh] they have no sincere & hearty sp[irit] of submission & abund[ance] yet out of fear they shall make as if they had." Jonathan Edwards, "365. Sermon on Ps 66:3 (August [6,] 1735)," in *Sermons, Series II, 1735*, vol. 50 of *WJEO*, L. 1r. And see his sermon on Ps 17:3, in which he preached the doctrine, "The manner of men[']s Behaviour in secret & when hid from the Eye of the World is a much greater Proof of their sincerity than what they do openly." Jonathan Edwards, "903. Sermon on Ps 17:3 (August 1748)," in *Sermons, Series II, 1748*, vol. 66 of *WJEO*, L. 1r.

148. Jonathan Edwards, "The Great Concern of a Watchman for Souls" (Heb 13:17), in *Sermons and Discourses 1743–1758*, ed. Wilson H. Kimnach, vol. 25 of *WJE* (2006), 63.

149. Edwards, "The Great Concern," 63. See also McClymond and McDermott, *The Theology of Jonathan Edwards*, 464–476.

150. Edwards made this point clear in a February 1735 sermon while discussing Ps 27:4, which shows that a person's salvation is the most important concern of life: "This seeking eternal life should not only be one concern that our souls are taken up about, with other things; but salvation should be sought as the 'one thing needful' (Luke 10:42). And as the 'one thing' that is 'desired' (Ps. 27:4)." Jonathan Edwards, "Pressing into the Kingdom of God" (Luke 16:16), in *Sermons and Discourses 1734–1738*, ed. M. X. Lesser, vol. 19 of *WJE* (2001), 276–277.

that Edwards, as a renowned awakening preacher, proclaimed the gospel forth-rightly, it may surprise some to see how clearly he preached the gospel from the book of Psalms. In Edwards' unified view of the Old and New Testaments, he had no reservation about speaking the message of salvation in Jesus Christ even from the Psalms. Not to do so would have shocked him. While we will treat Edwards' *concept* of the gospel in the Psalms at the end of this chapter, here we discuss his *practice* of preaching the gospel from the Psalter by examining five sermons on the Psalms.

In the winter of 1737, Edwards made an appeal directed at young people to respond to the gospel from Ps 71:5, "For thou art my hope, O Lord GOD: thou art my trust from my youth."[151] Earlier interpreters recognized the benefits of early piety but made less of this verse than Edwards.[152] He began his exposition by commenting that it was most likely penned on "the occasion of Absalom[']s Rebellion" for it was written when David was in "great trouble" with enemies (vv. 10–12) "in the time of old age," not during the earlier years of Saul's per-secution (v. 9).[153] Edwards observed that because God had been the object of David's hope from his youth, it was a "great comfort" to David when he faced new troubles in his old age "to think that he had long trusted in G[od] & so had much experience of God[']s faithfulness."[154] As Edwards extrapolated the larger theological point, it is always a comfort to persons that they had been "early pious & devoted thems[elves] to G[od] in their youth."[155] So he preached

151. Jonathan Edwards, "693j. Sermon on Ps 71:5 (n.d. [*c.* late 1730s])," Beinecke Rare Book and Manuscript Library, Yale University, New Haven, CT. On the dating of the sermon, Edwards mentioned in the sermon that it had been a year and a half since the revivals died down, so he likely preached it in the winter of 1737. Edwards, "693j. Sermon on Ps 71:5," L. 6v.

152. We should note that Edwards' sermons in this section differed from other exegetes com-pared here in part because he was preaching sermons while they were writing commentaries, but those commentaries were also used by preachers, and the thrust of Edwards' sermons yields an emphasis that was not as strong in the earlier tradition. As for the commentarial tradition on this verse, Henry similarly recognized how strong David's "confidence in GOD" was, since it was "supported and encourag'd by his Experiences," which "should ingage us to an early Piety" and should instruct us to "lose no time when we are capable." Henry, *Exposition*, [Ps 71:5]. Dickson briefly noted how beneficial "confidence in God" is, "specially when it is of long standing." Dickson, *Other fifty Psalmes*, 137. And Calvin described the great benefit of a "confidence" when joined with "experience," for "the remembrance of God's benefits" have a "powerful influence" in "nourishing his hope." Calvin, *Commentary*, 3:84. Poole and Trapp made only passing comments about having hope, without mentioning the speaker's remembrance of his youth. Poole, *Synopsis*, 959; Trapp, *Commentary*, 766.

153. Edwards, "693j. Sermon on Ps 71:5," L. 1r.

154. Edwards, "693j. Sermon on Ps 71:5," L. 1v.

155. Edwards, "693j. Sermon on Ps 71:5," L. 1v.

the doctrine, "It behooves Young Persons to seek that they may be converted while they are young," not only because it is their duty to give God their best and to begin all things with God but because it is in their own interest, giving them comfort in this world and eternal happiness in the next.[156] In his application, Edwards called young people to examine themselves and presented several reasons "not to spend their youth in sin but earnestly to seek that they may be converted now while young."[157] To those who had been converted, he exhorted them to thank God for distinguishing them not only from the unconverted but also from those who were converted in later years after wasting their youth in sin.[158]

In the months leading up to the 1740–1742 revivals, Edwards preached an awakening sermon on Ps 18:35, "Thou hast also given me the shield of thy salvation: and thy right hand hath holden me up, and thy gentleness hath made me great." The surviving manuscript includes only the text, a summary of the doctrine, and the application—most likely because the first part of this two-part sermon was separated from the rest of it. From the pages we have, we see that Edwards spoke not only of God's wrath to deter sinners but also of his gentleness to lure them to the gospel. He reminded his hearers that "[i]n the doctrinal handling of these words, I showed how this word David says of hims[elf] is applicable to all the saints and 1. I showed how they are become Great, and 2. How tis God[']s gentleness that hath made them so."[159] Earlier Reformed interpreters did not address this verse at length, and instead of proclaiming the gospel and Christ's gentleness, they focused on God's defense and preservation of David.[160] But Edwards, in his application, spent most of his time speaking to sinners, exhorting them "to do their utmost to obtain an Interest in [Christ]."[161] He first reminded them of the miserable state of sin they were in and that "you are in no wise able to deliver yourself" from God's "fury & fierceness."[162] But he went on, following Ps 18:35, to present

---

156. Edwards, "693j. Sermon on Ps 71:5," L. 2r.

157. Edwards, "693j. Sermon on Ps 71:5," L. 3r.–7v. Quotation on 3r.

158. Edwards, "693j. Sermon on Ps 71:5," L. 8r.

159. Jonathan Edwards, "693i. Sermon on Ps 18:35 (n.d. [*c.* 1739–1740])," Beinecke Rare Book and Manuscript Library, Yale University, New Haven, CT, L. 1r. Edwards repreached this sermon at Sutton on February 1, 1742.

160. Henry, *Exposition*, [Ps 18:35]; Trapp, *Commentary*, 619; Dickson, *First Fifty Psalms*, 95; Calvin, *Commentary*, 1:293.

161. Edwards, "693i. Sermon on Ps 18:35," L. 1r.

162. Edwards, "693i. Sermon on Ps 18:35," L. 1r., 1v., 3r.

a "matter of great Encouragemt to sinners that are sensible of their misery to come to [Christ]," and to partake of that gentleness described in the text, which is only available in Christ, who came down from his majesty on high to be the redeemer you need and who will "deal gently with you," "Heal your wounds," and "wipe Tears from your Eyes."[163] Edwards called them to consider how gentle Christ's invitations are, for "he don[']t speak in the gospel with that voice that he did from mt Sinai," where he made the earth tremble, but speaks with a voice that will "put life & courage & strength" into your soul, and he added, "you can't desire [Christ] to be more meek & more Gracious & ready to Receive sinners than he is."[164]

In his "Blank Bible" note on this verse, Edwards cited Poole, noting that the Hebrew word translated "gentleness" here, עֲנָוֶה, can mean "humiliation" or "affliction." He seems to have gleaned this point from Poole's discussion of the rabbinic doctors, who explained that this term "properly denotes *affliction, humiliation, poverty*."[165] Still, Edwards' final takeaway from this semantic discussion was to highlight the gospel: "This teaches that the exaltation of God's people is by the humiliation and suffering of their Savior."[166]

In June 1741, in the heat of the revivals, Edwards preached an awakening sermon that employed the imagery of sleep using Ps 13:3, "Consider and hear me, O LORD my God: lighten mine eyes, lest I sleep the sleep of death." Edwards noted that the text describes the psalmist's fear of sleeping the sleep of death and that the "means to prevent it is by his Eyes Enlightened."[167] Edwards observed the literal sense that David feared a temporal calamity, but he also noted that these words have a spiritual sense, signifying a prayer for "spiritual Life & a deliv[erance] from sp[iritual] sleep."[168] In fact, Scripture more often uses the metaphor of light to signify spiritual light, and here the psalmist's prayer "is much more naturally understood of the Enlighteneding of his mind with sp[iritual] Light."[169] Earlier Reformed exegetes focused on David's melancholy caused by lacking God's light, which felt like an encroaching death,

163. Edwards, "693i. Sermon on Ps 18:35," L. 6v., 7v.

164. Edwards, "693i. Sermon on Ps 18:35," L. 8v., 9r., 10r.

165. Poole, *Synopsis*, 618. The Latin reads, "propriè *afflictionem, humiliationem, paupertatem*."

166. Edwards, The "Blank Bible," 485.

167. Jonathan Edwards, "615. Sermon on Ps 13:3 (June 1741)," Beinecke Rare Book and Manuscript Library, Yale University, New Haven, CT, L. 1r.

168. Edwards, "615. Sermon on Ps 13:3," L. 1v.

169. Edwards, "615. Sermon on Ps 13:3," L. 1v.

but did not turn this observation to the Spirit's regenerating light, as Edwards did.[170] In his four-part doctrine, Edwards first noted that "[t]he soul is said to be asleep when it is insensible," and so persons are spiritually asleep when they are insensible of judgment or are "unawakened."[171] Second, Edwards noted that persons sleep the sleep of natural death either when they never wake up or when their sleep causes them to die because they do not sense impending danger. In the same way, persons sleep the sleep of spiritual death either by continuing "blind & senseless" despite means of grace until they are "finally given up by G[od] to Judicial blindness & hardness," or by straying so far that they "sleep thems[elves] into Hell."[172] In his third point Edwards noted that the sleep of death is prevented through enlightening the eyes, for "God[']s whole work in the soul is carried on by Light."[173] And fourth, the source of this light is only God, for humans are "insufficient thems[elves]" to enlighten themselves, but rather God, "the Father of Lights," is the source of enlightenment—a countercultural statement in the "Age of Lights."[174] In his application, Edwards sought to awaken souls who were still asleep, and he spoke in stark terms to his people at the height of the revivals: "how Confirmed is the sleep that many of you are in," for it has been continuing for so long, even during such great means of awakening, and "[h]ow often has [God] thundered aloud with his voice," yet his "Rumbling"

---

170. Henry interpreted the enlightening of the eyes as symbolizing refreshment of a weary soul whose eyes are darkened under "the cloud of Melancholy." Henry, *Exposition*, [Ps 13:3]. Trapp read the enlightenment of the eyes as a way to "chear up my drooping spirit," and the sleep of death served as a metaphor indicating the seriousness of the psalmist's spiritual condition. Trapp, *Commentary*, 601. Dickson similarly saw the lightening of the eyes as "some immediate comfort to uphold me in the hope of my delivery," for it is as death to a godly man "to be long without the sense of God[']s love." Dickson, *First Fifty Psalms*, 64. Likewise, Calvin said that enlightening the eyes means "to give the breath of life" and that the sleep of death represents David's expectation that, without God's light, he will be "immediately overwhelmed with the darkness of death." Calvin, *Commentary*, 1:184–185. Poole explored this passage in more complexity and in ways that mirrored Edwards. Like others he noted that the enlightening of the eyes indicates an enlivening of the spirit, dispelling the clouds of affliction. He also observed several ways that light is used in Scripture, noting that "*Light* often signifies *joy*" ("*Lux* saepe sign. *gaudium*") and that "ignorance is removed from the mind by the word and the Spirit of God" ("ignorantia per verbum & Spiritum Dei ex mente auferetur"). Poole further explored the many ways that the phrase "sleep of death" could be taken, whether to sleep to death, in death, or in accordance with death, while "death" could mean eternal or natural death. Poole, *Synopsis*, 574–575.

171. Edwards, "615. Sermon on Ps 13:3," L. 2v.

172. Edwards, "615. Sermon on Ps 13:3," L. 5r., 8r.

173. Edwards, "615. Sermon on Ps 13:3," L. 8v.

174. Edwards, "615. Sermon on Ps 13:3," L. 8v.

"failed of waking you."[175] Speaking "plainly," Edwards said that for those who still had not awakened, their case for going to hell was pretty strong: "if men don[']t look upon you likely to be damned[,] who is likely[?]"[176] And when you get to hell, he warned, "you'll wake up & you[']ll never sleep no more," for "it will be an everlasting waking."[177] Edwards closed his sermon with directions for those still asleep to remove any hindrances to God, to obey Christ's commands, and to "beg mightily of God to Enlighten your Eyes."[178] This Psalms passage provided Edwards with the ideal imagery of sleep for proclaiming a message of "awakening," a message demanded of a gospel minister caring for souls.

This gospel minister cared not only for the adults and young people in his congregation; he also directed his attention to the souls of children in a July 1741 sermon on Ps 34:11, "Come, ye children, hearken unto me: I will teach you the fear of the LORD." In this private meeting for children, Edwards noted from this text that "[c]hildren need to be taught the fear of the Lord"; that Christ "calls 'em & is ready to teach 'em"; and that "[h]e sends forth his ministers"—like Edwards—"to Call 'em & to teach 'em."[179] Having established his duty to teach them the truth, Edwards presented his doctrine: "Theref[ore] now I would improve this [scripture] to call upon you Children now to forsake your sins and seek the fear of G[od]."[180] Edwards' interpretation and application of this verse was rather unusual. While earlier Reformed exegetes did not present a unified interpretation of this verse, none of them attributed the psalmist's voice to Christ or used this verse to apply a gospel call to children.[181] But Edwards taught that "in this Ps[alm]" Christ calls to children, and Edwards, speaking in Christ's name, said, "I call upon you so often to seek an Interest in

---

175. Edwards, "615. Sermon on Ps 13:3," L. 10v., 11r.

176. Edwards, "615. Sermon on Ps 13:3," L. 12r.

177. Edwards, "615. Sermon on Ps 13:3," L. 12v.

178. Edwards, "615. Sermon on Ps 13:3," L. 18v.

179. Jonathan Edwards, "622. Sermon on Ps 34:11 (July 1741)," Beinecke Rare Book and Manuscript Library, Yale University, New Haven, CT, L. 1r.

180. Edwards, "622. Sermon on Ps 34:11," L. 1r.

181. Henry portrayed David as condescending to teach children, specifically to instill in them the fear of the Lord. Henry, *Exposition*, [Ps 34:11]. Poole made only a brief comment on this verse, noting that without the fear of the Lord, one will necessarily perish. Poole, *Synopsis*, 718. Trapp lauded the teacher as deserving of the name "father," for he gives his "wel-being." Trapp, *Commentary*, 669. Dickson identified the voice as God, who "offereth himself as a father ready to instruct his visible Kirk, or his children." Dickson, *First Fifty Psalms*, 223. Calvin took the term "children" not as a reference to actual children, but as "a gentle and courteous appellation" for God's people signifying the need for them to "be brought to a chastened and humble state." Calvin, *Commentary*, 1:566.

[Christ]" because "you must be Converted" since "you are miserable Creatures without [Christ]."[182] He then walked the children through a frightening procession of an unconverted child's death, asking them, how will it be if you live and die in a natural condition, and how is it for those children whose souls have already left their bodies? How will it be when your soul "goes down to Hell," "at the day of Judgm[en]t," and then "after the day of Judgm[en]t"?[183] He asked them to imagine what they would see if they went to observe "wicked chil[dren] that are gone to Hell" and urged them to hearken to him, noting that "[i]f you wont hearken" to me, then you "will go to Hell."[184]

It appears that Edwards was testing the limits of hellfire preaching in the summer of 1741. These two previous sermons certainly suggest so, as does the other renowned sermon he preached on July 8, 1741, at Enfield, Connecticut, "Sinners in the Hands of an Angry God." But as screeching as these words might sound to our twenty-first century ears, just as soothing were the words in Edwards' exposition of this verse a year earlier. In another sermon to children in July 1740, Edwards commented on Ps 34:11 by depicting Christ as a friend of children: "Never any in this world showed such wonderful condescension in taking notice of children" as Christ, who "graciously offers himself and all his great blessings that he has purchased by his death to them. He is willing to be theirs, so that they may say of this glorious King, 'This is my Jesus, this is my Redeemer, my friend, my portion, one that has given himself to me.'"[185] As Edwards cared for souls, he used both dread and delight to draw them to the gospel.

Edwards continued to call people to attend to eternal affairs and put themselves in the way of grace—that is, to use the means of grace while recognizing that only God in his sovereignty can bestow grace on anyone. And he used the Psalms to do so, as in his September 1742 sermon on Ps 126:5–6, "They that sow in tears shall reap in joy. He that goeth forth and weepeth, bearing precious seed, shall doubtless come again with rejoicing, bringing his sheaves with him." Edwards observed that the psalm's subject is "the Joyf[ul] notion of the turning the Captivity of Zion," or the church.[186] He "safely" understood this turning as "all that Redemption out of captivity

182. Edwards, "622. Sermon on Ps 34:11," L. 1r.

183. Edwards, "622. Sermon on Ps 34:11," L. 1v.

184. Edwards, "622. Sermon on Ps 34:11," L. 1v.

185. Jonathan Edwards, "Children Ought to Love the Lord Jesus Christ Above All" (Matt 10:37), in *Sermons and Discourses 1739–1742*, ed. Harry S. Stout and Nathan O. Hatch with Kyle P. Farley, vol. 22 of *WJE* (2003), 174.

186. Jonathan Edwards, "683. Sermon on Ps 126:5–6 (September 1742)," Beinecke Rare Book and Manuscript Library, Yale University, New Haven, CT, L. 1r.

which [Christ] works for his Elect Ch[urc]h whom he saved & gave hims[elf] for."[187] This psalm prescribes the means that "persons ought to use in order to their R[edemption] out of sp[iritual] captivity," namely the "precious seed," which "chiefly" signifies the Word of God.[188] People are to go forth and hear the Word, which will cause weeping, but after that, they will return with fruits and joy. Where Edwards differed from earlier exegetes was in applying these verses not only to the saint, as they did, but to the unawakened sinner.[189] In his doctrine Edwards compared the saints' spiritual work to the business of a husbandman: "The great work and business that we have to do in order to our sp[iritual] & Et[ernal] happiness is fitly represented by the business of an husbandman."[190] Edwards made several comparisons more explicit. Both require prudence, vigilance, care, and patience, and as the husbandman labors in the ground, so the divine Husbandman labors in human hearts, and the fruits come forth in a great variety. There is also "an agreement in the Causes of the Fruits," for while "men[']s labour is necessary," God is "the highest cause on which all depends."[191] In his application, Edwards gave directions for engaging in this spiritual work of husbandry by continuing the comparison with agriculture. "Take Heed," he warned, that "you don[']t take a Course to harden" your heart, that "instead of ploughing it & breaking it up you don[']t make it be like the hard beaten path."[192] You must also "observe & improve all special seasons," such as awakenings, times when you have "fair weather," a "time of rain," or a "time of harvest."[193] And you must "depend on the Influences of the Heavens," for just as a "Husbandman of hims[elf] can make nothing of the growth of the field," so can we make nothing of spiritual growth.[194] Edwards closed by noting how profitable for people's souls it is to compare the business of husbandry to spiritual growth, for, in Edwards' all-encompassing vision of God's

---

187. Edwards, "683. Sermon on Ps 126:5–6," L. 1r.

188. Edwards, "683. Sermon on Ps 126:5–6," L. 1v.

189. Poole, *Synopsis*, 1250–1252; Trapp, *Commentary*, 898; Dickson, *Last Fifty Psalmes*, 257; Calvin, *Commentary*, 5:101–103. Henry alone hinted at God's salvation: "They that sow in the Tears of godly Sorrow, shall reap in the Joy of a sealed Pardon, and a settled Peace." Henry, *Exposition*, [Ps 126:5–6].

190. Edwards, "683. Sermon on Ps 126:5–6," L. 2r.

191. Edwards, "683. Sermon on Ps 126:5–6," L. 3r.

192. Edwards, "683. Sermon on Ps 126:5–6," L. 5r.

193. Edwards, "683. Sermon on Ps 126:5–6," L. 6r.

194. Edwards, "683. Sermon on Ps 126:5–6," L. 7r.

communication of himself, "There are divine lessons in every thing."[195] And the divine lessons in this psalm led people to reflect on their progress toward redemption.[196]

Edwards' unified vision of the Bible gave him the grounds for using the Psalms to preach the good news that humanity can be reconciled to God through Christ. As we have seen from these five sermons, he used the Psalms in preaching to call adults, youth, and children to repentance; to employ the imagery of a voice, light, sleep, and husbandry in his appeal to attend to gospel duties; and to depict both the dangers of hell and the gentleness of God that his congregants' souls might dwell in God's holy heaven. In Edwards' view, the minister's duty was to preach the gospel using the primary means of God's Word, and the Psalter was well equipped for this purpose because it is full of gospel truth.

God's Work of Redemption

As we have seen throughout our exploration of Edwards' love affair with the Psalms, God's work of redemption served as a key organizing theme in Edwards' interpretation of the Psalms. This interpretive framework appears not only in the different elements of redemptive history that he emphasized in notes, sermons, and treatises but also in plain comments stating that the Psalms display God's redemptive-historical plan and testify to the gospel truth revealed more fully in the New Testament. We have explored the Holy Spirit's nature and role in salvation along with the promotion of that salvation doctrine in revivals and preaching and the need for discerning an authentic work of the Spirit—all from Edwards' engagement with the Psalms. In this final section of the chapter, we see these pieces come together in Edwards' broad conception of the gospel and the history of redemption as revealed in the book of Psalms.

Speaking of Edwards' "Harmony," Marsden observes that he "tried to view Scripture from God's perspective, as intricately designed luminously to reveal the great end of creation, God's redemptive love. God had built into Scripture,

---

195. Edwards, "683. Sermon on Ps 126:5–6," L. 9v.

196. See also Jonathan Edwards, "The Duty of Hearkening to God's Voice" (Ps 95:7–8), in *Sermons and Discourses 1720–1723*, vol. 10 of *WJE* (1992), 439, a sermon he repreached at Bolton and during his Yale tutorship (1724–1726) calling people "without any delay, to hearken to God's voice"; Edwards' entry on Ps 95:7–8 in *The "Blank Bible,"* 523; and Jonathan Edwards, "1004. Sermon on Ps 119:60(b) (September 1751)," Beinecke Rare Book and Manuscript Library, Yale University, New Haven, CT, in which he used the concept of time to urge a response to the gospel today.

as he had into nature and the rest of history, elaborate harmonies all resolved in the grand theme of Christ's love."[197] This harmonic view of Scripture enabled him to read the Psalms through the lens of redemptive history, since God had enshrined his grand plan within the whole Bible. Interpreting the Psalms with this teleological purpose in mind was not unlike Augustine, whose "constant concern was to make the mystery of redemption transparent through the biblical words."[198] Michael Fiedrowicz explains that Augustine interpreted the Psalms always within the analogy of faith: "Augustine's exposition is concerned to make the text of a psalm relevant in the sense that the Old Testament words can function fully as prayer in the epoch of the new covenant; they must be taken over into this definitive stage of salvation history in such a way that their meaning accords with the Church's faith."[199] Edwards held a similar approach, though basing his redemptive reading on the harmonic quality with which God had endowed the Scriptures, an outflow of his divinely intrinsic beauty and harmony.

As Edwards applied this thinking to the Psalms, he attributed a fullness of gospel doctrine to the book. During the months of his New York pastorate (August 1722–April 1723), Edwards preached "God's Excellencies," a sermon on Ps 89:6—"For who in the heaven can be compared unto the LORD? Who among the sons of the mighty can be likened unto the LORD?" He opened with this description of the Psalms:

> This book of Psalms has such an exalted devotion, and such a spirit of evangelical grace every[where] breathed forth in it! Here are such exalted expressions of the gloriousness of God, and even of the excellency of Christ and his kingdom; there is so much of the gospel doctrine, grace, and spirit, breaking out and shining in it, that it seems to be carried clear above and beyond the strain and pitch of the Old Testament, and almost brought up to the New. Almost the whole book of Psalms has either a direct or indirect respect to Christ and the gospel which he was to publish, particularly this Psalm wherein is our text.[200]

---

197. Marsden, *Jonathan Edwards: A Life*, 479.

198. Michael Fiedrowicz, "General Introduction," in *Expositions of the Psalms: 1–32*, trans. Maria Boulding and ed. John E. Rotelle, part III, vol. 15 of *The Works of Saint Augustine* (Hyde Park, NY: New City, 2000), 57.

199. Fiedrowicz, 27–28.

200. Jonathan Edwards, "God's Excellencies" (Ps 89:6), in *Sermons and Discourses 1720–1723*, ed. Wilson H. Kimnach, vol. 10 of *WJE* (1992), 415. Brackets are original to the Yale volume.

As is evident here, Edwards saw a unity that transcends the distinction between the two testaments. He did not deny a distinction, recognizing the "strain and pitch of the Old Testament," the veil through which God communicated his truths. Yet the Spirit so unifies them that Edwards could see not only the spirit of the gospel but the very grace and doctrine of the New Testament gospel clearly proclaimed in the Psalms. By making this bold assertion, Edwards stood in line with a long Christian tradition, including Thomas Aquinas, who said of the Psalms, "Everything which pertains to faith in the incarnation is so clearly treated in this work that it almost seems to be a gospel, rather than prophecy."[201]

Edwards held that "most of the Psalms" are "prophetical of the Messiah's days."[202] And in "Miscellanies" Entry No. 251, he reflected on the prophecies of the Old Testament, particularly those in the Psalms, and saw a connection with the gospel:

> There are many of the Psalms, and some other parts of Scripture, wherein the penmen immediately intended the affairs of the church of Israel. But these things being represented poetically, in those beautiful and exalted images, which a poetical genius and fire, excited and invigorated by an extraordinary exercise of grace and a holy and evangelical disposition, in which excitations there was the afflatus [or inspiration] of God's Spirit—their minds naturally conceived such poetical images of the Jewish church, as very exactly described the affairs of the gospel and the Christian church. They agreed much more properly with the latter than the former: for with [respect to] these they were tropical representations; but the fire of grace, together with a true poetical genius, naturally guided them to make use of such images *as almost literally described the affairs of the gospel*; of which all in the Jewish church was a shadow and representation, the most natural that could be, and representations so natural that a poetical genius, so exalted and animated by lively and vigorous grace, would by them be naturally led to the ideas of gospel things.[203]

---

201. Thomas Aquinas, *The Gifts of the Spirit: Selected Spiritual Writings*, ed. Benedict M. Ashley and trans. Matthew Rzeczkowski (Hyde Park, NY: New City, 1995), 96.

202. Jonathan Edwards, "Types of the Messiah," in *Typological Writings*, ed. Mason I. Lowance Jr. with David H. Watters, vol. 11 of *WJE* (1992), 216.

203. Edwards, *The "Miscellanies": Entry Nos. a–500*, 363–364. Italics mine.

Edwards stopped short of saying the gospel is explicitly revealed in the Psalms, but just barely. The Holy Spirit had a purpose in inspiring the Old Testament, pointing ultimately to the gospel of Christ. Edwards went on to argue that the more of a "gracious disposition" one has, the more one is able to recognize the gospel saturation of the Psalms, for the Holy Spirit planted these shadows in the Jewish church and "intended that gospel things should be represented by them" and that the later church should use them accordingly.[204]

Edwards believed that the Psalms, more so than any other book of the Old Testament, advanced the light of the gospel in God's outworking of the plan of redemption:

> The main subjects of these sweet songs were the glorious things of the gospel, as is evident by the interpretation that is so often put upon them and the use that is made of them in the New Testament. For there is no one book of the Old Testament that is so often quoted in the New as the book of Psalms. Joyfully did this holy man sing of those great things of Christ's redemption that had been the hope and expectation of God's church and people from the very beginning of the church of God on earth. And joyfully did others follow him in it, as Asaph, Heman, Ethan.[205]

Prior to the Psalms prophecies of Christ appeared only "here and there," but in the Psalms

> Christ is spoken of by his ancestor David abundantly in multitudes of songs, speaking of his incarnation, life, death, resurrection, ascension into heaven, his satisfaction, intercession, his prophetical, kingly, and priestly office, his glorious benefits in this life and that which is to come, his union with the church, and the blessedness of the church in him, the calling of the Gentiles, the future glory of the church near the end of the world, and Christ's coming to the final judgment. All

---

204. Edwards, *The "Miscellanies": Entry Nos. a–500*, 363–364. See also Edwards' "Miscellanies" Entry No. 378, "CHRISTIAN RELIGION," where he argued that the Psalms present clear evidence that "the Jews had the true worship and communion of the one great and holy God, and that no other nation upon earth had—it is as clear as the sun at noonday." Edwards, *The "Miscellanies": Entry Nos. a–500*, 448.

205. Jonathan Edwards, *A History of the Work of Redemption*, ed. John F. Wilson, vol. 9 of *WJE* (1989), 210.

these things and many more concerning Christ and his redemption are abundantly spoken of in the book of Psalms.[206]

In Edwards' view, prior to the revelation of Christ incarnate, God gave the greatest light about his plan of redemption in the Psalms. These various quotations show, in part, why Edwards relished the Psalms: More than any other Old Testament book, the Psalms aided him in thinking of Scripture through the interpretive lens of redemptive-history, the reigning paradigm in Edwards' thought for understanding the Bible. This paradigm captured for Edwards the excellency of God's salvation. As he observed that the Psalms speak often of singing a "new song" (Pss 33:1–3; 96:4; 98:1; 144:9; 149:1), he explained that this new song principally concerns "the glorious salvation of Christ and God's infinite grace and love in that work," which is "more excellent" and "more glorious" than anything before it.[207]

Edwards spoke much of redemptive-history in the Psalms, as is evident from his notebook on "Prophecies of the Messiah." His frequent reference to things besides the person of Christ in this notebook shows that he conceived of these prophecies as broadly referring to gospel times. For example, Edwards held that when the psalmist prays to God to "stir up thy strength, and come and save us" (Ps 80:2), he speaks of "the bringing of God's church out of captivity and bondage to foreign enemies," which is "agreeable to most other prophecies of the redemption of the Messiah; and 'tis also agreeable to other prophecies of the Messiah, that his redemption should be compared to the going forth of the children of Israel out of Egypt."[208] Similarly, he argued that Psalm 85 prophesied of "the redemption of the Messiah," for the "grand subject" of the psalm is "the bringing back the captivity of Jacob, and forgiving the iniquity of his people and covering all their sin, and taking away all his wrath and turning the people again to God; which is the description everywhere given of the Messiah's salvation."[209] Edwards held that the final group of Psalms (145–150) reveals the *ultimum* of the whole Psalter, the highest aim that unifies the entire book, namely the great redemption of God. Edwards explained that "[a] certain great salvation of the church is manifestly

206. Edwards, *A History of the Work of Redemption*, 210–211.

207. Jonathan Edwards, "They Sing a New Song" (Rev 14:3), in *Sermons and Discourses 1739–1742*, ed. Harry S. Stout and Nathan O. Hatch with Kyle P. Farley, vol. 22 of *WJE* (2003), 234.

208. Jonathan Edwards, "The Miscellanies: Entry No. 1067: Prophecies of the Messiah," Franklin Trask Library, Andover Newton Theological School, Newton, MA, §84.

209. Edwards, "Prophecies of the Messiah," §78.

the great subject of David's praise in these psalms" (Pss 145:4–6, 14, 18–20; 146:7–9; 147:2–3, 10–14; 148:14; 149:4–9), and in fact "[t]here surely is nothing that he ever speaks of in the book of Psalms, that his heart is more engaged [in] and his affections more raised [by]," for he "shuts up his whole book of Psalms" with this "grand subject" of God's salvation, which was "the sum of what engaged his mind, and his affections and praises."[210]

In his "Notes on Scripture" manuscript, Edwards developed an extensive discussion of the giving of the Law at Mt. Sinai as typifying God's redemptive work in Entry No. 210, based on Ps 68:8–9: "The earth shook, the heavens also dropped at the presence of God: even Sinai itself was moved at the presence of God, the God of Israel. Thou, O God, didst send a plentiful rain, whereby thou didst confirm thine inheritance, when it was weary."[211] Edwards argued that this passage, in connection with a number of others, reveals that God's glory was made manifest in such a dramatic way on the day he gave the Ten Commandments that its meteorological effects could be felt in the surrounding nations. The event was accompanied by "a great shower of rain upon the camp of Israel."[212] Then followed great thunder and lightning, and an earthquake, which explains the expressions in Ps 114:4 of "the mountains skipping like rams, and the little hills like lambs."[213]

Edwards developed a corollary from this historical discussion, that the giving of the law and all of its events on that day of Pentecost typified a greater event that took place on the day of Pentecost following Christ's death and resurrection.[214] Edwards parsed out a lengthy discussion of the parallels between the two: God's descent on Mt. Sinai compared with God's descent on "Mt. Sion" to his church at Jerusalem; God's revelation of the law compared with

---

210. Edwards, "Prophecies of the Messiah," §86. See also Edwards similar comments on Pss 89:11–12 and 107:1–7 in "Miscellanies" Entry Nos. 918 and 1124, respectively. Edwards, The "Miscellanies": Entry Nos. 833–1152, 166, 496.

211. This was an important note to Edwards as he cited it in ten "Blank Bible" entries: Exod 14:24–25; 19–20; Lev 23:15–17; Deut 16:9–11; Judg 5:4; Pss 68:8–9; 77:16; 78:25–26, Hab 3:3–6; 1 Cor 10:2. Edwards, The "Blank Bible," 225, 232, 258, 296, 330, 504, 512, 513, 806, 1046. He also cited this note in "Miscellanies," Entry No. 694. Edwards, The "Miscellanies": Entry Nos. 501–832, 276.

212. Edwards, Notes on Scripture, 135.

213. Edwards, Notes on Scripture, 135. Edwards employed the analogy of Scripture in this passage, referencing, inter alia, Judg 5:4; Hag 2:6–7; Heb 12:18.

214. Edwards also developed a second corollary explaining 1 Cor 10:2, "their fathers were all baptized unto Moses in the cloud and in the sea," which Edwards connected with Ps 68:8–9 and other passages to present "an argument for baptism by sprinkling or affusion." Edwards, Notes on Scripture, 139–140.

God's revelation of the gospel by his Spirit; God's voice uttered in thunder with lightning reaching the surrounding world compared with God's voice uttered in his Word as "his glorious gospel" shined forth in Jerusalem to enlighten the world; the cloud of glory as a symbol of God's presence compared with the voice of the gospel as the voice of Christ and the light as Christ's glory; the spread of God's voice and light to the nations around Mt. Sinai compared with the going out of "God's Word, and the powerful and glorious light of truth...spread abroad into Gentile nations"; the trumpet of Mt. Sinai compared with the trumpet of the gospel; the earthquake at Mt. Sinai compared with "the pouring out of the Spirit on the day of Pentecost"; the shaking of all nations by God's voice at Sinai compared with the shaking of the world by "God's voice in the gospel"; the terrifying of God's enemies in the surrounding nations at Sinai compared with "the amazement that Satan and the powers of darkness were put into by the sudden and wonderful spreading of the gospel"; the downpour of rain on the Sinai camp compared with "the great and abundant pouring out of the Spirit on the Christian church on the day of Pentecost, and on the world"; a "refreshing rain to the congregation of Israel" in the dry lands of Horeb compared with the "sweet influences of the Spirit of God on the soul"; and finally, God's presence in "the cloud of glory" giving rain and manna compared with the Father sending the Spirit as a refreshing rain and the Son as "the true bread from heaven."[215] Edwards read Ps 68:8–9 in light of the whole Bible, employing the analogy of Scripture to explain its meaning, and he read it in light of the history of redemption, employing the analogy of faith to keep him focused on the central message of the Bible. Edwards had confidence in this redemption because God's faithful character as described in the Psalms ensured he would fulfill his covenant promises.[216]

Another major element of the work of redemption that Edwards discussed from the Psalms was the expansive nature of God's kingdom, which would

---

215. Edwards, *Notes on Scripture*, 136–138.

216. See especially Edwards' sermon on Ps 111:5, "He hath given meat unto them that fear him: he will ever be mindful of his covenant," where he explained that "[t]he design of this Ps[alm] is to Celebrate the glo[rious] w[ork] of G[od] which G[od] had wrought on behalf of his Ch[urc]h," and preached the doctrine, "G[od] never fails in any Instance of faithfulness to the Cov[enant] Engagem[en]ts he has entered into on behalf of any of mankind," especially the covenant of redemption. Jonathan Edwards, "788. Sermon on Ps 111:5 (August 1745)," Beinecke Rare Book and Manuscript Library, Yale University, New Haven, CT, L. 1r., iv. See also Edwards' comment that "God has by many great, and precious, and positive promises engaged never to forsake his people; and he has confirmed it from time to time by his oath," as in Pss 89:3–4, 33, 35; and 110:4. Jonathan Edwards, "The Everlasting Love of God" (Jer 31:3), in *Sermons and Discourses 1734–1738*, ed. M. X. Lesser, vol. 19 of *WJE* (2001), 483–484. Quotation on 483.

reach beyond the Jews to the Gentiles. Psalm 87 was particularly instructive in this regard. Based on Ps 87:4, "I will make mention of Rahab and Babylon to them that know me: behold Philistia, and Tyre, with Ethiopia; this man was born there," Edwards saw a future time when the Messiah would bring unclean Gentile nations, the Jews' "most cruel and inveterate enemies," into the church to be "one holy society with Israel"—a common Reformed interpretation.[217] He also looked to verse 7, which says, "all my springs are in thee." Edwards argued that the term "springs" refers to "fountains of posterity," for God appears to say to Zion, "Although I have many children born in many places of many nations, yet thou art the mother of them all. Though I have many streams in many countries, yet the fountains from whence all those streams proceed are in thee. All are by the means of grace maintained in thee, and used by thee."[218] Edwards made similar observations on Psalms 65; 66; 86; and 145.[219] He also observed that, "[a]ccording to the prophecies, the Gentiles were not thus to be brought under the dominion of the Messiah to enslave them, but to enlighten and cleanse them, to save and bless them, and make them happy," as seen in several Psalms.[220] In fact, in Edwards' reading of the Psalms, spiritual cleanliness rather than Jewish heredity was the true identifying factor of God's people. Edwards interpreted Psalm 24 as speaking of the gospel call to the Gentiles to be

---

217. Edwards, "Types of the Messiah," 224. See Edwards' similar comment in "Prophecies of the Messiah," §59. Henry likewise saw this verse as "a Prophecy or Promise of bringing the *Gentiles* into the Church, and uniting them in one Body with the *Jews*." Henry, *Exposition*, [Ps 87:4]. Poole observed that even the greatest of enemies "will obtain grace from God, so as to be made members of the Church, dwelling with those who formerly blasphemed them" ("à Dei consequentur gratiam, ut membra fiant Ecclesiae, colentes eum quem antea blasphemaverunt"). Poole, *Synopsis*, 1053–1055. Trapp interpreted this verse as indicating that the enemy nations of the Jews would be "born a new, and so made free-denizens of the new *Jerusalem*, fellow-citizens with the Saints, and of the house-hold of God." Trapp, *Commentary*, 803. Dickson celebrated in this verse the "conversion of men from Paganism and Idolatry unto fellowship in the Covenant in the Church," which indicates "regeneration." Dickson, *Other fifty Psalmes*, 293. Calvin interpreted the verse to mean that "those who formerly were deadly enemies, or entire strangers, shall not only become familiar friends, but shall also be ingrafted into one body, that they may be accounted citizens of Jerusalem." Calvin, *Commentary*, 3:399–401. Quotation on 399.

218. Edwards, *The "Blank Bible,"* 518.

219. Edwards, "Prophecies of the Messiah," §82, §83, §80, §86.

220. Jonathan Edwards, "The Miscellanies: Entry No. 1068: The Fulfillment of the Prophecies of the Messiah," Franklin Trask Library, Andover Newton Theological School, Newton, MA, §136. Edwards cited Pss 72:17; 48:2; 65:5; 66:1; 67:2–5; 68:31–32; 89:11–12; 96:1; 97:1; 98:4; 100; 138:4–5; 145:9–10. See also Edwards' comment that, "It was foretold that the Gentiles should be brought under the dominion of the Messiah, and so under the visible dominion of the God of Israel," which agrees with Pss 2:8; 22:28–29; 45:12; 72:8–9; 96:10; 97:1, 5, 9. Edwards, "Fulfillment of the Prophecies," §135.

the people of God. When the psalm asks the question, "Who shall ascend into the hill of the LORD? or who shall stand in his holy place?" (Ps 24:3), the answer it gives is not a pureblood Jew but "He that hath clean hands, and a pure heart" (Ps 24:4). Internal purity makes a person part of "the generation of them that seek him" (Ps 24:6), and thus the psalm teaches that "the privileges of God's people shall not be confined to any particular family or generation of men, but whosoever have pure hearts and clean hands, of all that dwell upon the earth, are God's generation or nation, his Israel."[221] Reading verse 7, "Lift up your heads, O ye gates ... and the King of glory shall come in," Edwards saw a foreshadow of Christ's justifying grace, for "it seems to be implied that the King of glory here spoken, was in a peculiar manner free from sin, of clean hands and a pure heart, and therefore all others had a right to ascend God's holy hill and to stand in his holy place."[222] Christ's own righteousness made way for others to stand in his righteousness and enter God's holy haven. Edwards' understanding of the Bible as a harmony demanded that he read the Psalms as speaking prophetically of God's salvation and full redemptive work to include the Gentiles.

We find a revealing discussion on the work of redemption in Edwards' substantial treatment of Psalm 136, which he addressed in a "Blank Bible" entry, in "Miscellanies" Entry No. 702, and in a sermon on Ps 136:1. We focus on the sermon because it is the most expansive discussion and grows out of Edwards' two notebook entries.[223] In his sermon—which contains the longest text portion of all the sermons on the Psalms—Edwards argued that the subject of Psalm 136 is "The Eternity & Constancy of God[']s mercy to his People," a fairly common interpretation of the passage.[224] The text of the sermon, Ps 136:1,

---

221. Edwards, "Prophecies of the Messiah," §85.

222. Edwards, "Prophecies of the Messiah," §85.

223. Edwards, *The "Blank Bible,"* 537; "Miscellanies" Entry No. 702, "WORK OF CREATION. PROVIDENCE. REDEMPTION," in Edwards, *The "Miscellanies": Entry Nos. 501–832,* 283–309; Jonathan Edwards, "413. Sermon on Ps 136:1 (November 1736)," in *Sermons, Series II, 1736,* vol. 51 of *WJEO.* While we do not know the date of Edwards' "Blank Bible" entry, we know the approximate date of some of Edwards' "Miscellanies" entries; he wrote Entry No. 698 in August 1736, which makes it reasonable to suppose that he wrote Entry No. 702 before or around November 1736, when he preached this sermon. See Ava Chamberlain, ed., "Editor's Introduction, in *The "Miscellanies": Entry Nos. 501–832,* vol. 18 of *WJE* (2000), 42–48.

224. Edwards, "413. Sermon on Ps 136:1," L. 1r. Henry similarly noted that this psalm indicates God's mercy enduring from beginning to end in God's roles as creator of the world, God of Israel, Redeemer, and benefactor for all creation. Henry, *Exposition,* [Psalm 136]. Poole argued that the repeated clause in this psalm "signifies that all the benefits of God proceed from his mere benevolence and mercy" ("significat, omnia Dei beneficia à mera ejus bonitate & clementia proficisci"). Poole, *Synopsis,* 1275. Trapp interpreted the repeated clause in this psalm as a reference to God's "Covenant-mercy, that precious Church-priviledge," which

reads, "O give thanks unto the LORD; for he is good: for his mercy endureth for ever," and each subsequent verse of the psalm repeats the phrase "for his mercy endureth forever" in the second line. Edwards recognized that the term "endureth" seems to imply God's mercy going on into eternity future without speaking of it originating in eternity past, but he rejected this interpretation because the term "endureth" does not occur in the original Hebrew. Rather, he translated the Hebrew as, "mercy is in Eternity," signifying "from Eternity to Eternity."²²⁵ Edwards described these works as the "Great wonders" of creation, before the church had a being; of providence, during the "successive ages" of the church; and of redemption, or those works that are "common to all ages of the Ch[urc]h & of mankind."²²⁶ These works display the "Eternity & Constancy" of God's mercy to his people because they show his mercy beginning before the church was formed and because "God[']s mercy to his Ch[urc]h has never failed."²²⁷ So Edwards preached the doctrine, "That all Great works of G[od] from the beginning of the [world] to the End of it are works of mercy to his People."²²⁸

Edwards' concept of the work of redemption shone through in his doctrine section. He noted that "[a]ll the Great dispens[ations] of G[od] to the People of Is[rael] from moses to [Christ]" was a work of mercy, for all these things— from the exodus and the giving of the Law to the prophets, the establishment of David's royal family, and even the exile—"all were works of mercy to the Ch[urc]h[;] all were to make way for the Coming of [Christ] & the Introducing the Evangelical dispensation."²²⁹ Edwards explained that "all the Great things done in the Glo[rious] work of Redemption are works of mercy to God[']s

---

is "perpetuall to his people, and should perpetually shine in our hearts." Trapp, *Commentary*, 908. Dickson recognized that "the fountain of his mercy" flows "to the benefit of his owne people in special" and is seen in his work of creation, in the redemption of Israel, in mercy during the psalmist's day, and to all living creatures. Dickson also noted the "perpetuity of God[']s mercy" and that "the Lord is God by Covenant." Dickson, *Last Fifty Psalmes*, 291–293. Calvin observed that from this repeated clause we learn that "while God should be praised for all his works, it is mercy principally that we should glorify." Calvin, *Commentary*, 5:183.

225. Edwards, "413. Sermon on Ps 136:1," L. IV. In "Miscellanies" Entry No. 702, "WORK OF CREATION. PROVIDENCE. REDEMPTION," Edwards specifically noted that the Hebrew clause, לְעוֹלָם[חַסְדּוֹ, was literally translated as "his mercy is in eternity," which he interpreted to mean "his mercy to his church is from everlasting to everlasting, the same, unchangeable." Edwards, *The "Miscellanies": Entry Nos. 501–832*, 292.

226. Edwards, "413. Sermon on Ps 136:1," L. 3r., 3v.

227. Edwards, "413. Sermon on Ps 136:1," L. 3v., 4v.

228. Edwards, "413. Sermon on Ps 136:1," L. 6r.

229. Edwards, "413. Sermon on Ps 136:1," L. 11r.

People," and while the psalmist especially insists on God's redemption of Israel out of Egypt, this and the other events in Israel's history are "but types & shadows of the Great Redemption," for "[t]hose things that G[od] wrought in this work are the Greatest works of G[od] that ever were wrought and are spoken of in S[cripture] as much more Glo[rious] than the works of Creation."[230] Edwards thus traced God's work of mercy from creation to Christ to the final judgment to show that all God's works are works of mercy to his church, demonstrating that the work of redemption best encapsulates the purpose of all God's works. He argued from his treatment of Psalm 136 that "the work of Redemption must needs be Greatest of all God[']s works because we see by this doc[trine] that all other works are subordinated to it in that they are all subordinated to the Good & Happiness of the Redeemed."[231] In Edwards' reading of this psalm he detected the metanarrative God placed in Scripture, the history of his work of redemption.[232]

Conclusion

In the months before he died, Edwards was planning to write a work that would organize his theology around the history of redemption and, as we have seen, the book of Psalms was the preeminent Old Testament book for speaking in those terms. His description of this work, which he planned to title *A History of the Work of Redemption*, sheds light on how the concept of God's work of redemption guided Edwards' interpretation of the Psalms. The work was to be a "body of divinity," or systematic theology,

> in an entire new method, being thrown into the form of an history, considering the affair of Christian theology, as the whole of it, in each part, stands in reference to the great work of redemption by Jesus Christ; which I suppose is to be the grand design of all God's designs, and the *summum* and *ultimum* of all the divine operations and degrees;

---

230. Edwards, "413. Sermon on Ps 136:1," L. 11r.–11v. Edwards expounded on this point in "Miscellanies" Entry No. 702, noting that because God's mercy endures forever, so his work of redemption—not creation—stands as the superior work of God. Edwards, *The "Miscellanies": Entry Nos. 501–832*, 298.

231. Edwards, "413. Sermon on Ps 136:1," L. 22r.

232. Thus Paul Ramsey rightly observes that this sermon is, "in effect, a sketch of *History of Redemption*." Paul Ramsey, ed., in Jonathan Edwards, *Ethical Writings*, vol. 8 of *WJE* (1989), 510.

particularly considering all parts of the grand scheme in their historical order.[233]

Edwards went on to show that this historical order would begin in eternity past, continue through the "successive dispensations," culminate in the last judgment and "consummation of all things," and conclude with "that perfect state of things, which shall be finally settled, to last for eternity."[234] For Edwards, God's work of redemption included the whole of history, and it was the all-encompassing theological concept around which all others were oriented. McClymond and McDermott are thus right to note that "[o]ne of Edwards's governing theological ideas—and the concept that dominated much of his private reflection during his final years—is captured in the phrase 'history of redemption.'"[235] That concept propelled his interpretation of the Psalms.

We have seen that in Edwards' view, all God's works in Scripture and in history are subordinated to his work of redemption. The intra-Trinitarian covenant of redemption that God made explains the purpose of God's lesser works of creation and providence for it aims both at the glory of God and the happiness of the saints, two mutual ends toward which all history flows. This all-encompassing conceptual framework gave Edwards the interpretive lens through which to read the Psalms. The history of redemption model gave shape to Edwards' broad interpretation of the Psalms and is especially visible in the theological themes related to salvation. As we have observed in this chapter, Edwards used the Psalms to describe the Spirit's nature through the images of oil and light, which represented the Spirit as God's excellency, love, and joy, and to describe the Spirit's work, particularly his impartation of divine light and saving grace and his inspiration of the Psalms with the gospel message. The Spirit played a major role in Edwards' doctrine of salvation as articulated from the Psalms, especially with regard to his gracious influences in regeneration. Edwards also defended the doctrine of justification by faith using the Psalms to demonstrate the unity of the Old and New Testaments, which indicates that justification has always consisted in believers' dependent faith in God. In his practical outworking of his doctrines of the Spirit and salvation, Edwards used the Psalms to describe, promote, and

---

233. Jonathan Edwards to the Trustees of the College of New Jersey, October 19, 1757, in *Letters and Personal Writings*, ed. George S. Claghorn, vol. 16 of *WJE* (1998), 727–728.

234. Edwards to the Trustees, 728.

235. McClymond and McDermott, *The Theology of Jonathan Edwards*, 181. See their fuller treatment of the history of redemption on 181–190.

stake out a moderate position on revivals, warning both those who opposed them and those who took pride in them to support the work of God's Spirit with a humble posture. Still, he recognized the potential for false professions of faith, and he found the preeminent passage describing hypocrisy and the difficulty in discerning others' spiritual state in Ps 55:12–14. The Psalms also provided Edwards with biblical texts from which he could promote salvation among young and old by preaching the gospel, using its variegated imagery to awaken sinners and using both dread and delight to motivate people to put themselves in the way of grace.

In comparing Edwards to the Reformed exegetical tradition on the themes of the Holy Spirit and the gospel, we can recognize that he shared a number of affinities with them, particularly in describing the wickedness of false professions, in depicting the visible church as a mixed body, in emphasizing God's mercy, in describing God's plan of bringing the Gentiles into the church, and in a number of smaller exegetical details. However, of all the themes, Edwards was most innovative in the themes of this chapter. While Edwards was not unique in identifying the Spirit in the Psalms, he was much more willing to do so than his predecessors, and he did so more creatively by both developing types of the Spirit from the imagery of the Psalms and describing the Spirit's work of regeneration and inspiration from the Psalms. Again, this characteristic in Edwards' exegesis differentiates him from a strictly Christological way of reading the Psalter. Edwards was also unique in using the Psalms to argue that holy religious affections can be accompanied with bodily manifestations while at the same time developing the notion from Ps 55:12–14 that it is extremely difficult to discern another's spiritual state. Finally, Edwards preached the gospel more forcefully from the Psalms than the Reformed predecessors here described, and he did so from passages that were more obscure or in which the gospel message was less readily apparent. He also uniquely spoke from the Psalms of God's gentleness as a motivation for seeking God and directed his message of responding to Christ's gospel call to youth and children.

Was Edwards playing fast and loose with the Psalms, using it for his own purposes without boundaries? No. A better explanation, given his attestation to the authority of the Bible, is that he combed through the Psalms to decipher what Scripture had to say about the particular theological and ministerial challenges he was facing in his time, and it is clear that those particular challenges revolved around the Holy Spirit, discerning a true work of the Spirit, and what happens in revival and the salvation process. Edwards took these innovative directions with the Psalms both because of the particular circumstances he was facing and because the gospel was central to his ministry and theology.

Edwards employed the Psalms to describe the Holy Spirit, to explicate his doctrine of salvation, to promote revival, to discern between true and false religion, and to preach the gospel, and all these theological emphases fall under the rubric of the history of redemption. At this point, we can more clearly see that Edwards' exegesis of the Psalms was driven by his redemptive-historical understanding of Scripture, encompassing all of the triune God's works with the aim of proclaiming the gospel and glorifying God so the redeemed can participate in God's goodness and find true happiness. The unity of the two Testaments, the analogy of Scripture, and the analogy of faith all guided him in a redemptive-historical interpretation of the Psalms. Calling Edwards' exegesis "Christological" or "Christological typology" fails to capture the breadth of his engagement with the Psalms as he incorporated discussion about the Holy Spirit's person and work in salvation and the fullness of God's work of redemption. As for Edwards' theology, what is striking from this chapter is that he engaged the Psalms to explicate so many of his lifelong theological emphases, especially his driving aim of sparking revival and spreading the gospel. His theology grew not merely out of a response to a shifting theological context but from wrestling deeply with the Psalms—and Scripture generally—as he channeled his energy toward promoting God's glory and participating in God's grand work of redemption by advancing the gospel.

6

Christian Piety

One thing have I desired of the LORD, that will I seek after;
that I may dwell in the house of the LORD
all the days of my life,
to behold the beauty of the LORD,
and to enquire in his temple.
Psalm 27:4

IN EDWARDS' UNDERSTANDING of God's work of redemption, one of the key players in that history is the church. And in his unified conception of the Bible, Edwards found the Psalms to be replete with teaching on the nature and practice of the church both in its corporate expression and in its individual members. We discuss the corporate church in the next chapter, while here we confine ourselves to the individual Christian. In fact, Edwards spent far more time addressing individual Christian piety from the Psalms than a single chapter can encapsulate, but an abbreviated survey will provide a good sense of how he treated this topic from the Psalms.

Edwards interpreted the Psalms devotionally, reading the book in straightforward, literal ways that related to Christian piety and holiness. The degree to which Edwards interpreted the Psalms in relation to practical Christian piety militates against describing his overall method of interpretation as typological. In addition, as Edwards emphasized the nurturing of spiritual fruit and holy living as a pastor, we are reminded that the Psalms served as a key book for developing his understanding of this key theological theme in his ministry.

We begin by examining Edwards' use of the Psalms in his personal piety, followed by a discussion about his concept of the Psalms as one's language. Then we explore his emphasis on religious affections in the book of Psalms and close by discussing the Psalms as a book for Christian living. Edwards' engagement with the Psalms with respect to individual piety shows that he believed true religious affections are nurtured by imbibing Psalmistic language, and they issue forth in holy fruit seen in personal virtue, in relation to others, and in relation to God.

The Psalms in Edwards' Personal Piety

Jonathan Edwards had an appreciation for the delicacies and treasures of this world. The leaf of his sermon on Ps 118:6–9 records an accounting of items that Edwards' brother-in-law James Pierpont purchased for his family, probably in Boston, including four pounds of chocolate and three necklaces.[1] Still, in Edwards' view, the enjoyment of earthly things should never overshadow the pursuit of lasting things in the eternal world. As he pursued a life of piety, Edwards found help from the Psalms in aiding his growth in devotion to God.

We find glimpses of the Psalms in Edwards' personal piety in his "Diary," written mostly in the years 1723–1724, and his "Personal Narrative," a December 1740 letter to his future son-in-law, Aaron Burr, describing his spiritual journey.[2] Edwards believed he should prioritize worshiping with the Psalter, even when other matters pressed for attention. In a January 21, 1723, entry in his "Diary," he chided himself for devoting his time before sunrise to answering questions raised earlier in his diary and not to personal worship and repentance: "I ought to have spent the time in bewailing my sins, and in singing psalms, especially psalms or hymns of repentance; these duties being most suited to the frame I was in."[3] Later that summer, on August 28, 1723, Edwards charged himself, when he had "not very good books" to read, "not to spend time in reading them, but in reading the Scriptures, in perusing Resolutions, Reflections [i.e., his 'Miscellanies'], etc., in writing on types of the Scripture, and other things, in studying the languages, and in spending more time in private duties."[4] For Edwards the Psalms were integral to both

---

1. Jonathan Edwards, "1168. Sermon on Ps 118:6–9 (July 23, 1756)," Beinecke Rare Book and Manuscript Library, Yale University, New Haven, CT, L. iv., 2r.

2. For more on these writings, see George S. Claghorn, ed., *Letters and Personal Writings*, vol. 16 of *WJE* (1998), 741–752.

3. Jonathan Edwards, "Diary," in *Letters and Personal Writings*, ed. George S. Claghorn, vol. 16 of *WJE* (1998), 766.

4. Edwards, "Diary," 780. One book that Edwards deemed worthy of his time that summer was Thomas Manton's *One hundred and ninety Sermons on the Hundred and Nineteenth Psalm*. From Manton's sermon on Ps 119:22, Edwards gleaned that we must avoid the hypocrisy of dressing ourselves in "a garb of religion," but "in our own sight we should be the worst of men." That summer Edwards also wrote a resolution based on Manton's sermon on Ps 119:26: "Resolved, very much to exercise myself in this all my life long, viz. with the greatest openness I am capable of, to declare my ways to God, and lay open my soul to him: all my sins, temptations, difficulties, sorrows, fears, hopes, desires, and everything, and every circumstance." Edwards, "Resolutions," in *Letters and Personal Writings*, ed. George S. Claghorn, vol. 16 of *WJE* (1998), 758. See Thomas Manton, *One hundred and ninety Sermons on the Hundred and Nineteenth Psalm* (London: Tho. Parkhurst...; Jonathan Robinson...; Brabazon Aylmey...; and Benjamin Alsop..., 1681), 135–142, 162–170.

Scripture reading and private duties, and on September 22, 1723, Edwards recorded a resolution in his "Diary": "To praise God, by singing psalms in prose, and by singing forth the meditations of my heart in prose."[5]

As Edwards reflected on his earlier years in his "Personal Narrative," he remembered the strong yearning he had for God after his conversion: "I had vehement longings of soul after God and Christ, and after more holiness; wherewith my heart seemed to be full, and ready to break."[6] He turned to the Psalms for language to describe this experience, noting that Ps 119:28 often came to his mind, which Edwards paraphrased as, "My soul breaketh for the longing it hath."[7] Edwards explained how this longing "broke" his soul: "I often felt a mourning and lamenting in my heart, that I had not turned to God sooner, that I might have had more time to grow in grace."[8] When he faced physical brokenness, he also appropriated the language of the Psalms. In September 1725, Edwards came down with a severe illness on his way home to East Windsor that forced him to stop in North Village (now North Haven), Connecticut. Observing those who watched over him in the night and who waited eagerly for the morning to come "brought to my mind those words of the Psalmist, which my soul with sweetness made its own language, 'My soul waiteth for the Lord more than they that watch for the morning: I say, more than they that watch for the morning'" (Ps 130:6).[9] With the threat of death creeping upon him, Edwards found comfort in the Psalms.

Edwards gravitated to the Psalms for enriching his religious affections. So he said in his "Personal Narrative" that Ps 115:1, "Not unto us, O LORD, not unto us, but unto thy name give glory, for thy mercy, and for thy truth's sake," was a scripture that "has often been sweet to me."[10] While we do not have extensive details about Edwards' personal spirituality, we can see that the Psalms provided him the language for expressing his devotion to God. As a pastor, he wanted his people to learn this language as well.

---

5. Edwards, "Diary," 781.

6. Edwards, "Personal Narrative," in *Letters and Personal Writings*, ed. George S. Claghorn, vol. 16 of *WJE* (1998), 794.

7. Edwards, "Personal Narrative," 794. The KJV reads, "My soul melteth for heaviness."

8. Edwards, "Personal Narrative," 794.

9. Edwards, "Personal Narrative," 798.

10. Edwards, "Personal Narrative," 800.

Making the Psalms One's Language

Throughout his corpus, Edwards encouraged his people to make the Psalms their own language because that is a characteristic of the truly converted. In *Some Thoughts*, Edwards said that a joyful "Christian in a lively frame" makes the Psalms the "language" of his heart.[11] And in an August 1735 sermon, Edwards stated that Ps 45:2, "Thou art fairer than the sons of men," is "the language of the believer's soul concerning Christ."[12]

Just as Edwards used the language of the Psalms to describe the revivals, so he also called those converted in the revivals to embrace the Psalter's verbiage for themselves. In a November 1735 sermon on Isa 12:6, "God Amongst His People," Edwards concluded with a flourish of Psalms texts (Pss 33:1; 97:12; 22:23; 30:4; 132:9; 145:10–12; 68:13; 18:1–2; 118:6; 66:17, 19; 116:1–2; 40:2–3; 142:7; 34:1, 3) strung together all to exhort those who had experienced the special grace of God in the revivals to raise their voices up in praise to God. As the Psalms show, saints are especially expected to praise God because they are no more worthy than anyone else, yet God has distinguished them from others by delivering them from sorrows, temptations, and travails by his grace. So Edwards exhorted the saints, "Let that therefore be the language of your heart. Ps. 116, at the beginning, 'I love the Lord, because he hath heard the voice of my supplications. Because he hath inclined his ear unto me, therefore will I call upon him as long as I live.'"[13]

In another sermon, Edwards explained that to test one's position before God, people should ask themselves if they made Ps 115:1 their soul's language. If God's gracious work had truly affected them, they would abase themselves and uphold God's sovereignty:

> Is that the spirit that you are of, to desire with all your heart that Christ and his worthiness and his righteousness alone should be made mention of? Is God's footstool the place where you delight to be? Is that in Ps. 115:1—"Not to us, O Lord, not unto us, but unto thy name give glory, for thy mercy, and for thy truth's sake"—the natural language of your heart?[14]

11. Jonathan Edwards, *Some Thoughts Concerning the Revival*, in *The Great Awakening*, ed. C. C. Goen, vol. 4 of *WJE* (1972), 492.

12. Jonathan Edwards, "The Sweet Harmony of Christ" (John 10:4), in *Sermons and Discourses 1734–1738*, ed. M. X. Lesser, vol. 19 of *WJE* (2001), 440.

13. Jonathan Edwards, "God Amongst His People" (Isa 12:6), in *Sermons and Discourses 1734–1738*, ed. M. X. Lesser, vol. 19 of *WJE* (2001), 472.

14. Jonathan Edwards, "Like Rain upon Mown Grass" (Ps 72:6), in *Sermons and Discourses 1739–1742*, ed. Harry S. Stout and Nathan O. Hatch with Kyle P. Farley, vol. 22 of *WJE* (2003), 314.

Psalm 115:1 offered words that Christians should appropriate to describe their humility and gratitude for salvation in Christ. And they ought also to pray for Christ's return using the Psalms: "'Tis the language of the church of God, and the breathing of the soul of every true saint, that we have in Ps. 14:7. 'O that the salvation of Israel were come out of Zion! When the Lord bringeth back the captivity of his people, Jacob shall rejoice, and Israel shall be glad.' "[15] Praying the Psalms would help believers orient their lives to eternal matters, giving them the very language they needed to attune their hearts to God's ultimate aims.

To promote revivals Edwards also held up examples of saints under gracious influences who adopted the Psalms as their language, most notably David Brainerd, Edwards' preeminent model of a person with true religious affections.[16] Brainerd regularly weaved snippets from the Psalms into the narrative of his journal, as if they were an outflow of his day-to-day speech. We could mention many examples. On April 12, 1742, Brainerd wrote, "This morning the Lord was pleased to 'lift up the light of his countenance upon me' [Ps 4:6] in secret prayer."[17] And on October 6, 1744, he recorded that he "was enabled to 'pour out my heart before God' [Ps 62:8], for the increase of grace in my soul" and other ministry endeavors.[18] When burdened by guilt, he made "that prayer in the bitterness of my soul. 'O Lord, deliver me from bloodguiltiness' [Ps 51:14]."[19] And as he found spiritual refreshment, he described his release using the Psalms: "had some exercise of grace sensible and comfortable; my soul seemed lifted above the 'deep waters' [Ps 69:2, 14], wherein it has been so long almost drowned."[20] Brainerd interweaved the language of the Psalms with his words throughout his journal.

Like Edwards, Brainerd also described the Psalms as "sweet" to him. He recorded that "[t]hose words hung upon me with much divine sweetness,

---

15. Jonathan Edwards, *An Humble Attempt to Promote Explicit Agreement and Visible Union of God's People in Extraordinary Prayer for the Revival of Religion and the Advancement of Christ's Kingdom on Earth, Pursuant to Scripture-Promises and Prophecies Concerning the Last Time*, in *Apocalyptic Writings*, ed. Stephen J. Stein, vol. 5 of *WJE* (1977), 347.

16. Edwards also described Abigail Hutchinson as a model who reflected long on Ps 12:6. Jonathan Edwards, *A Faithful Narrative*, in *The Great Awakening*, ed. C. C. Goen, vol. 4 of *WJE* (1972), 193.

17. Jonathan Edwards, *The Life of David Brainerd*, ed. Norman Pettit, vol. 7 of *WJE* (1985), 160.

18. Edwards, *The Life of David Brainerd*, 268.

19. Edwards, *The Life of David Brainerd*, 203.

20. Edwards, *The Life of David Brainerd*, 204. He also used the phrase "deep waters" from Ps 69:2, 14 elsewhere. Edwards, *The Life of David Brainerd*, 198, 208, 278, 282.

Ps. 84:7"; that he "[w]as supported under my burdens, reading the 125th Psalm: Found that it was sweet and comfortable to lean on God"; and that "I enjoyed sweetness in secret prayer, and meditation on Ps. 73:28."[21] Brainerd spoke of a deep relish for God using the Psalms' language. He described his "secret prayer" one evening as "sweet and comfortable" for he longed for "the recovery of the divine image in my soul: 'Then shall I be satisfied, when I shall awake in God's likeness' [Ps 17:15], and never before."[22] Psalm 17:15, in fact, was "a precious text" to Brainerd, who quoted it often to describe his desire to become like Christ.[23] In fact, when he wrote his final letter, he used Ps 17:15 to describe the aim that his brother John should pursue: "Oh, my brother, pursue after holiness; press towards this blessed mark; and let your thirsty soul continually say, 'I shall never be satisfied till I awake in thy likeness.' "[24]

In his appendix, Edwards upheld Brainerd as "a very lively instance to see the nature of true religion," and described the fruit in his life using the Psalms: "delighting in God" (Ps 37:4), "rejoycing in the Lord" (Ps 33:1), "thirsting for God" (Ps 42:2), "the soul's 'breaking for the longing it hath to God's judgments'" (Ps 119:20), and "mourning for sin with 'a broken heart and contrite spirit'" (Ps 51:17).[25] Edwards exclaimed, "How full is the Book of Psalms, and other parts of Scripture, of such things as these!"[26]

In Edwards' view, Christians should embrace the Psalter as their own language because it gives them the words of true love for God. The Psalms offer the saints the language in which to express authentic religious affections, and Edwards employed the Psalms as the premier book for describing these affections he sought so hard to promote.

Religious Affections in the Psalms

McClymond and McDermott argue that for Edwards the affections "lay at the heart of his theological anthropology," which is why he "probed the affections and religious experience with an intensity unique to the eighteenth century

---

21. Edwards, *The Life of David Brainerd*, 163, 240, 381. Psalm 73:28 was a favorite for Brainerd; see Edwards, *The Life of David Brainerd*, 379, 382, 402, 405, 408, 416.

22. Edwards, *The Life of David Brainerd*, 184.

23. Edwards, *The Life of David Brainerd*, 186, 293, 295, 296, 497. Quotation on 293.

24. Edwards, *The Life of David Brainerd*, 497.

25. Edwards, *The Life of David Brainerd*, 500, 525.

26. Edwards, *The Life of David Brainerd*, 525.

and perhaps the centuries since."[27] The Psalms constituted a foundation in Edwards' treatment of the affections. He cited the Psalms 145 times in *A Treatise Concerning Religious Affections*, and his use of the Psalms in that work centered on the individual's spirituality, not on Christological, ecclesiological, or typological readings.[28] He offered the Psalms in general—and Psalm 119 in particular—as the exemplary places for understanding true religious affections.

Edwards' treatment of the affections with respect to the Psalms was not unlike Augustine's, who found in the Psalms a "regulation" of human affections; for Augustine, "the psalms demonstrated the right orientation of the affections, in conformity with God's order."[29] And like Edwards, Henry also said that the Psalter is "of singular use with that to convey Divine Life and Power, and a Holy Heat into our Affections. There is no one Book of Scripture that is more helpful to the Devotions of the Saints than this, and it has been so in all Ages of the Church."[30] Edwards similarly mined the Psalms to understand holy affections.

Edwards established his doctrine—that "[t]rue religion, in great part, consists in holy affections"—with the examples of the most eminent saints in Scripture, particularly David, Paul, and John, who consisted much in holy affections.[31] David, "that man after God's own heart," gave us "a lively portraiture of his religion, in the Book of Psalms."[32] Edwards showed that "[t]hose holy songs of his, he has there left us, are nothing else but the expressions and breathings of devout and holy affections," describing humility, love to God,

27. Michael J. McClymond and Gerald R. McDermott, *The Theology of Jonathan Edwards* (New York: Oxford University Press, 2012), 312, 320.

28. The Jonathan Edwards Center at Yale University, "WJE Online," http://edwards.yale.edu/archive (accessed August 23, 2010).

29. Michael Fiedrowicz, "General Introduction," in *Expositions of the Psalms: 1–32*, trans. Maria Boulding and ed. John E. Rotelle, part III, vol. 15 of *The Works of Saint Augustine* (Hyde Park, NY: New City, 2000), 40–41.

30. Matthew Henry, *An exposition of the five poetical books of the Old Testament; viz. Job, Psalms, Proverbs, Ecclesiastes, and Solomon's song*... (London: T. Darrack..., 1710), [Introduction to the Psalms].

31. Jonathan Edwards, *Religious Affections*, ed. John E. Smith, vol. 2 of *WJE* (1959), 95. McClymond and McDermott provide a helpful treatment of Edwards' definition of the affections, noting two common misunderstandings: ignoring the intellectual component and reducing affections to "emotions." In fact, Edwards' concept of the affections included both understanding/intellect and inclination/feeling, and he argued that they drive what a person, as a unitary human being, feels, thinks, and does. McClymond and McDermott, *The Theology of Jonathan Edwards*, 312, 314.

32. Edwards, *Religious Affections*, 108.

admiration, longings for God, joy, gratitude, triumph, delight in God's people and way, sorrow over sin, and zeal for God.[33] Because God enshrined them forever in the songbook of the church, "these expressions of holy affection" are "fitted to express the religion of all saints, in all ages, as well as the religion of the Psalmist," for David speaks as "the psalmist of Israel," "in the name of the church," and "in the name of Christ, as personating him in these breathings forth of holy affection."[34] Edwards made good on this observation by turning to the Psalms throughout *Religious Affections* for biblical insight into the affections.

As Edwards set forth his doctrine, he also made an explicit appeal to the language of Scripture: "The Holy Scriptures do everywhere place religion very much in the affections; such as fear, hope, love, hatred, desire, joy, sorrow, gratitude, compassion and zeal."[35] As he treated each of these particular affections, he used the Psalms frequently. For example, he noted that "[h]ope in the Lord is...frequently mentioned as the character of the saints," as attested by Ps 146:5, "Happy is he that hath the God of Jacob for his help, whose hope is in the LORD his God."[36] He also pointed to "holy desire, exercised in longings, hungerings and thirsting after God and holiness...as an important part of true religion," quoting, among other Psalms passages, Ps 27:4, "One thing have I desired of the LORD, that will I seek after; that I may dwell in the house of the LORD all the days of my life, to behold the beauty of the LORD, and to enquire in his temple."[37] Edwards saw the book of Psalms so full of describing the affections of gratitude and praise to God that he felt no need to mention particular texts.[38] In this opening section, he described several other affections using the Psalms to establish his point that holy affections lay at the core of true religion.[39]

---

33. Edwards, *Religious Affections*, 108. See Edwards' similar comment in *The "Miscellanies": Entry Nos. 1153–1360*, ed. Douglas A. Sweeney, vol. 23 of *WJE* (2004), 541.

34. Edwards, *Religious Affections*, 108–109.

35. Edwards, *Religious Affections*, 102.

36. Edwards, *Religious Affections*, 103. Edwards also quoted Ps 31:24.

37. Edwards quoted Pss 42:1–2; 63:1–2; 84:1–2; 119:20; and he cited Pss 73:25; 143:6–7. Edwards, *Religious Affections*, 104. Elsewhere, Edwards pointed to Ps 24:6, "This is the generation of them that seek him, that seek thy face, O Jacob," to emphasize that it is the character of saints to seek God. Edwards, *Humble Attempt*, 315; Jonathan Edwards, *The "Blank Bible,"* ed. Stephen J. Stein, vol. 24, part 1 of *WJE* (2006), 543.

38. Edwards, *Religious Affections*, 105.

39. He described religious fear and hope from Pss 33:18; 147:11; hatred of sin from Pss 97:10; 101:2–3; 119:104, 128; 139:21; joy from Pss 37:4; 97:12; 33:1; 149:2; 119:14; sorrow and

We could discuss much in *Religious Affections* to show Edwards' belief that if one appropriates the words of the Psalms as his or her own language, that person's heart will issue forth in springs of holy affections. But it will suffice to illustrate the place of the Psalms in *Religious Affections* by examining two of the twelve reliable signs that one's religious affections truly arise from the gracious influence of the Holy Spirit.[40]

Edwards stated his third positive sign as follows: "a love to divine things for the beauty and sweetness of their moral excellency, is the first beginning and spring of all holy affections."[41] The Psalms supported this notion because they speak of the "beauty of holiness," or moral goodness (Pss 29:2; 96:9; 110:3). It was in his treatment of the third sign that Edwards described Psalm 119 as the most robust segment of Scripture for evidence of true godliness: "I know of no part of the Holy Scriptures, where the nature and evidences of true and sincere godliness, are so much of set purpose, and so fully and largely insisted on and delineated, as the 119th Psalm." But the psalmist celebrated the beauty of holiness most:

> in this psalm the excellency of holiness is represented as the immedi-
> ate object of a spiritual taste, relish, appetite and delight, God's law, that
> grand expression and emanation of the holiness of God's nature, and
> prescription of holiness to the creature, is all along represented as the
> food and entertainment, and as the great object of the love, the appetite,
> the complacence and rejoicing of the gracious nature, which prizes God's

---

brokenness of heart from Pss 34:18; 51:17; and compassion from Ps 37:21. Edwards, *Religious Affections*, 103–106.

40. See also Edwards' treatment of the fourth sign, where he used Pss 43:3–4; 9:10; 119:18 to show that "[g]racious affections do arise from the mind's being enlightened, rightly and spiritually to understand or apprehend divine things"; the sixth sign, where he used Pss 34:18; 51:17; 138:6 to show that true religious affections "are attended with evangelical humili-ation"; the eighth sign, where he used Pss 133:1–2; 68:13; 74:19; 37:10–11; 147:6; 37:21, 26; 112:5, 9 to show that true religious affections "naturally beget and promote such a spirit of love, meekness, quietness, forgiveness and mercy, as appeared in Christ"; the ninth sign, where he used Pss 119:120; 2:1 to show that "[g]racious affections soften the heart, and are attended and followed with a Christian tenderness of spirit"; the tenth sign, where he used Pss 2:11; 33:18; 147:11; 112:7; 119:104, 128; 63:5–6 to show that "[a]nother thing wherein those affections that are truly gracious and holy, differ from those that are false, is beautiful symmetry and proportion"; and the eleventh sign, where he used Pss 24:6; 69:6, 32; 74:4 to show that with "gracious affections, the higher they are raised, the more is a spiritual appetite and long-ing of soul after spiritual attainments, increased." Edwards, *Religious Affections*, 266, 270, 280–281; 311–313; 345, 348–349, 353, 355; 357, 361; 365–366, 371, 375; 380–382. Edwards used the Psalms in coordination with other Scripture texts for these points.

41. Edwards, *Religious Affections*, 253–254.

commandments above gold, yea, the finest gold, and to which they are sweeter than the honey, and honeycomb; and that upon account of their holiness.[42]

Edwards compared the new "spiritual sense" to tasting honey, and with the new spiritual sense, a saint tastes the beauty of holiness, a beauty that the unregenerate cannot perceive. As the psalmist extolled the beauty of God's Word in Psalm 119, Edwards argued that he did so because he loved to magnify holiness and moral goodness.

The most important positive sign for Edwards was the twelfth sign, "Gracious and holy affections have their exercise and fruit in Christian practice."[43] Again, Edwards turned to the Psalms to elucidate this evidence of true holy affections. He established that these affections that issue in holy practice arise from God's gracious influences, as Ps 110:3 states, "Thy people shall be willing in the day of thy power."[44] He also explained "the essence of Christianity" as not only professing essential doctrines but also exhibiting essential attitudes and performing certain actions.[45] One of these attitudes is that "[t]hey ought to profess a willingness of heart to embrace religion with all its difficulties, and to walk in a way of obedience to God universally and perseveringly," a teaching affirmed by two Psalms passages expressing a verbal commitment to obey God's commands: Ps 119:57, "Thou art my portion, O LORD: I have said that I would keep thy words," and Ps 119:106, "I have sworn, and I will perform it, that I will keep thy righteous judgments."[46] In expounding the twelfth sign, Edwards posited that the Scriptures—especially the Psalms and the apostle John's writings—set forth Christian practice, not only as one evidence of grace but "as the main evidence of the truth of grace, not only to others, but to men's own consciences. It is not only more spoken of and insisted on than other signs, but in many places where it is

---

42. Edwards, *Religious Affections*, 260. See Edwards' similar comment on Psalm 119 in "The Way of Holiness" (Isa 35:8), in *Sermons and Discourses 1720–1723*, vol. 10 of *WJE* (1992), 473. In his "Signs of Godliness" notebook, penned in the late 1720s through the 1740s, Edwards listed as one sign, "[r]elishing, savoring and delighting in the Word of God," which "is spoken of in the Psalms, in places too many to be enumerated." Jonathan Edwards, "Signs of Godliness," in *Writings on the Trinity, Grace, and Faith*, ed. Sang Hyun Lee, vol. 21 of *WJE* (2003), 509.

43. Edwards, *Religious Affections*, 383.

44. Edwards, *Religious Affections*, 393.

45. Edwards, *Religious Affections*, 413–415.

46. Edwards, *Religious Affections*, 415.

spoken of, it is represented as the chief of all evidences."[47] Conversely, "unholy practice" is the Scripture's most "emphatical" expression to denote hypocrisy, as Edwards quoted Ps 125:5, "As for such as turn aside unto their crooked ways, the LORD shall lead them forth with the workers of iniquity: but peace shall be upon Israel."[48]

Edwards pointed to the Psalms to describe a number of specific affections, such as perseverance, fear, gratitude, gracious desires, hope, and joy.[49] Throughout *Religious Affections*, he explored insights into the nature of true religious affections using the book of Psalms, for it is saturated with gracious affections that delight in the beauty of holiness and issue forth in Christian fruit. Edwards called Christians to embrace the language of the Psalms as their own for it is a sure guide in speaking and living out the spiritual life, and in his final analysis, as Psalm 119 "chiefly insists upon," so "[h]oly practice is . . . the chief, and most important, and most distinguishing part" of Christian experience.[50]

The Psalms as a Book for Christian Living

Outside of *Religious Affections*, Edwards spoke at length about Christian practice and holy fruit using the book of Psalms. It was his firm belief that the Holy Spirit's gracious influences should issue forth in the fruit of the Spirit (Gal 5:22–23), and he employed the Psalms regularly in calling believers to Christian piety.

Christian obedience was even one of the aims of salvation. Reading Ps 119:145–146, "I cried with my whole heart; hear me, O LORD: I will keep thy statutes. I cried unto thee; save me, and I shall keep thy testimonies," Edwards explained that "Christ's salvation is a salvation from sin; and one end of it, and one benefit we have by it, is our obedience to God's commandments."[51] We see the same teaching in Ps 116:16, "O LORD, truly I am thy servant; I am thy servant,

---

47. Edwards, *Religious Affections*, 438. Edwards cited Pss 15; 24:3–4; 34:11–14; 119:1, 6. Edwards, *Religious Affections*, 440.

48. Edwards, *Religious Affections*, 440.

49. See Edwards' discussion of perseverance, using Pss 78:7–8, 10–11, 35–37, 41–42, 56, etc.; 106:3, 12–15; 125:4–5; 66:10; of holy fear of God, using Pss 34:11–14; 36:1; of thankfulness, using Pss 116:12; 50:14, 23; of gracious desires, using Pss 27:4; 63:1–2, 8; of hope, using Pss 119:166; 78:7; and of joy, using Ps 119:111–112, 14. Edwards, *Religious Affections*, 388–389, 430; 448; 448; 448; 449; 449.

50. Edwards, *Religious Affections*, 450–451.

51. Edwards, *The "Blank Bible,"* 532.

and the son of thine handmaid: thou hast loosed my bonds." Edwards showed
that as God freed the Jews from bondage to Pharaoh, so by freeing us from slavery to our enemies, God "has bound us to serve him," and by this "redemption," "he that procured the release of a captive, took him for his servant."[52] Thus
Edwards saw from this verse, paradoxically, that the saints should celebrate their
freedom in the gospel by becoming servants of God.

In a handful of sermons, Edwards preached from the Psalms to show
that human happiness is wrapped up with following God's moral code. In a
September 1745 sermon, around the time he was writing *Religious Affections*,
Edwards preached on Ps 37:3, "Trust in the LORD, and do good; so shalt thou dwell
in the land, and verily thou shalt be fed." Edwards' overarching observation for
the sermon was that "[t]he way to happiness lies in these two things, believing in
God and doing good"—a common reading of this passage among his Reformed
exegetical predecessors.[53] He explained that faith is not the "Cause," but rather
"brings the soul to G[od] the Fount of Happ[iness] through a Redeemer," while
doing good is not itself the righteousness but "is the appointed way to it," for
"it pleases G[od] so to ordain that these things shall succeed in this order" and

---

52. Edwards, *The "Blank Bible,"* 530.

53. Jonathan Edwards, "792. Sermon on Ps 37:3 (*c.* September 1745)," Beinecke Rare Book
and Manuscript Library, Yale University, New Haven, CT, L. 1r. It appears that the sermon
text truly is Ps 37:3 but that we only have the second part of perhaps a two-part sermon, the
part where Edwards picked up with the text and observation and continued in the course
of the sermon with point IV of the doctrine. As for the exegetical tradition, Henry similarly linked faith with active service: "The Life of Religion lies much in a believing Reliance
on GOD, his Favour, his Providence, his Promise, his Grace, and a diligent Care to serve
him and our Generation, according to his Will." Henry, *Exposition*, [Ps 37:3]. Trapp similarly identified works as the evidence of true faith: "True faith will trust in God, where it
cannot trace him; it will also work by love, and by doing good approve it self to be right."
John Trapp, *A Commentary or Exposition Upon the Books of Ezra, Nehemiah, Esther, Job, and
Psalms*...(London: T. R. and E. M. for Thomas Newberry..., 1657), 677. Dickson joined faith
and obedience as the way to God's blessing: "Continuance in the faith, and obedience of
God, whatsoever tentation we meet with, is the surest way to have God[']s blessing in this
life, and to have heaven...after this life" (David Dickson, *A Brief Explication of the first Fifty
Psalms* (London: T. M. for Ralph Smith..., 1652), 243. Calvin made the same connection, pri-
oritizing faith and demanding works: "Now, as David places faith first in order, to show that
God is the author of all good, and that by his blessing alone prosperity is to be looked for; so it
ought to be observed that he connects this with a holy life: for the man who places his whole
confidence in God, and gives himself up to be governed by him, will live uprightly and inno-
cently, and will devote himself to doing good." John Calvin, *Commentary on the Psalms*, trans.
from the Original Latin and Collated with the Author's French Version by James Anderson
(1843–1855; repr., Grand Rapids, MI: Eerdmans, 1963), 2:18–20. Poole, on the other hand,
only briefly contrasted this trust with the fear in verse 1. Matthew Poole, *Synopsis Criticorum
Aliorumque Sacrae Scripturae Interpretum et Commentarum, Summo Studio et Fide Adornata*,
vol. II: *Complectens Libros Jobi, Psalmorum, Proverbiorum, Ecclesiastis, & Cantici Canticorum*
(Francofurti ad Moenum: Balthasaris Christophori Wustii, 1678), 736.

to give happiness as "a free Reward."[54] We learn from this verse that it is "far from being a common thing for true saints to do more hurt in the [world] than good."[55] True faith issues in doing good, so if a person does more hurt than good, the genuineness of his faith is in question. True saints are "fruitful Branches," being in Christ, the good tree, and they are "like their Lord & master," having a "Beneficent Temper & Behavior," because they have something mere professors do not—God's grace.[56] Edwards thus called his people to examine themselves to see "whether your Faith works by Love to produce the fruit that has been spoken of viz. a Practice of doing Good."[57]

Edwards often challenged people to take their religious duties and spiritual life seriously because not only their temporal but their eternal happiness depended on the Spirit giving them a new heart, evidenced by spiritual fruit.[58] As he emphasized attending to holy duties, he highlighted that the true Christian seeks after them with a single-minded devotion, as we see in Ps 27:4: "One thing have I desired of the LORD, that will I seek after; that I may dwell in the house of the LORD all the days of my life, to behold the beauty of the LORD, and to enquire in his temple." Earlier Reformed interpreters likewise emphasized single-minded devotion like Edwards.[59] In his March 1741

---

54. Edwards, "792. Sermon on Ps 37:3," L. 1r.

55. Edwards, "792. Sermon on Ps 37:3," L. 1v.

56. Edwards, "792. Sermon on Ps 37:3," L. 3r.–3v. Quotation on L. 3r.

57. Edwards, "792. Sermon on Ps 37:3," L. 5v.

58. See Edwards' 1724 sermon on Ps 119:60, where he preached the doctrine, "[w]e ought to make religion our present and immediate business"; his August 1737 sermon on Ps 106:4–5, where he argued that those are blessed "above all others" who partake of God's electing love, find joy in God's merciful power in making them his nation, and exalt in God being their inheritance and they being his; and his November 1740 sermon on Ps 144:15, where he preached the doctrine, "The Interest of a People mainly consists in the Interest of Religion among them." Jonathan Edwards, "That We Ought to Make Religion Our Present and Immediate Business" [Ps 119:60(a)], in *The Blessing of God: Previously Unpublished Sermons of Jonathan Edwards*, ed. Michael D. McMullen (Nashville, TN: Broadman & Holman, 2003), 91; Jonathan Edwards, "442. Sermon on Ps 106:5 (August 1737)," in *Sermons, Series II, 1737*, vol. 52 of *WJEO*, L. 3r.; Jonathan Edwards, "580. Sermon on Ps 144:15 (November 1740)," Beinecke Rare Book and Manuscript Library, Yale University, New Haven, CT, L. 2v.

59. Henry similarly spoke of David having "an intire Affection to GOD and to his Ordinances." Henry, *Exposition*, [Ps 27:4]. Poole described the priority of being in the public worship of God: "*unum* is placed for the chief or first rank" ("*unum* ponitur pro primo seu primario"), for "I ask for this one thing before others" ("Unum hoc prae caeteris expeto"). Poole, *Synopsis*, 682. Trapp also noted the single-minded pursuit of David seeking after "[o]ne thing above the rest," for "he is resolved never to give it over, but to prosecute it to the utmost...till he had prevailed." Trapp, *Commentary*, 647. Dickson spoke of David's "very earnest desire" and his "[h]earty resolution" to pursue communion with God through his

sermon on this text, Edwards observed that all David's desires and resolutions, even under Saul's persecution, were about "sp[iritual] good," and he thus preached the doctrine, "Earnest desires and strong Resolutions should accompany one another in seeking spiritual and Eternal good."[60] He explained that "the heart should not be divided between many things" but should express a wholehearted pursuit of one thing.[61] Still, earnest desires are not enough; one must also make strong resolutions—as Edwards did as a teenager—for if strong desires are to be "profitable" and "answered," they must be accompanied by resolutions to forsake sin, keep duties, resist wicked companions, and "hold on & hold out" in difficulties.[62] Edwards added that saints must humbly depend on God in these resolutions because desires can only be attained when "our own insufficiency [is] joined with God[']s all sufficiency."[63]

Edwards felt deeply about the priority that should be given to religious duties, and he exhorted his people to devote themselves wholeheartedly to them. When Christians faithfully attend to religious duties while depending on God's grace to work in them, they should expect to abound in holy Christian fruit. Edwards treated several specific manifestations of this spiritual fruit throughout his corpus, and we consider them in three categories: living the Christian virtues, relating with people, and relating with God.

Living the Christian Virtues

In Edwards' view, the Psalms spoke at length about Christian virtues, and he turned to the Psalms to describe these virtues that he believed should issue from the Spirit's gracious influence, virtues such as faith, holiness, hope, joy, peace, humility, and love—a conglomeration that in many ways reflects the

---

ordinances. Dickson, *First Fifty Psalms*, 183. And Calvin described David's single-minded pursuit of God's house: "Under the word *one*, there is an implied antithesis, in which David, disregarding all other interests, displays his intense affection for the service of God; so that it was bitterer to him to be an exile from the sanctuary, than to be denied access to his own house." Calvin, *Commentary*, 1:453–454.

60. Jonathan Edwards, "601. Sermon on Ps 27:4(a) (March 1741)," Beinecke Rare Book and Manuscript Library, Yale University, New Haven, CT, L. 1r. Edwards repreached this sermon in July 1754, most likely to the white congregation in Stockbridge.

61. Edwards, "601. Sermon on Ps 27:4(a)," L. 1v. See also Edwards' "Signs of Godliness" notebook, where he argued that one sign of godliness is "[h]ungering and thirsting after spiritual good" (Pss 4:6–7; 27:4; 42:1–2; 63:1–2; 73:25; 84:1–3; 130:6; 143:6–7); Edwards, "Signs of Godliness," 488.

62. Edwards, "601. Sermon on Ps 27:4(a)," L. 3r. See also Edwards, "Resolutions," 753–759.

63. Edwards, "601. Sermon on Ps 27:4(a)," L. 3v.

triad of faith, hope, and love (1 Cor 13:13), as well as the fruit of the Spirit (Gal 5:22–23). Due to limited space, we discuss only faith, holiness, and love as examples of these virtues.[64]

Faith

In speaking of faith, Edwards gleaned from the Psalms that Christians place their trust in God to such a degree that they do not fear men, even when their circumstances look bleak. In his earliest extant sermon—and perhaps his "first formal sermon"[65]—Edwards used Ps 112:7–8 to describe the steadiness of a man who places his trust in God. He exhorted his listeners not to fear the troubles of this world, for Ps 112:7–8 says that the good man "shall not be afraid of evil tidings: his heart is fixed, trusting in the LORD. His heart is established, he shall not be afraid, until he see his desire upon his enemies." Edwards explained that a person has no need to fear men when God is his refuge, for after these afflictions end, "then you shall enjoy the greatest happiness without any interruption," for while here, "the firmer your faith is, the stronger your hope."[66]

Edwards likewise turned to the Psalms in his personal correspondence to encourage friends enduring difficult times to trust in God. He wrote letters citing the Psalms to encourage Rev. Benjamin Colman upon the death of his daughter (Ps 92:14); to encourage his Scottish friend William McCulloch on

---

64. On hope see Edwards' reading of Ps 39:7 in *The "Blank Bible,"* 494. On joy see Edwards' sermon on Ps 119:162. Jonathan Edwards, "943. Sermon on Ps 119:162 (November 1749)," in *Sermons, Series II, 1749*, vol. 67 of *WJEO*, L. 1r. On peace see Edwards, "Signs of Godliness," 495, and his sermon on Ps 23:2. Jonathan Edwards, "483. Sermon on Ps 23:2 (July 1738)," in *Sermons, Series II, 1738, and Undated 1734–1738*, vol. 53 of *WJEO*, L. 1r. On humility see his treatment of numerous psalms in Edwards, "Signs of Godliness," 502, 504; Jonathan Edwards, "Harmony of the Genius Spirit Doctrines and Rules of the Old Testament and the New," Beinecke Rare Book and Manuscript Library, Yale University, New Haven, CT, 219, 231, 251, 261, 265–266, 269, 274; Jonathan Edwards, *Charity and Its Fruits*, in *Ethical Writings*, ed. Paul Ramsey, vol. 8 of *WJE* (1989), 236, 239; Jonathan Edwards, "A Spiritual Understanding of Divine Things Denied to the Unregenerate" (1 Cor 2:14), in *Sermons and Discourses 1723–1729*, ed. Kenneth P. Minkema, vol. 14 of *WJE* (1997), 87, 88; and Jonathan Edwards, "God Glorified in Man's Dependence" (1 Cor 1:29–31), in *Sermons and Discourses 1730–1733*, ed. Mark Valeri, vol. 17 of *WJE* (1999), 214.

65. Wilson H. Kimnach, ed., *Sermons and Discourses 1720–1723*, vol. 10 of *WJE* (1992), 294.

66. Jonathan Edwards, "Christian Happiness" (Isa 3:10), in *Sermons and Discourses 1720–1723*, vol. 10 of *WJE* (1992), 306. On his discussion of having faith in God instead of fearing men from Pss 11:1; 37:5–7; 55:22; 127:2; and 118:6–9, see Jonathan Edwards, "Christian Safety" (Prov 29:25), in *Sermons and Discourses 1720–1723*, 462–463; Jonathan Edwards, "Profitable Hearers of the Word" (Matt 13:23), in *Sermons and Discourses 1723–1729*, ed. Kenneth P. Minkema, vol. 14 of *WJE* (1997), 271; Edwards, *The "Blank Bible,"* 534; Edwards, "Harmony," 8–9; and Edwards, "1168. Sermon on Ps 118:6–9," L. 1v., 2r.

the sufferings he endured from a sociopolitical uprising (Pss 91:1; 46:2); and to describe the healing work of Christ as showers that water the earth in a letter to Lady Mary Pepperell on the death of her son (Ps 72:6).[67] The Psalms served a practical purpose for dealing with the inevitable blows of trials in this life.[68]

Holiness

Another Christian virtue that Edwards highlighted in several sermons on the Psalms was holiness. He gravitated to Psalm 119, treating the theme of holiness in seven sermons on that psalm. We could discuss much on the virtue of holiness because it is such an encompassing theme but limit ourselves to one sermon from Psalm 119.[69]

---

67. Jonathan Edwards to the Reverend Benjamin Colman, July 27, 1745, in *Letters and Personal Writings*, ed. George S. Claghorn, vol. 16 of *WJE* (1998), 174; Jonathan Edwards to the Reverend William McCulloch, May 12, 1746, in *Letters and Personal Writings*, 208; Jonathan Edwards to Lady Mary Pepperell, November 28, 1751, in *Letters and Personal Writings*, 417. In addition to citing the Psalms to encourage correspondents in suffering, Edwards also turned to the Psalms to address theological and philosophical matters; to discuss the safe dwelling of God's people out of their enemies' reach in a theological discussion with William McCulloch (Pss 59:1; 69:29; 91:14; 107:41); to address the issue of worshipping with Psalms and hymns; to speak of God as a refuge and fortress in a theological discussion with overseas correspondent Thomas Gillespie (Pss 18:2; 46:1; 91:2, 9); to expound a philosophy of education to Sir William Pepperell; and to discuss a theological question with his friend and disciple Joseph Bellamy (Ps 82:6–8). Edwards cited the Psalms in his extant correspondence only in these eight letters. Jonathan Edwards to the Reverend William McCulloch, March 5, 1744, in *Letters and Personal Writings*, 140; Jonathan Edwards to the Reverend Benjamin Colman, May 22, 1744, in *Letters and Personal Writings*, 144–145; Jonathan Edwards to the Reverend Thomas Gillespie, April 2, 1750, in *Letters and Personal Writings*, 336; Jonathan Edwards to Sir William Pepperrell, November 28, 1751, in *Letters and Personal Writings*, 406–414; Jonathan Edwards to the Reverend Joseph Bellamy, December 1, 1757, in *Letters and Personal Writings*, 733–736.

68. Edwards believed true Christians would persevere through trials, and he compared false professors of religion to a "deceitful bow" (Ps 78:57). Edwards, *The "Blank Bible,"* 514; Jonathan Edwards, "704. Sermon on Ps 78:57 (June 1743)," in *Sermons, Series II, 1743*, vol. 61 of *WJEO*, L. 1v.; Edwards, *The "Miscellanies": Entry Nos. 501–832*, 254; and Jonathan Edwards, "Persevering Faith" (Heb 10:38–39), in *Sermons and Discourses 1734–1738*, ed. M. X. Lesser, vol. 19 of *WJE* (2001), 601–604.

69. See also these six other sermons touching on holiness. From Ps 119:2, Edwards preached the doctrine, "That the way to Recieve the Blessed fruits of Religion is to Practice it with our whole hearts." Jonathan Edwards, "146. Sermon on Ps 119:2 (Summer–Fall 1729)," in *Sermons, Series II, 1729*, vol. 44 of *WJEO*, L. 2r. From Ps 116:12, he preached the doctrine, "when Persons have Recieved signal mercies of G[od,] It becomes em to be Earnestly Inquisitive what they shall Render to the L[ord] for all his Benefits towards them," and he argued that "what G[od] Chiefly Looks at and will be most to his Glory" is bringing forth fruit. Jonathan Edwards, "378. Sermon on Ps 116:12 (February 1736)," in *Sermons, Series II, 1736*, vol. 51 of *WJEO*, L. 2r., 7v. From Ps 119:3, Edwards preached the doctrine, "The spirit that godly men are of, is a spirit to be perfectly holy," noting that "[t]hough they ben't actually perfectly holy," yet "[n]othing short of perfect holiness will satisfy the appetite and

In February 1745, Edwards preached a sermon on Ps 119:1–3, "Blessed are the undefiled in the way, who walk in the law of the Lord. Blessed are they that keep his testimonies, and that seek him with the whole heart. They also do no iniquity: they walk in his ways." Throughout the text, doctrine, and application portions of the sermon, Edwards confined himself wholly to Psalm 119, which makes this sermon essentially an extended reflection on the 119th psalm. In the text section, Edwards observed that in true piety there is "a sweet Harmony and agreem[en]t" between the "word of G[od] and the Heart of a true saint," a harmony that "appears in his Practice" and manifests "his sincere Holiness & true Piety."[70] This harmony is answerable to the image of the wax and the seal: "these two things are the two Grand subjects insisted on in this remarkable Psalm from one End of it to the other viz. The Law of G[od] & the sincere Piety of the saint[,] the one being the seal & the other the Impression on the wax."[71] Building from the expressions "undefiled in the way" (v. 1), "keep his testimonies" (v. 2), and "with the whole heart" (v. 2), Edwards developed a three-part doctrine that parallels each phrase: "as we would approve ourselves true saints we must obey God[']s Com[mands] universally perseveringly & with our whole Hearts."[72]

In his doctrine section, Edwards developed three propositions that paralleled these three descriptions of the saint's obedience. When Edwards said that true saints obey God's commands "universally," he meant that they obey with their whole selves (Ps 119:13, 46, 27, 15, 108); they obey every command (Ps 119:104, 128); they seek to know all of God's will (Ps 119:5, 12, 19, 26–27, 124–125); they esteem and cleave to all God's commands (Ps 119:6, 24, 105, 128); and they are "in a way of actually obeying all the Com[mands] of G[od]" (Ps 119:3,

---

craving of their souls." Jonathan Edwards, "Striving after Perfection" (Ps 119:3), in *Sermons and Discourses 1734–1738*, ed. M. X. Lesser, vol. 19 of *WJE* (2001), 683–684. He repreached this Ps 119:3 sermon in January 1757. Edwards preached a sermon in July 1744 and four additional times on Ps 119:140, delivering the doctrine, "Holy Persons Love Holy Things for their Holiness." Jonathan Edwards, "748. Sermon on Ps 119:140 (July 1744)," Beinecke Rare Book and Manuscript Library, Yale University, New Haven, CT, L. 1v. He also preached to the Stockbridge Indians on Ps 119:1–6, arguing that "He that is a good man walks in a holy way." Jonathan Edwards, "1112. Sermon on Ps 119:1–6 (March 1754)," Beinecke Rare Book and Manuscript Library, Yale University, New Haven, CT, L. 1r. Preaching to the Stockbridge Indians, Edwards upheld holiness using Ps 1:1, proclaiming that there is a "great diff[erence] between good men & wicked men." Jonathan Edwards, "1147. Sermon on Ps 1:1 (August 1755)," Beinecke Rare Book and Manuscript Library, Yale University, New Haven, CT, L. 1r.

70. Jonathan Edwards, "771. Sermon on Ps 119:1–3 (February 1745)," Beinecke Rare Book and Manuscript Library, Yale University, New Haven, CT., L. 1r.

71. Edwards, "771. Sermon on Ps 119:1–3," L. 1r.

72. Edwards, "771. Sermon on Ps 119:1–3," L. 2r.

101–102, 168).[73] Edwards explained that obeying "perseveringly" distinguishes the true saint from the unsteadiness and apostasy of hypocrites (Ps 119:31, 44, 112, 16, 93, 153, 176)—not that saints are perfect, for "They fail continually of Perfection," yet "[']tis his ordinary & Constant way & manner to have Respect to all God[']s Comm[ands]" (Ps 119:20, 117).[74] True saints persevere when they suffer for keeping their religious duties (Ps 119:83, 92, 143, 55); when they bear reproach from neighbors (Ps 119:22, 51, 69, 141); when they endure persecution rather than give up religion (Ps 119:78, 84, 95, 110, 157, 161); when following God will ruin their temporal interests or even take their lives (Ps 119:85–87, 109); or when they can "see no way" (Ps 119:81, 84, 123, 124).[75] Finally, Edwards showed that obeying with their "whole hearts" means that true saints do it from "an abiding Holy principle in the Heart" or "Inclination" (Ps 119:112) for they are "Free in their Relig[ion]" (Ps 119:30, 108, 173).[76] They approach religion "with delight of soul" (Ps 119:16, 24, 35, 47, 48, 70, 77, 92, 159, 174), an "inexpressible delight in holiness" (Ps 119:67, 97, 103), and "a sense of God[']s Excellency & the Excellency of his Com[mands]" (Ps 119:57, 128–129, 137–138, 142, 144, 151, 160, 172).[77] They "Love God[']s commands for their Holiness" (Ps 119:140, 119) and "have Earnest longings to do God[']s Com[mands] in a great degree" (Ps 119:5, 20, 40, 94, 131) and "with fervent zeal" (Ps 119:139).[78] They also obey with "full & fixed Resolutions" (Ps 119:8, 106, 115, 117) and devote themselves to obeying God's commands (Ps 119:38).[79]

As Edwards turned to his application, he called people to examine themselves using Psalm 119, for he believed that no other part of the Bible delineated the nature and evidences of holiness as this psalm did: "what a mercy of G[od] to us is it that he has been pleased to Leave us in his word such a Long & particular & full description" of the true saint's godliness, so much that all persons should judge themselves by "this touch stone" chapter in the Bible.[80] He exhorted all to seek that they might evidence universal, persevering, and wholehearted obedience to God. Be sure that "you belong to G[od] in that

73. Edwards, "771. Sermon on Ps 119:1–3," L. 2v.–4v. Quotation on L. 4v.

74. Edwards, "771. Sermon on Ps 119:1–3," L. 5r., 6r. Quotation on L. 5r.

75. Edwards, "771. Sermon on Ps 119:1–3," L. 7v.–9v.

76. Edwards, "771. Sermon on Ps 119:1–3," L. 10r., 10v.

77. Edwards, "771. Sermon on Ps 119:1–3," L. 10v., 11v., 12r.

78. Edwards, "771. Sermon on Ps 119:1–3," L. 12r.–12v.

79. Edwards, "771. Sermon on Ps 119:1–3," L. 12v., 13r.

80. Edwards, "771. Sermon on Ps 119:1–3," L. 13v.

G[od] has made you" (Ps 119:73), for God's goodness lays "great obligations" on you (Ps 119:65, 68).[81] Be careful you are not deceived, imagining yourself godly when these things are lacking (Ps 119:118), for those who say they are godly but lack these things will be "Rejected as dross" (Ps 119:118–119, 155).[82] If you obey universally, perseveringly, and with your whole heart, "you shall never be ashamed" (Ps 119:6) but will "enjoy true Liberty" (Ps 119:45), "have true Peace" (Ps 119:165), experience "inexpressible" privileges in this world (Ps 119:56), and be "pronounced Blessed Persons" by God (Ps 119:1–2).[83]

Edwards closed his sermon with lengthy instructions, still drawn from Psalm 119, for how to nurture universal, persevering, and wholehearted obedience: You must earnestly seek the holy divine principles that come only from God, not nature. Seek spiritual light (Ps 119:18, 34, 35) and spiritual life (Ps 119:25, 37, 40, 88, 159), and see to it that worldly-mindedness and pride are mortified (Ps 119:19, 36, 21) and holy fear embraced (Ps 119:120).[84] Pursue obedience "now without delay" (Ps 119:160), laboring to know God's mind and will by diligently searching the Scriptures (Ps 119:15, 48, 99).[85] Keep God's commands always in mind (Ps 119:11, 30, 98), and set the God who gave those commands always before you (Ps 119:168).[86] Heed your covenant with God (Ps 119:29, 106, 163), and "thoroughly believe the Principles of God[']s Word" (Ps 119:66, 74, 81, 89–92, 114, 152), "often examining your ways & Comparing them with the word of G[od]" (Ps 119:59, 105).[87] Speedily return to God, even daily, when you wander (Ps 119:9, 59, 176), and "as much as in you lies avoid Temptation" (Ps 119:37, 115) and keep company with those who appear holy (Ps 119:63).[88] Edwards warned that "you can never expect to" have the heart of a true saint in universal, persevering obedience "without care[,] watchfullness & diligence" (Ps 119:4, 9), while at the same time "you must not trust in your self but in G[od]" (Ps. 119:8, 17, 42, 116–117, 149, 156, 159), and so "Be much in prayer to G[od] for his Help" (Ps 119:10, 36, 133, 145).[89] Edwards' treatment of Psalm

---

81. Edwards, "771. Sermon on Ps 119:1–3," L. 15v.

82. Edwards, "771. Sermon on Ps 119:1–3," L. 15v., 16r.

83. Edwards, "771. Sermon on Ps 119:1–3," L. 16r.–16v.

84. Edwards, "771. Sermon on Ps 119:1–3," L. 17r., 18r., 18v., 20v.

85. Edwards, "771. Sermon on Ps 119:1–3," L. 22v., 24r.

86. Edwards, "771. Sermon on Ps 119:1–3," L. 25r., 26v.

87. Edwards, "771. Sermon on Ps 119:1–3," L. 28r.–29r.

88. Edwards, "771. Sermon on Ps 119:1–3," L. 29v.–30v.

89. Edwards, "771. Sermon on Ps 119:1–3," L. 27v., 31r.

119 illustrates his thematic approach to the Bible—not in a verse-by-verse treatment but in a theological synthesis—and reveals just how much the Psalms informed his understanding of spirituality. It also shows that he believed holiness was a key virtue in the Christian life.

Love

Edwards emphasized the virtue of love as a necessary characteristic of a true Christian. In fact, "True piety has its primary seat in the Heart, and true obedience is obedience from love, and with delight," a point Edwards gleaned from Ps 1:2, which says the blessed man's "delight is in the law of the LORD."[90] Also, following Ps 17:3, "Thou hast proved mine heart," Edwards stated that "[t]he essence of true piety is rectitude of heart."[91] In a sermon titled "Saving Faith and Christian Obedience Arise from Godly Love," Edwards argued that those who are in a state of salvation are characterized by having "divine love in their hearts."[92] The Psalms particularly demonstrate that "[t]he people of Christ are called those that love his name": Ps 69:36 shows that "loving God's name is spoken of as the distinguishing qualification of them that have a title to the spiritual inheritance"; Ps 5:11–12 establishes that loving God's name is described as "the character of all the righteous that trust in God, that are the objects of his favor, whom God will defend and bless"; Ps 145:20 divides all humanity into "those that love God, who shall be saved and preserved; and the wicked that shall be destroyed"; and Ps 97:10–11 likewise equates the "saints" with those who love the Lord.[93] Edwards concluded that "loving God's name is spoken of as the common character of such as shall obtain mercy of God," in keeping with Ps 119:132, "Look thou upon me, and be merciful unto me, as thou usest to do unto those that love thy name."[94]

Edwards connected love of God with a single-minded focus on God in two sermons on Ps 27:4, "One thing have I desired of the LORD, that will I seek after; that I may dwell in the house of the LORD all the days of my life, to behold

---

90. Edwards, "Harmony," 217.

91. Edwards, "Harmony," 222. See Edwards' similar comments on Pss 24:4; 36:10; 37:31; 51:6; 64:10; 78:8, 36–37; 101:2–4; 125:4–5. Edwards, "Harmony," 225, 231, 232, 238, 242, 251, 261, 273.

92. Jonathan Edwards, "Saving Faith and Christian Obedience Arise from Godly Love" (1 John 5:1–4), in *Sermons and Discourses 1743–1758*, ed. Wilson H. Kimnach, vol. 25 of *WJE* (2006), 521.

93. Edwards, "Saving Faith," 523–524.

94. Edwards, "Saving Faith," 524.

the beauty of the LORD, and to enquire in his temple." He preached the first in March 1752, when he argued that "[t]is the Heart of a truly good man to Love G[od] above all things."[95] Edwards' emphasis on loving God from this verse, while not unique, was less common in the Reformed exegetical tradition.[96] In this sermon Edwards portrayed the truly good man as one whose heart has been transformed, whose disposition bends first and foremost toward a love of God. He loves God as a child loves his father, and he loves God "above all for his own Beauty."[97] He loves religion as his happiness because he knows his goodness is never satisfactory but that righteousness is a means to communion with God. He delights in the Word of God because by it he can "see God[']s Beauty" and "Learn to do his will."[98] In his application, Edwards called all "to seek such a Heart" with this new disposition for those who love God above all things "have the best portion."[99] In this sermon Edwards focused on the individual's heart, that he might have "a Heart full of Love to [Christ,] Love to G[od] as a Father for his Beauty," for having a heart like this is ultimately the way to "dwell with G[od] in his House above & then to see Him Face to Face."[100]

In an October 1756 sermon on the same text, Edwards narrowed specifically on worship duties, a standard approach among his Reformed predecessors.[101]

---

95. Jonathan Edwards, "1031. Sermon on Ps 27:4(b) (March 1752)," Beinecke Rare Book and Manuscript Library, Yale University, New Haven, CT, L. 1r. See also Edwards' 1736 sermon on Ps 73:25, in which he preached the doctrine, "It is the spirit of a truly godly man, to prefer God before all other things, either in heaven or on earth." Jonathan Edwards, "God the Best Portion of the Christian" (Ps 73:25), in vol. 4 of *Works of President Edwards* (Worcester ed.), 8th ed. (1778; repr., New York: Leavitt & Allen, 1852), 540. Edwards repreached the Ps 73:25 sermon five times, in Boston, Windsor, Hadley, Stockbridge, and Canaan.

96. Henry and Dickson observed the importance of loving God from this verse. Henry noted that "[i]f our Hearts can witness for us that we delight in GOD above any Creature," it is "a sign we are those whom He protects as *his own*." Henry, *Exposition*, [Ps 27:4]. Dickson noted that "[t]he desire of communion with God, and love to his ordinances, where it is sincere, should have the chief place in the heart, above all earthly desires and delights whatsoever." Dickson, *First Fifty Psalms*, 183. But Poole, Trapp, and Calvin spoke not of loving God but of loving his ordinances. Poole, *Synopsis*, 682; Trapp, *Commentary*, 647; Calvin, *Commentary*, 1:453–455.

97. Edwards, "1031. Sermon on Ps 27:4(b)," L. 1r.

98. Edwards, "1031. Sermon on Ps 27:4(b)," L. 1v.

99. Edwards, "1031. Sermon on Ps 27:4(b)," L. 2r.

100. Edwards, "1031. Sermon on Ps 27:4(b)," L. 2v.

101. Henry observed that "[a]ll God's Children desire to *dwell in God's House*; Where should they dwell else?" Henry, *Exposition*, [Ps 27:4]. Poole noted that David asked for peace from his enemies not for ill motives, but "so he might more freely serve God" ("ut liberius Deo serviat") and participate in public worship. Poole, *Synopsis*, 682. Trapp showed that what David desired most was "the liberty of God[']s Sanctuary, and enjoyment of his publick

He preached the doctrine, "'Tis our duty to love the House of [God]."[102] If our duty is to love God, then we are also to "Love every thing [that] belongs to G[od]"—his word, day, people, and house—and we are particularly to love God's house because it is Christ's house and there we can "Hear the glo[rious] Gospel of [Christ]."[103] In his application, Edwards made the love of God's house the test for a changed heart. For "if we love to keep away from G[od]" now, how can we expect to desire to be near God in eternity, and "If you don[']t love God[']s House here How can you expect to be admitted to his House above."[104] In the end, Edwards exhorted his people, in keeping with his heart-based view of religion, to "Endeavour to get the Love of G[od] in your Heart."[105] For Edwards, love was the seed virtue in the Christian from which all the other virtues sprout into being, for love characterizes the redeemed heart whose affections have been reoriented and transformed by the gospel of Christ.

Relating with People

As Edwards engaged piety in the Psalms, he not only discussed virtues for the individual but also described specific ways the Psalms teach us about how Christians should relate with other people. Specifically, he discovered teaching on the family, living in unity within society, and the practice of benevolence.

Family

The Psalms informed Edwards' conception of the family. Standing in the stream of Puritanism, he believed like his predecessors that godly parents are charged with the spiritual instruction of their children.[106] He preached from

---

Ordinances." Trapp, Commentary, 647. Dickson said that "[t]he desire of communion with God, and love to his ordinances, where it is sincere, should have the chief place in the heart, above all earthly desires and delights whatsoever." Dickson, First Fifty Psalms, 183. And Calvin held that since God draws people to himself through temples and ordinances, these "deservedly ought to draw the affections and desires of the faithful to them," for "[t]he Word, sacraments, public prayers, and other helps of the same kind, cannot be neglected, without a wicked contempt of God, who manifests himself to us in these ordinances, as in a mirror or image." Calvin, Commentary, 1:455.

102. Jonathan Edwards, "1175. Sermon on Ps 27:4(c) (October 1756)," Beinecke Rare Book and Manuscript Library, Yale University, New Haven, CT, L. 1r.

103. Edwards, "1175. Sermon on Ps 27:4(c)," L. 1r.

104. Edwards, "1175. Sermon on Ps 27:4(c)," L. 2v.

105. Edwards, "1175. Sermon on Ps 27:4(c)," L. 2v.

106. On the New England Puritan expectation that parents should provide religious instruction to their children, see Allen Carden, Puritan Christianity in America: Religion and Life in

the Psalms on parents' duty to instruct their children in a February 1745 sermon on Ps 78:5–7:

> For he established a testimony in Jacob, and appointed a law in Israel, which he commanded our fathers, that they should make them known to their children: That the generation to come might know them, even the children which should be born; who should arise and declare them to their children: That they might set their hope in God, and not forget the works of God, but keep his commandments.

Edwards noted first "The duty required of Parents viz. that they make Known God[']s wonderful w[orks] to their Chil[dren]."[107] He described two aims in this duty: the "more Immediate End" of imparting "the Knowledge of these divine things in the Posterity of God[']s People from generation to gen[eration]," and "the more remote but principal End" that the posterity of God's people "be truly gracious & Holy Persons."[108] Thus in Edwards' doctrine he positioned this parenting duty within God's work of redemption: "The Relig[ious] Education of Chil[dren] is one of the principle means of grace that G[od] has appointed in his Church."[109] Earlier Reformed exegetes also emphasized God's preservation of his church through parents' duty of instruction.[110]

Seventeenth-Century Massachusetts (Grand Rapids, MI: Baker Book House, 1990), 174–180. Edwards also thought that the Psalter was a good starting place for children to learn how to read. Edwards to Sir William Pepperrell, 406–414.

107. Jonathan Edwards, "770. Sermon on Ps 78:5–7 (February 1745)," Beinecke Rare Book and Manuscript Library, Yale University, New Haven, CT, L. 1r. Edwards repreached this sermon in June 1755, presumably for his white congregation in Stockbridge.

108. Edwards, "770. Sermon on Ps 78:5–7," L. 1r., 1v.

109. Edwards, "770. Sermon on Ps 78:5–7," L. 1v.

110. Henry held that God "appointed that Parents should train up their Children in the knowledge of the Law," so that "as one Generation of GOD's Servants and Worshipers passeth away, another Generation may come, and *the Church, as the Earth*, may *abide for ever.*" Henry, *Exposition*, [Ps 78:5–7]. Italics original. Poole observed that God decreed this law for fathers so their posterity would know God's deeds. Poole, *Synopsis*, 1006. Trapp maintained that parents must convey God's truth to their children so that when they grow up they will "Succeed their Parents both in their place and office of teaching their posterity." Trapp, *Commentary*, 784. Dickson highlighted "the Lord's care of his Church, in giving them his Scriptures and revealed rule of faith and obedience, to be transmitted from one generation to another." David Dickson, *A Brief Explication of the other fifty Psalmes, From Ps. 50 to Ps. 100* (London: T. R. and E. M. for Ralph Smith…, 1653), 199. And Calvin upheld the duty of fathers diligently to instruct their children in the law and show their children that they had been "gathered into one body as his Church." Calvin, *Commentary*, 3:231.

As Edwards fleshed out this doctrine, he explained three aspects of the religious education of children: instruction, example, and government. First, it must include instruction of both the doctrines and duties of religion. Parents must teach children to avoid ill manners, use God's appointed means of grace, read, and sing—Edwards wanted them to be fully prepared to participate in corporate psalmody for the good of their souls.[111] He further aimed for children to embrace this learning with full understanding, for instruction includes "not only explaining things but applying them," as well as "Enquiring into the state of their souls."[112] Second, parents must set their children a good example, for as the psalmist resolves in Ps 101:2: "I will walk within my house with a perfect heart," so "Example has a greater & more powerf[ul] Influence on them than Precept."[113] Third, in the religious education of their children, parents must also exercise government. Since God has set them up "to Rule for G[od]," "Parents should take heed they don[']t Loose their authority," for refraining from this duty actually "tends to bring God's curse on a Family as appears in the Instance of Eli."[114] Edwards argued that all three of these aspects are necessary, for if one of them is lacking, the children will likely miss the benefits. Since religious education of children is one of God's primary means of grace, it may be argued that it is God's "Chief dispensation for establishing his Ch[urc]h in the [world]."[115] In his application, Edwards exhorted the heads of families to "be faithful" in the use of this means, for "These great means are committed to you," as is "the care of your Chil[dren]'s souls."[116] The Psalms helped Edwards explain God's plan to use families in the spread of the gospel.

The result of parents fulfilling their duties in religious education would be virtuous sons and daughters, as taught in Ps 144:12, "That our sons may be as plants grown up in their youth; that our daughters may be as corner stones, polished after the similitude of a palace." Edwards preached on this verse in a November 1744 sermon titled, "The Beauty of Piety in Youth," five months after the "Bad Book" culprits had made public confessions in church that they

---

111. On the rise of singing schools in New England and Edwards' support of the movement and belief that singing aided revival, see David W. Music, "Jonathan Edwards and the Theology and Practice of Congregational Song in Puritan New England," *Studies in Puritan American Spirituality* 8 (2004): 103–133.

112. Edwards, "770. Sermon on Ps 78:5–7," L. 2v.

113. Edwards, "770. Sermon on Ps 78:5–7," L. 4v.

114. Edwards, "770. Sermon on Ps 78:5–7," L. 5v., 6r. On Eli, see 1 Sam 3:11–14.

115. Edwards, "770. Sermon on Ps 78:5–7," L. 9v.

116. Edwards, "770. Sermon on Ps 78:5–7," L. 13v.

had apprehended a midwifery manual and teased girls about their anatomy—an issue that was likely still a sore point between Edwards and some of his parishioners.[117] In his treatment of the passage, Edwards first established that while the psalm refers on one level to God's deliverance of David and his people, it more properly speaks of the church.[118] He then noted that the primary subject was "the spiritual prosperity of a people, as appearing very much in the piety of their youth."[119] The emphasis on youth was because the "flourishing of religion" usually starts with young people, as Edwards had observed in the revivals in his own town, and because piety in youth is "beautiful," "a lovely sight to behold," which is why pious young men are compared to flourishing plants and pious young women are compared to polished cornerstones—"things that are beautiful and pleasant to the eye."[120] Edwards thus preached the doctrine, "'Tis a peculiarly lovely and pleasant sight to behold young people walking in the ways of virtue and piety."[121] Edwards argued that there is a "peculiar decency" in young piety because it is "most suitable" that people devote "the first of their time," the best part of their life, and "thereby the whole life" to God.[122] It also produces "good fruits" as it prevents much sin, promotes greater holiness, and makes persons more beneficial to society.[123] Based on this beauty, Edwards pleaded with young people to commit themselves to God in their youth and to avoid carnal sins because, as he said, "I desire your good, your happiness in this world and that which is to come."[124]

---

117. For more on the "Bad Book" episode, see Ava Chamberlain, "Bad Books and Bad Boys: The Transformation of Gender in Eighteenth-Century Northampton, Massachusetts," in *Jonathan Edwards at Home and Abroad: Historical Memories, Cultural Movements, Global Horizons*, ed. David W. Kling and Douglas A. Sweeney (Columbia: University of South Carolina Press, 2003), 61–81.

118. Edwards argued that it is spoken in the name of Christ more so than in David's name from the analogy of Scripture, comparing this psalm with Pss 22:22 and 69:9, which he then compared with Heb 2:12 and John 2:17. Jonathan Edwards, "The Beauty of Piety in Youth" (Ps 144:12), in *Sermons and Discourses 1743–1758*, ed. Wilson H. Kimnach, vol. 25 of *WJE* (2006), 105. See also Edwards' discussion of "excellent mothers" and "virtuous" daughters and sons from Ps 144:12. Edwards, *The "Blank Bible,"* 540.

119. Edwards, "The Beauty of Piety in Youth," 106.

120. Edwards, "The Beauty of Piety in Youth," 106.

121. Edwards, "The Beauty of Piety in Youth," 106.

122. Edwards, "The Beauty of Piety in Youth," 106.

123. Edwards, "The Beauty of Piety in Youth," 107.

124. Edwards, "The Beauty of Piety in Youth," 110.

At a time when men were asserting a greater sexual freedom than granted to women, Edwards may have sounded like a throwback to a bygone era.[125] But in Edwards' mind, he only sought the good of his people, offering them the best life they could experience in the temporal world but most importantly in the eternal world. So Edwards charged the youth in his congregation to devote themselves to piety and virtue, which would reflect the beauty of God's excellency in this world, and he urged parents to attend to their duty of religious instruction, for by this means of grace God advances his kingdom and establishes his church.

Living in Unity

Edwards' concern for the family was driven both by an interest in the good of souls individually and an interest in the good of the church and society corporately. As Edwards reflected on the society at large, he called for a unity based on the teaching of Ps 133:1, "Behold, how good and how pleasant it is for brethren to dwell together in unity!" While earlier Reformed interpreters applied this verse to the Christian church, Edwards applied it to "a society living together in peace and unity" and called for peace to reign in their midst: "O that there may be nothing but perfect amity and agreement! Let us therefore by all means abstain from anything that either directly or indirectly tends to contention."[126] Likewise, in a December 1729 sermon, Edwards described societal contention as "deplorable," for it means living "a disturbed and miserable life" and is "one of the greatest miseries that can befall a people."[127] But

---

125. George M. Marsden, *Jonathan Edwards: A Life* (New Haven, CT: Yale University Press, 2003), 300–301; Chamberlain, "Bad Books and Bad Boys," 61–81 (esp. 71–75); and esp. Cornelia Hughes Dayton, "Consensual Sex: The Eighteenth-Century Double Standard," in *Women before the Bar: Gender, Law, and Society in Connecticut, 1639–1789* (Chapel Hill: University of North Carolina Press, 1995), 157–230. Dayton observes, for example, that by the mid-eighteenth century, New England had adopted "a prosecutorial double standard for sexual behavior," favoring men and punishing women. In response to the changing times, and "[c]ontrary to what ministers might urge, middling and elite families increasingly claimed the right to keep private the premarital sexual lapses of their young people." Dayton, 159, 215.

126. Jonathan Edwards, "Living Peaceably One with Another" (Rom 12:18), in *Sermons and Discourses 1723–1729*, ed. Kenneth P. Minkema, vol. 14 of *WJE* (1997), 133. Reformed interpreters tended both to describe what this unity meant particularly to David, given the troubles and contentions he faced in his kingdom, and to call for unity among Christians, whether the invisible or the visible church. Henry, *Exposition*, [Ps 133:1]; Poole, *Synopsis*, 1268–1269; Trapp, *Commentary*, 905–906; David Dickson, *A Brief Explication of the last Fifty Psalmes, From Ps. 100 to the end* (London: T. R. and E. M. for Ralph Smith…, 1654), 280–281; Calvin, *Commentary*, 5:163–165.

127. Jonathan Edwards, "Sin and Wickedness Bring Calamity and Misery on a People" (Prov 14:34), in *Sermons and Discourses 1723–1729*, ed. Kenneth P. Minkema, vol. 14 of *WJE* (1997), 495.

from Ps 133:1, we learn that "[l]ove and peace is the cement of any society, and the happiness of human society does very much consist in it."[128] Again, in an August 9, 1730 sermon, Edwards called for people to live in unity in society from Ps 133:1, arguing that society's strength depends on the peacefulness of its citizens. For "the comfort of society very much consists in love and peace," but a society "full of contentions" is "like the company of the damned; for great part of the misery of hell consists in the reign of malice and spite there. And the more there is of love and peace, the more are they like heaven."[129] Here Edwards cast earthly societies as images of the two eternal societies, keeping the end of God's redemptive history in sight. By living in peaceful concord on earth, God's people give the world a picture of heaven in eternity.

Benevolence

Edwards was a firm proponent of the Christian duty of benevolence, and he argued that one of the true signs of godliness is "[m]ercy and liberality to the poor" (Pss 37:21, 26; 112:5, 9).[130] When we ask with the psalmist, "What shall I render unto the LORD for all his benefits toward me?" (Ps 116:12), we should answer that we will show good will toward humanity. Since we cannot fully express our gratitude to an infinite God in showing benevolence to him, Edwards prescribed a posture of gratitude that issues in benevolence toward humankind, for God "has appointed others to be his receivers, and to stand in his stead, as the objects of our beneficence; such are especially our indigent brethren."[131]

Edwards expressed these sentiments more fully in his January 1733 sermon on Deut 15:7–11, "Duty of Charity to the Poor," in which he presented the doctrine, "'Tis the most absolute and indispensable duty of a people of God to give bountifully and willingly for the supply of the wants of the needy."[132] In one of his points to motivate his people to this duty, he argued that "[t]his very thing is often mentioned in Scripture as an essential part of the character of a godly man," as we see in Pss 37:21, 26; 112:5, 9.[133] A further motivation was

---

128. Edwards, "Sin and Wickedness," 495.

129. Jonathan Edwards, "Envious Men" (James 3:16) in *Sermons and Discourses 1730–1733*, ed. Mark Valeri, vol. 17 of *WJE* (1999), 109.

130. Edwards, "Signs of Godliness," 491.

131. Jonathan Edwards, *Freedom of the Will*, ed. Paul Ramsey, vol. 1 of *WJE* (1957), 280.

132. Jonathan Edwards, "The Duty of Charity to the Poor" (Deut 15:7–11), in *Sermons and Discourses 1730–1733*, ed. Mark Valeri, vol. 17 of *WJE* (1999), 373.

133. Edwards, "The Duty of Charity to the Poor," 381.

God's faithfulness to those who are generous to the needy. Edwards warned that calamity comes upon anyone, being no respecter of persons, but to those who give to the poor to ameliorate their troubles, God will show pity and help when they fall on difficult times. So we learn from Ps 41:1–2, "Blessed is he that considereth the poor: the LORD will deliver him in time of trouble. The LORD will preserve him, and keep him alive; and he shall be blessed upon the earth: and thou wilt not deliver him unto the will of his enemies." So Edwards challenged his people, saying, "Such as have been merciful and liberal to others in their distress, God won't forget it, but will so order it that they shall have help when they are in distress; yea, their children shall reap the fruit of it in the day of trouble" (Ps 37:25).[134] With these clear teachings from the Psalms, Edwards upheld his belief that persons under the gracious influence of the Holy Spirit will embrace this duty of showing benevolence to the poor out of gratitude to God and in anticipation of God's care for their own lives.

Relating with God

In his reading of the Psalms, Edwards also emphasized four major ways that the Christian maintains his or her vertical relationship with God: self-examination, accepting chastisement, offering the best sacrifices, and prayer.

Self-Examination

The duty of self-examination featured prominently in Edwards' ministry, most clearly evidenced in his frequent homiletical call to his people to examine themselves throughout his sermon corpus.[135] Edwards' sermons on the Psalms regularly include a segment asking people to check themselves against the doctrinal discussion to see if they manifest the characteristics prescribed of Christians. The Psalms themselves also prescribed the practice of self-examination. So in one exhortation, Edwards appropriated the language of Ps 139:23–24 to show that the Scriptures require self-examination, calling his people to "be much in begging of God the judge, that he would search you and try you now, and discover you to yourself, that you may see if you are insincere, and lead you in the way everlasting; that if you are not upon a good foundation,

---

134. Edwards, "The Duty of Charity to the Poor," 389. Edwards also described God's rewards to those who serve the poor using Pss 18:25; 41:1; 112:5, 9, in Edwards, *Charity and Its Fruits*, 215–217.

135. On Edwards' emphasis on self-examination as a Christian practice, see Ted Rivera, *Jonathan Edwards on Worship: Public and Private Devotion to God* (Eugene, OR: Pickwick, 2010), 75–117.

that God would unsettle you and fix you on a better path."[136] Edwards preached on this topic in a March 1754 sermon on Ps 119:59–60, "I thought on my ways, and turned my feet unto thy testimonies. I made haste, and delayed not to keep thy commandments," from which he defended the doctrine, "men ought to be much in thinking of their own ways."[137] When thinking of their ways, if they discover that they are in a wrong way, they should immediately set about to get themselves in the way of God's commandments through repentance, confession, resolutions, forsaking sins, and prayer.[138] From this psalm, Edwards distilled a common principle in his ministry, that one of the key ways we relate to God is by comparing our thoughts, words, and actions to the standard laid out in Scripture because this reveals sins in our lives that may elude our sight.

Accepting Chastisement

It is difficult to convince a child that the discipline he is about to bear is for his good. Yet Edwards sought to convince his people of this very principle, that though they suffer God's chastisement, they must look upon it as a good work to teach them to turn from their sins and cling to God. He pursued this line of thought in a sermon on Ps 94:12, "Blessed is the man whom thou chastenest, O LORD, and teachest him out of thy law."[139] Edwards noted that Psalm 94 as a whole speaks of "the Persecutions which the Church suffers from wicked men," and it calls for God to act in vengeance on her enemies.[140] The sermon text begins a discussion of comforts for God's people under persecutions, and

136. Jonathan Edwards, "The Day of Judgment" (Acts 17:31), in *Sermons and Discourses 1723–1729*, ed. Kenneth P. Minkema, vol. 14 of *WJE* (1997), 540. Ps 139:23–24 reads, "Search me, O God, and know my heart: try me, and know my thoughts: And see if there be any wicked way in me, and lead me in the way everlasting."

137. Jonathan Edwards, "1113. Sermon on Ps 119:59–60 [60–61] (March 1754)," Beinecke Rare Book and Manuscript Library, Yale University, New Haven, CT, L. 1r. Edwards incorrectly listed the passage as Ps 119:60–61 on his manuscript, while the words he quoted on the manuscript are vv. 59–60.

138. Edwards, "1113. Sermon on Ps 119:59–60," L. 1r.–1v.

139. Jonathan Edwards, "207. Sermon on Ps 94:12(a) (August 1731–December 1732)," in *Sermons, Series II, 1731–1732*, vol. 46 of *WJEO*. See also Edwards' later sermon on Ps 94:12, in which he explained that God's chastening is the saints' "distinction" from the wicked because affliction is used for their good, while for the wicked the afflictions of this world are only "forerunners" of the eternal torments in the next. Jonathan Edwards, "808. Sermon on Ps 94:12(b) (February 1746)," Beinecke Rare Book and Manuscript Library, Yale University, New Haven, CT, L. 5r., 5v. See also Edwards' sermon on Ps 94:10, in which he argued that if God chastises the heathen, how much more will he chastise the sins of his own people. Jonathan Edwards, "537. Sermon on Ps 94:10 (February 1740)," in *Sermons, Series II, January–June 1740*, vol. 55 of *WJEO*, L. 2r., 8r.

140. Edwards, "207. Sermon on Ps 94:12(a)," L. 1r.

it shows that God is the one who orders their affliction. Though the suffer-ings of God's people "may be from the hand of men[,] may be the fruit of their malice & Cruelty or may be from other second Causes[,] Yet they are of the Ordering of G[od]," and we are called to consider them "God[']s Just & holy Chastenings" from which we must learn and grow.[141] Edwards went on to explain that while the world may reject this paradox, it is possible that peo-ple "may be blessed & Yet afflicted."[142] The necessary condition for chastened people to experience blessing is that when God chastens, he teaches them. So Edwards preached the doctrine, "He is a happy man tho[ugh] an afflicted one whom G[od] Chastends & teaches out of his word."[143] Earlier Reformed exegetes affirmed this paradox and highlighted the necessity of being taught in affliction.[144]

As Edwards fleshed out this doctrine, he showed how it is possible to be both happy and afflicted and that God's chastening can prepare people to accept further teachings, especially teachings leading to salvation. In fact, when God afflicts a person to teach and chasten him, he is "the object of the Love of G[od]," for such afflictions "are not from hatred" nor are they "the fruits of the Revenging wrath of G[od]" but are "the fruits of God[']s Love."[145] It makes a great difference if afflictions arise from God's love or wrath, for "more dread full is a little affliction that is the fruit of God[']s Hatred than the Greatest that Ever man suffered when it is from Love."[146] Thus Edwards called his people

---

141. Edwards, "207. Sermon on Ps 94:12(a)," L. 1r.–1v.

142. Edwards, "207. Sermon on Ps 94:12(a)," L. 1v.

143. Edwards, "207. Sermon on Ps 94:12(a)," L. 1v.

144. Henry similarly recognized God's goodness in afflicting the saints, for he "gives it another Name," chastening, which is "design'd for our Instruction, Reformation, and Improvement." He also distinguished between chastening alone and chastening with teach-ing: "'Tis not the *chastening* itself that *doth good*, but the *teaching* that goes along with it." Henry, *Exposition*, [Ps 94:12]. Poole understood God's chastenings as "ministers" ("minis-tros") for "either restraint or instruction or benefit" ("Castigatio enim vel coercitio est vel verbo, vel opere"). Poole, *Synopsis*, 1091–1092. Trapp likewise made a distinction between forms of chastening: "strike whiles thou pleasest, Lord; only to thy correction adde instruc-tion," for we want not only "Lashing," but also "lessoning." Trapp, *Commentary*, 818. Dickson differentiated between the end of condemnation for the wicked and the end of rest for the saints, and he explained that God's "chastising of his own, and his teaching them out of his law to make the right use of it, is the means whereby he doth save his own, that they perish not with the world in his wrath." Dickson, *Other fifty Psalmes*, 362. Calvin similarly highlighted the rest that God promises will come to his afflicted children, a rest that distin-guishes them from the world perishing around them. Calvin, *Commentary*, 4:20–22.

145. Edwards, "207. Sermon on Ps 94:12(a)," L. 11r.

146. Edwards, "207. Sermon on Ps 94:12(a)," L. 11r.

to examine themselves whether they have been taught through God's afflictions or merely punished for sin. He warned his parishioners: If you are not
taught in afflictions, you have reason to fear that "you have only been made
worse by them."[147] Edwards kept the gospel message in sight as he closed this
sermon: "Eye the hand of G[od] in afflictions[;] don[']t think of the afflictions
that Come upon You as a meer Chance that happend to you[.] Consider that
G[od] is he that wounds & that Heals," and turn to him to instruct you through
them for your eternal good.[148] As difficult as chastisement could be, Edwards
sought to guide his people in making good on it, not just in this world but,
most importantly, in the next.

Offering the Best Sacrifices

In the Old Testament Edwards encountered an intricate system of sacrifices
from ancient Israel that the people employed in their worship of Yahweh. As
he engaged this sacrificial system in the Psalms to describe proper worship
of God for the people of his time, he emphasized that the best sacrifices are
not external shows of ceremony or lip service but internal heart attitudes that
issue forth in active obedience. So when preaching a November 1744 thanksgiving sermon on Ps 119:108, "Accept, I beseech thee, the freewill offerings
of my mouth, O LORD, and teach me thy judgments," Edwards preached the
doctrine, "In a right Thanksgiving to God, Heart and mouth and practice all
go together."[149] He joined verbal praise with the act of obedience to show that
true thanksgiving is founded in heart religion.

Following this theme of heart-based sacrifices, Edwards preached a fast
day sermon in March 1733 on David's prayer of repentance over his adultery
with Bathsheba and murder of Uriah in Ps 51:17, "The sacrifices of God are
a broken spirit: a broken and a contrite heart, O God, thou wilt not despise."
His gospel-centered approach to this passage held much in common with
the Reformed tradition, and he shared particular parallels with Matthew
Henry.[150] Edwards observed that while sacrifices had been established since

---

147. Edwards, "207. Sermon on Ps 94:12(a)," L. 16v.

148. Edwards, "207. Sermon on Ps 94:12(a)," L. 17r.

149. Jonathan Edwards, "760. Sermon on Ps 119:108 (November 1744)," Beinecke Rare Book
and Manuscript Library, Yale University, New Haven, CT, L. 2r.

150. Edwards shared many parallels with Matthew Henry in this sermon, marked in the footnotes that follow, suggesting that Edwards might have used him as a source for developing
this sermon, though he did not explicitly say so. The other four exegetes also made similar
interpretations as Edwards. Poole described the psalmist's deep sorrow for sin and a sense
that he deserves God's anger, while he also begged God for mercy, a mercy available only
through Christ's sacrifice, for contrition "is described moreover by this reason, not a cause

the fall in the Garden of Eden and had been particularly "Revived" in the Law of Moses, even for the children of Israel, "these sacrifices were in them no way acceptable to G[od] in thems[elves] and upon their own Account."[151] So the preceding verse records, "For thou desirest not sacrifice; else would I give it: thou delightest not in burnt offering" (Ps 51:16).[152] David declares that God does not delight in legal sacrifices because he delights in what those sacrifices were typical of, namely "of [Christ] the Great sacrif[ice] & of spiritual sacrifices that the Godly man offers to G[od] viz...a broken sp[irit]."[153] The words of the text implied both that God accepts the sacrifice of a broken heart and that he will forgive even the greatest sins upon the offering of this sacrifice—"not that a broken H[eart] doth Expiate sin but tis the way to have the Benefit of [Christ's] Expiation."[154] So while rich and high men despise the lowly, the infinitely high God embraces the humble, penitent heart.[155] Thus

---

on account of which sins are remitted, which is only the death of Christ" ("Describitur autem hac ratione, non causa propter quam peccata remittantur, quae unica est mors Christi"). Poole, *Synopsis*, 834–835. Trapp noted that "such a person as with a self-condemning, self-crucifying, and sin-mortifying heart, humbly, and yet beleivingly [*sic*] maketh out for mercy and pardon in the blood of Christ, this, this is the man that God expects, accepts, and makes great account of." Trapp, *Commentary*, 725. Dickson similarly emphasized the gospel message: "The man who most renounceth his own works, worth, or merits, and despiseth all his own doings, as a broken earthen vessel is most acceptable in his approaches to God[']s free grace in the Mediatour...and that not for any worth in the matter of contrition, but because by contrition is expelled all conceit of self-worth, and so the man is most fit for receiving grace and free pardon from God." Dickson, *Other fifty Psalms*, 12. Calvin likewise observed from this passage that we can bring "nothing to God in the shape of compensation" but must rest our "whole dependence upon the satisfaction of Christ," for "the only way of obtaining the favour of God is by prostrating ourselves with a wounded heart at the feet of his Divine mercy." Calvin, *Commentary*, 2:304–306.

151. Jonathan Edwards, "275. Sermon on Ps 51:17 (March 1733)," in *Sermons, Series II, 1733*, vol. 48 of *WJEO*, L. 1r. Henry similarly said that God "had no *delight* in them [animal sacrifices] for any intrinsick Worth or Value they had." Henry, *Exposition*, [Ps 51:17]. Italics original.

152. Edwards also cited Ps 40:6 and many other "parallel places" that assert the insufficiency of ceremonial sacrifices. Edwards, "275. Sermon on Ps 51:17," L. 1r.

153. Edwards, "275. Sermon on Ps 51:17," L. 2r. Henry likewise reckoned these sacrifices as "Types of CHRIST." Henry, *Exposition*, [Ps 51:17].

154. Edwards, "275. Sermon on Ps 51:17," L. 2r. Henry echoed this gospel message: "The breaking of CHRIST's Body for Sin is the only Sacrifice of *Atonement*, for no Sacrifice but That could *take away Sin:* but the breaking of our Hearts for Sin is a Sacrifice of *Acknowledgement*," for "the broken Heart is acceptable to GOD only through JESUS CHRIST; there's no true repentance without Faith in Him." Henry, *Exposition*, [Ps 51:17]. Italics original.

155. Henry similarly said that "Men despise that which is broken, but GOD will not" and that the "proud Pharisee despised the broken-hearted Publican,...but God did not despise him." Henry, *Exposition*, [Ps 51:17].

Edwards preached the doctrine, "a broken H[eart] is an acceptable sacrifice to G[od]"[156]

Edwards went on to explain that a broken heart is a heart that has turned away from all creaturely helps; a heart that is wounded by a "Godly sorrow for sin" and grasps how excellent a being he has sinned against; "a sensible Tender Heart"; "a heart whose Pride is subdued & mortified & that is Graciously humbled"; and a heart "made Yieldable to G[od]."[157] This broken heart is properly called a sacrifice because it is "slain when tis thus Broken" and because it is "alwaies offered wholly & Entirely to G[od]."[158] A broken heart is acceptable to God because God looks not at outward appearances but at the soul, and a broken heart is the best disposition for abasing oneself and giving all the glory to God. In Edwards' description of the best sacrifices, he located them in the heart and united them with the evidence of holy practice.

Prayer

In his reading of the Psalms, Edwards also discussed the importance of prayer in the way true saints relate to God. He held that "[p]rayer is the expression of faith" from several Psalms (Pss 31:14–18; 32:6–7; 34:4–6; 57:1–2; 65:2; 71:1–7; 86:1–7; 91:15).[159] And he argued that God has ordained prayer to be a powerful agent in the outworking of his will: "The sincere and fervent prayers of God's people have that power to bring down spiritual showers; the prayers of God's people can call God down from heaven [and] cause him to 'bow the heavens and come down'" (Ps 144:5).[160]

In his engagement with the Psalms on prayer, Edwards emphasized that sin hinders prayers to God. He preached two distinct but similar sermons on Ps 66:18, "If I regard iniquity in my heart, the Lord will not hear me"—both

---

156. Edwards, "275. Sermon on Ps 51:17," L. 2v. Henry similarly emphasized "how acceptable true Repentance is to God," for it is "a Heart breaking with itself, and breaking from its Sin." Henry, *Exposition*, [Ps 51:17].

157. Edwards, "275. Sermon on Ps 51:17," L. 4v.–6v. Henry similarly described "a necessary Humiliation" and "a Heart subdu'd and brought into Obedience." Henry, *Exposition*, [Ps 51:17].

158. Edwards, "275. Sermon on Ps 51:17," L. 7r.

159. Edwards, "Harmony," 227, 228, 229, 240, 242, 246, 258. On Edwards' theology of prayer, see Peter Beck, *The Voice of Faith: Jonathan Edwards's Theology of Prayer* (Kitchener, ON: Joshua, 2010).

160. Jonathan Edwards, "The Dangers of Decline" (Rev 2:4–5), in *Sermons and Discourses 1730–1733*, ed. Mark Valeri, vol. 17 of *WJE* (1999), 98.

for public days of fasting, March 29, 1739, and April 12, 1744.[161] We focus our discussion on the first of these sermons. Edwards observed that Ps 66:18 teaches our "duty of Prayer," confirmed by the context of Ps 66:17–20, which speaks of crying out to God, of God attending to the psalmist's prayers, and of blessing God for not turning away from his prayers.[162] The "ill Qualification" for this duty of prayer is regarding iniquity in one's heart, which cannot refer to "the having of corrupt inclinations in the Heart" for "even the best of men have a principle of regard to sin in their hearts."[163] Regarding iniquity, then, is "the heart[']s consenting to it or the will[']s yielding to it & resting in it."[164] The consequence of willfully giving sin reign is that God will turn a deaf ear to our prayers. So Edwards preached this doctrine: "[']Tis in vain for any to expect to have their prayers heard as Long as they continue in the allowance of sin."[165] His discussion of prayer and what it means to regard sin in the heart, as described below, clearly mirrored the Reformed exegetical tradition.[166]

In fleshing out his doctrine, Edwards described what it means for God to hear prayer. First, it means that he accepts it, based largely on the person's posture of depending wholly on God. But second, it means that he answers it, which is manifested in two ways: (1) God gives some spiritual influences on the heart as a pledge to bestow future mercies in answer to the prayer, though people must beware that they do not confuse gut feelings with God's Spirit,

---

161. Jonathan Edwards, "507. Sermon on Ps 66:18(a) (March 29, 1739)," in *Sermons, Series II, 1739*, vol. 54 of *WJEO*; Jonathan Edwards, "736. Sermon on Ps 66:18(b) (April 12, 1744)," Beinecke Rare Book and Manuscript Library, Yale University, New Haven, CT.

162. Edwards, "507. Sermon on Ps 66:18(a)," L. 1r.

163. Edwards, "507. Sermon on Ps 66:18(a)," L. 1r.

164. Edwards, "507. Sermon on Ps 66:18(a)," L. 1r.

165. Edwards, "507. Sermon on Ps 66:18(a)," L. 1v.

166. Henry noted that "Iniquity regarded in the Heart will certainly spoil the Comfort and Success of Prayer," and he described this regard similarly to Edwards: "if I have favourable thoughts of it, if I love it, indulge it, and allow my self in it, if I treat it as a Friend and bid it welcome, make provision for it, and am loth to part with it, if I roll it under my Tongue as a sweet Morsel." Henry, *Exposition*, [Ps 66:18]. Poole described this regard of sin as looking on it "with approbation and affection" ("cum approbatione et affectu"), which renders such people hypocrites. Poole, *Synopsis*, 915. Trapp noted that "[h]e who chuseth to hold fast sin, doth, by his own election, forsake mercy." Trapp, *Commentary*, 755. Dickson stated that "[h]e is an upright man in God[']s accompt [i.e., account], who doth not entertain affection to any known sin." Dickson, *Other fifty Psalmes*, 95. Calvin described this regard of iniquity as being "bent upon the practice of iniquity," and he explained that "[w]hen the heart does not correspond to the outward conduct, and harbours any secret evil intent, the fair exterior appearance may deceive men; but it is an abomination in the sight of God." Calvin, *Commentary*, 2:478.

and (2) God answers prayer "by afterwards giving that mercy asked or something Equivalent"; in fact, "G[od] often times answer [*sic*] Prayer fully when the particular thing asked is not granted."[167] Having established what it means for God to hear prayer, Edwards described what is meant by allowing sin. Edwards recognized that, in some cases, people allow sin to reign in their heart's disposition, though outwardly they restrain themselves from sin because they fear punishment in hell—yet sin is still what they love most. In other cases, "they don[']t only allow sin in the Inward disposition of their hearts but they dare to Let it range abroad."[168] In his 1744 sermon, Edwards called this "an Habitual Predominant Love to sin & Choice of sin."[169] In either case, whether secretly cherishing sin or flagrantly disregarding any restraint on sin, no one should expect God to hear their prayers. Edwards believed that prayer was a powerful means of communicating with God that could lead him to bow the heavens and come down, but sin was a serious barrier to that relationship with God and had to be removed before a saint could expect God to act. Even then, the saint had to leave the answer in God's hands to deliver as he deemed best.

Conclusion

In this chapter we have observed Edwards' extensive discussion of Christian piety from the Psalms. The book of Psalms played a formative role in Edwards' own spirituality, and he believed it should do so in the lives of every Christian, arguing that true Christians make the words of the Psalms their very own language. He also believed the Psalter was the premier book in Scripture for describing religious affections, and thus he used the Psalms regularly as a guide for authentic Christian piety exhibited in Christian virtues and renewed ways of relating with humanity and with God, a piety arising from the gracious influence of the Holy Spirit that manifests itself in holy fruit.

This approach to the church in its individual members was largely in step with Edwards' Reformed predecessors. Like Edwards, the earlier exegetes discussed matters of Christian piety from the Psalms by expressing a concern for holy fruit that grows out of faith in Christ. Besides making a stronger emphasis on God's love from Ps 78:5–7 and applying Ps 133:1 to the broader society, we see little novelty in Edwards' discussion of piety using the Psalms.

---

167. Edwards, "507. Sermon on Ps 66:18(a)," L. 5v.

168. Edwards, "507. Sermon on Ps 66:18(a)," L. 7v.

169. Edwards, "736. Sermon on Ps 66:18(b)," L. 2r., 3r.

Edwards' extensive use of the Psalms to proclaim vital heart religion and Christian virtue shows us that he often read the Psalms quite plainly to mine their devotional value for Christian living. The high frequency with which he read the Psalms practically as they relate to Christian piety argues against any claim that confines him to a typological method of exegesis. Edwards engaged the Psalms for a variety of purposes, and one major purpose was to nurture the holy living of his people—a top priority throughout his ministry. In addition, the Psalms played a critical role not only in the weekly proclamation of faithful devotion to God but also in the fundamental way in which he understood holy affections and their connection to holy living. Again, we see that Edwards developed his theology through an extensive engagement with the Psalms.

All in all, the Psalms provided Edwards with an unending supply of insight into living the Christian life. He used the Psalms to nurture his personal piety and held that true believers will embrace the language of the Psalms as their very own because it models the proper affections of one whose heart has been reoriented by the Holy Spirit to love the things of God. The Psalms also described the holy fruit that issues from a regenerated heart, emerging in Christian virtues and transformed ways of relating with people and with God. For Edwards, the Psalms exhibited a model of authentic Christian piety for the redeemed church to display in its individual members.

7

Church and Eternity

The king's daughter is all glorious within:
her clothing is of wrought gold.
She shall be brought unto the king in raiment of needlework:
the virgins her companions that follow her
shall be brought unto thee.
With gladness and rejoicing shall they be brought:
they shall enter into the king's palace.
Psalm 45:13–15

EDWARDS WAS NOT merely interested in telling individual Christians to live
out the implications of their redemption in vital piety but also emphasized
that redemption is a corporate matter, and he used the Psalms to speak at
length about the church corporate, which he often described as the body of
Christ or the bride of Christ. His thinking on the church was also guided by
the teleological emphasis of his thought as he sought to work out the purpose
of all redemptive history, which is moving toward the end of the world and
the establishment of the new heavens and new earth. The Psalms, Edwards
showed, have much to teach us about what is to come.

In this chapter we see that Edwards interpreted the Psalms using typological, ecclesiological, and eschatological methods of exegesis. To the degree
that Edwards discussed the wicked and their eternal dwelling in hell, the term
"Christological" does not capture his engagement with the book of Psalms.
Rather, we see that some of the theological themes that Edwards discussed at
length in his career—the nature of the church, the end of the world, hell, and
heaven—were doctrines that he developed from his extensive engagement
with the book of Psalms. For Edwards the all-encompassing framework that
encapsulated these ideas was the history of redemption.

We first examine Edwards' understanding of the church in the Psalms
by discussing his ecclesiological interpretation of the Psalms as they portray Christ mystical and by describing his theology and practice of worship
from the Psalms. I also treat the imprecatory language in the Psalms in this

discussion on the church because Edwards portrayed David, in speaking these imprecations, as head of the church. In the second section we discuss the eternal hope of the church, from the advance of Christ's kingdom leading to the end of the world and culminating in future judgment for the wicked and future blessings for the saints.

The Church in the Psalms

Edwards' concept of the harmony of the Old and New Testament allowed him to describe the church as a corporate body in the Psalms.[1] Throughout his writings he spoke of Israel as the "Jewish church" because he saw great continuity between ancient Israel as the body of God's people and the Christian church as established after Christ's ascension. So as he came to the Psalms, it was no leap for him to identify the Christian church in the Old Testament, and in fact, he saw much in the Psalms that aided him in describing the church as "Christ mystical" and in defining proper modes of worship and praise. The harmony of the two testaments and Edwards' understanding of the church also helped him deal with the thorny interpretive problem of imprecatory language in the Psalms.

Christ Mystical

Edwards used the phrase "Christ mystical" to describe the church as the body of Christ with Christ as its head and also to describe the church as the bride of Christ, who is united with Christ. He applied the Psalms to the church throughout his corpus, and in his "Supplement to Prophecies of the Messiah" manuscript, Edwards made his clearest description of the church as Christ mystical:

> IN THE BOOK OF PSALMS in General the Psalmist speaks either in the Name of Christ or in the Name of the Church[.] And this is to be observed concerning a very great Part of this Book that the Psalmist speaks in the Name of Christ most comprehensively taken viz as including his Body or Members or in the Name of [Christ] mystical & even in some of those Psalms that seem to be the most direct and plain

---

1. On Edwards' ecclesiology, see Rhys S. Bezzant, *Jonathan Edwards and the Church* (New York: Oxford University Press, 2013); and Douglas A. Sweeney, "The Church," in *The Princeton Companion to Jonathan Edwards*, ed. Sang Hyun Lee (Princeton, NJ: Princeton University Press, 2005), 167–189.

Prophecies of [Christ,] some Parts of which are most applicable to the Head or [Christ] other Parts to the Body or the Church.[2]

Edwards based his argument in large part on the intermingling of singular and plural nouns and pronouns in a given psalm. That seeming confusion could be cleared up by explaining it as referencing the body, which could be discussed either as a singular whole or as its plural members. So, for example, in Psalm 25, the author prays earnestly for God's mercy to him as an individual but concludes in verse 22 with a singular pronoun to speak collectively of the nation, "Redeem Israel, O God, out of all his troubles." This final verse reveals that the writer "had been speaking as Head of the Ch[urc]h or that the Church it self had been speaking and not any particular Person or that the Prayer in this Psalm is uttered in the Name of the whole Body."[3] Edwards made similar observations on Psalms 3; 5; 22; 28; 40; 31; 64; 69; and 92.[4] In his "Prophecies of the Messiah" notebook, he stated this point succinctly: "because [in] most of the Psalms the Psalmist speaks in the name of the church or of Christ mystical, therefore in many of them the singular and plural numbers are used promiscuously."[5]

Edwards also made much of the psalmist speaking in the position of head of the church. He observed that in several psalms, the writer

> speaks as the Head of the People of God or one that had undertaken their Cause or led them in religious affairs whose Heart was most strictly united [to] them[,] whose Interest was the same with theirs and they most nearly concerned in his sufferings deliverance and Exaltation[.] And as one that was a Pattern of God[']s dealings with the righteous.[6]

From this observation about the psalmist's position, Edwards argued that several of the psalms should be read collectively as referring to the church.[7] To further

---

2. Jonathan Edwards, "Supplement to Prophecies of the Messiah," Franklin Trask Library, Andover Newton Theological School, Newton, MA. Edwards made a note at the beginning of his observations on the Psalms in his "Blank Bible" to see the "Supplement." Jonathan Edwards, *The "Blank Bible,"* ed. Stephen J. Stein, vol. 24, part 1 of *WJE* (2006), 475.

3. Edwards, "Supplement to Prophecies of the Messiah."

4. Edwards, "Supplement to Prophecies of the Messiah."

5. Jonathan Edwards, "The Miscellanies: Entry No. 1067: Prophecies of the Messiah," Franklin Trask Library, Andover Newton Theological School, Newton, MA, §60.

6. Edwards, "Supplement to Prophecies of the Messiah."

7. Edwards, "Supplement to Prophecies of the Messiah." The passages Edwards mentioned include Pss 7:7–8; 14:4; 16:1–3; 22:22–31; 25:2–3, 8–9, 12–14; 30:4; 34; 35:27; 40:3, 15–16;

support this idea, Edwards noted that the psalmist spoke as "a Publick Person either as Head of God[']s People or in the name of God[']s People" because he so regularly called them to praise God for his favor to his people.[8] Edwards even noted that several "whole Psalms are plainly & undeniably in the name of the Church," including Psalms 14; 33; 46; 47; 48; 53; 67; 68; 76; 85; 124; 125; 126; and 129.[9] In his "Prophecies" notebook he linked this observation to salvation. Whereas David, the king of Israel, often speaks in the Psalms "as head of the church and as he in whose interest the interest and salvation of God's people is involved," so in a similar manner, "it may be observed that in some psalms, where the church of God is represented speaking, she speaks of her king as her head, in whom all her interest is bound up, and in whose salvation, happiness and glory is their happiness and glory."[10] With a view toward Israel's purpose, the salvation of the elect, Edwards also made an extensive argument that when the Old Testament used names such as Jacob, Israel, Jerusalem, and Zion to identify the people who would live in the Messiah's kingdom, it intended the whole people of God, including both Jews and Gentiles.[11]

Edwards established the concept of "Christ mystical" in part by defining the encompassing boundaries of the godly in "Harmony of the Genius Spirit Doctrines and Rules of the Old Testament and the New." Speaking on Ps 4:3, "But know that the LORD hath set apart him that is godly for himself," Edwards saw evidence for an inclusive understanding of the church that held true in both testaments: "'Tis the godly, and not any particular whole nation, that God has separated from the rest of the world as his peculiar treasure."[12] Edwards continued this theme with eight other psalms as well.[13] This differentiation of

---

52:6; 59:11; 60:5; 63:11; 69:6, 31–36; 75:2–3; 89:1–5, 7, 15–20; 92; 108:6; 118:1–5, 21–29; 142:7; 144:13–15.

8. Edwards, "Supplement to Prophecies of the Messiah." Edwards mentioned Pss 9:14; 22:22–26; 26:7–12; 35:18; 40:9–10; 66:17; 109:30.

9. Edwards, "Supplement to Prophecies of the Messiah."

10. Edwards, "Prophecies of the Messiah," §60.

11. Edwards mentioned Pss 69:35–36; 22:22–23, 25–31; 24:1–4, 6; 47:9; 48:2; 50:5–7, 16; 96:6–10; 100; 102:21–22; 122:4. Jonathan Edwards, "The Miscellanies: Entry No. 1068: The Fulfillment of the Prophecies of the Messiah," Franklin Trask Library, Andover Newton Theological School, Newton, MA, §146.

12. Jonathan Edwards, "Harmony of the Genius Spirit Doctrines and Rules of the Old Testament and the New," Beinecke Rare Book and Manuscript Library, Yale University, New Haven, CT, 217.

13. The eight additional passages that Edwards mentioned include Pss 7:7; 14:5; 15; 22:22–23, 25–27; 24:3–6; 47:9; 69:36; 74:19. Edwards, "Harmony," 218, 220, 221, 224, 225, 235, 245,

the godly as a spiritual rather than a genetic status allowed Edwards to identify the church in the Psalms since the Psalms gave this broad definition. So he read from Ps 25:22, "Redeem Israel, O God, out of all his troubles," that the psalmist "speaks in the name of Christ or his church, or rather in the name of Christ mystical," which he does in "many of the psalms."[14] In Edwards' conception, Christ and the church are uniquely related, "for the church hath such an union and communion with Christ that almost all the same things that are predicated of Christ are also, in some sense, predicated of the church."[15] It was this mystical union of Christ and the church that promised the members of the body a hope of eternal life. Using Ps 16:10, "For thou wilt not leave my soul in hell; neither wilt thou suffer thine Holy One to see corruption," Edwards held out hope to Christians that "[w]hat came to pass with respect to the real body of Christ is what likewise comes to pass with respect to the church, the mystical body of Christ": while it "sometimes seems to be dead" and "is as it were hid in the grave," it will never be "wholly destroyed" but "shall come to life again."[16] Because of the unity of the Old and New Testaments, Edwards was able to use the Psalms to show the unity of Christ and the church, which established the true hope of Christians in God's work of redemption.

As Edwards engaged the Psalms from an ecclesiological viewpoint, he also employed typology to identify images in the Psalms with the church, such as a palm tree (Ps 92:12), "fruitful trees" (Ps 1:3), and a fountain (Ps 68:26).[17] He used the imagery of the Psalms primarily to describe the church's beauty, noting that "[u]nion is spoken of in Scripture as the peculiar beauty of the church of Christ," which agrees with Ps 122:3, "Jerusalem is builded as a city that is compact together."[18] He also described the beauty of the rainbow as a type of the beauty of the church using Pss 48:2; 50:2; and 122:3:

> The whole rainbow, composed of innumerable, shining, beautiful drops,
> all united in one, ranged in such excellent order, some parts higher and

250. See also Jonathan Edwards, "Christians a Chosen Generation" (1 Pet 2:9), in *Sermons and Discourses 1730–1733*, ed. Mark Valeri, vol. 17 of *WJE* (1999), 278–279, 285.

14. Edwards, *The "Blank Bible,"* 489–490. See also Edwards' comment on "Christ mystical" in Ps 72:6–7. Jonathan Edwards, *Notes on Scripture*, ed. Stephen J. Stein, vol. 15 of *WJE* (1998), 148–149.

15. Edwards, *Notes on Scripture*, 246.

16. Edwards, *The "Blank Bible,"* 483.

17. Jonathan Edwards, *Some Thoughts Concerning the Revival*, in *The Great Awakening*, ed. C. C. Goen, vol. 4 of *WJE* (1972), 318; Edwards, *Notes on Scripture*, 549.

18. Jonathan Edwards, *An Humble Attempt to Promote Explicit Agreement and Visible Union of God's People in Extraordinary Prayer for the Revival of Religion and the Advancement of Christ's*

others lower, the different colors, one above another in such exact order, beautifully represents the church of saints of different degrees, gifts, and offices, each with its proper place, and each with its peculiar beauty, each drop very beautiful in itself, but the whole as united together much more beautiful.[19]

While Edwards was often dissatisfied with the state of the visible church and sought to protect its purity, especially in the membership controversy that led to his dismissal, he did so because he believed the visible church ought to display the innate beauty of the invisible church. That is why, in his reading of Ps 50:2, "Out of Zion, the perfection of beauty, God hath shined," Edwards identified "the perfection of beauty" as a reference to the church.[20] He looked forward to a final purgation in Ps 68:14, "When the Almighty scattered kings in it, it was white as snow in Salmon," noting that when the church is delivered from the antichrist, "[t]o her shall be granted that she shall be clothed in fine linen, clean and white."[21]

Of all the passages in the Psalms that Edwards used to describe the church, Psalm 45 was the preeminent psalm. In Edwards' interpretation of the passage, he drew together themes already mentioned, including union and purity, and showed God's work of redemption as visible through the psalm. Edwards interpreted Psalm 45, the love song of the Psalms, in an ecclesiological sense, noting that the term "daughter" refers to "the church of Christ," which is here represented as "one holy person."[22] Edwards also pointed to Psalm 45 to show the Scripture's comparison of the "union and communion" between Christ and his church with that of a bridegroom and his bride; from this we know that for God's saints in heaven, "[t]here will be no restraint to his love" and "no restraint to their enjoyment of himself."[23] To experience this union, however,

Kingdom on Earth, Pursuant to Scripture-Promises and Prophecies Concerning the Last Time, in *Apocalyptic Writings*, ed. Stephen J. Stein, vol. 5 of *WJE* (1977), 365. See also Edwards' identification of Mount Zion as a type of the church. Edwards, *The "Blank Bible*," 504–505.

19. Edwards, *Notes on Scripture*, 331.

20. Jonathan Edwards, *The "Miscellanies": Entry Nos. a–z, aa–zz, 1–500*, ed. Thomas A. Schafer, vol. 13 of *WJE* (1994), 356.

21. Edwards, *The "Blank Bible*," 504.

22. Jonathan Edwards, *Original Sin*, ed. Clyde A. Holbrook, vol. 3 of *WJE* (1970), 368. Edwards likewise pointed to Pss 22:20; 35:17; 60:4–5; 74:19; 108:6; and 127:2, to give "confirmation" that the bride whom the Song of Solomon identifies as "'my love,' 'my dove,' 'my sister,' 'my spouse,' and the like" refers to "the church." Edwards, *Notes on Scripture*, 520.

23. Jonathan Edwards, *The "Miscellanies": Entry Nos. 501–832*, ed. Ava Chamberlain, vol. 18 of *WJE* (2000), 372. Edwards discussed Psalm 45 in this capacity alongside Psalm 21 and the Song of Solomon.

the church must first forsake her sin, and Edwards saw the church doing just that in Ps 45:10, "Hearken, O daughter, and consider, and incline thine ear; forget also thine own people, and thy father's house." As "[t]he spouse, in the 45th psalm, forgets her own people and father's house," so also "believers forsake sin and their lusts, that are natural to 'em, that they are born with, and are naturally dear to them...all for the sake of Christ."[24] Similarly, Ruth's story of forsaking her people for the God of Israel illustrates Ps 45:10 and "typifies the universal church, and the conversion of every believer," for "[w]e are all born in sin, as Ruth was born in Moab, and was born a Moabitess. A state of sin is as it were our father's house, and sinners are our own people. When we are converted, we forsake our own people and father's house, as the church in the 45th Psalm."[25] Here we see the process of salvation at work. Nature leaves us estranged from God, but when grace leads us away from sin, we are joined to Christ and transformed by his love.

The result of this grace is a God-given purity for the church. Psalm 45:13–14 says, "The king's daughter is all glorious within: her clothing is of wrought gold. She shall be brought unto the king in raiment of needlework." On the one hand, Edwards read "all glorious within" as a reference to both Moses' tabernacle and the church, both of mean external appearance but "inwardly beautiful and glorious."[26] On the other hand, he noted that this beautiful wedding garment, which denotes her purity, does not belong on the bodies of false professors, for "None, I suppose, will say, this righteousness that is so pure, is the common grace of lukewarm professors, and those that go about to serve God and Mammon."[27] Instead, the visible church should be set apart from the world.

24. Jonathan Edwards, "Apocalypse Series," in *Apocalyptic Writings*, ed. Stephen J. Stein, vol. 5 of *WJE* (1977), 132. See also Edwards' comment on Ps 45:10–11 identifying the bride's beauty with her "poverty of spirit." Edwards, *Notes on Scripture*, 520.

25. Edwards, *Notes on Scripture*, 85. See Edwards' similar comment on Ps 45:10 in "Ruth's Resolution" (Ruth 1:16), in *Sermons and Discourses 1734–1738*, ed. M. X. Lesser, vol. 19 of *WJE* (2001), 307. See also Edwards' parallel discussion of Ps 45:10–11 and Deut 21:11–13, where he identified God's instructions on the proper way for Jews to marry a woman taken captive in battle as "a type of the marriage of a soul to Christ," calling the soul an alien "captivated by divine grace...away from all the idols and enjoyments of its father's house and native country, to be espoused to Christ." Edwards, *The "Blank Bible,"* 298.

26. Edwards, *The "Blank Bible,"* 496.

27. Jonathan Edwards, *An Humble Inquiry into the Rules of the Word of God, Concerning the Qualifications Requisite to a Complete Standing and Full Communion in the Visible Christian Church*, in *Ecclesiastical Writings*, ed. David D. Hall, vol. 12 of *WJE* (1994), 230.

The church derives this purity from Christ, Edwards explained in a December 1743 sermon on Ps 45:9, "Kings' daughters were among thy honourable women: upon thy right hand did stand the queen in gold of Ophir." Edwards held that the church is represented by the queen and gains this honored appellation solely from "her [r]elation & union to so glorious a king."[28] Christ is this King of kings, appointed by the Father and promised a kingdom as heir of all things, and the church receives honor by association to this glorious king. The church is joined to him in marriage as a "partaker of his Royal glory & beauty," for there is "none so near & dear" to Christ than his bride, the church, and he "has shown more Love" to her than any other, even the angels.[29] Finally, the church's "clothing," described as "gold of Ophir," symbolizes its "preciousness," "Purity," and "beauty & lustre."[30] But this clothing is not her own. The glory is all Christ's, yet he shares it with his church, and so this gold clothing represents "the preciousness[,] beauty & glory of the clothing she ever has in her imputed & inherent righ[teousness]."[31]

For Edwards Psalm 45 exhibited God's redemptive work in his church, taking her out of sin by his grace, uniting her with Christ, and bestowing upon her his righteousness, all for the glory of Christ—an interpretation clearly in step with his Reformed predecessors.[32] Edwards' ecclesiological interpretation

---

28. Jonathan Edwards, "727. Sermon on Ps 45:9 (Dec. 1743)," Beinecke Rare Book and Manuscript Library, Yale University, New Haven, CT, L. 1r. We have only a fragment of this sermon; the "application" section is missing from the extant manuscript.

29. Edwards, "727. Sermon on Ps 45:9," L. 2r., 3r.–3v.

30. Edwards, "727. Sermon on Ps 45:9," L. 4v.

31. Edwards, "727. Sermon on Ps 45:9," L. 4v.

32. Henry, Poole, Trapp, Dickson, and Calvin all interpreted this passage as a reference to the mystical marriage of Christ and the church, and they drew the same comparison between the daughter leaving her father's house and sinners leaving their former ways of sin to be joined to Christ. Trapp also explicitly recognized that the church's members are "adorned not with their own proper attire" but "out of the King Christ[']s Wardrobe" (John Trapp, *A Commentary or Exposition Upon the Books of Ezra, Nehemiah, Esther, Job, and Psalms...*(London: T. R. and E. M. for Thomas Newberry..., 1657), 702–705. Quotation on 704. And Dickson described the church as one who receives the ornaments of "adoption, justification, sanctification" from Christ who has brought about her "redemption." David Dickson, *A Brief Explication of the first Fifty Psalms* (London: T. M. for Ralph Smith..., 1652), 303, 309–312. Quotation on 309–310. Matthew Henry, *An exposition of the five poetical books of the Old Testament; viz. Job, Psalms, Proverbs, Ecclesiastes, and Solomon's song...*(London: T. Darrack..., 1710), [Ps 45:9–15]; Matthew Poole, *Synopsis Criticorum Aliorumque Sacrae Scripturae Interpretum et Commentarum, Summo Studio et Fide Adornata, vol. II: Complectens Libros Jobi, Psalmorum, Proverbiorum, Ecclesiastis, & Cantici Canticorum* (Francofurti ad Moenum: Balthasaris Christophori Wustii, 1678), 788, 798–801; John Calvin, *Commentary*

of the Psalms displayed his typological exegesis within the overarching framework of the history of redemption.

Worship in the Church of God

In reflecting on the church in the Psalms, Edwards not only described it theologically as Christ mystical but also attended to the practical worship of God's people. We have already discussed Edwards' use of the Psalms in worship within the long history of the Psalter as the church's primary songbook in chapter 1. Here we examine how the Psalms themselves informed Edwards' theology of corporate worship.

As Edwards engaged the Psalms, he saw guidance for the proper approach to Sabbath observance and worship.[33] He strictly practiced Sabbath worship with his own family, singing a psalm to initiate family worship on Saturday evening "as an introduction to the sanctifying of the Sabbath."[34] He was also concerned that people treat the Lord's day with proper respect, largely because it represented so great a salvation. Thus much of his discussion about the Sabbath from the Psalms centered on a defense of Sunday, the day Christ redeemed his people, thus replacing the Jewish Sabbath. As Ps 81:1–7 shows that the "Israelites in all their solemn feasts were to remember and praise God for their redemption out of Egypt," Edwards argued, "[h]ow much more should Christians commemorate that infinitely greater redemption of Jesus Christ, of which the other was but a shadow, by keeping a holy day."[35] He added this observation on Psalm 92: "That the main design of the sabbath is to commemorate and celebrate God's works of mercy and salvation from enemies is manifest by the 92nd Psalm."[36] Psalm

---

on the Psalms, trans. from the Original Latin and Collated with the Author's French Version by James Anderson (1843–1855; repr., Grand Rapids, MI: Eerdmans, 1963), 2:173, 184–192.

33. He also defended his positions on the sacraments from the Psalms. On his defense of a closed communion table from Ps 26:4–5, see Edwards, *An Humble Inquiry*, 309. On his defense of infant baptism using Ps 22:10, see Edwards, *The "Blank Bible,"* 485.

34. Samuel Hopkins explained that Edwards conducted family worship every Saturday evening since he followed the Jewish accounting of days, starting each new day on sundown of the day before. Samuel Hopkins, *The Life and Character of the Late Reverend, Learned, and Pious Mr. Jonathan Edwards* (Northampton, MA: Andrew Wright, 1804), 47. He also used this time to teach his children the *Westminster Shorter Catechism.* Douglas A. Sweeney, *Jonathan Edwards and the Ministry of the Word: A Model of Faith and Thought* (Downers Grove, IL: IVP Academic, 2009), 65.

35. Jonathan Edwards, *The "Miscellanies": Entry Nos. 1153–1360*, ed. Douglas A. Sweeney, vol. 23 of *WJE* (2004), 131.

36. Edwards, *The "Miscellanies": Entry Nos. 1153–1360*, 131. See Edwards' similar comment in "Miscellanies" Entry No. 920, "Lord's Day," where he argued from Psalm 92 that "the

92:4 also showed that "the Jewish sabbath was a day of rejoicing," as it reads, "For thou, LORD, hast made me glad through thy work"; in like manner, Edwards expected Christians to treat the Sabbath as a joyful day remembering Christ's redemption—the greatest joy-giving event in history.[37]

Edwards furthered this thinking in his sermon, "Perpetuity and Change of the Sabbath," in which he devoted one of his fourteen points to Ps 118:22–24, "The stone which the builders refused is become the head stone of the corner. This is the LORD's doing; it is marvellous in our eyes. This is the day which the LORD hath made; we will rejoice and be glad in it." These verses instruct the church, he explained, to celebrate the day of Christ's resurrection with holy joy. The "stone" is Christ, and its rejection images his death, while the making of the cornerstone refers to his exaltation, beginning with his resurrection. Thus, "[w]hile Christ lay in the grave, then he lay as a stone cast by the builders; but when God raised him from the dead, then he became the head of the corner."[38] The application of this passage to Christ in Acts 4:10–11 gave Edwards further grounds for his interpretation, and he concluded that God made the day of Christ's resurrection "to be the day of the rejoicing of the church."[39] In this approach, Edwards stood firmly in line with Reformed exegesis.[40]

---

sabbath was always kept as a day of rejoicing, and in commemoration of God's wise, deep, mysterious and wonderful works of mercy and salvation towards his people." Jonathan Edwards, The "Miscellanies": Entry Nos. 833–1152, ed. Amy Plantinga Pauw, vol. 20 of WJE (2002), 167.

37. Edwards, The "Miscellanies": Entry Nos. 501–832, 392. See also his argument from Ps 111:4 that Christ's resurrection made Sunday holy. Edwards, The "Miscellanies": Entry Nos. 1153–1360, 235.

38. Jonathan Edwards, "Perpetuity and Change of the Sabbath" (1 Cor 16:1–2), in Sermons and Discourses 1730–1733, ed. Mark Valeri, vol. 17 of WJE (1999), 238.

39. Edwards, "Perpetuity and Change of the Sabbath," 238. See Edwards' similar discussion of Ps 118:22–24 in "Miscellanies" Entry No. 1051, "THE LORD'S DAY." Edwards, The "Miscellanies": Entry Nos. 833–1152, 392.

40. Henry, Poole, Trapp, Dickson, and Calvin all identified Christ from this passage, and while Dickson and Calvin did not explicitly link the day of rejoicing with the Christian Sabbath, Dickson connected it to Christ's resurrection and Calvin to Christ's "redemption of the Church." David Dickson, A Brief Explication of the last Fifty Psalms, From Ps. 100 to the end (London: T. R. and E. M. for Ralph Smith..., 1654), 157; Calvin, Commentary, 4:388–396. Quotation on 392. Henry, Poole, and Trapp all made explicit links to the Christian Sabbath based on Christ's resurrection and redemption. Henry argued that this passage speaks of the "Christian Sabbath, which we sanctifie in remembrance of CHRIST's Resurrection," for God made this day marvelous because "the Redemption he wrought out is the most amazing of all GOD's Works of Wonder." Henry, Exposition, [Ps 118:22–24]. Poole interpreted the day of rejoicing as "certainly the Lord's day, sanctified by the resurrection of Christ" ("nempe dominicus, resurrectione Christi sanctificatus"). Poole, Synopsis, 1201–1202. Quotation on 1202.

Edwards also had much to say about how the Psalms inform our praise of God as the church gathers for public worship.[41] At the foundation of his thinking was his belief that the salvation described in the Psalter is the same salvation offered in the New Testament. The book of Psalms contains "the language of Christ and the Christian church," as evidenced by the use of the Psalms both in the New Testament and "in the public worship in Christian assemblies, from the beginning of the Christian church."[42] Because God appointed the Psalter as the church's songbook, "the qualifications of the godly, and the way of their acceptance with God, and admission to his favor, and the fruits of it, are the same now under the Christian dispensation, as of old in David's time."[43] In fact, the Psalms served as "a glorious advancement of the affair of redemption as God hereby gave his church a book of divine songs for their use in that part of their public worship, viz. singing his praises throughout all ages to the end of the world."[44] Edwards traced their use in the Bible from David through the early church (Eph 5:19; Col 3:16) and showed that "they have been and will to the end of the world" be used in Christian worship, for they extol God and further his gospel.[45] As David Music observes, for Edwards singing was "a means of expressing the gospel" and thus was "an integral part of the renewal experience."[46]

Trapp identified this day of rejoicing with "the Christian Sabbath" or "the day of salvation by Christ exalted to bee the head-corner-stone," for "the great work of man[']s Redemption by Christ" is "especially" marvelous. Trapp, *Commentary*, 875.

41. Though practices varied by location, the order of worship in the New England Puritan tradition generally included two times of psalm singing, and Puritans gathered twice on Sunday for about three hours each time and once at a midweek service. Charles E. Hambrick-Stowe, *The Practice of Piety: Puritan Devotional Disciplines in Seventeenth-Century New England* (Chapel Hill: University of North Carolina, 1982), 96–100. See also Allen Carden, *Puritan Christianity in America: Religion and Life in Seventeenth-Century Massachusetts* (Grand Rapids, MI: Baker Book House, 1990), 115–117. On the strict observance of the Sabbath and its impact on seventeenth- and early eighteenth-century America, see Winton U. Solberg, *Redeem the Time: The Puritan Sabbath in Early America*, A Publication of the Center for the Study of the History of Liberty in America (Cambridge, MA: Harvard University Press, 1977). On Edwards' approach to congregational singing, see David W. Music, "Jonathan Edwards and the Theology and Practice of Congregational Song in Puritan New England," *Studies in Puritan American Spirituality* 8 (2004): 103–133.

42. Edwards, *The "Miscellanies": Entry Nos. 833–1152*, 116.

43. Edwards, *The "Miscellanies": Entry Nos. 833–1152*, 116.

44. Jonathan Edwards, *A History of the Work of Redemption*, ed. John F. Wilson, vol. 9 of *WJE* (1989), 211.

45. Edwards, *A History of the Work of Redemption*, 211.

46. Music, "Jonathan Edwards and the Theology and Practice of Congregational Song," 117.

The Psalms teach, in fact, that forgiveness precedes worship and that worship is in vain without forgiveness. As Ps 130:4 reads, "But there is forgiveness with thee, that thou mayest be feared," so "[i]f there was no forgiveness with God, it would be in vain for us to pretend to worship God, for the guilt of past sins and the sinful imperfections of our present worship would effectually prevent all acceptance."[47] On the other hand, true grace should issue in a strong delight in the external duties of religion: praying to God (Ps 55:17); singing praises to God (Pss 135:3; 147:1); hearing the Word of God preached as a joyful sound (Ps 89:15); and loving God's public worship (Pss 26:8; 27:4; 84:1–7, 10).[48] Sincerity ought to mark the worship of the visible church, for as both Pss 111:1 and 149:1 speak of people praising the Lord in the congregation, so it is "beautiful and becoming...for a congregation, a multitude, to join together in sincerely praising and magnifying the Most High God."[49] Gracious influences would engender a love for singing praise to God.

To nurture an appropriate posture in worship, Edwards preached on praising God from the Psalms, as he did in a November 10, 1726, sermon on Ps 147:1, "Praise ye the Lord: for it is good to sing praises unto our God; for it is pleasant; and praise is comely." In reflecting on this text, Edwards turned his thoughts to David, "the sweet psalmist of Israel" (2 Sam 23:1), and his role as a head worshipper of God. He "spent his life very much in God's praises," which led to the collection of the Psalms being "used ever since in the church."[50] The text of the sermon gives three reasons for David's diligence in praising God. First, it is "good" to praise God: "We are not to look upon that time lost that 'tis spent in worshipping God and magnifying him," for "[w]e cannot spend time better for our souls" as it "doth good to the heart in that manner to be

---

47. Edwards, The "Blank Bible," 535.

48. Jonathan Edwards, Religious Affections, ed. John E. Smith, vol. 2 of WJE (1959), 163–164. Edwards' emphasis on delight in worship duties from the Psalms supports Ted Rivera's argument that Edwards was ultimately concerned with heart worship, not external worship. Ted Rivera, Jonathan Edwards on Worship: Public and Private Devotion to God (Eugene, OR: Pickwick, 2010), 16.

49. Jonathan Edwards, "God Amongst His People" (Isa 12:6), in Sermons and Discourses 1734–1738, ed. M. X. Lesser, vol. 19 of WJE (2001), 470.

50. Jonathan Edwards, "It's a Very Decent and Comely Thing That Praise Should Be Given to God" (Ps 147:1), in The Glory and Honor of God: Volume 2 of the Previously Unpublished Sermons of Jonathan Edwards, ed. Michael D. McMullen (Nashville, TN: Broadman & Holman, 2004), 121–122. See also Edwards' sermon on Ps 33:1, in which he described the duty of praise, which is the "expression of Love[,] Joy & admiration in a sense of God[']s excellency & mercy." Jonathan Edwards, "112. Sermon on Ps 33:1 (Summer–Fall 1729)," in Sermons, Series II, 1729, vol. 44 of WJEO, L. 1r.–1v.

lifted up unto God."[51] Second, praising God is pleasant, for "the pleasures of this approach, the nearest of any to the joys of heaven."[52] And third, praising God is "a comely and amiable thing."[53] While many people will do something merely because it is profitable, pleasurable, or becoming, praising God consists in all three characteristics to a high degree. In his doctrine Edwards considered "wherein God's praise consists."[54] He defined "praise" as "an expression of a magnifying and exalting sense of God's greatness and goodness," for praising God's greatness is empty unless the worshipper "is affected with a sense of God's glory and grace."[55] People are to praise God both for his greatness, or the "infinite perfections" of his nature, and for his goodness, or his divine perfection "as it is exerted towards us."[56] So Edwards applied the doctrine by noting that "all such as have a discerning of spiritual beauties and excellencies will delight in praising God."[57] While Edwards' interpretation mirrored the exegesis of earlier Reformed interpreters, he stood out by connecting delight in praise with the fruit of God's gracious influence.[58] For Edwards, the supernatural grace bestowed on the elect would cause them to find enjoyment in praising God. So in a May 1752 sermon on Ps 84:10, he similarly exhorted his people not to "neglect to come to the House of G[od]" and not to "stay at home" on the Sabbath but to "worship in a right manner."[59]

---

51. Edwards, "It's a Very Decent and Comely Thing,"122.

52. Edwards, "It's a Very Decent and Comely Thing,"122.

53. Edwards, "It's a Very Decent and Comely Thing,"123.

54. Edwards, "It's a Very Decent and Comely Thing,"123.

55. Edwards, "It's a Very Decent and Comely Thing,"123.

56. Edwards, "It's a Very Decent and Comely Thing,"126.

57. Edwards, "It's a Very Decent and Comely Thing," 129.

58. Henry similarly interpreted this verse as describing our "Duty" of praising God, for it is good for us in that it is pleasant to the saints and becoming of those in covenant with God. Henry, *Exposition*, [Ps 147:1]. Poole noted that we must not be lacking in this duty of praise. Rather, it is "good" in that it is "beneficial in the highest degree" ("summe proficuum"); it is "pleasant" in that it is "sweet" (*"dulce"*); and it is "comely" in that it is "fitting" (*"decorum"*) or "decent" (*"decens"*). Poole, *Synopsis*, 1324. Italics in original. Trapp merely referred readers to his note on Ps 103:1. Trapp, *Commentary*, 831, 923. Dickson highlighted praise as the central aspect of worship and described these three motives as to "the believer[']s advantage" ("good"), "full of sweet refreshment" ("pleasant"), and *"honourable"* ("comely"). Dickson, *Last Fifty Psalmes*, 360. Calvin explained that the psalmist calls praise "good" and "pleasant" to motivate the church to "address itself to the praises of God with more alacrity," and "comely" to "teach men to take a delight in this religious exercise." Calvin, *Commentary*, 5:292.

59. Jonathan Edwards, "1038. Sermon on Ps 84:10 (May 1752)," Beinecke Rare Book and Manuscript Library, Yale University, New Haven, CT, L. 2v. In this sermon, Edwards preached

Edwards believed the Psalms provided a model of right worship and praise, especially for the church of God as it gathers together from Sabbath to Sabbath. It gathers as the church visible, and its Sabbath praise should be marked by sincerity and heartfelt devotion from a sense of God's greatness and goodness and especially because of the redemptive work of Christ on its behalf. Sunday is the new Sabbath because it commemorates the day when Christ secured redemption for his people. In light of God's grace and redemption, Edwards called all saints to delight in the praise of God.

Imprecatory Psalms

As Edwards' church gathered to sing the Psalms, they sang some of the most difficult passages to interpret in Scripture—the imprecatory psalms, pleas where the psalmist asks God to exact vengeance or inflict violence on his enemies. Since Edwards believed that David spoke as the head of the church in many of the psalms, this belief raised the question: In what way should the church appropriate the Psalter's imprecatory language? While some have chalked up imprecatory language to mere spite, Edwards regarded it not as personal vengeance but as a corporate matter for the church and as prophetic of both historical events and spiritual realities within God's plan of redemption. And he tempered these observations with love for one's enemies and hope for their repentance under the gospel.

Edwards on Imprecatory Language

Edwards' made his most extensive treatment of the imprecatory psalms in "Miscellanies" Entry No. 640, "LOVE OF ENEMIES. PRAYING AGAINST THEM," in which he made seven observations about David's imprecatory prayers against enemies. This entry provides a distillation of his multifaceted approach to the imprecatory language in the Psalms, though other passages in his corpus round out his treatment of the topic. First, Edwards denied that the psalmist expresses personal vengeance but held that he must hope for his enemies' conversion: "unless speaking in the name of the Lord, he is not to be understood as praying against any particular persons, that God would indeed execute

---

the doctrine, "a day spent in the House of G[od] in a right manner is beter than a Thous[and] spent in sin in the Enjoym[en]t of the things of the [world]." Edwards, "1038. Sermon on Ps 84:10," L. 1r. See also Edwards' sermon to the Stockbridge Indians on Ps 145:15–21, in which he preached the doctrine, "all Crea[tures] in H[eaven] & Earth have all their good things from G[od]" and charged his people to consider that "you are made to glorify G[od]." Jonathan Edwards, "1096. Sermon on Ps 145:15–21 (November 1, 1753)," Beinecke Rare Book and Manuscript Library, Yale University, New Haven, CT, L. 1r.

vengeance on such and such men, or that he did not desire that they should repent," for "David can be understood only as praying against his enemies continuing his enemies."[60] This point emerged as he sought to harmonize these imprecations with the injunction to love one's enemies, reading these psalms in light of the whole Bible so as to reflect the harmony of the Old and New Testaments. In "Miscellanies" Entry No. 600, Edwards explained that the Old Testament did not permit imprecations of personal vengeance and hatred against one's enemies but that prophets spoke these imprecations in the name of the Lord. And so, Edwards explained, "[w]e can't think that those imprecations we find in the Psalms and prophets were out of their own hearts, for cursing is spoken of as a very dreadful sin in the Old Testament."[61] Looking at David, although he prayed for vengeance on enemies more often than any others, "by the history of his life [he] was a man of a spirit very remote from a spiteful, revengeful spirit."[62] Edwards pointed to David's response to the deaths of Saul, Ishbosheth, and Abner—all enemies whom David mourned—and he showed that David even wished well on his enemies, did good to them (Ps 7:4), and prayed for them (Ps 35:13–14). When he cursed others, David was "far from a revengeful frame."[63] This discussion showed that "there is no inconsistence between the religion of the old testament and new in this respect."[64]

The second point Edwards made was that these psalms uphold God's justice. While David showed himself to be "wholly innocent and righteous," his enemies sought after his very life and proved themselves to be "all wicked men," indicating that a standard of righteousness does indeed apply to mankind.[65] This point comes in Edwards' treatment of perhaps the most notorious imprecatory verse in the Psalms, Ps 137:9, "Happy shall he be, that taketh and dasheth thy little ones against the stones." At the outset, Edwards noted that in this passage—and in the many passages describing the destruction of infants, such as in Sodom, the flood, Canaan, Egypt, Midian, Amalek, and Edom—we see God's burning anger toward sin, amplified by directing it even toward

---

60. Edwards, *The "Miscellanies": Entry Nos. 501–832*, 174.

61. Edwards, *The "Miscellanies": Entry Nos. 501–832*, 141.

62. Edwards, *The "Miscellanies": Entry Nos. 501–832*, 141.

63. Edwards, *The "Miscellanies": Entry Nos. 501–832*, 142.

64. Edwards, *The "Miscellanies": Entry Nos. 501–832*, 141. See also Edwards' use of the analogy of Scripture, pointing to Job 31:29–30, to make the same point. Edwards, *The "Blank Bible*," 458–459.

65. Edwards, *The "Miscellanies": Entry Nos. 501–832*, 174.

infants. He argued that since death is accompanied by a ghastly appearance, it "naturally suggests to our minds God's awful displeasure" and is peculiarly "a testimony of God's displeasure for sin."[66] In light of that observation, Edwards suggested that this verse supports the doctrine of original sin and children's "just exposedness to divine wrath": "We may well argue from these things, that infants are not looked upon by God as sinless, but that they are by nature children of wrath, seeing this terrible evil comes so heavily on mankind in infancy."[67]

In his "Blank Bible," Edwards explored the historical background of the verse to illustrate how it denounces sin. He read it in context with verse 8, "O daughter of Babylon, who art to be destroyed; happy shall he be, that rewardeth thee as thou hast served us." Thus Edwards argued that the passage refers historically to the dashing of Babylonian children against stones when Cyrus took the city and when the prophecy against Babylon in Isa 47:9 was fulfilled: "But these two things shall come to thee in a moment in one day, the loss of children, and widowhood: they shall come upon thee in their perfection for the multitude of thy sorceries, and for the great abundance of thine enchantments." For this historical background, Edwards relied on Humphrey Prideaux (1648–1724), who explained that when the city of Babylon was sieged by Darius, the Babylonians took "the most desperate and barbarous" measures to stay alive by killing "all unnecessary Mouths," "whether wives, sisters, daughters, or young children useless for the wars."[68] Edwards turned to the best historical scholarship in his day to show that this horrific sight could be explained by the horrendous wickedness of the Babylonians, whom God justly punished for their heinous evil. In Edwards' view, a discussion of the imprecatory psalms could not omit God's righteous judgment of sin.

Third, Edwards argued from the logic of divine election. David's enemies were a group of "exceedingly hardened and very implacable" men, and since they were a multitude, he "could not expect that they would all repent and be appeased."[69] This observation showed that love for enemies is not inconsistent

---

66. Edwards, *Original Sin*, 215. Edwards incorrectly cited Ps 137:4 in the text of his treatise but quoted verse 9. His quotation, "Happy shall he be that shall take thy little ones, and dash them against the stones," differs in word order from the KJV, likely indicating that Edwards was working from memory.

67. Edwards, *Original Sin*, 215–216.

68. Humphrey Prideaux, *The Old and New Testament Connected in the History of the Jews and Neighbouring Nations from the Declension of the Kingdoms of Israel and Judah to the Time of Christ*, 9th ed., part 1, vol. 1 (R. Knaplock in St. Paul's Church-Yard, and J. Tonson in the Strand, 1725), 265.

69. Edwards, *The "Miscellanies": Entry Nos. 501–832*, 174.

with prayers against them. And just as David prayed against his enemies "as a prophet in the name of the Lord," so Edwards extended the practice of praying against enemies to the church in his own day: "'tis not unlawful for the people of God, as the case may be, whether they speak as prophets or no, to pray *in general* that God would appear on their side, and plead and vindicate their cause, and punish those wicked men that are entirely and impenitently and implacably their enemies, in a righteous cause," for

> making such a prayer is not inconsistent with the love of *particular* persons, and earnestly desiring that they might repent and be appeased and be forgiven. For when our entire and resolved enemies are a multitude or some great party or combination of wicked men, we have no reason to expect that they will all repent and be reconciled. Especially is it not unsuitable thus to pray against our enemies, if the cause wherein they are our enemies is the cause of God, so that in being our enemies they are also directly God's enemies; and more especially still, if the enemies are public enemies and are enemies in God's cause too, and we pray against them as interested in the public. For here love to men don't only not hinder our praying for the punishment of our implacable enemies, but it inclines us to it, viz. our love to the public, to the people of God that we are chiefly obliged to love and should love more than wicked men; yea, and love to God too, as 'tis in the cause of God.[70]

In Edwards' ethics, love to "Being in general" required a love for the greatest good of society, and thus it was not wrong to pray against enemies—all the while hoping that they might repent and be reconciled.[71] But no one would expect that every enemy would answer the gospel call, so Edwards believed this difficult tension could be maintained by praying at the same time for repentance and, if a person refused to relent, for judgment.

Fourth, Edwards noted that David's cause was God's righteous cause, so he "prays against them not merely as his own, but as God's enemies."[72] In interpreting Ps 137:9, Edwards not only noted the historical background but also went beyond "literal Babylon" to the destruction of "spiritual Babylon." He explained, "They indeed will do God's work, and will perform a good work,

---

70. Edwards, *The "Miscellanies": Entry Nos. 501–832*, 173. Italics mine.

71. On Edwards' notion of "Being in general," see Jonathan Edwards, *Dissertation II: The Nature of True Virtue*, in *Ethical Writings*, ed. Paul Ramsey, vol. 8 of *WJE* (1989), 536–627.

72. Edwards, *The "Miscellanies": Entry Nos. 501–832*, 174.

who shall be God's instruments of the utter overthrow of the Church of Rome with all her superstitions, and heathenish ceremonies, and other cursed fruits of her spiritual whoredoms, as it were without having any mercy upon them."[73] In this way, Edwards interpreted the verse within the framework of the history of redemption, ultimately understanding it as describing the destruction of the greatest enemy to God's work. In another setting, Edwards saw in Ps 137:9 a reward of blessing for those who destroyed spiritual enemies: "what a blessing is pronounced on those which shall have any hand in the destruction of Babylon, which was the head city of the kingdom of Satan, and of the enemies of the church of God?"[74] Said another way, David and Christians are on the side of God and good, which justifies their posture toward the rebellious enemies of God.

Edwards' fifth and sixth points together showed that David must be understood as praying on behalf of the corporate body of God's people. In his fifth point, he noted that David prayed "as a public and not a private person," as "the head of the church and people of God" praying against "public enemies, enemies to the people of God, as in joint interest with them."[75] And in his sixth point he observed that, except when he cursed his enemies in the name of the Lord, David prayed not for the sake of their hurt but rather "as necessary for his own deliverance and safety, and the safety of God's people, and of religion itself, and for the vindication of his and their cause, and also of God's own cause."[76] For Edwards, there is a corporate element to David's prayers that makes their pleas more viable and palatable.

The historical books shed light on this point. One would expect that if David, who had written most of the imprecatory psalms, wanted to exact vengeance on Saul, he would have danced at his death. But David's response to Saul's death in 2 Sam 1:11–17 was to lament, indicating that his imprecatory statements in the book of Psalms were not tainted with hatred but derived from divine inspiration against God's enemies. For they "are not the expressions of a spirit of private revenge, but imprecations he put up in the name of Christ as head of the church against his and his church's enemies, and what he spake as a prophet in the name of the Lord."[77] Commenting on Ps 59:13,

---

73. Edwards, The "Blank Bible," 537.

74. Edwards, Some Thoughts, 369.

75. Edwards, The "Miscellanies": Entry Nos. 501–832, 174.

76. Edwards, The "Miscellanies": Entry Nos. 501–832, 175.

77. Edwards, The "Blank Bible," 360. Edwards cited this entry in his "Blank Bible" entry on Ps 69:22–28. Edwards, The "Blank Bible," 507.

"Consume them in wrath, consume them, that they may not be: and let them know that God ruleth in Jacob unto the ends of the earth," Edwards recognized that the occasion of David's prayer may have been "from the malice of his personal enemies, yet that the enemies he has respect to in his prayer are principally not those personal enemies that give the occasion of his prayer, but they are the enemies of the church of Christ."[78] Here Edwards gave credence to David's circumstances but redeemed him from sinful utterances by showing that the Spirit spoke through him of the church's enemies, for David identified his enemies as the "heathen" (Ps 59:5, 8), and spoke "as the head of the church and in the person of Christ, of whom he was the great type."[79]

Edwards' seventh point was to identify David's imprecatory statements as prophecies—an argument alluded to earlier: "'Tis questionable whether David ever prayed against his enemies, but as a prophet speaking in the name of the Lord. 'Tis evident by the matter of the Psalms that very frequently it was so."[80] Edwards stated in his "Notes on Scripture" notebook that "[w]hen we find passages of this kind in the Psalms or the Prophets, we are to look upon them as prophetical curses. They curse them in the name of the Lord, as Elisha did the children that mocked him, as Noah cursed Canaan."[81] In "Miscellanies" Entry No. 1033, "IMPRECATIONS OF THE OLD TESTAMENT," Edwards said it is "evident to anyone that carefully considers them" that "the imprecations that we have in the Psalms are what inspired persons uttered as prophets, and that they are a kind of prophecies."[82] Edwards then pointed to eight passages in the psalms where the imprecations are "mixed with express predictions of the destruction imprecated," which suggested that the psalmist spoke imprecations as prophecies in line with the psalm's explicit prophecies.[83] By comparing imprecations from the Psalms with other Old Testament imprecations (Gen 27:28–29; Deut 33:6–8, 24; Judg 9:20), Edwards noted, "It was an ancient way of prophecy to prophesy of future blessings and calamities in the language of prayer or

---

78. Edwards, *The "Blank Bible,"* 501.

79. Edwards, *The "Blank Bible,"* 501. Ps 59:5, 8 read, "Thou therefore, O LORD God of hosts, the God of Israel, awake to visit all the heathen: be not merciful to any wicked transgressors. Selah.... But thou, O LORD, shalt laugh at them; thou shalt have all the heathen in derision."

80. Edwards, *The "Miscellanies": Entry Nos. 501–832,* 175.

81. Edwards made this note in "Notes on Scripture" Entry No. 176, reflecting on Jer 12:3. Edwards, *Notes on Scripture,* 103. He also cited "Miscellanies" Entry No. 600, discussed below.

82. Edwards, *The "Miscellanies": Entry Nos. 833–1152,* 370.

83. Edwards, *The "Miscellanies": Entry Nos. 833–1152,* 370. The eight passages Edwards mentioned were Pss 5:6–12; 6:8–10; 7:6–17; 9:3–6; 10:15–18; 59:8–11; 69:22–36; 129:4–8.

petition."[84] Edwards did not drop the prayer aspect of the imprecations but joined it with a prophetic element. He also envisioned these prophecies as both calamities for the wicked and blessings for the righteous, for God would act both for his glory and for justice.[85]

Edwards further described the prophetic element of the imprecatory psalms in a discussion of Ps 58:6–10, which reads, [in part,] "Break their teeth, O God, in their mouth.... The righteous shall rejoice when he seeth the vengeance: he shall wash his feet in the blood of the wicked." Edwards argued that this passage could not refer to David's vengeance against Saul, for David "was so far from trampling on his blood that he greatly lamented his death, and condemned those that insulted him in his misery."[86] At the same time, verse 10 was "exactly parallel with many prophecies of the destruction of the enemies of the church in the days of the Messiah," an observation based on the analogy of Scripture (Isa 30:29, 32; Ps 68:23; Isa 26:5–6; Mic 7:10; Mal 4:3).[87] Edwards applied this language prophetically within the flow of redemptive history to the final judgment when Christ would crush his enemies under his feet.

Edwards dealt with the imprecatory passages of the Psalms by noting that the psalmist does not use them for personal vengeance but speaks as head of the church and as a prophet to highlight God's response of justice to sin, recognizing the limits of salvation as he speaks against God's enemies and pleads for the safety of the church against its enemies while looking toward the final fulfillment of these curses in the eschaton.

Reformed Exegetes on Imprecatory Language

How did Edwards compare to earlier Reformed interpreters on the imprecatory language of the Psalms?[88] Most of Edwards' approach is reflected in

---

84. Edwards, The "Miscellanies": Entry Nos. 833–1152, 370.

85. David P. Murray describes this dual aspect of the imprecatory psalms by noting that "blessing and cursing are two sides of the same coin. Real compassion for the wronged can exist only beside indignation against wrong-doing (Matt. 23). Both are beautiful qualities in God's sight." David P. Murray, "Christian Cursing?" in Sing a New Song: Recovering Psalm Singing for the Twenty-First Century, ed. Joel R. Beeke and Anthony T. Selvaggio (Grand Rapids, MI: Reformation Heritage Books, 2010), 117.

86. Jonathan Edwards, "The Miscellanies: Entry No. 1068: The Fulfillment of the Prophecies of the Messiah," Franklin Trask Library, Andover Newton Theological School, Newton, MA, §81.

87. Edwards, "Prophecies of the Messiah," §81. See also Edwards' identification of Ps 69:22 as a prophecy fulfilled in the Roman destruction of Jerusalem in AD 70. Edwards, The "Blank Bible," 507.

88. We focus on the Reformed exegetes' interpretation of Pss 58:6–10, 59:13, 137:7–9, the primary texts in Edwards' discussion. For an introduction to how the church interpreted

his Reformed predecessors. Like Edwards, they did not question the divine inspiration of these psalms. Calvin, for example, said of these psalms: "The Psalmist prays, under the inspiration of the Spirit, that God would practically demonstrate the truth of this prediction," which would remind the people of God's promised "avenging justice."[89] It was also common to interpret these psalms as prophecies, as Edwards did. Poole held that David wrote Psalm 137 "by a prophetic spirit," foretelling the destruction of Babylon, while Henry argued that imprecations are prophecies and Dickson saw the imprecatory prayer in Psalm 58 as a "prophecie and promise to the Church[']s comfort."[90]

While these exegetes saw prophecies in these passages, they interpreted their fulfillment in both historical and spiritual settings, as Edwards did. For example, most explained Ps 137:9 historically of the Medes and Persians fulfilling God's work of punishing the Babylonians who oppressed the Israelites. Dickson noted that while they were happy in their barbarous deeds, they acted from "corrupt intentions," but while they did not work as "religious servants," still they were "God[']s instruments, a good work of justice upon the oppressors of God[']s people, and a good work of delivery of the Lord[']s people."[91] These Reformed exegetes, like Edwards, also recognized spiritual and theological shades of meaning. It was widely held that imprecatory language was

---

the imprecatory psalms throughout the history of the church, see "Psalms and Curses," chapter 4 in John L. Thompson, *Reading the Bible with the Dead: What You Can Learn from the History of Exegesis That You Can't Learn from Exegesis Alone* (Grand Rapids, MI: William B. Eerdmans Publishing Co., 2007), 49–70. For an essay that describes many of the issues involved in interpreting the imprecatory psalms, written from a faith perspective, see Murray, "Christian Cursing?" 111–121. For an African perspective on the imprecatory psalms, which argues that Eurocentric interpretations emphasize the violence and darkness of these psalms while Africentric interpretations emphasize the protection and defense of these psalms, see David Tuesday Adamo, "The Imprecatory Psalms in African Context," in *Biblical Interpretation in African Perspective*, ed. David Tuesday Adamo (Lanham, MD: University Press of America, 2006), 142. For a modern take on the imprecatory psalms, see Nancy L. deClaissé-Walford, who casts these words as giving over our anger to the God of universal judgment and acknowledging our responsibility to move past the rage to work toward ending that rage, in "The Theology of the Imprecatory Psalms," in *Soundings in the Theology of Psalms: Perspectives and Methods in Contemporary Scholarship*, ed. Rolf A. Jacobson (Minneapolis, MN: Fortress Press, 2011), 77–92.

89. Calvin, *Commentary*, 5:196. See also David Dickson, *A Brief Explication of the other fifty Psalmes, From Ps. 50 to Ps. 100* (London: T. R. and E. M. for Ralph Smith…, 1653), 49.

90. Poole, *Synopsis Criticorum*, 1276; Henry, *Exposition*, [Ps 58:6]; Dickson, *Other fifty Psalmes*, 49. The Latin in Poole reads, "spiritu prophetico." See also Calvin, *Commentary*, 2:375; 5:196.

91. David Dickson, *Last Fifty Psalmes*, 304. Henry, Poole, and Calvin all recognized historical readings of this passage. Henry, *Exposition*, [Ps 137:8–9]; Poole, *Synopsis Criticorum*, 873; Calvin, *Commentary*, 5:197.

inspired by God to comfort his saints. Henry described two effects of sinners being destroyed in Psalm 58: "[t]hat Saints would be encourag'd and comforted by it" and "[t]hat Sinners would be convinc'd and converted by it."[92] Calvin also maintained that the promises in Psalm 137 of retribution give "hope and confidence" to God's people, reminding them that "it is well with us in our worst distresses, and that our enemies are devoted to destruction."[93]

A theological theme that Reformed interpreters employed that Edwards, surprisingly, did not was God's sovereignty and glory.[94] In his reading of Ps 59:13, Henry said that the psalmist prayed that "GOD would glorifie himself as *Israel's* GOD and King in their Destruction," for God's judgments confirm his sovereignty: "The Design of GOD's Judgments is to convince men that *the Lord reigns*, that he fulfills his own Counsels, gives Law to all the Creatures, and disposeth all things to his own Glory, so that the greatest of Men are under his Check, and he makes what use he pleases of them."[95] At the same time, a major theological theme that both Edwards and the Reformed exegetes employed with the imprecatory psalms was justice. Speaking on Ps 58:10, Poole explained that when the psalmist rejoices at the punishment of the wicked it is "from a zeal for Divine justice," and he also defended God's just character in Ps 137:9, noting that "God justly permitted this violence on the bloodthirsty Babylonians," who are lions that tear apart sheep.[96]

Of greater concern to most of these Reformed exegetes was guiding Christians in their appropriation of the imprecatory psalms, warning them, like Edwards, not to use them as justification for personal vengeance. Henry explained that when David made imprecations, he "acted by a publick Spirit in praying against them, and not by any private Revenge," so Christians "may

---

92. Henry, *Exposition*, [Ps 58:10–11].

93. Calvin, *Commentary*, 5:197. Poole and Dickson likewise saw comfort in the imprecatory psalms. Poole, *Synopsis Criticorum*, 873; Dickson, *Last Fifty Psalmes*, 304.

94. Perhaps the most likely reason that Edwards did not emphasize God's sovereignty and glory in his treatment of the imprecatory language of the Psalms is that he engaged this imprecatory language in his biblical notebooks for a particular purpose, to give an account for this violent language within the harmony of the Old and New Testaments. He sought to harmonize the calls for vengeance in the Psalms with the New Testament injunction to love one's enemies, and so God's sovereignty and glory were not at the forefront of his mind.

95. Henry, *Exposition*, [Ps 59:13]. See the similar emphasis on God's sovereignty and glory in Dickson, *Other fifty Psalmes*, 56.

96. Poole, *Synopsis Criticorum*, 872; the Latin reads, "non amore vindictae, sive...ob ultionem sui, sed ex zelo Divinae justitiae." Poole, *Synopsis Criticorum*, 1280; the Latin reads, "justè Deus permisit hanc saevitiem in crudeles Babylonios." Dickson and Calvin concurred. Dickson, *Other fifty Psalmes*, 50; Calvin, *Commentary*, 5:197.

in Faith pray against the Designs of the Church[']s Enemies, as the Prophet doth," but it must be a corporate, not a private interest.[97] Poole, speaking on Ps 58:10, argued that when the psalmist rejoices at the punishment of the wicked it is "not from a love of vengeance" or "revenge of himself" but "from a zeal for Divine justice."[98] Similarly, Dickson warned Christians that "[i]t is lawful for the godly to rejoyce in God[']s justice against the obstinate enemies of his people: provided their joy be indeed in God[']s justice, not in the destruction of the creatures."[99] In discussing Ps 137:7–9, Calvin also noted that praying for retribution must always be tempered by a desire for our enemies' redemption and by God's promise of judgment on the reprobate. We do not act out of our own revenge but out of God's while maintaining a pure spirit that waits on God's appointed timing: "To pray for vengeance would have been unwarrantable, had not God promised it, and had the party against whom it was sought not been reprobate and incurable; for as to others, even our greatest enemies, we should wish their amendment and reformation."[100]

This quotation by Calvin leads us to a final shared concern between Edwards and the Reformed tradition: hoping for enemies' repentance. Calvin, speaking on Ps 58:10, acknowledged the seeming inconsistency of saints rejoicing at the destruction of their enemies when they are to be vessels of mercy, but he showed that there is no inconsistency when we recognize the difference between hateful revenge and holy zeal:

> There is nothing absurd in supposing that believers, under the influence and guidance of the Holy Ghost, should rejoice in witnessing the execution of divine judgments. That cruel satisfaction which too many feel when they see their enemies destroyed, is the result of the unholy passions of hatred, anger, or impatience, inducing an inordinate desire of revenge. So far as corruption is suffered to operate in this manner, there can be no right or acceptable exercise. On the other hand, when one is led by a holy zeal to sympathize with the justness of that vengeance which God may have inflicted, his joy will be as pure in beholding the retribution

97. Henry, *Exposition*, [Ps 58:6, 8].

98. Poole, *Synopsis Criticorum*, 872. He also argued that Ps 137:9 cannot speak of revenge: "He desires this from an appetite, not of vengeance, but of justice, as the wicked parents are punished in their offspring, and as no posterity remains, so much as an impious race" ("Optat hoc ex appetitu, non vindictae, sed justitiae ut impii parentes puniantur in suis prolibus, et ut nulla posteritas remaneat tam impiae stirpis"). Poole, *Synopsis Criticorum*, 1280.

99. Dickson, *Other fifty Psalmes*, 50–51.

100. Calvin, *Commentary*, 5:196.

of the wicked, as his desire for their conversion and salvation was strong and unfeigned.[101]

Christians when guided by the Spirit must long for their enemies' salvation, but they will still rejoice when God's justice is carried out on those who refuse to repent. Henry sums up this thrust succinctly in his reading of the phrase "break their teeth" in Ps 58:6: not to "break their necks" but rather to "let them live to repent."[102]

We can see that Edwards was firmly in line with the Reformed stream of interpretation. Three elements distinguish Edwards' interpretation from theirs. For one, his willingness to use these passages to defend the doctrine of original sin was fairly original, though perhaps a logical outworking of the Reformed doctrine of original sin. Second, Edwards was more concerned, while discussing the imprecatory psalms, to establish the harmony of the Old and New Testaments, which was a stronger force in Edwards' dealing with these passages because he engaged them theologically in his "Miscellanies" notebook rather than exegeting the Psalms in canonical order in a commentary.[103] And finally, Edwards' redemptive-historical approach to the Bible comes out more clearly in his treatment of the imprecatory language in the Psalms than in the Reformed exegetes. While this concept is evident in all their discussions, Edwards even more so approached the imprecatory psalms with the question of how they fit into the grand scheme of God's redemptive plan. So we find more links with theological themes like original sin and biblical harmony but also a greater emphasis on the church with David speaking as its head and on prophecy and its fulfillment in God's culmination of all things. Edwards was a metanarrative-thinking theologian who sought to cast everything within God's purposeful plan of redemptive history.

Assessing Edwards on Biblical Violence

Little has been said in modern scholarship on Edwards' approach to the imprecatory language in the Psalms. Only Stephen Stein has addressed it, and he expresses deep reservations, arguing that "Edwards frequently celebrated the

---

101. Calvin, *Commentary*, 2:377–378.

102. Henry, *Exposition*, [Ps 58:6].

103. Only Poole spoke explicitly on this issue from the passages under consideration, noting in his treatment of Ps 137:9 that, given the harmony of the two testaments, "the moral laws are the same under the Old and New Testament" ("Eadem erant leges morales sub V. & N. T."). Poole, *Synopsis Criticorum*, 1280.

violence at the heart of the biblical accounts in ways that perhaps shaped the tradition of which he was a part and still does in our own day, sometimes with not so desirable results."[104] Stein calls Edwards' "justification" of the violent language of the imprecatory psalms by distinguishing between a personal enemy and an enemy of the church an "ethical rationalization" that is "casuistical."[105] By speaking in terms of "cultures" of biblical violence, Stein essentially presents Edwards as an ethnocentrist, who thought all cultures and religions were substandard to his. He concludes that Edwards' views on biblical violence "underscore the intense hostility he felt and expressed toward other religious traditions and those who were part of them."[106]

It should be noted, however, that for Edwards *all* cultures were substandard to God's measure of perfection. Stein seems to want to uphold a moral sensibility of peace, which he believes can only be maintained by acceptance of all cultures and religions. But Edwards wanted to uphold the peace that can only be attained through Christ, who by his death and resurrection made peace between God and humanity. It is this redemptive-historical framework that guided his interpretation of the imprecatory psalms.

Also, while it is undeniable that Edwards explored the violent language of Scripture, he balanced it with the command to love one's enemies—something Stein omits from his discussion. Edwards also refused to give individuals the freedom to decide whom they can curse. It is the Spirit-inspired speech of a prophet against the enemies of the church, while individual members of the church need to hope that those enemies will, by God's grace, become members of the church. It is thus God's place to judge and to inspire his prophets to speak prophetically of their destruction. For Edwards, the imprecatory language of the Psalms cannot be understood apart from the affirmation that there is indeed a day of vengeance coming. The church suffers at the hands of its enemies in this era, and it cries out for justice, but it does not exact justice on its enemies. Rather, God as sovereign judge will condemn in his time those enemies that remain his enemies, that is, those who do not repent and profess faith in Christ before their period of trial on this earth ends. Edwards' nuanced reading cast the violence in the Bible not in terms of cultural superiority but in terms of the gospel.

---

104. Stephen J. Stein, "Jonathan Edwards and the Cultures of Biblical Violence," In *Jonathan Edwards at 300: Essays on the Tercentenary of His Birth*, ed. Harry S. Stout, Kenneth P. Minkema, and Caleb J. D. Maskell (Lanham, MD: University Press of America, Inc., 2005), 56.

105. Stein, "Jonathan Edwards and the Cultures of Biblical Violence," 57–58.

106. Stein, "Jonathan Edwards and the Cultures of Biblical Violence," 63.

Edwards set the imprecatory language in the Psalms in redemptive history to make sense of it using the analogy of Scripture within his harmonic view of the Old and New Testaments.[107] He saw the innate wickedness of infants and God's wrath against enemies. He described these imprecations as prophetical curses realized in historical events but ultimately in the destruction of the church's enemies, particularly spiritual Babylon. He cast David as speaking in the name of Christ as head of the church who sought the greater good of the church and society. And he exhibited the harmony of the ethics in the Old and New Testaments, showing that individuals must never seek personal vengeance but that the church can appropriate the imprecatory psalms as prayers against the enemies of the church who remain enemies of the church, all the while praying for their repentance and redemption. These themes ultimately connected to the eternal destinies of God's enemies and the church.

The Eternal Hope of the Church

In the grand scheme of God's work of redemption, there is a beginning and an end. God had redeemed a remnant out of sinful humanity by the work of Christ and reoriented their affections by the work of the Spirit, and he planned to rescue his church from its enemies and bring it to live forever with Christ, its spouse, in heavenly bliss. This work would be accomplished in a series of events at the end of time. In Edwards' writings on the Psalms, he described the advance of Christ's kingdom on earth, the end of the world, and the final destinations of the wicked and the saints—hell and heaven.

The Advance of Christ's Kingdom

In Edwards' *An Humble Attempt to Promote Explicit Agreement and Visible Union of God's People in Extraordinary Prayer for the Revival of Religion and the Advancement of Christ's Kingdom on Earth, Pursuant to Scripture-Promises and Prophecies Concerning the Last Time,* he described his anticipation that the gospel would spread throughout the world. He believed that God had plans for a much greater "advancement" of Christ's kingdom since many promises in Scripture had not yet come to fruition, including certain messianic prophecies

---

107. It is interesting to note that Edwards preached no sermons on the imprecatory psalms and instead reflected on them in his personal notebooks. But it would be wrong to conclude that Edwards was afraid to discuss the imprecatory psalms in a public setting because the "Miscellanies" entries above show that he was working out how the imprecatory language of the Psalms fit into the harmony of the Old and New Testaments, and he clearly would have treated this material in his "Harmony of the Old and New Testament" had he lived to finish it.

from the Psalms: "all nations shall serve him" (Ps 72:11); "men shall be blessed in him: all nations shall call him blessed" (Ps 72:17); and "all flesh should come to him that hears prayer" (Ps 65:2).[108] Indeed, Edwards anticipated that "the whole world should finally be given to Christ, as one whose right it is to reign, as the proper heir of him, who is originally the king of all nations, and the possessor of heaven and earth," which was agreeable to Ps 2:6–8, in which God promised to set up his Son as king and give him "the heathen for thine inheritance and the uttermost parts of the earth for thy possession."[109]

As Edwards surveyed the limited extent of God's kingdom in human history, especially given the recent discovery of "a very great part of the world" (i.e., the Americas), he argued, "[t]hese things make it very evident, that the main fulfillment of those prophecies, that speak of the glorious advancement of Christ's kingdom on earth, is still to come."[110] Some of these prophecies emerged from the Psalms: Ps 48:2 spoke of Jerusalem being made "the joy of the whole earth," and Ps 72:7 of an "abundance of peace so long as the moon endureth."[111] When God's "future promised advancement of the kingdom of Christ" happens, it will be "[a] time wherein religion and true Christianity shall in every respect be uppermost in the world" and the poor be raised to the seat of princes (Ps 113:7–8); "[a] time wherein vital piety shall take possession of thrones" (Ps 45:12); "[a] time of wonderful union, and the most universal peace, love and sweet harmony" (Pss 46:9; 72:3); "[a] time wherein this whole great society shall appear in glorious beauty, in genuine amiable Christianity, and excellent order, as 'a city compact together' [Ps 122:3] and 'the perfection of beauty' [Ps 50:2]"; and "[a] time wherein the earth shall be abundantly fruitful" (Ps 67:6).[112]

As Edwards longed for this grand advancement of God's kingdom, he called for a transatlantic concert of prayer in keeping with the statement in the Lord's prayer, "Thy kingdom come" (Matt 6:10). Edwards argued that the churches throughout the world should appropriate the language of the Psalms in prayer, for the Psalms make it evident that "the prevalence of true religion in the latter days" will reach to "the utmost ends of the earth" (Ps 2:8) and "to all the ends of the earth" (Pss 22:27, 67:7, 98:3).[113] These "most strong

---

108. Edwards, *Humble Attempt*, 329–330.

109. Edwards, *Humble Attempt*, 330.

110. Edwards, *Humble Attempt*, 335.

111. Edwards, *Humble Attempt*, 336.

112. Edwards, *Humble Attempt*, 337–340. See also Edwards' related discussion of Ps 89:15. Edwards, *Humble Attempt*, 338.

113. Edwards, *Humble Attempt*, 331–332. Edwards also mentioned Pss 65:5, 8; 113:3.

expressions" denoting the inhabitable world in its farthest extent "signify the extent of the church of God in the latter days."[114] In fact, in one of Edwards' hyperbolic statements, he noted that the book of Psalms is mostly made up of prayers, prophecies, and praises for "the advancement of God's glory and kingdom of grace in the world":

> If we well consider the prayers that we find recorded in the book of Psalms, I believe we shall see reason to think, that a very great, if not the greater part of them, are prayers uttered, either in the name of Christ, or in the name of the church, for such a mercy: and undoubtedly the greatest part of that book of Psalms, is made up of prayers for this mercy, prophecies of it, and prophetical praises for it.[115]

Edwards' point here was not to say that the thrust of the Psalms can be exhausted by the concept of praying for the millennium, but this quotation does show again that Edwards thought globally about the Psalms, and "the advancement of God's glory and kingdom of grace in the world" is another way of saying that we should ask God to continue working out his plan of gracious redemption in human history as he leads it all to its final consummation in lifting up his glory and promoting the happiness of his saints.

In his *Humble Attempt*, however, Edwards did speculate about the possibility that God may soon set up his kingdom on earth, and he believed he would do it in response to prayer. He wondered if perhaps Ps 102:16–18 prophesied of a future generation whose prayers would spur God to usher in his kingdom. The passage reads, "When the LORD shall build up Zion, he shall appear in his glory. He will regard the prayer of the destitute, and not despise their prayer. This shall be written for the generation to come: and the people which shall be created shall praise the LORD." Edwards observed that his generation had come on spiritually destitute times, and he wondered if their humble prayers could change everything: "if God's people, in this time of great drought, were but made duly sensible of this calamity, and their own emptiness and necessity, and brought earnestly to thirst and cry for needed supplies, God would doubtless soon fulfill this blessed promise."[116] In fact, the words of verse 18 that speak of a "generation to come" signified to Edwards that "this promise should be left on record to encourage some future generation of God's people to pray

---

114. Edwards, *Humble Attempt*, 332.

115. Edwards, *Humble Attempt*, 350.

116. Edwards, *Humble Attempt*, 352.

and cry earnestly for this mercy, to whom he would fulfill the promise."[117] Edwards even posed the question, "Who knows but that the generation here spoken of may be this present generation?"[118] Edwards held that a 250-year period of revival would precede the millennium, but he believed the prayers of God's people could launch that preparatory period in his day.[119] To encourage people to pray, he described the benefits that those who prayed for a "great effusion of the Spirit of God" would receive: "those that are engaged in such prayer might expect the first benefit," just as in Ps 122:6, "[a] special blessing is promised to them that love and pray for the prosperity of the church."[120]

As Edwards reflected on the advancement of God's kingdom on earth, he also thought about the church in heaven, and in what McClymond and McDermott call "one of the more distinctive and unusual ideas in the whole of Edwards's theology," he believed that heavenly saints would gaze on earth, observing the unfolding of God's plan of redemption.[121] In fact, in the verses discussed below, earlier Reformed exegetes did not make an explicit connection to heavenly saints gazing on God's works on earth.[122] But Edwards pointed to the Psalms as support of this idea. In "Miscellanies" Entry No. 917, as he considered Ps 89:5, "And the heavens shall praise thy wonders, O LORD: thy faithfulness also in the congregation of the saints" (as well as Pss 19:1–2; 149:5), he argued that saints in heaven would be "very much in observing gospel wonders done on earth" because they would thus behold God's glory in his wondrous works on this earthly orb.[123] Discussing the saints in heaven in "Miscellanies" Entry No. 1089 from Ps 25:13,

---

117. Edwards, *Humble Attempt*, 352.

118. Edwards, *Humble Attempt*, 352.

119. For more on Edwards' millennial views, see Michael J. McClymond and Gerald R. McDermott, *The Theology of Jonathan Edwards* (New York: Oxford University Press, 2012), 572–577; Mark C. Rogers, "A Missional Eschatology: Jonathan Edwards, Future Prophecy, and the Spread of the Gospel," *Fides et Historia* 41, no. 1 (Winter/Spring 2009): 23–46.

120. Edwards, *Humble Attempt*, 356–357. Psalm 122:6 reads, "Pray for the peace of Jerusalem: they shall prosper that love thee."

121. McClymond and McDermott, *The Theology of Jonathan Edwards*, 306.

122. On Ps 89:5, see Henry, *Exposition*, [Ps 89:5]; Poole, *Synopsis*, 1062; Trapp, *Commentary*, 806; Dickson, *Other fifty Psalmes*, 309–310; Calvin, *Commentary*, 3:422–423. On Ps 25:13, see Henry, *Exposition*, [Ps 25:13]; Poole, *Synopsis*, 674; Trapp, *Commentary*, 643; Dickson, *First Fifty Psalms*, 145; Calvin, *Commentary*, 1:428–430. On Ps 50:4, see Henry, *Exposition*, [Ps 50:4]; Poole, *Synopsis*, 819–820; Trapp, *Commentary*, 717; Dickson, *First Fifty Psalms*, 342–343; Calvin, *Commentary*, 2:262–263.

123. Edwards, *The "Miscellanies": Entry Nos. 833–1152*, 166. See Edwards' similar comment on Ps 89:1–5 in "Miscellanies" Entry No. 1121. Edwards, *The "Miscellanies": Entry Nos. 833–1152*, 494.

"His soul shall dwell at ease; and his seed shall inherit the earth," Edwards argued that "the saints in heaven see and are concerned and interested in the prosperity of the church on earth."[124] And in "Miscellanies" Entry No. 1119, he cited Ps 50:4, "He shall call to the heavens from above, and to the earth, that he may judge his people," and claimed that "God so often calls the heavens to be witnesses of his dealings with men on earth" that one can argue from this that the saints in heaven can see what is happening on earth.[125] Edwards deduced that the heavenly saints bear witness to God's outworking of his plan of redemption on earth, and he thus called the earthly saints to work in concert with this plan through prayer, longing for that glorious, happy day when they would see God's kingdom spread to the farthest extent of the world.

The End of the World

As Christ's kingdom advanced more and more on earth, it would culminate in the subduing of all God's enemies, in Christ's millennial reign on earth, and eventually in the end of this world with a transition to the eternal realms of hell and heaven.

Edwards believed that Psalms 14, 47, and 53 prophesied of a time when God would take notice of the great wickedness on earth, subdue his enemies, and establish Christ's reign over all nations.[126] And several psalms intimated this final destruction of the wicked. Tracing the theme of "morning" through the Psalms (Pss 30:5; 49:14; 59:16; 143:8; 46:5) and other biblical passages, Edwards observed that God's various works occurring in the morning suggests that "the terrible destruction of the wicked is at the beginning of the glorious day wherein the Sun of Righteousness rises on the earth," or the millennium.[127]

---

124. Edwards, The "Miscellanies": Entry Nos. 833–1152, 474. Edwards cited Matt 19:27–30 and Prov 10:30 in concord with Ps 25:13 in this entry.

125. Edwards, The "Miscellanies": Entry Nos. 833–1152, 493. In addition, Edwards cited Deut 31:28; 32:1; 4:26; 30:19; and Isa 1:2.

126. Edwards, "Prophecies of the Messiah," §48, §51. See also Edwards' discussion of Psalm 50 as laying out the timeline of the dispensations of the church: the gospel goes to the Gentiles (vv. 1–2); Christ's kingdom is established (vv. 3–6); worship is instituted as spiritual service, not external forms (vv. 7–16); the wicked are "more effectually" shut out from God's people (vv. 17–20); wrath is poured out on the wicked (vv. 21–22); and the way to God's acceptance is described (v. 23). Edwards cited Poole in a later entry on this psalm. Edwards, The "Blank Bible," 498. See also Edwards' speculation that the gospel would arise out of the west, informed by his reading of Psalm 29. Edwards, The "Blank Bible," 490.

127. Edwards, Notes on Scripture, 344. Edwards cited this note in his "Blank Bible" entry on Ps 49:14. Edwards, The "Blank Bible," 497.

Edwards' typological reading of Psalm 72 gave further insight into Christ's millennial reign. Edwards interpreted Ps 72:8, "He shall have dominion also from sea to sea, and from the river unto the ends of the earth," both of Solomon's reign, when he ruled over "all countries conquered by David on this side [of] the river Euphrates to the Great Sea and Red Sea," and of Christ's coming reign, when he will rule over "all countries in the world, all continents contained between different parts of the ocean."[128] Similarly, following verse 11, "Yea, all kings shall fall down before him: all nations shall serve him," Edwards explained that as the reign of Solomon, whose name means "peace," was not established until David had subdued all his enemies, so Christ's peaceful reign does not begin until he subdues his enemies, for Solomon's "reign was a most eminent type of the millennium."[129]

When Christ's millennial reign is established, Edwards believed that God's saints "shall be made princes in all the earth, and shall then come to reign on earth" as princes and kings, comparing Rev 19:14 with Pss 45:16 and 113:7–8.[130] Likewise, as Ps 37:8–11 describes evildoers being cut off and those who wait on the Lord inheriting the earth, so Edwards interpreted this as Christ's millennial kingdom being set up on earth: "This evidently refers to the glorious times of the gospel, when the enemies of God's people shall be cut off, and the kingdom shall be given into the hands of the saints of the most high God, and they shall delight themselves in the abundance of peace."[131]

Edwards preached on the end of the world in a January or February 1728 sermon from Ps 102:25–26, "Of old hast thou laid the foundation of the earth: and the heavens are the work of thy hands. They shall perish, but thou shalt endure: yea, all of them shall wax old like a garment; as a vesture shalt thou change them, and they shall be changed."[132] Edwards recognized that the

128. Edwards, "Apocalypse Series," 180–181.

129. Edwards, "Apocalypse Series," 180.

130. Edwards, "Apocalypse Series," 209–210. Edwards also mentioned these passages: Judg 5:10; 1 Sam 2:8; Job 36:7; Dan 7:27; 1 Pet 2:9; Rev 1:6; 5:10; 20:4.

131. Edwards, *The "Miscellanies": Entry Nos. 833–1152,* 111. See Edwards' similar comment on Ps 37:6. Edwards, *The "Blank Bible,"* 493. On the joy of the saints when Christ establishes his kingdom, see Edwards, *The "Blank Bible,"* 541.

132. This sermon consists of two parts: The first part is available only on the Jonathan Edwards Center website, and the second part is available in Michael McMullen's edited volume of sermons by Edwards. Jonathan Edwards, "61. Sermon on Ps 102:25–26 (January or February 1728)," in *Sermons, Series II, 1728–1729,* vol. 43 of *WJEO;* Jonathan Edwards, "That This Present World Shall One Day Come to an End" (Ps 102:25–26), in *The Glory and Honor of God: Volume 2 of the Previously Unpublished Sermons of Jonathan Edwards,* ed. Michael D. McMullen (Nashville, TN: Broadman & Holman, 2004), 107–119.

title contextualizes the psalm as coming from one in affliction pouring out his complaint to God, and while it could apply to David at many times in his life, Edwards thought the Holy Spirit's "Principal aim" is "to Represent the Case of the Church of God" in "dark Circumstances."[133] While the psalmist speaks in the name of the church in its calamity, he comforts himself in that he committed his soul to God, and "seeing thou dost Continue and will Remain unchangeable forever, thy People also that trust in thee shall also be forever Preserved."[134] But the creation did not have that promise. Thus Edwards noted the text's plain assertion that the heavens and the earth shall meet their end, made clear from the comparison with a garment, for when a garment grows old, it is no longer useful since it has accomplished the ends God intended for it and so is disposed and a new one introduced. In the same way, "the present form and disposition of the world shall be Wholly destroyed and Another shall be Introduced."[135] Edwards moved from his treatment of the text to argue this doctrine: "That this Present world shall one day Come to An End"—an interpretation shared by his Reformed predecessors.[136]

Edwards went on in the doctrine section to explain what it means for the world to come to an end: "we don[']t mean that the whole Universe shall Come to An End but only this Part of it that we Are Concernd with in Our Present state"; that is, the earth, which is the "habitation of frail mortal Creature," will pass away, but heaven—"the habitation of Immortal beings," or the "highest heavens"—is made to last forever.[137] Coming to an end means not annihilation,

---

133. Edwards, "61. Sermon on Ps 102:25–26," L. 1r.

134. Edwards, "61. Sermon on Ps 102:25–26," L. 1v.

135. Edwards, "61. Sermon on Ps 102:25–26," L. 2r.

136. Edwards, "61. Sermon on Ps 102:25–26," L. 2r. Henry recognized the certain end of this world and observed that being "changed" means "not *annihilated*, but *alter'd*," emphasizing that God, who never changes, is the source of all true hope. Henry, *Exposition*, [Ps 102:25–27]. Italics original. Poole recognized the certainty that the heavens and earth shall perish and offered the understanding that the end of this world would issue forth in a new world: "The change will thus be not of natures, with the substance remaining, but clearly a production of new heavens and a new earth" ("Erit ergo immutatio non qualitatum, manentibus substantiis, sed novorum plane coelorum & novae terrae productio"). Poole, *Synopsis*, 1120. Trapp noted that "[t]hey shall change form and state, being dissolved by the last fire." Trapp, *Commentary*, 830. Dickson observed that the heavens and earth, being "subject to vanity," shall perish. Dickson, *Last Fifty Psalmes*, 19. Calvin contrasted the transience of this world with the permanence of God: "If the whole frame-work of the world is hastening to its end, what will become of the human race?... We ought therefore to seek stability no where else but in God." Calvin, *Commentary*, 4:123.

137. Edwards, "61. Sermon on Ps 102:25–26," L. 2v., 3r. Edwards, "That This Present World," 108. In a later "Miscellanies" note (Entry No. 931), Edwards commented on Ps 102:25–26 more clearly, that "the time will come when the whole *visible universe*, including the starry heavens,

but dissolution, akin to wood being burned, which does not annihilate the wood but changes it into smoke and ashes. Thus in an apocalyptic vision of the future, Edwards anticipated that the form and disposition of the earth will be made uninhabitable.[138] He explained that after the earth is shaken and the last judgment held, "the Present dispensation of Grace shall Cease forever," and "the means of Grace shall forever Cease," for "there shall be no more offers of a saviour."[139] Edwards drew together several elements of the end times when the world is dissolved: "the Good and the Bad will be Everlastingly separated one from another"; "The Righteous and the wicked shall be in exceeding different Conditions"; "Their Bodies will be Partakers in their happiness or misery"; "they will Recieve the perfection of their Reward & Punishments"; and "their state will be Eternal and unalterable."[140]

As Edwards applied this doctrine to his listeners, he emphasized that the weight of eternity should change how they live in this temporal realm. He exhorted them "not to set your heart upon this world, seeing that all these things are corruptible and will be dissolved," but to be diligent in preparing for the future judgment.[141] This call brings out the heart of what mattered to Edwards: joining oneself to God's kingdom, given the certain end of the redemptive-historical story. He then painted a terrifying mental picture of what it will be like for the unconverted on the final day of this temporal world: "How dreadful will the sentence be to you when it is pronounced, when you shall be damned to everlasting punishment," for "[w]hen the words are once passed, they shall never be recalled."[142] And "[w]hat cries will there be in that multitude when they are all thrown headlong into this great furnace, and the flames wrap themselves about their naked bodies, and the wrath of God scorches their souls."[143] But not only is the first day of hell so excruciating, for "if you should be one of those cursed, consider how it would be with you after

---

shall be destroyed and pass away, and be rolled together." Edwards, *The "Miscellanies": Entry Nos. 833–1152*, 176. Italics added.

138. In this understanding of the desolation of the earth, Edwards believed that heaven would be glorified and thus become a "new heaven" but would also constitute the "new earth" in the sense that the church will be taken there to dwell, making it their "new earth." McClymond and McDermott, *The Theology of Jonathan Edwards*, 578–579.

139. Edwards, "61. Sermon on Ps 102:25–26," L. 9v.

140. Edwards, "61. Sermon on Ps 102:25–26," L. 10r.–12v.

141. Edwards, "That This Present World," 114.

142. Edwards, "That This Present World," 117.

143. Edwards, "That This Present World," 118.

you had been in this condition for some thousands of years," for after that thousand years there will be another thousand, and another, and another, "and you would come never the nearer to an end."[144] Given this horrid reality when this world ends, Edwards called for conversion by shortening the time people had left: "consider also one thing more, and that is that the matter will soon be determined, whether the case will be thus with you at the end of the world or no."[145] And so in this sermon, Edwards crossed the hinge point from temporality to eternity, taking us from the end of the world when Christ subdues his enemies to the everlasting dwelling places of humanity, which leads us to his treatment of hell and heaven from the book of Psalms.

Future Judgment for the Wicked

It will come as no surprise that the preacher renowned for his sermon, "Sinners in the Hands of an Angry God," preached on a coming judgment for the wicked that will leave them eternally in hell—even from the Psalms. Edwards recognized that the future state and the resurrection were "great mysteries in Old Testament times," but even so, he stated that in Ps 49:3–15 the future state is "perhaps...more plainly spoken of than anywhere else in the Old Testament; the Psalmist really speaks right down plain about it."[146] Since "good and bad, and all, die," the reality of a future state, and "the misery of the wicked in comparison of the godly," makes it critical for people to take the future seriously and pursue godliness.[147] Even in the Old Testament book of Psalms, one could discover intimations about this future netherworld and God's coming judgment.

This judgment would be terribly dreadful. From Ps 78:38, "he...did not stir up all his wrath," we learn that God restrains his wrath for the present but that the "torments of hell" will consist of "God's full and unrestrained wrath."[148] And Ps 73:19 describes the intense sufferings of those in hell: "The utter sinking of the soul in its amazement and overbearing distress in hell,

144. Edwards, "That This Present World," 118.

145. Edwards, "That This Present World," 119.

146. Edwards, *Notes on Scripture*, 52–53. See his similar comment on Ps 49:4 in his "Blank Bible" entry on Ps 49:3–4, where he cited this entry. Edwards, *The "Blank Bible,"* 497.

147. Edwards, *Notes on Scripture*, 53.

148. Jonathan Edwards, "The Torments of Hell Are Exceeding Great" (Luke 16:24), in *Sermons and Discourses 1723–1729*, ed. Kenneth P. Minkema, vol. 14 of *WJE* (1997), 305.

and its being crushed as it were and quite destroyed, is livelily represented in Ps. 73:19, by their being 'utterly consumed with terrors.' "[149]

While the final judgment will consist of horrific torments, Edwards spoke from the Psalms to defend the justice of God's eschatological sentence. In the latter half of 1729, Edwards preached on Ps 18:26, "With the pure thou wilt shew thyself pure; and with the froward thou wilt shew thyself froward." Edwards contextualized this psalm from the title, by which he determined that David wrote it in his final days when God delivered him from all his enemies, including Saul, Absalom, the Philistines, and the Canaanite nations (2 Samuel 22). As David reflected on God's dealings with him over the years, he came to the conclusion recorded in the sermon text: As David was merciful, upright, and pure, God showed himself to be merciful, upright, and pure with David, but as his enemies were contrary, God showed himself contrary with them. Edwards observed that God gives rewards to mankind that are congruent to the "degree" and "Kind" of their works; he will show a proportionate recompense, whether it be mercy or contrariness.[150] He focused his sermon on the second half of the text and thus preached the doctrine, "They that Contend with G[od] Can expect no other than that G[od] will Contend with them."[151] Edwards sought to awaken wicked men, cautioning them against idle quarreling with God's sovereignty and warning them that in the end, God will have "either bent them or broke them."[152]

Edwards further explained the justice of God's judgment by comparing it to his glorious nature, a concept he gleaned from Ps 90:11, "Who knoweth the power of thine anger? even according to thy fear, so is thy wrath." Edwards saw a proportion between God's great majesty that he will reveal to his church and his awful wrath that he will pour out on the wicked. Earlier Reformed interpreters saw God's great wrath in this verse, and some also saw a call for awe, but Edwards' concern to defend God's justice via a proportionality between

---

149. Edwards, *The "Miscellanies": Entry Nos. 833–1152*, 324.

150. Jonathan Edwards, "111. Sermon on Ps 18:26 (Summer–Fall 1729)," in *Sermons, Series II, 1729*, vol. 44 of *WJEO*, L. 1v.

151. Edwards, "111. Sermon on Ps 18:26," L. 2r.

152. Edwards, "111. Sermon on Ps 18:26," L. 7v. See also Edwards' similar comments on Ps 18:26 in another sermon, arguing that God deals justly with people: "[s]urely 'tis but fair that you should be made to buy in the same measure in which you sell." Jonathan Edwards, "The Justice of God in the Damnation of Sinners" (Rom 3:19), in *Sermons and Discourses 1734–1738*, ed. M. X. Lesser, vol. 19 of *WJE* (2001), 352. Also see his comments on God's justice in judgment from Ps 50:1–4, 29. Jonathan Edwards, "True Grace, Distinguished from the Experience of Devils" (James 2:19), in *Sermons and Discourses 1743–1758*, ed. Wilson H. Kimnach, vol. 25 of *WJE* (2006), 619–620; Edwards, "Harmony," 237.

fear and wrath was unique.[153] He explained that "the wrath of God is dreadful according to the greatness and highness of God as he is in himself, that is, that it is infinitely dreadful, as it is, in that it is eternal."[154] Indeed, it is "fit there should be a visible proportion, for therein consists much of the majesty of God, viz. in his terribleness," and those in heaven will see God's majesty manifest in his judgment when they see "answerable proportionable discoveries" of God's awful majesty "in the misery of those that bear his wrath."[155] Edwards' high view of God's glory and his penchant for finding beauty in agreement, proportion, and symmetry led him to read this psalm as a fear-instilling statement on God's judgment. He anticipated that when the day of judgment comes and the wicked "see the immense and terrible greatness and awful majesty of God, and also see how exceedingly he abhors sin, and how he is provoked with them," then they will "expect" that "now their sufferings must be answerable to that great power, excited by fierceness of wrath."[156] While some may object to God inflicting "such an extreme degree of suffering," Edwards explained that on that day, "they shall be 'given over unto death' (Ps. 118:18). The creature will be utterly lost and thrown away of God. As to any concern God will have for it, God will have a concern for justice, but no sort of concern for the creature. This is evident, because he makes their sufferings eternal."[157] This last point Edwards defended from the Psalms elsewhere, noting that "[i]t was

153. Henry did not speak of proportion like Edwards did, but he did see an equality between fear and wrath and emphasized God's great wrath: "GOD's wrath is equal to the Apprehensions which the most thoughtful serious People have of it," for indeed, "what is *felt* in 'tother World, is infinitely worse than what is fear'd in this World." Henry, *Exposition*, [Ps 90:11]. Poole explained a number of interpretations, including a fear that is befitting God, a fear that causes tremors, a fear that leads people to draw back from sins, and a fear that shows God will begin his justice among his people. Poole, *Synopsis*, 1075–1076. Trapp similarly warned, "let a man fear thee never so much, he is sure to feel thee much more, if once he fall into thy fingers." Trapp, *Commentary*, 902. Dickson came closer to Edwards' approach in that he saw fear of God leading to awe: "Seeing men know not the power of God[']s wrath till it break upon them, it is wisdome to study his fear, that wrath may be prevented, and to take the measure of the power of God[']s wrath, by measuring his dreadful feare and terrible terror, and to stand in awe of him in time." Dickson, *Other fifty Psalmes*, 336. Calvin also linked fear with awe, noting that "it is a holy awe of God, and that alone, which makes us truly and deeply feel his anger," for while the faithful humble themselves in true devotion to God because they sense his wrath, the reprobate "are not touched with the feeling of God's wrath, because they do not stand in awe of him." Calvin, *Commentary*, 3:472–473.

154. Edwards, *The "Miscellanies": Entry Nos. a–500*, 535.

155. Edwards, *The "Miscellanies": Entry Nos. a–500*, 535.

156. Edwards, *The "Miscellanies": Entry Nos. 501–832*, 90.

157. Edwards, *The "Miscellanies": Entry Nos. 501–832*, 91.

foretold in the prophecies of the Old Testament, that everlasting burnings should be the punishment of the Messiah's enemies, and of all that refused to submit to and obey him" (Ps 21:9).[158] Edwards believed that the Scriptures make it clear both that God will cast the wicked out of the reach of his mercy and that in doing so he will uphold and display his infinite divine justice.

As Edwards preached on hell, he turned to the Psalms to teach his people about how serious it was. In fact, the third time Edwards preached "Sinners in the Hands of an Angry God," he switched his sermon text from Deut 32:35, "Their foot shall slide in due time," to Ps 7:11, "God judgeth the righteous, and God is angry with the wicked every day."[159] In the text segment of the sermon, he also used Ps 73:18, "Surely thou didst set them in slippery places: thou castedst them down into destruction," to support two points: that sinners are "*always* exposed to destruction, as one that stands or walks in slippery places is always exposed to fall," and that sinners are "always exposed to *sudden* unexpected destruction. As he that walks in slippery places is every moment liable to fall; he can't foresee one moment whether he shall stand or fall the next."[160] The Psalms illustrated for Edwards the precarious place of rebellious sinners before a holy God.

Edwards actually delivered sermons on both of these texts on other occasions. Sometime between fall 1730 and spring 1731, he preached on Ps 73:18–19, "Surely thou didst set them in slippery places: thou castedst them down into destruction. How are they brought into desolation, as in a moment! they are utterly consumed with terrors." He noted that in Psalm 73 the psalmist "stumbled" over the apparent prosperity of the wicked and wondered whether he had been sold a bill of goods and if it would not be better to set aside all religion and embrace the rewards of worldly living.[161] The psalmist almost lost the foundation of his faith in this conundrum but kept his footing because when he lacked understanding, he went into the sanctuary, seeking "Light & Instruction" from God.[162] In taking this path, he became aware

---

158. Edwards, "Fulfillment of the Prophecies," §181. See also Edwards' similar comments in support of eternal conscious punishment and against annihilationism from Pss 50:21; 17:13–14. Edwards, *The "Miscellanies": Entry Nos. 1153–1360*, 230, 591.

159. Harry S. Stout, Nathan O. Hatch, and Kyle P. Farley, eds., *Sermons and Discourses 1739–1742*, vol. 22 of *WJE* (2003), 403.

160. Jonathan Edwards, "Sinners in the Hands of an Angry God" (Deut 32:35), in *Sermons and Discourses 1739–1742*, ed. Harry S. Stout and Nathan O. Hatch with Kyle P. Farley, vol. 22 of *WJE* (2003), 404.

161. Jonathan Edwards, "168. Sermon on Ps 73:18–19 (Fall 1730–Spring 1731)," in *Sermons, Series II, 1729–1731*, vol. 45 of *WJEO*, L. 1r. Edwards possibly repreached this sermon at Southampton on March 9, 1743.

162. Edwards, "168. Sermon on Ps 73:18–19," L. 1v.

of "his own Ignorance & blindness" in questioning God's faithfulness for he then comprehended the "miserable Condition of wicked men notwithstanding their outward Prosperity" and the blessedness granted to the righteous.[163] In language that prefigured what Edwards would later preach in "Sinners in the Hands of an Angry God," he described the plight of the wicked from Ps 73:18–19:

> in our text the unhappy Case of the wicked is set forth by their danger. [T]hou hast set them in slippery Places[.] [T]ho[ugh] they seem to Live in Prosperity[,] yet they don't live at all safely[.] . . . [I]t is so unsafe a state as a man that walks in slippery Places is in continual danger of falling[.] [H]e knows not how soon he may have a fall[.] [H]e don[']t know when to expect it[.] . . . [W]hen a man falls that walks in slippery Places he falls suddenly & without warning[.] [S]o it is with wicked men as it follows in the next v[erse]. [H]ow are they brought into desolations in a moment so that before they are actually destroyed they are in a miserable Case inasmuch as they are in such Constant danger of it.[164]

Edwards continued by noting that God is the cause of their danger but not of their sin, and he preached this doctrine: "That those that are in a natural Condition have Reason to be alwaies in fear of being destroyed," for they are like a man walking on slippery ground—"he is never safe but is every moment in danger of falling."[165] In his doctrine section Edwards employed imagery that eerily echoes his later "Sinners" sermon, noting that the unconverted are constantly "in danger of dropping into hell," for it is "as if they hung over the Pit of hell by a thread that is Continually gnawed upon by moths & they don[']t know how Near it is being gnawed asunder."[166] This sermon shows that Edwards' development of "Sinners" occurred over years of reflection on the biblical text, stemming in part from the Psalms.

In February 1750 Edwards preached on Ps 7:11—the text he used for "Sinners" the third time he delivered it—which reads, "God judgeth the righteous, and God is angry with the wicked every day." He presented a two-part doctrine, showing first "What is God[']s anger" and second "How he is angry with the

163. Edwards, "168. Sermon on Ps 73:18–19," L. ɪᴠ.

164. Edwards, "168. Sermon on Ps 73:18–19," L. 2r.

165. Edwards, "168. Sermon on Ps 73:18–19," L. 2v.

166. Edwards, "168. Sermon on Ps 73:18–19," L. 4r.

w[icked] every day."[167] Edwards explained that what is described in the text is different than his anger toward his children, for his anger toward the wicked is "The Exercise of Infinite opposition of his Heart against sin tending to an answerable vengeance on the sinner."[168] As Edwards argued elsewhere, he reiterated here that the wicked person deserves an "answerable Punishm[en]t," so he dies "under the guilt of wickedness."[169] Edwards stated that God "tends not only to be angry with their sins but with their Persons," and he expresses his daily anger, which is "in constant Exercise," for God must "execute vengeance" and they have "obligations to suffer it."[170] Earlier Reformed exegetes also highlighted God's wrath, if not to the same degree that Edwards did.[171] Edwards went on to awaken sinners by describing several characteristics of God's anger, and he reminded them of the doctrine he preached in "Sinners" nearly a decade earlier: "nothing preserves you one moment from suffering this wrath but the meer pleasure of this angry G[od]."[172] He also pointed to the "one way of Escape" and "one Saviour."[173] For those in his Northampton congregation who thought they were converted, Edwards warned them, in the tumultuous months leading up to his dismissal, not to be deceived, for "There are many that flatter thems[elves]—who are indeed the Chil[dren] of wrath."[174]

---

167. Jonathan Edwards, "954. Sermon on Ps 7:11 (February 1750)," Beinecke Rare Book and Manuscript Library, Yale University, New Haven, CT, L. 1r.

168. Edwards, "954. Sermon on Ps 7:11," L. 1v.

169. Edwards, "954. Sermon on Ps 7:11," L. 2r.

170. Edwards, "954. Sermon on Ps 7:11," L. 2v.–3r.

171. Henry also described "the certain Destruction of wicked People" from this verse, noting "[a]s his *Mercies* are *new* every Morning towards his People, so his Anger is new every Morning against the wicked, upon the fresh Occasions given for it by their renew'd Transgressions." Henry, *Exposition*, [Ps 7:11]. Italics original. Poole discussed varied ways of reading this passage and noted that God "exercises his judgments every day, punishes the wicked, lest they promise themselves security" ("Judicia sua quotidie exercet, punit impios, ne sibi securitatem promittant"). Poole, *Synopsis*, 532. Trapp explained this verse as saying that "they are under the arrest of his wrath, and liable to the wrath to come." Trapp, *Commentary*, 584. Dickson contrasted justice and mercy: "neither justice against the wicked, nor mercy toward the godly is idle; for God[']s Word and Works do speak mercy to the one, and wrath to the other, every day; all things are working for the one[']s good, and for the other[']s damage continually." Dickson, *First Fifty Psalms*, 37. Calvin explained this verse as showing that although God exercises patience toward sinners, "as no time passes, yea, not even a day, in which he does not furnish the clearest evidence that he discerns between the righteous and the wicked, notwithstanding the confusion of things in the world, it is certain that he never ceases to execute the office of a judge." Calvin, *Commentary*, 1:86–87.

172. Edwards, "954. Sermon on Ps 7:11," L. 8r.

173. Edwards, "954. Sermon on Ps 7:11," L. 8v.

174. Edwards, "954. Sermon on Ps 7:11," L. 10v.

In Edwards' view, the Psalms spoke plainly about the impending eternal sufferings awaiting the unrepentant wicked and the justice of God in damning the wicked to hell as a manifestation of his glory, and he sought to awaken them out of their dream so they might realize their precarious state on slippery ground and turn to the one Savior who could rescue them from eternity in hell.[175] Apparently, in 1747 Edwards expressed some reservations about the nearly three decades' worth of hellfire sermons he had preached because they seemed to have "little apparent effect."[176] Wilson Kimnach, in reflecting on this comment and Edwards' later sermons, has argued that the "revivalist had seen the limitations of revival preaching," and "for the remainder of his career in Northampton and Stockbridge, Edwards was not to return to full-blown hellfire preaching."[177] But Edwards' 1750 sermon on Ps 7:11 (discussed above) and 1751 sermon on Ps 112:1 (discussed below) illustrate that even in the later years of his preaching, Edwards continued to preach on hell to awaken sinners from their deadly spiritual state.

Future Blessings for the Saints

Edwards preached so forcefully on hell because he wanted people to experience the lavish blessings of living eternally in the presence of the great and glorious God of heaven. This was the dual aim of God's work of redemption, to exalt the glory of God and to usher the saints into their eternal happiness as the body of Christ. And the Psalms aided Edwards in outlining a vision of this eternal abode.

He showed that the book of Psalms represents heaven as "God's dwelling house" (Pss 113:5; 123:1) or "God's palace," "the house of the great King of the Universe" that is home to "his throne" (Ps 11:4).[178] Heaven is God's eternal "fixed abode."[179] And this house is prepared for God's adoptees, for Ps 23:6,

---

175. See Edwards' comparison of God's judgment to waking from a dream, an image taken from Ps 73:20, "As a dream when one awaketh; so, O Lord, when thou awakest, thou shalt despise their image." Edwards, *The "Blank Bible,"* 510–511.

176. Jonathan Edwards, "Yield to God's Word, or Be Broken by His Hand," in *Sermons and Discourses, 1743–1758*, vol. 25 of WJE (2006), 220.

177. Wilson H. Kimnach, "Edwards as Preacher," in *The Cambridge Companion to Jonathan Edwards*, ed. Stephen J. Stein (New York: Cambridge University Press, 2007), 122. See a parallel argument in McClymond and McDermott, *The Theology of Jonathan Edwards*, 498–499.

178. Jonathan Edwards, "The Many Mansions" (John 14:2), in *Sermons and Discourses 1734–1738*, ed. M. X. Lesser, vol. 19 of *WJE* (2001), 738.

179. In support of this point, Edwards cited Pss 11:4; 20:6; 14:2; 53:2; 33:13–14; 57:3; 76:8; 80:14; 102:19; 68:4, 33; 123:1; 115:2–3; 113:5; 18:9; 144:5; 73:9. See also Edwards' similar discussion of

"I will dwell in the house of the Lord forever," signifies that we are adopted children, not mere guests: "Being there not merely as a servant, or as a guest kindly entertained for a little while…, but as a child adopted into the family."[180]

Being brought into this house, Edwards explained, is like being taken to a place of tremendous happiness. In reading Ps 49:15, "But God will redeem my soul from the power of the grave: for he shall receive me," Edwards noted that the Hebrew term לָקַח is translated "receive," while in Gen 5:24, the same term is translated "took": "And Enoch walked with God: and he was not; for God took him." This parallel use of the term via the analogy of Scripture suggested to Edwards that "the souls of the saints do not die when their bodies die but are received to a state of happiness in more perfect union and communion with God" in heaven.[181] Similarly, following Ps 37:16, "A little that a righteous man hath is better than the riches of many wicked," Edwards noted that "G[od] is the best portion," and the righteous have "the best Riches" stored up for them in heaven, for "In Heaven [they] shall alwaies be Rich."[182] This happiness will be an eternal, never-ending happiness. Thus Edwards noted that "[e]ternal life is often spoken of in the prophecies of the Old Testament, as the fruit of the Messiah's salvation" (Pss 22:26; 69:32).[183] And he made a comparison between the way of the wicked and the way of the righteous to argue for the eternality of heaven. As "way" in Ps 1:6, "the way of the ungodly shall perish," is a metonym for the wicked people themselves who walk in such a way, meaning that they will perish, so "way" in Ps 139:24, "lead me in the way everlasting," is a metonym for the people who walk in that way. They "shall never perish," and "[t]heir life, and peace, and happiness in this way shall be everlasting."[184] And the saints will also be fully conscious in eternity.[185]

Pss 132:7; 115:15–16; 103:19, 22; 45:6 in this same entry, "Miscellanies" Entry No. 743. Edwards, *The "Miscellanies": Entry Nos. 501–832*, 376–381. Quotation on 376.

180. Edwards, *The "Blank Bible,"* 488.

181. Edwards, *The "Blank Bible,"* 497.

182. Jonathan Edwards, "1161. Sermon on Ps 37:16 (April 1756)," Beinecke Rare Book and Manuscript Library, Yale University, New Haven, CT, L. 1v., 2v.

183. Edwards, "Fulfillment of the Prophecies," §180.

184. Edwards, *The "Blank Bible,"* 538. Edwards also pointed to other passages where the word "way" was used as a metonymy (Prov 2:8; Jer 12:1; Isa 1:12).

185. See Edwards' resolution to the apparent problem that people may be unconscious in the afterlife, raised by Ps 6:5, "For in death there is no remembrance of thee: in the grave who shall give thee thanks?" He recognized that "in death" could mean death "without God's salvation" or "temporal death," which ends the time for saints "to bring forth fruits to God's praise as in life." Edwards, *The "Blank Bible,"* 476–477.

In Edwards' "Harmony," he spoke at length on several passages from the Psalms about the hope that saints have in a future state in heaven. When the psalmist says, "Thou hast put gladness in my heart, more than in the time that their corn and their wine increased" (Ps 4:7), Edwards saw a picture of the saint truly affected by gracious affections: "The chief happiness of God's favorites consists not in earthly prosperity but in spiritual and heavenly good, in the enjoyment of God, in the manifestations of his glory and love."[186] Edwards similarly spoke of heavenly happiness from Ps 27:4, "One thing have I desired of the LORD, that will I seek after; that I may dwell in the house of the LORD all the days of my life, to behold the beauty of the LORD, and to enquire in his temple," saying, "The greatly and only happiness of God's people, which they choose and chiefly desire, is not any earthly happiness, but of a spiritual and divine nature, consisting in seeing God, union and communion with him, and serving him."[187] Speaking on Ps 31:19, "Oh how great is thy goodness, which thou hast laid up for them that fear thee," Edwards stated that "The chief happiness of the saints is future happiness."[188] He furthered this argument using Ps 89:46–48, "How long, LORD? wilt thou hide thyself for ever? shall thy wrath burn like fire? Remember how short my time is: wherefore hast thou made all men in vain? What man is he that liveth, and shall not see death? shall he deliver his soul from the hand of the grave?" Edwards explained that we can know there is a future state and that the "the chief reward of the saints is not in this life" because "Man's life is so short, that it was never worth the while to make such a creature as man only for so short an existence" and because "Man's life is so short and so full of trouble, that it is not worth the while to be born, only to live in such an evil world, and for so short a time."[189] Edwards spoke about a future state in similar ways in more than three dozen other passages from the Psalms, revealing that, in his thinking, the Psalms' extensive teaching on the future state for saints in heaven manifested the harmony of the Old and New Testaments.[190] Edwards' comment on Psalm 128 is

---

186. Edwards, "Harmony," 218.

187. Edwards, "Harmony," 226.

188. Edwards, "Harmony," 227.

189. Edwards, "Harmony," 256.

190. These passages include Pss 16:5–6; 17:14–15; 21:6; 23:6; 36:8–9; 37:18, 27–28; 39:5–7, 12; 41:1–4; 43:3–4; 49:6, 16–18; 52:7–9; 62:10; 63:1–8; 65:4; 72:14; 73:20, 22, 24, 25–26, 26–28; 84:1–7, 5–7, 10; 90; 91:1–16; 94; 102:3, 12–13, 16–17, 19–20; 107:39–43; 112:8–10; 116:15; 119:19, 54, 119; 140:11–13; 141:7–10; 145:20. Edwards, "Harmony," 221–224, 231–236, 239, 241–243, 247–250, 253–254, 256–259, 261, 264–265, 267, 269, 271, 276–277.

representative of the way he discussed the saints' hope in heaven from the Psalter:

> The promise here made of happiness and prosperity to them that fear the Lord, and their being "blessed out of Zion," and "seeing the good of Jerusalem" and "peace on Israel," is a clear evidence of happiness in another world, seeing that the life of the saints in this world is very commonly a life of great affliction and suffering, of persecution, as the matter is abundantly represented in this book of Psalms.[191]

Edwards' understanding of the harmony of the Old and New Testaments enabled him to speak at length about the happiness promised to the saints in the glorious heavenly abode.

Edwards described heaven at greater length in a March 1741 sermon on Ps 45:15: "With gladness and rejoicing shall they be brought: they shall enter into the king's palace." This verse brings us full circle to where we began this chapter talking about the church from Psalm 45, and again, Reformed exegetes commonly viewed this verse as representing the final presentation of the church to Christ at the marriage feast.[192] His six-part doctrine fleshed out his interpretation of the passage. First, he showed how heaven is the King's palace, either with respect to God the Father who sits on the throne or with respect to God the Son, who is "so Great a King" and for whom heaven is his "special place of abode" and the place of his royal throne.[193] Second, he described this great palace as "large & spacious," of "great magnificence," a place of "Beauty & pleasantness," a "paradise," full of light and "glorious," "precious," having "Beams of Love," "most beautifully adorned," "bespangled with gold & Jewels," ornaments that are "Chiefly spiritual."[194] It is "abundantly furnished with the Richest & most Excellent Provision," "a place of

---

191. Edwards, "Harmony," 273.

192. Henry identified the king's palaces as "the Heavenly Mansions" and this bringing in of the spouse as both the initial "Conversion of Souls to CHRIST" and "the Marriage of the Lamb," or "the compleating of the Mystical Body, and the Glorification of the Saints at the end of Time." Henry, *Exposition*, [Ps 45:15]. Poole described the church corporate being led to Christ. Poole, *Synopsis*, 801. Trapp emphasized the rejoicing at this marriage feast. Trapp, *Commentary*, 705. Dickson described the presentation of the completed church at the end of time to Christ as his bride. Dickson, *First Fifty Psalms*, 311–312. Calvin, though, did not comment on Ps 45:15. Calvin, *Commentary*, 2:191–192.

193. Jonathan Edwards, "731. Sermon on Ps 45:15 (Mar. [21,] 1744)," Beinecke Rare Book and Manuscript Library, Yale University, New Haven, CT, L. IV.

194. Edwards, "731. Sermon on Ps 45:15," L. 2v.–3r.

glorious Entertainm[en]t" and "feasting," and it is "unparalleled," "Inimitable,"
"Inconcievable," "Perfect," and "fortified with Infinite strength."¹⁹⁵ Third, he portrayed the character of those who enter the king's palace as "Holy persons" and
"pure" (Psalms 15; 24), people who are humble, strong in faith, "Hungering &
thirsting after R[ighteousness]," "compassionate, merciful, charitable, loving,"
"Followers of G[od] as dear Chil[dren]."¹⁹⁶ Fourth, he described the manner in
which people enter this palace, both at death, as God's angels take them to heaven
where they are "made welcome" and have a "Joyfull Reception" by Christ and the
Father; and at the day of judgment, when there will be a most "Joyfull & glorious
Entrance" into heaven, for on that day "[Christ] & all his angels shall Come forth
to bring them" to heaven, and God the Father shall give each individual "Perfect
Beauty of soul" and "glorious Beauty of Body" and shall "Present them in all their
Perfection & Glory" to Christ.¹⁹⁷ Fifth, Edwards explained that the saints will enter
the palace both "as the Chil[dren] of G[od] the F[ather] there to dwell with him
forever & ever" and receive his "Fatherly Love & Tenderness," and as the bride of
Christ, there to "everlastingly Enjoy his Love," to "Reign with him" and sit with
him on his throne, to "enjoy the most full & intimate communion with him," and
"to dwell in his Eternal Embraces."¹⁹⁸ Finally, Edwards exhorted all "to seek this
Great Priviledge."¹⁹⁹

We close this discussion of the future state with a February 1751 sermon in
which Edwards conjoined language from both "Sinners in the Hands of an Angry
God" and "Heaven Is a World of Love," illustrating his interest in promoting the

<hr />

195. Edwards, "731. Sermon on Ps 45:15," L. 5r.

196. Edwards, "731. Sermon on Ps 45:15," L. 7r., 8v.

197. Edwards, "731. Sermon on Ps 45:15," L. 9v.–10r.

198. Edwards, "731. Sermon on Ps 45:15," L. 10v., 11v. On the activity of the saints in heaven,
see Edwards' November 26, 1747, sermon on Ps 115:17–18, from which he preached the doc-
trine: "The blessedness [of saints in heaven] consists very much in praising & glorifying
G[od]." Jonathan Edwards, "880. Sermon on Ps 115:17–18 (November 26, 1747)," in Sermons,
Series II, 1747, vol. 65 of WJEO, L. 2v. See also Edwards' similar but distinct sermon, "Serving
God in Heaven," in which he used Rev 22:3 as his text in his March 14, 1731, preaching of
the sermon but Ps 115:17–18 in a second, undated preaching of the sermon. Mark Valeri, ed.,
Sermons and Discourses 1730–1733, vol. 17 of WJE (1999), 252. The doctrine he preached was
"The happiness of the saints in heaven consists partly in that they there serve God." Jonathan
Edwards, "Serving God in Heaven" (Rev 22:3), in Sermons and Discourses 1730–1733, ed. Mark
Valeri, vol. 17 of WJE (1999), 254.

199. Edwards, "731. Sermon on Ps 45:15," L. 11v. See also Edwards' note on this verse that
the church will receive a "glorious privilege" when she enters the king's palace in Notes on
Scripture, 526–527.

gospel both by dread and delight.²⁰⁰ He preached on Ps 112:1: "Praise ye the Lᴏʀᴅ. Blessed is the man that feareth the Lᴏʀᴅ, that delighteth greatly in his commandments," from which he developed the doctrine: "good men are Happy men."²⁰¹ Edwards explained that for good men, "G[od] has forgiven all their sins that ever they committed & is no more angry with them for their sins."²⁰² While God is an enemy of others, he is the friend of the forgiven man, and he is a Father who cares for and loves his children. With God and Christ as his friend and Savior, the good man need not fear death, war, or the devil, for his soul is protected from all danger. Even affliction in this world is no danger because Christ will use it "to make em beter men & to fit em more for Heaven."²⁰³ Edwards summed it up saying, "they who have the great G[od] for their Friend need to be afraid of nothing for nothing can Hurt them."²⁰⁴ Fear is wiped away by the hope of heaven, which is a "[world] of Love," where God will wipe away every tear and where saints will "drink of Rivers of pleasure."²⁰⁵ In contrast, the happiness of the wicked is a mere façade, for when they die, neither their wealth, military strength and prowess, royalty, finery, or exquisite fare will do these sinners any good before an angry God. In a passage reminiscent of "Sinners," Edwards stated, "all wicked men are mis[erable] whether they be Rich or poor because the great G[od] is angry with them," and "G[od] is not their F[ather] & friend but their Enemy," which means "they are in danger of going to Hell every day. They Hang over the Pit of Hell by a rotten string that is just ready to Break every moment."²⁰⁶ So Edwards exhorted his people to turn to God: "Theref[ore] now harken to me lest you go to Hell.... I this day make you a greater offer than if I offered you all the money in the whole [world.] I offer you G[od] & [Christ] & honor if you will forsake your sin & give your Hearts to J[esus] [Christ]."²⁰⁷

For Edwards, the Psalms described the future state of heaven quite clearly, portraying it as God's glorious house and beautiful palace, where adopted

---

200. Edwards, "Sinners," 400–435; Jonathan Edwards, "Heaven Is a World of Love" (2 Cor 13:8–10), in *Charity and Its Fruits*, in *Ethical Writings*, ed. Paul Ramsey, vol. 8 of *WJE* (1989), 366–397.

201. Jonathan Edwards, "981. Sermon on Ps 112:1 (February 1751)," Beinecke Rare Book and Manuscript Library, Yale University, New Haven, CT, L. 1r.

202. Edwards, "981. Sermon on Ps 112:1," L. 1r.

203. Edwards, "981. Sermon on Ps 112:1," L. 1v.

204. Edwards, "981. Sermon on Ps 112:1," L. 1v.

205. Edwards, "981. Sermon on Ps 112:1," L. 2r.

206. Edwards, "981. Sermon on Ps 112:1," L. 3r.

207. Edwards, "981. Sermon on Ps 112:1," L. 4r.

children are received with joy and warm welcome, where the greatest happiness is enjoyed not for a period but for eternity, where the saints experience both the tender love of God the Father and the most intimate communion with Christ as his beautiful, redeemed bride.

Conclusion

In this chapter we have seen a broad array of ways in which Edwards engaged the Psalms, all related to the church corporate and the final culmination of all things issuing forth in the permanent eternal state of both the redeemed and the wicked. Edwards' approach was largely in step with his Reformed predecessors. They shared a typological interpretation of the Psalms to describe the church, and they spoke on worship in a similar fashion as well. They also explained the imprecatory psalms using some of the same arguments, although Edwards' redemptive-historical emphasis emerged more clearly in his discussion. Looking at eternity, they envisioned the certain end of this world and the coming wrath of God on the wicked from the Psalms and also anticipated the glorious marriage feast that inaugurates an eternity of happiness with Christ. Edwards differed from earlier Reformed exegetes on the view he developed partly from the Psalms that heavenly saints gaze on the earth to see God's work of redemption unfold and in his aim to defend God's justice by showing the proportionality between God's majesty and wrath—the latter of which may reflect the time in which he lived, when attacks from reason on the Bible and God's justice proliferated. By and large, however, Edwards stood firmly in line with his Reformed predecessors in his interpretation of the Psalms on the church corporate and the eternal culmination of all things.

This chapter also shows that Edwards employed several exegetical methods in his interpretation of the Psalms. He used typology especially to describe the church corporate from the Psalms, but he also set the Psalms in their historical context to understand their relation to David's life, and that literal reading often formed the foundation for his ecclesiological and spiritual readings of the text. In addition, he interpreted the Psalms both apocalyptically and anagogically—that is, he spoke of the destruction of this world and the wicked and also of the hope of the world to come. Edwards' exegesis was so varied that any attempt to confine him to a typological method of exegesis simply does not do justice to the way he interpreted the Psalms day in and day out. And even if one defines "Christological" exegesis broadly to include the church corporate and in its individual members as the body of Christ, such a rendering does not take into account the place of the wicked and of hell in Edwards' discussion of the Psalms, while the concept of the history of redemption does.

We have also seen that Edwards used the Psalms as foundational, authoritative texts for developing and establishing some of the theological themes that concerned him at great length over the course of his ministry, from the nature of the church to the end of the world and the eternal dwelling places of hell and heaven. As we saw from the end of chapter 5, Edwards was concerned about all of these doctrines because of the way they fit into the overarching framework of God's work of redemption in history.

In this chapter we come to the end of the history of redemption, though it is also just the beginning of the eternal state, in which God will accomplish his ends in perfection, namely manifesting his glory and endowing the redeemed elect with eternal happiness. Christ's redemption focused on the church, a remnant of fallen humanity, whom God has saved out of their sins and out of hell to become the glorious bride of Christ. All the while Christ is advancing his kingdom more and more as we approach the end of the world and beginning of eternity, where the wicked will eternally display God's glorious justice in hell and the redeemed will eternally enjoy God's benefits and love in union with Christ. This chapter thus rounds out the long history of redemption, the interpretive framework that guided Edwards as he exegetically and theologically engaged the book of Psalms.

Conclusion

EDWARDS CONSISTENTLY SOUNDED the gospel and its encompassing themes in his treatment of the Psalms, and as we draw this study to a close, comparing two sermons on Psalm 89 at the beginning and end of his preaching career illustrates well the constant centrality of redemptive history in Edwards' engagement with the book of Psalms. During his earliest preaching years while serving at a New York congregation between summer 1722 and spring 1723, Edwards preached on Ps 89:6, "For who in the heaven can be compared unto the LORD? who among the sons of the mighty can be likened unto the LORD?" And as we saw in chapter 5, in this sermon he described the book of Psalms broadly by saying, "there is so much of the gospel doctrine, grace, and spirit, breaking out and shining in it, that it seems to be carried clear above and beyond the strain and pitch of the Old Testament, and almost brought up to the New" for "[a]lmost the whole book of Psalms has either a direct or indirect respect to Christ and the gospel."[1] He continued by noting that Ethan the Ezrahite, who penned the psalm, began by zeroing in on "the glorious excellencies, perfections, and works of God," which indicated to Edwards that it must have reference to Christ since "never were God's perfections manifested so gloriously as they have been manifested in the work of redemption; never did his infinite glories so brightly shine forth as in the face of Jesus Christ."[2]

In October 1756 Edwards returned to Psalm 89 to proclaim the gospel in what Wilson Kimnach calls his "last major homiletical effort."[3] While he certainly delivered dozens more sermons after that date, this sermon was apparently the last one he spent significant time developing and writing out. For this sermon he took as his text Ps 89:15, "Blessed is the people that know

---

1. Jonathan Edwards, "God's Excellencies" (Ps 89:6), in *Sermons and Discourses 1720–1723*, vol. 10 of *WJE* (1992), 415.

2. Edwards, "God's Excellencies," 415.

3. Wilson H. Kimnach, ed., *Sermons and Discourses 1743–1758*, ed. Wilson H. Kimnach, vol. 25 of *WJE* (2006), 698. He also preached this sermon again in Stockbridge that December.

the joyful sound: they shall walk, O LORD, in the light of thy countenance."[4] Edwards associated "the joyful sound" with the sound of the silver trumpets that were sounded during the festivals and feasts of the Jewish calendar. He said these "sacred trumpets" alluded to the year of jubilee, "the most joyful time when liberty was proclaimed throughout all the land to the Israelites that were in servitude."[5] And these joyful trumpets and the jubilee "undoubtedly represented" something further,

> the sound of the gospel by which that great spiritual and eternal feast is proclaimed that God has appointed for his people, and by which God proclaims liberty to captives and the opening of the prison to them that are bound, and proclaims that spiritual jubilee that the prophet Isaiah, chapter 61, at the beginning, calls "the acceptable year of the Lord."[6]

Edwards held that the preaching of the gospel of Christ was represented by the blowing of a trumpet, as in Isa 27:13, and that the Scripture made "innumerable representations" of the gospel with images agreeable to a joyful sound.[7] The context of Psalm 89 further supported this interpretation because its contents— God's covenant with David, glorious things for Jews and Gentiles, the fulfillment of that covenant—are principally related to "the gospel day."[8] Edwards moved from this exegesis to describe the glorious sounding of the gospel.

He developed this gospel theme through five points in the doctrine section of his sermon, arguing at length in his first point that "[t]he gospel of Jesus Christ is a joyful sound."[9] It is joyful because it proclaims deliverance from such "infinitely dreadful" evils, namely, "the guilt of sin, captivity and bondage to Satan, the wrath of God and perfect and everlasting ruin and misery."[10] The tidings are joyful because they offer humanity, in its "natural state" of

---

4. Edwards, "Of Those Who Walk in the Light of God's Countenance" [Ps 89:15(b)], in *Sermons and Discourses 1743–1758*, ed. Wilson H. Kimnach, vol. 25 of *WJE* (2006), 698–710. See also Edwards' bare outline of an earlier sermon on Ps 89:15, written on two leaves of paper. Jonathan Edwards, "677. Sermon on Ps 89:15(a) (July 1742)," Beinecke Rare Book and Manuscript Library, Yale University, New Haven, CT.

5. Edwards, "Of Those Who Walk," 701.

6. Edwards, "Of Those Who Walk," 701.

7. Edwards, "Of Those Who Walk," 701–702. For example, Luke 2:10 calls it "glad tidings of great joy."

8. Edwards, "Of Those Who Walk," 702.

9. Edwards, "Of Those Who Walk," 702.

10. Edwards, "Of Those Who Walk," 702.

imprisonment to sin and Satan, complete deliverance from the guilt of sin and "everlasting peace with God."[11] The gospel is also joyful because it ushers people into "an eternal mansion in the house of God," in the heavenly Zion, a paradise of pleasures receiving "peculiar favor" with God and love from Christ—an experience of "ineffable heights of glory in the heaven of heavens."[12] These good things are certain because they are "sealed with the blood of the Son of God," who is our Redeemer and judge and to whom we are "betrothed," for the down payment is that the "soul is united to God [through the] spirit of adoption as confirmation and assurance of a future marriage with the Lamb."[13] Finally, the gospel is a joyful sound because it "conveys joy unspeakable and full of glory into our hearts, actually communicating and administering that divine food to our souls wherein our happiness consists, and which is its most refreshing and satisfying and exquisitely delightful entertainment."[14] In this way the gospel displays "God's glorious beauty and love," which delivers the "most perfect happiness of the soul," for "God's love to us has [a] manifestation that is perfectly unparalleled."[15]

Edwards went on in the second point of his doctrine to describe what it means to know this joyful sound, both having "a spiritual and saving understanding of the great things" of the gospel and embracing those things as one's own.[16] Third, Edwards argued that all people who know this joyful sound are "strictly united one to another but greatly distinguished from all the world," describing the corporate body of the church.[17] For his fourth doctrinal point, Edwards held that this one body is a happy people due to the "greatness" and "grounds" of that joy.[18] He closed his doctrine section with this point: "The great and peculiar happiness of that blessed people may be summed up in their walking in the light of God's countenance."[19] Such people see and enjoy this light, which is "[t]he light of God's glory," for they anticipate the joy that

---

11. Edwards, "Of Those Who Walk," 703.

12. Edwards, "Of Those Who Walk," 704.

13. Edwards, "Of Those Who Walk," 704.

14. Edwards, "Of Those Who Walk," 705.

15. Edwards, "Of Those Who Walk," 705.

16. Edwards, "Of Those Who Walk," 706.

17. Edwards, "Of Those Who Walk," 707.

18. Edwards, "Of Those Who Walk," 707.

19. Edwards, "Of Those Who Walk," 707.

awaits them of seeing God's face in the world to come.[20] Those who walk in the light of God's countenance not only enjoy God's love and light, but they live under its influences, so that they "shine with the reflection of it."[21]

In his application, Edwards called his hearers to examine themselves and see whether or not they were people who know the joyful sound and embrace it and are truly united to the body of people who live in the light of God's countenance. And then he challenged them to live with happiness, knowing the joyful sound of the gospel will overcome misery in this world, even death itself. So the one who has confirmed the joy of living in the light of God's countenance can appropriate the language of the Psalms as his own, saying, "God is our refuge and strength, a very present help in trouble. Therefore will not we fear, though the earth be removed, and though the mountains be carried into the midst of the sea; Though the waters thereof roar and be troubled, though the mountains shake with the swelling thereof" (Ps 46:1–3). Edwards concluded his sermon with a call to piety, to make Christ's abode the aim of one's journey, to engage in spiritual warfare along the way, and "to hearken to the joyful sound as exhibited in the sweet invitations of the gospel."[22]

We rehearse Edwards' treatment of Ps 89:15 here because it encapsulates in one sermon at the end of his life so many of the themes that he emphasized over the course of his life in his engagement with the book of Psalms. He described the nature of humanity in bondage to sin and the work of Christ to redeem humanity by his blood. He proclaimed the hope of salvation and all its joyful benefits to those who embrace this joyful sound as their own. He portrayed the church as a corporate body that basks in the light of its Redeemer and spiritual husband and reflects that holy light in the piety of its individual members. He looked forward to dwelling eternally with Christ, enjoying his love and the light of God's eminent glory. And he drew these theological concepts together with the joyful noise of the gospel.

In this book, we have touched on all of these themes and others that are best encapsulated by the phrase "the history of redemption." Edwards lived in a time of new challenges to the Bible generally and the Psalms particularly, raising questions about how to interpret the Psalms in light of the new learning, the focus on historical background, and the debate between revealed and natural religion; questions about whether to preach on David's historical place or proclaim Christ and the gospel from the Psalms; and questions about the use

---

20. Edwards, "Of Those Who Walk," 707.

21. Edwards, "Of Those Who Walk," 707–708.

22. Edwards, "Of Those Who Walk," 708–710. Quotation on 710.

of the Psalter to sing of Christ and his redemption in worship. I have argued that, in light of his affirmation of the divine inspiration of the Psalms and the harmony of the Old and New Testaments, Edwards appropriated the book of Psalms to proclaim the gospel boldly, seeing it as layered with the theological truths that constitute the redemptive-historical work of the triune God. We see the concept of redemption history even from his earliest sermons on the Psalms but more fully fleshed out in his 1756 sermon on Ps 89:15 as he developed his understanding of the Psalter. While Edwards occasionally changed his thinking about exegesis of the Psalms on minor interpretive questions, the interpretive framework of the history of redemption served as a constant in his engagement with the Psalms throughout his life.[23] Sometimes he emphasized certain aspects of it more than others to fit the occasion as priorities in his ministry shifted over the years, but he never lost sight of the whole of redemption history as he sought to worship with, interpret, and preach the Psalms.

As historians continue to debate what constitutes the center of Edwards' theology, one thing is certain: Any discussion of Edwards' theology must incorporate the concept of the history of redemption. Recent works on Edwards have recognized this thrust. In his treatment of Edwards' view of the Christian life, Sean Michael Lucas sums up God's "grand design" by describing two levels of Edwards' theological vision: the cosmic level of "the grand narrative of the history of the work of redemption" and the personal level of the application of that work to the individual.[24] McClymond and McDermott likewise structure their massive volume, *The Theology of Jonathan Edwards*, around the history of redemption, and while they resist the call to simplify Edwards' theology to any single theme or center, given its complexity and his eclectic interest in so many theological and philosophical ideas, they nonetheless argue that "[o]ne of Edwards's governing theological ideas...is captured in the phrase 'history of redemption.' "[25] The concept of the history of redemption was not only the

---

23. For example, see his "Blank Bible" notes on Ps 16:9, where he interpreted the meaning of the term "glory" first as "soul" but later as "*logos*"; on Ps 45:8, where he understood the meaning of "ivory" first as "purity," but later as "heaven"; on Ps 126:4, where he interpreted the symbol of streams first as a reference to God's people but later as a symbol of refreshment; and on Psalms 145–150, where he first thought these six psalms constituted "one continued song" but later explained that Psalm 145 was an introduction to the latter five psalms. Jonathan Edwards, *The "Blank Bible,"* ed. Stephen J. Stein, vol. 24, part 1 of *WJE* (2006), 482–483; 495–496; 533–534; 540–541. Italics original.

24. Sean Michael Lucas, *God's Grand Design: The Theological Vision of Jonathan Edwards* (Wheaton, IL: Crossway, 2011), 14.

25. Michael J. McClymond and Gerald R. McDermott, *The Theology of Jonathan Edwards* (New York: Oxford University Press, 2012), 181. McClymond and McDermott similarly state,

key overarching and organizing theme for his theology; it also served Edwards as the broad encompassing interpretive framework for how he engaged the Psalms. And as such, it allowed him to focus his efforts on the issue that mattered most to Edwards in his ministry: the proclamation and advancement of the gospel.

The History of Biblical Interpretation

As we have compared Edwards to representative Reformed exegetes of the Psalms—Matthew Henry, Matthew Poole, John Trapp, David Dickson, and John Calvin—we have seen a number of differences and similarities. As earlier exegetes differed on some interpretive details in the Psalms, so Edwards differed on some smaller points as well, such as identifying "Cush the Benjamite" as Shimei in Psalm 7. But Edwards stood out from the Reformed tradition in three broader ways.

First, on a number of occasions he discussed the Psalms with a unique angle because of his particular context. In large part, these differences arose from questions raised by the new Enlightenment-era learning, leading him to discuss the authorship of the Pentateuch, comparative religion, and the existence of God as evidenced by design in nature. The differences also arose from circumstances particular to his time and place, including a military loss, the natural elements at Stockbridge, and bodily manifestations in the revivals. Because of new attacks on certain doctrines, Edwards also used the Psalms to address specific theological issues in ways that earlier exegetes did not, including doctrines such as original sin, justification by faith, God's justice in damning sinners, God's sovereignty, authentic signs of the Spirit's work, and the harmony of the Old and New Testaments. As he engaged new challenges to and questions about Christianity, he found answers in the Psalms for which his predecessors had not felt the need to look.

Second, Edwards differed from earlier Reformed exegetes in the *extent* to which he used typology. He saw more types of Christ in the Psalms than his predecessors, through images like manna and the river, and he found more depictions of Christ's life, including his incarnation, transfiguration, and prayer in the Garden of Gethsemane. From the imagery of the Psalms he also distinctively identified types of the Spirit, portrayed as oil, a river, a fountain, and dew, and types of humanity, portrayed as grass, a shaking leaf, and

---

"Perhaps the most-repeated theme of the thousands of entries in the Old Testament portion of Edwards's *Blank Bible* is that this or that person or event or teaching points to Christ and his redemption." McClymond and McDermott, *The Theology of Jonathan Edwards*, 249.

a withering flower. The point to note here is not that typology was unique to Edwards but rather that he pursued it further than earlier exegetes. Many of them clearly used typology frequently in their interpretation of the Psalms to identify Christ and the church, just as Edwards did, but in keeping with his expansive view of typology, Edwards saw biblical types in the Psalms that earlier Reformed interpreters did not identify.

Third, Edwards distinguished himself in making certain interpretations of the Psalms that highlighted the history of redemption. By describing a lower view of humanity compared to angels and hounding on the desperate sinfulness of mankind from the Psalms, he both highlighted his hearers' great need of a Redeemer and exalted God's glory in redeeming humanity. For Edwards, showing the lowness of human sin served all the more to raise up God's great excellency. He also saw redemptive symbols in the Psalms that earlier Reformed exegetes did not, such as linking Psalm 45 with the historical account of Solomon marrying Pharaoh's daughter, which spoke prophetically of the calling of the Gentiles or the redemptive union of Christ and the church. Edwards also more eagerly described the Spirit's work of regeneration and inspiration from the Psalms, showing that his broader, redemptive-historical view of the Psalter went beyond a merely Christological interpretation. His notion that the heavenly saints gaze upon the earth underscored the importance of witnesses to God's redemptive work. And he preached the gospel not only from psalms commonly identified as Christological, such as Psalms 2, 22, and 110, but also from passages in which the gospel was less readily apparent. Unlike the earlier Reformed exegetes, Edwards called sinners to wake up from their vain fantasies using Ps 10:6, made a gospel call to children from Ps 34:11, and described Christ's gentleness in Ps 18:35 to proclaim the gospel. Edwards' emphasis on the history of redemption distinguished him in the history of interpreting the Psalms.

But one should not conclude from these observations that Edwards stood miles apart from the Reformed tradition, for the comparison of Edwards to his predecessors shows that he stood firmly in line with them both in his interpretive approach to the Psalms and in his formulation of theological themes from the Psalms. He was certainly not identical to his exegetical forebears, but he shared core commitments with them on the foundational doctrines developed from the Psalter and on the multilayered methods of reading it within the whole canon of Scripture. From God's glory, sovereignty, mystery, and mercy to the divine inspiration of the Psalms; from the nature of humanity as a feeble creature to human depravity and the deceitfulness of sin; from the foretelling of Christ in types and prophecies to Christ's obedience, redemptive work, and kingly reign; from describing the evil of false professions in the mixed visible church to emphasizing God's mercy and the bringing in of the Gentiles; from describing worship and the church to explaining the imprecatory psalms and calling for Christian piety; from warning about the end of the world and judgment in hell to anticipating the final marriage feast in heaven—across these varied theological topics, Edwards shared strong affinities with the Reformed exegetical tradition.

In McClymond and McDermott's reading of Edwards, they state that "Jonathan Edwards is one of the great Christian thinkers who defies precise categorization. His thinking is recognizably Reformed but with a difference," which is visible because he "enjoyed tinkering with if not transforming his received Puritan and Reformed traditions."[26] This study bears out this judgment insofar as one understands that Edwards believed this "tinkering" was more faithful to the biblical witness, which speaks harmoniously across both testaments. And as he tweaked his theology while drinking deeply from the Psalms, he kept himself within the boundaries of the redemptive-historical framework of interpretation. This framework had long guided theologians in the Christian tradition. As John Thompson notes, "precritical" interpreters held a common parameter in exegetical decisions, namely, "keeping the Bible's redemptive intention constantly in mind as a key to unlock the meaning of Scripture."[27] This study suggests that Edwards stood within this stream of thought, and where he verged away from common Reformed interpretations of the Psalms—in part because he embraced and engaged the new enlightened learning of his age—he did so to emphasize redemptive history from the Psalms even more than those who came before him.

Edwards' Exegesis in Historical Assessment

How does this study of Edwards and the Psalms speak to scholars' previous descriptions of Edwards and the Bible? On one level, the discussion on Edwards and the Reformed exegetical tradition seems to corroborate Robert Brown's argument that Edwards was "modestly critical," adopting a "hybrid traditionalism, one modified in significant ways by his accommodations to the new learning."[28] He remained largely in step with the traditional interpretations of

---

26. McClymond and McDermott, *The Theology of Jonathan Edwards*, 663.

27. John L. Thompson, *Reading the Bible with the Dead: What You Can Learn from the History of Exegesis That You Can't Learn from Exegesis Alone* (Grand Rapids, MI: Eerdmans, 2007), 220–221.

28. Robert E. Brown, *Jonathan Edwards and the Bible* (Bloomington: Indiana University Press, 2002), xvii–xviii.

his predecessors, but was affected by the rise of the new learning as it caused him to bring new questions to the Psalms, all the while upholding the Bible as God's divinely inspired Word. He was interested in the meaning of Hebrew terms and in the historical background to David's psalms, and he addressed new critical questions, such as the Mosaic authorship of the Pentateuch, with input from the Psalms. How critical he was remains a matter of some debate, and this study suggests that while he certainly responded to the rising his-torical criticism by appropriating some of its methods and asking some of its questions, he exhibited a greater modesty *in the Psalms particularly* than Brown has found in his broader study focused on Edwards' engagement with the new criticism. Still, he engaged with the new learning enough to differentiate him from his Reformed predecessors, suggesting that, while he certainly had much in common with the precritical approach to the Bible, to call him strictly precritical, as Stephen Stein, Glenn Kreider, and Jeongmo Yoo have identified him, does not quite capture his approach to the Psalms.[29] Douglas Sweeney portrays this tension well in noting that while Edwards "was fully apprised of recent trends in modern critical thought," he also "spent a lot of time defend-ing Protestant orthodoxy in the face of new attacks," making Edwards "a fasci-nating example of a modern thinker with premodern sympathies."[30]

We must also consider McClymond and McDermott's argument that Edwards' biblical exegesis exhibited a "catholic tendency insofar as he embraced the medieval tradition of seeing multiple senses in scripture."[31] Similarly, Brandon Withrow argues that "[t]he language of deification and the spiritual reading of Scripture found in the writings of ancient Christians . . . clearly have a kindred spirit in the ideas of Edwards."[32] They are right to note continuity between Edwards and the medieval and patristic exegetical traditions in that

29. Stephen J. Stein, "The Spirit and the Word: Jonathan Edwards and Scriptural Exegesis," in *Jonathan Edwards and the American Experience*, ed. Nathan O. Hatch and Harry S. Stout (New York: Oxford University Press, 1988), 119; Glenn R. Kreider, *Jonathan Edwards's Interpretation of Revelation 4:1–8:1* (Dallas: University Press of America, Inc., 2004), 283; Jeongmo Yoo, "Jonathan Edwards's Interpretation of the Major Prophets: The Books of Isaiah, Jeremiah, and Ezekiel," *Puritan Reformed Journal* 3, no. 2 (2011): 164, 192.

30. Douglas A. Sweeney, "Edwards and the Bible," in *Understanding Jonathan Edwards: An Introduction to America's Theologian*, ed. Gerald R. McDermott (Oxford: Oxford University Press, 2009), 70; Douglas A. Sweeney, "Edwards, Jonathan (1703–1758)" in *Dictionary of Major Biblical Interpreters*, ed. Donald K. McKim (Downers Grove, IL: IVP Academic, 2007), 399.

31. McClymond and McDermott, *The Theology of Jonathan Edwards*, 175, 17.

32. Brandon G. Withrow, *Becoming Divine: Jonathan Edwards's Incarnational Spirituality within the Christian Tradition* (Eugene, OR: Cascade, 2011), 204.

they all found multiple senses in Scripture. My comparison of Edwards with earlier Reformed exegetes on the Psalms militates against associating multiple senses only with medieval Catholicism, for it shows that Reformed interpreters commonly saw multiple senses in the Psalms as well. But we should also recognize a distinction between these traditions. While some medieval exegetes showed interest in the historical meaning—especially those from the school of St. Victor—Reformed interpreters gave greater attention to the historical meaning and developed related typological or spiritual meanings differently, emphasizing that historical reality while avoiding allegory. And while medieval exegetes spoke of a fourfold sense (the *quadriga*), Protestant and Puritan exegetes spoke of the literal sense but debated what could be included in the literal sense, some accepting more typological interpretations than others. Protestant and Puritan exegetes intentionally avoided using the language of the fourfold sense to distinguish themselves from Roman Catholic interpreters, even if some of their interpretations within what they conceived as the literal sense functioned in similar ways to the fourfold sense. None of them explicitly retrieved the medieval Catholic *quadriga* in the formulaic way that earlier Catholics employed it.

As we have seen in this study, Edwards shared many of the same historical and spiritual readings of the Psalms as Reformed interpreters ranging from John Calvin to Matthew Henry. Edwards' interpretation owes more to this Reformed-Puritan typological vision of Scripture that grew out of Calvin's restrained, historical approach to the Psalms than to Catholics in the Middle Ages.[33] McClymond and McDermott's linking of Edwards with the medieval tradition supports their aim of presenting Edwards as the premier theologian for ecumenical dialogue, and Withrow similarly upholds Edwards as "a Protestant candidate for continuing interests in ecumenical dialogue between Western and Eastern Christians."[34] While they emphasize the *broad similarities* between Edwards, the Reformed interpreters, the medieval Catholic tradition, and the

---

33. Part of McClymond and McDermott's argument rests on their example of Edwards' interpretation of 2 Samuel 20, in which they observe that Edwards said "almost nothing regarding the historical situation that lay behind this text." McClymond and McDermott, *The Theology of Jonathan Edwards*, 177. But this example is misleading and misrepresentative of Edwards' interpretive practice, at least in the Psalms, where we have clearly seen that, in the text segment of his sermons, his common practice was to describe the historical setting of the passage at hand.

34. Withrow, *Becoming Divine*, 204. On McClymond and McDermott's argument that Edwards can serve as a bridge between Eastern and Western Christianity, between Protestants and Catholics, between liberals and conservatives, and between charismatics and non-charismatics, see McClymond and McDermott, *The Theology of Jonathan Edwards*, 718–728.

early church—similarities that do exist—my study suggests that the *differences* between these brands of multiple senses point to a gap between the Reformed tradition of typology, out of which Edwards developed his exegesis, and the Roman Catholic tradition of the *quadriga*—a gap that still merits recognition.

In addition, we must assess Stein's charge that Edwards did not remain within the Protestant tradition in his biblical interpretation. Stein argues that he used "immense hermeneutical latitude in his interpretation of the psalms"; that "[h]is pursuit of spiritual meaning in the texts knew no bounds"; that "the Bible did not function for him as a theological norm or source in any usual Protestant fashion because the literal sense of the text did not restrict him"; and that he pursued the spiritual sense "with abandon."[35] What this study on the Psalms shows is that Edwards did in fact place boundaries on his exegesis, in much the same way as his Protestant forebears. While he explored more types in the Psalms than his predecessors, he also spent much time seeking to understand the historical meaning of the Psalms, and when he did use typology or spiritual exegesis, he stood within the accepted practices of the Reformed traditions he inherited. We have also seen how frequently he interpreted the plain meaning of the Psalms in his call for Christian piety. More important, when he engaged in spiritual exegesis, he did so within the confines of a redemptive-historical framework, tempering his interpretation by the analogy of faith and the analogy of Scripture.[36] This assessment stands in line with Stephen R. C. Nichols' persuasive argument in his study of the relationship of the Old and New Testament in Edwards' theology that "Edwards is guided in his interpretation of types by the grammar book of that language, the Bible," and that the charges saying Edwards' typology was arbitrary do not take into account his "sophisticated biblical literacy."[37] Rather, given Edwards' reliance on the analogy of faith and the analogy of Scripture, Nichols concludes that "Stephen Stein's depiction of Edwards's poetic 'flights of exegetical fancy' must be rejected."[38] This study corroborates Nichols' assessment.

---

35. Stephen J. Stein, "Editor's Introduction," in *The "Blank Bible,"* ed. Stephen J. Stein, vol. 24 of *WJE* (2006), 34–35, 40; Stephen J. Stein, "The Quest for the Spiritual Sense: The Biblical Hermeneutics of Jonathan Edwards," *Harvard Theological Review* 70 (1977): 100–101, 113.

36. For a similar argument in a different book of the Bible, see my article, "'The Only Rule of Our Faith and Practice': Jonathan Edwards' Interpretation of the Book of Isaiah as a Case Study of His Exegetical Boundaries," *Journal of the Evangelical Theological Society* 52, no. 4 (2009): 811–829.

37. Stephen R. C. Nichols, *Jonathan Edwards's Bible: The Relationship of the Old and New Testaments in the Theology of Jonathan Edwards* (Eugene, OR: Pickwick, 2013), 85, 88.

38. Nichols, *Jonathan Edwards's Bible*, 84.

Finally, we consider Kreider and Stein's claims concerning Edwards' interpretive method in light of Edwards' gospel thrust in the Psalms.[39] There is some preliminary merit in Stein's observation that a "critical center" of Edwards' take on the Psalms *in the "Blank Bible"* was Christological—in the sense of either Christ the head or Christ mystical, his body the church—for in that notebook Edwards tended to speculate more with Christological readings of the Psalms than elsewhere. Yet even in the "Blank Bible," as Stein acknowledges, Edwards defies placement in only a Christological category. And clearly the whole of his corpus indicates that he was not bound by Christological and ecclesiological readings but that he held a much broader theological vision of the Psalms.

Kreider's definition of "Christological typology" as referring to Christ and his work of redemption on behalf of the church gets us closer, insofar as his definition embraces the gospel emphasis of Edwards' interpretation. Yet the label "Christological typology" does not immediately indicate this definition, for it emphasizes the narrower aspects of Christ and typology rather than the more encompassing category of redemption history. It also orients Edwards' interpretation around *Christ's* work of redemption, which is still too narrow for understanding his engagement with the Psalms.

Instead, I argue that Edwards' method of interpreting the Psalms is best understood not as being confined by the descriptions "Christological" or "Christological typology." The notion that Edwards' interpretive method is defined by his typology simply does not take into account the evidence of the multifarious ways he engaged the Psalms. And for Edwards, the Psalter is not *merely* Christological, even in the broad sense of referring to Christ and his body the church. It is Trinitarian, speaking of God the Father and God the Spirit, just as it speaks of God the Son, and it is gospel-oriented, warning sinners of judgment, preaching the mercy of God, proclaiming the Spirit's power to reorient the affections, and hailing the glories of heaven.

In short, I am not denying that Edwards was Christological or typological—he was both. But these were only two methods he used in his larger interpretive framework. Edwards clearly employed methods that grounded his exegesis of the Psalms in the text of Scripture—that is, examining the original Hebrew, exploring historical backgrounds, engaging technical questions, and employing the analogy of Scripture—but he also used other methods in concert with a historical-grammatical reading. He built from the foundation

---

39. Some of the material in this section is adapted from my article, "Making the Psalter One's 'Own Language': Jonathan Edwards Engages the Psalms," *Jonathan Edwards Studies* 2, no. 1 (2012): 3–29. Used with permission from *Jonathan Edwards Studies.*

of the text to interpret the Psalms theologically, the scaffolding of God's work of redemption giving him the framework—and boundaries—for exegesis. Within that frame he observed Christ, the church, and a multitude of types, but he also observed the sovereign God in all his glory, man steeped in sin, the gospel advanced by the Spirit, the devotion of the saints, and a culmination of the triune God's redemptive work in space and time. So to take into account Edwards' broad engagement with the Psalms throughout his life and across the varied genres of his corpus, all the while recognizing the complexity of his interpretation, it is more accurate and encompassing to describe Edwards' exegesis of the Psalms as "redemptive-historical," or governed by the Trinity's work of redemption in history.

By proposing this descriptive label, I am not saying that Edwards used a single method in the Psalms called the "redemptive-historical" method but that he interpreted the Bible in a variety of ways that were organized by his overarching redemptive-historical paradigm of thought, a paradigm that he believed guided him in unearthing the theological treasures contained within the divinely inspired book of Psalms. He did not strictly limit himself to, say, a typological method of exegesis, nor did he function with modern definitions of "method" or "hermeneutic" (an anachronistic term for Edwards' day). Instead, he was more organic in pulling on the various methods available to him to make good theological sense of the Psalms as a harmonious whole within a broad theological structure. Looking for a single category for Edwards from our categories today misleads us away from capturing the complexity of his exegesis of the Psalms day by day as he studied the Bible, prepared sermons, worshiped with his congregation and in private, nurtured his own spiritual life, and ministered pastorally to others. In these various activities, Edwards found many methods quite helpful in understanding the book of Psalms and employing it in ministry and theology. So he fluidly used grammatical-historical, scriptural-analogical, typological, Christological, ecclesiological, devotional, and theological methods of interpretation, but the organizing framework that governed his interpretation of the Psalms as he employed these diverse methods was the triune God's work of redemption in history.

The Foundations of Edwards' Theology

This study has also shown that the Bible undergirds Edwards' theological reflection and construction. Most of the theological emphases in his treatises and sermons—such as original sin, religious affections, God's glory, the holy fruit of the Spirit's influence, God's end in creating the world, and the work of redemption—resonate with his exegesis of the Psalms, and Edwards treated these theological themes throughout his life in Psalms sermons that range from his earliest preaching in New York to his mission years in Stockbridge. In many ways his writings on the Psalms provide a microcosm of his broad theological program—an observation that highlights his heavy reliance on Scripture as a foundation for his theology.

Recognizing the role of the history of redemption in Edwards' exegesis, McClymond and McDermott argue that "the real authority for his theological work was not the biblical text per se but his own imaginative construal of the story inscribed there, which he called the 'work of redemption.' "[40] Does this mean that he concocted a synthesis of the Bible's overarching story foreign to the Bible itself? Such a conclusion misses McClymond and McDermott's point that Edwards—like all biblical interpreters—read the Scriptures through some interpretive lens. Some embrace a historical-critical framework that seeks to understand the Bible as the record of an ancient people's culture or a reader-response framework that locates meaning not in the past or the text but in the individual reader's personal takeaway from the reading. Both of these frameworks—there are others—have their own boundaries and "rules" for reading, whether it be archeological findings or personal experience. Edwards had a framework too, but unlike these other frameworks, a redemptive-historical approach to the Psalms like the one that governed Edwards' interpretation had been employed for centuries by other Christian exegetes. For the history of redemption sums up the core Christian doctrines constructed from the Bible about God's nature and activity in relation to humanity, a synthesis enshrined in the early creeds of the church. The Apostles' Creed, an early condensation of the rule of faith, for example, speaks of God's creation, human sin, Christ's redemptive work and kingly rule, the Holy Spirit, the redeemed church, the forgiveness of sins, a coming judgment, and the life everlasting.

People coming from different faith and philosophical perspectives will debate which of these frameworks renders the best understanding of the Bible. What I am arguing is that Edwards did not force his redemptive-historical concept on the Psalms but that he interpreted the Psalms within a framework that had guided thousands of Christian interpreters since the earliest centuries of the church. He believed this framework did the best justice to the biblical text, and since he believed the Bible was divinely inspired and authoritative, he read the Psalms as a reliable guide to developing his theology, assuming he kept his interpretation within the confines of God's work of redemption.

---

40. McClymond and McDermott, *The Theology of Jonathan Edwards*, 146.

It would be reductionistic to conclude that Edwards forced his theology on the Psalms. Instead, Sweeney reminds us that he "knew the Bible's contents better than most scholars, past or present," and in fact "knew the bulk of them by heart," which led him to become "a dialectical biblical thinker, or one for whom Scripture yielded a theology that in turn he employed in interpretation."[41] Applied here, Edwards found in the Psalms the evidence for a redemptive-historical understanding of Scripture and indeed all of reality, and thus he read the Psalms within a redemptive-historical framework of interpretation.

As we have seen in this book, Edwards so imbibed the Psalms that they influenced his thinking on diverse theological topics and played an undeniable role in his theology. While scholars debate the influences on Edwards, a man who longed to soak up the latest learning, we do well to remember that none of his other interests, whether John Locke, Peter Van Mastricht, or Matthew Poole, could take the powerful place of the Scriptures. The Psalms uniquely provided guidance and fodder for Edwards' thought because they encapsulated the broad theology of the whole Bible—praising God's glory; warning of human weakness and depravity; proclaiming Christ's suffering, death, resurrection, and kingship; heralding the gospel and the hope of revival through the Holy Spirit; calling Christians to vital piety; describing the nature of the church; and warning of judgment while extending hope for future blessing.

This study shows that Edwards' theology was biblically saturated, for the Psalms functioned as a rich source for his theological development and as a starting point for understanding and explaining so many theological themes throughout his lifetime. That is why Edwards called the Scripture "the only rule of our faith and practice," and because of that conviction, he engaged the Psalms extensively in his development of theology and aimed to ground his theology in the Bible.[42]

Areas for Further Study

Exploring Edwards' writings on the Psalms clearly illustrates just how much biblical material fills his corpus. Since I confined my study of Edwards' biblical material to the Psalms in this project, that leaves much work still to be done in assessing his exegesis. The sheer mass of more than 1,200 sermons

---

41. Sweeney, "Edwards and the Bible," 71; Sweeney, "Edwards, Jonathan," 400.

42. Jonathan Edwards, *The "Miscellanies": Entry Nos. a–z, aa–zz, 1–500*, ed. Thomas A. Schafer, vol. 13 of *WJE* (1994), 310.

alone calls for close attention, and as the Jonathan Edwards Center makes the remaining sermons available digitally on its website, it will become that much easier to explore what Edwards said about the whole Bible. Edwards' personal manuscripts, especially the "Blank Bible," "Notes on Scripture," and "Miscellanies," also still deserve closer examination as we fill out our understanding of Edwards' private reflections and public discourse on the Bible. In addition, studying Edwards' use of the Scripture in his theological treatises will be important for understanding the relationship between the Bible and theology in Edwards' thought.

Happily, Douglas Sweeney is writing an overarching synthesis of Edwards' exegesis across his writings that considers his interpretation from Genesis to Revelation.[43] So the area that most needs study at this point is Edwards' interpretation of other books of the Bible. To date, scholars have discussed, to some extent, his treatment of the Psalms, Proverbs, Isaiah, Jeremiah, Ezekiel, James, and Revelation. While more could be said about Edwards' engagement with these books of the Bible, what is of greater need is to study other books, and especially other genres, of biblical literature. What can we say about Edwards's engagement with the Pentateuch, the Old Testament historical books, the Gospels, or the Pauline epistles?[44]

As these other genres are explored, it will be important to examine whether Edwards employed the redemptive-historical framework of interpretation across the board or whether it was unique to his engagement with the Psalter. Can this interpretive model explain his whole program of biblical exegesis? Or is it particularly applicable to the Psalms in a way that it is not applicable, say, to the book of Esther or Titus? Given the gospel thrust of Edwards' ministry and his emphasis on God's work of redemption in his theology, it is my suspicion that the redemptive-historical interpretive framework he followed in the Psalms will prove a constant across his interpretation of the Bible, but closer examinations will need to be performed to bear out this hypothesis.

One other area for further study is whether Edwards' engagement with the Psalms—or other books of the Bible—influenced later exegetes and theologians. Given the current state of research, it does not appear that Edwards'

---

43. Douglas Sweeney, *Edwards the Exegete: Biblical Interpretation and Anglo-Protestant Culture on the Edge of the Enlightenment* (New York: Oxford University Press, in press).

44. While John Gerstner, David Lovi, and Benjamin Westerhoff have compiled Edwards' comments on Romans and Hebrews, further analysis of these books and the epistle genre is warranted. John H. Gerstner, *The Rational Biblical Theology of Jonathan Edwards*, vol. 1 (Powhatan, VA: Berea, 1991), 247–479; David S. Lovi and Benjamin Westerhoff, eds., *The Power of God: A Jonathan Edwards Commentary on the Book of Romans* (Eugene, OR: Pickwick, 2013).

interpretation or preaching of the Psalms significantly influenced the way others employed the Psalms in their ministry. However, no one has done a dissertation on the sermons of his successors, the New Divinity pastors and theologians, and compared them to Edwards' sermons and biblical exegesis. Such a project could prove fruitful in showing lines of influence, similarity, and contrast.

A New Legacy for Edwards?

After Edwards' death, he gradually became an iconic figure, and in the nineteenth century, theologians fought over who was the true heir of Edwards. But they fought over his theology, not his exegesis proper—even though the two are inextricably linked.[45] The general perception of Edwards was that he was an impressive student of the Bible with a thorough understanding of Scripture, an observation that was taken for granted more than it was described in detail as a model to follow.[46] As we draw this study to a close, I would like to suggest that Edwards could have a new legacy in ways of thinking about the Psalms for today. His lifelong engagement with the Psalter can inform the worship, preaching, and exegesis of the twenty-first century.

In a Christian community that is often divided by "worship wars," it is helpful to remember that Edwards lived through a worship war in his own time. The rise of hymns in public worship caused quite a stir in New England, and even Edwards' credibility was called into question for modestly accepting hymns in Sunday afternoon summer gatherings. In today's worship wars, hymns have taken the place of psalms and contemporary praise songs have taken the place of hymns. Edwards accepted hymns as songs that related the gospel message and the truths of Christianity in new musical settings; today, he might caution Christians against rejecting all contemporary praise songs or hymns. He did not confine himself strictly to the Psalter but found benefit in new songs for the spiritual edification of his congregation. Still, as Edwards welcomed new hymns that his people enjoyed singing, he was concerned

---

45. On Edwards' theological legacy, see David W. Kling and Douglas A. Sweeney, eds. *Jonathan Edwards at Home and Abroad: Historical Memories, Cultural Movements, Global Horizons* (Columbia: University of South Carolina Press, 2003); and McClymond and McDermott, *The Theology of Jonathan Edwards*, 601–648.

46. See Samuel Hopkins, *The Life and Character of the Late Reverend Mr. Jonathan Edwards, President of the College of New-Jersey* (Boston: S. Kneeland, 1765), 40–41; Sereno E. Dwight, ed., *The Works of President Edwards: With a Memoir of His Life*, vol. 1 (New York: S. Converse, 1829–1830), 57.

that what they sang upheld orthodox Christian doctrine by rehearsing God's redemptive work, and here we may find a warning against creating a wall of separation between the disciplines of worship and theology. They can coexist and indeed ought to. Of greater import, however, is the near total loss of singing the Psalter in many churches in America—something Edwards would have lamented.[47] For what Edwards discovered was that singing the Psalms allowed people to know the words of this gospel-laden book and make these words their own language, which transformed their minds and nurtured true religious affections. The Psalter has been the songbook of the church for most of the church's existence, and Edwards found that singing the Psalms is beneficial not only in public worship but also in family devotions and individual spirituality. This study suggests that, for those within the Christian faith, the recovery of the Psalms alongside hymns and praise songs could provide the church with a songbook that orients Christian worship today to the broad redemptive history in which it finds its own being.

Edwards' approach to preaching the Psalms also suggests at least two recommendations for the homiletical arena today. First, his affinity for preaching from the book of Psalms in at least 108 sermons over the course of his lifetime stands as a challenge to pastors who have never chosen the Psalms as a sermon text and to those who visit the Psalms only on the rare occasion. Edwards might say to pastors today that they should embrace the Psalms as a key part of the Christian Bible and should develop messages from the Psalms that proclaim Christian truths within the history of redemption. Second, the frequency with which Edwards preached the gospel message and called people to examine whether they were truly converted from the Psalms challenges pastors today not only to preach from this book but to proclaim the gospel message of Christ from the Psalms. In his harmonic view of the Bible, Edwards saw clear presentations of gospel truths "breaking out and shining" in the book of Psalms, and he did not hesitate to sound the joyful noise of the gospel as he preached from this book. By following his example, preachers today may discover a trove of gospel treasure in the Psalter readily available to those who seek it.[48]

---

47. For modern pleas to revive psalm-singing, see Joel R. Beeke and Anthony T. Selvaggio, eds., *Sing a New Song: Recovering Psalm Singing for the Twenty-First Century* (Grand Rapids, MI: Reformation Heritage Books, 2010) and Michael LeFebvre, *Singing the Songs of Jesus: Revisiting the Psalms* (Fearn, Scotland: Christian Focus, 2010).

48. As pastors preach from the Psalms, they might consider consulting Edwards and other exegetes from Christian history as a way to approach the biblical text *with the church*. John Thompson argues that, instead of truncating input into the homiletical process by stopping

As for interpreting the Psalms, Edwards would likely respond to modern exegetes steeped in the historical-critical method by arguing that there is a place for typological, Christological, and ecclesiological interpretation of the Psalms when tempered by the redemptive-historical framework. This is not to say that Christians should interpret the Psalms exactly as Edwards—his typological propensity will likely cause many exegetes today to squirm. But his willingness to see elements of the gospel in the Psalms in light of the harmony of the Old and New Testaments and the analogy of Scripture and framed by the analogy of faith should cause Christians today to pause if they are unwilling to recognize those elements in the Psalter. A case in point is *The Essential Bible Companion to the Psalms: Key Insights for Reading God's Word*, a conservative evangelical book written by Brian L. Webster and David R. Beach. The authors are strikingly silent about Christ and his redemption in their overview of the book of Psalms and their description of the royal psalms generally. They even resist applying specific psalms to Christ, including those commonly associated with Christ in the Christian tradition, such as Psalms 2, 23, 45, and 110. And in their treatment of Psalm 22, while they recognize that Christ appropriated this psalm on the cross, they refuse to link any prophetic relationship between the psalm and the crucifixion event.[49] Edwards' work suggests that, perhaps, Christian interpreters should recognize greater unity between the testaments, which speak in a harmonic voice and link the Psalms prophetically and typologically with the New Testament world and the fullness of gospel doctrine. In Edwards' view, it is not only possible but quite appropriate to speak of Christ and the triune God's work of redemption even from the Psalms when comparing scripture with scripture and reading the Psalms within the boundaries of a redemptive-historical interpretive framework.

We also see from this study that Edwards exhibited what many today call theological interpretation.[50] While Edwards was interested in the historical and geographical background of the Psalms and its lexical and literary meaning, he

---

with modern commentaries, the proclamation of God's Word should be "connected with the largest community of interpretation possible—with the mind of the whole church as it has attempted to be faithful to the whole counsel of God," connecting us "with the life of God among the everlasting people of God." Thompson, *Reading the Bible with the Dead*, 227.

49. Brian L. Webster and David R. Beach, *The Essential Bible Companion to the Psalms: Key Insights for Reading God's Word* (Grand Rapids, MI: Zondervan, 2010), 11, 17, 38, 59, 80, 145, 58.

50. For an introduction to modern theological interpretation of the Bible, see Kevin J. Vanhoozer, "What Is Theological Interpretation of the Bible?" in *Dictionary for Theological Interpretation of the Bible*, ed. Kevin J. Vanhoozer, Craig G. Bartholomew, Daniel J. Treier, and N. T. Wright (Grand Rapids, MI: BakerAcademic, 2005), 19–25.

was most concerned about the book's theological meaning. One could argue that, at times, he failed to give due attention to the other interpretive issues involved in the flow of the text, but by and large Edwards stands as a model of theological interpretation who regularly sought out background and linguistic material, so much that Sweeney holds him up as "a prime example of the so-called theological interpretation of Scripture shaped by the best historical research of his day."[51] As Kevin Vanhoozer explains, "The principal thrust of theological interpretation is to direct the interpreter's attention to the subject matter of Scripture—God, the acts of God in history, the gospel," and as we have seen in this study, this is what Edwards did.[52] As he engaged the Psalms, Edwards did not get lost in the minute details of exegesis that might have distracted him from the overarching thrust of the Scriptures, but rather, by keeping the redemptive-historical vision in mind, he was able to discover spiritual and theological insight from the Psalms that emphasized the core doctrines of the Christian faith in a world changing due to Enlightenment challenges to the Bible and Christianity. Edwards' legacy with respect to the Psalms today could inspire more interpreters to think theologically about the Psalms.

JONATHAN EDWARDS LOVED the history of redemption. In his "Personal Narrative," he wrote, "I have loved the doctrines of the gospel: they have been to my soul like green pastures. The gospel has seemed to me to be the richest treasure; the treasure that I have most desired, and longed that it might dwell richly in me. The way of salvation by Christ, has appeared in a general way, glorious and excellent, and most pleasant and beautiful."[53] And as Edwards loved gospel doctrine, so he loved the Psalter, for he believed it was full of the gospel. It nurtured his spiritual life, his family, and his church. It provided the language of those truly under the gracious influences of the Holy Spirit, as well as the language of the church. As the world around him shifted, Edwards grasped onto the Psalms as divinely inspired songs given by God to proclaim the great truths of the gospel, from the sin and weakness of humanity to the sovereignty of God; from the redemptive work of Christ to the regenerating work of the Spirit; from the salvation of sinners to the piety of the saints; from God's justice in condemning the recalcitrant wicked to his mercy in raising up the church as Christ's bride; and from the blessed happiness God bestows

---

51. Sweeney, "Edwards and the Bible," 77.

52. Vanhoozer, "What Is Theological Interpretation of the Bible?", 24.

53. Jonathan Edwards, "Personal Narrative," in *Letters and Personal Writings*, ed. George S. Claghorn, vol. 16 of *WJE* (1998), 799.

on the saints forever in heaven to the magnificent glory of God displayed in the long history of redemption. Edwards firmly believed that we should make our theology biblical and our Bible reading theological. So as he engaged the Psalms day in and day out, he listened for the resonant, joyful sounding of the gospel. And he heard it loud and clear.

Jonathan Edwards' Sermons on the Psalms

The table below presents all 104 of Edwards' extant sermons on the book of Psalms, organized canonically. The following abbreviations mark where these sermons are available:

BRBML   Nontranscribed sermons available at the Beinecke Rare Book and Manuscript Library of Yale University

Dw   Published in the Dwight edition of Edwards' works (1829): http://www.archive.org/stream/workspresidente06dwiggoog#page/n6/mode/2up (vol. 6); http://www.archive.org/stream/workspresidente04dwiggoog#page/n6/mode/2up (vol. 7)

FTL   Nontranscribed sermons available at Andover Newton Theological Seminary's Franklin Trask Library

JEC   Transcribed by the Jonathan Edwards Center at Yale University but not available on their website

MDM   Published in one of Michael D. McMullen's two volumes of previously unpublished sermons: Jonathan Edwards, *The Blessing of God: Previously Unpublished Sermons of Jonathan Edwards*, ed. Michael D. McMullen (Nashville, TN: Broadman & Holman, 2003), and Jonathan Edwards, *The Glory and Honor of God: Volume 2 of the Previously Unpublished Sermons of Jonathan Edwards*, ed. Michael D. McMullen (Nashville, TN: Broadman & Holman, 2004)

WJE   Published by Yale University Press in *The Works of Jonathan Edwards*

WJEO	Transcribed sermons available in *The Works of Jonathan Edwards Online* at the Jonathan Edwards Center at Yale University website: http://edwards.yale.edu/research/sermon-index/canonical? book=19
Wor	Published in the Worcester edition of Edwards' works: http://www.archive.org/stream/worksofpresident041852edwa#page/n5/mode/2up
r	= repreached

WEIGHTING OF SERMON DOCTRINES BY SEVEN CATEGORIES

Doctrinal Category	Number of Sermons
Piety	22
Nature, Character, and Glory of God	16
Sin/Wickedness/Judgment	16
Christ	15
Spiritual Benefits for the Church/Saints	13
Human Nature/Brevity of Life	13
Awakening/Light/Repentance	9

Text	Title/Doctrine/Subject	Date	JEC #	Publication Location	Doctrinal Category
Ps 1:1	There is a "great diff[erence] between good men & wicked men."	Aug. 1755	1147	BRBML	Sin/ Wickedness/ Judgment
Ps 1:3 (a)	"[Christ] is to the Heart of a saint like a River to the Root of a tree that is planted by it."	*c.* 1742	693c	FTL	Christ
Ps 1:3 (b)	"Christ is to the heart of a true saint like a river to the roots of a tree that is planted by it."	Aug. 1751	999	*WJE*, vol. 25, 600–604	Christ
Ps 2:3–4	"However wicked men oppose God[']s Rule over them & Endeavour to cast it off all their attempts will be in vain for G[od] will still Rule over them."	July 1744	747	BRBML	Sin/ Wickedness/ Judgment
Ps 2:6	"Kingly office of [Christ]."	June 1744; r. Mar. 1755	745	*WJEO*, vol. 62	Christ

(Continued)

Continued

Text	Title/Doctrine/Subject	Date	JEC #	Publication Location	Doctrinal Category
Ps 5:4–5	"The infinite evil of sin."	Mar. 1752	1030	BRBML	Sin/ Wickedness/ Judgment
Ps 7:8	"'Tis a blessed thing to some persons that God is to be their judge."	Oct. 1736	411	MDM, vol. 2, 53–65	Nature and Character of God
Ps 7:11	"I. What is God[']s anger. II. How he is angry with the w[icked] every day."	Feb. 1750	954	BRBML	Nature and Character of God
Ps 8:4–5	"man is a creature who in his nature is vastly Inferior to the Angels."	Feb. 1745	769	BRBML	Human Nature
Ps 10:6	"Wicked men ben't apt to be sensible but that it will always be with them as it is now."	Sum.–Fall 1729	144	MDM, vol. 2, 66–76	Sin/ Wickedness/ Judgment
Ps 10:17	"God's manner is first to prepare men's hearts and then to answer their prayers."	Mar. 1735	352	MDM, vol. 2, 77–106	Nature and Character of God
Ps 13:3	"1. I would show when the souls of persons may be said to be asleep… 2. How that there are some persons that do sleep the sleep of death. 3. How this is prevented by Person[']s Eyes being Enlightened. 4. That tis G[od] that gives Persons this Light."	June 1741	615	BRBML	Awakening/ Repentance
Ps 14:1 (a)	"A principle of atheism possesses the hearts of all ungodly men."	Sum.–Fall 1729	145	*WJE*, vol. 17, 45–56	Sin/ Wickedness/ Judgment
Ps 14:1 (b)	"There certainly is a God."	Dec. 1752	1059	BRBML	Nature and Character of God
Ps 17:3	"The manner of men[']s Behaviour in secret & when hid from the Eye of the World is a much greater Proof of their sincerity than what they do openly."	Aug. 1748	903	*WJEO*, vol. 66	Human Nature

(Continued)

Continued

Text	Title/Doctrine/Subject	Date	JEC #	Publication Location	Doctrinal Category
Ps 18:26	"They that Contend with G[od] Can expect no other than that G[od] will Contend with them."	Sum.–Fall 1729	111	*WJEO*, vol. 44	Sin/ Wickedness/ Judgment
Ps 18:35	"In the doctrinal handling of these words, I showed how this word David says of hims[elf] is applicable to all the saints and 1. I showed how they are become Great, and 2. How tis God[']s gentleness that hath made them so."	n.d. [c. 1739–1740]; r. Feb. 1, 1742	693i	BRBML	Spiritual Benefits for the Church/ Saints
Ps 19:7–10	"The good that is obtained by the word of G[od] lasts forever."	undated [c. 1750s]	1179	BRBML	Spiritual Benefits for the Church/ Saints
Ps 19:12	"Tis an Exceeding hard thing for men to be sensible that are sinfull & offensive to G[od]."	Sept. 1739	517	*WJEO*, vol. 54	Sin/ Wickedness/ Judgment
Ps 21:4	"God never begrutches his people anything they desire, or are capable of, as being too good for 'em."	May 1738	473	*WJE*, vol. 19, 768–792	Nature and Character of God
Ps 23:2	"The sp[iritual] Enjoym[en]ts that believers have through [Christ] are attended with quietness & Rest of soul."	July 1738	483	*WJEO*, vol. 53	Christ
Ps 24:7–10	"Jesus [Christ] Entring his Glory after he suff[ered] was a sight worthy to be beheld with Great Admiration."	Jan. 1739	499	*WJEO*, vol. 54	Christ
Ps 25:11	"If we truly come to God for mercy, the greatness of our sin will be no impediment to pardon."	undated	266	Wor, vol. 4, 422–428	Spiritual Benefits for the Church/ Saints

(Continued)

Continued

Text	Title/Doctrine/Subject	Date	JEC #	Publication Location	Doctrinal Category
Ps 27:4 (a)	"Earnest desires and strong Resolutions [and humble dependence] should accompany one another in seeking spiritual and Eternal good."	Mar. 1741; r. July 1754	601	BRBML	Piety
Ps 27:4 (b)	"'Tis the Heart of a truly good man to Love G[od] above all things."	Mar. 1752	1031	BRBML	Piety
Ps 27:4 (c)	"'Tis our duty to love the House of [God]."	Oct. 1756	1175	BRBML	Piety
Ps 33:1	"That the Righteous Above other men have Reason to Praise God."	Sum.–Fall 1729	112	*WJEO*, vol. 44	Piety
Ps 34:11	"Theref[ore] now I would improve this S[cripture] to call upon you Children now to forsake your sins and seek the fear of G[od]."	July 1741	622	BRBML	Awakening/ Repentance
Ps 36:2	"Wicked men generally flatter themselves with hopes of escaping punishment, till it actually comes upon them."	undated	267	Wor, vol. 4, 322–329	Sin/ Wickedness/ Judgment
Ps 36:7	"I. the Lovingkindness G[od] sends men through J[esus] [Christ] is transcendently excellent. II. this great Excellency is the good in which the Chil[dren] of man put their Trust under the shadow of God[']s wings."	Mar. 1751; r. 1751	989	FTL	Christ
Ps 37:3	"Observation: The way to happiness lies in these two things, believing in God and doing good."	*c.* Sept. 1745	792	BRBML	Piety
Ps 37:16	"Riches of the wicked can do 'em no good."	Apr. 1756	1161	BRBML	Sin/ Wickedness/ Judgment

(*Continued*)

Continued

Text	Title/Doctrine/Subject	Date	JEC #	Publication Location	Doctrinal Category
Ps 39:4	"It would be a thing that would tend much to men[']s Spiritual profit & advantage if they would be much on Considering their own mortality."	July 1733	289	*WJEO*, vol. 48	Human Nature
Ps 39:5	"The Time men have to spend in this [world] is very short."	Mar. 1753	1071	BRBML	Human Nature
Ps 40:6–8	"The sacrifice of Christ is the only sacrifice that is upon its own account acceptable to God."	Sum.–Fall 1729	113	*WJE*, vol. 14, 437–457	Christ
Ps 45:3–5	"The L[ord] J[esus] [Christ] is a glorious Conqueror."	Aug. 1750; r. 1751	963	BRBML	Christ
Ps 45:9	"Supposing therefore her that is here spoken of to be the Ch[urc]h of [Christ]." (fragment sermon)	Dec. 1743	727	JEC	Spiritual Benefits for the Church/ Saints
Ps 45:15	"1. show how Heaven is the King[']s Palace. 2. give some Caref[ul] description of this great palace. 3. describe the Character of the People that shall Enter there. 4. describe the manner of their Entrance. 5. show in what Quality & to what purpose they shall Enter. 6. Conclude with an agreeable Exh[ortation]."	Mar. [21,] 1744	731	BRBML	Spiritual Benefits for the Church/ Saints
Ps 46:10	"Hence the bare consideration *that God is God,* may well be sufficient to still all objections and opposition against the divine sovereign dispensations."	undated	360	Dw, vol. 6, 293–303	Nature and Character of God

(*Continued*)

Continued

Text	Title/Doctrine/Subject	Date	JEC #	Publication Location	Doctrinal Category
Ps 51:17	"a broken H[eart] is an acceptable sacrifice to G[od]."	Mar. 1733	275	*WJEO*, vol. 48	Awakening/ Repentance
Ps 55:12–14	"men are not sufficient to positively determine the state of the souls of others that are of God[']s visible People."	Sept. 1741	633	JEC	Human Nature
Ps 60:9–12	Four propositions: "I. If God be pleased to forsake a people and not to go forth with their armies, defeat and con- fusion is like to be the consequence...."	Aug. 28, 1755	1148	*WJE*, vol. 25, 685–697	Sin/ Wickedness/ Judgment
Ps 61:2	"Christ is as an high Rock on which Persons may stand above the Floods that other wise would overwhelm Them."	July 1747	867	*WJEO*, vol. 65	Christ
Ps 65:2	"That it is the character of the Most High, that he is a God who hears prayer."	Jan. 1736; r. Mar. 1752	374	Wor, vol. 4, 561–572	Nature and Character of God
Ps 65:9	"God, by the exercises of his common bounty towards men, shows that he has an all-sufficiency for the supply of their wants."	Nov. 13, 1729	114	*WJE*, vol. 14, 471–483	Nature and Character of God
Ps 65:11	"That we Ought to Praise God for Annual blessings."	Nov. 7, 1728	75	*WJEO*, vol. 43	Piety
Ps 66:3	"all That natural men do in Religion is altogether forced."	Aug. 6, 1735	365	*WJEO*, vol. 50	Human Nature
Ps 66:5	"That 'tis to the Glory of G[od] that he is terrible in his doings towards the Children of men."	Spr.–Fall 1729	98	JEC	Nature and Character of God

(*Continued*)

Continued

Text	Title/Doctrine/Subject	Date	JEC #	Publication Location	Doctrinal Category
Ps 66:18 (a)	"Tis in vain for any to expect to have their prayers heard as Long as they continue in the allowance of sin."	Mar. 29, 1739	507	*WJEO*, vol. 54	Piety
Ps 66:18 (b)	"1 show when a person may be said in the sense of the text to Regard Iniq[uity] in His heart/& then in the 2. Place proceed to the Consideration of that which is asserted in the text of such."	Apr. 12, 1744	736	BRBML	Sin/ Wickedness/ Judgment
Ps 71:5	"It behooves Young Persons to seek that they may be converted while they are young."	n.d. [c. late 1730s]	693j	BRBML	Awakening/ Repentance
Ps 72:6	"Christ, in communicating himself and dispensing his benefits, does as it were come down as the rain on the mown grass."	Jan. 1741	589	*WJE*, vol. 22, 298–318	Christ
Ps 73:18–19	"That those that are in a natural Condition have Reason to be alwaies in fear of being destroyed."	Fall 1730– Spr. 1731; poss. r. Mar. 9, 1743	168	*WJEO*, vol. 45	Sin/ Wickedness/ Judgment
Ps 73:25	"It is the spirit of a truly godly man, to prefer God before all other things, either in heaven or on earth."	Apr. 1736; r. 5x [no dates]	386	Wor, vol. 4, 540–547	Piety
Ps 78:5–7	"The Relig[ious] Education of Chil[dren] is one of the principle means of grace that G[od] has appointed in his Church."	Feb. 1745; r. June 1755	770	BRBML	Spiritual Benefits for the Church/ Saints
Ps 78:25	"Those that spiritually feed on [Christ,] they Eat Angel[']s food."	Aug. 1731– Dec. 1732; r. July 1757	206	*WJEO*, vol. 46	Christ

(*Continued*)

Continued

Text	Title/Doctrine/Subject	Date	JEC #	Publication Location	Doctrinal Category
Ps 78:36–37	"[']Tis hanous wicked-ness to make a false Profession of Relig[ion] when the Heart is not Right[eous] & not to be steadfast in God[']s Cov[enant]."	Dec. 1751	1013	BRBML	Sin/ Wickedness/ Judgment
Ps 78:57	"The Backsliding of such as are the visible People of God."	June 1743	704	*WJEO*, vol. 61	Sin/ Wickedness/ Judgment
Ps 82:6–7	"that Great men are as Liable to death as others."	Spr.–Fall 1729	99	*WJEO*, vol. 44	Human Nature
Ps 84:3	"[Christ] is the Believer[']s Home."	Apr. 1747	860	BRBML	Christ
Ps 84:10	"a day spent in the House of G[od] in a right manner is beter than a Thous[and] spent in sin in the Enjoym[en]t of the things of the [world]."	May 1752	1038	BRBML	Spiritual Benefits for the Church/ Saints
Ps 89:6	"God is infinitely exalted in gloriousness and excellency above all cre-ated beings."	Sum. 1722–Spr. 1723; r. [uncertain date]	8	*WJE*, vol. 10, 413–435	Nature and Character of God
Ps 89:15 (a)	"Blessed are the people that know the Joyfull sound."	July 1742	677	BRBML	Spiritual Benefits for the Church/ Saints
Ps 89:15 (b)	Five Propositions: "I. The gospel of Jesus Christ is a joyful sound...."	Oct. 1756; r. Dec. 1756	1176	*WJE*, vol. 25, 698–710	Christ
Ps 90:5–6	"man is fitly Compared to Grass that in the morning Green & flour-ishing but in the Evening Cut down & withered."	Apr. 1734; r. June 1753, July 1757	319	*WJEO*, vol. 49	Human Nature
Ps 90:12	"Our time here is so short and Uncertain that we had Great need wisely to Improve it."	Spr. 1728	67	*WJEO*, vol. 43	Awakening/ Repentance

(Continued)

Continued

Text	Title/Doctrine/Subject	Date	JEC #	Publication Location	Doctrinal Category
Ps 94:8–11	"That there is an extreme and brutish blindness in things of religion, which naturally possesses the hearts of mankind."	Feb. 1740	536	Dw, vol. 7, 3–30	Human Nature
Ps 94:10	"Those that are of God[']s own People have much more Reason to fear God[']s Chastisem[en]ts for their sins than others."	Feb. 1740	537	WJEO, vol. 55	Sin/ Wickedness/ Judgment
Ps 94:12 (a)	"He is a happy man tho an afflicted one whom G[od] Chastends & teaches out of his word."	Aug. 1731– Dec. 1732	207	WJEO, vol. 46	Piety
Ps 94:12 (b)	"God[']s dealings with the Righ[teous] & wicked are here compared."	Feb. 1746	808	BRBML	Nature and Character of God
Ps 95:7–8	"It is our great duty forthwith, without any delay, to hearken to God's voice."	Sum. 1722– Spr. 1723; r. 1724–1726	9	WJE, vol. 10, 436–450	Awakening/ Repentance
Ps 102:25– 26	"This present world shall one day come to an end."	Feb. 1728	61	MDM, vol. 2, 107–119; WJEO, vol. 43	Awakening/ Repentance
Ps 106:5	"They above all others are blessed ones that are admitted to see the Good of God[']s chosen. & to rejoice in the gladness of God[']s nation & to glory with his inheritance."	Aug. 1737	442	WJEO, vol. 52	Spiritual Benefits for the Church/ Saints
Ps 108:4	"G[od] is a being of Transcendent mercy."	July–Aug. 1731	195	WJEO, vol. 46	Nature and Character of God
Ps 110:2	"[Christ] shall Rule in the midst of his Enemies."	May 1733	282	WJEO, vol. 48	Christ
Ps 110:4	"Christ[']s Priestly office."	June 1744; r. Mar. 1755	746	WJEO, vol. 62	Christ

(Continued)

Continued

Text	Title/Doctrine/Subject	Date	JEC #	Publication Location	Doctrinal Category
Ps 111:5	"G[od] never fails in any Instance of faithfulness to the Cov[enant] Engagem[en]ts he has entered into on behalf of any of mankind."	Aug. 1745	788	BRBML	Nature and Character of God
Ps 112:1	"good men are Happy men."	Feb. 1751	981	BRBML	Piety
Ps 113:6	"The subject I intend to insist on from these words is God[']s Humbling himself to behold the things that are in Heaven."	Nov. 11, 1742	685	BRBML	Nature and Character of God
Ps 115:1	"It is the spirit and temper of those that are truly godly, to delight to exalt God and to lay themselves low before him."	Fall 1723	25	MDM, vol. 1, 71–87	Piety
Ps 115:17– 18	"The blessedness [of saints in heaven] consists very much in praising & glorifying G[od]."	Nov. 26, 1747	880	*WJEO*, vol. 65	Spiritual Benefits for the Church/ Saints
Ps 116:12	"when Persons have Recieved signal mercies of G[od] It becomes em to be Earnestly Inquisitive what they shall Render to the L[ord] for all his Benefits towards them."	Feb. 1736	378	*WJEO*, vol. 51	Piety
Ps 118:6–9	"I. How men are apt to trust in men."	July 23, 1756	1168	BRBML	Human Nature
Ps 119:1–3	"as we would approve ourselves true saints we must obey God[']s Com[mands] universally perseveringly & with our whole Hearts."	Feb. 1745	771	BRBML	Piety
Ps 119:1–6	"I. He that is a good man walks in a holy way...."	Mar. 1754	1112	BRBML	Piety

(*Continued*)

Continued

Text	Title/Doctrine/Subject	Date	JEC #	Publication Location	Doctrinal Category
Ps 119:2	"That the way to Recieve the Blessed fruits of Religion is to Practice it with our whole hearts."	Sum.–Fall 1729	146	*WJEO*, vol. 44	Piety
Ps 119:3	"The spirit that godly men are of, is a spirit to be perfectly holy"	May 1737; r. Jan. 1757	431	*WJE*, vol. 19, 680–703	Piety
Ps 119:18	"I. men are naturally blind so that they don[']t [see] the main things in the word of G[od].... ."	Oct. 1751	1007	BRBML	Human Nature
Ps 119:56	"when Person have strictly [adhered to] their duty they commonly afterwards find that Benefit & Reward of it that makes Glad that they have done so."	Sept. 1740	568	*WJEO*, vol. 56	Spiritual Benefits for the Church/ Saints
Ps 119:60–61 [actually vv. 59–60]	"men ought to be much in thinking of their own ways."	Mar. 1754	1113	BRBML	Awakening/ Repentance
Ps 119:60 (a)	"We ought to make religion our present and immediate business."	Sum. 1724	32	MDM, vol. 1, 89–105	Awakening/ Repentance
Ps 119:60 (b)	"man is made to differ from all the Bruit Cre[atures] in that Resp[ect] that he is capable of Knowing G[od] & Knowing his will."	Sept. 1751	1004	BRBML	Human Nature
Ps 119:108	"In a right Thanksgiving to God, Heart and mouth and practice all go together."	Nov. 1744	760	BRBML	Piety
Ps 119:140	"Holy Persons Love Holy Things for their Holiness."	July 1744; r. Apr. 1754	748	BRBML	Piety
Ps 119:162	"The Joy that is experienced by by [sic] soul that spiritual Good exhibited in the word of G[od] is like the Joy of him that finds great spoil in war."	Nov. 1749	943	*WJEO*, vol. 67	Spiritual Benefits for the Church/ Saints

(Continued)

Continued

Text	Title/Doctrine/Subject	Date	JEC #	Publication Location	Doctrinal Category
Ps 126:5–6	"The great work and business that we have to do in order to our sp[iritual] & Et[ernal] happiness is fitly repre-sented by the business of an husbandman."	Sept. 1742	683	BRBML	Piety
Ps 127:2	"That those that Trust in thems[elves] & seek satisfaction & Rest for their souls in their own strength weary thems[elves] with many vain attempts."	May 1736	390	*WJEO*, vol. 51	Human Nature
Ps 136:1	"That all Great works of G[od] from the begin-ning of the [world] to the End of it are works of mercy to his People."	Nov. 1736	413	*WJEO*, vol. 51	Nature and Character of God
Ps 139:7–10	"God is everywhere present."	Wint. 1728	44	MDM, vol. 1, 107–121	Nature and Character of God
Ps 139:23–24	"All men should be much concerned to know whether they do not live in some way of sin."	Sept. 1733	297	Dw, vol. 6, 328–364	Sin/ Wickedness/ Judgment
Ps 144:12	"'Tis a peculiarly lovely and pleasant sight to behold young people walking in the ways of virtue and piety."	Nov. 1744	761	*WJE*, vol. 25, 103–110	Piety
Ps 144:15	"The Interest of a People mainly consists in the Interest of Religion among them."	Nov. 1740	580	BRBML	Piety
Ps 145:15–21	"all Crea[tures] in H[eaven] & Earth have all their good things from G[od]."	Nov. 1, 1753	1096	BRBML	Spiritual Benefits for the Church/ Saints
Ps 147:1	"It's a very decent and comely thing that praise should be given to God."	Nov. 10, 1726	39	MDM, vol. 2, 120–134	Piety

Bibliography

PRIMARY SOURCES FOR JONATHAN EDWARDS

Edwards, Jonathan. "Apocalypse Series." In *Apocalyptic Writings*, edited by Stephen J. Stein, 125–218. Vol. 5 of *The Works of Jonathan Edwards*. New Haven, CT: Yale University Press, 1977.

———. *Apocalyptic Writings*. Edited by Stephen J. Stein. Vol. 5 of *The Works of Jonathan Edwards*. New Haven, CT: Yale University Press, 1977.

———. *The "Blank Bible."* Edited by Stephen J. Stein. Vol. 24, Parts 1 and 2 of *The Works of Jonathan Edwards*. New Haven, CT: Yale University Press, 2006.

———. *The Blessing of God: Previously Unpublished Sermons of Jonathan Edwards*. Edited by Michael D. McMullen. Nashville, TN: Broadman & Holman, 2003.

———. *Catalogues of Books*. Edited by Peter J. Theusen. Vol. 26 of *The Works of Jonathan Edwards*. New Haven, CT: Yale University Press, 2008.

———. *Charity and Its Fruits*. In *Ethical Writings*, edited by Paul Ramsey, 123–402. Vol. 8 of *The Works of Jonathan Edwards*. New Haven, CT: Yale University Press, 1989.

———. "'Controversies' Notebook: Justification." In *Writings on the Trinity, Grace, and Faith*, edited by Sang Hyun Lee, 328–413. Vol. 21 of *The Works of Jonathan Edwards*. New Haven, CT: Yale University Press, 2003.

———. "Diary." In *Letters and Personal Writings*, edited by George S. Claghorn, 759–789. Vol. 16 of *The Works of Jonathan Edwards*. New Haven, CT: Yale University Press, 1998.

———. "Discourse on the Trinity." In *Writings on the Trinity, Grace, and Faith*, edited by Sang Hyun Lee, 109–144. Vol. 21 of *The Works of Jonathan Edwards*. New Haven, CT: Yale University Press, 2003.

———. *Dissertation I: Concerning the End for Which God Created the World*. In *Ethical Writings*, edited by Paul Ramsey, 403–536. Vol. 8 of *The Works of Jonathan Edwards*. New Haven, CT: Yale University Press, 1989.

———. *The Distinguishing Marks*. In *The Great Awakening*, edited by C. C. Goen, 213–288. Vol. 4 of *The Works of Jonathan Edwards*. New Haven, CT: Yale University Press, 1972.

———. *Ecclesiastical Writings*. Edited by David D. Hall. Vol. 12 of *The Works of Jonathan Edwards*. New Haven, CT: Yale University Press, 1994.

———. "Efficacious Grace, Books I–III." In *Writings on the Trinity, Grace, and Faith*, edited by Sang Hyun Lee, 198–290. Vol. 21 of *The Works of Jonathan Edwards*. New Haven, CT: Yale University Press, 2003.

———. *Ethical Writings*. Edited by Paul Ramsey. Vol. 8 of *The Works of Jonathan Edwards*. New Haven, CT: Yale University Press, 1989.

———. "Exposition on the Apocalypse." In *Apocalyptic Writings*, edited by Stephen J. Stein, 97–124. Vol. 5 of *The Works of Jonathan Edwards*. New Haven, CT: Yale University Press, 1977.

———. "Faith." In *Writings on the Trinity, Grace, and Faith*, edited by Sang Hyun Lee, 414–468. Vol. 21 of *The Works of Jonathan Edwards*. New Haven, CT: Yale University Press, 2003.

———. *A Faithful Narrative*. In *The Great Awakening*, edited by C. C. Goen, 144–211. Vol. 4 of *The Works of Jonathan Edwards*. New Haven, CT: Yale University Press, 1972.

———. *Freedom of the Will*. Edited by Paul Ramsey. Vol. 1 of *The Works of Jonathan Edwards*. New Haven, CT: Yale University Press, 1957.

———. *The Glory and Honor of God: Volume 2 of the Previously Unpublished Sermons of Jonathan Edwards*. Edited by Michael D. McMullen. Nashville, TN: Broadman & Holman, 2004.

———. *The Great Awakening*. Edited by C. C. Goen. Vol. 4 of *The Works of Jonathan Edwards*. New Haven, CT: Yale University Press, 1972.

———. "Harmony of the Genius Spirit Doctrines and Rules of the Old Testament and the New." Jonathan Edwards Collection. Beinecke Rare Book and Manuscript Library, Yale University, New Haven, CT.

———. "Hebrew Idioms." Jonathan Edwards Collection. Beinecke Rare Book and Manuscript Library, Yale University, New Haven, CT.

———. *A History of the Work of Redemption*. Edited by John F. Wilson. Vol. 9 of *The Works of Jonathan Edwards*. New Haven, CT: Yale University Press, 1989.

———. *An Humble Attempt to Promote Explicit Agreement and Visible Union of God's People in Extraordinary Prayer for the Revival of Religion and the Advancement of Christ's Kingdom on Earth, Pursuant to Scripture-Promises and Prophecies Concerning the Last Time*. In *Apocalyptic Writings*, edited by Stephen J. Stein, 307–436. Vol. 5 of *The Works of Jonathan Edwards*. New Haven, CT: Yale University Press, 1977.

———. *An Humble Inquiry into the Rules of the Word of God, Concerning the Qualifications Requisite to a Complete Standing and Full Communion in the Visible Christian Church*. In *Ecclesiastical Writings*, edited by David D. Hall, 167–348. Vol. 12 of *The Works of Jonathan Edwards*. New Haven, CT: Yale University Press, 1994.

———. "Images of Divine Things." In *Typological Writings*, edited by Wallace E. Anderson, 49–135. Vol. 11 of *The Works of Jonathan Edwards*. New Haven, CT: Yale University Press, 1992.

———. *Letters and Personal Writings*. Edited by George S. Claghorn. Vol. 16 of *The Works of Jonathan Edwards*. New Haven, CT: Yale University Press, 1998.

———. *The Life of David Brainerd*. Edited by Norman Pettit. Vol. 7 of *The Works of Jonathan Edwards*. New Haven, CT: Yale University Press, 1985.

———. *The "Miscellanies": Entry Nos. a–z, aa–zz, 1–500*. Edited by Thomas A. Schafer. Vol. 13 of *The Works of Jonathan Edwards*. New Haven, CT: Yale University Press, 1994.

———. *The "Miscellanies": Entry Nos. 501–832*. Edited by Ava Chamberlain. Vol. 18 of *The Works of Jonathan Edwards*. New Haven, CT: Yale University Press, 2000.

———. *The "Miscellanies": Entry Nos. 833–1152*. Edited by Amy Plantinga Pauw. Vol. 20 of *The Works of Jonathan Edwards*. New Haven, CT: Yale University Press, 2002.

———. "The Miscellanies: Entry No. 1067: Prophecies of the Messiah." Jonathan Edwards Papers. Franklin Trask Library, Andover Newton Theological School, Newton, MA.

———. "The Miscellanies: Entry No. 1068: The Fulfillment of the Prophecies of the Messiah." Jonathan Edwards Papers. Franklin Trask Library, Andover Newton Theological School, Newton, MA.

———. *The "Miscellanies": Entry Nos. 1153–1360*. Edited by Douglas A. Sweeney. Vol. 23 of *The Works of Jonathan Edwards*. New Haven, CT: Yale University Press, 2004.

———. *Notes on Scripture*. Edited by Stephen J. Stein. Vol. 15 of *The Works of Jonathan Edwards*. New Haven, CT: Yale University Press, 1998.

———. *Original Sin*. Edited by Clyde A. Holbrook. Vol. 3 of *The Works of Jonathan Edwards*. New Haven, CT: Yale University Press, 1970.

———. "Personal Narrative." In *Letters and Personal Writings*, edited by George S. Claghorn, 790–804. Vol. 16 of *The Works of Jonathan Edwards*. New Haven, CT: Yale University Press, 1998.

———. *Religious Affections*. Edited by John E. Smith. Vol. 2 of *The Works of Jonathan Edwards*. New Haven, CT: Yale University Press, 1959.

———. "Resolutions." In *Letters and Personal Writings*, edited by George S. Claghorn, 753–759. Vol. 16 of *The Works of Jonathan Edwards*. New Haven, CT: Yale University Press, 1998.

———. *Scientific and Philosophical Writings*. Edited by Wallace E. Anderson. Vol. 6 of *The Works of Jonathan Edwards*. New Haven, CT: Yale University Press, 1980.

———. *Sermons and Discourses 1720–1723*. Edited by Wilson H. Kimnach. Vol. 10 of *The Works of Jonathan Edwards*. New Haven, CT: Yale University Press, 1992.

———. *Sermons and Discourses 1723–1729*. Edited by Kenneth P. Minkema. Vol. 14 of *The Works of Jonathan Edwards*. New Haven, CT: Yale University Press, 1997.

———. *Sermons and Discourses 1730–1733*. Edited by Mark Valeri. Vol. 17 of *The Works of Jonathan Edwards*. New Haven, CT: Yale University Press, 1999.

———. *Sermons and Discourses 1734–1738*. Edited by M. X. Lesser. Vol. 19 of *The Works of Jonathan Edwards*. New Haven, CT: Yale University Press, 2001.

——. *Sermons and Discourses 1739–1742*. Edited by Harry S. Stout and Nathan O. Hatch with Kyle P. Farley. Vol. 22 of *The Works of Jonathan Edwards*. New Haven, CT: Yale University Press, 2003.

——. *Sermons and Discourses 1743–1758*. Edited by Wilson H. Kimnach. Vol. 25 of *The Works of Jonathan Edwards*. New Haven, CT: Yale University Press, 2006.

——. "Signs of Godliness." In *Writings on the Trinity, Grace, and Faith*, edited by Sang Hyun Lee, 469–510. Vol. 21 of *The Works of Jonathan Edwards*. New Haven, CT: Yale University Press, 2003.

——. *Some Thoughts Concerning the Revival*. In *The Great Awakening*, edited by C. C. Goen, 289–530. Vol. 4 of *The Works of Jonathan Edwards*. New Haven, CT: Yale University Press, 1972.

——. "Subjects of Inquiry." In *Minor Controversial Writings*. Vol. 28 of *The Works of Jonathan Edwards Online*. Jonathan Edwards Center at Yale University, 2008. http://edwards.yale.edu/archive?path=aHRocDovL2Vkd2FyZHMueWFsZS5lZHUvY2dpLWJpbi9uZXdwaGlsby9nZXRvYmplY3QucGw/Yy4yNzo1LndqZW8 (accessed June 14, 2011).

——. "Supplement to Prophecies of the Messiah." Jonathan Edwards Papers. Franklin Trask Library, Andover Newton Theological School, Newton, MA.

——. "Table to the 'Miscellanies.'" In *The "Miscellanies": Entry Nos. a–z, aa–zz, 1–500*, edited by Thomas A. Schafer, 125–150. Vol. 13 of *The Works of Jonathan Edwards*. New Haven, CT: Yale University Press, 1994.

——. "Treatise on Grace." In *Writings on the Trinity, Grace, and Faith*, edited by Sang Hyun Lee, 149–197. Vol. 21 of *The Works of Jonathan Edwards*. New Haven, CT: Yale University Press, 2003.

——. "Types." In *Typological Writings*, edited by Wallace E. Anderson, 143–153. Vol. 11 of *The Works of Jonathan Edwards*. New Haven, CT: Yale University Press, 1992.

——. "Types of the Messiah." In *Typological Writings*, edited by Mason I. Lowance Jr. with David H. Watters, 187–324. Vol. 11 of *The Works of Jonathan Edwards*. New Haven, CT: Yale University Press, 1992.

——. *Typological Writings*. Edited by Wallace E. Anderson and Mason I. Lowance Jr. with David H. Watters. Vol. 11 of *The Works of Jonathan Edwards*. New Haven, CT: Yale University Press, 1992.

——. *Writings on the Trinity, Grace, and Faith*. Edited by Sang Hyun Lee. Vol. 21 of *The Works of Jonathan Edwards*. New Haven, CT: Yale University Press, 2003.

EDWARDS' 104 EXTANT SERMONS ON THE PSALMS

Edwards, Jonathan. "61. Sermon on Ps 102:25–26 (January or February 1728)." In *Sermons, Series II, 1728–1729*. Vol. 43 of *The Works of Jonathan Edwards Online*. Jonathan Edwards Center at Yale University, 2008. http://edwards.yale.edu/archive?path=aHRocDovL2Vkd2FyZHMueWFsZS5lZHUvY2dpLWJpbi9uZXd

waGlsby9nZXRvYmplY3QucGw/Yy4oMTozLndqZW8 (accessed June 28, 2011).
[N.B.: The second half of this sermon was published as, "That This Present
World Shall One Day Come to an End" (listed below).]

——. "67. Sermon on Ps 90:12 (Spring 1728)." In *Sermons, Series II, 1728–1729*.
Vol. 43 of *The Works of Jonathan Edwards Online*. Jonathan Edwards Center at
Yale University, 2008. http://edwards.yale.edu/archive?path=aHRocDovL2Vkd2
FyZHMueWFsZS5lZHUvY2dpLWJpbi9uZXdwaGlsby9nZXRvYmplY3QucGw/
Yy4oMTo4LndqZW8 (accessed July 2, 2011).

——. "75. Sermon on Ps 65:11 (November 7, 1728)." In *Sermons, Series II, 1728–1729*.
Vol. 43 of *The Works of Jonathan Edwards Online*. Jonathan Edwards Center at
Yale University, 2008. http://edwards.yale.edu/archive?path=aHRocDovL2Vkd2
FyZHMueWFsZS5lZHUvY2dpLWJpbi9uZXdwaGlsby9nZXRvYmplY3QucGw/
Yy4oMToxNy53amVv (accessed July 2, 2011).

——. "98. Sermon on Ps 66:5 (Spring–Fall 1729)." Jonathan Edwards Collection.
Beinecke Rare Book and Manuscript Library. Yale University. New Haven, CT.

——. "99. Sermon on Ps 82:6–7 (Spring–Fall 1729)." In *Sermons, Series II, 1729*.
Vol. 44 of *The Works of Jonathan Edwards Online*. Jonathan Edwards Center at
Yale University, 2008. http://edwards.yale.edu/archive?path=aHRocDovL2Vkd2
FyZHMueWFsZS5lZHUvY2dpLWJpbi9uZXdwaGlsby9nZXRvYmplY3QucGw/
Yy4oMjo1Mi53amVv (accessed July 5, 2011).

——. "111. Sermon on Ps 18:26 (Summer–Fall 1729)." In *Sermons, Series II, 1729*.
Vol. 44 of *The Works of Jonathan Edwards Online*. Jonathan Edwards Center at
Yale University, 2008. http://edwards.yale.edu/archive?path=aHRocDovL2Vkd2
FyZHMueWFsZS5lZHUvY2dpLWJpbi9uZXdwaGlsby9nZXRvYmplY3QucGw/
Yy4oMjoxMS53amVv (accessed July 5, 2011).

——. "112. Sermon on Ps 33:1 (Summer–Fall 1729)." In *Sermons, Series II, 1729*.
Vol. 44 of *The Works of Jonathan Edwards Online*. Jonathan Edwards Center at
Yale University, 2008. http://edwards.yale.edu/archive?path=aHRocDovL2Vkd2
FyZHMueWFsZS5lZHUvY2dpLWJpbi9uZXdwaGlsby9nZXRvYmplY3QucGw/
Yy4oMjoxMi53amVv (accessed July 6, 2011).

——. "146. Sermon on Ps 119:2 (Summer–Fall 1729)." In *Sermons, Series II, 1729*.
Vol. 44 of *The Works of Jonathan Edwards Online*. Jonathan Edwards Center at
Yale University, 2008. http://edwards.yale.edu/archive?path=aHRocDovL2Vkd2
FyZHMueWFsZS5lZHUvY2dpLWJpbi9uZXdwaGlsby9nZXRvYmplY3QucGw/
Yy4oMjooNi53amVv (accessed July 6, 2011).

——. "168. Sermon on Ps 73:18–19 (Fall 1730–Spring 1731)." In *Sermons, Series II,
1729–1731*. Vol. 45 of *The Works of Jonathan Edwards Online*. Jonathan Edwards
Center at Yale University, 2008. http://edwards.yale.edu/archive?path=aHRoc-
DovL2Vkd2FyZHMueWFsZS5lZHUvY2dpLWJpbi9uZXdwaGlsby9nZXRvYmpl
Y3QucGw/Yy4oMzoyMS53amVv (accessed July 6, 2011).

——. "195. Sermon on Ps 108:4 (July–August 1731)." In *Sermons, Series II, 1731–
1732*. Vol. 46 of *The Works of Jonathan Edwards Online*. Jonathan Edwards Center

at Yale University, 2008. http://edwards.yale.edu/archive?path=aHRocDovL2Vkd
2FyZHMueWFsZS5lZHUvY2dpLWJpbi9uZXdkwaGlsby9nZXRvYmplY3Qu
cGw/Yy4oNDo5LndqZW8 (accessed July 11, 2011).

——. "206. Sermon on Ps 78:25 (August 1731–December 1732)." In *Sermons, Series II, 1731–1732*. Vol. 46 of *The Works of Jonathan Edwards Online*. Jonathan Edwards Center at Yale University, 2008. http://edwards.yale.edu/archive?path=aHRoc-DovL2Vkd2FyZHMueWFsZS5lZHUvY2dpLWJpbi9uZXdkwaGlsby9nZXRvYmpl Y3QucGw/Yy4oNDoyMC53amVv (accessed July 11, 2011).

——. "207. Sermon on Ps 94:12(a) (August 1731–December 1732)." In *Sermons, Series II, 1731–1732*. Vol. 46 of *The Works of Jonathan Edwards Online*. Jonathan Edwards Center at Yale University, 2008. http://edwards.yale.edu/archive?p-ath=aHRocDovL2Vkd2FyZHMueWFsZS5lZHUvY2dpLWJpbi9uZXdkwaGlsby9 nZXRvYmplY3QucGw/Yy4oNDoyMS53amVv (accessed July 11, 2011).

——. "275. Sermon on Ps 51:17 (March 1733)." In *Sermons, Series II, 1733*. Vol. 48 of *The Works of Jonathan Edwards Online*. Jonathan Edwards Center at Yale University, 2008. http://edwards.yale.edu/archive?path=aHRocDovL2Vkd2Fy ZHMueWFsZS5lZHUvY2dpLWJpbi9uZXdkwaGlsby9nZXRvYmplY3QucGw/ Yy4oNjo3LndqZW8 (accessed July 12, 2011).

——. "282. Sermon on Ps 110:2 (May 1733)." In *Sermons, Series II, 1733*. Vol. 48 of *The Works of Jonathan Edwards Online*. Jonathan Edwards Center at Yale University, 2008. http://edwards.yale.edu/archive?path=aHRocDovL2Vkd2Fy ZHMueWFsZS5lZHUvY2dpLWJpbi9uZXdkwaGlsby9nZXRvYmplY3QucGw/ Yy4oNjoxMy53amVv (accessed July 12, 2011).

——. "289. Sermon on Ps 39:4 (July 1733)." In *Sermons, Series II, 1733*. Vol. 48 of *The Works of Jonathan Edwards Online*. Jonathan Edwards Center at Yale University, 2008. http://edwards.yale.edu/archive?path=aHRocDovL2Vkd2Fy ZHMueWFsZS5lZHUvY2dpLWJpbi9uZXdkwaGlsby9nZXRvYmplY3QucGw/ Yy4oNjoyMC53amVv (accessed July 12, 2011).

——. "319. Sermon on Ps 90:5–6 (April 1734)." In *Sermons, Series II, 1734*. Vol. 49 of *The Works of Jonathan Edwards Online*. Jonathan Edwards Center at Yale University, 2008. http://edwards.yale.edu/archive?path=aHRocDovL2Vkd2Fy ZHMueWFsZS5lZHUvY2dpLWJpbi9uZXdkwaGlsby9nZXRvYmplY3QucGw/ Yy4oNzo5LndqZW8 (accessed July 12, 2011).

——. "365. Sermon on Ps 66:3 (August [6,] 1735)." In *Sermons, Series II, 1735*. Vol. 50 of *The Works of Jonathan Edwards Online*. Jonathan Edwards Center at Yale University, 2008. http://edwards.yale.edu/archive?path=aHRocDovL2Vkd2Fy ZHMueWFsZS5lZHUvY2dpLWJpbi9uZXdkwaGlsby9nZXRvYmplY3QucGw/ Yy4oODoxNy53amVv (accessed July 13, 2011).

——. "378. Sermon on Ps 116:12 (February 1736)." In *Sermons, Series II, 1736*. Vol. 51 of *The Works of Jonathan Edwards Online*. Jonathan Edwards Center at Yale University, 2008. http://edwards.yale.edu/archive?path=aHRocDovL2Vkd2Fy

ZHMueWFsZS5lZHUvY2dpLWJpbi9uZXdwaaGlssby9nZXRvYmplY3QucGw/
Yy4oOTo1LndqZW8 (accessed July 13, 2011).

———. "390. Sermon on Ps 127:2 (May 1736)." In *Sermons, Series II, 1736*. Vol. 51 of *The Works of Jonathan Edwards Online*. Jonathan Edwards Center at Yale University, 2008. http://edwards.yale.edu/archive?path=aHRocDovL2Vkd2Fy ZHMueWFsZS5lZHUvY2dpLWJpbi9uZXdwaGlssby9nZXRvYmplY3QucGw/ Yy4oOToxNy53amVv (accessed July 13, 2011).

———. "413. Sermon on Ps 136:1 (November 1736)." In *Sermons, Series II, 1736*. Vol. 51 of *The Works of Jonathan Edwards Online*. Jonathan Edwards Center at Yale University, 2008. http://edwards.yale.edu/archive?path=aHRocDovL2Vkd2Fy ZHMueWFsZS5lZHUvY2dpLWJpbi9uZXdwaGlssby9nZXRvYmplY3QucGw/ Yy4oOTozOC53amVv (accessed July 14, 2011).

———. "442. Sermon on Ps 106:5 (August 1737)." In *Sermons, Series II, 1737*. Vol. 52 of *The Works of Jonathan Edwards Online*. Jonathan Edwards Center at Yale University, 2008. http://edwards.yale.edu/archive?path=aHRocDovL2Vkd2Fy ZHMueWFsZS5lZHUvY2dpLWJpbi9uZXdwaGlssby9nZXRvYmplY3QucGw/ Yy41MDoyMi53amVv (accessed July 15, 2011).

———. "483. Sermon on Ps 23:2 (July 1738)." In *Sermons, Series II, 1738, and Undated 1734–1738*. Vol. 53 of *The Works of Jonathan Edwards Online*. Jonathan Edwards Center at Yale University, 2008. http://edwards.yale.edu/archive?path=aHRoc-DovL2Vkd2FyZHMueWFsZS5lZHUvY2dpLWJpbi9uZXdwaGlssby9nZXRvYmpl Y3QucGw/Yy41MToyMC53amVv (accessed July 14, 2011).

———. "499. Sermon on Ps 24:7–10 (January 1739)." In *Sermons, Series II, 1739*. Vol. 54 of *The Works of Jonathan Edwards Online*. Jonathan Edwards Center at Yale University, 2008. http://edwards.yale.edu/archive?path=aHRocDovL2Vkd2Fy ZHMueWFsZS5lZHUvY2dpLWJpbi9uZXdwaGlssby9nZXRvYmplY3QucGw/ Yy41MjoxLndkZW8 (accessed July 19, 2011).

———. "507. Sermon on Ps 66:18(a) (March 29, 1739)." In *Sermons, Series II, 1739*. Vol. 54 of *The Works of Jonathan Edwards Online*. Jonathan Edwards Center at Yale University, 2008. http://edwards.yale.edu/archive?path=aHRocDovL2Vkd2 FyZHMueWFsZS5lZHUvY2dpLWJpbi9uZXdwaGlssby9nZXRvYmplY3QucGw/ Yy41Mjo4LndkZW8 (accessed July 19, 2011).

———. "517. Sermon on Ps 19:12 (September 1739)." In *Sermons, Series II, 1739*. Vol. 54 of *The Works of Jonathan Edwards Online*. Jonathan Edwards Center at Yale University, 2008. http://edwards.yale.edu/archive?path=aHRocDovL2Vkd2Fy ZHMueWFsZS5lZHUvY2dpLWJpbi9uZXdwaGlssby9nZXRvYmplY3QucGw/ Yy41MjoxOC53amVv (accessed July 19, 2011).

———. "537. Sermon on Ps 94:10 (February 1740)." In *Sermons, Series II, January–June 1740*. Vol. 55 of *The Works of Jonathan Edwards Online*. Jonathan Edwards Center at Yale University, 2008. http://edwards.yale.edu/archive?path=aHRoc-DovL2Vkd2FyZHMueWFsZS5lZHUvY2dpLWJpbi9uZXdwaGlssby9nZXRvYmpl Y3QucGw/Yy41MzozLndkZW8 (accessed July 19, 2011).

——. "568. Sermon on Ps 119:56 (September 1740)." In *Sermons, Series II, July–December 1740*. Vol. 56 of *The Works of Jonathan Edwards Online*. Jonathan Edwards Center at Yale University, 2008. http://edwards.yale.edu/archive?path=aHRocDovL2Vkd2FyZHMueWFsZS5lZHUvY2dpLWJpbi9uZXdaXdwaGlssby9nZXRvYmplY3QucGw/Yy41NDo3LndqZW8 (accessed July 19, 2011).

——. "580. Sermon on Ps 144:15 (November 1740)." Jonathan Edwards Collection. Beinecke Rare Book and Manuscript Library. Yale University. New Haven, CT.

——. "601. Sermon on Ps 27:4(a) (March 1741)." Jonathan Edwards Collection. Beinecke Rare Book and Manuscript Library. Yale University. New Haven, CT.

——. "615. Sermon on Ps 13:3 (June 1741)." Jonathan Edwards Collection. Beinecke Rare Book and Manuscript Library. Yale University. New Haven, CT.

——. "622. Sermon on Ps 34:11 (July 1741)." Jonathan Edwards Collection. Beinecke Rare Book and Manuscript Library. Yale University. New Haven, CT.

——. "633. Sermon on Ps 55:12–14 (September 1741)." Jonathan Edwards Collection. Beinecke Rare Book and Manuscript Library. Yale University. New Haven, CT.

——. "677. Sermon on Ps 89:15(a) (July 1742)." Jonathan Edwards Collection. Beinecke Rare Book and Manuscript Library. Yale University. New Haven, CT.

——. "683. Sermon on Ps 126:5–6 (September 1742)." Jonathan Edwards Collection. Beinecke Rare Book and Manuscript Library. Yale University. New Haven, CT.

——. "685. Sermon on Ps 113:6 (November 11, 1742)." Jonathan Edwards Collection. Beinecke Rare Book and Manuscript Library. Yale University. New Haven, CT.

——. "693c. Sermon on Ps 1:3(a) (*c.* 1742)." Jonathan Edwards Papers. Franklin Trask Library, Andover Newton Theological School. Newton, MA.

——. "693i. Sermon on Ps 18:35 (n.d. [*c.* 1739–1740])." Jonathan Edwards Collection. Beinecke Rare Book and Manuscript Library. Yale University. New Haven, CT.

——. "693j. Sermon on Ps 71:5 (n.d. [*c.* late 1730s; probably winter 1737])." Jonathan Edwards Collection. Beinecke Rare Book and Manuscript Library. Yale University. New Haven, CT.

——. "704. Sermon on Ps 78:57 (June 1743)." In *Sermons, Series II, 1743*. Vol. 61 of *The Works of Jonathan Edwards Online*. Jonathan Edwards Center at Yale University, 2008. http://edwards.yale.edu/archive?path=aHRocDovL2Vkd2FyZHMueWFsZS5lZHUvY2dpLWJpbi9uZXdwaGlssby9nZXRvYmplY3QucGw/Yy41OToxLndqZW8 (accessed July 20, 2011).

——. "727. Sermon on Ps 45:9 (December 1743)." Jonathan Edwards Collection. Beinecke Rare Book and Manuscript Library. Yale University. New Haven, CT.

——. "731. Sermon on Ps 45:15 (March [21,] 1744)." Jonathan Edwards Collection. Beinecke Rare Book and Manuscript Library. Yale University. New Haven, CT.

——. "736. Sermon on Ps 66:18(b) (April 12, 1744)." Jonathan Edwards Collection. Beinecke Rare Book and Manuscript Library. Yale University. New Haven, CT.

——. "745. Sermon on Ps 2:6 (June 1744)." In *Sermons, Series II, 1744*. Vol. 62 of *The Works of Jonathan Edwards Online*. Jonathan Edwards Center at Yale

University, 2008. http://edwards.yale.edu/archive?path=aHRocDovL2Vkd2Fy
ZHMueWFsZS5lZHUvY2dpLWJpbi9uZXXdwaGlssby9nZXRvYmplY3QucGcw/
Yy42MDooLndqZW8 (accessed July 20, 2011).

——. "746. Sermon on Ps 110:4 (June 1744)." In *Sermons, Series II, 1744.* Vol. 62
of *The Works of Jonathan Edwards Online.* Jonathan Edwards Center at Yale
University, 2008. http://edwards.yale.edu/archive?path=aHRocDovL2Vkd2Fy
ZHMueWFsZS5lZHUvY2dpLWJpbi9uZXXdwaGlssby9nZXRvYmplY3QucGcw/
Yy42MD01LndqZW8 (accessed July 20, 2011).

——. "747. Sermon on Ps 2:3–4 (July 1744)." Jonathan Edwards Collection. Beinecke
Rare Book and Manuscript Library. Yale University. New Haven, CT.

——. "748. Sermon on Ps 119:140 (July 1744)." Jonathan Edwards Collection.
Beinecke Rare Book and Manuscript Library. Yale University. New Haven, CT.

——. "760. Sermon on Ps 119:108 (November 1744)." Jonathan Edwards Collection.
Beinecke Rare Book and Manuscript Library. Yale University. New Haven, CT.

——. "769. Sermon on Ps 8:4–5 (February 1745)." Jonathan Edwards Collection.
Beinecke Rare Book and Manuscript Library. Yale University. New Haven, CT.

——. "770. Sermon on Ps 78:5–7 (February 1745)." Jonathan Edwards Collection.
Beinecke Rare Book and Manuscript Library. Yale University. New Haven, CT.

——. "771. Sermon on Ps 119:1–3 (February 1745)." Jonathan Edwards Collection.
Beinecke Rare Book and Manuscript Library. Yale University. New Haven, CT.

——. "788. Sermon on Ps 111:5 (August 1745)." Jonathan Edwards Collection.
Beinecke Rare Book and Manuscript Library. Yale University. New Haven, CT.

——. "792. Sermon on Ps 37:3 (*c.* September 1745)." Jonathan Edwards Collection.
Beinecke Rare Book and Manuscript Library. Yale University. New Haven, CT.

——. "808. Sermon on Ps 94:12(b) (February 1746)." Jonathan Edwards Collection.
Beinecke Rare Book and Manuscript Library. Yale University. New Haven, CT.

——. "860. Sermon on Ps 84:3 (April 1747)." Jonathan Edwards Collection. Beinecke
Rare Book and Manuscript Library. Yale University. New Haven, CT.

——. "867. Sermon on Ps 61:2 (July 1747)." In *Sermons, Series II, 1747.* Vol. 65
of *The Works of Jonathan Edwards Online.* Jonathan Edwards Center at Yale
University, 2008. http://edwards.yale.edu/archive?path=aHRocDovL2Vkd2Fy
ZHMueWFsZS5lZHUvY2dpLWJpbi9uZXXdwaGlssby9nZXRvYmplY3QucGcw/
Yy42MzoxNC53amVv (accessed July 20, 2011).

——. "880. Sermon on Ps 115:17–18 (November 26, 1747)." In *Sermons, Series II,
1747.* Vol. 65 of *The Works of Jonathan Edwards Online.* Jonathan Edwards Center
at Yale University, 2008. http://edwards.yale.edu/archive?path=aHRocDovL2Vkd
2FyZHMueWFsZS5lZHUvY2dpLWJpbi9uZXXdwaGlssby9nZXRvYmplY3QucGu
cGcw/Yy42MzoyNy53amVv (accessed January 28, 2011).

——. "903. Sermon on Ps 17:3 (August 1748)." In *Sermons, Series II, 1748.* Vol.
66 of *The Works of Jonathan Edwards Online.* Jonathan Edwards Center at Yale
University, 2008. http://edwards.yale.edu/archive?path=aHRocDovL2Vkd2Fy

ZHMueWFsZS5lZHUvY2dpLWJpbi9uZXdadGdssby9nZXRvYmplY3QuccGw/
Yy42NDoxOS53amVv (accessed July 20, 2011).

——. "943. Sermon on Ps 119:162 (November 1749)." In *Sermons, Series II, 1749.*
Vol. 67 of *The Works of Jonathan Edwards Online.* Jonathan Edwards Center at
Yale University, 2008. http://edwards.yale.edu/archive?path=aHRocDovL2Vkd2
FyZHMueWFsZS5lZHUvY2dpLWJpbi9uZXdadGdssby9nZXRvYmplY3QuccGw/
Yy42NToyNC53amVv (accessed January 28, 2011).

——. "954. Sermon on Ps 7:11 (February 1750)." Jonathan Edwards Collection.
Beinecke Rare Book and Manuscript Library. Yale University. New Haven, CT.

——. "963. Sermon on Ps 45:3–5 (August 1750)." Jonathan Edwards Collection.
Beinecke Rare Book and Manuscript Library. Yale University. New Haven, CT.

——. "981. Sermon on Ps 112:1 (February 1751)." Jonathan Edwards Collection.
Beinecke Rare Book and Manuscript Library. Yale University. New Haven, CT.

——. "989. Sermon on Ps 36:7 (March 1751)." Jonathan Edwards Papers. Franklin
Trask Library, Andover Newton Theological School. Newton, MA.

——. "1004. Sermon on Ps 119:60(b) (September 1751)." Jonathan Edwards
Collection. Beinecke Rare Book and Manuscript Library. Yale University. New
Haven, CT.

——. "1007. Sermon on Ps 119:18 (October 1751)." Jonathan Edwards Collection.
Beinecke Rare Book and Manuscript Library. Yale University. New Haven, CT.

——. "1013. Sermon on Ps 78:36–37 (December 1751)." Jonathan Edwards Collection.
Beinecke Rare Book and Manuscript Library. Yale University. New Haven, CT.

——. "1030. Sermon on Ps 5:4–5 (March 1752)." Jonathan Edwards Collection.
Beinecke Rare Book and Manuscript Library. Yale University. New Haven, CT.

——. "1031. Sermon on Ps 27:4(b) (March 1752)." Jonathan Edwards Collection.
Beinecke Rare Book and Manuscript Library. Yale University. New Haven, CT.

——. "1038. Sermon on Ps 84:10 (May 1752)." Jonathan Edwards Collection.
Beinecke Rare Book and Manuscript Library. Yale University. New Haven, CT.

——. "1059. Sermon on Ps 14:1(b) (December 1752)." Jonathan Edwards Collection.
Beinecke Rare Book and Manuscript Library. Yale University. New Haven, CT.

——. "1071. Sermon on Ps 39:5 (March 1753)." Jonathan Edwards Collection.
Beinecke Rare Book and Manuscript Library. Yale University. New Haven, CT.

——. "1096. Sermon on Ps 145:15–21 (November 1, 1753)." Jonathan Edwards
Collection. Beinecke Rare Book and Manuscript Library. Yale University. New
Haven, CT.

——. "1112. Sermon on Ps 119:1–6 (March 1754)." Jonathan Edwards Collection.
Beinecke Rare Book and Manuscript Library. Yale University. New Haven, CT.

——. "1113. Sermon on Ps 119:59–60 [60–61] (March 1754)." Jonathan Edwards
Collection. Beinecke Rare Book and Manuscript Library. Yale University. New
Haven, CT.

——. "1147. Sermon on Ps 1:1 (August 1755)." Jonathan Edwards Collection.
Beinecke Rare Book and Manuscript Library. Yale University. New Haven, CT.

————. "1161. Sermon on Ps 37:16 (April 1756)." Jonathan Edwards Collection. Beinecke Rare Book and Manuscript Library. Yale University. New Haven, CT.

————. "1168. Sermon on Ps 118:6–9 (July 23, 1756)." Jonathan Edwards Collection. Beinecke Rare Book and Manuscript Library. Yale University. New Haven, CT.

————. "1175. Sermon on Ps 27:4(c) (October 1756)." Jonathan Edwards Collection. Beinecke Rare Book and Manuscript Library. Yale University. New Haven, CT.

————. "1179. Sermon on Ps 19:7–10 (undated, c. 1750s)." Jonathan Edwards Collection. Beinecke Rare Book and Manuscript Library. Yale University. New Haven, CT.

————. "The Beauty of Piety in Youth" (Ps 144:12). In *Sermons and Discourses 1743–1758*, edited by Wilson H. Kimnach, 103–110. Vol. 25 of *The Works of Jonathan Edwards*. New Haven, CT: Yale University Press, 2006.

————. "Christ Is to the Heart Like a River to a Tree Planted by It" [Ps 1:3(b)]. In *Sermons and Discourses 1743–1758*, edited by Wilson H. Kimnach, 600–604. Vol. 25 of *The Works of Jonathan Edwards*. New Haven, CT: Yale University Press, 2006.

————. "The Duty of Hearkening to God's Voice" (Ps 95:7–8). In *Sermons and Discourses 1720–1723*, edited by Wilson H. Kimnach, 436–450. Vol. 10 of *The Works of Jonathan Edwards*. New Haven, CT: Yale University Press, 1992.

————. "God the Best Portion of the Christian" (Ps 73:25). In vol. 4 of *Works of President Edwards* (Worcester ed.), 540–547. 8th ed. 1778. Reprint, New York: Leavitt & Allen, 1852.

————. "God's All-Sufficiency for the Supply of Our Wants" (Ps 65:9). In *Sermons and Discourses 1723–1729*, edited by Kenneth P. Minkema, 471–483. Vol. 14 of *The Works of Jonathan Edwards*. New Haven, CT: Yale University Press, 1997.

————. "God's Excellencies" (Ps 89:6). In *Sermons and Discourses 1720–1723*, edited by Wilson H. Kimnach, 413–435. Vol. 10 of *The Works of Jonathan Edwards*. New Haven, CT: Yale University Press, 1992.

————. "God's Manner Is First to Prepare Men's Hearts and Then to Answer Their Prayers" (Ps 10:17). In *The Glory and Honor of God: Volume 2 of the Previously Unpublished Sermons of Jonathan Edwards*, edited by Michael D. McMullen, 77–106. Nashville, TN: Broadman & Holman, 2004.

————. "God's People Tried by a Battle Lost" (Ps 60:9–12). In *Sermons and Discourses 1743–1758*, edited by Wilson H. Kimnach, 698–710. Vol. 25 of *The Works of Jonathan Edwards*. New Haven, CT: Yale University Press, 2006.

————. "Great Guilt No Obstacle to the Pardon of the Returning Sinner" (Ps 25:11). In vol. 4 of *Works of President Edwards* (Worcester ed.), 422–428. 8th ed. 1778. Reprint, New York: Leavitt & Allen, 1852.

————. "It's a Very Decent and Comely Thing That Praise Should Be Given to God" (Ps 147:1). In *The Glory and Honor of God: Volume 2 of the Previously Unpublished Sermons of Jonathan Edwards*, edited by Michael D. McMullen, 120–134. Nashville, TN: Broadman & Holman, 2004.

——. "Like Rain upon Mown Grass" (Ps 72:6). In *Sermons and Discourses 1739–1742*, edited by Harry S. Stout and Nathan O. Hatch with Kyle P. Farley, 298–318. Vol. 22 of *The Works of Jonathan Edwards*. New Haven, CT: Yale University Press, 2003.

——. "Man's Natural Blindness in the Things of Religion" (Ps 94:8–11). In vol. 7 of *The Works of President Edwards*, edited by Sereno E. Dwight, 3–30. New York: S. Converse, 1829.

——. "The Most High a Prayer-Hearing God" (Ps 65:2). In *The Works of Jonathan Edwards*, edited by Edward Hickman, 113–118. Vol. 2. 1834. Reprint, Edinburgh: Banner of Truth Trust, 1974.

——. "The Necessity of Self-Examination" (Ps 139:23–24). In vol. 6 of *The Works of President Edwards*, edited by Sereno E. Dwight, 328–364. New York: S. Converse, 1829.

——. "Of Those Who Walk in the Light of God's Countenance" [Ps 89:15(b)]. In *Sermons and Discourses 1743–1758*, edited by Wilson H. Kimnach, 698–710. Vol. 25 of *The Works of Jonathan Edwards*. New Haven, CT: Yale University Press, 2006.

——. "Practical Atheism" (Ps 14:1). *Sermons and Discourses 1730–1733*, edited by Mark Valeri, 45–58. Vol. 17 of *The Works of Jonathan Edwards*. New Haven, CT: Yale University Press, 1999.

——. "The Sacrifice of Christ Acceptable" (Ps 40:6–8). In *Sermons and Discourses 1723–1729*, edited by Kenneth P. Minkema, 437–457. Vol. 14 of *The Works of Jonathan Edwards*. New Haven, CT: Yale University Press, 1997.

——. "The Sole Consideration, that God Is God, Sufficient to Still All Objections to His Sovereignty" (Ps 46:10). In vol. 6 of *The Works of President Edwards*, edited by Sereno E. Dwight, 293–303. New York: S. Converse, 1829.

——. "Striving after Perfection" (Ps 119:3). In *Sermons and Discourses 1734–1738*, edited by M. X. Lesser, 680–703. Vol. 19 of *The Works of Jonathan Edwards*. New Haven, CT: Yale University Press, 2001.

——. "The Terms of Prayer" (Ps 21:4). In *Sermons and Discourses 1734–1738*, edited by M. X. Lesser, 768–791. Vol. 19 of *The Works of Jonathan Edwards*. New Haven, CT: Yale University Press, 2001.

——. "That God Is Everywhere Present" (Ps 139:7–10). In *The Blessing of God: Previously Unpublished Sermons of Jonathan Edwards*, edited by Michael D. McMullen, 107–121. Nashville, TN: Broadman & Holman, 2003.

——. "That It Is the Temper of the Truly Godly to Delight to Exalt God and to Lay Themselves Low" (Ps 115:1). In *The Blessing of God: Previously Unpublished Sermons of Jonathan Edwards*, edited by Michael D. McMullen, 71–87. Nashville, TN: Broadman & Holman, 2003.

——. "That This Present World Shall One Day Come to an End" (Ps 102:25–26). In *The Glory and Honor of God: Volume 2 of the Previously Unpublished Sermons of Jonathan Edwards*, edited by Michael D. McMullen, 107–119. Nashville, TN: Broadman & Holman, 2004. [N.B.: This is the published second half of sermon no. "61. Sermon on Ps 102:25–26 (January or February 1728)" (listed above).]

———. "That We Ought to Make Religion Our Present and Immediate Business" [Ps 119:60(a)]. In *The Blessing of God: Previously Unpublished Sermons of Jonathan Edwards*, edited by Michael D. McMullen, 89–105. Nashville, TN: Broadman & Holman, 2003.

———. "That Wicked Men Be Not Apt to Be Sensible but That It Will Always Be with Them As It Is Now" (Ps 10:6). In *The Glory and Honor of God: Volume 2 of the Previously Unpublished Sermons of Jonathan Edwards*, edited by Michael D. McMullen, 66–76. Nashville, TN: Broadman & Holman, 2004.

———. "The Vain Self-Flatteries of the Sinner" (Ps 36:2). In vol. 4 of *Works of President Edwards* (Worcester ed.), 322–329. 8th ed. 1778. Reprint, New York: Leavitt & Allen, 1852.

———. "'Tis a Blessed Thing to Some Persons That God Is to Be Their Judge" (Ps 7:8). In *The Glory and Honor of God: Volume 2 of the Previously Unpublished Sermons of Jonathan Edwards*, edited by Michael D. McMullen, 53–65. Nashville, TN: Broadman & Holman, 2004.

NONEXTANT SERMONS ON THE PSALMS

Sermon on Ps 2:11. Mentioned in Jonathan Edwards, *The "Miscellanies": Entry Nos. a–z, aa–zz, 1–500*, ed. Thomas A. Schafer, vol. 13 of *The Works of Jonathan Edwards*. New Haven, CT: Yale University Press, 1994, 510.

Sermon on Ps 18:25. Mentioned in Joseph Tracy, *The Great Awakening: A History of the Revival of Religion in the Time of Edwards and Whitefield*. Boston: Charles Tappan, 1845, 204.

Sermon on Ps 90:11. Mentioned in Jonathan Edwards, *The "Blank Bible,"* ed. Stephen J. Stein, vol. 24 of *The Works of Jonathan Edwards*. New Haven, CT: Yale University Press, 2006, 520.

Sermons on Ps 94:6–10. Mentioned in Jonathan Edwards, "Miscellanies" Entry No. 1156, in *The "Miscellanies": Entry Nos. 1153–1360*, ed. Douglas A. Sweeney, vol. 23 of *The Works of Jonathan Edwards*. New Haven, CT: Yale University Press, 2004, 67.

OTHER SERMONS BY EDWARDS

Edwards, Jonathan. "344. Thanksgiving Sermon on Rev 14:2 (Nov. 7, 1734)." In *Sermons, Series II, 1734*. Vol. 49 of *The Works of Jonathan Edwards Online*. http://edwards.yale.edu/archive?path=aHR0cDovL2Vkd2FyZHMueWFsZS5lZ

HUvY2dpLWJpbi9uZXdwaGlsbsby9nZXRvYmplY3QucGw/Yy40oNzozNi53amVv (accessed December 6, 2013).

——. "398. Sermon on Col 3:16 (June 17, 1736)." In *Sermons, Series II, 1736*. Vol. 51 of *The Works of Jonathan Edwards Online*. http://edwards.yale.edu/archive?path=aHRocDovL2Vkd2FyZHMueWFsZS5lZHUvY2dpLWJpbi9uZXdwaGlsbsby9nZXRvYmplY3QucGw/Yy40oOToyNS53amVv (accessed December 6, 2013).

——. "433. Sermon on 2 Cor 9:15 (May 1737)." In *Sermons, Series II, 1737*. Vol. 52 of *The Works of Jonathan Edwards Online*. http://edwards.yale.edu/archive?path=aHRocDovL2Vkd2FyZHMueWFsZS5lZHUvY2dpLWJpbi9uZXdwaGlsbsby9nZXRvYmplY3QucGw/Yy41MDoxNy53amVv (accessed October 16, 2012).

——. "743. Sermon on Deut 18:18 (June 1744)." In *Sermons, Series II, 1744*. Vol. 62 of *The Works of Jonathan Edwards Online*. http://edwards.yale.edu/archive?path=aHRocDovL2Vkd2FyZHMueWFsZS5lZHUvY2dpLWJpbi9uZXdwaGlsbsby9nZXRvYmplY3QucGw/Yy42MDozLndqZW8 (accessed January 27, 2011).

——. "All God's Methods Are Most Reasonable" (Isa 1:18–20). In *Sermons and Discourses 1723–1729*, edited by Kenneth P. Minkema, 161–197. Vol. 14 of *The Works of Jonathan Edwards*. New Haven, CT: Yale University Press, 1997.

——. "Children Ought to Love the Lord Jesus Christ Above All" (Matt 10:37). In *Sermons and Discourses 1739–1742*, edited by Harry S. Stout and Nathan O. Hatch with Kyle P. Farley, 167–180. Vol. 22 of *The Works of Jonathan Edwards*. New Haven, CT: Yale University Press, 2003.

——. "Christ the Spiritual Sun" (Mal 4:1–2). In *Sermons and Discourses 1739–1742*, edited by Harry S. Stout and Nathan O. Hatch with Kyle P. Farley, 48–63. Vol. 22 of *The Works of Jonathan Edwards*. New Haven, CT: Yale University Press, 2003.

——. "Christ's Sacrifice an Inducement to His Ministers" (Acts 20:28). In *Sermons and Discourses 1743–1758*, edited by Wilson H. Kimnach, 653–675. Vol. 25 of *The Works of Jonathan Edwards*. New Haven, CT: Yale University Press, 2006.

——. "Christian Happiness" (Isa 3:10). In *Sermons and Discourses 1720–1723*, edited by Wilson H. Kimnach, 294–301. Vol. 10 of *The Works of Jonathan Edwards*. New Haven, CT: Yale University Press, 1992.

——. "Christian Safety" (Prov 29:25). In *Sermons and Discourses 1720–1723*, edited by Wilson H. Kimnach, 451–464. Vol. 10 of *The Works of Jonathan Edwards*. New Haven, CT: Yale University Press, 1992.

——. "Christians a Chosen Generation" (1 Pet 2:9). In *Sermons and Discourses 1730–1733*, edited by Mark Valeri, 273–328. Vol. 17 of *The Works of Jonathan Edwards*. New Haven, CT: Yale University Press, 1999.

——. "The Curse of Meroz" (Judg 5:23). In *Sermons and Discourses 1739–1742*, edited by Harry S. Stout and Nathan O. Hatch with Kyle P. Farley, 490–508. Vol. 22 of *The Works of Jonathan Edwards*. New Haven, CT: Yale University Press, 2003.

——. "The Danger of Corrupt Communication among Young People" (Eph 4:29). In *Sermons and Discourses 1739–1742*, edited by Harry S. Stout and Nathan O. Hatch with Kyle P. Farley, 156–166. Vol. 22 of *The Works of Jonathan Edwards*. New Haven, CT: Yale University Press, 2003.

——. "The Dangers of Decline" (Rev 2:4–5). In *Sermons and Discourses 1730–1733*, edited by Mark Valeri, 87–100. Vol. 17 of *The Works of Jonathan Edwards*. New Haven, CT: Yale University Press, 1999.

——. "The Day of Judgment" (Acts 17:31). In *Sermons and Discourses 1723–1729*, edited by Kenneth P. Minkema, 506–541. Vol. 14 of *The Works of Jonathan Edwards*. New Haven, CT: Yale University Press, 1997.

——. "A Divine and Supernatural Light" (Matt 16:17). In *Sermons and Discourses 1730–1733*, edited by Mark Valeri, 405–426. Vol. 17 of *The Works of Jonathan Edwards*. New Haven, CT: Yale University Press, 1999.

——. "The Duty of Charity to the Poor" (Deut 15:7–11). In *Sermons and Discourses 1730–1733*, edited by Mark Valeri, 369–404. Vol. 17 of *The Works of Jonathan Edwards*. New Haven, CT: Yale University Press, 1999.

——. "Envious Men" (James 3:16). In *Sermons and Discourses 1730–1733*, edited by Mark Valeri, 101–120. Vol. 17 of *The Works of Jonathan Edwards*. New Haven, CT: Yale University Press, 1999.

——. "The Everlasting Love of God" (Jer 31:3). In *Sermons and Discourses 1734–1738*, edited by M. X. Lesser, 473–490. Vol. 19 of *The Works of Jonathan Edwards*. New Haven, CT: Yale University Press, 2001.

——. "The Excellency of Christ" (Rev 5:5–6). In *Sermons and Discourses 1734–1738*, edited by M. X. Lesser, 560–594. Vol. 19 of *The Works of Jonathan Edwards*. New Haven, CT: Yale University Press, 2001.

——. "Extraordinary Gifts of the Spirit Are Inferior to Graces of the Spirit" (1 Cor 13:8–13). In *Sermons and Discourses 1743–1758*, edited by Wilson H. Kimnach, 275–311. Vol. 25 of *The Works of Jonathan Edwards*. New Haven, CT: Yale University Press, 2006.

——. "False Light and True" (2 Cor 11:14). In *Sermons and Discourses 1734–1738*, edited by M. X. Lesser, 120–142. Vol. 19 of *The Works of Jonathan Edwards*. New Haven, CT: Yale University Press, 2001.

——. "Glorious Grace" (Zech 4:7). In *Sermons and Discourses 1720–1723*, edited by Wilson H. Kimnach, 388–399. Vol. 10 of *The Works of Jonathan Edwards*. New Haven, CT: Yale University Press, 1992.

——. "Glorying in the Savior" (Isa 45:25). In *Sermons and Discourses 1723–1729*, edited by Kenneth P. Minkema, 458–470. Vol. 14 of *The Works of Jonathan Edwards*. New Haven, CT: Yale University Press, 1997.

——. "God Amongst His People" (Isa 12:6). In *Sermons and Discourses 1734–1738*, edited by M. X. Lesser, 451–472. Vol. 19 of *The Works of Jonathan Edwards*. New Haven, CT: Yale University Press, 2001.

——. "God Glorified in Man's Dependence" (1 Cor 1:29–31). In *Sermons and Discourses 1730–1733*, edited by Mark Valeri, 196–216. Vol. 17 of *The Works of Jonathan Edwards*. New Haven, CT: Yale University Press, 1999.

——. "The Great Concern of a Watchmen for Souls" (Heb 13:17). In *Sermons and Discourses 1743–1758*, edited by Wilson H. Kimnach, 59–81. Vol. 25 of *The Works of Jonathan Edwards*. New Haven, CT: Yale University Press, 2006.

——. "Heaven Is a World of Love" (2 Cor 13:8–10). In *Charity and Its Fruits*. In *Ethical Writings*, edited by Paul Ramsey, 366–397. Vol. 8 of *The Works of Jonathan Edwards*. New Haven, CT: Yale University Press, 1989.

——. "Heeding the Word, and Losing It" (Heb 2:1). In *Sermons and Discourses 1734– 1738*, edited by M. X. Lesser, 37–57. Vol. 19 of *The Works of Jonathan Edwards*. New Haven, CT: Yale University Press, 2001.

——. "Honey from the Rock" (Deut 32:13). In *Sermons and Discourses 1730–1733*, edited by Mark Valeri, 121–138. Vol. 17 of *The Works of Jonathan Edwards*. New Haven, CT: Yale University Press, 1999.

——. "The Importance and Advantage of a Thorough Knowledge of Divine Truth" (Heb 5:12). In *Sermons and Discourses 1739–1742*, edited by Harry S. Stout and Nathan O. Hatch with Kyle P. Farley, 80–102. Vol. 22 of *The Works of Jonathan Edwards*. New Haven, CT: Yale University Press, 2003.

——. "The Importance of a Future State" (Heb 9:27). In *Sermons and Discourses 1720– 1723*, edited by Wilson H. Kimnach, 351–376. Vol. 10 of *The Works of Jonathan Edwards*. New Haven, CT: Yale University Press, 1992.

——. "The Justice of God in the Damnation of Sinners" (Rom 3:19). In *Sermons and Discourses 1734–1738*, edited by M. X. Lesser, 336–376. Vol. 19 of *The Works of Jonathan Edwards*. New Haven, CT: Yale University Press, 2001.

——. "Justification by Faith Alone" (Rom 4:5). In *Sermons and Discourses 1734–1738*, edited by M. X. Lesser, 143–242. Vol. 19 of *The Works of Jonathan Edwards*. New Haven, CT: Yale University Press, 2001.

——. "Light in a Dark World, a Dark Heart" (2 Pet 2:19). In *Sermons and Discourses 1734–1738*, edited by M. X. Lesser, 704–733. Vol. 19 of *The Works of Jonathan Edwards*. New Haven, CT: Yale University Press, 2001.

——. "Living Peaceably One with Another" (Rom 12:18). In *Sermons and Discourses 1723–1729*, edited by Kenneth P. Minkema, 116–133. Vol. 14 of *The Works of Jonathan Edwards*. New Haven, CT: Yale University Press, 1997.

——. "The Many Mansions" (John 14:2). In *Sermons and Discourses 1734–1738*, edited by M. X. Lesser, 734–746. Vol. 19 of *The Works of Jonathan Edwards*. New Haven, CT: Yale University Press, 2001.

——. "Mary's Remarkable Act" (Mark 14:3). In *Sermons and Discourses 1739–1742*, edited by Harry S. Stout and Nathan O. Hatch with Kyle P. Farley, 378–399. Vol. 22 of *The Works of Jonathan Edwards*. New Haven, CT: Yale University Press, 2003.

——. "Of God the Father" (1 Cor 11:3). In *Sermons and Discourses 1743–1758*, edited by Wilson H. Kimnach, 142–154. Vol. 25 of *The Works of Jonathan Edwards*. New Haven, CT: Yale University Press, 2006.

——. "Perpetuity and Change of the Sabbath" (1 Cor 16:1–2). In *Sermons and Discourses 1730–1733*, edited by Mark Valeri, 217–250. Vol. 17 of *The Works of Jonathan Edwards*. New Haven, CT: Yale University Press, 1999.

——. "Persevering Faith" (Heb 10:38–39). In *Sermons and Discourses 1734–1738*, edited by M. X. Lesser, 595–608. Vol. 19 of *The Works of Jonathan Edwards*. New Haven, CT: Yale University Press, 2001.

——. "Praying for the Spirit" (Luke 11:13). In *Sermons and Discourses 1739–1742*, edited by Harry S. Stout and Nathan O. Hatch with Kyle P. Farley, 211–223. Vol. 22 of *The Works of Jonathan Edwards*. New Haven, CT: Yale University Press, 2003.

——. "Pressing into the Kingdom of God" (Luke 16:16). In *Sermons and Discourses 1734–1738*, edited by M. X. Lesser, 272–304. Vol. 19 of *The Works of Jonathan Edwards*. New Haven, CT: Yale University Press, 2001.

——. "Profitable Hearers of the Word" (Matt 13.23). In *Sermons and Discourses 1723–1729*, edited by Kenneth P. Minkema, 243–277. Vol. 14 of *The Works of Jonathan Edwards*. New Haven, CT: Yale University Press, 1997.

——. "Quæstio: Peccator Non Iustificatur Coram Deo Nisi Per Iustitiam Christi Fide Apprehensam." In *Sermons and Discourses 1723–1729*, edited by Kenneth P. Minkema and translated by George G. Levesque, 47–66. Vol. 14 of *The Works of Jonathan Edwards*. New Haven, CT: Yale University Press, 1997.

——. "Ruth's Resolution" (Ruth 1:16). In *Sermons and Discourses 1734–1738*, edited by M. X. Lesser, 305–320. Vol. 19 of *The Works of Jonathan Edwards*. New Haven, CT: Yale University Press, 2001.

——. "Saving Faith and Christian Obedience Arise from Godly Love" (1 John 5:1–4). In *Sermons and Discourses 1743–1758*, edited by Wilson H. Kimnach, 494–535. Vol. 25 of *The Works of Jonathan Edwards*. New Haven, CT: Yale University Press, 2006.

——. "Serving God in Heaven" (Rev 22:3). In *Sermons and Discourses 1730–1733*, edited by Mark Valeri, 251–261. Vol. 17 of *The Works of Jonathan Edwards*. New Haven, CT: Yale University Press, 1999.

——. "Sin and Wickedness Bring Calamity and Misery on a People" (Prov 14:34). In *Sermons and Discourses 1723–1729*, edited by Kenneth P. Minkema, 484–505. Vol. 14 of *The Works of Jonathan Edwards*. New Haven, CT: Yale University Press, 1997.

——. "Sinners in the Hands of an Angry God" (Deut 32:35). In *Sermons and Discourses 1739–1742*, edited by Harry S. Stout and Nathan O. Hatch with Kyle P. Farley, 400–435. Vol. 22 of *The Works of Jonathan Edwards*. New Haven, CT: Yale University Press, 2003.

——. "A Spiritual Understanding of Divine Things Denied to the Unregenerate" (1 Cor 2:14). In *Sermons and Discourses 1723–1729*, edited by Kenneth P. Minkema, 67–96. Vol. 14 of *The Works of Jonathan Edwards*. New Haven, CT: Yale University Press, 1997.

——. "The Suitableness of Union in Extraordinary Prayer for the Advancement of God's Church" (Zech 8:20–22). In *Sermons and Discourses, 1743–1758*, edited by

Wilson H. Kimnach, 197–206. Vol. 25 of *The Works of Jonathan Edwards*. New Haven, CT: Yale University Press, 2006.

———. "The Sweet Harmony of Christ" (John 10:4). In *Sermons and Discourses 1734–1738*, edited by M. X. Lesser, 435–450. Vol. 19 of *The Works of Jonathan Edwards*. New Haven, CT: Yale University Press, 2001.

———. "They Sing a New Song" (Rev 14:3). In *Sermons and Discourses 1739–1742*, edited by Harry S. Stout and Nathan O. Hatch with Kyle P. Farley, 224–244. Vol. 22 of *The Works of Jonathan Edwards*. New Haven, CT: Yale University Press, 2003.

———. "The Threefold Work of the Holy Ghost" (John 16:8). In *Sermons and Discourses 1723–1729*, edited by Kenneth P. Minkema, 371–436. Vol. 14 of *The Works of Jonathan Edwards*. New Haven, CT: Yale University Press, 1997.

———. "The Torments of Hell Are Exceeding Great" (Luke 16:24). In *Sermons and Discourses 1723–1729*, edited by Kenneth P. Minkema, 297–328. Vol. 14 of *The Works of Jonathan Edwards*. New Haven, CT: Yale University Press, 1997.

———. "True Christian's Life a Journey" (Heb 11:13–14). In *Sermons and Discourses 1730–1733*, edited by Mark Valeri, 427–446. Vol. 17 of *The Works of Jonathan Edwards*. New Haven, CT: Yale University Press, 1999.

———. "True Grace, Distinguished from the Experience of Devils" (James 2:19). In *Sermons and Discourses 1743–1758*, edited by Wilson H. Kimnach, 605–640. Vol. 25 of *The Works of Jonathan Edwards*. New Haven, CT: Yale University Press, 2006.

———. "Undeserved Mercy" (Ezek 20:21–22). In *Sermons and Discourses 1734–1738*, edited by M. X. Lesser, 628–655. Vol. 19 of *The Works of Jonathan Edwards*. New Haven, CT: Yale University Press, 2001.

———. "The Way of Holiness" (Isa 35:8). In *Sermons and Discourses 1720–1723*, edited by Wilson H. Kimnach, 465–479. Vol. 10 of *The Works of Jonathan Edwards*. New Haven, CT: Yale University Press, 1992.

OTHER PRIMARY SOURCES

Ainsworth, Henry. *Annotations upon the Five Bookes of Moses, the Booke of the Psalmes, and the Song of Songs, or, Canticles, Wherein the Hebrew Words and Sentences are compared with, and explained by the ancient Greeke and Chaldee Versions, and other Records and Monuments of the Hebrews: But chiefly by conference with the holy Scriptures, Moses, his words, lawes, and ordinances, the Sacrifices, and other legall Ceremonies heretofore commanded by God to the Church of Israel, are explained.* London: M. Parsons for John Bellamie, 1639.

Athanasius. "A Letter of Athanasius, Our Holy Father, Archbishop of Alexandria, to Marcellinus on the Interpretation of the Psalms." In *The Life of Antony and the Letter to Marcellinus*, 101–129. Translated by Robert C. Gregg. New York: Paulist Press, 1980.

Augustine. *The Confessions of St. Augustine*. Translated by John K. Ryan. New York: Image Books, 1960.

———. *Expositions of the Psalms*. Translated by Maria Boulding and edited by John E. Rotelle. Part III, vols. 15–20 of *The Works of Saint Augustine*. Hyde Park, NY: New City, 2000–2004.

The Bay Psalm Book. 1640. Reprint, Chicago: University of Chicago Press, 1956.

Bedford, Arthur. *The Scripture Chronology Demonstrated by Astronomical Calculations, and also by The Year of Jubilee, and the Sabbatical Year among the Jews: or, An Account of Time From the Creation of the World, to the Destruction of Jerusalem; as it may be proved from the Writings of the Old and New Testament*. London: James and John Knapton, Daniel Midwinter and Aaron Ward, Arthur Bettesworth, Francis Favram, John Pemberton, John Osborn and Tho. Longman, Charles Rivington, Francis Clay, Jeremiah Batley, and Richard Hett, 1730.

Buxtorf, Johannis. *Lexicon Hebraicum et Chaldaicum Complectens Omnes Voces, Tam Primas quam Derivatas, quae in Sacris Bibliis, Hebraea, & ex parte Chaldea lingua scriptis, extant: Interpretationes Fide, Exemplorum Biblicorum copia, Locorum plurimorum difficilium ex variis Hebraeorum Commentariis explicatione, auctum & illustratum. Accessit Lexicon Breve Rabbini, co-Philosophicum, communiora vocabula continens, quae in Commentariis passim occurrunt. Cum Indice Locorum Scripturae & Vocum Latino*. 10th ed. Basileae: Francisci Plateri & Joh. Philippi Richteri, 1698.

Byles, Mather. *The character of the perfect and upright man; his peaceful end described; and our duty to observe it laid down: In a discourse on Psalm XXXVII. 37*. Boston: S. Gerrish, 1729.

Calvin, John. *Commentary on the Psalms*. Translated from the original Latin and collated with the author's French version by James Anderson. 5 vols. 1843–1855. Reprint, Grand Rapids, MI: Eerdmans, 1963.

———. *Institutes of the Christian Religion*. Edited by John T. McNeill and translated by Ford Lewis Battles. 2 vols. Louisville, KY: Westminster John Knox, 2006.

Charnock, Stephen. *Several discourses upon the existence and attributes of God*. London: D. Newman, T. Cockerill, Benj. Griffin, T. Simmons, and Benj. Alsop, 1682.

Chauncy, Charles. *Marvellous things done by the right hand and holy arm of God in getting him the victory: a sermon preached the 18th of July 1745: being a day set apart for solemn thanksgiving to almighty God for the reduction of Cape-Breton by His Majesty's New-England forces, under the command of the Honourable William Pepperrell, Esq., lieutenant-general and commander in chief, and covered by a squadron of His Majesty's ships from Great Britain, commanded by Peter Warren, Esq*. Boston: J. Fleet, 1745.

Chrysostom, John. *Commentary on the Psalms*. 2 vols. Translated with introduction by Robert Charles Hill. Brookline, MA: Holy Cross Orthodox Press, 1998.

Clark, Peter. *Religion to be minded, under the greatest perils of life. A sermon on Psal. cxix. 109. Containing a word in season to soldiers. Preach'd on April 6. 1755. Being the Lord's-Day, before muster of a number of soldiers in the North-Parish in Danvers, who had enlisted in the publick service of the King and country, in the intended expedition. Published at the request of the hearers. By Peter Clark, A.M. Pastor of the First Church in Danvers.* Boston: S. Kneeland, 1755.

Cotton, John. *Singing of Psalmes a gospel-ordinance.* London: M.S. for Hannah Allen, at the Crowne in Popes-head-alley, and John Rothwell at the Sunne and fountaine in Pauls-church-yard, 1647.

Cruden, Alexander. *A Complete Concordance to the Holy Scriptures of the Old and New Testaments.* London: D. Midwinter, A. Buttesworth and C. Hitch, J. and J. Pemberton, R. Ware, C. Rivington, R. Ford, F. Clay, A. Ward, J. and P. Knapton, J. Clarke, T. Longman, R. Hett, J. Oswald, L. Wood, A. Cruden, and J. Davidson, 1738.

Davies, Samuel. *A Sermon, Preached before the Reverend Presbytery of New-Castle, October 11, 1752.* Philadelphia, PA: B. Franklin and D. Hall, at the New Printing Office, in Market street, 1753.

Dickson, David. *A Brief Explication of the first Fifty Psalms.* London: T. M. for Ralph Smith, at the Bible in Cornhill, neer the Royal Exchange, 1652.

———. *A Brief Explication of the last Fifty Psalmes, From Ps. 100 to the end.* London: T. R. and E. M. for Ralph Smith, at the Bible in Cornhill, near the Royal Exchange, 1654.

———. *A Brief Explication of the other fifty Psalmes, From Ps. 50 to Ps. 100.* London: T. R. and E. M. for Ralph Smith, at the Bible in Cornhill, near the Royal Exchange, 1653.

Diodore of Tarsus. "Commentary on the Psalms, Prologue." In *Biblical Interpretation in the Early Church*, edited by Karlfried Froehlich, 82–86. Sources of Christian Thought Series. Philadelphia, PA: Fortress, 1984.

A Directory for the Public Worship of God in the Three Kingdoms. Reprinted in *Scripture and Worship: Biblical Interpretation and the Directory for Public Worship*, by Richard A. Muller and Rowland S. Ward, 141–175. The Westminster Assembly and the Reformed Faith Series, edited by Carl R. Trueman. 1645. Reprint, Phillipsburg, NJ: P & R, 2007.

Doddridge, Philip. *The family expositor; or, a paraphrase and version of the New Testament. With critical notes, and a practical improvement of each section.* 6 vols. London: John Wilson, 1739–1756.

Duchal, James. *Presumptive arguments for the truth and divine authority of the Christian religion; in ten sermons: to which is added a sermon upon God's moral government.* London: A. Millar, 1753.

Dwight, Sereno E., ed. *The Works of President Edwards: With a Memoir of His Life.* 10 vols. New York: S. Converse, 1829–1830.

Evans, John. *Practical discourses concerning the Christian temper: being thirty eight sermons upon the principal heads of practical religion, especially as injoined and inforced by Christianity.* London: John and Barham Clark; Eman. Matthews; and John Morley, 1723.

Gale, Theophilus. *Court of the Gentiles: or A Discourse touching the Original of Human Literature, both Philologie and Philosophie, From the Scriptures & Jewish Church, Part 1, Of Philologie.* 2d ed. Oxon: H. Hall for Tho. Gilbert, 1672.

Glas, John. *Some Notes on Scripture-Texts, Shewing the Import of these Names of Jesus Christ, the Son of God and the Word of God; With an Account of The Image of God in Man.* Edinburgh: W. Sand, A. Murray, and J. Cochran, 1747.

———. *Notes on Scriptures-Texts, in Seven Numbers.* In vol. 3 of *The Works of Mr. John Glas*, 1–344. 2d ed. Perth: R. Morison and Son, 1782.

Grotius, Hugo. *De Veritate religionis Christianae.* [S.I.]: Excudebat L. L[ichfield] impensis G. Webb, 1639.

Henry, Matthew. *An exposition of the five poetical books of the Old Testament; viz. Job, Psalms, Proverbs, Ecclesiastes, and Solomon's song. Wherein The Chapters and Psalms are sum'd up in Contents, the sacred Text inserted at large, in Paragraphs, or Verses, and each Paragraph, or Verse, reduc'd to its proper Heads, the Sense given, and largely illustrated With Practical Remarks and Observations.* London: T. Darrack, for T. Parkhurst, at the Bible and Three Crowns in Cheapside, J. Robinson, at the Golden Lion in St. Paul's Church-Yard, and J. Lawrence, at the Angel in the Poultrey, 1710.

Hervey, James. *Theron, Paulinus, and Aspasio; or, Letters and Dialogues, upon the Nature of Love to God, Faith in Christ, Assurance of a Title to Eternal Life. Containing Some Remarks on the Sentiments of the Revd. Messieurs Hervey and Marshal, on These Subjects.* 3 vols. London, 1755.

Homer. *The Odyssey.* In *The Complete Works of Homer: The Iliad and The Odyssey.* Translated by S. H. Butcher and Andrew Lang. New York: The Modern Library, 1935.

Hopkins, Samuel. *The Life and Character of the Late Reverend Mr. Jonathan Edwards, President of the College of New-Jersey.* Boston: S. Kneeland, 1765.

Howe, John. *The blessedness of the righteous opened, and further recommended from the consideration of the vanity of this mortal life: in two treatises, on Psal. 17.15, Psal. 89.47.* London: A. Maxwell, for Sa. Gellibrand, at the Ball in St. Pauls Church-yard, 1673.

Hugh of St. Victor. *The Didascalicon of Hugh of St. Victor.* Translated by Jerome Taylor. 1961. Reprint, New York: Columbia University Press, 1991.

Kidder, Richard. *A Demonstration of the Messias. In which The Truth of the Christian Religion Is Proved, against all the Enemies thereof; But especially against the Jews. In Three Parts.* 2d ed. corr. London: John Osborn and Thomas Longman in Pater-Noster Row; Richard Ford in the Poultry; Aaron Ward in Little Britain; and Samuel Billingsley in Chancery Lane, 1726.

Leigh, Edward. *Annotations on Five Poetical Books of the Old Testament: (viz.) Job, Psalmes, Proverbs, Ecclesiastes, and Canticles.* London: A. M. and T. Pierpont, E. Brewster, and M. Keinton, 1657.

Lewes, Daniel. *The sins of youth, remembred with bitterness: As represented in a sermon at a private meeting of a society of young men for religious exercise, on the evening after the Lord's-Day, in Boston, Feb. 14. 1724, 5. upon Psalm XXV. 7.* Boston: S. Kneeland, 1725.

Luther, Martin. *First Lectures on the* Psalms I. Edited by Hilton C. Oswald. Vol. 10 of *Luther's Works*. St. Louis: Concordia, 1974.

———. *First Lectures on the Psalms II*. Edited by Hilton C. Oswald and translated by Herbert J. A. Bouman. Vol. 11 of *Luther's Works*. St. Louis, MO: Concordia, 1976.

———. *Reading the Psalms with Luther*. St. Louis, MO: Concordia, 2007.

Manton, Thomas. *One hundred and ninety Sermons on the Hundred and Nineteenth Psalm*. London: Tho. Parkhurst at the Bible and Three Crowns at the Lower End of Cheapside; Jonathan Robinson at the Golden Lion in St. Pauls Church-yard; Brabazon Aylmey at the Three Pigeons in Cornhil over against the Royal Exchange; and Benjamin Alsop at the Angel and Bible in the Poultrey, 1681.

Mather, Cotton. *Addresses to Old Men, and Young Men, and Little Children*. Boston: R. Pierce, for Nicholas Buttolph, 1690.

———. *Psalterium Americanum*. Boston: 1718.

———. "Psalms 1–30 of Cotton Mather's *Biblia Americana*." In "Cotton Mather's *Biblia Americana* Psalms and the Nature of Puritan Scholarship," edited by Cheryl Rivers, 213–451. PhD diss., Columbia University, 1977.

———. *Biblia Americana*. Boston, MA: Massachusetts Historical Society, n.d.

Mather, Samuel. *The Figures or Types of the Old Testament*. Edited with an introduction by Mason I. Lowance, Jr. Series in American Studies, edited by Joseph J. Kwiat. 1705 (2d ed.). Reprint, New York: Johnson Reprint Corporation, 1969.

Origen. "Commentary on Psalms 1–25, Fragment from Preface." In *Origen*, edited and translated by Joseph W. Trigg, 69–72. The Early Church Fathers Series. New York: Routledge, 1998.

Origène. *Philocalie, 1–20 sur les Écritures*. Edited and translated by Margerite Harl. La Tour-Maubourg, France: Les Éditions du Cerf, 1983.

Owen, John. *An Exposition of the Epistle to the Hebrews: Hebrews 8–10*. Vol. 23 in *The Works of John Owen, D.D.*, edited by William H. Gould. London: Johnstone and Hunter, 1855.

Poole, Matthew. *Synopsis Criticorum Aliorumque Sacrae Scripturae Interpretum et Commentarum, Summo Studio et Fide Adornata*. Volume II: Complectens Libros Jobi, Psalmorum, Proverbiorum, Ecclesiastis, & Cantici Canticorum. Francofurti ad Moenum: Balthasaris Christophori Wustii, 1678.

Pope, Alexander, trans. *The Odyssey of Homer*. Vol. 10 of *The Poems of Alexander Pope*, edited by Maynard Mack. New Haven, CT: Yale University Press, 1967.

Prideaux, Humphrey. *The Old and New Testament Connected in the History of the Jews and Neighbouring Nations from the Declension of the Kingdoms of Israel and Judah to the Time of Christ*. 9th ed. Part 1, Vol. 1. London: R. Knaplock in St. Paul's Church-Yard, and J. Tonson in the Strand, 1725.

Prince, Thomas. *Earthquakes the works of God and tokens of his just displeasure: Two sermons on Psal. xviii. 7. At the particular fast in Boston, Nov. 2. and the general thanksgiving, Nov. 9. Occasioned by the late dreadful earthquake. Wherein among other things is offered a brief account of the natural causes of these operations in the hands of God: with a relation of some late terrible ones in other parts of the world, as well as those that have been perceived in New-England since it's [sic] settlement by English inhabitants.* Boston: D. Henchman, 1727.

———. *Precious in the sight of the Lord is the death of his saints: a sermon upon the death of Mrs. Elizabeth Oliver, relict of the Honourable Daniel Oliver, Esq: Wednesday May xxi, 1735, aetatis 58: delivered at the South Church in Boston, on the Lord's Day after* [Ps 116:15]. Boston: S. Kneeland & T. Green, 1735.

———. *The pious cry to the Lord for help when the godly and faithful fail among them: a sermon occasion'd by the great and publick loss in the death of the Honourable Thomas Cushing, Esq, speaker of the Honourable House of Representatives of the province of the Massachuesetts-Bay in New-England, April 11, 1746: delivered at the South Church in Boston, the Lord's Day after his funeral* [Ps 12:1]. Boston: T. Rand, 1746.

Rawlin, Richard. *Christ the Righteousness of his People; or, The Doctrine of Justification by Faith in Him. Represented in several Sermons, Preached at the Merchants Lecture at Pinner's-Hall.* London: R. Hett and J. Oswald, 1741.

Roberts, Francis. *Clavis Bibliorum. The Key of the Bible, Unlocking the Richest Treasury of the Holy Scriptures. Whereby The Order, Names, Times, Penmen, Occasion, Scope, and Principall Parts, Containing the Subject-Matter of every Book of Old and New Testament, are familiarly and briefly opened: For the help of the weakest capacity in the understanding of the whole Bible.* London: T. R. and E. M. for George Calvert, 1648.

Rolle, Richard. *Richard Rolle: The English Writings.* Edited and translated by Rosamund S. Allen. Classics of Western Spirituality. New York: Paulist, 1988.

Shuckford, Samuel. *The sacred and prophane history of the world connected, from the creation of the world to the dissolution of the Assyrian empire at the death of Sardanapalus, and to the declension of the kingdoms of Judah and Israel, under the reigns of Ahaz and Pekah.* 3 vols. London: R. Knaplock and J. Tonson, 1728–1730.

Stapfer, Johann Friedrich. *Institutiones Theologiæ Polemicæ Universæ, Ordine Scientifico dispositæ.* 5 vols. 3d ed. Tiguri: Heideggerum et Socios, 1757.

Taylor, John. *The Scripture-Doctrine of Original Sin Proposed to Free and Candid Examination.* London: J. Wilson, at the Turk's-Head in Gracechurch-street, 1740.

———. *The Hebrew Concordance, Adapted to the English Bible; Disposed after the Manner of Buxtorf.* 2 vols. London: J. Waugh and W. Fenner, at the Turk's Head in Lombard-Street, 1754–1757.

Tennent, Gilbert. *The danger of forgetting God describ'd. And the duty of considering our ways explain'd: In a sermon on Psalm L. 22: Preach'd at New-York, March 1735.* New York: John Peter Zenger, 1735.

———. *The necessity of thankfulness for wonders of divine mercies: a sermon preached at Philadelphia April 15th 1744: on occasion of the important and glorious victory obtain'd by the British arms in the Mediterranean, under the conduct of Admiral Matthews, over the united fleets of France and Spain, and likewise the frustrating a detestable attemt to invade England, by a popish pretender.* Philadelphia, PA: William Bradford, 1744.

——. *A sermon preach'd at Burlington in New-Jersey, November 23, 1749: being the day appointed by His Excellency the Governor, with the advice of His Majesty's Council, for a provincial thanksgiving: before the Governor and others, upon texts chosen by His Excellency: with a prefatory address to Philip Doddridge, D.D.* Philadelphia, PA: W. Bradford, 1749.

Thomas Aquinas. *Sancti Thomae Aquinatis Doctoris Angelici Ordinis Praedicatorum Opera Omnia.* Tomus XIV. Parma ed. 1852–1873. Reprint, New York: Musurgia, 1949.

——. *The Gifts of the Spirit: Selected Spiritual Writings.* Edited by Benedict M. Ashley and translated by Matthew Rzeczkowski. Hyde Park, NY: New City, 1995.

Trapp, John. *A Commentary or Exposition Upon the Books of Ezra, Nehemiah, Esther, Job, and Psalms, Wherein the Text is Explained, some Controversies are Discussed, sundry Cases of Conscience are Cleared, and many Remarkable Matters hinted, that had by former Interpreters been pretermitted. In all which divers other Texts of Scripture, which occasionally occurre, are fully Opened, and the whole so intermixed with pertinent Histories, as will yield both pleasure and profit to the Judicious Reader.* London: T. R. and E. M. for Thomas Newberry at the three Golden Lions at Cornhil, near the Royal Exchange, and Joseph Barber at the Holy Lamb in the New Rents in St. Pauls Church-yard, 1657.

Tucker, John. *God's goodness, amidst his afflictive providences, a just ground of thankfulness and praise: a discourse on Psalm CXVIII, 18,19: delivered November 25, 1756, being a day appointed by authority, for a publick thanksgiving thro' this province.* Boston: S. Kneeland, 1757.

Van Mastricht, Peter. *Theoretica-practica theologia: qua, per singula capita theologica, pars exegetica, dogmatica, elenchtica & practica, perpetuâ successione conjugantur, accedunt Historia ecclesiastica, plena quidem, sed compendiosa, Idea theologiae moralis, Hypotyposis theologiae asceticae &c., proin opus quasi novum.* Trajecti ad Rhenum: Ex officina Thomae Appels, 1699.

Watts, Isaac. *The Glory of Christ as God-Man Display'd, in Three Discourses. viz. Disc. I. A Survey of the visible Appearances of Christ, as God before his Incarnation, with some Observations on the Texts of the Old Testament apply'd to Christ. Disc. II. An Enquiry into the Extensive Powers of the Human Nature of Christ in its present glorify'd State, with several Testimonies annex'd. Disc. III. An Argument tracing out the early Existence of the Human Soul of Christ, even before the Creation of the World. With an Appendix, Containing an Abridgement of Dr. Thomas Goodwin's Discourse of the Glories and Royalties of Christ, in his Works in Folio, Vol. II. Book 3.* London: J. Oswald, at the Rose and Crown near the Mansion-House; and J. Buckland, at the Buck in Pater-noster Row, 1746.

——. *The Psalms of David imitated in the language of the New Testament, and apply'd to the Christian state and worship with the preface, or, an enquiry into the right way of fitting the Book of Psalms for Christian worship, and notes.* 1719. Reprint, Boston: D. Kneeland, for Thomas Leverett, in Corn-Hill, 1770.

Wells, Edward. *An historical geography of the Old Testament, in Three Volumes.* 3 vols. London: James Knapton, 1711–1712.

The Westminster Confession of Faith, A.D. 1647. In *The Evangelical Protestant Creeds, with Translations.* Vol. 3 of *The Creeds of Christendom, with a History and Critical Notes,* edited by Philip Schaff. New York: Harper & Brothers, 1877.

Whitefield, George. *Britain's mercies and Britain's duty: represented in a sermon preach'd at the new-building in Philadelphia, on Sunday August 24, 1746: occasioned by the suppression of the late unnatural rebellion.* Boston: S. Kneeland and T. Green, 1746.

Winder, Henry. *Critical and Chronological History of the Rise, Progress, Declension, and Revival of Knowledge, Chiefly Religious.* Vol. 2. 2d ed. London: J. Waugh and W. Fenner at the Turk's-Head, in Lombard-Street, 1756.

SECONDARY SOURCES

Abernethy, Andrew T. "Jonathan Edwards as Multi-Dimension[al] Bible Interpreter: A Case Study from Isaiah 40–55." *Journal of the Evangelical Theological Society* 56, no. 4 (December 2013): 815–830.

Adamo, David Tuesday. "The Imprecatory Psalms in African Context." In *Biblical Interpretation in African Perspective,* edited by David Tuesday Adamo, 139–153. Lanham, MD: University Press of America, 2006.

Anderson, Wallace E. "Editor's Introduction to 'Images of Divine Things' and 'Types.'" In *Typological Writings,* edited by Wallace E. Anderson and Mason I. Lowance, Jr., with David Watters, 3–48. Vol. 11 of *The Works of Jonathan Edwards.* New Haven, CT: Yale University Press, 1992.

Austern, Linda Phyllis, Kari Boyd McBride, and David L. Orvis, eds. *Psalms in the Early Modern World.* Burlington, VT: Ashgate, 2011.

Ayabe, John A. "A Search for Meaning: Principles of Literal and Spiritual Exegesis in Jonathan Edwards' 'Notes on Scripture.'" MA thesis, Trinity Evangelical Divinity School, 2001.

Bainton, Roland H. *Here I Stand: A Life of Martin Luther.* New York: Meridian, 1977.

Barshinger, David P. "'The Only Rule of Our Faith and Practice': Jonathan Edwards' Interpretation of the Book of Isaiah as a Case Study of His Exegetical Boundaries." *Journal of the Evangelical Theological Society* 52, no. 4 (2009): 811–829.

——. "Making the Psalter One's 'Own Language': Jonathan Edwards Engages the Psalms," *Jonathan Edwards Studies* 2, no. 1 (2012): 3–29.

Beck, Peter. *The Voice of Faith: Jonathan Edwards's Theology of Prayer.* Kitchener, Ontario: Joshua, 2010.

Becker, Laura L. "Ministers vs. Laymen: The Singing Controversy in Puritan New England, 1720–1740." *New England Quarterly* 55 (March 1982): 79–96.

Beeke, Joel R. "Psalm Singing in Calvin and the Puritans." In *Sing a New Song: Recovering Psalm Singing for the Twenty-First Century*, edited by Joel R. Beeke and Anthony T. Selvaggio, 16–40. Grand Rapids, MI: Reformation Heritage Books, 2010.

Beeke, Joel R., and Anthony T. Selvaggio, eds. *Sing a New Song: Recovering Psalm Singing for the Twenty-First Century*. Grand Rapids, MI: Reformation Heritage Books, 2010.

Bercovitch, Sacvan, ed. *Typology and Early American Literature*. Amherst, MA: University of Massachusetts Press, 1972.

——, ed. *The American Puritan Imagination: Essays in Revaluation*. New York: Cambridge University Press, 1974.

Beuttler, Fred W. "Jonathan Edwards and the Critical Assault on the Bible." MA thesis, Trinity Evangelical Divinity School, 1988.

Bezzant, Rhys S. *Jonathan Edwards and the Church*. New York: Oxford University Press, 2013.

Blaising, Craig A., and Carmen S. Hardin, eds. *Ancient Christian Commentary on Scripture: Old Testament: Psalms 1–50*. Vol. 7. Downers Grove, IL: InterVarsity, 2008.

Bombaro, John J. "Jonathan Edwards's Vision of Salvation." *Westminster Theological Journal* 65 (2003): 45–67.

Bonomi, Patricia U. Under *the Cope of Heaven: Religion, Society, and Politics in Colonial America*. New York: Oxford University Press, 1986.

Bradshaw, Paul F. The *Search for the Origins of Christian Worship: Sources and Methods for the Study of Early Liturgy*. New York: Oxford University Press, 1992.

Bray, Gerald L. "Poole, Matthew (1624–1679)." In *Dictionary of Major Biblical Interpreters*, edited by Donald K. McKim, 840–842. Downers Grove, IL: InterVarsity Press, 2007.

Brekus, Catherine A. *Sarah Osborn's World: The Rise of Evangelical Christianity in Early America*. New Directions in Narrative History. New Haven, CT: Yale University Press, 2013.

Brown, Robert E. "Edwards, Locke, and the Bible." *Journal of Religion* 79, no. 3 (1999): 361–384.

——. *Jonathan Edwards and the Bible*. Bloomington: Indiana University Press, 2002.

——. "The Bible." In *The Princeton Companion to Jonathan Edwards*, edited by Sang Hyun Lee, 87–102. Princeton, NJ: Princeton University Press, 2005.

——. "The Sacred and the Profane Connected: Edwards, the Bible, and Intellectual Culture." In *Jonathan Edwards at 300: Essays on the Tercentenary of His Birth*, edited by Harry S. Stout, Kenneth P. Minkema, and Caleb J. D. Maskell, 38–53. Lanham, MD: University Press of America, Inc., 2005.

Brown, Susan Tara. *Singing and the Imagination of Devotion: Vocal Aesthetics in Early English Protestant Culture.* Studies in Christian History and Thought. Milton Keynes, UK: Paternoster, 2008.

Brumm, Ursula. *American Thought and Religious Typology.* New Brunswick, NJ: Rutgers University Press, 1970.

Burton-Christie, Douglas. *The Word in the Desert: Scripture and the Quest for Holiness in Early Christian Monasticism.* Oxford: Oxford University Press, 1993.

Butler, Jon. "Enthusiasm Described and Decried: The Great Awakening as Interpretive Fiction." *The Journal of American History* 69, no. 2 (1982), 305–325.

Cady, Edwin H. "The Artistry of Jonathan Edwards." *New England Quarterly* 22 (1949): 61–72.

Cabaniss, Allen. "Background of Metrical Psalmody." *Calvin Theological Journal* 20, no. 2 (1985): 191–206.

Caldwell, Patricia. *The Puritan Conversion Narrative: The Beginnings of American Expression.* New York: Cambridge University Press, 1983.

Caldwell, Robert W., III. *Communion in the Spirit: The Holy Spirit as the Bond of Union in the Theology of Jonathan Edwards.* Studies in Evangelical History and Thought. Eugene, OR: Wipf & Stock, 2007.

Carden, Allen. *Puritan Christianity in America: Religion and Life in Seventeenth-Century Massachusetts.* Grand Rapids, MI: Baker Book House, 1990.

Carrick, John. *The Preaching of Jonathan Edwards.* Carlisle, PA: Banner of Truth Trust, 2008.

Chamberlain, Ava. "Editor's Introduction." In *The "Miscellanies": Entry Nos. 501–832,* edited by Ava Chamberlain, 1–48. Vol. 18 of *The Works of Jonathan Edwards.* New Haven, CT: Yale University Press, 2000.

———. "Bad Books and Bad Boys: The Transformation of Gender in Eighteenth-Century Northampton, Massachusetts." In *Jonathan Edwards at Home and Abroad: Historical Memories, Cultural Movements, Global Horizons,* edited by David W. Kling and Douglas A. Sweeney, 61–81. Columbia: University of South Carolina Press, 2003.

Cheever, George B. "The Manuscripts of President Edwards." *Independent* 4 (1852): 208.

Cherry, Conrad. "Symbols of Spiritual Truth: Jonathan Edwards as Biblical Interpreter." *Interpretation* 39, no. 3 (July 1985): 263–271.

Cho, Hyun-Jin. *Jonathan Edwards on Justification: Reformed Development of the Doctrine in Eighteenth-Century New England.* Lanham, MD: University Press of America, 2012.

Claghorn, George S., ed. *Letters and Personal Writings.* Vol. 16 of *The Works of Jonathan Edwards.* New Haven, CT: Yale University Press, 1998.

deClaissé-Walford, Nancy L. "The Theology of the Imprecatory Psalms." In *Soundings in the Theology of Psalms: Perspectives and Methods in Contemporary Scholarship,* edited by Rolf A. Jacobson, 77–92. Minneapolis, MN: Fortress, 2011.

Conforti, Joseph. "The Invention of the Great Awakening, 1795–1842." *Early American Literature* 26, no. 2 (1991): 99–118.

Cooper, Derek. "The Analogy of Faith in Puritan Exegesis: Scope and Salvation in James 2:14–26." *Stone-Campbell Journal* 12 (Fall 2009): 235–250.

Corrigan, John. *The Prism of Piety: Catholick Congregational Clergy at the Beginning of the Enlightenment*. New York: Oxford University Press, 1991.

Costley King'oo, Clare. *Miserere Mei: The Penitential Psalms in Late Medieval and Early Modern England*. South Bend, IN: Notre Dame University Press, 2012.

Crocco, Stephen D. "Edwards's Intellectual Legacy." In *The Cambridge Companion to Jonathan Edwards*, edited by Stephen J. Stein, 300–324. New York: Cambridge University Press, 2007.

Crookshank, Esther Rothenbusch. "'We're Marching to Zion': Isaac Watts in Early America." In *Wonderful Words of Life: Hymns in American Protestant History and Theology*, edited by Richard J. Mouw and Mark A. Noll, 17–41. Calvin Institute of Christian Worship Liturgical Studies Series. Grand Rapids, MI: Eerdmans, 2004.

Crump, David. "The Preaching of George Whitefield and His Use of Matthew Henry's *Commentary*." *Crux* 25, no. 3 (September 1989): 19–28.

Davies, Horton. *The Worship of the English Puritans*. Westminster: Dacre, 1948.

——. *The Worship of the American Puritans, 1629–1730*. New York: Peter Lang, 1990.

——. *Worship and Theology in England: From Watts and Wesley to Martineau, 1690–1900*. Grand Rapids, MI: Eerdmans, 1996.

Dayton, Cornelia Hughes. *Women before the Bar: Gender, Law, and Society in Connecticut, 1639–1789*. Chapel Hill: University of North Carolina Press, 1995.

Davis, Thomas J., ed. *John Calvin's American Legacy*. New York: Oxford University Press, 2010.

Davis, Thomas M. "The Traditions of Puritan Typology." In *Typology and Early American Literature*, edited by Sacvan Bercovitch, 11–45. Amherst: University of Massachusetts Press, 1972.

Dell, Katharine J. "Psalms." In *The Oxford Handbook of the Reception History of the Bible*, edited by Michael Lieb, Emma Mason, and Jonathan Roberts, 37–51. New York: Oxford University Press, 2011.

Dolezal, James E. "A Practical Scholasticism: Edward Leigh's Theological Method." *Westminster Theological Journal* 71 (2009): 337–354.

Duncan, J. Ligon. "Christ in the Psalms." *Modern Reformation* 11 (November 2002): 30–34.

Dyer, Joseph. "Monastic Psalmody of the Middle Ages." *Revue Bénédictine* 99 (1989): 41–74.

Earle, Morse Alice. *The Sabbath in Puritan New England*. New York: Charles Scribner's Sons, 1891.

Fabiny, Tibor. "Edwards and Biblical Typology." In *Understanding Jonathan Edwards: An Introduction to America's Theologian*, edited by Gerald R. McDermott, 91–108. Oxford: Oxford University Press, 2009.

Fiedrowicz, Michael. "General Introduction." In *Expositions of the Psalms: 1–32*, translated by Maria Boulding and edited by John E. Rotelle, 13–66. Part III, vol. 15 of *The Works of Saint Augustine*. Hyde Park, NY: New City, 2000.

Fiering, Norman. *Jonathan Edwards's Moral Thought and Its British Context*. Chapel Hill: University of North Carolina Press, 1981.

Foote, Henry Wilder. *Three Centuries of American Hymnody*. Hamden, CT: Shoe String Press, 1961.

Flynn, William T. "Liturgical Music." In *The Oxford History of Christian Worship*, edited by Geoffrey Wainwright and Karen B. Westerfield Tucker, 769–792. Oxford: Oxford University Press, 2006.

Froehlich, Karlfried. "Christian Interpretation of the Old Testament in the High Middle Ages." In *Hebrew Bible/Old Testament: The History of Its Interpretation*, edited by Magne Sæbø, 496–558. 2 vols. Göttingen: Vandenhoeck & Ruprecht, 1996.

———. "Thomas Aquinas (1224/25–1274)." In *Dictionary of Major Biblical Interpreters*, edited by Donald K. McKim, 979–985. Downers Grove, IL: IVP Academic, 2007.

Gates, J. Terry. "A Comparison of the Tune Books of Tufts and Walter." *Journal of Research in Music Education* 36, no. 3 (Autumn 1988): 169–193.

Gay, Peter. *The Enlightenment: An Interpretation*. 2 vols. New York: W. W. Norton, 1966–1969.

Gerstner, John H. "Jonathan Edwards and the Bible." *Tenth* 9 (1971): 1–71.

———. "The Church's Doctrine of Biblical Inspiration." In *The Foundation of Biblical Authority*, edited by James Montgomery Boice, 23–58. Grand Rapids, MI: Zondervan, 1978.

———. "The View of the Bible Held by the Church: Calvin and the Westminster Divines." In *Inerrancy*, edited by Norman L. Geisler, 383–410. Grand Rapids, MI: Zondervan, 1980.

———. *The Rational Biblical Theology of Jonathan Edwards*. 3 vols. Powhatan, VA: Berea, 1991–1993.

Gillingham, Susan E. *Psalms Through the Centuries*. Vol. 1. Blackwell Bible Commentaries. Malden, MA: Blackwell, 2008.

Goldman, Shalom. "Introduction." In *Hebrew and the Bible in America: The First Two Centuries*, edited by Shalom Goldman, xi–xxx. Hanover: University Press of New England, 1993.

———. "Edwards as Hebraist." Paper read at Edwards Conference, Bloomington, IN, June 1994.

———. *God's Sacred Tongue: Hebrew & the American Imagination*. Chapel Hill: University of North Carolina Press, 2004.

Goodell, Charles LeRoy. "A Puritan Commentator." *Methodist Review* 99 (Jan 1917): 63–74.

Goodwin, Gordon. "Leigh, Edward (1602–1671)." In Vol. 11 of *The Dictionary of National Biography*, edited by Leslie Stephen and Sidney Lee, 873–874. London: Oxford University Press, 1917.

Gordis, Lisa. *Opening Scripture: Bible Reading and Interpretive Authority in Puritan New England*. Chicago: University of Chicago Press, 2003.

de Greef, Wulfert. "Calvin as Commentator on the Psalms." Translated by Raymond A. Blacketer. In *Calvin and the Bible*, edited by Donald K. McKim, 85–106. New York: Cambridge University Press, 2006.

———. "Calvin's Understanding and Interpretation of the Bible." Translated by David Dichelle. In *John Calvin's Impact on Church and Society, 1509–2009*, edited by Martin Ernst Hirzel and Martin Sallmann, 67–89. Grand Rapids, MI: Eerdmans, 2009.

Hagen, Kenneth. "*Omnis homo mendax:* Luther on Psalm 116." In *Biblical Interpretation in the Era of the Reformation: Essays Presented to David C. Steinmetz in Honor of His Sixtieth Birthday*, edited by Richard A. Muller and John L. Thompson, 85–102. Grand Rapids, MI: Eerdmans, 1996.

Hall, Christopher A. *Reading Scripture with the Church Fathers*. Downers Grove, IL: InterVarsity, 1998.

Hambrick-Stowe, Charles E. *The Practice of Piety: Puritan Devotional Disciplines in Seventeenth-Century New England*. Chapel Hill: University of North Carolina, 1982.

Haraszti, Zoltan. *The Enigma of the Bay Psalm Book*. Chicago: University of Chicago Press, 1956.

Heine, Ronald E. *Reading the Old Testament with the Ancient Church: Exploring the Formation of Early Christian Thought*. Grand Rapids, MI: Baker Academic, 2007.

Himmelfarb, Gertrude. *The Roads to Modernity: The British, French, and American Enlightenments*. New York: Vintage, 2004.

Hirzel, Martin Ernst, and Martin Sallman, eds. *John Calvin's Impact on Church and Society, 1509–2009*. Grand Rapids, MI: Eerdmans, 2009.

Hobbs, R. G. "How Firm a Foundation: Martin Bucer's Historical Exegesis of the Psalms." *Church History* 53 (1984): 477–491.

Holladay, William L. *The Psalms through Three Thousand Years: Prayerbook of a Cloud of Witnesses*. Minneapolis, MN: Fortress, 1993.

Israel, Jonathan I. *Enlightenment Contested: Philosophy, Modernity, and the Emancipation of Man, 1670–1752*. Oxford: Oxford University Press, 2006.

Jenson, Robert W. *America's Theologian: A Recommendation of Jonathan Edwards*. New York: Oxford University Press, 1988.

Johnson, Lawrence J. *Worship in the Early Church: An Anthology of Historical Sources*. 4 vols. Collegeville, MN: Liturgical Press, 2009.

Johnson, Terry. "The History of Psalm Singing in the Christian Church." In *Sing a New Song: Recovering Psalm Singing for the Twenty-First Century*, edited by Joel R. Beeke and Anthony T. Selvaggio, 41–60. Grand Rapids, MI: Reformation Heritage Books, 2010.

Johnson, Thomas H. "Jonathan Edwards' Background of Reading." *Publications of the Colonial Society of Massachusetts* 28 (1931): 193–222.

The Jonathan Edwards Center at Yale University. "A Chronological List of Jonathan Edwards's Sermons and Discourses." 2007.

———. "Sermon Index (Chronological)." http://edwards.yale.edu/research/sermon-index (accessed January 26, 2009).

———. "Search WJE Online." http://edwards.yale.edu/archive (accessed April 28, 2010).

Kidd, Thomas. *The Great Awakening: The Roots of Evangelical Christianity*. New Haven, CT: Yale University Press, 2007.

Kimnach, Wilson H. "General Introduction to the Sermons: Jonathan Edwards' Art of Prophesying." In Jonathan Edwards. *Sermons and Discourses 1720–1723*, edited by Wilson H. Kimnach, 3–258. Vol. 10 of *The Works of Jonathan Edwards*. New Haven, CT: Yale University Press, 1992.

———. "Edwards as Preacher." In *The Cambridge Companion to Jonathan Edwards*, edited by Stephen J. Stein, 103–124. New York: Cambridge University Press, 2007.

Kling, David W., and Douglas A. Sweeney, eds. *Jonathan Edwards at Home and Abroad: Historical Memories, Cultural Movements, Global Horizons*. Columbia: University of South Carolina Press, 2003.

Knight, Janice. "Typology." In *The Princeton Companion to Jonathan Edwards*, edited by Sang Hyun Lee, 190–209. Princeton, NJ: Princeton University Press, 2005.

Kolb, Robert. "The Doctrine of Christ in Nikolaus Selnecker's Interpretation of Psalms 8, 22, and 110." In *Biblical Interpretation in the Era of the Reformation: Essays Presented to David C. Steinmetz in Honor of His Sixtieth Birthday*, edited by Richard A. Muller and John L. Thompson, 313–332. Grand Rapids, MI: Eerdmans, 1996.

Kreider, Glenn R. *Jonathan Edwards's Interpretation of Revelation 4:1–8:1*. Dallas, TX: University Press of America, Inc., 2004.

Lambert, Barbara, ed. *Music in Colonial Massachusetts, 1630–1820, Vol. II: Music in Homes and Churches*. Vol. 54 of the Publications of the Colonial Society of Massachusetts. Boston: The Society, 1985.

Lambert, Frank. *Inventing the "Great Awakening."* Princeton: Princeton University Press, 1999.

Laurence, David Ernst. "Religious Experience in the Biblical World of Jonathan Edwards: A Study in Eighteenth-Century Supernaturalism." PhD diss., Yale University, 1976.

LeFebvre, Michael. *Singing the Songs of Jesus: Revisiting the Psalms*. Fearn, Scotland: Christian Focus, 2010.

Lesser, M. X. *Reading Jonathan Edwards: An Annotated Bibliography in Three Parts, 1729–2005*. Grand Rapids, MI: Eerdmans, 2008.

Levesque, George G. "Introduction" to Edwards' "Quæstio." In *Sermons and Discourses 1723–1729*, edited by Kenneth P. Minkema, 47–53. Vol. 14 of *The Works of Jonathan Edwards*. New Haven, CT: Yale University Press, 1992.

Logan, Samuel T., Jr. "The Hermeneutics of Jonathan Edwards." *Westminster Theological Journal* 43, no. 1 (1980): 79–96.

Lovi, David S., and Benjamin Westerhoff, eds. *The Power of God: A Jonathan Edwards Commentary on the Book of Romans.* Eugene, OR: Pickwick, 2013.

Lowance, Mason I., Jr. "Typology and the New England Way: Cotton Mather and the Exegesis of Biblical Types." *Early American Literature* 4 (1969): 15–37.

———. "'Images or Shadows of Divine Things' in the Thought of Jonathan Edwards." In *Typology and Early American Literature*, edited by Sacvan Bercovitch, 209–244. Amherst: University of Massachusetts Press, 1972.

———. *The Language of Canaan: Metaphor and Symbol in New England from the Puritans to the Transcendentalists.* Cambridge, MA: Harvard University Press, 1980.

Lowance, Mason I., Jr., and David H. Watters. "Editor's Introduction to 'Types of the Messiah.'" In Jonathan Edwards. *Typological Writings*, edited by Wallace E. Anderson and Mason I. Lowance Jr. with David H. Watters, 157–182. Vol. 11 of *The Works of Jonathan Edwards.* New Haven, CT: Yale University Press, 1992.

Lucas, Sean Michael. *God's Grand Design: The Theological Vision of Jonathan Edwards.* Wheaton, IL: Crossway, 2011.

MacDougal, Hamilton C. *Early New England Psalmody: An Historical Appreciation, 1620–1820.* Brattleboro, VT: Stephen Daye, 1940.

Manley, Johanna, ed. *Grace for Grace: The Psalter and the Holy Fathers: Patristic Christian Commentary, Meditations, and Liturgical Extracts Relating to the Psalms and Odes.* Menlo Park, CA: Monastery Books, 1992.

Marsden, George M. "Can Jonathan Edwards (and His Heirs) Be Integrated Into the American History Narrative?" *Historically Speaking: The Bulletin of the Historical Society* 5 (July–August 2004): 13–15.

———. *Jonathan Edwards: A Life.* New Haven, CT: Yale University Press, 2003.

———. "The Quest for the Historical Edwards: The Challenge of Biography." In *Jonathan Edwards at Home and Abroad: Historical Memories, Cultural Movements, Global Horizons*, edited by David W. Kling and Douglas A. Sweeney, 3–15. Columbia: University of South Carolina Press, 2003.

Marshall, Madeleine Forell and Janet Todd. *English Congregational Hymns in the Eighteenth Century.* Lexington: University of Kentucky Press, 1982.

McClymond, Michael J. *Encounters with God: An Approach to the Theology of Jonathan Edwards.* New York: Oxford University Press, 1998.

McClymond, Michael J., and Gerald R. McDermott. *The Theology of Jonathan Edwards.* New York: Oxford University Press, 2012.

McDermott, Gerald R. "Jonathan Edwards, Deism, and the Mystery of Revelation." *Journal of Presbyterian History* 77, no. 4 (Winter 1999): 211–224.

———. *Jonathan Edwards Confronts the Gods: Christian Theology, Enlightenment Religion, and Non-Christian Faiths.* New York: Oxford University Press, 2000.

——. "Alternative Viewpoint: Edwards and Biblical Typology." In *Understanding Jonathan Edwards: An Introduction to America's Theologian*, edited by Gerald R. McDermott, 109–112. Oxford: Oxford University Press, 2009.

——, ed. *Understanding Jonathan Edwards: An Introduction to America's Theologian*. Oxford: Oxford University Press, 2009.

McKim, Donald K., ed. *Dictionary of Major Biblical Interpreters*. Downers Grove, IL: InterVarsity, 2007.

McKinnon, James. "Desert Monasticism and the Later Fourth-Century Psalmodic Movement." *Music and Letters* 75 (1994): 505–521.

Miller, Patrick D., Jr., *Interpreting the Psalms*. Philadelphia, PA: Fortress, 1986.

Miller, Perry. *Jonathan Edwards*. The American Men of Letters Series. New York: William Sloane Associates, 1949.

Minkema, Kenneth P. "The East Windsor Conversion Relations, 1700–1725." *Connecticut Historical Society Bulletin* 51 (Winter 1986): 9–63.

——. "A Great Awakening Conversion: The Relation of Samuel Belcher." *William & Mary Quarterly* 44, no. 1 (January 1987): 121–126.

——. "The Lynn End 'Earthquake' Relations of 1727." *New England Quarterly* 69, no. 3 (September 1996): 473–499.

——. "The Other Unfinished 'Great Work': Jonathan Edwards, Messianic Prophecy, and 'The Harmony of the Old and New Testament.'" In *Jonathan Edwards's Writings: Text, Context, Interpretation*, edited by Stephen J. Stein, 52–65. Bloomington: Indiana University Press, 1996.

——. "Jonathan Edwards in the Twentieth Century." *Journal of the Evangelical Theological Society* 47, no. 4 (2004): 659–687.

Moody, Josh. *Jonathan Edwards and the Enlightenment: Knowing the Presence of God*. Lanham, MD: University Press of America, 2005.

——, ed. *Jonathan Edwards and Justification*. Wheaton, IL: Crossway, 2012.

Morimoto, Anri. *Jonathan Edwards and the Catholic Vision of Salvation*. University Park, PA: Penn State Press, 1995.

Mouw, Richard J., and Mark A. Noll, eds. *Wonderful Words of Life: Hymns in American Protestant History and Theology*. Calvin Institute of Christian Worship Liturgical Studies Series. Grand Rapids, MI: Eerdmans, 2004.

Mowinckel, Sigmund. *The Psalms in Israel's Worship*. 1962. Reprint, Grand Rapids, MI: Eerdmans, 2004.

Muller, Richard A. "Biblical Interpretation in the Era of the Reformation: The View from the Middle Ages." In *Biblical Interpretation in the Era of the Reformation: Essays Presented to David C. Steinmetz in Honor of His Sixtieth Birthday*, edited by Richard A. Muller, and John L. Thompson, 1–22. Grand Rapids, MI: Eerdmans, 1996.

——. *Holy Scripture: The Cognitive Foundation of Theology*. Vol. 2 of *Post-Reformation Reformed Dogmatics: The Rise and Development of Reformed Orthodoxy, ca. 1520 to ca. 1725*. 2d ed. Grand Rapids, MI: Baker Academic, 2003.

——. "Biblical Interpretation in the Sixteenth and Seventeenth Centuries." In *Dictionary of Major Biblical Interpreters*, edited by Donald K. McKim, 22–44. Downers Grove, IL: IVP Academic, 2007.

——. "Scripture and the Westminster Confession." In Richard A. Muller and Rowland S. Ward. *Scripture and Worship: Biblical Interpretation and the Directory for Public Worship*, 1–82. The Westminster Assembly and the Reformed Faith Series, edited by Carl R. Trueman. Phillipsburg, NJ: P & R, 2007.

Muller, Richard A., and John L. Thompson, eds. *Biblical Interpretation in the Era of the Reformation: Essays Presented to* David C. Steinmetz *in Honor of His Sixtieth Birthday*. Grand Rapids, MI: Eerdmans, 1996.

Muller, Richard A., and Rowland S. Ward. *Scripture and Worship: Biblical Interpretation and the Directory for Public Worship*. The Westminster Assembly and the Reformed Faith Series, edited by Carl R. Trueman. Phillipsburg, NJ: P & R, 2007.

Munk, Linda. "His Dazzling Appearance: The Shekinah in Jonathan Edwards." *Early American Literature* 27, no. 1 (1992): 1–30.

Murray, David P. "Christian Cursing?" In *Sing a New Song: Recovering Psalm Singing for the Twenty-First Century*, edited by Joel R. Beeke and Anthony T. Selvaggio, 111–121. Grand Rapids, MI: Reformation Heritage Books, 2010.

Music, David W. "Jonathan Edwards and the Theology and Practice of Congregational Song in Puritan New England." *Studies in Puritan American Spirituality* 8 (2004): 103–133.

——. "'An Holy Duty of God's Worship': John Cotton's *Singing of Psalms a Gospel Ordinance*." *The Hymn* 56, no. 1 (Winter 2005): 7–15.

Nassif, Bradley. "Antiochene θεωρία in John Chrysostom's Exegesis." In *Ancient & Postmodern Christianity: Paleo-Orthodoxy in the 21st Century: Essays in Honor of Thomas C. Oden*, edited by Kenneth Tanner and Christopher A. Hall, 49–67. Downers Grove, IL: InterVarsity, 2002.

Neele, Adriaan. *Petrus Van Mastricht (1630–1706): Reformed Orthodoxy: Method and Piety*. Brill Series in Church History. Leiden: Brill, 2009.

Nichols, Stephen R. C. *Jonathan Edwards's Bible: The Relationship of the Old and New Testaments in the Theology of Jonathan Edwards*. Eugene, OR: Pickwick, 2013.

Noll, Mark A. "The Defining Role of Hymns in Early Evangelicalism." In *Wonderful Words of Life: Hymns in American Protestant History and Theology*, edited by Richard J. Mouw and Mark A. Noll, 3–16. Calvin Institute of Christian Worship Liturgical Studies Series. Grand Rapids, MI: Eerdmans, 2004.

——. "The Significance of Hymnody in the First Evangelical Revivals, 1730–1760." In *Revival, Renewal, and the Holy Spirit*, edited by Dyfed Wyn Roberts, 45–64. Studies in Evangelical History and Thought. Milton Keynes, UK: Paternoster, 2009.

Noll, Mark A., and Edith L. Blumhofer, eds. *Sing Them Over Again to Me: Hymns and Hymnbooks in America*. Tuscaloosa: University of Alabama Press, 2006.

Old, Hughes Oliphant. *Moderatism, Pietism, and Awakening.* Vol. 5 of *The Reading and Preaching of the Scriptures in the Worship of the Christian Church.* Grand Rapids, MI: Eerdmans, 2004.

——. "Henry, Matthew (1662–1714)." In *Dictionary of Major Biblical Interpreters,* edited by Donald K. McKim, 520–524. Downers Grove, IL: InterVarsity, 2007.

Old, Hughes Oliphant, and Robert Cathcart. "From Cassian to Cranmer: Singing the Psalms from Ancient Times until the Dawning of the Reformation." In *Sing a New Song: Recovering Psalm Singing for the Twenty-First Century,* edited by Joel R. Beeke and Anthony T. Selvaggio, 1–15. Grand Rapids, MI: Reformation Heritage Books, 2010.

Opie, John, ed. *Jonathan Edwards and the Enlightenment.* Problems in American Civilization Series. Lexington, MA: D. C. Heath and Co., 1969.

Outram, Dorinda. *The Enlightenment.* 2d ed. New Approaches to European History. Cambridge: Cambridge University Press, 2005.

——. *Panorama of the Enlightenment.* Los Angeles, CA: J. Paul Getty Museum, 2006.

Pak, G. Sujin. *Judaizing Calvin: Sixteenth-Century Debates over the Messianic Psalms.* Oxford Studies in Historical Theology. New York: Oxford University Press, 2010.

Parsons, Michael. *Martin Luther's Interpretation of the Royal Psalms: The Spiritual Kingdom in a Pastoral Context.* Lewiston, NY: Edwin Mellen, 2009.

Pfeiffer, Robert Henry. "The Teaching of Hebrew in Colonial America." *Jewish Quarterly Review* 45, no. 4 (1955), 363–373.

Phillips, Christopher N. "Cotton Mather Brings Isaac Watts' Hymns to America; or, How to Perform a Hymn without Singing It." *The New England Quarterly* 85, no. 2 (June 2012): 203–221.

Plantinga Pauw, Amy. *The Supreme Harmony of All: The Trinitarian Theology of Jonathan Edwards.* Grand Rapids, MI: Eerdmans, 2002.

Pool, David de Sola. "Hebrew Learning among the Puritans of New England Prior to 1700." 1911. In *Early American History: The Marrow of American Divinity,* edited by Peter Charles Hoffer, 1–53. New York: Garland, 1988.

Porter, Bertha. "Trapp, John (1601–1669)." In Vol. 19 of *The Dictionary of National Biography,* edited by Leslie Stephen and Sidney Lee, 1082. London: Oxford University Press, 1917.

Puckett, David L. *John Calvin's Exegesis of the Old Testament.* Louisville, KY: Westminster John Knox, 1995.

Quitsland, Beth. *The Reformation in Rhyme: Sternhold, Hopkins and the English Metrical Psalter, 1547–1603.* St. Andrews Studies in Reformation History. Aldershot: Ashgate, 2008.

Reventlow, Henning Graf. *The Authority of the Bible and the Rise of the Modern World.* Philadelphia, PA: Fortress, 1984.

——. "English Deism and Anti-Deist Apologetic." In Vol. 2 of *Hebrew Bible, Old Testament: The History of Its Interpretation,* edited by Magne Sæbø, 851–874. Göttingen: Vandenhoeck & Ruprecht, 2008.

Rhinelander McCarl, Mary. "Thomas Shepard's Record of Relations of Religious Experience, 1648–1649." *William and Mary Quarterly*, third series, 48, no. 3 (July 1991): 432–466.

Rivera, Ted. "Jonathan Edwards's 'Hermeneutic': A Case Study of the Sermon 'Christian Knowledge.'" *Journal of the Evangelical Theological Society* 49, no. 2 (2006): 273–286.

———. *Jonathan Edwards on Worship: Public and Private Devotion to God*. Eugene, OR: Pickwick, 2010.

Rivers, Cheryl. "Cotton Mather's *Biblia Americana* Psalms and the Nature of Puritan Scholarship." PhD diss., Columbia University, 1977.

Rivett, Sarah. *The Science of the Soul in Colonial New England*. Omohundro Institute of Early American History and Culture. Chapel Hill: University of North Carolina Press, 2011.

Rogers, Mark C. "A Missional Eschatology: Jonathan Edwards, Future Prophecy, and the Spread of the Gospel." *Fides et Historia* 41, no. 1 (Winter/Spring 2009): 23–46.

Ryan, Thomas F. *Thomas Aquinas as Reader of the Psalms*. Notre Dame, IN: University of Notre Dame Press, 2000.

Sæbø, Magne. "From the Renaissance to the Enlightenment—Aspects of the Cultural and Ideological Framework of Scriptural Interpretation." In Vol. 2 of *Hebrew Bible, Old Testament: The History of Its Interpretation*, edited by Magne Sæbø, 21–45. Göttingen: Vandenhoeck & Ruprecht, 2008.

———, ed. *Hebrew Bible/Old Testament: The History of Its Interpretation*. 2 vols. Göttingen: Vandenhoeck & Ruprecht, 1996, 2008.

Scholes, Percy. *The Puritans and Music in England and New England*. 1934. Reprint, New York: Russell & Russell, 1962.

Selderhuis, Herman J. *Calvin's Theology of the Psalms*. Texts and Studies in Reformation and Post-Reformation Thought. Grand Rapids, MI: Baker Academic, 2007.

Selement, George, and Bruce C. Woolley, eds. *Thomas Shepard's Confessions*. Vol. 58 of Publications of the Colonial Society of Massachusetts Collections. Boston: Colonial Society of Massachusetts, 1981.

Senn, Frank C. *Christian Liturgy: Catholic and Evangelical*. Minneapolis, MN: Fortress, 1997.

Smalley, Beryl. *The Study of the Bible in the Middle Ages*. 3d ed. 1964. Reprint, Notre Dame, IN: University of Notre Dame Press, 1978.

Smith, Lesley. *The Glossa Ordinaria: The Making of a Medieval Bible Commentary*. Vol. 3 of *Commentaria: Sacred Texts and Their Commentaries: Jewish, Christian and Islamic*, edited by Grover A. Zinn, et al. Leiden: Brill, 2009.

Smolinski, Reiner. "Cotton Mather's *Biblia Americana*: America's First Bible Commentary," *Uncommon Sense* 129 (Winter/Spring 2011): 9–12. http://oieahc. wm.edu/uncommon/129/mather.cfm (accessed September 8, 2011).

Smolinski, Reiner, and Jan Stievermann, eds. *Cotton Mather and* Biblia Americana—
America's First Bible Commentary: Essays in Reappraisal. Tübingen: Mohr Siebeck,
2010.

Solberg, Winton U. *Redeem the Time: The Puritan Sabbath in Early America.* A
Publication of the Center for the Study of the History of Liberty in America.
Cambridge, MA: Harvard University Press, 1977.

Sorkin, David. *The Religious Enlightenment: Protestants, Jews, and Catholics from
London to Vienna.* Princeton, NJ: Princeton University Press, 2008.

Stein, Stephen J. "Jonathan Edwards and the Rainbow: Biblical Exegesis and Poetic
Imagination." *New England Quarterly* 47 (1974): 440–456.

——. "The Biblical Notes of Benjamin Pierpont." *Yale University Library Gazette* 50
(1976): 195–218.

——. "Editor's Introduction." In *Apocalyptic Writings*, edited by Stephen J. Stein,
1–93. Vol. 5 of *The Works of Jonathan Edwards.* New Haven, CT: Yale University
Press, 1977.

——. "The Quest for the Spiritual Sense: The Biblical Hermeneutics of Jonathan
Edwards." *Harvard Theological Review* 70 (1977): 99–113.

——. "Providence and Apocalypse in the Early Writings of Jonathan Edwards." *Early
American Literature* 13, no. 3 (1978–1979): 250–267.

——. "'For Their Spiritual Good': The Northampton, Massachusetts, Prayer Bids of
the 1730s and 1740s." *William and Mary Quarterly*, third series, 37, no. 2 (April
1980): 261–285.

——. "'Like Apples of Gold in Pictures of Silver': The Portrait of Wisdom in
Jonathan Edwards's Commentary on the Book of Proverbs." *Church History* 54
(1985): 324–337.

——. "The Spirit and the Word: Jonathan Edwards and Scriptural Exegesis." In
Jonathan Edwards and the American Experience, edited by Nathan O. Hatch and
Harry S. Stout, 118–130. New York: Oxford University Press, 1988.

——. "Editor's Introduction." In *Notes on Scripture*, edited by Stephen J. Stein, 1–46.
Vol. 15 of *The Works of Jonathan Edwards.* New Haven: Yale University Press,
1998.

——. "Jonathan Edwards and the Cultures of Biblical Violence." In *Jonathan Edwards
at 300: Essays on the Tercentenary of His Birth*, edited by Harry S. Stout, Kenneth
P. Minkema, and Caleb J. D. Maskell, 54–64. Lanham, MD: University Press of
America, 2005.

——. "Editor's Introduction." In *The "Blank Bible,"* edited by Stephen J. Stein, 1–117.
Vol. 24 of *The Works of Jonathan Edwards.* New Haven, CT: Yale University Press,
2006.

——. "Edwards as Biblical Exegete." In *The Cambridge Companion to Jonathan
Edwards*, edited by Stephen J. Stein, 181–95. Cambridge: Cambridge University
Press, 2007.

——. "Cotton Mather and Jonathan Edwards on the Epistle of James: A Comparative Study." In *Cotton Mather and* Biblia Americana—*America's First Bible Commentary: Essays in Reappraisal,* edited by Reiner Smolinski and Jan Stievermann, 363–382. Tübingen: Mohr Siebeck, 2010.

——, ed. *The Cambridge Companion to Jonathan Edwards.* New York: Cambridge University Press, 2007.

Steinmetz, David C. "The Superiority of Precritical Exegesis." *Theology Today* 37, no. 1 (1980): 27–38.

Stephens, Bruce M. "An Appeal to the Universe: The Doctrine of the Atonement in American Protestant Thought from Jonathan Edwards to Edwards Amasa Park." *Encounter* 60, no. 1 (Winter 1999): 55–72.

Stetina, Karin Spiecker. *Jonathan Edwards' Early Understanding of Religious Experience: His New York Sermons, 1720–1723.* Lewiston, NY: Edwin Mellen, 2011.

Stevenson, Robert. *Protestant Church Music in America: A Short Survey of Men and Movements from 1564 to the Present.* New York: W. W. Norton & Company, 1966.

Stievermann, Jan. "Cotton Mather and 'Biblia Americana'—America's First Bible Commentary: General Introduction." In *Cotton Mather and* Biblia Americana—*America's First Bible Commentary: Essays in Reappraisal,* edited by Reiner Smolinski and Jan Stievermann, 1–58. Tübingen: Mohr Siebeck, 2010.

Stout, Harry S. "Liturgy, Literacy, and Worship in Puritan Anglo-America, 1560–1670." In *By the Vision of Another World: Worship in American History,* edited by James D. Bratt, 11–35. Grand Rapids, MI: Eerdmans, 2012.

——. *The New England Soul: Preaching and Religious Culture in Colonial New England.* New York: Oxford University Press, 1986.

Studebaker, Steven M. *Jonathan Edwards' Social Augustinian Trinitarianism in Historical and Contemporary Perspectives.* Gorgias Studies in Philosophy and Theology 2. Piscataway, NJ: Gorgias, 2008.

Studebaker, Steven M., and Robert W. Caldwell, III. *The Trinitarian Theology of Jonathan Edwards: Text, Context, and Application.* Farnham, UK: Ashgate, 2012.

Sweeney, Douglas A. *Nathaniel Taylor, New Haven Theology, and the Legacy of Jonathan Edwards.* Oxford: Oxford University Press, 2003.

——. "The Church." In *The Princeton Companion to Jonathan Edwards,* edited by Sang Hyun Lee, 167–189. Princeton, NJ: Princeton University Press, 2005.

——. "'Longing for More and More of It'? The Strange Career of Jonathan Edwards's Exegetical Exertions." In *Jonathan Edwards at 300: Essays on the Tercentenary of His Birth,* edited by Harry S. Stout, Kenneth P. Minkema, and Caleb J. D. Maskell, 25–37. Lanham, MD: University Press of America, Inc., 2005.

——. "Edwards, Jonathan (1703–1758)." In *Dictionary of Major Biblical Interpreters,* edited by Donald K. McKim, 397–400. Downers Grove, IL: IVP Academic, 2007.

——. "Edwards and the Bible." In *Understanding Jonathan Edwards: An Introduction to America's Theologian,* edited by Gerald R. McDermott, 63–82. Oxford: Oxford University Press, 2009.

———. *Jonathan Edwards and the Ministry of the Word: A Model of Faith and Thought.* Downers Grove, IL: IVP Academic, 2009.

———. "Justification by Faith Alone? A Fuller Picture of Edwards's Doctrine." In *Jonathan Edwards and Justification*, edited by Josh Moody, 129–154. Wheaton, IL: Crossway, 2012.

———. "The Biblical World of Jonathan Edwards." *Jonathan Edwards Studies* 3, no. 2 (2013): 207–254.

———. *Edwards the Exegete: Biblical Interpretation and Anglo-Protestant Culture on the Edge of the Enlightenment.* New York: Oxford University Press, forthcoming.

Sweeney, Douglas A., and Brandon G. Withrow. "Jonathan Edwards: Continuator or Pioneer of Evangelical History?" In *The Advent of Evangelicalism: Exploring Historical Continuities*, edited by Michael A. G. Haykin and Kenneth J. Stewart, 278–301. Nashville, TN: Broadman & Holman Academic, 2008.

Taylor, Jerome. "Introduction." In *The Didascalicon of Hugh of St. Victor.* 1961. Reprint, New York: Columbia University Press, 1991.

Thompson, John L.. *Reading the Bible with the Dead: What You Can Learn from the History of Exegesis That You Can't Learn from Exegesis Alone.* Grand Rapids, MI: Eerdmans, 2007.

———. "A Finding Guide to English Translations of Commentary Literature Written 1600–1700." Fuller Theological Seminary. http://purl.oclc.org/net/jlt/exegesis/ (accessed November 28, 2009, September 16, 2011).

Thuesen, Peter J. "Edwards' Intellectual Background." In *The Princeton Companion to Jonathan Edwards*, edited by Sang Hyun Lee, 16–33. Princeton, NJ: Princeton University Press, 2005.

———. "Editor's Introduction." In Jonathan Edwards. *Catalogues of Books*, edited by Peter J. Thuesen, 1–113. Vol. 26 of *The Works of Jonathan Edwards.* New Haven, CT: Yale University Press, 2008.

Tomas, Vincent. "Edwards' Master Was the Bible, Not Locke." In *Jonathan Edwards and the Enlightenment*, edited by John Opie. 36–38. Lexington, MA: D. C. Heath and Company, 1969.

Tooman, William A. "Edwards' Ezekiel: The Interpretation of Ezekiel in the Blank Bible and Notes on Scripture." *Journal of Theological Interpretation* 3, no. 1 (Spring 2009): 17–38.

Tracy, Joseph. *The Great Awakening: A History of the Revival of Religion in the Time of Edwards and Whitefield.* Boston: Charles Tappan, 1845.

Turnbull, Ralph G. "Jonathan Edwards—Bible Interpreter." *Interpretation* 6 (1952): 422–435.

Van der Woude, Joanne. "'How Shall We Sing the Lord's Song in a Strange Land?': A Transatlantic Study of the *Bay Psalm Book*." In *Psalms in the Early Modern World*, edited by Linda Phyllis Austern, Kari Boyd McBride, and David L. Orvis, 115–134. Burlington, VT: Ashgate, 2011.

Vanhoozer, Kevin J. "What Is Theological Interpretation of the Bible?" In *Dictionary for Theological Interpretation of the Bible*, edited by Kevin J. Vanhoozer, Craig

G. Bartholomew, Daniel J. Treier, and N. T. Wright, 19–25. Grand Rapids, MI: Baker Academic, 2005.

Van Lieburg, Fred. "Interpreting the Dutch Great Awakening (1749–1755)." *Church History* 77, no. 2 (June 2008): 318–336.

Wainwright, Geoffrey, and Karen B. Westerfield Tucker, eds. *The Oxford History of Christian Worship*. Oxford: Oxford University Press, 2006.

Webster, Brian L., and David R. Beach. *The Essential Bible Companion to the Psalms: Key Insights for Reading God's Word*. Grand Rapids, MI: Zondervan, 2010.

Weisheipl, James A. *Friar Thomas D'Aquino: His Life, Thought, and Work*. Garden City, NY: Doubleday & Co., Inc., 1974.

Wesselschmidt, Quentin F., ed. *Ancient Christian Commentary on Scripture: Old Testament: Psalms 51–150*. Vol. 8. Downers Grove, IL: InterVarsity, 2007.

Westerfield Tucker, Karen B. "North America." In *The Oxford History of Christian Worship*, edited by Geoffrey Wainwright and Karen B. Westerfield Tucker, 586–632. Oxford: Oxford University Press, 2006.

Wheeler, Rachel. "'Friends to Your Souls': Jonathan Edwards' Indian Pastorate and the Doctrine of Original Sin." *Church History* 72, no. 4 (2003): 736–765.

White, James F. Introduction *to Christian Worship*. Nashville, TN: Abingdon, 1981.

Winslow, Ola Elizabeth. *Jonathan Edwards, 1703–1758: A Biography*. 1940. Reprint, New York: Octagon Books, 1973.

Withrow, Brandon G. "'Full of Wondrous and Glorious Things': The Exegetical Mind of Jonathan Edwards in His Anglo-American Cultural Context." PhD diss., Westminster Theological Seminary, 2007.

——. *Becoming Divine: Jonathan Edwards's Incarnational Spirituality within the Christian Tradition*. Eugene, OR: Cascade, 2011.

Wodrow, Robert. "Short Account of the Life of the Author." In vol. 1 of David Dickson. *A Brief Explication of the Psalms*, xvii–xxv. 1726. Reprint, Glasgow: John Dow, 1834.

Yeager, Jonathan M. *Enlightened Evangelicalism: The Life and Thought of John Erskine*. New York: Oxford University Press, 2011.

Yoo, Jeongmo. "Jonathan Edwards's Interpretation of the Major Prophets: The Books of Isaiah, Jeremiah, and Ezekiel." *Puritan Reformed Journal* 3, no. 2 (2011): 160–192.

Zakai, Avihu. *Jonathan Edwards' Philosophy of History: The Reenchantment of the World in the Age of Enlightenment*. Princeton, NJ: Princeton University Press, 2009.

Index

Scripture Index

40:15–16 311n7
40:16 232, 237n84
40:17 55
41:1 300n134
41:1–2 300
41:1–4 350n190
41:11 11n38
42:1 12n40
42:1–2 280n37, 286n61
42:2 278
42:5 11, 237n84
42:11 237n84
43:3–4 281n40, 350n190
43:5 237n84
44 184n81
44:26 87
45 142, 169, 178–182, 182n74, 314–
    317, 314n23, 351, 362, 374
45:2 11n38, 179, 180, 181, 276
45:3 169
45:3–4 243, 243n108
45:3–5 196–197, 197n131
45:4 214
45:5 11n38
45:6 169n21, 170n23, 349n179
45:7 180, 188, 221
45:8 360n23
45:9 316, 316n28, 316n32
45:10 142, 182n74, 315, 315n25
45:10–11 315nn24–25
45:11 180
45:12 266n220, 335
45:13 81, 178, 180, 180n67, 182n74
45:13–14 315
45:13–15 309
45:15 351–352, 351nn192–193,
    352n199
45:16 339
46 90
46:1 88, 288n67
46:1–3 85, 92, 92n72, 169, 359
46:2 288

46:4 88
46:5 338
46:6–9 89
46:7 85
46:8–9 90
46:9 335
46:10 88, 89, 89n55, 90
47:1 85
47:9 205n176, 312n11, 312n13
48:2 266n220, 312n11, 313, 335
48:7 47
48:8 84
48:9 185
48:11–14 85
49:3–4 45, 342n146
49:3–15 342
49:4 48, 48n91, 342n146
49:6 350n190
49:11–14 143
49:14 338, 338n127
49:15 46, 349
49:16–18 350n190
49:20 155, 155n139
50 198, 338n126
50:1–2 338n126
50:1–4 343n152
50:2 313, 314, 335
50:3–6 338n126
50:4 337, 339
50:5 232
50:5–7 312n11
50:7–16 338n126
50:14 283n49
50:15 11n38, 107
50:16 249, 312n11
50:17 249
50:17–20 338n126
50:21 151–152, 225, 339n158
50:21–22 338n126
50:22 11n38, 56n115
50:23 283n49, 338n126
51 55

78:41–42 283n49
78:42–43 106
78:43 44n71, 52n101
78:56 283n49
78:57 249, 288n68
78:67–72 170n22
78:69 170n26
79 184n81
79:9 84, 86, 86n42
80 184n81
80:2 263
80:14 348n179
80:17 55
81:7 102n114, 317
81:10 11n38, 111, 111n160
81:12 92n70
82 132, 175
82:6–7 132–134, 132n34, 132n36,
    133n42
82:6–8 175–176, 288n67
82:8 176nn49–50
84:1 238
84:1–2 280n37
84:1–3 286n61
84:1–7 320, 350n190
84:2 245
84:3 203–204, 203n166, 204n169
84:4 43n68
84:5–7 237n85, 350n190
84:7 278
84:8–9 237nn84–85
84:10 62n139, 320, 321, 321n59,
    350n190
84:11 86
84:11–12 234n72
84:12 237n84
85 184n81, 263
85:9 233
85:10 106, 216
85:10–11 239
86:1–7 237n84, 305
86:2 236n82

86:4–5 107
86:11 226n37
87 266
87:3 81
87:4 266, 266n217
87:7 266
88:9–11 150
88:15 150
89 170, 170n24, 356–357
89:1–2 104–105
89:1–5 312n7, 337n123
89:2–3 170n23
89:3–4 265n216
89:5 337, 337n122
89:6 44n72, 58, 82–83, 83n24, 83n26,
    85, 260, 260n200, 356, 356n1
89:7 312n7
89:8–9 187
89:11–12 119, 264n210, 266n220
89:14–29 214
89:15 85, 320, 335, 356–360, 357n4
89:15–20 312n7
89:18 85
89:19 169, 169n21
89:20 169
89:20–21 170n23
89:25 170n23
89:27 169n21, 211n201
89:33 265n216
89:34 42n67
89:35 265n216
89:36–37 170n23
89:37 173n35
89:46–48 350
90 55, 131, 149–150, 350n190
90:3 136, 149
90:5–6 61n137, 129, 135–138,
    136n53, 136n55
90:5–9 44n71
90:5–12 149
90:8 11n38
90:9 136

Jonathan Edwards and the Psalms